Ex Líbrís

Randy Manning

B212 © APCo

ANNALS OF COMMUNISM

Each volume in the series Annals of Communism will publish selected and previously inaccessible documents from former Soviet state and party archives in the framework of a narrative text that focuses on a particular topic in the history of Soviet and international communism. Separate English and Russian editions will be prepared. Russian and American scholars select and annotate the documents for each volume; together they explain the selection criteria and discuss the state of relevant research and scholarly interpretation. Documents are chosen not for their support of any single interpretation but for their particular historical importance or their general value in deepening understanding and facilitating discussion. The volumes are designed to be useful to students, scholars, and interested general readers.

ment but to allow readers to ponder, to interpret, and, if they wish, to judge these events, the revolution as a whole, and the main players. The evidence must be selected without prejudice, but also read critically, even skeptically. The facts are not as straightforward as most writers would have us think. Like all historical documents, these texts are ambiguous, lend themselves to varied readings, or intentionally deceive or remain silent about important facts. And some documents have vanished. Thus, for example, we cannot be absolutely certain whether Moscow directly ordered the murder of the tsar and his family; this often-asserted "fact" is likely true, but no direct proof has ever surfaced.[5] Many writers have allowed themselves to speculate about facts that lie frustratingly beyond the reach of documentary evidence and to uncritically accept statements in archival documents or memoirs (especially when these concur with their own presumptions and judgments). The official cloak of secrecy behind which many documents were concealed cannot be taken as proof of their truthfulness—a truism often forgotten in the enthusiasm that has followed the opening of the Soviet archives. Secrets and truths are not identical.

The documents in this collection are authentic historical records, but they remain texts whose authors stand between us and the past. Memory, understanding, motive, and intent shroud simple fact. Yet it is especially here, in the traces of these authors' vision, that the documents are most eloquent. In introductory texts, I have presented the historical and intellectual contexts in which these documents were written and examined many issues concerning their meanings and veracity. Although the documents, even at face value, are often richly vocal about human experience during the revolution, readers will be most rewarded who engage these texts thoughtfully and listen critically to how things are said as much as to what is said and who pay as much attention to the offhand remarks and the seemingly trivial details as to the main narrative.

The image of Nicholas II that dominates historical memory is of a weak and witless ruler, ill equipped to cope with the challenges of bringing Russia into the modern age. This picture has been sustained by the obvious failure of the autocratic monarchy during the long trial of World War I, although it originated in views held before the revolution by many liberal-minded Russians. A contemporary joke held that Russia did not need a limited (that is, constitutional) monarchy, for it already had a limited monarch. Somewhat more generously, many historians and biographers have portrayed Nicholas as a man with little understanding of how to govern an increasingly complex and changing Russia, a man who preferred to hunt, hike, play tennis, swim, bicycle, row, ride, watch soldiers march, or keep company with his beloved family.

This image is not altogether false. Nicholas often spoke—in his diaries, in letters, and in conversation—of his love of sport and exercise, his desire to be with his wife and family, and his distaste for tiresome official meetings and piles of papers to review.[6] It is clear, too, that he was not as intellectually sophisticated or as broadminded as many educated Russians would have liked or as Russia perhaps needed. This is not to say that Nicholas was poorly educated. Private tutors had instructed him in a wide range of subjects, including foreign languages (English, French, and German), history, geography, mathematics, and chemistry. From the age of seventeen on, he was introduced to leading political, military, and academic figures, who were brought in to instruct him in subjects necessary for governance, such as political economy, finance, international and civil law, and military science. The tutors lectured him, assigned readings, and sometimes gave examinations. By all accounts, he was an intelligent and able student. Even Sergei Witte, who served Nicholas II as both finance minister and chairman of the Council of Ministers and who generally had little positive to say about the emperor in his memoirs—especially in comparison with Nicholas's father, Alexander III, whom Witte admired—acknowledged that Nicholas was "far superior to his father in intelligence and ability as well as in education."[7]

Whatever Nicholas's natural abilities, his development was hindered by a formalistic education that emphasized knowledge of facts over facility with ideas and by a familial and social milieu that placed little value on intellectual accomplishment, much less imagination. Contemporaries close to the court recorded the commonplace, trivial, and even vulgar talk often heard from Alexander III and his family and the general absence of any serious aesthetic or intellectual interests.[8] In Nicholas's own writings and speeches, as well as the memoirs of those who worked with him, we can see revealed a narrow and conventional intelligence. Nicholas was unique neither to his class nor to Russia, of course. He reflected in his character "a cultural and intellectual decline common to late nineteenth-century royalty and aristocracy as a whole."[9] Against the background of an increasingly educated public in Russia this decline appeared dramatic and dangerous.

The conventional image of Nicholas as tragically ignorant and weak is not so much false as simplistic, obscuring beliefs and values that shaped his reign and brought revolution closer. The real tragedy of Nicholas's rulership perhaps lay less in the absence of ideas or in the often-described clash between the political needs of his time and his personal preoccupation with family and personal pleasure than in the conflict between his convictions and values, on the one hand, and the need for reasoned change, on the other. The conflict was complicated by a strong tension in Nicholas's own mind between competing ideals of political authority. Alexandra's contribution to this tragic history similarly lay less in the pull toward domestic life that she exerted over Nicholas, or even in her damaging interference in government administration, than in her encouragement of Nicholas's anachronistic political convictions. His worldview was not static but deepened over time and in response to experiences. In the face of Russia's urban and industrial development, growing public pressures for democratic change, and a revolutionary upheaval in 1905 that forced the tsar to grant limited constitutional reforms, Nicholas and Alexandra grew more and more convinced that traditional social and political relationships, values, and structures were necessary for Russia's survival and happiness.

Nicholas II's political philosophy was built on moral judgments and religious faith, and it is with these that we must begin. Moral lessons were central even to his formal education. One recent historian has sarcastically but accurately observed that General Grigory Danilovich, who supervised Nicholas's education from the time the boy was ten, was "better known for his military discipline and plodding uprightness than for the brilliance of his mind or the breadth and tolerance of his views."[10] The point, however, is that self-discipline and high moral principle were understood to be essential virtues to instill in the future monarch. All of the evidence indicates that Nicholas took these lessons to heart.

Orderliness was a cardinal virtue for Nicholas. His diaries, terse chronicles of appointments and activities often cited as evidence of his intellectual shallowness, were not his medium for reflection or for expressing ideas—Nicholas articulated his ideas often enough in conversation, speeches, and letters. The diaries were foremost an exercise in self-discipline. From the first, he used his diaries to record the daily routines that structured his existence. Orderliness, systemization, and self-discipline carried over into his work as emperor. As a matter of personality and principle, Nicholas maintained a rigid and unvarying work schedule: meals, review of reports, meetings with courtiers and ministers, physical exercise, and time with the family were all by the clock.[11] In a similar spirit, Nicholas insisted on doing all of his own secretarial work—which undoubtedly kept him from devoting more time to questions of policy. But Nicholas seems to have found satisfaction in the discipline and orderly control that went with this labor. Even in the smallest details of his life, Nicholas was, according to those who knew his personal habits, "the tidiest, most systematic of men," who diligently kept every pen and pencil on his desk and every item in his bathroom in perfect order.[12] The high value that he placed on rational order and discipline in his personal life extended to his standards for society and politics.

These ideals were in many respects military virtues. In Russia, as elsewhere, service in the military was the conventional finishing school for highborn men—a place for imbibing the military code of command and obedience and for enjoying comradeship, parades, banquets, and women. This was all part of Nicholas's upbringing, and he clearly found great pleasure in his years as a young officer. At a deeper level, the exposure to military customs, ceremonies, and symbols reinforced in his mind the traditional centrality of the military in Russian political culture. Much of the history of the Russian state, especially since its emergence from Tatar domination, was a history of military preparations and expansion. As many historians have shown, military needs and experiences have been paramount in shaping political institutions and even economic and social policies in Russia since the sixteenth century.

At a symbolic and ornamental level, the importance of the military in tsarist political culture was reflected in the militarization of much of the public life of Nicholas and his family. As a matter of custom, he, his wife, his four daughters, and his son were honorary commanders of various elite regiments. They were given the appropriate uniforms and always wore them, evidently with pride and pleasure, in the presence of "their" soldiers. Nicholas devoted a great deal of time to attending military reviews and inspections and observing maneuvers—always in uniform, often on horseback, and frequently accompanied by his son and heir as Aleksei grew older. Nicholas never complained about this burden of office. On the contrary, he wrote of these affairs with pleasure. "A white sea of soldiers in a pretty country on a warm summer day—nothing can be finer for me, except a squadron of large ships."[13] He repeatedly remarked on the "beauty" of military dress, ceremony, and practice, finding emotional and spiritual satisfaction in military culture.[14] When he observed large maneuvers near Kursk in 1902, he wished that Alexandra could share with him the "good healthy feelings" and sense of "calm" that he was enjoying. At the end of the revolutionary year 1905, he confessed to his mother after attending the fiftieth anniversary celebration of the imperial family's rifle battalion that "it has been a long time since I felt so rested in my soul."[15]

Even war retained for some time a romantic aura in Nicholas's mind. During the ill-fated Russo-Japanese War of 1904–1905 he wrote of the "joy" with which many officers left behind their beloved families "for their Country's sake & for the glory of our army," and he often addressed troops returning from battle with fervent praise for their "heroism," "honor," and "glorious exploits" (*blestiashchie podvigi*).[16] In 1914 he viewed the approach of war with confidence, insisting that a "righteous war" would stimulate national feeling and make Russia stronger and better than ever.[17] During the war itself, he wrote frequent letters home exuding romantic enthusiasm for the heroism and beauty of warriors and combat. The following, from March 1916, is typical: "You can imagine my agreeable surprise when I rode up to the troops for the large review, to see our dear cossacks, who beginning by [*sic*] Zhukov to the last man were simply grinning & showing their teeth. . . . I gave them your compliments & greetings fr. the girls! They had just come from the *okopy* [trenches]. . . . The next day, which was yesterday—I saw a newly formed division . . . it looked simply magnificent—splendid tall men—like the guards."[18]

Nicholas's prohibition of the sale of alcohol during the war—notwithstanding the huge revenues the state normally received from its monopoly on spirits and the desperate need for cash to pursue the war—reflected his sense of war as an affair of honor.[19] For him the military tradition was a tradition of honor, duty, discipline, and service to the nation. His last public speech, made after his abdication in March 1917, was an address reminding the troops of these values (Document 39).

A belief in the virtues of physical fitness and outdoor activity—a military ideal but also an echo of the Victorian and Edwardian ethic of a sound body—was another essential part of Nicholas's moral temperament. This was a family tradition. His father, Alexander III, was a large, vigorous man often seen hunting game, chopping and sawing wood, clearing snow from paths, and cutting ice. He made a point of teaching his children the virtues of shoveling snow and cutting dead wood from trees on the palace grounds and, more broadly, an appreciation of nature and exercise.[20] Nicholas embraced this ideal and passed it on to his children. After coming home from a vigorous walk "soaked through and through," he wrote to his mother: "It reminds me so much of dear Papa, how he loved to sweat from physical activity, and now I love this too."[21] During the world war, when Nicholas was commanding the army from Staff Headquarters, he sought every opportunity to engage in physical activity outdoors. On one occasion, after a heavy nighttime snow, he wrote to Alexandra about his delight in having found a wooden spade in the garden with which to clear a pathway.[22] In 1917–1918 physical labor and exercise were a major part of the life of the imperial family while they were under arrest and in exile, and a major cause of complaint when it was denied them. For Nicholas, outdoor activity was more than a pleasant diversion. It was essential to his personal and moral life. We can perceive in his many remarks on the exhilarating pleasure and usefulness of outdoor physical activity both the expression of sensual need—paralleling his physical passion for his wife, often voiced in his wartime correspondence—and a judgment of moral virtue.[23]

Notions about the virtues of work were entwined with these values. In a semiofficial account of Nicholas's reign published in 1913, which conveyed to the public the way Nicholas wished to be seen and perhaps in large measure the way he saw himself, a chapter was devoted to "the crowned worker" (*ventsenosnyi truzhenik*). In this account Nicholas's refusal to use a personal secretary was portrayed as a reflection of his ethic of hard work. Similarly presented were the many hours that Nicholas spent fulfilling the duties of his office. "I do the work of three men. Let everyone learn to do the work of at least two," Nicholas reportedly pronounced.[24]

When sport, exercise, and labor were family activities, they were both more pleasurable and more meaningful. Family was a principal value for Nicholas. His letters were filled with adoring love for his wife, children, mother, and siblings, and this closeness to family was sustained to the end of his life. He liked to repeat the Russian proverb "It is good to go visiting, but it is better to be at home."[25] Whenever he was away from his family—to observe maneuvers or inspect troops, to make an occasional journey abroad, or to command the army during the First World War (when his absences were longer than ever before)—his letters to them were filled with expressions of tender love for his wife and children, sadness about departing after a visit home, warm memories of time spent together, and a longing to return.

Nicholas and Alexandra were well aware of the infidelities and divorces that plagued so many aristocratic and royal marriages—indeed, they often expressed dismay and disgust at the loose morals of their family and class[26]—and reveled in their many years of marital bliss. Their letters to one another are filled with sentimental diminutives, invariably written in English. To Nicholas, Alexandra was Sunny (her childhood nickname), sweety-mine, darling little wify, lovebird, my sweetest girlie, and lovykins; Nicholas was, in turn, Nicky (his childhood name), huzy, precious one, treasure, angel, sweetheart, and Blue Boy (from a favorite sentimental novel by Florence Barclay that they both read). They kissed one another's letters, sent flowers, and recalled moments of passion. Alexandra was unrestrained: she often recalled "loving caresses," proclaimed their love "undying through all eternity," and described herself covering Nicholas with kisses "passionately" and "with infinite tenderness."[27] Nicholas responded in kind, though by nature he was more phlegmatic (he admitted that "I never show my feelings," and Alexandra even chided him for being "shy" about voicing passion except in letters and "in the dark").[28] "How I miss your sweet kisses—yes, beloved One, *you know* how to give them—oh! how naughtily! B——y hops from remembrances."[29] One benefit of abdication, Nicholas recognized, was that he could spend "much more time with my sweet family than in more normal years" (Document 56 [6 May 1917]).

That Nicholas would rather be shoveling paths or enjoying the company of his wife and children than governing the country has typically been interpreted as evidence of his detachment from his role as tsar. This logic is much too simple. Whatever his personal preferences, Nicholas felt a strong sense of public duty and responsibility. Indeed, duty was a prime virtue for Nicholas, and he often judged himself and others by this measure. His own labors as tsar, as he saw them, were required not just by the political necessities of the moment but by "feelings of duty or, as dear Papa liked to say, *verfluchte Schuldigkeit* [damned duty]."[30] He believed that others should feel the same responsibility for their work. During the revolution of 1905–1906, Nicholas expressed his certainty that social disorder could be contained "if the authorities fulfill their duties honestly," and he appealed constantly to workers and peasants to devote themselves to the "honest labor" that was their duty.[31]

Most important, Nicholas was convinced that it was his duty to preserve Russia's autocratic system. As he told the minister of internal affairs, Prince Pyotr Sviatopolk-Mirsky, during high-level discussions of constitutional reform in 1904, "I am not holding on to autocracy for my own pleasure. I act in this spirit only because I am certain that this is necessary for Russia. If it were only for myself, I would with pleasure have turned away from all of this."[32] Autocracy was not to be preserved for his own sake, Nicholas often asserted, but for Russia, God, his ancestors, and his heirs. Just as he liked to remind soldiers that they were continuing the "service" of their "ancestors,"[33] so, too, did he often speak of his own duty to continue along the path followed by his father, to preserve the traditions of autocracy.[34] Failure to maintain national traditions, he believed, was a fundamental cause of the decline of nations. As he declared in a speech on 21 June 1905 (4 July on the Western calendar) to representatives of various classes and social organizations, "Only that state which preserves the heritage of its past [*zavet proshlogo*] is strong and firm. We ourselves have sinned against this, and God is perhaps punishing us."[35] In Nicholas's thinking, the upsurge of civic protest in 1905 was not a political sign of the need for democratic reform but a divine sign of the need to return to a purer autocracy.

The same sense of moral duty and national service led Nicholas to take command of the Russian army in 1915, against the advice of his ministers, his wife, and even the famous court mystic, Rasputin. In 1904, during the war with Japan, Nicholas had likewise sought to join his troops at the front: "My conscience has at times been troubling me that I am sitting here and am not there to share the suffering, deprivation, and hardships of battle together with the army." But he had been advised that his "presence there is not needed in this war."[36] In 1915 the arguments against his taking personal command of the war or even spending long periods at Headquarters were made forcefully: doing so would compromise his authority by associating him personally with failures at the front and by leaving daily political control in the hands of subordinates. But Nicholas felt that his presence would inspire the troops. Besides, being with his army was his duty. Like many tsars before him, he felt that he belonged with his troops at such a time of national "trial" (a term that recurs in his letters), that he should share the soldiers' sufferings and victories.[37] He repeatedly emphasized this sense of duty in his letters to Alexandra. "It is hard to separate again, after having spent only 6 days together. *Duty!* that is the reason." "Our separation is *our own* personal sacrifice for our country in this serious time and this thought makes it much easier to bear."[38] Paradoxically, the same sense of duty to country may have made it possible for Nicholas to agree to abdicate. As he wrote in his diary on 2 March 1917, "My abdication is needed . . . in the name of saving Russia and maintaining calm in the army at the front" (Document 30).[39]

Nicholas's preoccupation with moral behavior was shaped by his religious attitudes. These were shaped, in turn, by people close to him: his mother, Maria Fyodorovna (born Princess Dagmar of Denmark), a Protestant convert to Orthodoxy who strove to inculcate strong faith and encourage regular ritual practices in her children; Konstantin Pobedonostsev, chief procurator of the Holy Synod (lay head of the church), one of Nicholas's tutors and later a close adviser, who constantly reminded Nicholas that the tsar was anointed by God and was a divinely inspired source of wisdom and order; and his wife, Alexandra, also a Protestant convert to Orthodoxy, who encouraged Nicholas's mysticism and his faith in God's omnipotence and personal guidance.

Nicholas found increasing comfort in religious practice and faith. In 1900 he began regularly celebrating Easter with his family in Moscow's ancient Kremlin churches and cathedrals. During this first Holy Week in Moscow, Nicholas wrote to his mother, "I never knew I could be in such a state of *religious ecstasy* as I have experienced this Lent. . . . Everything here makes for prayer and spiritual peace."[40] Over time, his religious feeling grew deeper. During World War I, Nicholas repeatedly expressed faith that God would protect the Russian army and that the presence of sacred icons, such as the Vladimir Mother of God, sustained and inspired the troops.[41]

The rites and images were Orthodox, but Nicholas's faith was more broadly Christian and pietistic. Together with Alexandra, he read a variety of religious literatures, both Western and Eastern. According to Anna Vyrubova, a close friend, Nicholas and Alexandra "believed that it was possible outside the church and without the aid of regularly ordained bishops and priests to hold communion with God and with His Spirit."[42] They believed, further, that there were holy men to whom God gave mystical powers of healing and prophecy. During 1902–1903, Nicholas and Alexandra welcomed into the palace a French mystic, Philippe Nizier-Vachod, who had been operating a popular spiritualist medical practice in Lyons and had a reputation as a healer, spiritual guide, and clairvoyant.[43] To Nicholas and Alexandra, he was "our Friend" and an important source of prophecy and comfort.[44] Several years later, another lay mystic and healer, Grigory Rasputin, gained Nicholas's and Alexandra's confidence. Nonclerical religious teachers and healers were a well-established part of the Russian religious tradition, although the relationship between the established church and these holy men, who were usually peasants, was uneasy. But Nicholas seemed to believe that God worked and spoke through them.

Nicholas did not heed all of Rasputin's copious advice. He ignored his dire warnings in 1914 that war would bring "God's punishment" upon Russia and "great destruction and grief without end," despite the likely victory over Germany.[45] He ignored his counsel against taking personal command of the army. He ignored some recommended appointments to the government—"our Friend's ideas about men are sometimes queer," he wrote to Alexandra— and most of his military suggestions.[46] But Nicholas also ignored warnings that Rasputin's presence at court was discrediting his own authority. He found Rasputin's presence, prayers, and words "most comforting."[47] "When I am worried, or doubtful, or vexed, I only have to talk to Grigory for five minutes to feel myself immediately soothed and strengthened."[48] Rasputin's evident power to heal Aleksei's hemophiliac bleeding seemed to prove that God worked through him. And Nicholas's instincts, which he trusted above all other sources of knowledge, seemed to tell him that this holy man of the people, from the depths of rural Russia, could be relied on.

Religious faith gave Nicholas the assurance that all would be well, but it also helped him to accept failure and adversity. What many have described as Nicholas's weakness, his apparent inability to demonstrate determination and flexibility in resolving crises and his tendency to "slip away [*uskol'zaet*] from every unpleasantness,"[49] was not simply a matter of a flabby will or a distracted mind but of a fatalistic spirituality. Nicholas viewed all misfortune as the will of God. Like Christ in his Passion, whose story especially moved him,[50] and the many Orthodox saints distinguished by their submissive suffering, Holy Russia, Nicholas seemed to believe, ought to accept the trials that God chose to impose on it. Faced with misfortune or unpleasantness of any kind he was likely to declare, "God knows what is good for us, we must bow down our heads & repeat the sacred words 'Thy will be done.'"[51] Thus, during the

1905 revolution, Nicholas, foreshadowing his emotions and behavior during 1917–1918, repeatedly insisted that this "ordeal" was God's will. His foreign minister, Aleksandr Izvolsky, was amazed at Nicholas's calm reception of a report on the naval mutiny at the Kronstadt Fortress near St. Petersburg: "If you find me so little troubled, it is because I have the firm and absolute faith that the destiny of Russia, my own fate, and that of my family are in the hands of Almighty God, who has placed me where I am. Whatever may happen, I shall bow to His will."[52]

This pervading personal "serenity," as Izvolsky called it, was seen by many as a political flaw. His uncle Grand Duke Sergei, for example, considered Nicholas's calmness amid crises "painful and pitiful! He is in a blissful state of . . . fatalism."[53] The leitmotif that whatever happened was God's will was woven through Nicholas's life. He voiced this faith when the unexpected death of his father brought him to the throne.[54] He voiced the same faith when the revolution forced him from that throne. As he implied in the manifesto announcing his abdication, the revolution was much more than a historical or political event: "The Lord God saw fit to send down upon Russia a harsh new ordeal" (Document 26). In the months that followed his abdication, he continued to view historical events as part of a divine plan. Revolutionary turmoil, Bolshevik power, and preparations for a separate peace with Germany evoked—even in Nicholas's terse diary entries—expressions of anguish at Russia's suffering, but also the inevitable fatalistic counterpoint: "And still there is none like God! May His holy will be done!" (Document 97, entry of 2 [15] March 1918). Tellingly, in these months of captivity and exile, Nicholas decided to reread the entire Bible, together with works like *La sagesse et la destinée* (Wisdom and destiny), Maurice Maeterlinck's book of stoic reflections on happiness, love, sacrifice, and death.[55]

All these elements of Nicholas's intellectual worldview—his moral idealization of discipline, physical activity, family, and duty, and the comfort and certitude he found in his faith in God's power and will—were coupled with his political beliefs. Nicholas did not rule by whim and certainly not by bending with the political wind, but according to a distinct philosophy of kingship and of his own proper identity, role, and duty. At the heart of this political philosophy was an inherited tradition of political myth—a body of idealized, justificatory, and inspiring images of the tsar.

This ruler myth was not stable or uniform. In the two centuries preceding Nicholas II's reign, justifications of autocracy had become increasingly "modern." The traditional image of the sovereign as *tsar' batiushka* (tsar-father), an all-powerful autocrat who ruled solely on the basis of his personal will, divine inspiration, pious morality, and love for his people, was joined by more secular, rational, and legalistic conceptions of autocratic state power. These emphasized the secular necessities of strong state authority for national security and progress, the need for the state to mediate rationally among the particularistic interests of class and party, and the embodiment of these goals in impersonal laws and institutions.[56] Such innovations, especially when brought to life in changing political practices, were not met silently. Conservatives inside and outside the government warned that institutionalizing the personal authority of the tsar in legal mandates and bureaucratic bodies—not to mention the participatory civic institutions that many in society were demanding—would weaken the tsar's sacred moral absolutism, which Russia needed to survive and remain strong.

In Nicholas II's time, the most articulate and influential voice of this Russian traditionalism was that of Konstantin Pobedonostsev, chief procurator of the Holy Synod and tutor and adviser to both Alexander III and Nicholas. In a direct challenge to the rationalist worldview of the Enlightenment, Pobedonostsev, like other nineteenth-century European conservatives, asserted the primacy of faith, feeling, spirituality, morality, community, and tradition over and against the false ideals of abstract theory, rationalism, intellectual speculation, legality, individualism, popular sovereignty, and reform. Inspired by divine wisdom, the true tsar must not allow laws or institutions, which merely embody human folly and weakness, to restrict his personal authority, nor permit any influence other than his sense of morality and duty to compel or limit his actions. Pobedonostsev's ideas reflected not only his faith in divine guidance but also his contempt, characteristic of nineteenth-century conservatives, for human wisdom. The most dangerous fallacy in modern thought, Pobedonostsev believed, was the idea that human beings are endowed with reason and that with reason they can create a more perfect society. He insistently taught instead that human beings are by nature morally weak, selfish, and vicious. Russians, as an uncultured people, were especially weak. The only hope for the survival of human society (Pobedonostsev sometimes seemed skeptical about human destiny under any conditions) was to subordinate human will to some sacred moral power, like that represented by the autocratic tsar.[57]

Nicholas embraced this myth of the tsar's authority as sacred and moral. He shared Pobedonostsev's epistemological rejection of the primacy of rational sources of truth in favor of understanding true knowledge as beyond reason. Nicholas believed, as Dominic Lieven has stated, "that the wisdom which sprang from the instincts and heart of a tsar was superior to any purely secular reasoning."[58] Nicholas was certain that God spoke through him, and this certainty helped to define his behavior as ruler. "I never prepare what I am going to say in audience," he liked to observe, "but, praying to the Lord God, I speak what comes into my mind."[59] Important political decisions were also decided in consultation with the divine voice. Thus, in 1906, Nicholas explained to the new chairman of the Council of Ministers, Pyotr Stolypin, that he had to reject a recommendation (to extend equal rights to Jews) made by the entire council because "an inner voice more and more firmly repeats to me not to accept this decision. To date, my conscience has *never* deceived me. . . . I know you also believe that 'the heart of the tsar is in the hand of God.' So be it."[60] He pointed to the same guidance several years later in his decision, against all advice, to take command of the army: "I remember so well that while I was standing opposite our Saviour's big picture upstairs in the big church [Fyodorovsky Cathedral at Tsarskoe Selo], an interior voice seemed to tell me to make up my mind & write about my decision at once to Nik. [Nikolai Nikolaevich, the commander in chief]." Once that decision was made, he reportedly felt God's presence, "a sort of feeling after the Holy Communion!"[61]

More than any of his modern predecessors, Nicholas II attached himself and the future of his dynasty to the besieged myth of *tsar' batiushka*—specifically, the myth of the tsar as saintly prince. When his father died, Nicholas commented in his diary, "This was the death of a saint!"[62] Although this is far from the harsh, authoritarian image of Alexander III that most historians or contemporaries would invoke, the words reflected not just Nicholas's admiration for his father but his ideal of the good tsar. With similar intent and meaning, Nicholas named his son and heir, born in 1904, after the ancestor he most admired: the first Tsar Aleksei, father of Peter the Great (the ruler whom Nicholas least admired).[63] Nicholas evoked his memory as an expression of his own political ideal. Tsar Aleksei, who reigned from 1645 to 1676, was called *tishaishii,* or "most gentle," and was conventionally portrayed as a saintly and pious man, whose personal goodness was the source and legitimation of his authority as tsar. This image evidently had less to do with Aleksei's actual personal qualities than with the promotion and dominance of a certain traditional myth of the good tsar.[64]

This ideal found many echoes in Nicholas's political self-image. His apparent preference for spending time with his family or outdoors rather than ruling the country—a preference exemplified by his often-quoted declaration upon hearing of his father's death in 1894, "I am not prepared to be tsar, I never wanted to become one,"[65] and by his frequent complaints about the burdens of office—at least partly reflected the myth of the tsar-saint, who typically disdained his own secular power and the profane work of everyday government. Most important was that the tsar-saint was close to God, who inspired his actions and words and to whom the tsar was ultimately responsible. By tradition, a tsar-saint was also ready to suffer and even sacrifice himself for God and for Russia.[66]

Like many conservative Russians, Nicholas looked nostalgically back to pre-Petrine Muscovy—the time before Peter the Great's efforts to modernize and westernize Russia—as an age of social harmony, piety, morality, and unity between tsar and people. In Nicholas's time, when conflicts between the emperor and his subjects and demands for a new relationship (voiced even by some of his own ministers) had reached unprecedented levels, Nicholas retreated into the past, adopting a romantic image of himself as a Muscovite tsar, as a saintly *tsar' batiushka.* This ruler myth was the touchstone that guided Nicholas in his responses to demands for reform and to conflicting ideas.

Central to the myth was the idea of a special bond uniting tsar and *narod*—the common people but also the nation and its social foundations. Certain images of the *narod* were especially vibrant in his mind, and they remained little changed to the end of his life. In the fall of 1902, in a letter to Alexandra, Nicholas wrote of driving through the countryside in a troika on the way to view military maneuvers: "We passed through large villages, where the good peasants presented simple bread & salt & all went down on their knees, showing such a touching childish joy."[67] Nicholas was convinced that the common people were as devoted to him as he believed he was to them. Indeed, the further away from him that large numbers of educated Russians and other dissenting groups seemed to move, the stronger grew his faith in the sacred bonds that united him with ordinary Russians, and the stronger grew his insistence on these bonds as the only definition of Russian nationhood. Nicholas's embrace of this myth, it can be argued, was a major obstacle to administrative and constitutional reform in Russia.

The myth was at the heart of the popular notion of a bureaucratic barrier between ruler and ruled, of self-serving bureaucrats and advisers interfering with the tsar's ability to know the needs of his people and to care for them. The folk idea—expressed in the saying "If only the tsar knew!"—had its official equivalent. Nicholas certainly showed his distrust of, and even contempt for, his own officials and willfully ignored their considered advice. Like his father, who, it is said, once drank a toast to the obliteration of his entire administration,[68] Nicholas believed in the personal, patriarchal rule of the monarch.[69] Faith in his own personal rulership helped Nicholas to face revolution with calm confidence, but it also encouraged him to resist proposals for constitutional reform—whether made by civic institutions like the zemstvos, the local rural assemblies whose modest pleas for democratic representation he dismissed as "senseless dreams," or by his minister of internal affairs Sviatopolk-Mirsky, who suggested similar reforms at the end of 1904—for such reforms would have placed elected representatives of the population between the tsar and his people.[70]

Even when Nicholas agreed in February 1905, when faced with massive public unrest, to allow a national representative assembly, or Duma, to be elected and to participate in drafting laws, he explained his decision in traditional terms: not as the acceptance of a constitutional limitation on his personal autocratic power but as the revival of a custom and as a means to better hear the voice of the *narod*. His speech to a delegation of zemstvo and town council representatives in June was typical in evoking as justification of reform the traditional ideal of the tsar united with his people: "Let there be established, as in olden times, the union between Tsar and all Rus' [an archaic term evoking old Russia], the communion [*obshchenie*] between Me and the people of the land [*zemskie liudi*], which lies at the foundation of an order that corresponds to unique Russian principles."[71]

Throughout 1905 and in the years following, Nicholas insistently evoked this traditional ideal in resisting plans for reform. Indeed, as the defiant behavior of many elected representatives to the State Duma increased his skepticism about the benefits of electoral representation, Nicholas focused ever more intently on his own role as the people's guardian. Thus, in advising Stolypin, chairman of the Council of Ministers, on how to explain the proroguing of the first State Duma in July 1906, he insisted that "henceforth all of my concern, like that of a father for his children, will be directed toward the just provision of land to the peasants." When addressing representatives of the people directly, he insisted that "your needs are dear to Me and they are My constant concern," that the "needs closest to My heart are those of the peasantry, of enlightening the people and advancing their well-being," and that his "most fervent wish is to see My people happy."[72] "The *narod* must know," he wrote to Stolypin in 1911, "that their sorrows and their joys are dear to the tsar."[73] During World War I, Nicholas described as "sickening" the thought that war brought so much suffering to the people.[74] Even at the moment of his abdication he insisted that his actions were guided by his devotion to the "good of the people" (*blago naroda*; Document 26).

The most symbolically expressive effort to evoke and confirm the unity of tsar and *narod* was the celebration of the three-hundredth anniversary of the Romanov dynasty in 1913. With enthusiasm, Nicholas retraced the journey of the first Romanov tsar, Mikhail, through the Russian heartland from Kostroma to Moscow. His reception in Moscow and especially as he traveled along the Volga, when thousands stood along the banks and waded into the river to greet him, confirmed the opinion of many traditionalists, including the imperial family, that the Russian people still adored their tsar.[75] Even Nicholas II's chairman of the Council of Ministers at that time, Vladimir Kokovtsov, who did not share these sentiments, perceived that for Nicholas these events were ideologically meaningful as enactments of the traditional myth of personal rule against modern notions of institutionalized authority: "The concepts of state and government were to be pushed into the background and the personality of the Tsar was to dominate the scene. The current attitude seemed to suggest that the government was a barrier between the people and their Tsar, whom they regarded with blind devotion as anointed by God. . . . The Tsar's closest friends at court became persuaded that the Sovereign could do anything by relying on the unbounded love and utter loyalty of the people."[76]

Their faith seemed vindicated by the enthusiastic demonstrations of popular support for war during the summer of 1914. On the day that war was declared, Nicholas and Alexandra went onto the balcony of the Winter Palace to greet the multitude filling the palace square. The emperor bowed his head to the crowd, a traditional gesture of devotion to his people, and the mass of people answered by falling to their knees and singing the national hymn, "God Save the Tsar, Strong and Mighty." The tsar and tsaritsa crossed themselves and reportedly wept.[77] This enactment of the myth of the unity of tsar and *narod* seemed to erase all memories of conflict and to confirm Nicholas's traditionalist ideological vision. He was now all the less likely to yield to demands for constitutional reform.

Popular riots, revolutionary violence, and even the destruction of his own rule did not seem to diminish Nicholas's romantic faith in the common people. As readers of the documents collected here will observe, and as those who spent time with Nicholas during his captivity often noted, sometimes with amazement, Nicholas retained and reiterated his confidence that the "good, virtuous, and kind *narod*" would soon "come to their senses" and then all would be well.[78]

Nicholas's traditionalist political vision contained a strong dose of nationalism. Like other romantic conservatives, he believed that a political and social system must emerge organically from a nation's character and history. That is why Nicholas felt great antipathy toward Peter the Great, who uncritically "admired European culture" and mistakenly "stamped out all the pure Russian customs."[79] Speaking of the direction of his own policies, Nicholas repeatedly spoke of the need for social and political structures to conform to "unique Russian principles" (*samobytnye russkie nachala*) and, generally, for loyalty to Russia's "historical foundations."[80] With a less sophisticated argument than that offered by other ideologists of autocracy, Nicholas nonetheless accurately echoed well-established traditionalist and romantic views when he asserted Russia's unique genius and spirit and its historical, cultural, and even moral distinctiveness from western Europe, a distinctiveness represented by the love and shared faith uniting people and tsar.

When political dissent challenged his traditionalist faith, as it increasingly did, Nicholas intensified the nationalism of this political myth. Authorized portrayals of his life and reign dwelled on his "Russianness"—his preference for Russian cuisine (suckling pig, *borshch, kasha,* and *bliny* were said to be his favorite dishes and *kvas* his favorite drink); his love of classical Russian literature, music, and theater; his many hours spent reading Russian history; his desire to have "Russian people" in responsible positions (people of western European ancestry were numerous in Russian state service); and generally, his "preference for all things Russian."[81] His liking for English and French romantic literature (documented in his diaries) and the predominant use of English in his conversation and correspondence with his wife were not mentioned. Nicholas's nationalism was not merely symbolic, of course; it was a key component of his political judgments and policies.

Nicholas understood loyalty and opposition in national terms. As opposition grew, and especially after the political trauma of open revolution in 1905, Nicholas was drawn to the views of those who attributed disorder to people whose national spirit, perhaps even their nationality and religion, was organically alien. Nicholas increasingly associated opposition with national—and, by extension, moral—otherness. Thus, during the Russo-Japanese War and the 1905 revolution, Nicholas insisted both publicly and privately that all "true Russian people" (*istinno-russkie liudi*) were devoted to the struggle against the enemy and loyal to the crown.[82] During World

War I he asserted that if one went outside the cosmopolitan capital cities and into the real heart of Russia, where the true Russian people lived, one would find that the people had "no doubt" about fighting to achieve complete victory. "The only two exceptions are Petrograd and Moscow—two needle-dots on the map of our country!"[83]

Nationality and morality were closely linked in Nicholas's arguments. When commenting in 1905–1906 on railroad strikes and threats of terrorism, for example, Nicholas seemed less troubled by the political threat than by the "shame" and "disgrace" such behavior brought upon Russia.[84] Similarly, during the First World War he evidently viewed opposition to the war and to the regime more with contempt than with fear. Because he viewed opposition in moral and national rather than in political terms, he saw little reason to respond to it politically.[85]

Of all the groups living permanently in the Russian Empire, Jews were most likely to be seen by nationalists as morally, spiritually, and politically un-Russian.[86] We can fairly assume that Nicholas shared the nearly universal opinion of his contemporaries that Jews bore a moral stain for their responsibility in crucifying Jesus and for their failure to accept the true Christian faith and church. From this presumed moral defect, many felt, came national and political alienness. The involvement of many Jews in revolutionary parties in Russia seemed to confirm assumptions that domestic rebellion had un-Russian origins. Nicholas apparently agreed with such views. In late October 1905 he wrote to his mother that "in the first days after the [October] manifesto bad elements strongly raised their heads, but then came a strong reaction and the whole mass of loyal people rose up. . . . The people were angered by the brazenness and insolence of the revolutionaries and the socialists, and since $\frac{9}{10}$ of them are yids, their whole fury turned against them—hence the Jewish pogroms." Nicholas believed that other moral faults also produced rebellion: "Harm befell not only the yids but also Russian agitators, engineers, lawyers, and all other bad people."[87] Looking back on these events a few months later, Nicholas reiterated his view that the revolution had been organized by outsiders—"Poles and yids"— and that whatever opposition remained by the end of 1906 was the work of "the Jewish clique [*zhidovskaia klika*], which again begins to work in order to sow disorder [*smuta*]."[88] Nicholas was always gratified when the "true Russian people" voiced their indignation against such "bad" and alien elements.[89] His refusal to remove any of the legal restrictions on the rights of Russia's Jewish population, as his Council of Ministers proposed in 1906 in order to pacify the nonrevolutionary majority of Jews, must be understood in this light.[90] For Nicholas, social order was primarily a moral problem, so political concessions to inherently "bad" people could hardly be expected to do much good.

During and after the 1917 revolution, Nicholas continued to blame spiritually alien elements for Russia's sufferings. In November 1917, as we can see from the list he attached to a letter to his sister, Nicholas was impressed by apparent evidence that behind the Russian pseudonyms of the revolutionary leaders were Jews or other non-Russians (Document 72). In March 1918, Nicholas's suspicions about Jews were reinforced by reading an edition of the infamous book by Sergei Nilus describing a supposed international Jewish-Masonic conspiracy to destroy Holy Russia. A large part of the text was the fabricated "Protocols of the Elders of Zion," which Nilus first published in Russia in 1905. "Very timely reading matter," Nicholas wrote in his diary on 27 March (9 April) 1918 (Document 110).[91]

Symbolically and sometimes literally, Nicholas expressed his political philosophy by turning away from Peter the Great's imperial capital.[92] For him, as for other traditionalists, St. Petersburg represented the new rationalistic ideal of the state and the un-Russianness that seemed to be the source of Russia's deepening crisis. Deliberately planned, geometrically arranged in lines, grids, squares, and triangles, and built in a neoclassical style that consciously opened an aesthetic window onto Europe, St. Petersburg was easily seen as the symbolic center of the new Petrine autocracy with its rationalizing, transforming, and westernizing aspirations.

Traditionalists recognized this symbolism and pointedly avowed their greater love for medieval Moscow, the historical, religious, and truly national capital—Russia's "heart," which Peter I separated from its brain when he built his new administrative center. Pobedonostsev emphasized the philosophical conflict between the two capitals when he titled the major statement of his political and religious views *Moskovskii sbornik* (Moscow collection). Nicholas, like his father, disliked Peter's capital on symbolic, moral, and political grounds: it was too Western, too decadent, and too disloyal and bureaucratic. In reaction, he tried "to bring Moscow into his own life and the life of the Petersburg court."[93] He spent as little time as possible in the Winter Palace in St. Petersburg, preferring nearby but distinctly provincial Tsarskoe Selo, where, for good measure, he had a new church, Fyodorovsky Cathedral, built in the Muscovite style, rather than in the Petrine or Catherinian styles that typified church architecture in and around St. Petersburg. He devoted a portion of his leisure to reading accounts of early Russian history and even studied old documents.[94] In 1903, Nicholas even ordered that a great ball be held in the Winter Palace at which all guests were to wear Muscovite costume (Nicholas dressed, appropriately, as Tsar Aleksei). Nicholas was so pleased with this symbolic performance that he reportedly considered making seventeenth-century dress mandatory at court.[95] At the start of World War I, Nicholas took another symbolic step in russifying St. Petersburg—changing its name from the European-sounding Sankt Peterburg to the Slavic Petrograd. The renaming, usually seen as simply a patriotic step occasioned by war with Germany, must also be understood as a symbolic and ideological gesture, a continuation of the traditionalist hostility toward the capital as an emblem of Petrine Westernism.

Beyond bringing Moscow into St. Petersburg, Nicholas brought the court more often to Moscow. He initiated an annual Easter pilgrimage to Moscow, which he represented as a symbolic return of the tsar to the sacred center of Holy Russia: here the tsar could enter into communion with the *narod,* "with the true children of our beloved Church, pouring into the temples . . . [and,] in the unity in prayer with My people, draw new strength for serving Russia." Nicholas claimed to feel "more at home in Moscow, peaceful and confident."[96]

Nicholas's philosophical and political traditionalism was a source of reassuring strength and hope at a time of national change and crisis. But it was also a source of uncertainty, for the traditionalist ideal of the tsar's power as sacred, moral, and personal—the ideal that Nicholas sought to realize and with which he resisted efforts to rationalize and institutionalize his authority—was itself a fractured image. The tsar was imagined as both awesome in power and might—*groznyi*, the epithet given to Ivan the Terrible—and pious, saintly, gentle (*tishaishii*), as Aleksei had been called. Nicholas was conscious of this divided tradition, acknowledging that he ought to be, by right and necessity, both *groznyi* and *tishaishii*. But his personality, instincts, and values—and perhaps his recognition of the need to legitimize his besieged authority—led him to emphasize the image of the saintly tsar.

Nicholas's personal struggle to reconcile these two roles can be seen in his own statements and writings, especially during times of crisis. In the wake of the revolution of 1905, Nicholas was quite ready to have opponents of the autocracy arrested, beaten, exiled, and hanged—which earned him the epithet Nicholas the Bloody among revolutionaries. His letters to his mother during 1905–1907 ring with an unflinching determination to use force against opponents. Hearing of unrest in Siberia in 1906, for example, he thought it an "excellent idea" to send "troops, gendarmes, and machine gunners" to "restore order at [railroad] stations and in the cities, seizing all rebels and punishing them without hesitating to be severe."[97] Nicholas's willingness for blood to be shed was sustained by his faith, already described, that his enemies were not "true Russians" or "good" people.[98] On the very eve of revolution at the end of 1916, he continued to believe that the major cause of social turmoil was that "the ministers are as weak as usual"[99] and, for his own part, promised to be "firm," "sharp and biting," even "cutting and disagreeable."[100] Even after his abdication, Nicholas still insisted that Russia's salvation lay in "discipline" and "order" (Document 56 [25 July 1917]).

Nicholas often revealed his discomfort with this harsh aspect of the tradition of the Russian tsar, however. Even in private, as I have mentioned, he liked to speak of his compassion for the common people and his anguish over the sufferings caused by the war. Although he certainly expressed no sympathy for the sufferings that he caused his enemies, he regretted that such methods had to be used. Repression was needed, he told his mother in 1905, but its effects were "sad and painful."[101] Similarly, for all his distrust of Jews and sympathy for the motives of those who perpetrated pogroms, he pointedly reminded representatives of the Union of Russian People and other right-wing organizations that "it is a great sin" to "kindle angry passions and mutual enmity."[102]

The empress Alexandra constantly appealed to Nicholas to act the part of the *groznyi* tsar. In the early years of his reign, she was already urging him to be both "friendly and severe" in dealing with people so that the person he was addressing "realizes he dare not joke with you—that is the *Chief* thing."[103] During the crisis of the world war, she begged Nicholas to demonstrate his "power of will & decisiveness," to show that he is "the *Samoderzh.* [autocrat] without wh. Russia cannot exist."[104] But Alexandra also saw that Nicholas hesitated to assume the mantle of the *groznyi* tsar even when fighting for the survival of his regime. She recognized his "marvelously gentle character," his "angelic kindness, forgiveness & patience," his need to be "more selfsure."[105] She appealed to him to overcome these saintly weaknesses: "Ah my Love, when *at last* will you thump with your hand upon the table & scream at Dzhunk. [Dzhunkovsky] & others when they act wrongly—one does not fear you—& one *must.* . . . Oh, my Boy, make one tremble before you—to love you is not enough." And, "Show to *all,* that you are the *Master* & *your* will *shall* be obeyed—the time of great indulgence & gentleness is over—now comes yr. reign of will & power, & they shall be *made* to *bow down* before you and listen to yr. orders. . . . You have spoiled them by yr. kindness & allforgivingness." And again, "Be Peter the G., John [Ivan] the Terrible, Emp. Paul—crush them all under you—now dont you laugh, naughty one."[106]

Nicholas's response to this political pleading was sometimes appreciative and grateful (on at least one occasion, he even kept Alexandra's written instructions on questions to ask in front of him during a meeting with his minister of internal affairs),[107] but very often he gently demurred. "What you write about being firm—the master—is perfectly true. I do not forget it—be sure of that, but I need not bellow at the people right & left every moment. A quiet sharp remark or answer is enough very often to put the one or the other into his place" (Document 2). Most often, he was simply silent before her appeals, ignoring them, as he ignored so much advice directed at him, or dismissing them with gentle irony. "Loving thanks for your strong reprimanding letter. I read it with a smile because you speak like to a child," "ever your very own poor little huzy with a tiny will."[108] Irony notwithstanding, Nicholas was unwilling to appear to his people as a *groznyi* tsar. Thus, even when he decided in December 1916 to close down the Duma, he was determined that someone else, the chairman of the Council of Ministers, should do the "dirty business," so that "all the responsibility & difficulty fall on his shoulders."[109] Nicholas's reluctance to be Peter the Great, Ivan the Terrible, Emperor Paul reflected not so much his weakness as the strength of his self-identification with— or at least his desire to be seen as—the mythic ideal of the gentle, *tishaishii* tsar, of the tsar as "saint."

As this dialogue about power suggests, Alexandra Fyodorovna brought her own ideas and values to Russia's ruling house. The stereotypical image of Alexandra as the "German tsaritsa," which was widespread in Russia on the eve of the revolution and afterward, reveals more about popular national and political attitudes than about Alexandra herself. Alexandra's Germanness was slight even before she left her native Germany to marry the heir to the Russian throne. In upbringing and education, she was more English than German. And although she was born in Germany, it would be more accurate to describe her national origin and identity as Hessian. She was born Princess Alix of Hesse-Darmstadt, on 6 June 1872 (25 May on the Russian calendar) in a Germany that had been united only the previous year. Her own small grand duchy of Hesse-Darmstadt entered the new empire with considerable hostility toward the dominant Prussia. During the Austro-Prussian War in 1866, Hesse-Darmstadt had sided with Austria. In retaliation, the victorious Prussia had annexed a sizable slice of Hessian territory. That Alexandra long retained a self-conscious identity as Hessian and, with it, an enmity toward Prussia was especially evident during World War I. In conversations and letters she identified the enemy as Prussia rather than Germany. When the war began, she blamed its outbreak on the "idiotic pride and insatiable ambition" of the Hohenzollerns. She declared bluntly that "Prussia has meant Germany's ruin," both by starting the war and, more generally, by degrading Germany morally: Prussia had instilled in Germans "feelings of hatred and revenge which are quite foreign to their nature."[110] As the war continued, Alexandra portrayed small German states as victims in the conflict and blamed "Prussian troops" for outrages committed by soldiers.[111]

Alexandra's alienation from the German Empire was due not only to her identity and experiences as a Hessian princess but also to her rather British upbringing and education. Alexandra's mother, Queen Victoria's second daughter, Princess Alice, brought a pervasively English spirit to her new household after she married Prince Louis of Hesse. A new palace was built in the English style with English decorations and gardens. An English governess, Mary Anne Orchard, was brought to Hesse to help Alice raise her children (the governess would later go to Russia to care for Alexandra's children). Visits to England were a regular part of Alexandra's childhood. After 1878, when Alice died of diphtheria and Queen Victoria took charge of supervising the children's education—even demanding written reports from each of the tutors—Alix and the other children visited England more often and for longer periods than before.[112]

After her marriage to Nicholas—for which she had to convert to Russian Orthodoxy and be rechristened with a Russian name—and after many years in Russia, English culture was still a vital part of Alexandra's life and thus of the life of the Russian imperial family. Although Alexandra knew German well (indeed, she criticized Russian wartime propaganda for its "abominable" German grammar)[113] and learned adequate Russian, her everyday tongue was English. Nicholas and Alexandra wrote and usually spoke to one another in English (and addressed their children in both English and Russian).[114] Alexandra also corresponded and spoke with her closest friends, Anna Vyrubova and Sofia Buksgevden, mostly in English. The family often read English literature together, sometimes aloud, and performed English (as well as French) plays for entertainment. During the world war and in captivity, as letters and diaries attest, she and Nicholas both found great pleasure in reading (and sometimes rereading) English novels. Her memories, sentiments, and aesthetic tastes, like her mother's, were intensely English. Alexandra Fyodorovna might well have been called the English empress rather than the German tsaritsa. But this simple label does little to convey Alexandra's complex intellectual, moral, and spiritual self.

Somewhat closer to the mark was Aleksandr Kireev's observation in 1904 that Alexandra was a practical Englishwoman on the surface and a mystical Russian underneath (though her mysticism was more cosmopolitan and universalizing than the nationalist Kireev appreciated).[115] Alexandra's practical Englishness may be seen, for example, in her devotion to orderly routines (in keeping with what she had been taught in Mary Anne Orchard's nursery and in keeping, too, with her husband's inclinations, the family's activities always followed a precise schedule), in her involvement in charitable work (like her mother, Alexandra was active in promoting hospitals in particular), and, especially, in her intense work ethic.

Alexandra feared and despised idleness. She shared her mother's belief that "life is meant for work and not for pleasure."[116] According to her friend Anna Vyrubova, she hated to see her daughters sitting around "with idle hands" and encouraged them to occupy themselves with needlework and embroidery, charitable work, reading, and correspondence. Alexandra herself kept constantly busy. Soon after coming to Russia, she unsuccessfully tried to establish a society of women from court and aristocratic circles who would with their own hands make three garments a year to give to the poor.[117] She valued work as a moral principle but also as a personal comfort. Troubled by the suffering caused by the world war, Alexandra declared that "work is the only remedy."[118] She threw herself into hospital work (joined by her older daughters, Olga and Tatiana, and by Anna Vyrubova) and even trained as a nurse so that she might not only comfort the wounded but assist in operations and treatment.[119] "I think I never saw her happier," Vyrubova remarked about the day Alexandra received the diploma of a certified war nurse.[120]

Viewing Russian high society through this moralistic lens, Alexandra judged her surroundings to be intolerably decadent. She made every effort to keep her family, particularly her daughters, isolated from the "idle and listless" lives, the "foolish and often vicious gossip," and the "unwholesomely precocious . . . outlook on life" that she saw among Russian aristocrats and even among many members of the House of Romanov.[121] She frequently told Nicholas of her dismay at the pervasive "dirt" in the personal lives of upper-class Russians, including Nicholas's own cousins and brothers: "Oh these young men of the family with bad health & love of pleasure instead of duty!"[122] Alexandra's disdain for high society, in turn, encouraged the Russian elite's perception of her as haughty and cold. As this perception spread to the larger Russian population and evolved into an image of Alexandra as alien and even treasonous, it did much to undermine the personal prestige and authority of the tsar and his family.

Among all of Alexandra's practical occupations, nursing was doubtless the most emotionally laden and may help us better to understand her. Alexandra was drawn to nursing not only by her ethic of practical work and her family tradition of charity but also by a sensitivity and even attraction to suffering. Alexandra's closest friends noted this trait as central to her psychological makeup: "Sickness and suffering were always sure keys to the Empress's heart"; "suffering always made a strong appeal to the Empress."[123] In the eyes of her friends and in her self-description, Alexandra was "motherly" and a "born nurse."[124] This inclination was intensified by her son's hemophilia, which frequently caused him excruciating pain, and her own ill health. Alexandra devoted much of her life to nursing people in pain: her children and her friends during their illnesses (such as the measles that afflicted much of the royal household during the February Revolution); her often-bedridden son; Anna Vyrubova, who was nearly killed in a train crash (Alexandra's friendship with Vyrubova, the daughter of the head of Nicholas's private chancellery, began when Vyrubova was dangerously ill with typhoid); and the wounded during the war. In her wartime letters, Alexandra regularly expressed sympathy for suffering soldiers on both sides, especially for the wounded men whom she treated. It gratified her, for it suited her self-image, when the bishop of Kovno, modifying the Russian word for nurse (*sestra miloserdiia*, "sister of mercy"), called her a "mother of mercy."[125]

If Alexandra's preoccupation with suffering was emotional and personal, it was also religious and moral and thus integral to the way she evaluated and responded to her world. In part, she believed that suffering reminded people to turn to God: "When I get hold of people alone who I know suffer much," she wrote to Nicholas in

1914 about her efforts to encourage soldiers to take Holy Communion, "I always touch this subject . . . making them understand that it is a possible and good thing to do & it brings relief and peace."[126] But she also viewed suffering itself as sacred and redemptive. Looking around at the "lowness of humanity—Sodom and Gomorrah, verily," she hoped that the suffering caused by the war might transform people.[127] Indeed, she tended to view the war as a holy war—not because of its military or political aims but because of the catharsis it brought: a "healthy" experience that awakened people's positive feelings and values.[128]

In her view, the revolution also brought virtue through suffering. During February and early March 1917, Alexandra assured Nicholas that God would reward him for his anguish and humiliation (Documents 1, 31, 34). When she and her family were confined and forcibly relocated, these themes became more pronounced. Suffering, she wrote, bound the souls of sufferers together, allowed them to "gaze a little into yonder world," and would be "valued" and "rewarded" by God, just as he cherished and recompensed Job (Documents 52, 57, and 83). To suffer patiently, like Job (on whose Holy Day Nicholas was born) and like so many Russian saints—to accept suffering as God's will and to wait for God's reward—was the highest virtue. Alexandra encouraged all around her, including Nicholas, to emulate this model. For her, as for Nicholas, fatalism was a moral and existential precept, a sacrament. "Life is difficult to understand—'*tak i nado—poterpi* [so it must be, have patience]'—thats all one can say."[129] As here, Alexandra and Nicholas often interjected Russian words or phrases into their English letters when expressing an idea that seemed somehow culturally Russian.

It is difficult to separate Alexandra's personality from her philosophical and political attitudes. Unlike Nicholas, who by all accounts was controlled in his emotions and laconic in speech and writing, Alexandra was effusive and even ecstatic. She was the first to acknowledge her emotional and verbal expansiveness (and Nicholas's frustrating, but also calming, self-restraint): "I cant put all in three words, I need heaps of pages to pour all out"; "God gave me such a heart, wh. fills up my whole being."[130] Every corner of her life seemed to be touched by this intense emotional spirit—her friendships, her love for Nicholas, her care for her children, her judgments about people, her sensitivity to suffering, her devotion to Russia's autocratic political traditions, her faith in God.

It was religious faith that gave direction to her feelings and, in turn, gave meaning to experiences and answers to questions. When she was a young woman, Alexandra was a devout Lutheran, like her mother. Unlike many other European princesses required to change religious affiliation for the purposes of dynastic marriage, she agonized over the requirement that she convert to Orthodoxy. Having only recently been confirmed, she considered conversion hypocritical. Long, heartrending discussions with relatives could not convince her to convert. Nicholas's effort—a "very difficult conversation," lasting more than two hours, he wrote to his mother—was received with tears, punctuated from time to time with a whispered "no, I cannot." After several days of discussions and inner struggle, she capitulated. One argument that may have helped was made by Alexandra's sister Ella, who herself had voluntarily converted in order to marry Nicholas's uncle Sergei. Ella suggested that Orthodoxy was really not so different in its Christian essence.[131]

Once Alexandra agreed to convert, she brought the same emotional intensity to Orthodoxy that she had devoted to Lutheranism. Indeed, the struggle over conversion, the challenges of her new life, and her love for Nicholas combined to enhance the ardor of her religious life. Alexandra became passionate and devout in Orthodox practice; she prayed and went to church daily, venerated saints and their relics, and nurtured a strong faith in the healing power of icons. Her letters, including those in this collection, abundantly testify to the power and centrality of religion in her life. But no less evident is the shape of Alexandra's faith—its particular emotional, cultural, and theological construction.

The echoes of Lutheran pietism persisted in Alexandra's religious sensibilities long after her conversion: the individual's relationship to God, personal responsibility for sin and goodness, the striving for moral self-perfection, the need to practice scriptural values in daily life, and the inclination to view Christian belief as grounded not in theology or ethical philosophy but in the heart. Her attitudes reflected the influence of Western pietism, but they may also have reflected the larger religious ferment under way in Russia (as in western Europe). More and more Russians, especially among the educated (particularly in St. Petersburg), were "seeking God," as contemporaries often described it—not only in Orthodoxy but also through mysticism, the occult, theosophy, spiritualism, Eastern philosophies, the exaltation of the unconscious and the mythic, and various forms of popular spirituality.[132] Although Alexandra was disdainful of the "spiritualism, table-tipping, or alleged materializations from the world beyond" that attracted many,[133] she shared with the many other Russian God-seekers of her time an inclination toward mysticism and wide-ranging spiritual exploration.

Alexandra's religiosity was as ecumenical as it was intense. According to Anna Vyrubova, "Both the Emperor and the Empress were profoundly interested in the religious life and expressions of the whole human race. They read with sympathy and understanding the religious literature not only of Christendom but of India, Persia, and the countries of the Far East."[134] Alexandra sometimes sought spiritual guidance and help from unorthodox mystics and healers, like the French mystic Philippe Nizier-Vachod, Alexandra and Nicholas's first "dear Friend," and Rasputin. Although Rasputin's influence has commonly been attributed to his apparent ability to relieve Aleksei's hemophiliac sufferings and to his promise that the boy would be healed, Philippe was brought into the palace in 1902, before Aleksei was born. The presence of Philippe at Tsarskoe Selo gave fresh encouragement to Alexandra's developing spirituality: "How unbearable all would be without Him," she wrote to Nicholas in 1902; "how life has changed since we know him."[135]

In later years Alexandra appropriately chose the swastika as her personal "sign" (Document 83). A symbolic talisman promising "well-being" (the literal meaning of the Sanskrit word *svastika*), the swastika once pervaded Indo-European culture. Alexandra drew swastikas in her letters, painted them on cards, embroidered them on fabrics, and, in 1918, inscribed them on the jamb of a window and on a wall when arriving in the house in Yekaterinburg where she would be killed.[136] According to her friend Lili Den, Alexandra saw in the swastika a universal symbol of divinity.[137] Universality was certainly part of its appeal. Although she drew the swastika with its arms turned in either direction, she most often chose not the right-facing (clockwise) swastika, the crux gammata—which is usually found in early and medieval Christian art, tombs, and vestments—but the left-facing swastika typically used by Buddhists, Hindus, and Jainas in India.

The swastika was only one sacred symbol among many. Alexandra also drew crucifixes in her letters and, wherever she lived or traveled, surrounded herself and her family with icons and other Christian images. She accepted the Orthodox faith in icons as sacred means through which God, Christ, the Virgin, and the saints can heal and help people. She regularly attended church services and took communion, venerated and sought the aid of certain icons, and, whenever she could, visited Orthodox holy places and holy men. Even when sailing on the imperial yacht, the *Shtandart,* Alexandra—together with her daughters and Anna Vyrubova—sometimes sang hymns.[138] The emotionalism and mysticism of Orthodoxy appealed to Alexandra and stimulated her personal inclinations. She found especially attractive, no doubt, the Orthodox reverence for suffering as an experience that enriches the spirit, testifies to one's devotion and faith, and brings one closer to Christ and his Passion.

Alexandra's emotional epistemology was not confined to religion. Like Nicholas but even more intensely, she saw knowledge and truth residing not in cold reason but in the instincts of the heart. In her letters to Nicholas, she often drew the distinction between brain and soul, making it clear that having "strong feeling" was more important than having wit or reason.[139] Besides shaping her judgments on religion—"our Church needs . . . soul & not brain,"[140] this epistemology also framed her approach to politics. Alexandra constantly urged Nicholas to be guided by his "instinct" and "soul" and assured him that her own political advice, which God wished her to give, was wiser than that of most of Nicholas's advisers because her "feeling" was strong.[141] This feeling, Alexandra believed, was God's voice. She was certain, too, that when Nicholas listened to his soul, he was hearing God speaking to his anointed tsar: "God will inspire you with the right words"; "you were inspired from above to give that order."[142]

Rasputin encouraged this romantic, instinctive way of reasoning, as Alexandra often mentioned in her letters. And his presence and influence at court reflected Alexandra's (and Nicholas's) certitude that this uneducated and almost wholly illiterate man was close to God and hence to truth precisely because of his charismatic spirituality. Again and again Alexandra told Nicholas that "God has given [Rasputin] more insight, wisdom & enlightenment" than all of the tsar's advisers and experts.[143] Under the circumstances of war and approaching revolution, Alexandra's rejection of formal knowledge and rationality was hazardous, especially because it encouraged Nicholas's own tendency to rely on a divine inner voice and to disregard reasoned political appeals from many educated Russians and from many of his own counselors and ministers.

Alexandra's instincts, like Nicholas's, conveyed a specific political message (which Rasputin reassured them was God's wisdom): constitutional reform was unnecessary and dangerous. This political certainty was moralistic and absolutist in tone and logic—like Nicholas, she constantly condemned critics of the tsarist regime as "bad" and "false" people—and it was politically aggressive. I have already noted Alexandra's appeals to Nicholas to be more authoritarian and repressive, to "crush" his opponents in the tradition of *groznyi* tsars like Peter the Great and Ivan the Terrible. During the war Alexandra voiced her "hatred" of members of Nicholas's government who were not absolutely loyal—especially those on "the left," by whom she meant not the revolutionaries of the socialist parties (she seems to have barely noticed them before 1918) but the liberals in the Duma and in influential civic organizations like the Union of Zemstvos and even the Union of the Nobility (whom she judged to be "vile, utterly revolutionary").[144] Toward the end of 1916 she advised "war" against the Duma and urged Nicholas to shut down the legislature, treat all opposition as "high treason," and send the Duma leaders Georgy Lvov, Pavel Miliukov, and Aleksandr Guchkov "to Siberia."[145] She even proposed, half in jest perhaps, that Nicholas's enemies be summarily executed: "Guchkov needs to be on a high tree"; "I could hang Tr. [Aleksandr Trepov, chairman of the Council of Ministers] for his bad consels." She acknowledged ruefully that Nicholas did not always see things this way.[146]

Like Nicholas, Alexandra was certain that ordinary Russians, the *narod*, loved and trusted their tsar. Even more bitterly than Nicholas, she contrasted the decadent and disloyal upper classes (whom she knew best) with the decent and loyal masses (whom she knew not at all). "The future of Russia lay, she thought, with the peasants—with the classes that were still untainted by the poison of civilization."[147] Like Nicholas, she was convinced that the capital was not characteristic of the country as a whole. Thus, in 1905, she wrote to her eldest sister, Victoria, princess of Battenberg, that "Petersburg is a rotten town, not an atom Russian. The Russian people are deeply and truly devoted to their Sovereign."[148] She retained this conviction to the very eve of the 1917 revolution: "All true Russians" see a constitution as "Russia's ruin."[149] Symptomatically, of all the many civic organizations that had emerged in Russia over the years, Alexandra viewed the reactionary and marginal Union of the Russian People—widely known as the Black Hundreds—as the true voice of "healthy, rightthinking" Russians.[150]

Alexandra's notion of political true Russianness, which encouraged and justified her opposition to constitutional reform, reflected not only her acceptance of Nicholas's traditionalist and romantic image of a special relationship between tsar and *narod* but also a particular cultural stereotype about Russians. "How long, years, people have told me the same—'Russia loves to feel [the] whip'—its their nature—tender love & then the iron hand to punish & guide."[151] In the very midst of revolution, she warned that Russians were not fit for constitutional democracy. "How many have told me—[']we want to feel the whip'—its strange, but such is the Slave [Slav] nature" (Document 1).

This condescending judgment was not meant as contempt. "I love my new country," she wrote to her sister Victoria in 1905. "It's so young, powerful, and has so much good in it, only utterly unbalanced and childlike."[152] She said much the same in letters in 1917 and 1918. Alexandra's maternal relationship with people, including her friends and husband, extended to Russia as a nation. She found it impossible to believe that Russia might have outgrown such controlling solicitude. Her views echoed and reinforced Nicholas II's own perceptions of the Russian people as simple, devoted, and "childish."[153] As this simple political idea was challenged by the events of 1917–1918, Alexandra and Nicholas held all the more tightly to their larger existential faith that God would set things right. Nicholas would never have abdicated if he had thought that the outcome of events depended on him alone.

If one must speak of tragedy in the fate of Nicholas and Alexandra, the usual story of a weak and warmhearted tsar and his innocent family falling victim to cruel revolutionaries is too simplistic and morally stark. The fall of the Romanovs is also a story of moral contradiction and fatal certainties. Blind faith in an ideology that had long outlived its vitality and plausibility fell beneath the feet of men and women proclaiming a new faith in the Communist myth of universal freedom and justice arising from class struggle. The false promises (and premises) of this new ideology were still to be discovered.

ᕔ 1 ᕗ

Revolution

ELL before the revolutionary upheavals of 1917, the democratic challenge to traditional structures of power in Russia worried Russian conservatives, among them Nicholas II. At the very beginning of his reign, Nicholas acknowledged the growth in Russian society of "senseless dreams of participation . . . in matters of internal administration."[1] Inspiring these dreams were powerful and dangerous ideas about inalienable rights and the moral and political necessity of civil liberty. Since the late eighteenth century, liberal ideas of the European Enlightenment had increasingly found a place in the thinking of Russia's educated elite, including many state officials. As the number and social influence of the educated grew—especially as economic development in the late nineteenth and early twentieth centuries fostered the development of a professional and commercial middle class—views about the need for civil liberties and public representation also spread.[2]

Even more troubling to the guardians of the traditional order, the poor also began to make use of the language of democratic rights and equality. Worse still, they often wove together demands for political inclusion with expectations of social justice and equality.[3] The peasants' dream of possessing all the land—necessary, they believed, to remedy their poverty and deserved because they were the ones who worked the land—had always touched on politics: the land would be theirs, peasants said, when a just ruler proclaimed to the peasant majority that they should take back from the rich landowners what rightfully belonged to them. Similarly, when industrial workers (most of them peasants in origin and many retaining village ties) spoke of freedom and democracy, they typically understood these ideas not only as means of ensuring civil liberties and political representation but also as means of remedying poverty and ending harsh and humiliating treatment by those in authority. Government labor policies, which combined paternalistic efforts to ameliorate the lot of the poor with firm measures for maintaining order and control, tended, for their part, to encourage workers to see the state, and thus politics, as the key to economic and social change.

For lower-class discontent to erupt into open protest, however, peasants and workers needed to see their sufferings not as the inevitable lot of the poor but as correctable wrongs. They needed moral notions of social right and standards of justice and a belief that alternatives existed. In the decades preceding the revolution, such ideas were increasingly in evidence in the thinking of lower-class Russians. Growing literacy and a burgeoning popular press and literature were particularly potent influences. Journals, newspapers, pamphlets, and books did much to spread ideas about universal rights, the natural equality of all human beings, and the mutability of every political order. More subtle but no less subversive, the very act of reading and becoming more "cultured" gave many commoners a sense of self-esteem that made the ordinary humiliations and hardships of lower-class life harder to endure.

Popular discontent was about more than justice, democracy, and rights. It was also an expression of anger and resentment. Once aroused to open protest, as in 1905–1906 and 1917–1918, many lower-class Russians showed not only a desire to be treated as social and political equals—"as human beings," they liked to say—but also a desire to punish and humiliate, even to dehumanize, those who stood above them and whom they blamed for their sufferings. In this spirit, workers put foremen or employers into wheelbarrows, dumped trash on their heads, and rolled them out of shops and into the street or, less ceremoniously, beat them, occasionally to death.

Peasants broke into the mansions of the gentry, smashed belongings, and burned what remained. Poverty had bred dreams of revenge and reversal as well as justice.[4] Nicholas and Alexandra and their children—living symbols of the old order—would feel the coarse edge of these feelings. They neither expected nor understood this plebeian rage.

During Nicholas II's reign, organized opposition to the autocracy was fragmented into dozens of legal and illegal parties and groups, many of which would play parts in the upheaval of 1917–1918 and in the fate of the tsar and his family. On the left stood varieties of socialists. Populist socialism, the oldest radical tradition, was organized in the prewar years by the Socialist Revolutionary (SR) Party and represented in the Duma, or legislature, by the Trudovik (Laborist) faction. Populists viewed the whole *narod*, the common people, as their constituency, and socialism as an order based on the ethical values of community and liberty. Marxists, who became numerous and influential, were organized mainly around the Russian Social-Democratic Workers' Party (RSDRP). They believed that they possessed a more "scientific" and rationalistic ideology than the populists. For them, socialism was historically destined to succeed capitalism as a more rational and progressive order, and the industrial proletariat was the class whose interests and struggles would bring the new order into being.

In real political life, socialists were divided far more intricately than these general descriptions of their dogmas reveal. Populists differed among themselves over such issues as the use of terror, the importance of peasant communalism, and the formation of an alliance, if any, with liberals. Marxists differed among themselves—often with rancor—over questions of organization (for example, how centralized and authoritarian the party should be), tactics (whether workers should ally with other classes), strategy (whether Russia was ready for socialism), and philosophy (how important ethics and revolutionary faith were compared with scientific reason). Many of these disagreements among Marxists led to the split in the Russian Social-Democratic Workers' Party between Mensheviks and Bolsheviks in 1903. But even these two groups were divided into factions, and many intermediary groupings stood between them.[5]

The liberal opposition was also a formidable but divided force.[6] In the years after the 1905 revolution, the Octobrist Party—formally, the Union of 17 October—represented the moderate wing of organized liberalism. Established by liberals who accepted as sufficient the limited political concessions that Nicholas II offered in his manifesto of 17 October 1905, Octobrists generally cooperated with the tsar's government. On the eve of World War I, however, even the Octobrists were at odds with Nicholas's policies, and they could often be heard criticizing the government in the Duma, where they formed the largest single bloc of deputies. This shift toward the opposition provoked a split among Octobrist deputies. Conservatives, led by Mikhail Rodzianko, challenged the more liberal leadership of Aleksandr Guchkov, as a result of which Rodzianko replaced Guchkov as Duma chairman. But by the end of 1916, even Rodzianko was turning against Nicholas II and his government.[7]

To the left of the Octobrist Party was the Constitutional Democratic Party, typically abbreviated to Kadet Party, but sometimes known by its formal name, the Party of the People's Freedom. The party leader was a Moscow history professor, Pavel Miliukov. The Kadets viewed the semi-constitutional order created after the 1905 revolution as unfinished and inadequate. Though not opposed in principle to a monarchical system, the Kadets insisted that a government should be responsible to a democratic parliament. Instead of the current system, which gave the tsar unlimited authority to appoint and dismiss ministers, they sought a political structure in which ministers were subject to parliamentary approval. And instead of the existing electoral law, which gave different social groups unequal electoral weight in selecting deputies to the Duma, they called for universal, direct, equal, and secret suffrage.

The Kadets also sought social reforms to improve the lives of ordinary Russians. The product of more than social conscience or political maneuvering, their social concern was essential to their political idealism. Unlike most Octobrists, who were especially solicitous of the needs of landowners, or the Progressists, members of another liberal party, who spoke for the interests of large-scale industry and finance, and certainly unlike the socialists, who represented labor, the Kadets refused to represent the interests of any one class. They insisted that they were "above class" and even "above party." This ideal may have been partly self-delusion, but it also reflected their ideas about government and nation. Although Kadets were devoted to the liberal idea of individual rights, they saw a nation as founded on free social community and patriotic solidarity, with unity overshadowing both individual and class, and they saw the democratic state as properly acting in this civic spirit.[8] These assumptions would have great political consequence. They nurtured noble political dreams and practical political courage. But they also bred an intolerance of—even an inability to understand—the class anger and class struggles that were so pervasive in Russia.

The outbreak of the world war temporarily quieted political and social protest, focusing resentment on an external enemy.[9] But the fragile patriotic unity did not last long. As the war dragged on, it exacerbated most of the problems in Russian life. The economy strained to keep up in a war that mobilized an unprecedented amount of human and material resources. Shortages of all sorts became epidemic—military equipment and supplies, fuel and raw materials for factories, food for the cities and for the troops—and prices soared. At the front, the army performed poorly and soldiers suffered from shortages of necessities ranging from boots and food to guns and shells. Carnage at the front and economic hardship in the rear helped revive and intensify civic protest.

At the very start of the war, liberals appealed to the tsar to establish a "government of national confidence." In line with their traditions, they also organized public voluntary associations to aid the war effort. In July 1914 (according to the Russian calendar, war was declared on 19 July), Duma members established a Provisional Committee for the Relief of Wounded and Sick Soldiers (under the leadership of Rodzianko). At the same time and for the same purpose, urban and rural councils of local administration, in which liberal professionals played a very large role, organized the All-Russian Union of Zemstvos and the All-Russian Union of Town Councils. In 1915 these unions merged to form the All-Russian Union of Zemstvos and Town Councils (known by the abbreviation Zemgor), headed by a Progressist, Prince Georgy Lvov. Also organized in 1915, to coordinate military production, was the Central

Military-Industrial Committee, which had branches in many cities and included representatives of business, labor, government, and the professions. It was chaired by the Octobrist leader, Guchkov.

These associations, which the government encouraged, were important sources of organizational experience and strength for liberals, but they also signified something deeper and more consequential: the development of organized civic involvement in public affairs. The autocracy's dismissive disregard of this emergent civil society was a major reason that the old regime was swept away by revolution in February 1917. Not coincidentally, many leaders of these civic organizations would soon take their places in the first post-Romanov government.

During the summer of 1915 a Progressive Bloc of Duma deputies formed, uniting Kadets, Octobrists, Progressists, Progressive Nationalists, and other liberal groups. Representing a large majority of Duma deputies, the bloc demanded a cabinet of ministers that would enjoy "the confidence of the public"—a moderate demand, given that many liberals were already calling for a "responsible" cabinet. In reply, the Council of Ministers, aware of the need for concessions, expressed willingness to work out a compromise. But Nicholas II was determined not to make the same mistake that he had made in 1905, when he had submitted to the advice of some of his ministers and agreed to establish a Duma. Instead, he ordered the Duma prorogued. When this decision was reported to the Council of Ministers, at a meeting on 2 September 1915, the foreign minister, Sergei Sazonov, said that he feared political upheaval: "Tomorrow blood will flow in the streets, and Russia will plunge into the abyss!"[10] Although his prediction was premature, it is plausible to argue that had Nicholas II conceded to the moderate demands of the Duma majority—and accepted the advice of his own ministers—the coming revolution might have been avoided or at least its fury might have been abated.

Against this background of social change, rising political discontent, autocratic immobility, and national crisis, the manifestation of autocratic willfulness that contemporaries dubbed "ministerial leapfrog"—the appointment and firing of ministers in rapid succession—seemed particularly outrageous. The tsar's absolute power to appoint ministers was the most conspicuous limitation of the Duma's authority. Insult was added to injury during the world war, especially after the tsar went to the front as commander in chief, when the power to appoint the government seemed to fall into the hands of the "German" empress, Alexandra, and her "dissolute" holy man, Rasputin. The description by a leading historian of Russia accurately echoes the opinion of many contemporaries: "A narrow-minded, reactionary, hysterical woman and an ignorant, weird peasant . . . had the destinies of an empire in their hands."[11] The abysmal quality of the appointments—rumors were rife that Interior Minister Aleksandr Protopopov was demented from advanced syphilis—made the political unaccountability of the ministers all the more grating.

Meanwhile, worsening economic conditions and growing popular frustration with the war provoked more strikes and provided fertile ground for the arguments of socialist activists. Nicholas and Alexandra's letters suggest only a slight awakening to the seriousness of public discontent and a persistent tendency to trivialize its causes. By the fall of 1916, Nicholas briefly recognized the political dangers inherent in the fact that "the people are beginning to starve."[12] Throughout these final months of the old regime, government officials, notably those responsible for public order (especially the secret security police), repeatedly warned that economic hardship—shortfalls in fuel and raw materials, which idled thousands of workers; increasing prices, which pushed the poor to the brink of starvation; and bread and other food shortages—were fostering a dangerous public mood.[13]

By the beginning of 1917, reports from police agents—who lived and worked among various classes of the population and whose reports were regularly summarized for higher officials—abundantly described the popular threat to social and political order: meetings in and around factories at which speakers complained about high prices and the persistent shortage of bread, about the war, and about the lack of a democratic government; demands for, and work stoppages in support of, higher wages and direct provision of bread; factories shutting down when workers declared that they were too hungry to work and needed to search for food; the dissemination of subversive leaflets and proclamations by an astonishing variety of parties, unions, and committees; street demonstrations, complete with red flags and revolutionary songs and banners; scattered violence against police and cossacks; assaults on businesses, especially food shops; and the appearance of guns and other weapons in workers' hands. Also reported were numerous muggings, robberies, suicides, and fires. Agents employed to keep under surveillance "the progressively inclined and oppositional segment of the capital's society" similarly reported, in January 1917, "a wave of animosity against those in authority in wide circles of the population." Among the working-class women who stood out in the cold on the lengthening bread lines in Petrograd, the mood was especially tense. According to a February report by an agent of the Petrograd Okhrana, "These mothers, exhausted from standing endlessly in lines and having suffered so much in watching their half-starving and sick children, are perhaps much closer to a revolution than Messrs. Miliukov, Rodichev, and Co. [leaders of the Kadet Party], and of course they are much more dangerous."[14]

Conservatives and liberals alike sought to halt the approach of revolution by forcing reform. As Alexandra angrily noted in her letters to Nicholas, liberal attacks on the government in both the Duma and the press grew more impassioned and hostile. Talk of a palace coup became common in the highest social circles by the end of 1916—among the grand dukes, among monarchist members of the State Council, in aristocratic salons, and in the officers' corps.[15] The only echo of these discussions in practice was the murder of Rasputin in December 1916, the result of a conspiracy uniting a leading rightist politician, a prince related by marriage to the imperial family, and one of Nicholas II's cousins.

In the face of a deepening crisis, liberals hesitated to defy the tsar's authority. Most liberals—notably in the Progressive Bloc, which retained a firm majority in the Duma—were immobilized by their own political logic: Although they foresaw a political upheaval if nothing changed, they were committed to principles of legality and thus opposed to a revolutionary challenge to the power of the tsarist regime; they were also justifiably afraid of provoking real revolution in the streets. Thus, when the Duma reconvened on 14 February 1917, a day marked also by strikes aimed at reminding the Duma of public discontent, the leader of the Progressive Bloc, the Kadet Pavel Miliukov, spoke against those in the Duma who demanded revolutionary action; he insisted that "the word and the vote" must remain their only weapons. The war of words launched in the Duma seemed only to underscore the powerlessness of the body as long as it remained within its legal mandates. Many liberal Duma deputies felt a tragic foreboding: "The deputies wander around like emaciated flies. Nobody believes in anything. Everyone has lost heart. Everyone feels and knows their powerlessness. The situation is hopeless."[16] Only when revolution broke out in the streets were liberals compelled to take serious political action.

On 22 February 1917, after spending two months in Petrograd and at the palace in Tsarskoe Selo, Nicholas II returned to Staff Headquarters at Mogilyov, near the front (Map 1). He did so confident that no serious challenges threatened his authority. He accepted the assurances of his minister of internal affairs, Aleksandr Protopopov (a trusted favorite who had been supported by Rasputin) that the situation was under control. By contrast, he was unmoved by the steady stream of supplicants who had been coming to the palace since the start of the new year—grand dukes, provincial nobles, and conservative and liberal members of the Duma—to convince him that revolution was impending if political changes were not made. Even the army's acting chief of staff, General Vasily Gurko (General Mikhail Alekseev was ill), reportedly warned Nicholas, "Your Imperial Majesty, you are willfully preparing yourself for the gallows. Do not forget that the mob will not stand on ceremony."[17]

On Thursday, 23 February (8 March) 1917, thousands of women textile workers in Petrograd shut down their factories, partly in commemoration of International Women's Day but mainly to protest bread shortages, thus adding to the already large number of men and women on strike. Strikers marched through the streets shouting "Give us bread" (*Daite khleb* and *Khleba, khleba*). Crowds headed toward the city center. Demonstrators—who were in a nasty mood, according to police reports—broke store windows, halted streetcars, and forced other workers to join them. During the next two days, encouraged by hundreds of experienced rank-and-file socialist activists, workers in factories and shops throughout the capital went on strike.

By the 25th virtually every industrial enterprise in Petrograd was

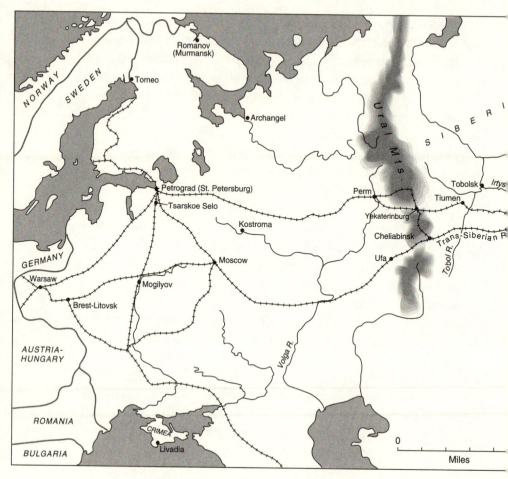

Map 1. European Russia and western Siberia.

shut down, as were many commercial and service enterprises. The demands—visible on banners and audible in the shouts of demonstrators and in speeches at rallies—escalated, again with the encouragement of activists, from demands for bread to appeals to end the war and abolish the autocracy. Demonstrators marched and protested all the more boldly when police and cossacks, under orders to show restraint, hesitated to stop them. Students, white-collar workers, and teachers joined workers in the streets and at public meetings. Although the protests and meetings were generally peaceful, the potential for mass violence was barely contained: some workers carried sticks, nuts, bolts, screws, pieces of metal, and, occasionally, pistols; crowds smashed shop windows, especially the windows of food and bread stores; looters became more common; demonstrators attacked and beat police officers—fatally on a couple of occasions. Although socialist activists condemned the violence and vandalism, the outbreaks became more frequent. Meanwhile, liberal and socialist deputies in the Duma shrilly denounced the current government and again demanded a responsible cabinet of ministers.

Nicholas received ambiguous information about the seriousness of events. Reports were also partially overshadowed by news that his children had been stricken with measles just after he left Tsarskoe Selo. On the 24th and 25th, word of the disturbances reached him at Headquarters—in Alexandra's letters (Documents 3, 5) and in telegrams from War Minister Mikhail Beliaev, Minister of Internal Affairs Protopopov, and the military commander of Petrograd, General Sergei Khabalov. Alexandra discounted the disturbances: "Its a *hooligan* movement, young boys & girls running about & screaming that they have no bread, only to excite—& then the workmen preventing others fr. work—if it were very cold they wld. probably stay in doors. But this will all pass & quieten down—if the *Duma* wld. only behave itself" (Document 5). Although the official reports were more thorough in describing the scale of the disturbances—the spreading strikes, the demands for bread, the mass demonstrations on Nevsky Prospect (Petrograd's main throughfare and the symbol of its urbanity), and the attacks on police officers— they also assured Nicholas that the police and the army were having no difficulty in controlling the disorders.[18] This was far from accurate.

About 9:00 P.M. on 25 February, General Khabalov received a telegram from Nicholas that was decisive in setting in motion actions that would transform the unrest into revolution: "I command you tomorrow to stop the disorders in the capital, which are unacceptable in the difficult time of war with Germany and Austria."[19] Meeting with his unit commanders an hour later, Khabalov ordered them to use all necessary force to disperse crowds, including firing at demonstrators, and he issued a proclamation to the population, posted the next morning, banning demonstrations and warning that this order would be enforced with arms. He also publicly warned strikers that they would be conscripted and sent to the front if they did not return to work by the 28th. That evening, on 25 February, the Council of Ministers was informed of the tsar's command to use military force to restore order. A majority of the ministers dismissed Protopopov's sanguine assurances that all would be well and suggested forming a new cabinet in consultation with the Duma as the only way to end the disorders. They delegated two members to begin negotiations with the Duma.[20]

On 26 February, as demonstrators again poured into the streets of Petrograd, police and soldiers, as commanded, fired systematically into the crowds, wounding and killing many. The show of force convinced many socialist leaders that the regime was determined and able to restore order.[21] It also convinced the Council of Ministers to abandon efforts to achieve a political compromise with the Duma—that no longer seemed necessary. Instead, the council recommended to Nicholas that he again prorogue the Duma, which he did. After the confident and effective use of force, the telegram from the chairman of the Duma to Nicholas on the night of 26 February (Document 6) insisting that "state authority is totally paralyzed and utterly unable to reimpose order" seemed to conflict with the facts, and thus the pleas for a cabinet responsible to the Duma hardly seemed worth answering. Indeed, Nicholas dismissed the warning: "That fat Rodzianko has written all sorts of nonsense to me, to which I will not even reply."[22] That night Rodzianko was handed the order proroguing the Duma. But the tsar's confidence was premature.

Leaders of the rebellion and of the government both underestimated the psychological and moral effect on the soldiers themselves of the order that they shoot at demonstrating civilians. Most obeyed the order on the 26th. But as they returned to their barracks, they thought and talked about whether to follow orders or their consciences the following day. The answer soon emerged in regiment after regiment: mutiny. On the morning of the 27th, workers in the streets, many now armed and ready for combat with troops, were joined by insurgent soldiers, often with red ribbons tied to their bayonets. With the disintegration of military authority in the capital, effective civil authority collapsed. The streets became a theater of revolution: workers and soldiers broke into weapon factories and arsenals and armed themselves; they liberated revolutionaries from prisons and also a great number of ordinary criminals; they invaded police stations, including central police headquarters, and set them ablaze; they assaulted policemen. "Requisitioned" trucks and cars crammed full of rebels sped around the streets. Everywhere soldiers, workers, and students were walking and driving about, sometimes draped in cartridge belts, carrying weapons, often more than one, and firing into the air. Numerous accidental injuries and deaths occurred along with deliberate ones. Looting and pillaging were also common: wine stores were broken into, store windows were smashed, goods were stolen from various businesses, and the homes of the rich were burglarized.

Increasingly aware of the gravity of the situation, Khabalov appealed to the tsar and the military command to "quickly send reliable units from the front."[23] Although the war minister, Beliaev, was still cabling Staff Headquarters his assurances that "calm will soon arrive" (Document 9), by evening he, too, was urgently informing Headquarters that "the situation in Petrograd has become extremely serious" and appealing for troops from the front.[24] Nicholas was not ill informed about the seriousness of events. As he wrote to Alexandra on the 27th, "I saw many faces here with frightened expressions" (Document 11). In response, he announced his own departure for the capital and ordered the transfer of reliable troops there, under the command of General Nikolai Ivanov, to restore order by force (Documents 10, 12).

Although Nicholas remained calm, panic spread through his

government, and pressure mounted for him to make concessions. When Khabalov went before the Council of Ministers on the afternoon of 27 February to report on the situation in the capital, witnesses reported that he visibly trembled.[25] Meeting at 7:00 that evening, the council again decided to seek an agreement with the Duma, although it also proposed a temporary military dictatorship to restore order. To signal the Duma of its readiness to work out a deal, the council forced Protopopov to resign. A few hours later, more and more fearful, the entire cabinet submitted their resignations to Nicholas—who rejected them in vain—and again proposed a temporary military dictatorship, suggesting the leadership of Grand Duke Mikhail Aleksandrovich.[26] Fearing violence, the ministers did not wait for Nicholas's answer but fled to their homes or into hiding.

Nicholas was also under pressure from his military commanders to make major concessions. In the afternoon and evening of 27 February, two top commanders—General Aleksei Brusilov, commander of the southwestern front, and General Nikolai Ruzsky, commander of the northern front, both of whom had received telegrams from Rodzianko—wired Nicholas their advice that he "adopt urgent measures to appease the population," establish a cabinet responsible to the Duma, and avoid "aggravating the situation" with repressive measures. Meanwhile, Rodzianko himself sent off yet another telegram to Nicholas; he pleaded with him to revoke his order closing the Duma, concluding ominously, "The hour in which your fate and that of the motherland will be decided has arrived. Tomorrow may be too late."[27]

Next it was the turn of leading Romanovs to turn against Nicholas. At 10:30 P.M., Grand Duke Mikhail Aleksandrovich, having conferred with both the frightened Council of Ministers and Rodzianko, wired Headquarters and added his voice to the chorus of appeals. He, too, pleaded with Nicholas to replace the entire cabinet with ministers who enjoyed the respect of a broad range of classes. He even offered to serve as Nicholas's intermediary and recommended Prince Georgy Lvov to head the new cabinet. The tsar, speaking through General Alekseev, rejected his brother's suggestions and reiterated his confidence that order would be restored by the troops who were approaching Petrograd from the front.[28]

Shortly thereafter, around 11:00 P.M., the telegram arrived from the chairman of the Council of Ministers, Nikolai Golitsyn, offering the cabinet's resignation. Alekseev presented the telegram to Nicholas personally, expressing his own support for the proposal for a new ministry.[29] At 2:20 A.M. yet another appeal for political compromise arrived: from members of the normally conservative State Council (Document 14). But Nicholas remained adamant about defending his power and the traditions of autocracy.

In the Tauride Palace in Petrograd, where the Duma had met and toward which the crowds began to turn for guidance on the 27th, two political forces tried to fill the vacuum in civic power. The first emerged out of the old Duma, though with considerable reluctance and even self-doubt. Although the leaders of the Progressive Bloc, Rodzianko especially, remained attached to principles of formal legality and thus could not defy the tsar's order that had prorogued the Duma—they hoped instead to convince Nicholas to cancel his decree—still, a third of the Duma's deputies, determined not to let chaos spread, assembled for a "private meeting." At 2:30 in the afternoon they met at the Tauride Palace, pointedly in a room other than the Duma's regular meeting hall. Rejecting proposals to declare this rump Duma a new government or even a constituent assembly that would lay the groundwork for new elections and a legitimate government, they decided to declare themselves a politically vague Provisional Committee of Members of the State Duma for the Restoration of Order in the Capital and for the Establishment of Relations with Public Organizations and Institutions. Faced with increasing civil disorder, however, and the appearance of another body claiming authority—the Soviet of Workers' and Soldiers' Deputies, led by socialists—the members of this Provisional Committee of the State Duma announced on the morning of the 28th that they found themselves "forced to take into their own hands the reimposition of state and social order" (Document 13).

During the next few days the Provisional Committee of the State Duma named new ministers but still hesitated to call itself a government, even a provisional one. It was continually pressured into asserting state authority, however, sometimes in directions that it had not intended. On 28 February, for instance, insurgent crowds began arresting tsarist ministers and other officials, often tracking them down in their apartments. The new minister of justice, the socialist Aleksandr Kerensky (a leader of the Trudovik faction in the Duma), personally sanctioned these arrests, although the other new ministers hesitated. By 1 March, as arrests continued, the emerging new government decided to endorse Kerensky's initiative in order to exercise some control over the process.[30]

The Provisional Duma Committee took power hesitantly, doubting the legitimacy of its authority and acting largely to forestall the spread of anarchy and popular power. Only late in the day on 2 March did the new ministers begin to refer to themselves as the government. The new Council of Ministers of the Provisional Government acknowledged that a "political revolution" (*gosudarstvennyi perevorot*) had occurred and, according to the minutes of its first formal meeting, that it now had to admit "the necessity of defining the scope of the powers of the Provisional Government precisely." Although the new government judged the old laws of the Russian state to be void, it considered that a new constitutional order would have to await the convening of a constituent assembly.[31] In the months that followed, this spirit of political hesitation would persist, undermining the government's ability to control events— specifically, to halt the coming to power of Bolshevik-led radicals.

The effective power of the Provisional Duma Committee, and later of the Provisional Government, was challenged by the authority of an institution that claimed to represent the will of workers and soldiers and could, in fact, mobilize and control these groups during the early months of the revolution: the Petrograd Soviet of Workers' and Soldiers' Deputies, an organization that would strongly shape the course of events and the fate of the Romanovs. Calls to establish a soviet (council) of elected workers' deputies were heard from the moment the strikes began on 23 February. The model for the soviet was the workers' councils established in scores of Russian cities during the 1905 revolution, including St. Petersburg. In February 1917 striking workers elected deputies to represent them, and socialist activists began organizing a citywide council in which representatives of the socialist parties would also participate. On 27 February, socialist Duma deputies, mainly Mensheviks and Socialist Revolutionaries, took the lead in calling for elections in all factories and, in recognition of the key role in the revolution played by soldiers, inviting "troops that have gone to the side of the people" to elect a deputy from each company.[32] That evening, the first meeting of the Petrograd Soviet took place in the Tauride Palace, the same place where the government organized by the Provisional Duma Committee was taking shape.

The leaders of the Petrograd Soviet did not consider taking state power into their own hands. They believed that Russia was not ready for socialism, that it was still too underdeveloped economically, socially, and culturally. Socialists from almost all of the parties represented in the Petrograd Soviet agreed that what Russians needed were democratic rights. Taking western Europe as their model (and, for many, Marx's writings on capitalism, the bourgeoisie, and history as their ideological guide), they assumed that the liberals of the Duma (the "democratic bourgeoisie") were destined, and most qualified, to bring democracy to semi-feudal Russia. Indeed, the leaders of the Petrograd Soviet, who formed an Executive Committee and met on 1 March to discuss the question of state power, decided that their most urgent task was precisely to compel the hesitant "bourgeoisie" to take power and introduce extensive democratic reforms (the replacement of the monarchy with a republic, guaranteed civil rights, democratic control of the police and army, abolition of religious and ethnic discrimination, elections to a constituent assembly, and so on).[33] The Soviet met in the same building as the Duma Committee, not to compete for state power but to exert pressure on the emerging government, to act, in other words, as a popular democratic lobby.

Late at night on 1 March, representatives of the Petrograd Soviet's Executive Committee met with representatives of the Provisional Duma Committee to discuss the question of power. The Duma leaders understood that the Soviet could control the crowd, whereas they could not, so they sought the Soviet's endorsement of their state authority. The leaders of the Petrograd Soviet, in turn, wished to influence the policies of the new government, so they came to the meeting prepared to bargain. The Duma representatives agreed almost immediately to most of the Soviet's terms and further conceded that the new government would "take into account the opinions of the Soviet of Workers' Deputies," though the Duma representatives were also determined to prevent "interference in the actions of the government," which would create "an unacceptable situation of dual power."[34]

The representatives of the Duma Committee also had reservations about two of the Soviet's demands. They balked at the Soviet's insistence that soldiers be given full civil rights, including the right to elect officers, arguing that this would destroy the army. And they refused to accept the Soviet's demand for a democratic republic. The first point was settled by compromise: the Soviet agreed to drop the demand for the election of officers, and the Duma Committee agreed to grant soldiers other civil rights. But on the question of the monarchy the Duma Committee was intractable.

Pavel Miliukov, speaking on behalf of the Duma Committee, vehemently argued that the form of government should not be preemptively decided by the Soviet or by the Duma Committee but should reflect the decision of the Russian people as expressed through a properly elected constituent assembly. He also insisted that the immediate abolition of the monarchy, which had been the basis of Russia's legal and institutional order for centuries, would result in chaos and turmoil, a new Time of Troubles, like the one that had afflicted Russia during the last dynastic crisis, in the seventeenth century, and he noted that monarchist sentiments remained strong outside Petrograd. Instead, Miliukov proposed preserving the monarchy, with Nicholas's son, Aleksei, as tsar and Nicholas's brother, Grand Duke Mikhail Aleksandrovich, as regent. The Soviet representatives decided not to make an issue of this point, agreeing that the form of government could be decided by a constituent assembly. The Soviet representatives were even willing to let the new government continue efforts to establish a constitutional monarchy, but they themselves intended to continue agitating for a democratic republic and even for Nicholas II's exile or arrest (Document 27).[35] The fate of the monarchy was not decided by debates between liberals and socialists over principle, however.

At 5:00 in the morning of 28 February, Nicholas left Staff Headquarters at Mogilyov confident that his presence in the capital and the arrival of loyal troops would restore order (Document 15). While he was en route to Tsarskoe Selo—indirectly via Smolensk and Bologoe, leaving the direct route, via Vitebsk and Dno, free for General Ivanov and his troops (Map 2)—news arrived that rebels

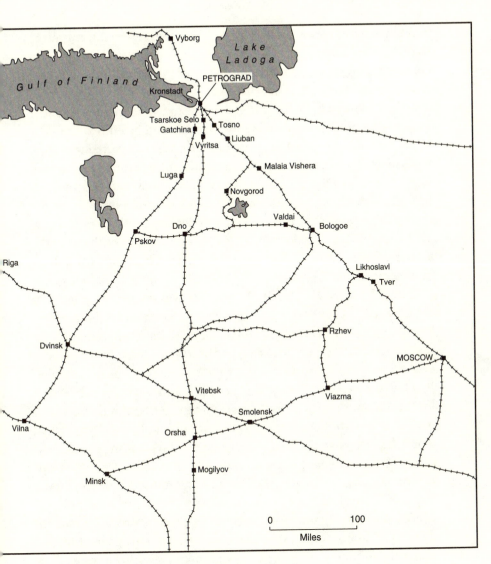

Map 2. Northwestern Russia.

had captured stations along any line that the imperial train might use to get to Tsarskoe Selo. Railway administrators, who were in contact with the Duma Committee and Rodzianko, deliberately exaggerated the threat in order to keep Nicholas away from Tsarskoe Selo, where his stubborn resistance to proposals for a responsible ministry was likely to be reinforced by Alexandra. The effort was effective, and the imperial train was redirected to Pskov, headquarters of the northern front. Rodzianko arranged a meeting with the tsar at Dno station, on the way to Pskov, but sentiment in the Provisional Duma Committee against leaving Nicholas on the throne at all prevented Rodzianko, who was still seeking only a new cabinet, from leaving the capital.[36] On the evening of 1 March, the tsar arrived in Pskov—after pacing the platform at Dno for half an hour waiting for Rodzianko.

Nicholas's arrival was ill omened. He was met at the station by the governor of Pskov, but the customary inspection of the guard of honor had not been arranged, and General Ruzsky and other important officers from the northern front headquarters in Pskov arrived several minutes late. According to a member of the tsar's suite, Ruzsky showed up with a hostile glare and wearing rubber galoshes, an apparent gesture of disrespect.[37] Although this account may be true, it may also reflect a loyalist's point of view: Ruzsky had a baneful influence on Nicholas during the days leading to his abdication. Ruzsky was the most politically dissident of all the front commanders: he had been the first to align himself with the Duma opposition, and, as we have seen, he spoke out early for political concessions and against repression. As a recent historian has commented, "Nicholas thus spent the most crucial two days of his life under the influence of the military commander who was most decisively against the emperor."[38] Ruzsky was only the tip of the iceberg of military disloyalty to Nicholas. As news arrived at Staff Headquarters that the soldiers' mutiny in the rear had spread to Moscow, and as Duma representatives continued to make their case to the military command that only a government established by the Provisional Duma Committee could bring calm to Russia and avoid a catastrophic defeat in the war, Russia's military leaders almost unanimously abandoned Nicholas.

By the evening of 1 March, when the emperor met with Ruzsky, he was bending under the pressure—but only slightly. He told Ruzsky that he was willing to allow Rodzianko to form a new government but insisted that the ministers remain responsible to him and not to the Duma. Ruzsky, given leave by the tsar to speak his mind, argued at length in favor of a cabinet of ministers responsible to the Duma. Ruzsky recalled that Nicholas refused this suggestion "calmly, coolly, and with a feeling of deep conviction."[39] But Nicholas's calm resistance to abandoning his autocratic prerogatives was coming under exceptional fire. Ruzsky reported the mutiny spreading through the army in the rear, including Moscow, and the desire for political concessions expressed by many other generals. Nicholas had at hand evidence that Ruzsky's report was true. Among the many telegrams that Nicholas probably saw when he arrived in Pskov was General Alekseev's cable to General Ivanov, whose army had already massed at Tsarskoe Selo to suppress the revolution with force. The telegram from the army chief of staff informed Ivanov that the tsar was likely to agree to "the wishes of the people" for a new government, which would naturally "change your manner of action."[40] This bordered on insubordination. Then, at 10:20 P.M., a figurative bombshell arrived directly from Alekseev: a telegram informing Nicholas of the spread of the revolution and even proposing the text of a manifesto, drafted at Staff Headquarters, establishing not merely a government enjoying the confidence of the nation but a cabinet of ministers responsible to the Duma and headed by Rodzianko (Document 19). Nicholas was now ready to concede: he would sign Alekseev's manifesto. He sent a telegram to General Ivanov ordering him to "undertake no measures before my arrival and your report to me."[41]

Nicholas's decision to sign a manifesto granting a responsible ministry was a dramatic and historical event, but the political process was outpacing Nicholas. In the predawn hours of 2 March, after Nicholas went to bed, Ruzsky began a four-hour dialogue by direct wire with Rodzianko in Petrograd, informing him that the tsar was ready to sign a manifesto granting a responsible ministry. Now it was Ruzsky's turn to feel overwhelmed by events. Rodzianko informed him that the situation had changed drastically:

It is obvious that His Majesty and you have not taken what is happening here into account. One of the most terrible revolutions has begun, which it will not be so easy to overcome. . . . The people's passions are so inflamed that it will hardly be possible to contain them; troops are completely demoralized—they not only disobey but murder their officers; hatred of Her Majesty the Empress has reached extremes. To avoid bloodshed we were forced to imprison all the ministers, except for war and navy, in the Peter and Paul Fortress. I very much fear that I will meet the same fate, because protests are directed against any whose demands are more moderate or limited. I consider it necessary to inform you that what you have proposed is already insufficient and that the dynastic question has been raised point-blank.

Ruzsky responded that no one at the front realized that things were so out of hand, and asked what solution to the dynastic question was being proposed. Rodzianko answered:

With pain in my heart I will now answer you, Nikolai Vladi-mirovich. I repeat once more, hatred of the dynasty has reached its limit. . . . Everywhere troops have gone to the side of the Duma and the people, and the terrible demand for abdication in the name of the son, under the regency of Mikhail Aleksandro-vich, has become definite.[42]

While Nicholas slept, General Alekseev, who was telegraphed a copy of this conversation, sent a circular telegram to all of the commanders at the front informing them of the conversation and expressing his own view that Nicholas's abdication in favor of his son, with Mikhail as regent, was the only means of saving the army, the country, and the dynasty. He asked the commanders to send their views to the tsar at Pskov, with copies to him.[43] This amounted to a mutiny of the military command.

Alekseev advised Ruzsky to awaken the tsar; matters were serious enough "to dispense with all etiquette."[44] At 10:00 A.M., Ruzsky read to Nicholas the text of his conversation with Rodzianko. After hearing it, Nicholas silently stood and stared out the window. He then informed Ruzsky that he had had his own doubts that the planned manifesto would help; further, "if it is necessary for the good of Russia that I should step aside, then I am prepared to do so."[45] While Nicholas was pondering these questions, the messages from the commanders responding to Alekseev's circular telegram began arriving; almost all favored abdication. In the early afternoon, Alekseev forwarded to Nicholas his own copies of the generals' appeals for abdication and reiterated his own support for it (Document 20).

Nicholas could dismiss the pleas of politicians, for whom he felt great contempt. But when his generals advised him to step down, appealing to his spirit of selfless patriotism, he could less easily refuse. After reading their telegrams and listening again to the arguments of Ruzsky and other generals present at Pskov, the tsar retired to his railroad car and wrote out two telegrams. To Staff Headquarters he wrote, "For the sake of the well-being, peace, and salvation of Russia, which I passionately love, I am prepared to abdicate from the throne in favor of my son. I ask you all to serve him truly and sincerely." To Rodzianko he wrote, "There is no sacrifice that I would not make for the sake of the true well-being and salvation of our own mother Russia. For that reason I am prepared to renounce the throne in favor of my son, assuming that he will remain with me until his coming of age, under the regency of my brother Grand Duke Mikhail Aleksandrovich."[46] He wired Alekseev at Headquarters to have an abdication manifesto drafted. The writing of it was delegated to Nikolai Bazili, chief of the diplomatic chancellery at Headquarters, who had also written the earlier manifesto proposed by Alekseev. After making a few changes in wording, Alekseev forwarded the draft to Pskov, where it was received at 7:40 P.M., shortly before the arrival of emissaries from the Provisional Duma Committee.[47]

Although Rodzianko's efforts were instrumental in provoking the responses by the generals that caused Nicholas to concede defeat, Rodzianko's own political star was declining, unbeknownst to any of the army's leaders. Considered too conservative by the liberals in the Provisional Duma Committee, whose support was needed to form a new government, and by the Petrograd Soviet, he was replaced as prospective chairman of the Council of Ministers by Prince Georgy Lvov. When the Duma Committee sought an emissary to present their arguments for abdication to the tsar, Rodzianko was not selected because many feared that he might strike a deal with Nicholas and the generals. Thus, on the morning of 2 March, after the successful negotiations with the leaders of the Petrograd Soviet, the Duma Committee dispatched two representatives, Aleksandr Guchkov and Vasily Shulgin, to go to Pskov and persuade the tsar to abdicate in favor of his son with Mikhail as regent. These delegates, however, were totally unaware of Rodzianko's communications with Ruzsky and the events that these had set in motion. Even Rodzianko and Ruzsky did not know that the tsar had in the meantime decided to alter the terms of his agreement with them. After meeting with his physician, who told him that there was no medical hope that Aleksei would ever recover from his hemophilia, Nicholas resolved to abdicate in favor of his brother Mikhail.

When Shulgin and Guchkov arrived at 9:45 P.M. to what they assumed would be resistance and even risk of arrest, they were astonished to hear that the tsar had already decided to abdicate. After a discussion, Nicholas retired to his private car and, as agreed, revised the manifesto sent to him by Alekseev to designate Mikhail as successor, not Aleksei. The Duma delegates asked Nicholas to make one significant addition, to which he also agreed. To the words "We entrust OUR Brother to conduct state affairs in complete and unshakeable unity with the representatives of the people in the legislative institutions, according to principles they will determine," Nicholas added, "and on this to take an inviolable oath." He signed the manifesto of abdication on 2 March 1917 at 11:40 P.M. By mutual agreement 3:00 P.M. was marked as the time of signing—that was when Nicholas had actually decided to abdicate—in order to make it clear that he had not signed under pressure from the deputies from the Provisional Duma Committee. In every way possible, the Duma Committee was seeking to acquire as much juridical legitimacy as it could. This concern to acquire formal legitimacy also motivated Guchkov and Shulgin to have Nicholas sign orders asking Prince Lvov to form a new government and appointing Grand Duke Nikolai Nikolaevich commander in chief of the army. Until the abdication was formalized, these Duma liberals still recognized the tsar as the source of legitimate state authority (Documents 25, 26).[48]

In deciding to abdicate also on behalf of his son and in favor of his brother, Nicholas demonstrated his fatherly affection for Aleksei and, more important, his persistent conception of the monarchy as personal autocratic power. As Shulgin and Guchkov immediately recognized and openly worried about, Nicholas had absolutely no legal authority to offer the throne to Mikhail: the Fundamental Laws of the Russian state allowed only the eldest son, if alive, to succeed the father, and a minor could not renounce his own rights.[49] Designating Mikhail as heir was, in fact, doubly illegal. When Mikhail married a commoner (a divorcée at that)—a choice that had outraged Nicholas and his mother—he was made to renounce any rights to succeed to the throne. Even in abdicating, then, Nicholas acted according to his notion of the absolute personal authority of the tsar.

We cannot know Nicholas's thoughts and feelings at the moment of his abdication. In the company of officers and public figures, he remained, as always, calm and restrained, even "serene."[50] But within the close and loyal circle of his own suite and in his private diary, he revealed something of the emotions that he likely felt. On the afternoon of 2 March, when his palace commandant, Vladimir Voeikov, burst into Nicholas's railway car to express his disbelief and dismay at the abdication, Nicholas pointed to the pile of telegrams on his desk and declared, "What else could I have done when everyone has betrayed me? And first among them Nikolasha [Grand Duke Nikolai Nikolaevich]."[51] He expressed the same sentiment in his diary at day's end: "All around me is treachery, cowardice, and deceit!" (Document 30).

The fate of the monarchy was still far from settled. Events and political considerations were making the agreement obsolete even before Nicholas signed it. On 2 March, in the wake of the deal between the Petrograd Soviet and the Provisional Duma Committee, and with Guchkov and Shulgin on their way to Pskov to seek the tsar's abdication, the Duma leaders prepared to announce the formation of the Provisional Government. To test the reaction of workers and soldiers, their spokesman, Pavel Miliukov, first announced the news informally in the Catherine Hall in the Tauride Palace, where anyone who wished to address "the people" appeared before a virtually round-the-clock meeting of workers and soldiers. When someone from the crowd questioned Miliukov about the fate of the dynasty, he announced that "the old despot who has brought the country to the edge of ruin will voluntarily renounce the throne or be deposed. Power will pass to a regent, the Grand Duke Mikhail Aleksandrovich. Aleksei will be the successor." Even before Miliukov could finish, however, his words were interrupted by indignant outcries, prolonged shouting, and cries of "Long live the republic!" and "Down with the dynasty!" Faced with this verbal onslaught, Miliukov assured the crowd that nothing had been decided in advance—the form of government would ultimately be decided by a constituent assembly. As news of Miliukov's comments spread, pressure mounted on the Provisional Government to abandon its hope of preserving the monarchy in some form. Delegations of soldiers, workers, and others made their way to the Tauride Palace to protest the preservation of the monarchy. Miliukov was compelled to state publicly that his speech was only an expression of personal opinion.[52]

The new government's retreat from efforts to preserve the monarchy was hastened by the news, late that night, that Nicholas II had abdicated in favor of his brother. As Rodzianko fearfully told Ruzsky in their conversation on the morning of 3 March, the proclamation of Mikhail as emperor would "pour oil onto the fire, and a merciless destruction of all that it is possible to destroy will begin" (Document 28). Guchkov had told Nicholas, "We had counted on the figure of little Aleksei Nikolaevich having a softening effect on the transfer of power" (Document 25).[53] Partly influenced by the arguments of Rodzianko and other Duma Committee members, the leaders of the military, including Grand Duke Nikolai Nikolaevich, now again commander in chief, were beginning to share the view that the transfer of the throne to Mikhail would lead to bloodshed.[54]

On 3 March, members of the Provisional Duma Committee and the Provisional Government met to debate the problem of the monarchy. Miliukov alone defended the need to preserve the throne, reminding his colleagues that the radicalism of the Petrograd masses did not reflect attitudes in the country as a whole. For the Provisional Government to be accepted by all of Russia until a constituent assembly could be elected, he argued, a symbolic, historical, and legal source of legitimacy was needed. The Romanov dynasty provided this. Kerensky vehemently countered that, given the mood of the masses (which he always claimed, as the only socialist in the government, to know best), any preservation of the monarchy would lead to further unrest and thus to further harm to the war effort and to Russia. The debate continued later that night for the benefit of Mikhail himself, who was to decide whether to accept the throne. The point that apparently made the most impression on Mikhail was Kerensky's: "I cannot vouch for the life of Your Highness." Even Miliukov admitted that there was considerable personal risk, though he added that "such a risk must be taken in the interests of the fatherland." Mikhail asked Prince Lvov, the new minister president, and Rodzianko, with whom he had the closest ties among the Duma leaders, whether they could guarantee his safety if he accepted the crown. They said they could not. In the end, Mikhail declined the offer.[55] He had little real choice: virtually the entire Duma Committee and even most of the other grand dukes were opposed to his becoming emperor. Two jurists, Boris Nolde and Vladimir Nabokov, drafted his manifesto of abdication. Mikhail signed it at 6:00 P.M. on the evening of 3 March 1917 (Document 29). Only four years after celebrating its three-hundredth anniversary with exceptional pomp, the Romanov dynasty quietly expired.

· 1 ·

Letter from Alexandra to Nicholas, 22 February 1917.
Original English text.

———

No: 644.   *Ts.S.*   Feb: 22nd 1917.[1]

My very Own precious One,

WITH anguish & deep pain I let you go—alone, without sweet Baby's[2] tender, warming, sunny companionship! And such a hard time as the one we are going through now. Being apart makes everything so much harder to bear—no possibility of giving you a gentle caress when you look weary, tormented. Verily God has sent you a terrible hard cross to bear & I do so long to help you carry the burden. You are brave & patient, but my soul feels & suffers with you **far** more than I can say. I can do nothing but pray & pray & Our dear Friend[3] does so in yonder world for you—there he is yet nearer to us—tho'

one longs to hear his voice of comfort and encouragement.—God will
help, I feel convinced, & send yet the great recompense for all you go
through—but how long to wait still! It seems as tho' things were taking a
better turn—only my Love be firm, show the master hand, its that what
the Russian needs. Love & kindnesses you have **never** failed to show—
now let them feel yr. fist at times. They ask for it themselves—how many
have told me—["]we want to feel the whip"—its strange, but such is the
Slave [Slav] nature, **great** firmness, hardness even—& warm love. Since
they now have begun to "feel" you & *Kalinin*[4] they begin to quieten down.
They must learn to fear you,—love is not enough. A child that adores its
father must still have fear to anger, displease or disobey him—one must
play with the reins, let them loose & draw them in, always let the master-
hand be felt; then they also far more value kindness—only gentleness they
do not understand.—Russian hearts are strange & not tender or suscepti-
ble in the higher classes, strange to say. They need decided treatment,
especially now.—I am sad we cannot be alone our last luncheon, but they
are yr. own who also want to see you. Poor little Xenia,[5] with such boys &
her daughter married into that wicked family—& with such a false
husband[6]—I pitty her deeply.—There is so much sorrow & grief all over
the world—one great pain in one's heart wh. gnaws at one unceasingly—
such a yearning for rest & peace, just to get a wee bit of strength to go on
fighting & struggling along this thorny road towards the shining goal.

   I hope you will have no difficulties or bothers with *Alekseev*[7] & that
you can come back **very** soon—its not fr. pure selfish longing that I speak,
but because I too well see how "the screaming mass" behave when you are
near—they fear you still & must yet more, so that whereever you are, they
should have the same quaver. And for the ministers you are **such** a strength,
& guide—come back soon—you see I don't beg for myself & Baby even—
because that you always know. I understand where duty calls—& that is
just now **more** here than there. So just set things going & do be home in ten
days—til times are really as they should be.—Yr. wall, wify, remains
guarding here in the rear, tho' she can do but little, but the good ones know
she is yr. staunch upholder.—My eyes ache for crying,—from the station
shall go straight to *Znamenia,*[8] even if have been there with you before—
to get calm & strength & pray for you my Angel—ah God, **how** I love
you!—Ever increasingly, deep as the sea, fathomless in tenderness. Sleep
calmly, dont cough,—may the change of air make you quite well again.
Holy Angels guard you, Christ be near you, & the sweet Virgin never fail
you—our Friend left us to her—*Znamenia.*—I bless you +,[9] clasp you
tightly in my arms & rest yr. weary head upon my breast. Ah the loneliness
of the nights to come—no Sunny near you—& no Sunshine [Aleksei]

either. All our love, burning & warming envelops you, my Huzy, my one & all, the light of my life, the treasure given to me by God Almighty. Feel my arms encircling you, feel my lips tenderly pressed upon yours—always together, never alone.—Farewell Lovy Sweet, come soon back again—to your very own old

Sunny

+

Please go to the "Virgin" as soon as you can—I have prayed **so much** for you there.

    1. Alexandra numbered her letters to Nicholas. Tsarskoe Selo (now Pushkin) is fifteen miles from Petrograd (named St. Petersburg until World War I), the capital of imperial Russia. Before the February Revolution, the Aleksandrovsky Palace in Tsarskoe Selo was the chief residence of Nicholas and his family.

    2. Aleksei Nikolaevich, the tsarevich (or caesarevich, as he was then called), son of Nicholas and Alexandra, was the heir to the throne. He was born in 1904. During 1915 and 1916 he spent many months at Headquarters with his father.

    3. Grigory Yefimovich Rasputin, the court seer, killed by aristocrats in December 1916.

    4. Aleksandr Dmitrievich Protopopov (1866–1918), known in Tsarskoe Selo as General Kalinin. Protopopov was a member of the Octobrist Party, deputy to the third State Duma, and deputy chairman of the fourth State Duma. On 18 September 1916, with Rasputin's help, he was named minister of internal affairs. One of Nicholas and Alexandra's most trusted advisers.

    5. Ksenia Aleksandrovna, grand duchess, Nicholas's elder sister.

    6. In 1914, Ksenia Aleksandrovna's daughter Irina married Prince Feliks Yusupov, who in 1916 took part in the murder of Rasputin—hence Alexandra's condemnation.

    7. Mikhail Vasilievich Alekseev, adjutant general. From August 1915 to March 1917 he was chief of staff to the commander in chief of the Russian army.

    8. Znamensky Church, located next to the lyceum in Tsarskoe Selo, was built in 1747 for the icon of Our Lady of the Sign (Ikona Znameniia Bozh'ei Materi). Alexandra especially venerated this image of the Virgin with Christ in her womb, which was also guardian of the House of Romanov and renowned for miraculous healing.

    9. Alexandra frequently inscribed the sign of the cross in her letters and diaries.

· 2 ·

Letter from Nicholas to Alexandra, 23–24 February 1917. Original English text.

G. [*General*] *Headquarters* Feb. 23ᵈ 1917.

My own beloved Sunny,

LOVING thanks for your precious letter—you left in my compartment—I read it greedily before going to bed. It did me good, in my solitude, after two months being together, if not to hear your sweet voice, at least to be comforted by those lines of tender love!

I never went out until we arrived here. Today I feel much better, the voice is not hoarse & the cough is much less strong.

It was a sunny but cold day & I was met by the usual people—*Alekseev* at their head. He really looks alright & the face has an expression of rest & calm, which I have long not seen. We had a good talk for an hour; after that I arranged my rooms & got your wire about Olga's[1] & Baby's [Aleksei's] measles. I could not believe my eyes—so unexpected was that news, especially after his own telegram where he says that he is feeling well! Anyhow it is very tiresome & rather troublesome for you, my Lovebird. Perhaps you will put off receiving so many people, as that is a lawful reason not to see so many, on account of their families.

In the 1st & 2d Cadet corps the number of boys who have got the measles is steadily rising.

I saw all the foreign generals at dinner—they were very sad to hear that news. It is so quiet in this house, no rumbling about, no excited shouts! I imagine he [Aleksei] is asleep in the bedroom! All his tiny things, photos & toys are kept in good order in the bedroom & in the bow window-room!
Enough![2]

On the other hand what a luck that he did not come with me **now** only to fall ill & lie in that small bedroom of our's. God grant the measles may continue with no complications & better all the children at once have it!

I miss my half an hour's work at the puzzle every evening. If I am free here I think I will turn to the domino again, because this silence around me is rather depressing—of course if there is no work for me.

Old *Ivanov*[3] was amiable & kind at dinner; my other neighbour was Sir H. Williams,[4] who was delighted to have seen so many countrymen lately.

What you write about being firm—the master—is perfectly true. I do not forget it—be sure of that, but I need not bellow at the people right & left every moment. A quiet sharp remark or answer is enough very often to put the one or the other into his place.—

Now, Lovy-mine, it is late. Good-night, God bless your slumber, sleep well without the animal-warmth.
Febr. 24th.

It is a grey windy day with snow falling thick, nothing like spring. Just got your wire about the children's health. I do hope they will all get it this time. I am sending you & *Aleksei* each a decoration from the Queen & the King of Belgians—in commemoration of the war. You better thank her yourself. Won't he be pleased to have a new cross!

God bless you my beloved Darling! I kiss you & the dear children ever so tenderly. In thoughts & prayers ever with you all.

Your own huzy

Nicky

1. Olga Nikolaevna, Nicholas and Alexandra's eldest daughter.
2. Russian *Ne nado!* (literally "Don't!"). Nicholas often used this expression as if appealing to himself for greater self-control when he was beginning to complain or get overly sentimental.
3. Nikolai Iudovich Ivanov, adjutant general. From July 1914 to March 1916 he was commander of the southwestern front; later, after Nicholas took command, he was attached to Headquarters.
4. Sir John Hanbury-Williams, British attaché at General Headquarters.

· 3 ·

Letter from Alexandra to Nicholas, 24 February 1917.

Original English text.

———

No: 646.   *Tsarskoe Selo.* Feb. 24th 1917.

My own precious One,

MILDER weather, $4\frac{1}{2}$[°C; 40°F].—Yesterday there were rows on the *V.* [Vasilievsky] *Island* & *Nevsky* [Prospect] because the poor people stormed the bread shops—they smashed *Filipov* completely & the cossacks were called out against them.[1] All this I know unofficially. Baby was cheery yesterday evening & I read Helen's babies[2] to him—or *P.V.P.*[3] read to him, 38.1[4] at 9—at 6—38.3. Olga both times 37.7.—She looks less well & tired.—He slept well & has 37.7.—At 10 went over to sit with Ania[5] (she looked like measles 37.7, cough strong, throat ache, may be *angina*) & then with *Lili, N.P.* & *Rodionov*[6] whom she had for dinner in the corridor whilst she was in bed.—so, after all the *Variag* leaves for England for 6 months, probably today. She [Lili Den] of course is brave, but one sees how sad & disappointed & anxious for the journey.—How awfully lonely yr. first night must have been—cannot imagine you there without Baby, my poor sweet Angel.—

I hope one will hang *Kedrinsky*[7] of the *Duma* after that horrible speech of his, its the only thing (military law time of war) & an example. One longs & entreats for **yr** firmness to be seen.

I wish you could have found out that story (wh. we know as true & there are artillery officers ready to swear to it) about *Andrei* & *Kutaisov*,[8] so as to punish *Andr:* for daring to forbid off. [officers] receiving yr. a.d.c. [aide-de-camp] because he fulfilled his duty. Oh, were but Fred:[9] fresher; its his buiseness [*sic*]. I think *Kut:* will soon be on duty with you, but I hope you can return before.—Remember to write to Georgie about Buchanan,[10] don't put it off.—Well, Ania has the measles, at 3 she had 38.3—*Tatiana*[11] too & also 38.3. Al. [Aleksei] *Olga*—37.7, 37.9. I wander from one sick room to the other—have made Marie & Anastasia[12] go back to their rooms. Mr Gibbs[13] in a *dressing gown* reads to *Aleksei,* his room has only a few curtains drawn, but O, & T. quite [*sic*], so I write near a lamp (on the sopha). Received for 1½ hours, Belgian, Siamese, Dane, Persian, Spaniard, 2 Japanese—*Korf, Benkendorf,*[14] my 2 pages, Nastinka[15] who leaves tomorrow for the Caucasus as her sister is very ill—& Isa[16] (without touching her) & *Groten*[17] fr. *Kalinin* [Protopopov]—worse disorder at 10, at 1 less, its in *Khabalov's*[18] hands now. See your *Mufti* at 6 & a lady too.

Went in a moment to place candles for all of you my treasures—air seemed lovely. Could not take *M. & A.* as their throats (& *Shura's*)[19] show decided signs "*suspicious,*" as the 4 D^{rs} said—so they sat with Ania. I go to her in the morning for an hour & an hour in the evening—such a journey to the other end of the house—but I get wheeled;—she coughs colossally.—So does Tatiana & her head aches. Olga has her face strongly spotted, Baby most on his legs. I saw *Bezobrazov* yesterday, hopes **very** much that you wont forget him—I said certainly not, but he must wait a little so as to get a good place. Excuse dull letter but my days are so fidgety & lots of talks by telephone besides.—

The children all kiss you very tenderly. Baby kisses you, & asks how you feel & what is *Kulik (the supervisor)* doing. Must end now, my Sunshine, God bless ✝ & protect you. Kiss you without end, with tender true devotion, burning love. Yr. own old

Wify

✝

Do find out about *N.P.'s* cross. He dines today with *Maklakov, Kalinin, Rimsky-Kors:* etc: at *Burdiukov's.*

1. Not only was Nevsky Prospect the main commercial street in Petrograd, but for many middle- and upper-class Russians it was a symbol of the capital's wealth and civilization. Violence and protests that took place here were always seen as especially challenging. Similarly, the Filippov bakery (Alexandra misspelled the name) was a well-known, respectable establishment.

2. John Habberton, *Helen's Babies: With Some Account of Their Ways Innocent, Crafty, Angelic, Impish, Witching, and Repulsive* (Boston, c. 1876). Juvenile fiction.

3. Pyotr Vasilievich Petrov, the tsarevich Aleksei's tutor for Russian language and literature. Petrov also taught Nicholas and Alexandra's daughters.

4. On the Celsius scale, 37° is considered a normal temperature, the equivalent of 98.6° Fahrenheit.

5. Anna Aleksandrovna Vyrubova (born Taneeva), lady-in-waiting and close companion of Alexandra's.

6. Lili Den (also Dehn; Yulia Aleksandrovna Den, born Smonskaia), wife of Karl Akimovich Den, captain of the cruiser *Variag*. She was very close to Alexandra and to Anna Vyrubova.

Nikolai Pavlovich Sablin, admiral, commander of the Guards Equipage Naval Battalion, then captain of the imperial yacht *Shtandart*.

Nikolai Nikolaevich Rodionov, senior lieutenant of the Guards Equipage.

7. Alexandra means Aleksandr Fyodorovich Kerensky, a politician, lawyer, deputy to the fourth State Duma, and leader of the Trudovik (Laborist) faction.

8. Andrei Vladimirovich, grand duke, Nicholas's cousin.

Konstantin Pavlovich Kutaisov, count, Nicholas's aide-de-camp. After Rasputin was murdered, Kutaisov accompanied Grand Duke Dmitry Pavlovich, one of the assassins, into exile at the Persian front.

9. Vladimir Borisovich Frederiks, count, adjutant general in the imperial suite, wealthy landowner, member of the State Council, minister of the imperial court and domain. One of Nicholas's closest advisers.

10. George V, king of Great Britain.

Sir George Buchanan, ambassador to Russia (1910–1918).

11. Tatiana Nikolaevna, Nicholas and Alexandra's second daughter.

12. Maria Nikolaevna, Nicholas and Alexandra's third daughter.

Anastasia Nikolaevna, Nicholas and Alexandra's fourth daughter.

13. Sidney Ivanovich Gibbs, an Englishman who, in 1908, was invited to teach English to Nicholas and Alexandra's children.

14. Pavel Pavlovich Korf, baron, master of ceremonies in the imperial court.

Pavel Konstantinovich Benkendorf (Benkendorff), count, adjutant general, trusted adviser to the tsar's family.

15. Anastasia Vasilievna Gendrikova, countess, lady-in-waiting to Alexandra.

16. Sofia Karlovna Buksgevden (Buxhoeveden), baroness, lady-in-waiting to Alexandra.

17. Pavel Pavlovich Groten, aide-de-camp, major general in the imperial suite, commander of the Life Guards Horse Grenadiers Regiment. In 1916–1917, Groten was temporarily brought to Tsarskoe Selo to serve as palace commandant.

18. Sergei Semyonovich Khabalov, lieutenant general, commander of the Petrograd military district from 5 to 28 February 1917.

19. Aleksandra Aleksandrovna Tegleva, member of the hereditary nobility, nanny to Nicholas and Alexandra's children.

· 4 ·

Letter from Nicholas to Alexandra, 24–25 February 1917. Original English text.

———

G. Headquarters   Febr. 24th 1917.

My darling Sunny-dear,

MANY hearty thanks for your beloved letter. So there we are with three children & Ania lying with measles! Do try & let Marie & Anastasia catch it too, it would be so much simpler & better for all of them & for you also!

And this all happened since I left—only two days ago. *Serg. Petr.*[1] is very interested how the illness will develope. He finds it absolutely necessary for the children & Alexei especially a change of climate after their complete recovery—soon after Easter. When I asked him what place he was place he was thinking of [*sic*]—he said it was the Crimea. He told me he has a son (never knew it) who got the measles & for a year the boy continued coughing until he was sent to the south which cured him promptly. He had tears in his eyes while he was talking upon this subject.

I must say I think his advice an excellent one—& what a rest it would be for you! Besides the rooms at *Tsarskoe* [Selo] must be disinfected later & you would not care probably going to Peterhof, so where is to live? We will think it over quietly when I come back, which I hope won't take long!

My brain feels rested here—no ministers & no fidgety questions to think over—I think it does me good, but only the brain. The heart suffers from being separated & this separation I hate, during such times especially! I won't be long away—only to put all things as much as possible to rights here & then my duty will be done.

2) Febr. 25th

Just got your morning telegram—thank God no complications as yet. The first days the temp. is always high & decreases slowly towards the end. Poor Ania—I can imagine what she feels & how much worse than the children!

Now at 2.30 before driving out for my walk I will peep into the monastery & pray for you & them to the Virgin!

The last snowstorms, wh. ended yesterday along all our southwestern railway lines, have placed the armies into a critical situation. If the trains cannot begin moving at once—in 3 or 4 days real famine will break out among the troops. Quite horribly anguishing!

Good-bye, my own Love, my beloved little Wify, God bless you & the children. With tender love ever your own huzy

Nicky

1. Sergei Petrovich Fyodorov, attending physician to the tsar and tsarevich at Head-quarters.

· 5 ·

Letter from Alexandra to Nicholas, 25 February 1917. Original English text.

———

No: 647.   Feb. 25th *1917.*

Precious, beloved Treasure,

8° [46°F] & gently snowing—so far I sleep very well, but miss my Love **more** than words can say.—The rows in town and strikes are more than provoking. I send you *Kal:*'s [Kalinin = Proto-popov] letter to me, the paper is not worth while, & you will get a more detailed one for sure fr. the *police chief.* Its a *hooligan* movement, young boys & girls running about & screaming that they have no bread, only to excite—& then the workmen preventing others fr. work—if it were very cold they wld. probably stay in doors.[1] But this will all pass & quieten down—if the *Duma* wld. only behave itself—one does not print the worst speeches but I find that antidynastic ones ought to be **at once** very severely punished as its time of war, yet more so.—I had the feeling when you go, things wld. not be good.—Do have *Batiushin*[2] cleared out, remember that *Alekseev* stands up very firmly for him. *Bat:* chose an aid now a *colonel* who was quite poor—his wife brought him 15,000 [rubles] and now he has become very rich—strange! *Batiushin* also frightens people into pay-ing him big sums so as not to be sent out (tho' innocent)—get rid of him my lovy dear, of *Bat:* I mean & quicker. How do you find *Alekseev.* Will you get good *Golovin* to come instead of the new man you do not care for? Have **yr.** wishes fulfilled first darling.—Hard not to be together.—Ania [Vyrubova] sends much love—she is the worst, suffers awfully & a terrible cough day & night, the rash is inside & burns so. This morning she has 38.6 too. Olga 37.6. *T.* [Tatiana] 37.1.—Baby still sleeps. Give me a message for Ania, it will do her good. Kind *Lili* came again & later when

DOCUMENT 5. First page of letter from Alexandra to Nicholas, 25 February 1917.

we left A. at 11 she sat with me & took tea til the train left. Nuisance receiving. Have the Chinese, Portugese with 2 daughters—the Greek, Argentine with wife. *Boisman* for Crimea—hope he will suit.—Do go in a moment to the Virgin & pray there quietly for yr. sweet self to gain strength for our big & little family. Our *Kniazhevich*'s brother died in Moscou, he was the help in my *sklad* [war relief storehouse]. And old Mme *Min* died in town, but is being buried here.—I thought Anastasia wld. get it to-day, she looked suspicious yesterday—the D^{rs} find the throats doubtful, but temp: so far quite normal. *Akilina* looks after Ania—all the D^{rs} too.—

I am just reading an account of the Sweedish [*sic*] Pastor Neander who visited our prisoners in Germany & Austria. Now he has come again, here to continue, shall see him next week. The former Gov. of Penza *Gen. Gorainov* asked him to visit his son's grave at Friedland, & he did so & found it in order under a birch cross made by our soldiers on a German property. Several died there, as ours arranged hospital in that house 25 Aug: til Sept. 8. 1914. The family asked birthday & namesday so as to put wreathes. Then he went to the town cemetry & found there many of our graves & one: *Gen: Major Makovsky, Commander Saint-Petersb. Regiment fallen to the glory of Russian arms on the field of battle near Friedl. 2nd June 1807.*

Ania sent for me as she felt bad & could not breathe well, so went over 10$\frac{1}{2}$ [10:30]–12—later I calmed her & she felt quieter, begs for your "pure prayers"—always gets so frightened. At 1 Baby had 38.5. Olga 38.1. T. 37.4. Sit with all change about. Am writing by a dark lamp on Olga's sopha. Just placed candles at *Znamenia* [church]—tired after reception, talk with Apraksin & *Boisman*.[3] Of course the latter says one ought to have had a real cavalry reg. here wh. wld. have put order at once, & not the *Reserves:* wh. consists of Petersburg people—therefore *Gurko*[4] wld. not have yr. lancers here, cld. always have found place *Groten* said. *Boisman* proposes *Khabalov* shld. take military ~~kitchens~~ ovens & have at once bread baked, as *B.* [Boisman] also says there is enough flower [*sic*]. Some baker shops have also striked. One ought at once to have made order now every day it gets worse. I told *B:* to go to *Kalinin* & tell him to speak ~~the~~ with *Khabalov* about the military ovens because to-morrow Sunday will be yet worse. Cant understand why they don't have the card system [for rationing]—& why not have all fabrics [factories] military, then there will be no disorder, the strikers said not to provoke those, because they wld. be sent to the front or severely punished.—No shooting is required—only order & not let them cross the bridges as they do.—That food question is

madning. Excuse dull letter, but so much worry all around.—Kiss & bless
you +. Ever yr. own old

Wify.

+

None feel too bad—Ania suffers & coughs most. **All** kiss you 1000 times.

   1. After weeks of bitterly cold weather, the temperature in Petrograd rose above freezing
on 24 February, reaching a high of 8°C (46°F) by the 25th and remaining there for several
days.
   2. Nikolai Stepanovich Batiushin, major general. During the war, he was chief army
investigator on the northern front and then chairman of the commission investigating wartime financial abuses and speculation in the rear.
   3. Apraksin and Boisman were aristocratic members of the imperial suite.
   4. Vasily Iosifovich Gurko, cavalry general. In August 1916 he was named commander
of the "special army." While General Mikhail Alekseev was ill, Gurko carried out the duties
of chief of staff to the commander in chief.

· 6 ·

Telegram from Mikhail Rodzianko,[1] chairman of the State Duma, to Nicholas II on the
start of revolutionary outbreaks in Petrograd, 26 February 1917.

───────

Sent from Petrograd on 26 February 1917 at 21:52
Received at Headquarters on 26 February 1917 at 22:40

To His Imperial Majesty, Army in the Field
Headquarters of the Commander in Chief

   Your most faithful servant reports to Your Majesty that popular uprisings, having begun in Petrograd, are taking on uncontrollable and threatening dimensions. Their cause is a shortage of baked bread and poor
delivery of flour, which is sowing panic, but the main reason is the absolute
distrust of the authorities, who are not competent to lead the country out
of its difficult situation. Because of this, events will certainly unfold that
can be temporarily held at bay at the expense of innocent citizens' spilled
blood but that will be impossible to contain in the event of a repetition.
Outbreaks could spread to the railways, and then the life of the country
will come to a standstill at the worst possible moment. Factories working
for the military in Petrograd are shutting down for lack of fuel and raw
materials, the workers are left with nothing to do, and the hungry, unem-
ployed throng is starting down the path of elemental and uncontrollable
anarchy. In all of Russia, railway communications are in total disorder.
Out of 63 blast furnaces in the south, only 28 are working because of the
lack of fuel deliveries and necessary raw materials. Out of 92 blast furnaces in the Urals, 44 are at a standstill and the production of pig iron is

shrinking from day to day, which threatens a major reduction in the production of shells. Fearing the inept orders of the authorities, the people do not take their grain products to market, bringing the mills to a stop and threatening the army and the rest of the population with the full force of flour shortages. State authority is totally paralyzed and utterly unable to reimpose order. Your Majesty, save Russia; she is threatened with humiliation and disgrace. In these circumstances, the war cannot be brought to a victorious conclusion because the ferment has already spread to the army and threatens to grow if a decisive end cannot be put to anarchy and governmental disorder. Your Majesty, urgently summon a person in whom the whole country can have faith and entrust him with the formation of a government that all the people can trust. Having been reinspired by faith in themselves and their leaders, all of Russia will heed such a government. In this terrible hour, unprecedented in its ghastly consequences, there is no other way out and to delay is impossible.

Chairman of the State Duma,
Mikhail Rodzianko

1. Mikhail Vladimirovich Rodzianko, one of the leaders of the Octobrist Party, a landowner in Yekaterinoslav province, a member of the State Council (1906–1907), deputy to and chairman of the third State Duma, and chairman of the fourth State Duma (1912–1917). Rodzianko also sent telegrams containing virtually the same text to General Alekseev and to commanders at the front (see *Krasnyi arkhiv* 21 [1927]: 5–6, 7n2, 13).

· 7 ·

Letter from Alexandra to Nicholas, 26 February 1917.
Original English text.

———

No: 648.　　　　　　　　　　　*Ts. S.* [Tsarskoe Selo]　Feb. 26th 1917.

Beloved sweet One,

WHAT a joy, at 9 this morning I found yr. sweet letter of the 23–24th.—Fancy only how long it went. Thanks over & over again for it—I covered it with kisses & shall do so yet very often. Its so lonely without you—**nobody** to speak to really, as Ania is very suffering indeed, coughs so high temp:—must have been even up to 40[1] I think one time, scarcely sleeps a wink, this morning already 39.8. Any amount of nurses around her, *Akilina, Fedosia Stepanovna, sister Tatiana* (fr. my train,) they change about 2 at a time & *Mania* & *Zhuk* (the children's 4 D[rs] in the morning) then *Yevg. Serg.* & *Vl. Nik.*[2] 2 to 3 times a day & her D[r] whom she loves & who loves her even spent this night near her. The children 3 times a day, I twice, *Lili* in the evening sweet creature. You know how difficult & capricious she is as a patient, but she really suffers & now luckily the spots are beginning to cover her whole face and chest, its better when they come out. I went to *Znam:* [Znamensky church] yesterday & will to-day again—to go to service all alone, being tired & their needing me—I think I need not—God sees my prayers here. The children are cheery, Anastasia & Marie call themselves the *assistant nurses [sidel'ki]*—chatter without end & telephone right & left—they are most useful—wonder if they too will break down. *Zhilik*[3] is still very weak & only pays Baby visits—Mr Gibbs is with him. All dark rooms is depressing tho' Baby's dark room with drawn curtains is still lighter.—To-day I wont receive anybody, cant continue like that—to-morrow however must again.— *Boisman* spoke very well—only fright *Kniazhevich* will be elected Mar. de Noblesse, as that will complicate matters. Told me much about the disorder in town (I think over 200,000 people)—finds one does not keep good order. But I wrote all this yesterday, forgive me, I am foolish. But **one ought** to arrange card system for bread (as in every country now) as one has it for sugar some time & all are quiet & get enough. Our people are idiots. Obolensky wld. not do it, tho' their Medem[4] wished to, as it succeeded at *Pskov*. A poor G. d Arme [gendarme] officer was killed by the crowd—a few other people too. That gaping public does harm, well dressed people, wounded soldiers & so on—*girl students* etc. who egg on others. *Lili* speaks to the *cabbies* to get news. They said students came to them & said if they come out in the morning they will be shot. Such rotten types, of course *cabbies* & traindrives consequently strike, but they say its not like 95 [1905], because all adore you & **only** want bread. *Lili* talked for me to *Groten,* as I could not leave Ania. Now at last I can take my drops again.— Such mild weather—bore the little ones cant even go in a shut motor.— Kind *Rodionov* sent O, T & Ania each a flowerpot with lilies of the valley—the *Equipage;* luncheon at the rifles did not take place, as the reg: were to be ready in case of need.—

Yr. loneliness must be awful, just that great stillness around is so depressing, poor beloved one.—

$3\frac{1}{2}$ [3:30]. Just got yr. dear letter of yesterday, fondest thanks—my sweetheart. Yes, certainly a change of air would be good after—only *Livadia* [in the Crimea] wld. be too painful & too much fuss now—well, one can think all over still.—The little ones are the whole time with the others & Ania—they may still catch it. Tatiana coughs awfully, 37.8.—O. 39.1. Al. 39.6. Ania 40.1.—I just took Marie to *Znamenia* to place candles, went to our Friend's grave—now the Church so high that I could kneel & pray there calmly for you all without being seen by the *orderly*. We went to *Aleks:* stopped & talked to M. *Ivanov, Khvoshchinsky,* to new ones & D^r.—Mild, very sunny;—I brought you this bit of wood just over his grave, where I knelt.—

Things were very bad yesterday in town—one made arrests 120—& 30 people, chief leaders & *Lelianov*[5] drawn to account for speeches in the *City Duma*. The ministers & some right members of the *Duma* had a council last night (*Kalinin* wrote at 4 in the morning) to take severe measures—& they are full of hope that to-morrow it will be calm, they had intended to set up barricades etc. Monday—I read a vile proclamation—but it seems to me it will be alright—the sun shines so brightly—I felt such peace & calm on His dear grave—He died to save us.—*Burdiukov* insists to see me to-day—I did so hope to see nobody. Nastinka [Gendrikova] leaves to-night for *Kislovodsk*—Miechen [Grand Duchess Maria Pavlovna] is reigning there one says. Baby is one rash, covered like a leopard—Olga—big flat spots, Ania too all over, all their eyes & throats ache. Ania had 6 D^rs & two nurses, & *Zhuk*, Marie & me. Madning—but she likes it, it soothes her nervousness—Becker came to her. It does not feel at all like Sunday.—

I must go back to them in their darkness now + Blessings & kisses without end.—God grant the frost may cease in the South, my Rieman's train got off the rails because of the ice near *Kiev*.—God will help—this seems the climax. Faith & trust. So quiet you went to that dear Image.

Ever, sweet Nicky, yr. own old

Sunny

+

1. On the Celsius scale, 37° is considered a normal temperature, the equivalent of 98.6° Fahrenheit.
2. Yevgeny Sergeevich Botkin, personal physician to Nicholas and his family.
    Vladimir Nikolaevich Derevenko, physician treating the tsarevich Aleksei.
3. Pierre Gilliard, Swiss citizen who taught the imperial children French and was the tsarevich Aleksei's governor.
4. Aleksandr Nikolaevich Obolensky, prince. From July 1914 through November 1916, Obolensky was police chief (*gradonachalnik*) of Petrograd.
    Nikolai Nikolaevich Medem, former governor of Pskov and, until May 1916, governor of Petrograd.
5. Pavel Ivanovich Lelianov, first guild merchant, head of the Petrograd City Duma (1908–1912 and 1916–1917).

· 8 ·

Letter from Nicholas to Alexandra, 26 February 1917.
Original English text.

———

G. *Headquarters*   Febr. 26th 1917.

My own beloved One,

THE trains are again all wrong; your letter came yesterday after 5.0, but today the last one N° 647 arrived exactly before lunch time. Tender kisses for it. Please do not overtire yourself running accross [*sic*] among the invalids. See often Lili Den—a good reasonable friend.

I went yesterday to the virgin's image & prayed hard for you my Love, for the dear children & our country, also for Ania. Tell her that I saw her broach fastened to the image & rubbed it with my nose while kissing!

Last evening I was in church; the old mother of the Bishop thanked for the money we gave.

This morning during service I felt an excruciating pain in the middle of my chest, wh. lasted for a quarter of an hour. I could hardly stand & my forehead was covered with beads of sweat. I cannot understand what it was, as I had no heart beating, but it came & left me at once, when I knelt before the virgin's image!

If it happens once more I will tell it to *Fyodorov*. I hope *Khabalov* will know how to stop those street rows quickly. *Protopopov* ought to give him clear and categorical instructions.

Only that old *Golitsyn*[1] does not lose his head!

Tell *Aleksei* that *Kulik* & *Glina*[2] are well and think of him.

God bless you my Treasure, our children & her!

I kiss you all very tenderly.

Ever your own,
Nicky

1. Nikolai Dmitrievich Golitsyn, prince. From 27 December 1916 to 27 February 1917 he was chairman of the last Council of Ministers.
2. The cadets Yevgeny Makarov (Kulik, "Sandpiper") and Vasily Ageev (Glina, "Clay"), playmates of the tsarevich Aleksei.

· 9 ·

Telegram from War Minister Mikhail Beliaev to General Mikhail Alekseev, chief of staff
to the commander in chief, on the adoption of measures to bring order to Petrograd,
27 February 1917.

Sent 27 February [1917] at 13:15
Received 27 February [1917] at 13:20

Starting this morning, companies and battalions remaining loyal to their duty are firmly and energetically putting down disturbances in some military units. It has not yet been possible to crush the rebellion, but I am firmly convinced that calm will soon arrive. Ruthless measures are being adopted to achieve this. The authorities remain totally calm.

Beliaev

· 10 ·

Telegram from Nicholas II to the chairman of the Council of Ministers, Prince Nikolai
Golitsyn, on measures undertaken to quell the demonstrations in Petrograd,
27 February 1917.

Sent 27 February at 23:25

To the chairman of the Council of Ministers. Petrograd.

I have given an order to my chief of staff concerning a chief military commander for Petrograd with instructions to come immediately to the capital.[1] Also in relation to the troops. I personally bestow upon you all the necessary powers for civil rule. Regarding changes in the personal staff, under the current circumstances I consider them inadmissible.

Nicholas

1. The Georgievsky Battalion, composed of soldiers and officers who had distinguished themselves in battle and had been awarded the St. George Cross "for service and bravery," was sent from Headquarters to Petrograd together with General Nikolai Ivanov.

G. Crovka. Feb. 27th
1917.

My own Treasure,

Tender thanks for your
dear letter. This will
be my last one. How
happy I am at the thought
of meeting you in two days.
I had much to do & there-
fore my letter is short.
After the news of yester-
day from town - I saw
many faces here with fright
and expressions. Luckily
nervousity is calm, but finds
a very energetic man must

be named to make the
ministers work for the
food question, coal, railways
etc. That is right of course.
The disorders among the
troops come from the same
bezobrazniyner according
to news I got. I wonder
what Paul is doing? He
ought to keep them in hand.
You then you my beloved
Funny! I cover your sweet
face with kisses, also the
children. Give her my love.

Ever your own
Nicky

DOCUMENT II Letter from Nicholas to Alexandra

· 11 ·

Letter from Nicholas to Alexandra, 27 February 1917.
Original English text.

———

G. *Headquarters* Febr. 27th 1917.

My own Treasure,

TENDER thanks for your dear letter. This will be my last one. How happy I am at the thought of meeting you in two days. I had much to do & therefore my letter is short.

After the news of yesterday from town—I saw many faces here with frightened expressions. Luckily *Alekseev* is calm, but finds a very energetic man must be named to make the ministers work for the food question, coal, railways etc. That is right of course.

The disorders among the troops come from the *companies of the convalescents* [soldiers recovering from injuries sustained at the front] according to news I got. I wonder what Paul[1] is doing? He ought to keep them in hand.

God bless you my beloved Sunny! I cover your sweet face with kisses, also the children. Give her my love.

Ever your own
Nicky

1. Pavel Aleksandrovich, grand duke, youngest son of Alexander II, adjutant general in the imperial suite. On 28 May 1916 he was made commander of the Life Guards corps, later inspector of the Guards.

· 12 ·

Telegram from Nicholas to Alexandra, 27 February 1917.
Original English text.

———

Sent from Headquarters of the Commander in Chief, 27 February 1917, 19:06.
Received at Tsarskoe Selo, 1917, 20:02.

TO HER MAJESTY

Many thanks letter. Leave tomorrow 2.30. Guard Cavalry from Nov [Novgorod] ordered at once for town [Petrograd]. God grant ~~vicissim~~

disorders[1] [among] troops shall soon be stopped. Always near you. Tender love to all.

Niki

1. The code word *vicissim* has been crossed out and deciphered on the original by hand.

· 13 ·

Declaration by the Provisional Committee of the State Duma on assuming state power,
28 February 1917.

Facing grave conditions of internal economic ruin, the Provisional Committee of members of the State Duma found themselves forced to take into their own hands the reimposition of state and social order. Accepting full responsibility for this decision, the committee expresses the certainty that the population and the army will help it in the difficult task of forming a new government that corresponds to the wishes of the population and that can enjoy its trust.

Chairman of the State Duma,
Rodzianko

· 14 ·

Telegram from the elected members of the State Council[1] to Nicholas II at Headquarters concerning the country's internal state and the necessity for "a government of trust,"
28 February 1917.

Sent from Petrograd on 28 February 1917 at 1:35
Received at Headquarters on 28 February 1917 at 2:20

TO THE SOVEREIGN EMPEROR AT ARMY HEADQUARTERS
IN THE FIELD

YOUR IMPERIAL MAJESTY. We, the undersigned elected members of the State Council, recognizing the terrible danger advancing on the motherland, appeal to YOU in order to fulfill our duty of conscience before YOU and before Russia. Mills and factories have come to a total standstill owing to the complete disruption of transportation and the absence of necessary materials. Forced unemployment and an extreme intensification of the food crisis, caused by the very same disruption of transportation, have driven the masses of people to despair. This feeling is heightened by that hatred of the government and those grave suspicions of the authorities that have become deeply ingrained in the people's soul. All this has welled up into popular disturbances [*narodnaia smuta*] of elemental force, and the troops are now joining in. The government, never having enjoyed Russia's trust, is utterly discredited and completely powerless to deal with the grave situation. MAJESTY, the continued stay in power of the present government means the complete collapse of legal order and carries with it an inescapable defeat in war, the death of the dynasty and the greatest disaster for Russia. We consider the last and only means to be decisive change by YOUR IMPERIAL MAJESTY in the direction of internal politics in accordance with the repeatedly expressed desire for popular representation of estates and social organizations, the immediate convocation of the houses of the legislature, the resignation of the current Council of Ministers, and YOUR assigning, MAJESTY, a person who deserves all the people's trust to confirm a list of new cabinet members capable of governing the country in total accord with popular representation. Every hour counts. Further delays and vacillations threaten untold misfortunes.

YOUR IMPERIAL MAJESTY'S faithful members of the State Council: Baron Meller-Zakomelsky, Grimm, Guchkov, Yumashev, Savitsky, Vernadsky, Krym, Count Tolstoy, Vasiliev, Glebov, Zubashev, Laptev, Oldenburg, Diakonov, Veinshtein, Prince Trubetskoy, Shumakher, Stakhovich, Stakheev, Komsin, Shmurlo, Prince Drutskoy-Sokolinsky, Marin

1. The State Council was the upper house in the bicameral constitutional system established in Russia in 1906. It functioned as a conservative counterweight to the Duma.

· 15 ·

Telegram from Nicholas to Alexandra, 28 February 1917.
Original English text.

Sent from Viazma on 28 February 1917 at 15:00
Received at Tsarskoe Selo on 28 February 1917 at 16:49

TO HER MAJESTY

Left this morning at 5 Thoughts always together Glorius [*sic*] weather Hope are feeling well and quiet Many troops sent from front Fondest love
Niki

· 16 ·

Diary of Alexandra, 28 February 1917. Original English text.

———

February
28th
Tuesday

12 [°C; 54°F]
O: [Olga] 39.1.[1] *T:* [Tatiana] 39.5½. *Al:* [Aleksei]
37.7. An: [Anastasia] 37.7.
Sat with A. [Anna Vyrubova].—*Benkend:* [Ben-
kendorf] *Groten—Borisov*
upstairs. *Linevich—*
1 o'clock. Al. 37.3[2] O. 29.8½ *T:* 39.8—
Isa
6 o'clock. O. 40.3. *T.* 39.4. *Al:* 37.1
whole day upstairs meals with M. O. *Lili* [Den]
who sleeps again here.
9 o'clock. O. 40.2. *T.* 39.7 *Al:* 36.7. Ania 40.1.
passed the troops in the garden.

1. On the Celsius scale, 37° is considered a normal temperature, the equivalent of 98.6°
Fahrenheit.
2. The last digit is followed by the superscript abbreviation *ch.* for "o'clock," apparently
an error.

———

· 17 ·

Telegram from Alexandra to Nicholas, 1 March 1917.

———

To His Majesty, imperial train
From Tsarskoe Selo [Aleksandrovsky] Palace
Received 1 March 1917 at 11:50

Thoughts [and] prayers do not leave you. The Lord will help. The
children's temperatures are still high; they have a bad cough. We all kiss
you warmly.

Alix

———

· 18 ·

Manifesto of the grand dukes, 1 March 1917.[1]

———

The Grand Dukes have decided to present this act, fully approved by
them, to Your Imperial Majesty Sovereign Emperor for signing.

By the grace of God
We Nicholas the Second

Emperor and All-Russian Autocrat, Polish King,
Grand Duke of Finland, etc., etc., etc.

Announce to all our faithful subjects:

With the firm intention of reconstructing governmental administration in the empire on the basis of broad, popular representation, we propose to coordinate the introduction of a new state structure with the day of the war's end. Our former government, which considered it undesirable to establish the responsibility of ministers before the fatherland in the form of legislative institutions, found it possible to delay this step indefinitely. The events of the past several days, however, have shown that the government, which does not rely on a majority in the legislative institutions, could not foresee the disturbances that have arisen and could not firmly avert them.

Our sorrow is great that in the days when Russia's fate is being decided on the field of battle, internal strife has overtaken the capital and diverted defense efforts that are so very necessary for a victorious end to the war.

This strife has not been sown without the intrigues of a crafty enemy, and Russia is now subjected to a grave ordeal. But, firmly putting our trust in the help of God's Providence, we are quite sure that the Russian people, on behalf of the good of their homeland, will overcome this strife and will not allow enemy intrigues to triumph.

Making the sign of the cross, We grant the Russian State a constitutional order and decree resumption of the activities of the State Council and State Duma, which were stopped by our order. We empower the chairman of the State Duma to appoint immediately a provisional cabinet that enjoys the trust of the country and will, in accord with us, see that a legislative assembly is convoked to promptly examine a draft of new fundamental laws for the Russian Empire that can be introduced by the government.

May this new state order serve the highest success, glory, and happiness of our dear Russia.

Delivered in Tsarskoe Selo, the first day of March, in the year of Our Lord 1917, in the 23d year of our reign.

Signed:

Grand Duke Mikhail Aleksandrovich[2]
Grand Duke Kirill Vladimirovich[3]
Grand Duke Pavel Aleksandrovich

This act is to be transmitted to the Provisional Committee of the State Duma by Barrister Nikolai Ivanov.

Grand Duke Mikhail

Grand Duke Pavel

Grand Duke Kirill

Verified copy submitted to the Provisional Committee of the State Duma on 1 March 1917, faithfully—P. Miliukov[4]

1. This manifesto was the work of Grand Prince Pavel Aleksandrovich, Nicholas's uncle; Rodzianko; Nikolai Nikiforovich Ivanov, lawyer and aide to Rodzianko; and Prince Mikhail Putiatin. The plan, worked out on 28 February, was to present the manifesto to Nicholas when he arrived at Tsarskoe Selo. When Pavel learned that Nicholas's train had detoured to Pskov, he sought Alexandra's endorsement of the manifesto. She refused and reported to Nicholas about Pavel's "idiotical manifest about constit: after the war" (Document 24). By the time the manifesto was brought to the Duma for preliminary approval on 1 March, and before it was taken to Nicholas (it is the Duma's copy of the document presented here), Ivanov and Rodzianko both recognized that it was already too late.

2. Mikhail Aleksandrovich (Misha), Nicholas's younger brother and heir to the throne from 1899 until 1904, when tsarevich Aleksei was born.

3. Kirill Vladimirovich, Nicholas's first cousin. During the February Revolution, Kirill supported the Provisional Government.

4. Pavel Nikolaevich Miliukov, political figure, historian, publicist, one of the organizers of the Kadet Party and, starting in 1907, chairman of its Central Committee. Miliukov was also editor of the newspaper *Rech'* (Speech) and a member of the third and fourth State Dumas. During the February Revolution, he advocated the preservation of the monarchy. Minister of foreign affairs in the Provisional Government's first cabinet (until 2 May 1917).

· 19 ·

Telegram from General Alekseev to Nicholas II, 1 March 1917.

———

Sent 1 March at 22:20

TO HIS IMPERIAL MAJESTY

The constantly growing danger of anarchy spreading to the whole country, the continued disintegration of the army, and the impossibility of continuing the war in the present situation urgently require the immediate issuance of an imperial act that can even now calm minds. That can be accomplished only by convoking a responsible ministry and by assigning its formation to the chairman of the State Duma. Incoming reports give reason to hope that Duma statesmen, led by Rodzianko, can even now stop the general collapse and that we may be able to work together. But any wasting of time reduces our last chances to preserve and restore order and enables the seizure of power by extreme left elements. In light of this, I vigorously beg Your Imperial Majesty to deign to immediately publish from Headquarters the following manifesto:

"We announce to all our faithful subjects: A fearsome and cruel enemy is gathering his last strength for a battle with our motherland. The decisive hour is near. Russia's fate, that of our heroic army, the happiness of our people, the entire future of our dear fatherland—all demand that the war be brought to a victorious conclusion at all costs. In an effort to unite all popular forces more solidly to achieve a quick victory, I have found it necessary to assemble a ministry responsible to the people's representatives and have assigned its formation to Rodzianko, the chairman of the State Duma, who will select persons enjoying the trust of all Russia.

"I trust that all of Russia's faithful sons, having solidly united around the throne and the people's representatives, will amicably help our glorious army complete its great exploit. In the name of our beloved motherland, I summon all Russian people to the fulfillment of their holy duty before her, in order that it may be once again shown that Russia is just as indestructible as ever and that no enemy intrigues can overcome her. May the Lord God help us."

Adjutant General Alekseev

1 March 1917

· 20 ·

Preserved portion of telegram to Nicholas II from General Mikhail Alekseev, chief of staff to the commander in chief, sent from Headquarters and received in Pskov, 2 March 1917.

[Received at 14:30]

Your most faithful servant presents YOUR IMPERIAL MAJESTY with these telegrams received by myself in the name of YOUR IMPERIAL MAJESTY:

FROM GRAND DUKE NIKOLAI NIKOLAEVICH[1]

"Adjutant General Alekseev reports to me on the unprecedentedly fateful situation that has developed and asks me to support his view that a victorious end to the war, so very necessary for the happiness and future of Russia and the salvation of the dynasty, calls for the adoption of extraordinary measures. According to the duty and spirit of my oath as a loyal subject, I think it is necessary to beg YOUR IMPERIAL MAJESTY upon bended knee to save Russia and YOUR heir, knowing YOUR feeling of holy love for Russia and for him. Having made the sign of the cross over yourself, transfer to him YOUR legacy. There is no other way out. As never before in my life, with particularly fervent prayer, I beseech God to fortify and to guide YOU.

Adjutant General Nikolai"

FROM ADJUTANT GENERAL BRUSILOV[2]

"I ask you to report to His Imperial Majesty my request as a most faithful subject, based on my loyalty and love for the motherland and the tsar's throne, that at this moment the only way to save the situation and create the possibility of continuing to fight the external enemy, without which Russia will perish, is to abdicate the throne in favor of His Majesty's heir tsarevich with Grand Duke MIKHAIL ALEKSANDROVICH as regent. There is no other way out. But it is necessary to hurry in order that the flames of popular unrest, which have already grown large, may be more quickly extinguished; otherwise this situation will have no end of catastrophic consequences. This act will save the dynasty itself in the person of the rightful heir.

Adjutant General Brusilov"

FROM ADJUTANT GENERAL EVERT[3]

"Your IMPERIAL MAJESTY. YOUR MAJESTY'S chief of staff has informed me of the situation that has arisen in Petrograd, Tsarskoe Selo, the Baltic Sea, and Moscow and the result of talks between Adjutant General Ruzsky[4] and the chairman of the State Duma. YOUR MAJESTY, counting on the army, as presently constituted, to repress internal disorders is impossible. The army can be held together only in the name of saving Russia from undoubted enslavement by the country's worst enemy should it become impossible to carry on the fight. I am taking all measures to prevent information about the real state of affairs in the capital cities from penetrating the army in order to guard against inevitable unrest. There are no means whatsoever of stopping a revolution in the capital cities. It is necessary to come to an immediate decision that could put a stop to disorders and could preserve the army for the fight against the enemy. Given the situation that has arisen and seeing no other way out, YOUR MAJESTY'S limitlessly loyal subject begs YOUR MAJESTY, in the name of saving the motherland and the dynasty, to make a decision in line with that advocated by the chairman of the State Duma to Adjutant General Ruzsky as the only effective way to stop the revolution and save Russia from the horrors of anarchy.

Adjutant General Evert"

Having faithfully reported these telegrams to YOUR IMPERIAL MAJ-ESTY, I beg you to make the decision without delay that the Lord God conveys to YOU. Procrastination threatens Russia with death. We have managed to save the army from the disease that has overtaken Petrograd, Moscow, Kronstadt, and other cities. But one cannot vouch for the further preservation of the highest discipline. Any involvement of the army in the business of internal politics will mean an unavoidable end to the war, Russia's disgrace, and her collapse. YOUR IMPERIAL MAJESTY, passionately love the motherland and for the sake of her unity and independence, for the sake of achieving victory, deign to make a decision that can lead to a peaceful and favorable way out of the more than grave situation that has arisen. I await further orders. 2 March 1917. No. 1878.

Adjutant General Alekseev

1. Nikolai Nikolaevich, Nicholas I's grandson, the tsar's first cousin once removed, commander in chief (20 July 1914–23 August 1915). Dismissed at the insistence of Alexandra, who feared his growing influence. Commander of the Caucasus armies and the tsar's governor-general in the Caucasus (24 August 1915–1 March 1917). After Nicholas II abdicated, he served again as commander in chief (2–11 March 1917) but was soon obliged to resign under pressure from the Petrograd Soviet and the Provisional Government.

2. Aleksei Alekseevich Brusilov, cavalry general, commander of the southwestern front starting in March 1916.

3. Aleksei Yermolaevich Evert, infantry general, commander of the western front starting in August 1915.

4. Nikolai Vladimirovich Ruzsky, infantry general, commander of the northern front from August 1915 to April 1917.

· 21 ·

Letter from Grand Duke Pavel Aleksandrovich to the chairman of the State Duma, Mikhail Rodzianko, on saving the throne, [2 March] 1917.

1917

Much-esteemed Mikhail Vladimirovich,

AS the only living son of the Tsar-Liberator, I entreat you to do **all** that is in your power to preserve the constitutional throne for the tsar. I know that you are passionately devoted to him and that any of your deeds are full of deep patriotism and love for the dear motherland. I would not disturb you at such a moment if I had not read the speech by Miliukov, minister of for. affairs, and his words about the regency of Grand Duke Mikh. Alek., in [the newspaper] *Izvestiia*. I find this thought about the total removal of the monarch oppressive. [After this are crossed out the words: "and poisonous. Think about the army at the front that is deeply loyal to him. This could crea [create]."] Given a constitutional form of government and proper supplies for the army, the sovereign will doubtless lead the troops to victory. I would come to see you, but my motorcar has been requisitioned, and I haven't the strength to come on foot. May the Lord help you and save our dear tsar and our motherland.

> Sincerely, respectfully, and
> loyally yours,
> G.D. Pavel Aleks.

· 22 ·

Letter from Grand Duke Pavel Aleksandrovich to Grand Duke Kirill Vladimirovich
concerning his attitude toward the regency, 2 March 1917.

2 March 1917

Dear Kirill,

YOU know that I am constantly in touch with the State Duma through Nik. Nikif. Ivanov. I thoroughly disliked last night's new idea of appointing Misha [Mikhail Aleksandrovich] regent. This is intolerable, and it may just be one of Brasova's intrigues.[1] P. [Perhaps] these are just rumors, but we must be on our guard and do everything that we can to save the throne for Niki. If Niki signs the manifesto that we sanctioned about a constitution, then this will meet all the demands of the people and the Provisional Government. Discuss it with Rodzianko and show him my letter. I very much count on your help and embrace you and Ducky[2] tightly.

> Your uncle P.

1. Natalia Sergeevna Brasova (previously Vulfert), countess, morganatic spouse of Grand Duke Mikhail Aleksandrovich, daughter of Sergei Sheremetevsky, the famous Moscow lawyer.
2. Viktoria Fyodorovna (Ducky), grand duchess. In her first marriage, she was the wife of Grand Duke Ernst of Hesse-Darmstadt (Alexandra's brother). She married Grand Duke Kirill Vladimirovich in 1905 without the customary permission of the tsar as head of the dynasty. Nicholas recognized the marriage in 1907.

· 23 ·

Letter from Grand Duke Kirill Vladimirovich to Grand Duke Pavel Aleksandrovich
concerning the attitude of Grand Duke Mikhail Aleksandrovich toward the regency,
2 March 1917.

———————

2 March 1917

Dear Uncle Pavel!

I HAVE heard only rumors concerning the question
that worries you. I completely agree with you, but
Misha, despite my insistent requests that he clearly
and single-mindedly work with our family, hides and communicates in
secret only with Rodzianko. I was completely alone during these difficult
days, and I take full responsibility before Niki and the motherland for
trying to save the situation and for recognizing the new government.

I embrace you,
Kirill

· 24 ·

Letter from Alexandra to Nicholas, 2 March 1917. Original English text.

———————

No: 650.   March 2nd 1917.

My own beloved, precious Angel, light of my life.

M Y heart breaks, thinking of you all alone going through all this
anguish, anxiety, & we know nothing of you & you neither of
us, so am sending off *Soloviev* & *Gramotin* each with letter,
trusting one may reach you at least. I wanted to send an aeroplane, but the
men have gone. The young men will tell you **everything**, so that I wont say
anything about the situation. Its all so abnormally hideous & the rapidity
colossal with wh. events go. But I have the firm belief, wh. **nothing** can
shake that all **will be** well somehow, especially since I got yr. wire this
morning the first ray of sunshine in this swamp. Not knowing yr. where-
abouts was making at last through the *Headquarters. Rodz:* [Rodzianko]
pretending he did not know why one stopped you. Its clear [he] does, only
not to get you to join with me before you have signed some paper of theirs,
constitution or some such horror. And you, who are alone, no army behind
you, caught like a mouse in a trap, what can you do? Thats the lowest,
meanest thing unknown in history, to stop ones sovereign.—Now P. [Pro-

topopov] cant reach you because of *Luga* [railway station] wh. the rev: [revolutionaries] have in hand, they stopped, took & unarmed the *But:* reg: [regiment] & spoiled the line.—Perhaps you will show yourself to the troops at *Pskov* & beyond & get them around you. If you are forced into concessions—you are **never** required to keep them, because the manner is beyond & below criticism. Paul [Pavel Aleksandrovich], after getting a colossal headmashing fr. me for doing **nothing** with the guard, tries to work hard now, & he is going to save us all, very grand & foolish. Has worked out idiotical manifest about constit: after the war etc. *Boris*[1] off to the *Headquarters,* I saw him in the morning, in the evening he left, as tho' urgent orders for the *Headquarters*—purest panick. *Georgy*[2] at *Gatchino* does not dream of giving any news or coming. Kirill Xenia Misha cant get out of town. Yr. little family worthy of their Father—by degree have told now all the situation to the big ones, the Cow [Vyrubova]—they were far too ill before—a horribly strong measles, such sickness, coughs. Acting before him was trying—Baby [Aleksei] I say the half. He has 36.1[3] & so bright only all wretched you have not come. *Lili* [Den] an angel unseperable, sleeps in the bedroom, Maria with me, in our *dressing gowns* & hair done. Whole day seeing people. *Groten perfect* & *Resin*[4] quiet. Old couple *Benk:* [Benkendorf] sleep in the house & Apr: [Apraksin][5] get through here in civil dress. Used *Linevich,*[6] fear they have kept him too in town. None of ours can come. Sisters [nurses], women, civils, wounded get through—only can teleph. to W. [Winter] Palace; *Rataev*[7] behaves admirably.—We are all up in spirits, uncrushed by circumstances, only in anguish for you & humiliated beyond words for you patient Saint. God Almighty help you.—Saw *Ivanov* last night 1 til 2½. he remains in his train here for the moment, I thought he cld. have gone with his train to you over Dno [station], but can he get through? He hoped yr. train wld. have followed his.—One burned Fred: [Frederiks's] house, his family are in the hosp. of G. à Cheval. They have taken Grünwald & Stackelberg.[8] Shall give a paper for them to bring you we got fr. *N. P.* [Nikolai Pavlovich Sablin] through a man we sent to town. He neither can get out—*on account of* [*na uchete*]. Two currents—*Duma* & revolutionists—two snakes who I hope will eat off each others heads, that wld. be the saving of the situation. I feel God will do something. Such bright sun today—only to get you here!—the pain that the *Equip:* [Guards Equipage] even left us this night—they understand **absolutely** nothing, a microbe sits in them. I'll save that paper for *Voeik:*[9] to read, it will hurt you as it did me, *Rodz.* [Rodzianko] not even once mentions you—but when one hears you are not let on, the troops then will rage & stand up against all. They believe the *Duma* means to be with & for you. Well, *let* [*puskai*] they make order &

show themselves fit for something—but they made a too big fire & how to put it out now.—The children lie quite in the dark, Baby lies with them for several hours after lunch and sleeps. I spent my days upstairs & receive there too—the lift does not work since 4 days, a pipe burst.—Olga 37.7. T. 38.9 & ear begins to ache—*An.:* 37.2 because of med. they gave her for her head, pyramidon. Baby still sleeping, Ania 36.6—their illness has been very heavy—God for sure sent it for the good somehow—they are so brave the whole time.—I shall go out and say good morning to the soldiers now in front of the house.—Don't know what to write, too many impressions, too much to say. Heart aches very much, but I don't heed it, my spirits are quite up and I am like a cock. Only suffer too hideously for you.—Must end & write the other letter in case you dont get this, & small for them to hide in their boots or burn.—God bless & protect you—send His Angels to guard & guide you—never away fr. you, *Lili* & *Ania* send tenderest **love** & prayers. We all kiss, & kiss & bless + you without end. God will help, will help & yr. glory will come—this is the climax of the bad. The horror before our Allies!! & the enemies joy!!—Can advise nothing, be only yr. precious self. If you have to give into things, God will help you to get out of them. Ah my suffering Saint. I am one with you, inseparably one.

Old Wify.

+

May this image I have kissed bring you my fervent blessings, strength, help. Wear his [Rasputin's] cross the whole time even if uncomfortable—for **my** peace's sake.

I don't send Image, they can easier crumble up the paper without.

1. Boris Vladimirovich, grand duke, Nicholas's cousin.
2. Georgy Mikhailovich, grand duke, son of Grand Duke Mikhail Nikolaevich, infantry general who served at Headquarters of the commander in chief during World War I.
3. On the Celsius scale, 37° is considered a normal temperature, the equivalent of 98.6° Fahrenheit.
4. Aleksei Alekseevich Resin, commander of His Majesty's Combined Infantry Regiment in Tsarskoe Selo starting on 14 August 1914, retainer to the imperial family.
5. Pyotr Nikolaevich Apraksin, comptroller of the household of the empress.
6. Aleksandr Nikolaevich Linevich, aide-de-camp in the tsar's suite, lieutenant in the Life Guards Horse Artillery.
7. Ivan Dmitrievich Rataev, prince, chief of police at the Winter Palace.
8. Artur Aleksandrovich fon Grinvald (von Grünwald), cavalry general in charge of the court stables.
Konstantin Karlovich Shtakelberg (Stackelberg), baron, lieutenant general in the Life Guards, director of the court orchestra.

9. Vladimir Nikolaevich Voeikov, major general in the tsar's suite, palace commandant beginning on 25 December 1913. He was expelled from Headquarters by the Provisional Government during the February Revolution and later arrested.

· 25 ·

Protocol of talks between deputies of the State Duma Aleksandr Guchkov[1] and Vasily Shulgin[2] and Nicholas II in Pskov concerning the signing of an act of abdication from the throne, 2 March 1917.

On 2 March, at approximately 10 o'clock at night, Guchkov, member of the State Council, and Shulgin, member of the State Duma, arrived in Pskov. They were immediately invited into the salon car of the imperial train where by that time [the following people] had gathered: commander of the northern front, Adjutant General Ruzsky; minister of the imperial court, Count Frederiks; and Major General Naryshkin,[3] chief of the military campaign office of His Imperial Majesty's suite. After walking into the salon, His Majesty graciously greeted the assembled and, asking them all to be seated, readied himself to listen to the deputies who had arrived.

MEMBER OF S.C. [State Council] GUCHKOV: I arrived with member of the State Duma Shulgin to report to you what has happened in Petrograd these past days and also to consult about measures that could save the situation. The situation is extremely threatening: First the workers and then the troops went into action, and the disturbances spread to the outskirts of town. Moscow is restless. This is not the result of some conspiracy or coup planned in advance, but a movement that sprang from the very ground and instantly took on an anarchical cast and left the authorities fading into the background. I went to General Khabalov's deputy, General Zankevich, and asked him if he had some reliable unit or at least some individuals of lower rank who could be counted upon. He told me that he had no such people and that all the units arriving on the scene were immediately taking the side of the rebels. Since it was terrifying that the mutiny was taking on an anarchical form, we formed the so-called Provisional Committee of the State Duma and began to take measures to try to reinstate officers to command the lower ranks. I personally visited many units and tried to convince the lower ranks to keep calm. The committee of the workers' party [the Petrograd Soviet of Workers' and Soldiers' Deputies] has also convened at the Duma and we find ourselves under its control and censorship. If Petrograd descends into anarchy, the danger is that we moderates will be swept aside, because this movement is already beginning to overwhelm us. Their slogans are for proclaiming a social republic. This movement is embracing the lower classes and even soldiers to whom it promises to give land. The second danger is that the movement will spread to the front where the slogan is, "Sweep away your commanders and elect whom you please." The same incendiary material is there, and the fire could spread to the whole front, for there isn't a single military unit that isn't immediately infected by the atmosphere of the movement. Yesterday, representatives of the Combined Infantry Regiment, the Railway Regiment, Your Majesty's Convoy, and court police appeared at the Duma and announced that they had joined the movement. They were told that they must continue to guard the persons they were assigned to protect, but the danger still exists, for the mob is now armed.

The people profoundly believe that the situation was caused by the mistakes of those in authority, in particular the highest authority, and this is why some sort of legal act is needed that would work upon the popular consciousness. The only path is to transfer the burden of supreme rulership to other hands. Russia can be saved, the monarchical principle can be saved, the dynasty can be saved. If you, Your Majesty, announce that you are transferring your power to your little son, if you assign the regency to Grand Duke Mikhail Aleksandrovich, and if in your name or in the name of the regent instructions are issued for a new government to be formed, then perhaps Russia will be saved. I say perhaps because events are unfolding so quickly that at present Rodzianko, myself, and other moderate members of the Duma are considered traitors by extreme elements. Of course, they are against such a maneuver, for they see in it the possibility of preserving our age-old principles. Thus, Your Majesty, only under these conditions can we make an attempt to establish order. This is what Shulgin and I were entrusted to tell you. Of course, before deciding to do this, you should think it over well, pray, but make a decision no later than tomorrow, because by that time we will no longer be in a position to give advice if you ask it of us, since there is reason to fear the aggressive outbreaks of the mob.

HIS MAJESTY: Through the morning, before your arrival and after Adjutant General Ruzsky's conversation with the Duma chairman over the direct line, I thought it over, and for the sake of the good, peace, and preservation of Russia, I was ready to abdicate from the throne in favor of my son. But now, having again thought the situation over, I have come to the conclusion that, in light of his illness, I should abdicate in my name and his name simultaneously, as I cannot be separated from him.

MEMBER OF S.C. GUCHKOV: We had counted on the figure of little Aleksei Nikolaevich having a softening effect on the transfer of power.

ADJUTANT GENERAL RUZSKY: His Majesty is worried that if the

throne is transferred to his successor then His Majesty will be separated from him.

MEMBER OF S.D. [State Duma] SHULGIN: I cannot give a categorical answer to that, because we came here to propose just what we did.

HIS MAJESTY: Having given my consent to abdication, I must be sure that you have considered what impression this will make on all of the rest of Russia. Will this not carry dangerous consequences?

MEMBER OF S.C. GUCHKOV: No, Your Majesty, the danger is not in that. We are afraid that if a republic is announced, there will be civil strife.

MEMBER OF S.D. SHULGIN: Allow me to somewhat clarify under what circumstances the Duma must work. On the 26th, a mob came into the Duma and, together with armed soldiers, occupied the whole right side while the left side was occupied by the public. We saved only two rooms where the so-called committee huddles together. All the arrested are being dragged here, and it's a good thing for them that the soldiers do this, for it spares them from mob justice; we free some of the arrested immediately. We are preserving the symbol of governance of the country, and only thanks to that is some semblance of order retained, with the railways operating uninterruptedly. These are the conditions in which we work; it's hell at the Duma, a madhouse. We are going to have to begin a decisive battle with leftist elements, and we need some sort of basis to do this. Concerning your plan, let us think about this for at least a quarter of an hour. This plan has the advantage of containing no thought of separation and, on the other hand, can contribute to furthering calm if your brother, Grand Duke Mikhail Aleksandrovich, as full monarch, swears to the constitution while simultaneously assuming the throne.

MEMBER OF S.C. GUCHKOV: All the workers and soldiers who have taken part in these disturbances are sure that restoring the old order means reprisals against them and that therefore a total change is needed. The popular imagination needs to be struck with a whip in such a way as to change everything. I think that the legal act upon which you have settled should be accompanied by the appointment of Prince Lvov[4] as chairman of the Council of Ministers.

HIS MAJESTY: I would like to have a guarantee that my departure serves as neither the reason nor the excuse for more unnecessary spilling of blood.

MEMBER OF S.D. SHULGIN: Elements that will lead the battle against the new order may engage in such acts, but these elements should not be feared. For example, Kiev, a city that I know well and that always supported the monarchy, has undergone a total change.

HIS MAJESTY: And you don't think that there could be disturbances in the cossack districts?

MEMBER OF S.C. GUCHKOV: No, Your Majesty, the cossacks are all on the side of the new order. Your Majesty, the human feeling of a father spoke in you, and politics has no place here, so we can make no objection to your proposal.

MEMBER OF S.D. SHULGIN: It is only important that it be stated in Your Majesty's act that your successor is obliged to swear to the constitution.

HIS MAJESTY: Would you like to think it over some more?

MEMBER OF S.C. GUCHKOV: No, I think that we can accept your proposal at once. When would you be able to prepare the final draft of the act? Here is a draft that could be of use to you if you wanted to take something from it.

His Majesty, having answered that the draft was already written, withdrew to his chamber, where he corrected by hand the manifesto of abdication that had been prepared in the morning to read that the throne was assigned to Grand Duke Mikhail Aleksandrovich and not to Grand Duke Aleksei Nikolaevich. Having ordered it to be rewritten, His Majesty signed the manifesto, entered the salon car at 11:40, and gave it to Guchkov. The deputies asked that the phrase stating that the new emperor swear to uphold the constitution be inserted, which His Majesty immediately did. His Majesty simultaneously wrote out in his own hand the edicts to the Ruling Senate on the appointment of Prince Lvov as chairman of the Council of Ministers and the appointment of Grand Duke Nikolai Nikolaevich as commander in chief. So it would not seem as if the act was executed under pressure from the deputies present, and since His Majesty had already made the actual decision to abdicate from the throne earlier in the day, on the advice of the deputies the time of signing was marked down on the manifesto as 3 P.M., and as 2 P.M. on the edicts to the Ruling Senate. Also present, in addition to the above-named persons, were General Danilov, chief of staff to [the commander of] the armies of the northern front who was summoned by Adjutant General Ruzsky.

In conclusion, Duma member Shulgin asked His Majesty about his further plans. His Majesty answered that he was getting ready to go to Headquarters, perhaps to Kiev to say good-bye to Her Majesty the [Dowager] Empress Maria Fyodorovna, and then would stay at Tsarskoe Selo until his children had recovered. The deputies said that they would do everything possible to facilitate His Majesty's fulfillment of his further plans. The deputies also asked that a duplicate of the manifesto be signed that would remain in the hands of General Ruzsky in case any misfortune befell them. His Majesty bid farewell to the deputies and dismissed them, after which he also bid farewell to the commander of the armies of the northern front and his chief of staff, kissed them, and thanked them for working with him. Within approximately one hour, a duplicate of the manifesto was presented to His Majesty for signing, after which all four signatures by His Majesty were countersigned by Count Frederiks, minister of the imperial court.

   1. Aleksandr Ivanovich Guchkov, major industrialist; founder and leader of the Union of October 17, or Octobrist Party; member and chairman of the third State Duma; chairman of the Central Military-Industrial Committee from 1915 to 1917; member of the State Council from 1915 to 1917; minister of war and navy in the first Provisional Government (March–May 1917).
   2. Vasily Vitalievich Shulgin, publicist, one of the leaders of the nationalists in the State Duma, member of the Provisional Committee of the State Duma.
   3. Kirill Anatolievich Naryshkin, Nicholas's childhood friend, major general in the tsar's suite.
   4. Georgy Yevgenievich Lvov, prince, lawyer, head of the All-Russian Union of Zemstvos and Town Councils for Relief to Wounded and Sick Soldiers, Moscow City Duma member, minister president in the first two cabinets of the Provisional Government after the February Revolution (prior to July 1917).

· 26 ·

Nicholas II's manifesto of abdication from the throne, 2 March 1917.

————

Headquarters

To the chief of staff:

   In these days of great struggle with an external enemy who has tried to enslave our country for nearly three years, the Lord God saw fit to send down upon Russia a harsh new ordeal. The developing internal popular disturbances threaten to have a catastrophic effect upon the future conduct of the relentless war. The fate of Russia, the honor of our heroic army, the good of the people, the whole future of our dear fatherland demand that the war be brought to a victorious end no matter what. A cruel enemy is summoning his last strength, and the hour is near when our valiant army, together with our renowned allies, can completely smash the enemy. During these decisive days for the life of Russia, WE considered it a duty of conscience to facilitate OUR people's close unity and the rallying of all popular forces in order to achieve victory as quickly as possible, and, in agreement with the State Duma, WE consider it to be for the good to abdicate from the Throne of the Russian State and to surrender supreme

Ставка

Начальнику Штаба.

Въ дни великой борьбы съ внѣшнимъ врагомъ, стремящимся почти три года поработить нашу родину, Господу Богу угодно было ниспослать Россіи новое тяжкое испытаніе. Начавшіяся внутреннія народныя волненія грозятъ бѣдственно отразиться на дальнѣйшемъ веденіи упорной войны. Судьба Россіи, честь героической нашей арміи, благо народа, все будущее дорогого нашего Отечества требуютъ доведенія войны во что бы то ни стало до побѣднаго конца. Жестокій врагъ напрягаетъ послѣднія силы и уже близокъ часъ, когда доблестная армія наша совмѣстно со славными нашими союзниками сможетъ окончательно сломить врага. Въ эти рѣшительные дни въ жизни Россіи, почли МЫ долгомъ совѣсти облегчить народу НАШЕМУ тѣсное единеніе и сплоченіе всѣхъ силъ народныхъ для скорѣйшаго достиженія побѣды и, въ согласіи съ Государственною Думою, признали МЫ за благо отречься отъ Престола Государства Россійскаго и сложить съ СЕБЯ Верховную власть. Не желая разстаться съ любимымъ Сыномъ НАШИМЪ, МЫ передаемъ наслѣдіе НАШЕ Брату НАШЕМУ Великому Князю МИХАИЛУ АЛЕКСАНДРОВИЧУ и благословляемъ Его на вступленіе на Престолъ Государства Россійскаго. Заповѣдуемъ Брату НАШЕМУ править дѣлами государственными въ полномъ и ненарушимомъ единеніи съ представителями народа въ законодательныхъ учрежденіяхъ, на тѣхъ началахъ, кои будутъ ими установлены, принеся въ томъ ненарушимую присягу. Во имя горячо любимой родины призываемъ всѣхъ вѣрныхъ сыновъ Отечества къ исполненію своего святого долга передъ Нимъ, повиновеніемъ Царю въ тяжелую минуту всенародныхъ испытаній и помочь ЕМУ, вмѣстѣ съ представителями народа, вывести Государство Россійское на путь побѣды, благоденствія и славы. Да поможетъ Господь Богъ Россіи.

Г. Псковъ.

2 Марта 15 час. мин. 1917 г.

Николай

Министръ Императорскаго Двора
Генералъ Адъютантъ Графъ Фредериксъ

DOCUMENT 26. Nicholas II's manifesto of abdication, 2 March 1917.

power. Not wishing to part with OUR beloved son, WE name as OUR successor OUR Brother, OUR Grand Duke MIKHAIL ALEKSANDROVICH, and bless his assumption to the Throne of the Russian State. We entrust OUR brother to conduct state affairs in complete and unshakeable unity with the representatives of the people in the legislative institutions according to principles they will determine, and on this to take an inviolable oath. In the name of our deeply beloved homeland, we call all faithful sons of the fatherland to fulfill their holy duty to this land in obedience to the tsar in this difficult moment of national trials and to help HIM, together with the representatives of the people, to lead the Russian State along the path of victory, prosperity, and glory. May the Lord God help Russia.

NICHOLAS

Town of Pskov
2 March (15:00) 1917
Minister of the Imperial Court, Adjutant General Count Frederiks

· 27 ·

From the minutes of the first session of the Council of Ministers of the
Provisional Government, on evicting the Romanovs, 2 March 1917.

———

On the question of the future fate of the members of the former imperial family, minister of foreign affairs [P. N. Miliukov] reported that the Soviet of Workers' Deputies asserted the necessity of evicting them beyond the borders of the Russian state, both for political reasons as well as for the safety of their future residence in Russia. The Provisional Government thought that extending this measure to all members of the family of the House of Romanov was not entirely justified, but that such a measure is completely necessary and urgent in relation to the abdicated former emperor Nicholas II and in relation to Grand Duke Mikhail Aleksandrovich, as well as to their families. Concerning the place of residence of these persons, there is no need to insist on eviction outside Russia, and should they wish to remain in our state, it is necessary only to limit their place of residence within known boundaries, equally limiting the possibility of their movement.

· 28 ·

Conversation by direct telegraph between General Nikolai Ruzsky in Pskov and Mikhail Rodzianko and Prince Georgy Lvov in Petrograd, concerning the transfer of the throne to Grand Duke Mikhail Aleksandrovich, 3 March 1917.

8:45

[RUZSKY:] General Ruzsky on the line.

[RODZIANKO:] Hello, Your Excellency. It is extremely important that the manifesto of abdication [and] the transfer of power to Grand Duke Mikhail Aleksandrovich not be published until such time as I let you know. The fact of the matter is we have managed to contain the revolutionary movement within more or less tolerable limits only with great effort, but the situation has still not righted itself, and a civil war is entirely possible. A regency of the grand duke with the accession to the throne of the caesarevitch [Tsarevich Aleksei] might be accepted, but his accession as emperor would be absolutely unacceptable. We ask that you take all measures that you can to bring about a delay.

[LVOV:] Rodzianko has stepped away. Prince Lvov is on the line.

[RUZSKY:] All right, instructions will be given, but I can't say whether it will be possible to hold up the news, because too much time has elapsed. I very much regret that the deputies sent yesterday were not adequately informed about their role and, in general, about why they had come. In any event, everything humanly possible will be done. I ask that you give me a full account right now of what took place yesterday and of what the consequences of this may be in Petrograd.

[RODZIANKO:] Rodzianko on the line. Again, the fact is that the deputies aren't to blame. A soldiers' mutiny suddenly flared up, the likes of which I've not seen, and these aren't really soldiers, of course, but just ordinary muzhiks [peasants] who have found it useful now to voice their muzhik demands. The only thing heard in the crowd was "Land and freedom," "Down with the dynasty," "Down with the Romanovs," "Down with the officers." The beating up of officers started in many units; the workers joined in, and anarchy reached its apogee. After lengthy negotiations with deputies from the workers, it was possible only this evening to come to a partial agreement that consists of convening in the near future a constituent assembly so the people can convey their views on a form of government. Only then did Petrograd breathe freely, and the night passed relatively calmly. Little by little, the troops were brought to order during the night. But pronouncing Grand Duke Mikhail Aleksandrovich emperor will pour oil onto the fire, and a merciless destruction of all that it is possible to destroy will begin. We will lose and let go of all power, and there will be no one to suppress popular unrest. In its proposed form, a return of the dynasty cannot be ruled out, and it is desirable that the Supreme Council and the Provisional Government, which is now working with us, continue to operate until approximately the end of the war. I am absolutely certain that under these circumstances, things can be quickly calmed down and a decisive victory provided for, as doubtless patriotic feeling will swell; everything is moving at a heightened pace, and a victory can probably be achieved.

[RUZSKY:] I have given all instructions, but it is extremely difficult to promise that the information won't get out, for what we had in mind with this measure was to give the army a chance to achieve calm more quickly at the home front. Yesterday, or more precisely today, because events were unfolding at night, the imperial train left for Headquarters via Dvinsk, and thus the center of further negotiations about this important matter must be transferred there, because by law the chief of staff stands in for and acts in the name of the commander in chief when the latter is absent. Besides this, Yuza [telegraph] apparatuses must be installed where the new government holds session in Petrograd to provide for the convenience of the quickest possible communications with Headquarters and with me. I also ask that I be briefed twice a day at a set time on the state of affairs either in person or through proxies whose names I should like to know.

[RODZIANKO:] I will do exactly as you request, and the Yuza apparatus will be installed, but in case the news of the manifesto breaks and reaches the public and the army, I ask that you at least not rush to have the troops swear allegiance. By tonight, I will give you and all the top commanders an update, and I will keep you informed on how things are going twice a day. Tell me, please, when Guchkov departed?

[RUZSKY:] Guchkov left from Pskov tonight around 3 o'clock. Yesterday in Pskov, I already gave instructions about holding up the swearing of allegiance. I will immediately let the army on my front and at Headquarters know. Prince Lvov was on the line, I believe? Does he wish to speak to me?

[RODZIANKO:] Nikolai Vladimirovich, everything's been said, Prince Lvov can't add anything. We are both firmly counting on God's help, on Russia's greatness and strength, on the valor and determination of the army, and notwithstanding any obstacles, on a victorious end to the war. Good-bye.

[RUZSKY:] Mikhail Vladimirovich. Tell me whether I understood correctly. So, for now everything remains the same no matter what is happening with the manifesto or with Prince Lvov's instructions on forming a ministry. I would also like to know your opinion concerning the appointment of Grand Duke Nikolai Nikolaevich as commander in chief on the orders of His Majesty, given yesterday in a separate decree by the sovereign emperor. These decrees were made widely known yesterday at the request of the deputies, even in Moscow and, of course, in the Caucasus.

[RODZIANKO:] Today we have formed a government with Prince Lvov as its head, about which all commanders at the front were notified by telegram. Until the question of a constitution is decided by the Constituent Assembly, everything remains in this form: the Supreme Council, a responsible ministry, and functioning legislative houses. We have nothing against the dissemination of decrees about the appointment of Grand Duke Nikolai Nikolaevich as commander in chief. Good-bye.

[RUZSKY:] Tell me who heads the Supreme Council.

[RODZIANKO:] I am mistaken: it is the Provisional Committee of the State Duma, under my chairmanship, not the Supreme Council.

[RUZSKY:] Okay. Good-bye. Don't forget to keep Headquarters informed, because further negotiations must be conducted at Headquarters; I need only be informed about the course and results of all this.

· 29 ·

Act (manifesto) of abdication of Mikhail Aleksandrovich Romanov from the throne, 3 March 1917.

By my brother's will, a heavy burden was placed upon me when I was assigned the All-Russian Imperial Throne during a time of unprecedented war and popular unrest.

Inspired, together with all the people, by the single thought that the good of our motherland is above all else, I have firmly resolved to assume supreme power only if that should be the will of our great people who will be required by popular vote, through their representatives in the Constituent Assembly, to create a form of government and new fundamental laws for the Russian State.

Therefore, in appealing for God's blessing, I ask all citizens of the Russian Empire [*Derzhava*] to obey the Provisional Government, which arose at the initiative of the State Duma and was vested with full power, until such time as the Constituent Assembly expresses the will of the people concerning their preferred form of government after being convened in the shortest time possible and by holding a general, direct, equal, and secret vote.

Mikhail

3 March 1917
Petrograd

66.

командующаго войсками на Валахѣ.
Я и вылѣзъ, гдѣ остановился на нетъ.
Видѣлъ Рузскаго, Д[?], Данилова и
Саввича. Затянулъ и Луга занята
тоже ехали замѣшкались и скоро въ
поѣздъ. Долженъ до Царскаго не
чудесно. Я жалѣлъ и думалъ, что
будетъ того! Какъ Богъ дастъ. Время же
должно быть милостиво день прошед -
быть все это событiй! потомъ
нашъ готовъ!

2-го Марта. Четвергъ.
Утромъ пришелъ Рузскiй и прочелъ
свой длиннѣйшiй разговоръ по аппарату
съ Родзянко. По его словамъ положенiе
въ Петроградѣ таково, что теперь
министерство изъ Думы будто бы безсильно

67.

что-либо сдѣлать, т. к. съ нимъ
борется соц. дем. партiя въ лицѣ рабочаго комитета. Нужно моё отреченiе.
Рузскiй передалъ этотъ разговоръ въ
Ставку, а Алексѣевъ всѣмъ главно-
командующимъ. Къ 2½ ч. пришли
отвѣты отъ всѣхъ. Суть та, что
во имя спасенiя Россiи и удержанiя
армiи на фронтѣ въ спокойствiи нужно
рѣшиться на этотъ шагъ. Я согласился.
Изъ Ставки прислали проектъ манифеста.
Вечеромъ изъ Петрограда прибыли Гучковъ
и Шульгинъ, съ кот. я переговорилъ и
передалъ имъ подписанный и переделанный
манифестъ. Въ часъ ночи уѣхалъ изъ
Пскова съ тяжелымъ чувствомъ пережитаго.
Кругомъ измѣна и трусость и обманъ!

76

DOCUMENT 30. Diary of Nicholas II, 2 March 1917.

· 30 ·
Diary of Nicholas II, 27 February–3 March 1917.

27 February. Monday.   Disorders in Petrograd began a few days ago. To my sorrow, troops also began to take part. It is such a horrible feeling to be so far away and to receive fragments of bad news! I spent a short time with a report. Took an afternoon walk along the highway leading to Orsha. The weather stayed sunny. After dinner, decided to hurry over to Ts.S. [Tsarskoe Selo] and at 1 A.M. made it onto the train.

28 February. Tuesday.   Went to sleep at 3:15, as I had talked a long time with N. I. Ivanov whom I am sending to Petrograd with troops to establish order. Slept until 10:00. We left Mogilyov at 5 in the morning. The weather was frosty, sunny. During the day, we passed Viazma and Rzhev, and we went past Likhoslavl at 9 o'clock.

1 March. Wednesday.   During the night, we turned back from M. [Malaia] Vishera because Liuban and Tosno turned out to be occupied by rebels. We went to Valdai, Dno, and then Pskov, where we spent the night. I saw Ruzsky. He, Danilov, and Savvich[1] were dining together. It turned out that Gatchina and Luga were also occupied. What shame and disgrace! We couldn't make it all the way to Tsarskoe. But my thoughts and feelings are constantly there! How hard it must be for poor Alix to live through these events alone! God help us!

2 March. Thursday.   Ruzsky came in the morning and read me the text of an extremely lengthy conversation with Rodzianko over the [telegraph] apparatus. By his account, the situation in Petrograd is such that now the Duma ministry will be powerless to do anything because the soc.-dem. [social-democratic] party, in the form of the workers' committee, is fighting against it. My abdication is needed. Ruzsky transmitted this conversation to Headquarters, and Alekseev transmitted it to all the division commanders. At 2:30 answers came from everyone. The essence is that in the name of saving Russia and maintaining calm in the army at the front it is necessary to take this step. I agreed. The draft of the manifesto was sent from Headquarters. That evening Guchkov and Shulgin arrived from Petrograd; I discussed things with them and gave them the signed and revised manifesto. At 1:00 in the morning I left Pskov with a heart heavy from suffering over this.

All around me is treachery, cowardice, and deceit!

3 March. Friday.   Slept long and soundly. Woke up far past Dvinsk. The day was sunny and frosty. Talked with people close to me about yesterday's events. Read a lot about Julius Caesar. At 8:20 arrived in Mogilyov. All the ranking officers from Headquarters were on the platform. Received Alekseev in the railcar. At 9:30 made it into the house. Alekseev came with the latest news from Rodzianko. It turns out Misha renounced the throne. His manifesto ends with a flourish about elections to the Constituent Assembly within six months. Lord knows who gave him the idea to sign his name to such a disgusting thing! The disorders have ceased in Petrograd—if only this can keep up.

  1. Georgy Nikiforovich Danilov, general, chief of staff to the commander of the northern front (General Ruzsky).
   Sergei Sergeevich Savvich, infantry general, chief of supplies for the northern and northwestern fronts.

· 31 ·

Letter from Alexandra to Nicholas, 3 March 1917. Original English text.

———

No. 652.   March 3rd 1917

BELOVED, Soul of my Soul, my own wee one—ah, how my heart bleeds for you—madning knowing absolutely nothing except the vilest *rumors* wh. drive one wild. Wonder if the 2 youngsters reached you to-day with my letters. An officer's wife brings this—oh for a line of life! No knowledge whatsoever about you, only heart-rending things—& you no doubt hear the same. Won't tell anything in a letter. Is Nini's husband [Voeikov] alive?—My, our 4 invalids go on suffering—only M. is up & about—calm & my help growing thin as shows nothing of what she feels. We all go ~~up~~ about as usual, each buries the anguish inside—the heart bursts fr. pain for you & yr utter solitude. I am afraid of writing much, as don't know, whether any letter can pass, if they wont search her on the way—to such a degree all are mad.—In the morning I make my round with M. through the cellar to see all our men—it does one good. A. [Aunt] Olga & Hélène came to ask for news—very loving.— Ducky's husband [Kirill Vladimirovich] abominable in town, tho' pretends is working for Sovereign & Country.—Ah my Angel, God is above all—I only live by my complete trust in Him—He is our only hope. "*God Himself is merciful and will save them*" on the big Image.—Had a lovely *Te Deum* & *akathistos* with the Z. [Znamenie] Virgin brought into their green bedroom—where they all lay, did one such good—confided them & you into Her Holy care—then She passed through all rooms & stopped in the Cows [Vyrubova's] where I was then.—Love, my Love—it will go well, it must & I dont waver in my faith. Sweet Angel, ah me loves you so—always together, night & day—I feel what you are going through—& yr poor heart. God have mercy, give you strength & wisdom—He **wont** forsake you—He will help, recompense this mad suffering & separation at such a time when one needs being together. Yesterday came a packet for you with maps fr. Headquarters, I have them safe & a promotion recompense list fr. *Beliaev*.[1]—Ah, whenever shall will [*sic*] be together again—utterly cut off in every way. Yet, their illness perhaps is a saving, one cant move him.—Don't fear for him, we'll all fight for our Sunshine [Aleksei];—we are all at our places. Pauline well & calm tho' suffers beyond words, lives in the house with her too;—as do the Cow's parents.—*Zhilik* [Gilliard] is again well & faithful companion & playmate—*Sig* [Gibbs] comes up & down when trains allowed to go. Blooming they have arrested & his 2 helps, & red cap too & his aide who bows to the ground always. *Lizochka* [Naryshkina?] behaves well. You understand I can't write properly—too much on heart & soul. Famille Benoiton kiss without end & suffer for sweet Father—*Lili* & Cow send love. Sunny [Alexandra] blesses + & prays, bears up by faith & for her Martyr's sake;—she mixes into **nothing,** has seen nobody of "those", & never asked to, so don't believe if one tells you. She is now only mother with ill children. Can do nothing for fear of harming, as has no news from her Sweetheart. Such sunny weather, no clouds—that means trust & hope—all is pitch black around but God is above all; we know not His ways nor how He will help—but He will hearken unto all prayers. Know nothing of the war, live cut off fr. the world—always new, madning news—the last, that Father [Nicholas II] declined to keep the place in wh. he occupies 23 years. One might loose one's reason—but we wont—she shall believe in a future of sunshine yet on earth, remember that.—Paul just came—told me **all—I fully** understand yr. action—my own heroe! I **know** you could not sign against what you swore at yr. coronation—we know each other through & through & need no words—&, as I live, we shall see you back upon yr. throne, brought back by yr. people & troops to the glory of your reign. You have saved yr. son's reign & the country & yr. saintly purity && (**Judas** *Ruzsky*) you will be crowned by God on this earth in yr. country. I hold you tight, tight in my arms & will never let them touch your shining Soul, I kiss, kiss, kiss & bless you & always understand you. **Wifey.**+

1. Mikhail Alekseevich Beliaev, infantry general, minister of war from 3 January to 27 February 1917.

· 32 ·

From the protocol of a session of the Executive Committee of the Petrograd Soviet, on the arrest of the Romanovs, 3 March 1917.

———

About the arrest of Nicholas and other members of the Romanov dynasty.
RESOLVED:

1. To inform the [Soviet of] Workers' Deputies that the Executive Committee of the Soviet of W. and S. D. [Workers' and Soldiers' Deputies] has resolved to arrest the Romanov dynasty and to suggest that the Provisional Government carry out the arrest jointly with the Soviet of Workers' Deputies. In case they refuse, to inquire how the Provisional Government would view it if the Executive Committee carried out the arrest itself. The response of the Provisional Government will be discussed a second time in the Executive Committee's session.

2. In relation to Mikhail, to arrest him but to announce that he is officially only under surveillance by the revolutionary army.

3. In relation to Nikolai Nikolaevich, given the danger of arresting him in the Caucasus, to preliminarily summon him to Petrograd and to institute strict surveillance while he is on the way.

4. To arrest the women of the House of Romanov gradually, depending on the role each played in the activities of the old regime.

The question of how to undertake and organize the arrests is to be assigned to the military commission of the Soviet of Workers' Deputies. Chkheidze and Skobolev[1] are to inform the government about the enacted resolution of the Executive Committee of the Soviet of Workers' Deputies.

1. Nikolai Semyonovich Chkheidze, Menshevik leader, deputy from Tiflis province to the third and fourth State Dumas. From February to August 1917, Chkheidze was chairman of the Executive Committee of the Petrograd Soviet; later, chairman of the first All-Russian Central Executive Committee of Soviets (VTsIK).
    Matvei Ivanovich Skobolev, Menshevik leader, deputy from the Caucasus to the fourth State Duma, deputy chairman of the Executive Committee of the Petrograd Soviet, minister of labor (April–September 1917).

· 33 ·

Note from Nicholas to General Alekseev intended for the Provisional Government, 4 March 1917.

———

Request from the Provisional Government the foll. [following] guarantees:

1. That I and accompanying persons not be hindered as we travel to Tsarskoe Selo.

2. That the stay in Tsarskoe Selo be safe and secure until the children accompanying the above persons are fully well.

3. That the trip to Romanov [Murmansk] on Murman with the same persons not be hindered.

4. That, at war's end, we come back to Russia for permanent residence in the Crimea—at Livadia.

· 34 ·

Letter from Alexandra to Nicholas, 4 March 1917. Original English text.

———

No: 653.   4.III.1917

Sweet, beloved Treasure—

THE lady leaves today instead of yesterday, so have occasion to write again.— **What** relief & joy it was to hear your precious voice, only one heard so badly & one listens now to all conversations. And yr. dear wire this morning. I wired to you yesterday evening about 9½ [9:30] & this morning before 1. Baby leans over the bed & tells me to kiss you—all 4 are lying in the green room in the dark, Marie & I are writing, scarcely seeing anything with the curtains drawn.—**This** morning only read the manifest & later another fr. M. [Mikhail]—People are besides themselves with misery & adoration for my Angel. A movement is beginning amongst the troops. Fear nothing fr. Sunny, she does not move & does not exist.—Only I feel & foresee glorious sunshine ahead.—Am utterly disgusted with Ducky's husband!!—One shuts up people right & left, officers of course. God knows what goes on—here rifles choose their own commanders & behave abominably to them, don't salute, smoke in the faces of their officers.—Don't want to write all that goes on, so hideous it is.—N. P. [Sablin] shut up at the *Equipage* in town. Sailors came to fetch the others. The invalids upstairs & downstairs know nothing of yr decision—fear to tell them, & also as yet unnecessary. *Lili* [Den] has been an angel & helps one being like iron & we have not once broken down. You my Love my Angel dear, cannot think of what you have & are going through—makes me mad—oh God, of course He will recompense 100 fold for all yr suffering. I wont write on that subject, one cant—how one has humiliated you sending those two brutes [Guchkov and Shulgin] too—

I did not know til you told me wh. of them had been.—I feel that the Army will stand up.—.

Revolution in Germany, W. [Wilhelm] killed, son wounded,—one sees all over the fremasons' movement.—Now *An:* temp. 38.6 & spots coming more out. Olga has *pleurisy,* Cow too. *T*'s ears better, Sunbeam [Aleksei] better, cheery—how I wish you had them around you,—but they cannot move yet, & I doubt one wld. ever let us pass anywhere here. Gibbs saw Emma, Nini[1] & their mother in one room in an officers hosp: (English.) Their rooms completely burned down; old woman very ill. Red Cap still shut up.—Live with you, love & adore you. Kiss & embrace so tenderly fondly. God bless + & keep you now & ever.—Get somebody to bring a line—have you plans more or less for the moment?—

God on high will help, & new *krestopoklonnaia* [fourth week of Lent] coming.—Hold you tight, tight. Yr. very own
Wifey

Only **this morning** we knew that all given over to *M.* [Mikhail] & Baby now safe—such comfort.

1. Emma Vladimirovna Frederiks, countess, lady-in-waiting, daughter of the minister of the imperial court and domain.
Yevgenia Vladimirovna Voeikova (born Baroness Frederiks), former lady-in-waiting, sister of Emma Frederiks, wife of the palace commandant Vladimir Voeikov.

· 35 ·

From the protocol of a session of the Executive Committee of the Petrograd Soviet, on the adoption of measures to arrest Nicholas, 6 March 1917.

---

7. [Chairman] Chkheidze's statement.

Chkheidze reports on his negotiations with the Provisional Government concerning the arrest of the House of Romanov.

The government has still not given a definitive answer. A communication has been received through General Alekseev in Nicholas Romanov's name about his desire to go to Tsarskoe Selo. It appears that the Provisional Government has nothing against this. One of the ministers stated that if the Executive Committee of the Soviet of W. and S.D. definitely decides to arrest Nicholas, the Provisional Government will do everything to facilitate the Executive Committee's fulfillment of this task.

The Executive Committee **resolved** to immediately inform the military commission of the Soviet of W. and S.D. about the adoption of measures to arrest Nicholas Romanov.

· 36 ·

Declaration by eighty-five members of the Petrograd Soviet directed to the Executive
Committee with the demand that the Provisional Government arrest all members of the
House of Romanov, 7 March 1917.

The undersigned members of the Soviet of Workers' and Soldiers'
Deputies declare the following to the Executive Committee:

1. Extreme indignation and alarm exists among the broad masses of
workers and soldiers who gained freedom for Russia, because the deposed
Nicholas II the Bloody; his traitorous wife; his son, Aleksei; his mother,
Maria Fyodorovna, as well as all the other members of the House of
Romanov, are still completely free and travel around Russia even into the
theater of military operations. This is completely inadmissible and dangerously hinders the restoration of normal order and calm in the country and
in the army and the successful progress of defending Russia from an external enemy.

2. We propose that the Executive Committee immediately demand
that the Provisional Government **without delay** adopt the most decisive
measures to assemble all the members of the House of Romanov in one
designated location under the dependable guard of the People's Revolutionary Army.

3. We demand that this declaration be immediately put to a vote in the
present session of the Soviet of Soldiers' and Workers' Deputies.

Petrograd
7 March 1917

[85 signatures]

· 37 ·

From the minutes of the tenth session of the Provisional Government, on the arrest of
Nicholas and Alexandra, 7 March 1917.

HEARD: On depriving the abdicated Emperor Nicholas II and his spouse of
freedom [*lishenie svobody*].

RESOLVED:

1. To agree to deprive the abdicated Emperor Nicholas II and his
spouse of their freedom and to deliver the abdicated emperor to Tsarskoe
Selo.

2. To charge General Mikhail Vasilievich Alekseev with assigning a detachment to guard the abdicated emperor that will be at the disposal of Duma members posted to Mogilyov: Aleksandr Aleksandrovich Bublikov, Vasily Mikhailovich Vershinin, Semyon Fyodorovich Gribunin, and Savely Andreevich Kalinin.

3. To require members of the State Duma assigned to accompany the abdicated emperor from Mogilyov to Tsarskoe Selo to submit a written report about their completed mission.

4. To publish this decree.

· 38 ·

Aleksandr Kerensky's speech to the Moscow Soviet, [7 March 1917].

───────────

Nikolai Nikolaevich will not be commander in chief. As for Nicholas II, the former tsar himself turned to the new government with a request for protection. Now, Nicholas II is in my hands, in the hands of the general procurator! And I'll tell you, comrades: the Russian Revolution happened bloodlessly, and I will not allow anything to overshadow this. I will never be the Marat of the Russian Revolution. But in the shortest time possible, under my personal supervision, Nicholas II will be taken to the harbor and will leave from there for England by ship.

· 39 ·

Order no. 371 of the chief of staff to the commander in chief, General Mikhail Alekseev, on Nicholas's parting words to the troops, 8 March 1917.

───────────

Before leaving the army in the field, the abdicated Emperor Nicholas II addressed the troops with the following farewell:[1]

"Fervently beloved troops, I address you for the last time. After my abdication from Russia's throne on behalf of myself and my son, power has been transferred to the Provisional Government established at the initiative of the State Duma. May God help it lead Russia on the path of glory and prosperity. May God also help you, valiant troops, defend our homeland from the evil enemy. During the course of the past two and a half years you have constantly borne the burden of military service, much blood has been spilled, much effort has been expended, and the hour is near when Russia, tied to its valiant allies by a single common striving toward victory, will smash the last efforts of the opponent. This unprecedented war must be brought to a complete victory.

"Whoever thinks now of peace, whoever wishes it, is a turncoat to the fatherland, a traitor. I know that every honest fighting man believes this. Fulfill your duty, valiantly defend our great homeland, obey the Provisional Government, heed your superiors, remember that any weakening of military order only plays into the hands of the enemy.

"I firmly believe that boundless love for your great homeland has not gone out in your hearts. May the Lord God bless you, and may the Martyred Victor, St. George, lead you to victory.

Nicholas"

8 March 1917
Headquarters
Signed: Chief of Staff, General Alekseev

1. At the direction of the Provisional Government, army units at the front were not widely informed of Nicholas II's farewell address to the troops.

· 40 ·

Diary of Nicholas II, 8 March 1917.

8 March. Wednesday.   The last day in Mogilyov. At 10:15, I signed the farewell order to the armies. At 10:30, went to the duty house, where I took leave of all the officers of the Headquarters' staff and administration. At home I said good-bye to the officers and cossacks of the Convoy and Combined Regiment—my heart nearly broke! At 12 o'clock, I went to Mama in the salon car, lunched with her and her retinue, and sat with her until 4:30. I said good-bye to her, Sandro,[1] Sergei,[2] Boris, and Alek.[3] They didn't let poor Nilov[4] go with me. At 4:45 I left Mogilyov; a touching crowd of people saw me off. Four members of the Duma are co-travelers in my train!

I've left for Orsha and Vitebsk.

The weather is frosty and windy.

It's miserable, painful, and depressing.

1. Aleksandr Mikhailovich, grand duke, Nicholas I's grandson, husband of Grand Duchess Ksenia Aleksandrovna, vice admiral.

2. Sergei Mikhailovich, grand duke, son of Grand Duke Mikhail Nikolaevich, artillery general. In January 1916, he was appointed the commander in chief's inspector general of field artillery.

3. Aleksandr Petrovich Oldenburgsky, prince, adjutant general of the imperial suite, infantry general in the Life Guards.

4. Konstantin Dmitrievich Nilov, adjutant general in the imperial suite, admiral, flag captain. Belonged to Nicholas II's inner circle. He was sent away from the imperial family after the abdication.

༄ 2 ༄

Under Arrest at Tsarskoe Selo

I NSPIRED by divergent ideas about the meaning and purposes of the revolution, the Provisional Government and the powerful nationwide network of soviets of workers' and soldiers' deputies viewed the fate of the abdicated tsar and his family differently. The liberals in the government held an embracing notion of citizenship that disregarded class and position. They were committed to promoting national unity and concord rather than conflict and hesitated to punish former enemies. Their political vocabulary was filled with references to nation, morality, law, duty, and rights. When considering the fate of the former imperial family, these liberals tended to view them as citizens and individuals and thus to be concerned mainly with their personal safety. By contrast, the socialist leaders of the soviets, and especially the urban lower-class public—the soviets' constituency, whom the moderate socialist intellectuals who led the soviets were constantly endeavoring to restrain—viewed the revolution as an opportunity to right past inequities and to challenge and punish their oppressors. Aleksandr Kerensky, the only socialist minister in the first Provisional Government cabinet, was cognizant of the clash between popular and official understandings of the February Revolution when he declared before the Moscow Soviet, whose members were demanding Nicholas II's arrest and punishment, that he refused to be "the Marat of the Russian Revolution" (Document 38). Such analogies to the French Revolution were common among political activists of all camps. Indeed, with that model in mind, the liberals of the Provisional Government feared that their revolution, too, would slide from the reasoned humanism of 1789 to the social revolution of 1792—from the liberty cap to the guillotine. Preventing this slide, paradoxically perhaps, required making concessions to the soviets and the radical public in order to preserve the liberal authority of the government. Policy toward the tsar and his family was at the center of this politics of maneuver and restraint.

The government largely ignored Nicholas II for the first few days following his abdication. He was free to travel to General Headquarters at Mogilyov, where he spent several days and even gave a brief speech (Document 39). Demands from the public and the soviets for the arrest of him and his family began almost immediately, however (Documents 32, 35, 36). As in much else, the Provisional Government had to act against its initial wishes in order to maintain authority and keep some control over events. On 7 March it ordered that Nicholas and Alexandra "be deprived . . . of their freedom" and confined at the family's residence at Tsarskoe Selo (Document 37).

In the months ahead, the fate of the deposed tsar and his family was one of the many sources of tension between the government and the soviets, as well as a source of troubled uncertainty within the government itself. Two issues, in particular, rankled during the early months of the revolution: the conditions of their confinement and their permanent fate. Decisions about the fate of the Romanovs, of course, would affect how they were treated in the short term. These issues—and the conflicting notions of revolutionary politics and justice that underlay them—pervade the documents that follow.

The Provisional Government, sensitive to popular fury toward the old regime and hoping to keep the revolution free of harshness and bloodshed, saw protection as the government's main responsibility toward the family. Confining them at Tsarskoe Selo was necessary both to satisfy demands for their arrest and to keep them out of harm's way. But the proximity of the palace to the revolutionary capital and the government's uncertain control over rebellious troops and workers made the removal of the family from Russia seem like the only sure way to guarantee their safety. On 2 March the Petrograd Soviet itself had suggested exiling the family and had also mentioned concern for their safety (Document 27). As a destination, England was the obvious choice: Britain was an ally, its government had immediately voiced support for the revolution, and King George was cousin to both Nicholas and Alexandra.

Nicholas seemed prepared to leave the country. On 4 (17) March he requested that the government allow him, his family, and his suite safe return to Tsarskoe Selo, residence there until his children recovered from their illness, and then unhindered passage to the northern port of Romanov (Murmansk). Although Nicholas did not say so, traveling to Romanov implied the intention to leave for England; Romanov was significant mainly as Russia's chief wartime shipping connection to England. Nicholas also wished to make it clear, however, that he considered exile temporary: the fourth point in his list of requests was that he be allowed to return to Russia at the end of the war for "permanent residence in the Crimea—at Livadia" (Document 33). General Mikhail Alekseev, to whom Nicholas gave the list, represented Nicholas before the government at Nicholas's request. When Alekseev forwarded the requests to the minister president (chairman of the Council of Ministers), Prince Georgy Lvov, he left off the final point, perhaps considering it naive. At any rate, two days later, on 6 (19) March, Lvov responded that the Provisional Government had agreed to the three requests.[1]

The next day, safe passage for the former tsar to Tsarskoe Selo was translated into his arrest and transport under the guard of government commissars assigned to accompany him. But the agreement to allow Nicholas and his family to leave for England remained unchanged. Indeed, faced with increasing public threats against members of the deposed dynasty, departure was treated as an urgent necessity. On 6 March, the new Russian foreign minister, Pavel Miliukov, informed the British ambassador, George Buchanan, of Nicholas's request to be allowed to reach Romanov and asked whether the British government was making the necessary arrangements to take the family from there to England. Two days later, the British Foreign Office passed on the diffident answer: His

Majesty's government was very much concerned for the safety of the tsar, but no invitation was being made. Instead, Buchanan was asked to inquire whether Denmark or Switzerland might not be better destinations. In fact, the Foreign Office knew from the report of a conversation that Britain's military attaché had had with Alexandra on 6 March that the former empress, fearing a long sea voyage, had herself stated a preference for Denmark. But the Provisional Government worried that these countries were too close to Germany and that Nicholas could fall into the hands of the Germans, who might send him back to Russia at the head of a German-backed counterrevolutionary force.

When informed of the British response on 8 (21) March, Miliukov pleaded even more insistently with Buchanan. He emphasized the need to be certain that Nicholas remained in England until the end of the world war and underscored his "anxiety" about the tsar's safety, warning, according to Buchanan, of the great danger from "Extremists" who "were exciting opinion against His Majesty." Buchanan endorsed Miliukov's appeal, advising the British government that "the departure of the Emperor would certainly strengthen the Russian government and help matters to settle down." The following day, 9 (22) March, the foreign secretary cabled the embassy in Petrograd that the British government had agreed to let Nicholas and his family come to England for the duration of the war, as long as the Russian government would pay their expenses.[2] Buchanan informed Miliukov of his government's decision on 10 (23) March.[3] But by this time the urgency had faded, and Miliukov showed no haste in taking up the English offer.

When the Petrograd Soviet heard of the plan to evacuate Nicholas and his family to England, a storm of protest broke out. The Soviet's leaders were sensitive to public opinion and had by now abandoned their initial support for exiling the tsar and his family. The Executive Committee discussed these rumors as their first order of business on 9 March and decided to mobilize workers and soldiers to occupy the railway stations through which Nicholas might be traveling, seize him, and imprison him in the Peter and Paul Fortress in Petrograd (Document 41). Urgent bulletins to this effect were sent out.[4] Later that day, however, the chairman of the Soviet, Nikolai Chkheidze, reported that a delegation from the Executive Committee had met with Kerensky and other government representatives, who assured them that Nicholas was already at Tsarskoe Selo (he had, in fact, arrived late that morning). Chkheidze assured the other leaders of the Soviet that the government representatives had promised, "under pressure from the Executive Committee," not to allow Nicholas to leave for England or anywhere else without the agreement of the Executive Committee (Document 41). Given the strong anti-Romanov mood in the soviets, such an agreement was not likely. When, on the following day, Buchanan informed Miliukov of his government's offer of refuge—stipulating that the Russian government must bear the cost, an item that was likely to aggravate public opinion—Miliukov undoubtedly already knew that his hands were tied.

Meanwhile, the agreement with England was coming undone because of internal British politics. Rumors of the offer of asylum spread quickly and ignited opposition. As a result, both the cabinet and the king came to feel that the political disadvantages of being associated with the deposed Russian emperor and empress far outweighed any potential benefits. On 6 April (24 March) the king's private secretary, Arthur Stamfordham, informed the British foreign secretary that "His Majesty receives letters from people in all classes of life, known or unknown to him, saying how much the matter is being discussed, not only in clubs, but by working men." Stamfordham dispatched a more insistent letter that evening, forwarding the king's request that the foreign secretary inform the prime minister that "from all he [King George] hears and reads in the press, the residence in this country of the ex-Emperor and Empress would be strongly resented by the public, and would undoubtedly compromise the position of the King and Queen." The king advised asking Buchanan to notify Miliukov that "we must be allowed to withdraw from the consent previously given to the Russian government's proposal."[5] The cabinet probably shared the king's concerns about public opinion; the Liberal prime minister, David Lloyd George, made his lack of sympathy for the deposed Russian monarch quite clear.[6] So, on 31 March (13 April), Buchanan received a telegram from the Foreign Office informing him that the offer of asylum had been withdrawn—though suggesting that he inform Miliukov of this fact only if the Russians themselves raised the matter again, to avoid alienating an ally unnecessarily.[7] Democratic pressures in both England and Russia prevented Nicholas and his family from leaving the country.

The conditions of confinement at Tsarskoe Selo represented a shifting mix of revolutionary vigilance and liberal generosity. Kerensky, who as justice minister was officially responsible for handling the family's arrest, would later emphasize the humaneness of the government's treatment, using the high moral language often heard in his speeches during the revolution: "I wanted this man to know that the Revolution was magnanimous and humane to its enemies, not only in word but in deed. I wished that for once in his life he should feel ashamed of the horrors that had been perpetrated in his name. This was the only revenge worthy of the Great Revolution, a noble revenge, worthy of the sovereign people."[8] But the circumstances of Nicholas's captivity were also shaped by public and soviet demands for strict, even punitive, treatment, by the government's need to retain popular confidence, and by the everyday behavior of the soldiers assigned to guard the family.[9]

On 8 March, General Lavr Kornilov, the new commander of the Petrograd military district, accompanied by the new commandant of the Tsarskoe Selo guard, Colonel Yevgeny Kobylinsky, and the new palace commandant, Captain Pavel Kotsebu, arrived at the palace to inform Alexandra of her arrest and to announce the conditions under which she and her family would live. The palace guard was to be replaced by troops loyal to the new government. Kornilov told members of the palace suite that they were free to leave but that those who voluntarily remained would be considered under arrest; the majority left. The doors of the Aleksandrovsky Palace, where the family resided, would be sealed except for the main entrance and the kitchen door, which would be under armed guard. Kornilov originally intended to forbid the prisoners to leave the palace at any time, though Pavel Benkendorf, chief marshal of the court, convinced him to allow the family a portion of the park for taking walks accompanied by guards. All letters going in and out of the palace were to be first examined by the palace commandant, and telephones were off limits (Document 41), though this rule was later modified so that the prisoners could talk on a telephone in the guard room, but only in Russian and in the presence of a guard.[10] These rules were spelled out in detail in the instructions to the guards issued a week later (Document 44).

Concerns about the guards' loyalty to the new regime and public complaints about the mildness of the terms of imprisonment resulted in periodic tightening of the rules. When Kerensky visited the palace for the first time, on 21 March, he ordered that Alexandra's close friend Anna Vyrubova—who had been vilified in the press as Rasputin's mistress and as his chief accomplice in his alleged occultism and debauchery in the palace—be removed from Tsarskoe Selo and imprisoned in Petrograd. He also announced the appointment of a trusted commandant, his personal friend Pavel Korovichenko, a military lawyer who had specialized in defending people accused of political offenses against the old regime. Later that day, another of the empress's confidantes, Lili Den, was arrested and removed from the palace. Though freed within a few days, Den was not allowed to return to Tsarskoe Selo. On 27 March, a week after the first visit, Kerensky returned and informed Nicholas and Alexandra that they had to be separated, except for brief meetings at mealtimes and during religious services. This was in response to demands from the radical public that Alexandra's dangerous influence over Nicholas be restricted. The separation lasted only a couple of weeks, but there were other harassments: in April the right to boat on the pond was revoked and the palace's stock of vodka was destroyed. When Kobylinsky replaced Korovichenko as palace commandant in May, however—Korovichenko was promoted to a more responsible military post—many of these restrictions were lifted. Kobylinsky, an officer in the Life Guards, was noticeably more sympathetic to his prisoners (Document 52).[11] Under his watch, correspondence and visitors were less rigorously controlled, the pond and a small island were again made available (Aleksei, in particular, enjoyed swimming), certain decisions by the guards, such as confiscating Aleksei's toy gun, were countermanded, and treatment of the family was more respectful and solicitous.

The life of the family and their suite in captivity at Tsarskoe Selo, especially after Kobylinsky's appointment as commandant, was characterized above all by quiet and tedious monotony. In the words of Aleksei's tutor, Pierre Gilliard, written in his diary in June, "The days follow one another, all alike, divided between lessons and walks."[12] Starting in April, Nicholas and Alexandra had begun to give lessons to their children—Nicholas teaching his favorite subjects, history and geography, and Alexandra taking charge of religious instruction. The family and their suite also put in a small kitchen garden near the palace and, after that work was done, cut firewood in preparation for winter. Alexandra embroidered and tatted, for she was not healthy enough for garden work. Much time was spent reading, mostly for pleasure and distraction but also for information about political affairs (they were allowed to receive newspapers). Every evening Nicholas read aloud to the family. Religious services were held in the palace and, during Holy Week, at the palace chapel. The entire family wrote letters, some of which passed, as required, through the commandant's hands, while others were smuggled out of the palace, sometimes with the help of trusted soldiers.

The revolution made itself felt in this calm life. From the newspapers, now virtually uncensored, the prisoners learned of the deepening turmoil in the cities. More painfully, they were confronted by a flood of hostile press reports featuring unrestrained stories about the private and public lives of the tsar and tsaritsa—"filth" and slander, Alexandra called them (Document 52). But they did not have to read the papers to witness the angry anti-authoritarianism of many ordinary Russians. Although some of the soldiers who guarded them were kind and respectful—addressing them as Your Majesties and even working beside them in the garden[13]—others found ways to express their hostility to the old regime.

Many of the soldiers of the guard engaged in what amounted to a spontaneous everyday theater of defiance, much as was occurring in factories, villages, and streets throughout Russia. In dress, manner, and speech, these soldiers acted out their new sense of power and liberty, with the former tsar, his family, and the suite as audience and target. To the family, these performances seemed like little more than crude ill-discipline. "The soldiers of the new guard were horrible to look at; untidy, noisy, quarrelling with everybody. . . . They were all impregnated with new ideas, and they spared nothing in order to show that they were the masters." And, "They were slovenly in their dress, their crushed caps were set awry on huge mops of unkempt hair, their coats were half-buttoned, and their nonchalant

manner of performing their military duties was a continual irrita-
tion to the Emperor."[14] Soldiers reportedly walked at will around
the palace and even entered the family's rooms unannounced; they
stood about in "slovenly" dress even while on duty; they complained that their officers were too respectful of the deposed sovereign; and they criticized the servants for wearing livery and for
pushing Alexandra about in the wheelchair that she now often
resorted to because of her weak heart and painful legs. (According
to Sofia Buksgevden, "The men seemed to be particularly irritated
by [Alexandra's] chair and her sad face, and swore loudly at her for
not being *made* to walk.") The soldiers scribbled insulting graffiti
on benches and walls and were generally, as Benkendorf recalled in
1919, "so rude that it was impossible to speak to them."[15] With few
exceptions, the guards made a point of either wholly ignoring polite
greetings from the family or responding with hostility (Document
72). Meanwhile, as a sort of crude backdrop to these performances,
crowds regularly gathered at the palace fence—"gapers," Nicholas
derisively called them in his diary on 3 April—to whistle and shout
insults or simply stare whenever the former emperor or empress
appeared (Document 56).

There were little scenes in this theater of defiance. When Nicholas first returned to Tsarskoe Selo from the front, for example, some
guards staged what Benkendorf aptly called an "offensive comedy."
The head of the palace guard pretended not to know who was
arriving until the sentry shouted "Nicholas Romanov."[16] There
were also big revolutionary performances, like the ceremonial burial,
on Maundy Thursday (30 March), of victims of the revolution
along the avenue leading to the palace and, on May Day (18 April
according to the Russian calendar), a procession to lay wreaths on
the graves. There were also small carnivalesque performances of
social reversal: on one occasion, soldiers knocked Nicholas off his
bicycle by sticking a bayonet into the spokes as he rode by, and then
laughed raucously as the former emperor picked himself up; and
another time one of the sentries on duty in front of the palace
arranged to sit at his post on a gilded armchair, complete with
pillows and footstool, all of which had been carried down from the
palace.[17]

1. Nicholas II in seventeenth-century dress for a masked ball,
St. Petersburg, 1903.

2. Nicholas II posing by a tennis court near the coast of Finland, 1912.
Photograph by Anna Vyrubova.

3. Alexandra writing a letter in bed, Tsarskoe Selo, 1910 or 1911. Photograph by Anna Vyrubova.

4. Nicholas II in cossack uniform at Spala, 1912. Photograph by Anna Vyrubova.

5. Nicholas II blessing troops leaving for the front in the Russo-Japanese War, Peterhof, 1905.

6. Nicholas II receiving bread and salt from representatives of the people during celebrations for the tercentenary of the House of Romanov, Kostroma, 1913.

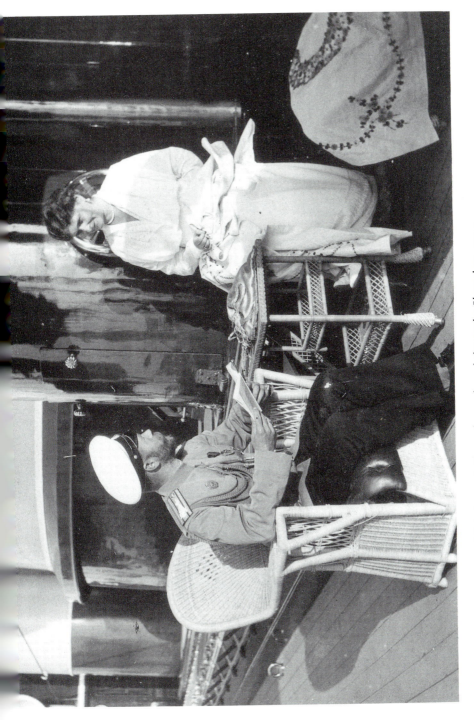

7. Nicholas and Alexandra on board the yacht *Shtandart*, 1914.

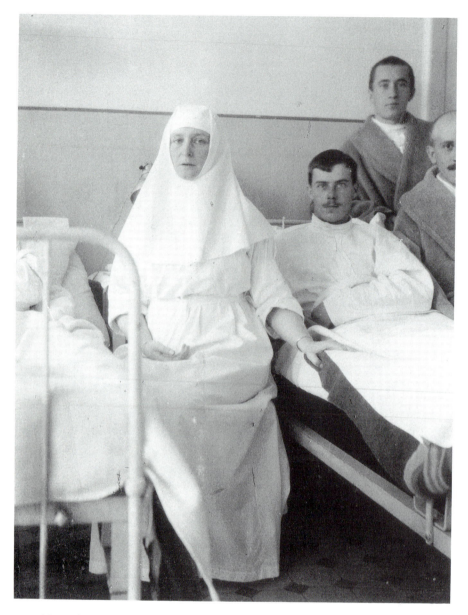

8. Alexandra as war nurse with recovering soldiers, Tsarskoe Selo, 1914 or
1915.

9. Alexandra and Nicholas under arrest in the palace at Tsarskoe Selo, 1917.

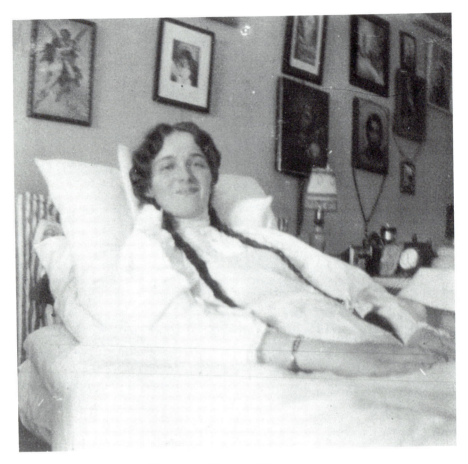

10. Alexandra in bed amid her icons, Tsarskoe Selo, 1917.

11. Nicholas clearing snow from a pathway, Tsarskoe Selo, March 1917.

12. Aleksei and Nicholas breaking ice in front of the palace at Tsarskoe Selo, March 1917.

13. Aleksei in uniform, Tsarskoe Selo, March 1917.

14. Olga, Aleksei, Anastasia, and Tatiana resting after working in the garden, Tsarskoe Selo, March 1917.

15. Alexandra embroidering while the family (not shown) prepares a vegetable garden, Tsarskoe Selo, April 1917.

16. Tatiana, holding a pet dog, and Anastasia with a guard and servants in the background, Tsarskoe Selo, June 1917. Photograph by Maria.

17. Nicholas and Alexandra in the palace garden, Tsarskoe Selo, June 1917.
Photograph by Maria.

18. Nicholas smoking in the palace park, Tsarskoe Selo, June 1917.
Photograph by Maria.

19. The children with their heads shaved after measles caused hair loss, June 1917. *From left to right,* Tatiana, Anastasia, Aleksei, Olga, and Maria. Photograph by Pierre Gilliard.

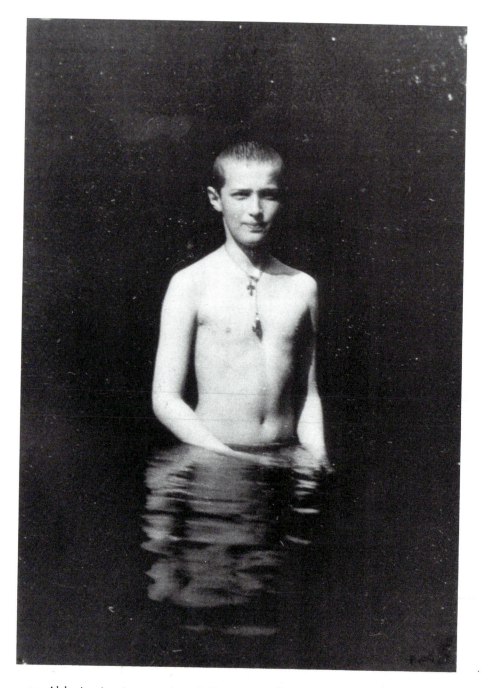

20. Aleksei swimming near the "children's island" in the palace pond, Tsarskoe Selo, July 1917. Photograph by Maria.

21. Tatiana and Anastasia with guards, Tsarskoe Selo, July 1917.

22. Aleksei with a guard, Tsarskoe Selo, July 1917.

23. Nicholas posing by the stump of a tree that he helped fell, with guards standing behind him, Tsarskoe Selo, July 1917.

24. Former Governor's House in Tobolsk, with palisade fence under construction, August 1917. The imperial family was imprisoned here from August 1917 to April 1918.

25. Soldier of the guard posing by the front entrance of the Governor's House, Tobolsk, winter 1917–1918.

26. Soldiers of the guard posing beside the Governor's House, Tobolsk, winter 1917–1918.

27. Nicholas and Aleksei sawing wood, Tobolsk, winter 1917–1918.

28. Nicholas with daughters on the roof of the greenhouse at the Governor's House, Tobolsk, early 1918.

29. Ipatiev house in Yekaterinburg during the first days that Nicholas and his family were imprisoned there, spring 1918, before the construction of the second fence.

30. Ural Regional Soviet of Workers' and Soldiers' Deputies, Yekaterinburg, 1917. *In the first row, on the far right, Filipp Goloshchekin; second from the left, Aleksandr Beloborodov.*

31. Filipp Goloshchekin, military commissar of the Ural Regional Soviet.

32. Aleksandr Beloborodov, chairman of the Ural Regional Soviet.

33. Yakov Yurovsky, commandant of the House of Special Purpose
(Ipatiev house), July 1918.

A more serious challenge to the conditions under which the family was confined came from outside—from the soviets and their public. The arrest and incarceration of the imperial family at their home and the suspension of plans to allow them to leave the country did not end public appeals for more secure and punitive confinement. Groups of workers and soldiers, local soviets, and even the entire workers' section of the Petrograd Soviet petitioned the Soviet to imprison the former tsar and his family in the garrison prison at the Kronstadt naval base (Kronstadt sailors were famous for their revolutionary militance) or in the Peter and Paul Fortress (where the tsarist regime had imprisoned many political prisoners) and to put them on trial for their crimes. Many found it unjust that "Nicholas the Bloody," said to be responsible for the sufferings of so many, should live comfortably and unpunished (Documents 47, 50, 51).[18] Aggravating public opinion—and reflecting it—were the rumors in circulation about the lenient conditions of confinement. Officers of the guard were said to regularly drink with the former tsar. It was also believed that some guards were monarchist agents. Kerensky, the Provisional Government, the commanders directly responsible for the family, and even the Petrograd Soviet had to constantly defend their handling of the Romanovs (Document 45).[19]

Even the socialist leaders of the soviets, who were generally finding it harder and harder to contain and represent the anger of their constituents, tried to quiet the growing demands for punishment. Acknowledging the widespread "dissatisfaction with the extremely gentle treatment by the victorious revolution of the person who was the bitterest enemy of the people," the newspaper of the Petrograd Soviet reminded its readers that "the revolution would have disgraced itself if it had followed in the footsteps of tsarism in the matter of punishing its enemies. . . . The magnanimity [*velikodushie*] of the victorious people stems from the fact that they do not fear their toppled enemies; they despise them too profoundly to stoop to their level. . . . The revolution has no intention of making martyrs out of its enemies. And least of all do its plans include making a martyr out of the former tsar, Nicholas Romanov."[20]

It was against this background of rising criticism that the Provisional Government decided to remove the family from Tsarskoe

Selo and relocate them in an isolated town on the far side of the Ural Mountains. The threat of radicalism, which Kerensky and the Provisional Government repeatedly insisted was their principal reason for moving the family, was certainly real. By the second week in July, when the decision to move the family was evidently made (Documents 55, 56), armed insurrection had erupted in Petrograd.

The Provisional Government accomplished a great deal in its months in power. In a matter of weeks, it freed thousands of political prisoners and welcomed back exiles; proclaimed freedom of speech, press, assembly, and association and the right to strike; abolished flogging, exile to Siberia, and the death penalty; removed legal restrictions on the rights of national and religious minorities; prepared for elections to a constituent assembly on the basis of universal, secret, direct, and equal suffrage; and started work on land reform. But the war continued—the government and its supporters saw it as a fight against tyranny at the side of democratic allies—and the economy continued to disintegrate, partly because the liberal government was even less willing than the autocracy to forcibly control prices and ensure production. Equally important, land reform remained only a promise, for the government insisted that any redistribution be carried out in a deliberate and legal fashion. Not surprisingly, discontent deepened.

The first major outbreak challenging the new government came in late April 1917, when the Petrograd Soviet and the public learned, two days after the fact, of a diplomatic note that Foreign Minister Miliukov had sent to the Allies on 18 April (1 May).[21] Miliukov assured the Allies that Russia was still fighting for "decisive victory" and intended to "fully observe" the treaty obligations worked out with them by the tsarist government. He also spoke of readiness to impose "guarantees and sanctions" after the war. These statements were widely understood as implying, among other things, that Russia still intended to demand control of Constantinople and the Dardanelles Strait; Miliukov had already openly supported this war aim, which the Allies had accepted in 1915. Miliukov's note directly contradicted the foreign policy that the Petrograd Soviet had been insisting on: for the short term, acceptance of the war only to defend the revolution against German militarism and, for the long term, "peace without annexations or indemnities." The terms of the note also seemed to contradict the government's own Declaration on War Aims of 27 March, worked out with the Petrograd Soviet, in which Russia formally renounced "domination over other nations" and "seizure of their national possessions."[22] Many thought that the note proved that the declaration was an act of political deceit and hypocrisy. Left-wing newspapers said as much in blistering attacks on 20–21 April. By 21 April large crowds of protesters (including soldiers with arms) were in the streets of Petrograd and Moscow denouncing "Miliukov-Dardanelsky," all of the "capitalist ministers," and the "imperialist war." Smaller demonstrations were held in support of the government and the war, and the two sides occasionally clashed violently. The upheaval caused both Miliukov, the foreign minister, and Guchkov, the minister of war, to resign at the beginning of May, but it also altered the political terrain in more fundamental ways.

In the face of the first big political crisis since the fall of the autocracy, the socialist leaders on the Executive Committee of the Petrograd Soviet, which had already begun to function as a shadow government, agreed, on 2 May, to enter into an open coalition government with the liberals. Unwilling to take state power directly into their own hands—most Mensheviks and Socialist Revolutionaries still believed that Russia was not ready for a worker-based socialist government—the leaders of the Petrograd Soviet resolved to accept ministerial appointments in the Provisional Government. They hoped to bolster the government's flagging public support but also to increase the left's influence on policy without embarking on a dangerous experiment in soviet state power. After negotiations between the Executive Committee and the Provisional Government, six socialists entered the government, on 5 May. At the same time, Kerensky replaced Guchkov as minister of war, and the nonparty liberal Mikhail Tereshchenko replaced Miliukov as foreign minister.

From this moment, the discontented lower classes faced a government in which the soviets were now complicit. The policy of participation was sanctioned at the first congress of deputies from soviets throughout Russia, in early June, at which a national Central Executive Committee of Soviets was also elected. Participation by representatives of the soviets in the Provisional Government had potent political consequences. After the entry of moderate socialists into the government, discontented workers and soldiers looked to the only major national party that refused to join the "bourgeois" government—the Bolshevik party. The party swelled in membership after April, and major Bolshevik gains were recorded in elections in grass-roots organizations like factory committees, soldiers' committees, and neighborhood soviets.

With the continued fracturing of power throughout society, the Bolshevik party gained strength, and the government's authority eroded further. Authority was subverted and seized by people in the places where they lived and worked. Crowds of workers and other townspeople, only loosely controlled by political organizations, regularly took over city streets in mass meetings and demonstrations, especially in Petrograd. In factories, workshops, and other businesses, workers and employees demanded control over work rules, wages, and even hiring and firing. Often workers directly defied established authority, sometimes merely being rude to supervisors and employers, sometimes refusing to obey orders, and sometimes physically assaulting those with power over them. Soldiers, too, disregarded orders, mocked officers (or beat them up), organized soldiers' committees, and sometimes even elected their own officers. They also deserted in increasingly large numbers. In the countryside, peasants seized land—from the gentry and richer peasants alike—without waiting for legal sanction; cut wood in private forests; stole seed and tools; and occasionally looted and burned landlords' houses. Alongside these acts of social defiance, and not unrelated, was a good deal of public drunkenness, hooliganism, robbery, and criminal violence.[23]

On 3–4 July this political and social crisis blossomed into insurrection. A machine-gun regiment garrisoned in Petrograd took to the streets with arms in hand—joined by thousands of workers and soldiers—to demand that the Provisional Government be overthrown and that all state power go to the soviets. The Bolsheviks nurtured the defiance and rebellion. The leaders of the soviets eventually persuaded the crowds to end their demonstrations, and the government responded to the "July Days" by arresting leading Bolsheviks. But no one thought that the troubles were over. The day before the demonstrations broke out, the Kadet ministers in the Provisional Government had already announced their collective resignation to protest the left-leaning policies of the government and the failure to restore discipline and order to army and society. The socialist ministers saw in the Kadet resignations and in the outburst of popular protest an opportunity to reorient the government's program further to the left—a necessity, they believed, if they were to undermine Bolshevik popularity. On 7 July, Minister President Lvov accepted the resignations of the Kadet ministers; then he himself resigned. In announcing his decision, on 8 July, Lvov castigated the socialist ministers for "sacrificing national and moral values to the masses . . . as a play to the galleries."[24] Lvov asked Kerensky, who was viewed as standing between the socialist left and the liberal right, to succeed him as minister president and organize a new government. Three days later, on 11 July, Kerensky traveled to Tsarskoe Selo to inform the former tsar that he and his family and retainers would have to move farther from the "uneasy capital" (Document 56).

Kerensky told Nicholas that they would probably be sent south, to Livadia. The British ambassador had already heard, however, that the more likely destination was the Siberian town of Tobolsk or Tomsk (Document 55). Siberia had obvious advantages in keeping the family safe and secure. Kerensky himself explained that he "chose Tobolsk because it was an out-and-out backwater, especially in winter (not being on a railway), had a very small garrison, no industrial proletariat, and a population which was prosperous and contented, not to say old-fashioned." Also, as a regional administrative center, Tobolsk had a governor's residence suitable for housing the former imperial family. Kerensky later took pains to insist that his choice of Tobolsk was not a concession to the left.[25] Still, transporting the former emperor under guard to Siberia appealed to many as a symbolically just retribution. Some of the people close to the family certainly perceived this symbolism: "What a trial and what humiliation!" (Document 58). Tobolsk was, however, close to Rasputin's native village of Pokrovskoe. To Alexandra, the proximity seemed a good sign (Documents 57, 58).

· 41 ·

From the protocol of a session of the Executive Committee of the Petrograd Soviet, on adopting measures to stop Nicholas from departing for England and on the need for his arrest, 9 March 1917.

----

1. On the arrest of Nicholas Romanov.

[RESOLVED:] In light of information received—that the Provisional Government decided to give Nicholas Romanov the opportunity to leave for England and that at present he is on the way to Petrograd—the Executive Committee decided immediately to adopt extraordinary measures for his detention and arrest. Orders have been given for our troops to occupy all train stations, and commissars with emergency powers have been dispatched to the Tsarskoe Selo, Tosno, and Zvanka train stations. In addition, it has been decided to send radiotelegrams to all cities with instructions to arrest Nicholas Romanov and in general to adopt a series of extraordinary measures. Together with this, it has been decided to announce immediately to the Provisional Government the unbending will of the Executive Committee not to allow Nicholas Romanov to leave for England, and to arrest him. It has been decided to house Nicholas Romanov in the Trubetskoy bastion of the Peter and Paul Fortress, replacing for this purpose the officers posted there with new ones. It has been decided to arrest Nicholas Romanov no matter what, even if this threatens to break off relations with the Provisional Government.

. . .

3. [Chairman of the Executive Committee] Chkheidze's report on the visit by Executive Committee delegates to the Provisional Government.

Com. Chkheidze reports that Nicholas Rom. has already arrived in Tsarskoe Selo. Under pressure from the Executive Committee, the Provisional Government has rejected the idea of allowing Nicholas Romanov to leave for England without the special consent of the Executive Committee. He has been temporarily left at Tsarskoe Selo. The Provisional Government and Minister of Justice Kerensky guarantee that he will not go anywhere. The Provisional Government agrees that the Executive Committee appoint its own surveillance commissar at Tsarskoe Selo so that Nicholas II will not go anywhere. In the future, the question about Nicholas Romanov will be decided together with the Executive Committee.

Having heard this report, the Executive Committee has resolved to remove guards from all train stations except the Tsarskoe Selo station, to send commissars to Tsarskoe Selo and to the Tosno station, to definitively discuss the question of Nicholas Romanov, and to make a decision tomorrow. Besides this, it was decided to adopt measures that would allow a faster mobilization of military units in the future.

. . .

13. Report of the representative dispatched to Tsarskoe Selo.

The guarding of the palace is in the hands of revolutionary troops. An order has been given not to allow anyone in or out of the palace. All telephones and telegraphs are shut off. Nicholas Romanov is under vigilant surveillance. **There are around 300 soldiers there.** The guard is drawn from the second contingent of the Third Rifle Regiment. An officer of the Mikhailovsky riding school refused to issue armored cars, not considering the signature of the Executive Committee to be sufficient without the countersignature of Karaulov.[1] At the palace and also considered under arrest are Naryshkin, Benkendorf, and Dolgorukov.[2] All letters and telegrams are delivered to the guardhouse. A representative went to the inner chambers and personally saw Nicholas Romanov. The regiment asked to let you know that it will continuously stand guard in order not to let him out. The officers guarding the palace regard it as completely acceptable for the committee to post its own representatives to supervise guarding him. They refused to deliver up Nicholas Romanov, considering it their duty to fulfill Gen. Kornilov's[3] order commanding them not to give him up. Being sure of the guards' reliability, the representatives think it possible to leave Nicholas as is. The riflemen insist on the withdrawal of the **entirely untrustworthy** Combined Regiment from Tsarskoe Selo. In the report of the representative of the officer-activists, a doctor at Tsarskoe Selo is quoted as saying that agitation is under way against the Soviet of W. and S.D. in the First Reserve Regiment. The troops support a constitutional monarchy. The officers especially insist upon it.

Having discussed this information, the Executive Committee **resolved** to post S. D. Maslovsky[4] as the Executive Committee's commissar to monitor [*kontrol'*] the guards and the organization of the whole matter.

1. Mikhail Aleksandrovich Karaulov, member of the second and fourth State Dumas, cossack *ataman* (commander).

2. Kyrill Naryshkin was not at the palace. Vasily Aleksandrovich Dolgorukov, prince, major general in the imperial suite, chief marshal of the imperial court. Dolgorukov was at Headquarters with Nicholas II during World War I.

3. Lavr Georgievich Kornilov was appointed commander of the Petrograd military district by the Provisional Government. He was assigned to personally arrest Alexandra at Tsarskoe Selo. He replaced General Mikhail Alekseev as commander in chief on 21 May (3 June) 1917.

4. Sergei Dmitrievich Maslovsky, left Socialist Revolutionary; after the February Revolution, commissar of the Petrograd Soviet. He tried to arrest Nicholas II at Tsarskoe Selo and send him to the Peter and Paul Fortress.

· 42 ·

Diary of Alexandra, 8–9 March 1917. Original English text.

March
8th
Wednesday

14. [°C; 57°F]
O: 36.1½[1] T: 37.1 M. 38.9.
An: 36.6 *Al:*   Ania 36.8.
Gen: Kornilov Commandant Ts.S. [Tsarskoe Selo]
Kobylinsky.[2]—*Korn:* announced we are shut up
2 *o'clock.* A.D.C. *Benkendorf.*
Zhilik. From now on are considered pris: shut up—may see nobody fr. outside
Benkend: Aprak: Nastinka
V. E. *Zborovsky* said goodbye.
Burned letters with *Lili.*
3 *o'clock.* O: 37. T: 37.1. M: 38.8.
An: 36.8 *Al:* 36.5
sat with Ania
Resin—
Lazarev—} both said goodbye.
6. O: 37 T 37. M. 39.8. *An:* 37.1½ *Al:* Isa
9 *o'clock.* O: 37.2½ T. 37.2½ M. 39.8
An: 37.7
Sat with Ania.

March
9th
Thursday

10. [°C; 50°F]
O: 36.3 T: 37. M. 37.2 *An:* 36.5 *Al:* 36.2 Ania 36.8
11¾ N. arrived.
lunched with N. & *Aleksei* in *playroom*—
3 *o'clock.* O: 36.8 T: 37 M. 37.6 *An:* 36.8.
Went to Ania whilst I was in the garden.
Lili takes her meals with Ania.
6 *o'clock.* O: 37.1½ T: 37.2 M. 38.6 *An:* 36.9
Al: burned letters with *Lili*
Mme Zizi.[3]
Isa & Nastinka.
dined with N. in *playroom.*
9 *o'clock* O: 37. T: 37. M. 39.

An: 37. Al: 36.4.
We both sat with Ania & then with the
Benkendorf & Isa, Zizi, Nastinka,
Valia, Apraksin

1. On the Celsius scale, 37° is considered a normal temperature, the equivalent of 98.6°
Fahrenheit.
2. Yevgeny Stepanovich Kobylinsky, colonel, appointed head of the guard at Tsarskoe
Selo in March 1917.
3. Yelizaveta Alekseevna Naryshkina, chief comptroller of the household of the empress.

· 43 ·

Telegram from the Soviet of Workers' Deputies at the Konstantinovsky factories to
Nikolai Chkheidze, chairman of the Petrograd Soviet, concerning the immediate arrest of
all the members of the House of Romanov, 13 March 1917.

———

Petrograd. Received on 22 March at 20:05
Delayed by a backlog [in] Kharkov

Because we want to ensure that the numerous victims in the struggle for
freedom have not fallen in vain, because we realize that only a democratic
republic answers to the immediate tasks of the proletariat, because the
gravity of this crucial moment is clear to us, we urgently call for the
immediate arrest of the entire Romanov dynasty so that the possibility of
restoring the monarchy may be nipped in the bud. We call for dealing with
traitors as military spies.

Soviet of Workers' Deputies of
the Konstantinovsky factories

· 44 ·

Instructions from the commander of the Petrograd military district to the head of the
garrison in the town of Tsarskoe Selo concerning the guarding of the Aleksandrovsky
Palace, 17 March 1917.

———

1. Rotate the sentries who will guard the Aleksandrovsky Palace
from all reserve regiments and battalions of the garrison entrusted to you.
In addition to the guard detail, assign a duty officer to the palace on a daily
basis who will strictly follow the directions stated in the instructions.
2. From the former Convoy of His Majesty, assign only mounted
patrols to guard the town of Tsarskoe Selo and the nearest vicinity for
which districts are to be established.

3. Immediately remove from their posts the palace police who guarded the palaces and performed other services for the former ministry of the court up until 8 March.

4. Allow the abdicated emperor and the former empress to go out onto the large palace balcony and into parts of the park directly adjacent to the palace at hours of their choosing in the time period between 8 o'clock in the morning and 6 o'clock in the evening. During these designated hours, the duty officer will accompany the abdicated emperor and former empress and, according to the chief of the guard's directions, will reinforce the external guarding of the palace.

Entrances: The middle entrance and nos. 2 and 3 for entering or exiting the palace are to be closed.

Entrances nos. 1 and 4 are to be left open and admission posts are to be established there.

5. All persons from the former suite whose names appear on the attached list and who desire by their own will to remain temporarily in the Aleksandrovsky Palace do not have the right to leave the palace and must submit to following the rules established by the present instructions relating to entering the park.

6. No meetings with individuals held in the Aleksandrovsky Palace are to be allowed without my permission.

7. Written dealings with all individuals inside the palace are to be allowed only through Staff Captain Kotsebu,[1] who is in charge of subjecting all letters, notes, and telegrams to a strict inspection and allowing through, on an independent basis, only those necessary for taking care of housekeeping matters and [providing] news of health, medical help, and so forth. All the rest are subject to presentation by yourself to district headquarters.

8. Telephones located in the palace's inner chambers are to be disconnected; telephone conversations are to be allowed only on the telephone in the duty officer's room in his presence or in that of Staff Captain Kotsebu.

9. In case doctors or specialists from Tsarskoe Selo or Petrograd need to be summoned to render medical help, they should be allowed into the palace by the duty officer, who will accompany them at all times.

10. All provisions delivered to the palace must be handed over to a servant remaining in the palace, in the presence of the duty officer or Staff Captain Kotsebu, whose duties include not allowing any conversations concerning persons inside the palace to take place.

11. The engineers Shvede and Legovich and the quartermaster Donini, who live apart from the palace, are to be allowed inside the palace only in

cases where it is necessary to inspect the premises, but only when accompanied by the duty officer, in which case their interactions with Count Benkendorf are to be allowed exclusively in the presence of Staff Captain Kotsebu or the duty officer.

12. The palace commandant is under orders to report to me about all events and, moreover, to immediately report by telephone.

Signed: Commander of the troops in the Petrograd military district, Lieutenant General Kornilov

1. Pavel Pavlovich Kotsebu, officer of Her Majesty's Life Guards Lancers Regiment. After the February Revolution, Kotsebu was appointed commandant of the Aleksandrovsky Palace in Tsarskoe Selo. After complaints about lax conditions of confinement for the imperial family began to circulate, he was replaced by Pavel Korovichenko on Aleksandr Kerensky's orders.

· 45 ·

"A. F. Kerensky before the Soviet of Soldiers' Deputies," from *Kavkazskii krai* (Land of the Caucasus), 29 March 1917.

Petrograd. 27 March. Recently, in the *Izvestiia* [News] *of the Soviet of Workers' and Soldiers' Deputies,* articles have appeared criticizing Kerensky's actions toward the tsar and his family and expressing distrust of the Provisional Government on account of General [Nikolai] Ivanov's release. *Izvestiia* printed a small item on the incomprehensibility of liberating such a dangerous enemy of the people without previously notifying the Executive Committee of the Soviet of Workers' and Soldiers' Deputies.

On 26 March, Kerensky appeared at a session of the Soviet of Soldiers' Deputies in the Tauride Palace and addressed them as follows:

EXPRESSION OF DISTRUST

"I came here after hearing that people are showing up who dare to express their distrust of me. I and the Provisional Government are being reproached for indulging the old government and members of the tsar's family. I warn you all that I will not allow myself to be distrusted and will not allow Russian democracy, in my person, to be insulted. I ask you either to exclude me from your midst or trust me unconditionally. You accuse me of allowing certain persons from the tsar's family to remain at liberty. Know that only those who protested against the old tsarism and fought against it, as you did, have remained free. Dmitry Pavlovich[1] has remained free, for he was the first to fight against tsarism, preparing the conspiracy that murdered Rasputin. He has every right to remain an ordinary officer in the ranks of the Russian army in Persia.

"I freed General Ivanov upon my own authority. He remains under my supervision in a private apartment. He was freed because he is sick and old and the doctors insist that he won't survive even three days in the place where he was originally held."

WHAT DOES THE GOVERNMENT STAND FOR?

"Comrade soldiers and officers! The work of the Provisional Government is vast and urgent. Remember that the Provisional Government stands to the last for freedom, law, and Russian independence. All of us bear the same responsibility for the fate of our homeland and, in the name of our duty to it, we must all work together in a closely united fashion. There should be no place for distrust. I was at Tsarskoe Selo. The palace commandant is someone with whom I am well acquainted.[2] I trust him completely. The garrison at Tsarskoe Selo promised to follow my orders alone. All that takes place in Tsarskoe Selo is done with my knowledge." (applause)

"I will not leave this post without being firmly convinced that there will be no other order in Russia except a democratic republic. In all the world, no army is as free now as the Russian one. A soldier is now a free citizen and enjoys all rights.

"On March 27 it will be exactly a month since the moment that I led the first unit of revolutionary troops into the Tauride Palace[3] and posted an honor guard."

REPRESENTING THE INTERESTS OF DEMOCRACY

"I joined the cabinet of the Provisional Government as a representative of your interests, and the Provisional Government has heeded your voice. In the next few days, a document will appear stating that Russia renounces military conquest as an aim. I am working as hard as I can as long as I am trusted and as long as people are honest with me."

WE MUST WORK TOGETHER

"In the name of our duty to our homeland, we must work together, and now, when rumors have begun that are aimed at sowing discord in our midst, I must make this announcement: If you want I will work with you, if you don't—I will leave.

"I want to know whether you trust me or not. Otherwise, I cannot work with you."

The minister pronounced these last words with great animation. The hall shook with applause. Cries rang out: "We ask you to work with us!" "Work with us!" "We believe you!" "The entire multimillion-man army trusts you, Aleksandr Fyodorovich!"

"I came here," Kerensky concluded, "not to justify myself, but only to say that I will not act in a manner that would bring all of Russian democracy's suspicion upon me!" (thunderous applause)

CHAIRMAN'S ANNOUNCEMENT

On behalf of the soldiers' deputies, the meeting chairman declared that there was no question about trust. Speeches by certain individuals who spoke of distrust were quickly cut off. ["]The army trusts you, as does all of Russian democracy in general.["]

At the palace, Kerensky began to feel faint and let himself down onto a chair. When he had recovered, the minister said:

"I am more than satisfied with what took place here. I will use my last strength to work for your well-being. In instances of doubt, come to me day or night and we will reach an accord."

People swept Kerensky up and carried him out of the hall on a chair, to thunderous salutations.

1. Dmitry Pavlovich, grand duke, son of Grand Duke Pavel Aleksandrovich. He was exiled to Persia after taking part in Rasputin's murder.

2. Pavel Aleksandrovich Korovichenko, military lawyer, colonel, friend of Kerensky's. From 21 March to 27 May 1917, he was commandant of the Aleksandrovsky Palace.

3. The Provisional Committee of the State Duma and the Petrograd Soviet were both located in the Tauride Palace during the February Revolution. Kerensky was a member of both organizations.

· 46 ·

Diary of Archpriest Afanasy Beliaev, dean at the Fyodorovsky Cathedral in Tsarskoe Selo, 2–31 March 1917.[1]

2 March 1917. Dmitry Nikolaevich Loman, churchwarden at the Fyodorovsky Cathedral, visited me and said that I had been invited to come to the Znamensky Church, to take the miracle-working icon of the Heavenly

Tsaritsa and to go with Her to the Aleksandrovsky Palace to hold a service in the children's section of the palace, where the tsar's children are lying sick with measles. A car was sent, which took me to the Znamensky Church. Having entered the church, I met Father, Archpriest, and Dean Ioann F. Speransky, who had already arranged for the vestments to be prepared, the Icon readied, and people to be gathered together to carry Her. So I immediately donned the robes, took the cross, and sang, together with the Znamensky Church parish clergy as we set out for the palace, the festal hymn "We Your Servants Have You, All-Pure Virgin, as an Unbreachable Wall and Fountain of Wonders." Admission to the palace was accomplished with ease, despite its being guarded by the Combined Infantry Regiment. We went through the first entrance up to the second floor to the children's section and, having walked through a row of bright rooms, came into a large, half-dark room where the sick children were lying down in simple, separate beds. We put the Icon on the table that had been prepared for it. The room was so dark that I could hardly see those present in it. The empress, dressed as a nurse, was standing beside the bed of the heir; not far from her stood other nurses and nannies. A few thin wax candles were lit before the icon. The thanksgiving service began. Oh, what a terrible, unexpected sorrow has befallen the tsar's family! The news came that the Sovereign, called to Tsarskoe Selo by the empress and already hurrying from Headquarters back to his dear family, has been detained on the road and arrested, and it is even possible that he has abdicated from the throne. Something terrible is going on in Petrograd: houses are being destroyed and burned; soldiers have betrayed the tsar and, having joined with the popular mob of workers, are smashing police stations, removing and arresting their bosses and former representatives of the authorities, letting criminals out of the prisons, and declaring complete freedom for all who proclaim a republic. On Nevsky [Prospect], rifle shots rumble and innocent victims fall. A fierce battle between the troops and the police has begun. Even Tsarskoe Selo is uneasy. In the Sofiisky part of town, where the troops are stationed, noise and frenzied cries can be heard; the rapid fire of arms is ongoing; soldiers are destroying and smashing wineshops and stores; police buildings are being burned down; they have set prisoners free from the jail. One can imagine what circumstances the helpless empress finds herself in, a mother with five such seriously sick children of her own. Suppressing her womanly feebleness and all her bodily ailments, dedicating herself in a heroic, self-assured manner to looking after the sick, with full trust in the help of the Heavenly Tsaritsa, she decided first of all to pray before the miracle-working icon of Our Lady of the Sign [*Znamenie Bozh'ei Materi*], instructing that the icon be brought into the chambers of the sick children. Fervently, on her knees, with tears in her eyes, the earthly tsaritsa asked the Heavenly Tsaritsa for help and intervention. Venerating the icon and coming to stand beneath it, she asked to bring it also to the sickbeds so that all the sick children could also touch their lips to the miracle-working Icon. Holding out the cross to be kissed, I said: "Fortify yourself and be brave, Your Majesty, for the dream is terrible, but God is merciful. In all things, rely upon His divine will. Believe, trust, and don't stop praying." The holy icon was taken into all the children's rooms; we went downstairs and came to a separate, isolated room where Anna A. Vyrubova, sick with measles and covered with a rash, was lying down. There I only read a prayer before the icon of the Mother of God, at which time the sick person, fervently pressing her flushed head to the holy icon, did not want to let it out of her hands for a long time. The empress, having come downstairs from the children's rooms by the direct, inner staircase, stood next to the sickbed and also fervently prayed. When we left with the icon, the palace was already cordoned off by troops, and it turned out that all those within were under arrest.

11 and 12 March. Saturday and Sunday.   When the Sovereign arrived at Tsarskoe Selo from Headquarters on 9 March, I was invited by a telephone call from the Aleksandrovsky Palace to come and conduct the vigil [*vsenoshnaia*] and a long liturgy in the palace church together with members of the court staff: archdeacon, psalm-reader, and choristers (four). When we arrived at the palace, we were met by the commandant and the guard on duty. After entering the corridor of the lower floor where Their Majesties' chambers were located, the Sovereign's valet came up to me and said: "His Majesty asks that you come into his room. He wants to say a few words to you about the forthcoming service in the palace church." In response to those words, the young ensign accompanying us said: "That is not allowed," and, addressing me, stated: "Be so kind as to go into the church; it is forbidden to talk with him." The astonished valet objected: "Allow this or I will inform His Majesty," but the stern guard was categorical: "I don't care. I cannot allow any meetings with anyone whomsoever—no contacts." And thus we were led into the church without stopping and in total silence. After a few minutes, still before the start of the service, Marshal of the Imperial Court Benkendorf came into the church hall and, in the name of the Sovereign, asked me to hold services in the palace church on Sundays and holidays. After the end of the vigil, I appealed to the palace commandant with a request to explain: Were there some sort of instructions for us concerning how to conduct services and how to act—for exam-

ple, how to answer the Sovereign if he were to ask about something? How should he be addressed? How should he be referred to during services and so forth and, in general, how should one comport oneself with all the employees of the palace? To this the commandant answered: "There are no instructions, but of course questions on the part of the Sovereign should be answered, although the conversation must not be political and must be in the presence of the guard on duty. It's better to avoid addressing him, although I call him 'Your Majesty.' Decline personal meetings in his rooms, and in general the less reason for reprimands on the part of the guard, the better it will be for the arrested." And truly, the Sovereign and his wife are so refined and grateful that they come to services themselves when we stand already robed at the altar and leave the church after services before anyone else does. They stand in church completely separately behind screens, taking up a rather small space in the corner with a separate entrance. The first time in the presence of the Sovereign, after the great entrance [a central part of the liturgy], when it was necessary to talk of the Russian State and the Provisional Government instead of the Devout Autocrat Sovereign Emperor and so on, I could not at first find the strength and almost started weeping. With a cracking voice, stumbling over the words, I finished the commemorations. On 24 and 25 March I conducted the vigil and the liturgy, and I conducted the vigil again on Sunday. After the vigil, I gave each person one very small twig of the consecrated willow branch. Even in this, the disrespect and penal conditions were evident.

May God bless.

. . .

29 March.   Rose at 7 in the morning, prayed to God and read the preparatory prayers for communion. I wait for the liturgy. It turned out that Schneider's rooms are next to mine and that Vyrubova's servants, who thirst for freedom, are on the other side. The liturgy is performed in the presence of three persons. The last time, there were great bows. After the liturgy, I read prayers for the confessors and gave a brief sermon on how to approach repentance. Confession for the servants is set for 2 o'clock in the afternoon. At 1 o'clock, lunch is served: shredded cabbage with pickles and potatoes, fish, and *kisel* [blancmange]. The confession began at 2 o'clock and lasted until 5 o'clock. There were fifty-four people confessing; the rest of those still fasting in preparation for communion were left until Saturday. At half past 6, I began matins with festal singing: "When the Glorious Disciples." Four soloists from the court choir dressed in crimson tailcoats sing at all the services. By 8 o'clock the service was over.

Today at 5 o'clock I was visited by the palace commandant [Korovichenko]. He turned out to be a wonderful, altogether humane and noble person. He informed me that I was a free person, that I can walk the palace halls freely and talk with all persons who live at court, and can even walk out into the garden to breathe the fresh air. After vigil, I saw [Doctor] Botkin and talked with him. Dinner was served at 8 o'clock at night—soup with mushrooms, fish, and dry biscuits in sweet syrup with a slice of pineapple. I received the newspaper *Novoe vremia* [New times].

30 March. I walked the palace halls and was amazed at the luxury and richness. From the windows of the round hall I saw how the graves were being prepared for those who died during the days of the wineshop riots in Tsarskoe Selo. The site for the graves was opposite the palace on an open field.[2] The liturgy, at which the tsar's family fervently prayed and all took communion, was over around 12 o'clock. Those fasting approached the holy chalice modestly, and I said a few words to them that could also be heard by all those present in the church. After the liturgy the footman told me that the father confessor, via Anichkov, agreed, despite his sickly state, to appear at the palace for the confession of Their Majesties, but he was answered that he need not trouble himself to come, for everything could be done without him. But nobody knew who would be invited to replace the father confessor, and there were no instructions yet issued on the matter. It appeared that everything was going smoothly and the service was satisfying everyone. They brought a small but wondrous Shroud of Christ from the Fyodorovsky Cathedral and a special table for it, a large book of the Gospels, and festal Easter vestments. The altar and table of oblation were covered for now in black vestments, and black chasubles were readied for the clergy. The vigil and reading of the Gospels was set for 6 o'clock in the evening. At 1 o'clock, luncheon was served: rice cutlets with white mushrooms, fried smelt, and fruit compote. At 4 o'clock, I opened the window and [now I] hear military music; the "Marseillaise" and funeral marches are being played. From the window many soldiers can be seen. It is impossible to make out what is being done at the graves because of the distance, although all this is taking place by the palace opposite the round hall, not far from the church. And this on Holy Thursday during Holy Week. Verily, they know not what they do. At 6 o'clock the service began with the twelve Gospel readings. The devout are all the same, one hundred people all told, including the suite and servants, in the presence of the guard on duty. The choristers sang beautifully—the four soloists from the court choir— especially "The Wise Thief." The service was reverential and moving, although it was shortened considerably: the Gospels were read, and after each reading, one hymn was sung. The whole service lasted for 1 hour and

40 minutes. Their Majesties listened to the whole service while standing. Folding lecterns on which the Gospels rested were placed before them so that they could follow along with the reading the entire time. Everyone stood to the end of the service and left through the common hall for their rooms, which they had never done before. One has to see for oneself, be near enough to understand and be convinced of how fervently the former tsar's family pray to God, in an Orthodox manner and often upon their knees. They stand at worship with such obedience, meekness, and humility, giving themselves up completely to the will of God. And I, a sinner and unworthy servant of the altar of the Lord, feel my heart stop beating, the tears flow; and despite the oppressive difficulty of seclusion, the Lord's abundance fills my soul, and the words of prayer flow, freely reaching and penetrating the hearing of the devout. At 8 o'clock, dinner is served: cabbage soup with mushrooms, roast meat, and raspberry gelatin. At 9 o'clock in the evening, I get ready for Friday; there will be the bearing-out of the Shroud of Christ; I think about what to say before the grave of the innocent sufferer-Saviour of ours. I read marvelous hymns in Russian translation designated for Good Friday and am moved by their content. What will tomorrow bring? How many and which people are getting ready to confess?

31 March. 9 o'clock in the morning. I got up early and spent the night anxiously. The wonderful conditions and all conveniences notwithstanding—it's clean, bright, warm, and cozy—sleep still wouldn't come. I washed for a long time and wet my head with cold water, prayed to God, and began to write some words for the bearing-out of the Shroud of Christ. At 12 o'clock, I went to the church to hear confession from those readying themselves for communion. There turned out to be forty-two at confession, including two doctors: Botkin and Derevenko. At half past 1, I received notification that I am expected at half past 5 in the children's section to take confession from the three sick princesses and the former heir and ready them for communion. At 2 o'clock, vespers began and the shroud was borne out to the middle of the church. A place for the shroud was adorned with rugs, and whole bushes of blooming white and red lilacs were brought, and many roses, and a wonderful, elegant flower bed of live flowers was made. The table brought from the Fyodorovsky Cathedral for the placing of the shroud was put in the center of the flower bed. Their Majesties, two princesses, and the suite appeared in deep mourning—all of them in black dress. Vespers passed in a decorous and rather ceremonial manner. The shroud was brought to the center of the church. I said a few words: "What a sad, ceremonial, holy act is now performed in all Ortho-

dox churches! The bearing-out of the shroud. Before us is the grave with the sacred image of the Divine Sufferer who died for the sins of all people. Oh, how strongly, irrepressibly I, a sinner, am drawn to cling to this coffin and, in place of the sacramentally anointed one, to shed tears of repentance upon His most pure body. Oh, how clearly I hear His last words, spoken from the cross. I also hear that death cry rending the soul, addressed to the Heavenly Father: 'My God, my God, why hast Thou forsaken Me!' And what a bottomless well of grief is heard in this cry! 'Let people leave Me, abandon Me—may friends and acquaintances turn away from Me. Let my near and dear leave me. But You, My Heavenly Father, why are You so angry with Me? Why have You averted Your wondrous, bright, and loving gaze?' And what a terrible, unheard-of occurrence. From the heavens there is no voice, no command. From that heaven where the voice of the Heavenly Father was always heard, 'This is My Beloved Son, listen to Him,' not a sound now comes—a terrible condition, to feel, to see oneself in an unbearably difficult moment of grief abandoned by God. And this for the only-begotten Son of God. Oh, what a great mystery! A mystery that is beyond human comprehension. But the wondrous power of God appears in what is inaccessible to the mind of man. And thus, in this inscrutable mystery of redemption we understand that God is the greatest, most eternal and boundless Love. There are those who love God. This love moved the Son to accept suffering and death; this love forced the Father to abandon his Son in the moment of His most unbearably difficult sufferings. Divine Love did all this to draw to itself all suffering, persecuted, and equally repentant sinners. O, Lord, my Saviour! What consolation You pour into my defeated heart with Your sufferings and death. I feel deeply that in all my sorrows I am not alone. For You, Lord, are with me. And walking with You, I fear not evil nor to be in the valley of death." These words spoken in the church by the shroud made many cry. One of the princesses' nannies was led away to another hall to be calmed. These words made a deep impression on the tsar—so he told me after confession. The hour of confession came for the tsar's children as well. The footman came and announced: "It's time to go; they are already waiting." I donned the stole, took the cross and the Gospels into my hands, and went upstairs after the footman, who showed the way to the children's rooms. These rooms are decorated in an amazing Christian manner. In a corner of her room, each princess has placed a real iconostasis filled with many icons of different sizes and with depictions of the especially venerated saints. Before the iconostasis is a folding table covered with a towel, and upon it are placed the prayer books and liturgical books, as well as the Holy Gospels and cross. The rooms' furnishings and their entire arrangement reflect an innocent, clean, chaste childhood unaware of worldly filth. In order to listen to prayers before confession, all four [ill] children were in one room, where the sick Olga Nikolaevna lay. Aleksei Nikolaevich sat in a chair dressed in a little light-blue robe sewn along the edges with a patterned braid. Maria Nikolaevna was half lying down in a large chair that was on wheels, which Anastasia Nikolaevna easily moved about. After the reading of prayers and a brief word before confession, only Olga Nikolaevna remained in the room. The heir exited by himself, and Anastasia Nikolaevna took Maria Nikolaevna away. Then I went to another room to hear confession from the rest: Aleksei, Maria, and Anastasia Nikolaevna. I will not say how the confession went. My general impression was as follows: Lord, let all children be morally as upright as the children of the former tsar. Such mildness, restraint, obedience to their parents' wishes, such absolute devotion to God's will, cleanliness in their lodgings, and complete ignorance of worldly filth—either passionate or sinful—amazed me and I was totally at a loss: as a confessor, do I need to remind them of sins that perhaps they do not know, and how do I dispose them to confessing sins unknown to them? Hearing confession from all four of them took 1 hour and 20 minutes. At half past 7, the Saturday matins began. I read the so-called lamentations over the shroud, and the religious procession with the bearing-out of the shroud was completed by carrying it through and behind the altar, coming to the altar by the north doors and leaving by the south, walking around the rooms near the walls of the round hall, and returning to the church and the royal doors [on the altar] and [going] back again to the middle of the church. Prince Benkendorf and Doctors Botkin and Derevenko carried the shroud; behind them came Nicholas Aleksandrovich, Alexandra Fyodorovna, Tatiana and Anastasia Nikolaevna, the suite, and a servant with lit candles. Matins ended at 8 o'clock in the evening, and the confession of the ladies of the suite began: Naryshkina, Dolgorukova, Gendrikova, and Buksgevden. The footman appeared and announced that Their Majesties are waiting to confess in their bedroom at 10 o'clock. I sat in my room from 9 to half past. The time went by quickly. At 9:40, I went to the church, prayed at the holy altar, venerated the shroud, donned my stole, took the cross and the Gospels, and followed the footman to Their Majesties' chambers. There a female servant took me through the rooms into the bedroom, where one wide bed stood, and pointed to a small room in the corner, a chapel where Their Majesties would be confessing. No one was in the room yet. Not two minutes had passed when the former Sovereign walked in with his wife and Tatiana Nikolaevna. The Sovereign greeted me, presented Her Majesty and, indicating his daughter, said: "This is our daughter, Tatiana. You, Father, start

the prayers that are read prior to confession and we will pray together."
The chapel room is very small and is filled from top to bottom with
hanging or standing icons. Lamps burn before the icons. Deeper, in the
corner, stands a special iconostasis with carved columns and places for
famous icons, and before it stands a folding table upon which has been
placed an ancient altar Gospels and cross and many prayer books. I did not
know where to put the cross and Gospels that I had brought and so put
them right down on the books that were already there. After the reading of
the prayers, the Sovereign and his wife left and Tatiana Nikolaevna stayed
for confession. After her, Her Majesty came in an agitated state, evidently
having prayed fervently and decided, in accordance with Orthodox rites
and in full consciousness of the greatness of the sacrament, to confess the
illnesses of her heart before the holy cross and Gospels. His Majesty came
for confession after her. Taking confession from all three lasted for 1 hour
and 20 minutes. Oh, how unspeakably happy I am that I was favored by
God's grace to become the mediator between the Heavenly Ruler and the
earthly one. Beside me was standing the one above whom no one else living
on earth rises superior. Until this time, this was our God-given Anointed
Sovereign, a Russian Orthodox tsar who reigned for twenty-three years by
the law of succession to the throne. And now Nicholas, a humble slave of
God, like a meek lamb, benevolent toward all his enemies, harboring no
offense, fervently praying for Russia's prosperity, believing deeply in her
glorious future, on bended knee, gazing at the cross and Gospels, in the
presence of my unworthiness, tells the Heavenly Father the innermost
secrets of his unfortunate life and, prostrating himself before the greatness
of the Heavenly Tsar, tearfully asks forgiveness for his voluntary and
involuntary sins. After the reading of the final prayer and the kissing of the
cross and Gospels, what clumsy words of comfort and consolation, what
joy could I instill in the heart of this person who was maliciously taken
away from his people and who remains to this moment completely certain
of the rightness of his actions, which were directed toward the good of his
beloved motherland? When I said: "Ah, Your Majesty, what good You
would have done for Russia had You granted in Your time a full Constitution, thereby fulfilling the wish of the people. Everyone would have hailed
You as the Angel of good, love, and peace." To this he responded in
amazement: "That may be true! Yes, everyone betrayed me. I was told that
there was anarchy in Petrograd and rebellion, and I decided to go: not to
Petrograd, but to Tsarskoe Selo, and so from the Nikolaevsky line headed
to Pskov, but the railroad was already cut off. I decided to return to the
front, but that line also turned out to be cut. And so alone, without a close
adviser, deprived of freedom like a captive criminal, I signed the act of

abdication from the throne for myself and my son and heir. I decided that if this is needed for the good of the motherland I was ready for anything. It is sad for my family!" And burning tears fell from the eyes of the weak-willed sufferer. Later there was a general conversation. Alexandra Fyodorovna asked how Father Aleksandr's health was and I answered that despite all his desire to be in Tsarskoe Selo and officiate, he still was unable to do this because his nerves were badly upset. Her Majesty said: "I am very sorry. Give him our regards and wishes for good health, as you are his close relative." The tsar conveyed the same wishes for good health, also asked after the health of Father Vasiliev, and added: "We all came to love him so very much. The reason for his nerves being upset I partly attribute to the loss of his son, whom we also all knew and over whose death we grieved. Please give him my kind regards." And Nicholas Aleksandrovich asked me: "You no longer officiate in the Yekaterinburgsky Cathedral, but what about the Fyodorovsky? I was very happy when I learned that you had agreed to officiate for us here in the Fyodorovsky Cathedral. And what is happening at present, what is the condition of this wonderful cathedral?" I answered that all the buildings of the Fyodorovsky settlement, together with the cathedral, are temporarily entrusted to the management of commissar Golovin. For a few minutes the conversation continued about family life. Incidentally, Her Majesty said: "I was misunderstood. I only wanted to do good."

1. Afanasy Ivanovich Beliaev, archpriest, senior priest at the Fyodorovsky Cathedral at Tsarskoe Selo. From March to July 1917, he replaced Aleksei Vasiliev, confessor to the tsar's family, who had fallen ill. The Fyodorovsky Cathedral in Tsarskoe Selo was built in 1912 with the imperial family's direct assistance. The cathedral was noted for its ancient Russian style.

2. "Victims in the Revolution" were buried along the avenue leading to the Aleksandrovsky Palace, within sight of the windows, in a ceremony on Maundy Thursday, 30 March 1917.

· 47 ·

Telegram from the residents of Kuragino to the Petrograd Soviet and the minister of justice, Aleksandr Kerensky, protesting the proposed departure of the tsar and his family to England, 5 April 1917.

———

Received on 6 April 1917 at 8:27

The Kuragino[1] general assembly protests the departure of Nicholas Romanov with his wife for England without a trial in light of the proof that they betrayed the fatherland. The committee on security is amazed that

Sukhomlinov[2] is on trial if exceptions are allowed for those in charge who ought to have more to answer for. Constitutional guarantees are null and void for the former tsar because he violated the constitution. We call for supporting this demand: Hand over Nicholas and his spouse to Kerensky's impartial court of justice.[3]

1. Kuragino is a small industrial town in Kaluga province in central Russia.

2. Vladimir Aleksandrovich Sukhomlinov, cavalry general, minister of war, 1909–1915. In the summer of 1915, he was dismissed from his post after being accused of committing crimes against the state, and the matter was submitted for investigation. From April to October 1916, he was held in the Peter and Paul Fortress. In 1917 he was sentenced to life imprisonment.

3. On 5 March 1917, the Provisional Government founded the Extraordinary Investigatory Commission (ChSK) to review the activities of former tsarist ministers and high officials for violations of the law.

· 48 ·

Statement by Cavalry Sergeant Major Aleksandr Danilov to the Petrograd Soviet concerning violations of the regimen for guarding the imperial family in the Aleksandrovsky Palace at Tsarskoe Selo, 7 April 1917.

STATEMENT

by Cavalry Sergeant Major Aleksandr Petrovich Danilov, deputy from the 180th Infantry Reserve Regiment. A private from the Fourth Company of the Second Rifle Res. [Reserve] Battalion appealed to him with the request that he mention that their unit has a very important piece of news. Nepomiluev of the Second Rifle Res. Battal. reported it. In Tsarskoe Selo the guards at the Aleksandrovsky Palace remain temporarily at their posts.

1. Nicholas II greets the guards, and they answer him just as they did before.

2. The posted guards (their number was not indicated) allowed in an unidentified civ. [civilian], who spoke with Nicholas II for a few hours.

3. As far as we know, Colonel Artobolevsky allowed in a gentleman in civilian clothes.

4. The chief of the guards was drunk; we weren't told the last name, but the guards that were with him could say.

5. Soldiers from the Second Battalion arrested an officer from the Fourth Company for daring to say: "We'll walk up to our knees in blood, but we'll bring back the old order." The officer was sent to the town council, but someone set him free, and they say that he went on leave to the countryside.

This information was given personally to the Exec. Commission [Committee] of the Sov. of S. [Soldiers'] Dep.

> Deputy from the Commission on
> Agitation in the 180th Infantry
> Res. Regiment,
> Cavalry Sergeant Major
> Aleksandr Petrovich Danilov

· 49 ·

Poem by Olga, dedicated to her mother, Alexandra, 23 April 1917.

———

Tsarskoe Selo   23 April 1917

> You are filled with anguish
> For the suffering of others.
> And no one's grief
> Has ever passed you by.
> You are relentless
> Only toward yourself,
> Forever cold and pitiless.
> But if only you could look upon
> Your own sadness from a distance,
> Just once with a loving soul—
> Oh, how you would pity yourself.
> How sadly you would weep.

To My Beloved Mama

· 50 ·

Resolution from the crew of the cruiser *Rossia* (Russia) on the transfer of Nicholas to Kronstadt adopted at the general assembly of sailors, 20 May 1917.

———

1. We join in supporting the resolution, passed by the command of the battleships *Zaria svobody* (Dawn of freedom) and *Respublika* (Republic), with an amendment after the words "We demand that the Soviet of S. and W.D. [Soldiers' and Workers' Deputies] compel the coalition ministry to immediately transfer all lands and inventory to them for placement under the jurisdiction of peasant committees"—after which we consider it necessary to add: "For the immediate, free use by the peasants and for final partition according to the legislation of the Constituent Assembly."

2. The second point of the resolution by the above-listed ships is adopted unanimously.

3. Having discussed the conditions for guarding Nicholas the Bloody and his henchmen [*oprichniki*], we find them to fall short of their purpose. We deem their comfortable life inadmissible. In the fight for the holy cause of the revolution, our comrades passed through prisons, languished for decades in the Shlisselburg and Peter and Paul fortresses, were starved and tortured in every conceivable manner during the reign of the above-mentioned Nicholas the Bloody and his henchmen, and death sentences for our comrades were carried out within twenty-four hours. But our demands for the transfer of the above-mentioned Nicholas the Bloody and his henchmen to Kronstadt have, for some reason, not been met for the past two months.

Recognizing that the refusal of the Provisional Government to fulfill our demands is an attempt to go against our will, we demand for the last time that the Provisional Government immediately send Nicholas the Bloody and his henchmen to the Kronstadt Fortress upon receiving our resolution.

We do not consider it superfluous to add to our resolution the following:

Recognizing that the allocation of thousands of pensions to the families of our former tyrant-ministers is a sign of generosity toward them, we demand the immediate cancellation of the above-mentioned allocations and, for our part, find it unnecessary even to give out the rations that reservists' families receive.

We ask other ships to join in supporting our resolution.

· 51 ·

Telegram from the soldiers of the Nikolaevsky Maritime Battery at the Ochakovsky Fortress to the Executive Committee of the Petrograd Soviet demanding the imprisonment of the tsar and his family in the Peter and Paul Fortress, 21 May 1917.

———

Received on 30 May 1917 at 6:40
Petrograd from Ochakov

The following was placed in *Odesskie novosti* [Odessa news] [no.] 10421: "Nicholas Romanov's guards drink wine and, together with them, the sailors themselves take Alexandra on outings." The soldiers of the Nikolaevsky Maritime Battery are highly upset by this and ask for the immediate transfer of Nicholas, Alexandra, and their family to the Peter and Paul Fortress in order to institute strict surveillance and to prosecute all those sympathetic to the Romanovs as traitors to the freedom of the Russian state. Friendship with Nicholas, just like fraternization at the front, is fatal for the motherland.

· 52 ·

Letter from Alexandra to Aleksandr Syroboiarsky,[1] 29 May 1917.

———————

Tsarskoe Selo   29 May

MAMA [Maria Syroboiarskaia] wrote out a good prayer for me that She Herself reads every day. It is so very touching. I don't know why she loves me so. Be tender with her and don't be shy about sharing your thoughts with her a bit more. It's hard for her, you know. It has to be. You say that you don't know how, but that's not the case. You're just out of practice and don't want to confide in her about the hardships of life. You want to protect her, but a mother has a keen heart and her soul suffers along with you. Knowing your character, I know that it isn't easy for you and that is why the house is empty. Different interests, thoughts, dreams. She writes that her heart has gotten better and I am so glad. It is so hard to read the papers. Where are we? Where have we ended up? But God will save Russia yet. I believe that strongly. But where has discipline gone? They write so much filth about Him [Nicholas II]: a weak mind and so forth. It gets worse and worse, I throw the papers down, it hurts, it hurts all the time. Everything good is forgotten, it is so hard to read curses against the person you love most, the unfairness of people, and never a single kind word. They don't let it be printed, of course, but you understand what kind of pain [I feel]. When they write filth about Me—let them, they started tormenting me long ago, I don't care now, but that they slander Him, throw dirt on the Sovereign Anointed by God, that is beyond the bearable. Long-suffering Job.[2] At least God values Him and will reward Him for his gentleness. How greatly he suffers inside, seeing the ruin. No one sees this. As if He would show anyone what goes on inside Him. You see, it's terrifying to love your homeland. How can you avoid your soul hurting when you see what goes on. I never thought there could be so much anarchy within three months, but I need to bear it through to the end and to pray. Pray that He saves everything. And the army—it makes you want to cry, I can't read about it, I throw it all down and remember the suffering of the Saviour; He died for us sinners and perhaps he will still be mollified. I shouldn't write all this down, but it isn't going through the mail, and I believe that the new commandant censor [Colonel Kobylinsky] won't reprove me for it. Don't you lose faith, you mustn't, you simply mustn't, or there just won't be enough strength left to live. They'll see for themselves that discipline and order are needed, that one shouldn't fear being stronger than the bad, destructive forces that only try to hurry Russia's death. They are not patriots and there is nothing holy in them. They await an offensive and then delay again. Oh, my soul is filled with pain, with pain, but He will save us, help us, will hear the prayers of those who love Russia. Forgive me that I write all this; perhaps they'll tear this page up. Make your poor mother happy with your presence. You know that she needs you—isn't that good? I lost my mother when I was six years old, and my father at eighteen. It is such consolation to have them, to know that she always waits for you with love and prays with all her strength for you. She needs you. It's a great pity that I can't see you and have the possibility of speaking with you. Your mood is so sad, dark, a hopeless outlook on everything. If we occasionally saw each other, then maybe I could help a little, help relieve things and clear things up, but I can't do it on paper, don't know how to write; it doesn't come out right and seems so empty. I want so much to help and try to clear the gloom. You mustn't look at everything this way, not all is lost, God will save our dear homeland yet. We will have to wait patiently (of course, folding one's hands is the most difficult thing), but this has to end. You talk of history. Yes, it all happened before and will happen again, everything repeats itself, but sometimes the Lord God uses different means to save a people. You know that I have nearly lost all faith in people, and yet My whole being is in God, and no matter what happens, this faith cannot be taken away. I don't understand, but I do know that He understands and that He does everything for the better. People have become worse and worse. It's Sodom and Gomorrah in the capital and what about the front? It's scarcely better in the cities. Because of this there is punishment, and many of those people have already suffered. All those (from among the good, but stupid and silly) who judged and cursed everything—see what a stew they've cooked up [*kashu zavarili*], and now they fear that the peasants are taking everything from them. That seems unfair to them because it really hurts. This is good for the soul. For those who strongly believe in God, this will be (I can't find the right word here) as a trial for perfecting their souls; for others it will be a trial— God will reward them, believe me. I know an old man who spent a long time (in jail); they let him out and in he went again, and he became pure, deeply faithful, and never lost his love for His M. [Majesty] and faith in

Him and in God.[3] If reward is not here, then it is there, in the other world, and this is what we live for. Everything here passes, and there—pure eternity. Oh, believe in this! You're young, it's hard for you to think about this, but suffer once in life and you will find consolation in this. Everyone needs trial and tribulation, but one must show firmness in everything and suffer through it all with a strong and faithful soul. There is no such adversity that does not pass. God promised us this in His endless mercy, and we know what unimaginable bliss He readies for those who love Him. Let Him help all these to humbly accept His divine will. "Night shall not cover the sky forever; perhaps there will be a ray of sun." His road has remained so that we may walk upon it. The way is thorny, but He walked it before us—let us also each bear our cross, as He did. I'm no good at writing, but pray fervently that He will lighten your suffering on behalf of others, that He may console and strengthen you. Remember how your dear father bore all cruelty and unfairness. Yes, sometimes life and health can't withstand it, but the spirit must. You know me well and understand my true wish to help you. People are bad and He punishes, punishes by example. A kingdom of evil is now on earth. But He is above all things; He can make everything turn out for the better. We will see better days. You are young, you will still see other things, don't be fainthearted. Whoever has a clean conscience bears slander and unfairness more easily. We live not for ourselves but for others, for our homeland (that is how we understood it). More than He [Nicholas II] did is impossible. But they said it was for the general good. But I don't believe that the Lord won't reward this. And those who acted so despicably, their eyes will be opened—for many that is already the case. The psychology of the masses is a terrible thing. Our people are really very uncultured; because of this they follow the wave like a herd of sheep. But give them to understand that they are deceived—and everything could go a different direction. These people are able but ignorant, they understand nothing. Let the people who are good try to save the country, since everywhere the bad ones are working on behalf of destruction. Our first duty is to rid ourselves of the external enemy—but with such troops it has become terribly difficult, though not completely hopeless—there are real patriots, there is God. And we at the home front must pray with all our weakened powers—and beg Him to save Russia. And He will hear and be mollified. There is much that we will still have to bear. The bad will not become better, but then somewhere there are good people, but, of course, they are weak "drops in the sea," as you call them, but, in time, all together they could be a stream of cleansing water and could wash away all the dirt.

I must end. I pray for you always. Everyone sends warmest regards.

May God preserve you. All the very, very best, a speedy recovery and spiritual peace.

Old Sister A.

1. Aleksandr Vladimirovich Syroboiarsky. During World War I, Syroboiarsky, an officer in the Russian army, was injured and sent to the hospital at Tsarskoe Selo, where Alexandra took a particular interest in him. Their extensive correspondence dated from that time.

2. Nicholas was born on the day the Russian Orthodox Church honors the prophet Job.

3. General Sukhomlinov, the former minister of war, was imprisoned in the Peter and Paul Fortress from April to October 1916 and was again arrested after the February Revolution and sentenced to life imprisonment.

· 53 ·

Letter from Olga to Pyotr Petrov, 19 June 1917.

Tsarskoe Selo   19 June 1917

Dear old P. V. P.,

THANK YOU very much for your letter. How glad I am that you are finally well, and once again in Tsarskoe. After foul Petrograd, of course, the air here will bring you health and quickly replenish your strength. You probably heard from Zhilik [Gilliard] about how we spend our days. We walk every day from 2 to 5. We work in the garden. If it isn't too stifling, Mama also comes out and lies on a couch under a tree by the water. Papa walks (with many others) to the outer reaches of the garden, where they chop and saw dry trees. Aleksei plays on the "children's island," runs barefoot, and sometimes swims. Never unbending her back, Trina [Shneider] weeds and waters the flower beds. Sometimes we also do the watering, including the roses that we planted nearby, opposite Grandmother's [Dowager Empress Maria Fyodorovna's] windows. Studies are taking their own course. Maria and I study English together. She reads to me aloud and, if it's not too hot, takes dictation. She and I study history two times a week. Russian history according to Nechvolodov's book.[1] He describes everything really well and in detail. Right now, we've stopped on the folk heroes (epics). Two times a week, Anastasia and I read about the history of the Middle Ages according to Konst. Amn.'s textbook. Though that's a lot harder, since my memory for all these events is atrocious, but hers is no better. I divided up my own hours (the free ones) for reading (boring things), history of art, French hist., general hist., and Russian lit. according to

Galakhov. There! I think that's all. Mama sends you regards, happy that you are better and so forth. Everyone sends greetings.

All the best to you,

Your pupil No. 1 O. N.

Thanks!

No. 4 A. N.

[Anastasia Nikolaevna]

1. Aleksandr Dmitrievich Nechvolodov, *Skazaniia o russkoi zemle* (Tales of the Russian Land), 4 vols. (St. Petersburg, 1909–1913). This was a popular illustrated history of Russia.

· 54 ·

Letter from Olga to her aunt Olga Aleksandrovna, 21 June 1917.

21 June 1917

My darling, dear Godmother,

A M terribly touched by your sweet letter and heartfelt words. I wanted to have a heart-to-heart talk with you when you were with us in Kiev, but there wasn't the opportunity.

Poor Mama is terribly bored; can't at all get used to the new life and the circumstances here, although on the whole we can all be grateful that we will be together and in the Crimea.[1] So horribly sad to think about our dear nieces and their parents and about our homeland. Little Dolls!! Now it's doubly hard for you, my darling Aunt Olga. May God preserve you.

A kiss to you and Mitia. Love you sincerely and with all my heart.

Your loving Goddaughter,

Olga

1. During the summer of 1917, the family still expected to be sent to Livadia, the family estate in Crimea.

· 55 ·

Deciphered telegrams from British Ambassador George Buchanan in Petrograd to London concerning the transfer of the tsar's family to Tobolsk, 11 (24) and 12 (25) July 1917. Original English text.

CIRCULATED TO THE KING AND THE WAR CABINET.

Decypher. Sir G. Buchanan (Petrograd)

D. [Dispatched]. 9.50 P.M. July 24th.1917.

R. [Received]. 11.48 A.M. July 25th.1917.

Personal.

Minister for Foreign Affairs [Mikhail Tereshchenko][1] told me confidentially to-day that it had been decided to send the Emperor and his family for greater safety to Siberia probably either to Tobolsk or to Tomsk. They would live in the Governor's House and be happier than at Tsarskoe as they would have more personal liberty. Reason which had prompted the Government to take this step was fear in the event of an attempt at a counter Revolution their lives might be in danger.

CIRCULATED TO THE KING AND THE WAR CABINET.

RUSSIA.

Decypher. Sir G. Buchanan (Petrograd)

D. July 25th.1917.

R. July 26th.1917. 6.30

Personal.

My telegram personal of yesterday.

Minister for Foreign Affairs told me to-day K. [Kerensky] who had seen Emperor yesterday had arranged for him to leave to-night for Tobolsk. His Majesty would have preferred to have gone to Crimea but seemed quite pleased with the proposed change of residence.

I expressed hope that when he was in Siberia Emperor's movements would not be so restricted as at Tsarskoe Selo and that he would be allowed to go out driving. In spite of many faults which he had committed and his weak character Emperor was not a criminal and deserved to be treated with as much consideration as possible. Minister for Foreign Affairs replied that K. quite acknowledged this and was anxious to do (? what he [note by cypher officer]) could to meet His Majesty's wishes. He had given him permission to chose [*sic*] those whom he wished to accompany him and he would have very comfortable house with large garden. Whether he would be able to drive out would depend a good deal on state of public feeling in Tobolsk. At Tsarskoe Selo it would have been dangerous for him to have done so.

Real reason of removal of Emperor is undoubted fear of Counter Revolution which is gaining ground among socialists.

I told Minister for Foreign Affairs ([code] group undecypherable) fear was in my opinion unfounded so far as restoration of Dynasty was concerned. There was however decided reaction in favour of order and strong Government but this was quite a different thing.

Minister for Foreign Affairs replied that he personally quite agreed with me.

1. Mikhail Ivanovich Tereshchenko. After the February Revolution, Tereshchenko was finance minister in the Provisional Government. After Pavel Miliukov's resignation, he became minister of foreign affairs and tried to arrange for the tsar and his family to go to England.

· 56 ·

Diary of Nicholas II, 9 March–31 July 1917.

9 March. Thursday.   Made it to Tsarskoe Selo quickly and safely at 11:30. But God, what a difference, guards are on the street and inside the park surrounding the palace, and some sort of ensigns are inside the entrance! Went upstairs and there saw my darling Alix and the dear children. She looked cheerful and healthy, and they were all lying down in the dark room. But everyone feels well except for Maria, who just recently came down with measles. We breakfasted and dined in Aleksei's playroom. Saw kind Benkendorf. Went for a walk with Valia Dolg. [Dolgorukov] and worked with him in the garden, as it was not possible to go any farther! After tea I unpacked my things. In the evening we made the rounds of all those living on the other side [of the palace] and found them all together.

10 March. Friday.   We slept well. Despite the conditions in which we now find ourselves, the thought that we are all **together** gladdens and consoles. In the morning, received Benkendorf, next looked through, put in order, and burned papers. Sat with the children until 2:30. Went for a walk with Valia Dolg. escorted by those same two ensigns. Today they were more courteous. We worked well in the snow. The weather stayed sunny. Spent the evening together.

. . .

21 March. Tuesday.   Kerensky came unexpectedly today; the present min. of justice walked through all the rooms, wished to see us, talked with me some five minutes, presented the new commandant of the palace, and then left. He ordered that poor Ania be arrested and taken to town together with Lili Den. This took place while I was out walking between 3 and 4 o'clock. The weather was revolting and corresponded to our mood! Maria and Anastasia slept practically all day. After dinner, we quietly spent the evening together, the four of us with Olga and Tatiana.

. . .

23 March. Thursday.   The day brightened up after 2 o'clock and there was a thaw. I walked briefly in the morning. I put my things and papers in order and started putting aside everything that I want to take with me if we have to leave for England. After breakfast I took a walk with Olga and Tatiana and worked in the garden. We passed the evening as usual.

. . .

27 March. Monday.   We began to fast, but this fast was not to bring us the usual joy. After liturgy, Kerensky came and asked us to limit our meetings to mealtime and to sit apart from the children; it seems that he needed this to keep the famous Soviet of Workers' and Soldiers' Deputies calm! Had to submit to avoid any sort of violence.

Went for a walk with Tatiana. Olga slept again because her throat was hurting. The rest feel well. At 9:45, went to my room. Tatiana sat with me until 10:30. After that, read, drank tea, took a bath, and went to sleep on my ottoman!

. . .

2 April. Blessed Christ's Resurrection.   Paschal matins and liturgy ended at 1:40. I broke fast with everyone—numbering around 16 people. Didn't go to bed immediately as I had eaten heartily. Got up around 10 o'clock. The day was splendid, truly a day for a holiday. Took a walk in the morning. Before breakfast, exchanged a triple kiss [*khristosovalsia*] with all the servants, and Alix gave them porcelain eggs that were left over from former reserves. There were only 135 people. In the daytime, we began to work at the bridge [breaking up the ice], but soon a crowd of idlers had gathered beyond the grating to gape—had to leave and pass the rest of the time in boredom in the garden. Aleksei and Anastasia came outside, into the fresh air, for the first time.

Vespers was finished upstairs in the playroom at 7 o'clock. After supper we all parted at 10 o'clock; I read aloud to Tatiana in my room. Went to bed early.

3 April. Monday.   A fine, sunny day. At 10 o'clock went for a walk with Valia D. [Dolgorukov]. At 11 o'clock went to liturgy with T. [Tatiana] and An. [Anastasia]. After breakfast, I went out with them and Aleksei to the park and spent the whole time breaking ice at our summer pier; a crowd of gapers was again standing at the grating and doggedly observed us from beginning to end. The sun warmed us well. After tea, sorted through a

mass of previously received postcards. In the evening, played "mill" with Alix upstairs and then read aloud awhile in my room to Tatiana.

. . .

8 April. Saturday. Quietly celebrated the 23d anniversary of our engagement!

The weather stayed sunny and warm. In the morning, walked for a long time with Aleksei. We found out why yesterday's guards were so nasty; they were all drawn from the ranks of soldiers' deputies. But then they were relieved by a good guard from the res. batt. [reserve battalion] of the Fourth Infantry Regiment. We worked at the pier because of the crowd and delighted in the warm sun. At 6:30 we went to vigil with T., An., and Al. Spent the evening as usual.

. . .

18 April. Tuesday. It is 1 May abroad today—that's why our blockheads [*bolvany*] decided to celebrate this day with processions in the streets with choruses of music and red flags. Apparently, they came into our park and brought wreaths to the graves![1]

The weather turned bad just at the time we were being so honored—a wet, thick snow began to fall! Went out for a walk at 3:45, after everything was over and the sun peeked out. Worked for an hour and a half with Tatiana. In the evening began reading *A Millionaire Girl* out loud to all the children.

. . .

22 April. Saturday. A fine, sunny day. Went for a walk with Aleksei from 11 o'clock to 12 o'clock; he played on the island while the riflemen stood on the other side in the garden and watched.

During the day we worked on our previous spot. The sun was good and hot. At 6:30, the whole family went to vigil. Before supper, Alix received modest presents from the "arrested," as Maria so aptly put it. In the evening, I read aloud.

23 April. Sunday. Dear Alix got marvelous weather for her name day. Before liturgy, the ladies and gentlemen living in the palace, as well as the people close to us, came with their congratulations. We breakfasted, as always, upstairs. At 2 o'clock, the **whole family** went out into the garden. We worked on the pond surrounding the "children's" island, broke up and dispersed all the ice. Returned home at 4:30.

I read in my room before supper and in the evening out loud. At 9 o'clock, the rain started falling.

24 April. Monday. It turned cold again overnight. It was a blustery day with sun and wet snow. Took a walk in the morning while Aleksei played on the island. Next, I gave him a geography lesson. During the day we worked on the ponds; the ice from the night before melted easily. We spent the evening as usual.

. . .

1 May. Monday. A marvelous, warm day. Had a good walk in the morning. Aleksei had a geography lesson starting at 12 o'clock. During the day we worked again on our vegetable garden. The sun really beat down, but the work is moving along well. Read before supper and aloud in the evening.

Last night we learned about General Kornilov's departure from his position as commander of the Petrog. milit. dist. and tonight of Guchkov's resignation, all for the same reason: the irresponsible meddling with and commanding of military power by the Sov. of Work. Deputies and other such organizations that are even more to the left.

What does Providence have in store for poor Russia? May God's will protect us! +

. . .

6 May. Saturday. I've turned 49. It's not far to the half-century mark! My thoughts were particularly with dear Mama. It is hard not even to be in a position to write to each other. I know nothing about her except from stupid or vile articles in the newspapers. The day passed like a Sunday: liturgy, breakfast upstairs, *puzzle!* Harmonious work in the vegetable garden: we began to dig beds. After tea the vigil, supper, and evening reading—am spending much more time with my sweet family than in more normal years.

. . .

14 May. Sunday. We spent the 21st anniversary of the coronation in different circumstances!

The weather was excellent—15 degrees [60°F] in the shade. Before liturgy, I went for a walk with Aleksei. We spent from 2 to 4:30 in the afternoon in the garden; canoed, rowed, worked on the vegetable garden, where new beds are being readied, and some more on the island. Read after tea and in the evening too.

. . .

17 May. Wednesday. A terrifically hot day—20 degrees [68°F] in the shade and 33 degrees [91°F] in the sun, with a light southerly breeze. Walked for more than an hour with Aleksei and then I gave him a history lesson. During the day we walked, worked, rowed on the pond, and sat on its bank. Before supper, rode bicycles with my daughters. Around 9:30, clouds gathered and poured onto the ground the life-giving moisture that it needs.

. . .

22 May. Whit Monday. A warm, gray day. Went walking until 11 o'clock with Olga, Anastasia, and Aleksei. We dined at 12 o'clock. During the day, we spent three hours in the garden, on the island, and on the pond. Toward the end, the rain started, and lasted until 8 o'clock. An amazing aroma came through the window.

Today was the anniversary of the beginning of the army's offensive on the southwestern front! What the mood was then and what it is now!

. . .

3 June. Saturday. After morning tea, Kerensky unexpectedly came from town in a car. He didn't stay with me long: he asked that certain papers or letters related to internal politics be sent to the commission of inquiry. After a walk and before dinner, I helped Korovichenko sort these papers. During the day, he continued this together with Kobylinsky. Finished sawing tree trunks where we had started. It was then that *the indiscretion* [*peché*] took place with Aleksei's rifle; he was playing with it on the island; the riflemen who were walking in the garden saw it and asked an officer to take it and then they took it off to the guardhouse. Later, it turned out that they sent it to the town council for some reason!

Quite some officers, who didn't dare say no to the lower ranks!

We were at vigil. Evening—as usual.

. . .

9 June. Friday. It's exactly three months since I came from Mogilyov and since we have been sitting here like prisoners. It's hard to be without news from my dear Mama, but I am indifferent toward everything else. Today the day was even hotter—25 degrees [77°F] in the shade and 36 degrees [97°F] in the sun. There was a strong smell of burning again. After a walk, I gave Aleksei a history lesson in my new office, since it is cooler there. We worked well in the same place as usual. Alix did not come out. Before supper, the five of us walked.

June 10. Saturday. During the night and until 3 o'clock the heat and stuffiness continued. In the morning, I took a long walk. Ate, as we did yesterday, in the children's dining room. We worked on the same spot during the day. A thunderstorm skirted us, there were a few drops of rain. Fortunately, it became cooler. At 6:30, we went to vigil. Around 11 o'clock at night a shot was fired in the garden. After a quarter of an hour the sentry chief asked to come in and explained that the guard had fired because it seemed to him that a signal was being given with a red lamp from the child. bedroom. Having examined the placement of the electric lights, and seeing the movements of Anastasia's head as she sat by the window, one of the noncommissioned officers who had come in with him figured out the problem and, excusing themselves, they left.

. . .

19 June. Monday. The weather was relatively cool. The day passed as always. Right before dinner, good news came about the start of an offensive on the southwestern front. After two days of art. [artillery] fire in the Zolochovsky sector, our troops broke through enemy positions and took prisoner around 170 officers and 10,000 people, [and captured] 6 pieces of ordnance and 24 machine guns. Thanks be to God! May God grant good luck! I felt entirely different after this joyous news.

20 June. Tuesday. The battle went well yesterday: in just two days our troops have taken 18,600 people prisoner. A service of thanks was conducted in the field church before breakfast.

During the day, we chopped down four dry trees beyond the tennis court and then briefly worked on the vegetable garden until 4:30. All day, the weather became more and more overcast, and a beneficial rain began at 4 o'clock. I read the whole time before supper.

. . .

25 June. Sunday. Went out with Aleksei in the morning. The weather was cool. We went to liturgy. We went for a walk at 2 o'clock. A few short showers didn't soak us. We chopped down and then sawed up one fir tree. We watched how our people cut the grass. We sat by the vegetable garden and returned home at our own pace. Read a lot before supper.

26 June. Monday. The day was magnificent. Our good commandant, Colonel Kobylinsky, asked me not to offer my hand to the officers in front of strangers and not to greet the riflemen. Prior to this, there were a few

instances when they would not respond. I gave Aleksei a geography lesson. We sawed down an enormous fir tree not far from the grating beyond the greenhouse. The riflemen themselves wished to help us in the work. In the evening, I finished reading *Le Comte de Monte-Cristo*.

June 27. Tuesday.   I forgot to note down that on 26 June our troops made a new breakthrough and captured 131 officers, 7,000 from the lower ranks, 48 ordnance pieces, among them 12 heavy artillery pieces. In the morning, all the daughters came out to gather the mowed grass. Took my usual walk.

During the day we worked where we did the day before. We cut down and sawed up two firs. Before supper we spent half an hour in the vegetable garden. In the evening, I began reading aloud *Arsène Lupin contre Sherlock Holmes*.

28 June. Wednesday.   Last night, we took Galich: 3,000 prisoners and around 30 pieces of ordnance.

Thank God!

The weather stayed gray and warm, with a breeze. After a walk, I gave Aleksei a history lesson. Worked at the same place; cut down three firs. Read from tea until supper.

. . .

5 July. Wednesday.   It rained all morning but by 2 o'clock the weather cleared up; it became cooler toward evening. We spent the day as always. In recent days, there have been disorders and shooting in Petrograd. Yesterday many soldiers and sailors arrived from Kronstadt to go against the Provisional Govt.! It's a total muddle. And where are the people who could take this movement in hand and stop the strife and bloodshed? The root of all evil is in Petrograd and not in Russia itself.

6 July. Thursday.   Fortunately, the overwhelming majority of troops in Petrograd remained loyal to their duty, and order has been restored to the streets.[2]

The weather was marvelous. Took a good walk with Tatiana and Valia. In the daytime, we worked well in the forest—we chopped down and sawed up four firs. In the evening I began *Tartarin de Tarascon*.

. . .

8 July. Saturday.   A nice, hot day. Walked around the park with Tatiana and Maria. During the day we worked in the same places. Yesterday and today

the guards from the Fourth and First Rifle Regiments were meticulous in performing their duties and refrained from wandering around the garden during our walk. There has been a change in the composition of the govt.: Prince Lvov resigned and Kerensky will be the chairman of the Coun. of Min. [Council of Ministers], remaining as min. of war and navy and also taking over management of the min. of trade and ind. [industry].

This person plays a positive role in his current position; the more power he has, the better things will be.

. . .

11 July. Tuesday. I took a walk with Aleksei in the morning. When I came back home, I learned of Kerensky's arrival. In our conversation, he mentioned that we would likely go south, given the proximity of Tsarskoe Selo to the uneasy capital.

We went to services to mark Olga's name day. After breakfast, we worked well in the same place; cut down two firs—we're nearly up to sixty sawed-up trees. Finished reading the third part of Merezhkovsky's trilogy, *Peter;* it's well written but makes a grim impression.

. . .

13 July. Thursday. There has been bad news from the southwestern front in recent days. After our attack at Galich, many units, infected throughout with base, defeatist teachings, not only refused to go forward but in some places retreated even without any pressure from the enemy. Using this favorable circumstance to their advantage, the Germans and Austrians even broke through to southern Galicia without having to use much force, which could cause the whole southwest. front to retreat to the east.

What disgrace and despair! Finally, the Prov. Govt. announced today that the death penalty will be applied to anyone in the milit. theater exposed as a traitor to the state. If only this measure isn't coming too late.

The day stayed gray and warm. We worked in the same place, along the sides of the forest clearing. We cut down three and sawed up two of the felled trees. I am starting to clean up things and books little by little.

. . .

19 July. Wednesday. Germany declared war against us three years ago; it seems as though a whole lifetime has been lived these past three years! Lord, help and preserve Russia!

It was very hot. Walked with T., M., and A. Again there was a whole convoy made up of guards from the Third Rifle Regiment. Worked on the same spot. Felled four trees and finished up the firs felled yesterday. Now I'm reading Merezhkovsky's novel *Alexander I*.

. . .

July 21. Friday.   A perfect day from morning on, and a wonderful moonlit night as well. For some reason, I was expecting Kerensky in the morning. I want to find out once and for all where and when we're to go. We did the usual walk from 11 to 12 o'clock. Worked at the same spot and finished up four felled trees. After tea, finished the first volume of *Alexander I*.

Before supper, Maria got presents.

. . .

25 July. Tuesday.   The new Provisional Govt. has been formed with Kerensky at its head. We'll see whether his affairs will go better. The very first task concerns tightening up army discipline and lifting the army's spirits and also putting Russia's domestic situation into some kind of order!

The weather was very warm.

We worked at the same place; chopped down four firs and sawed up the same amount.

Finished reading Merezhkovsky's *Alexander I*. The last guards were good ones, thanks to the return from the front of 300 men from each rifle regiment and many draft companies leaving the reserve battalions.

. . .

28 July. Friday.   A marvelous day; took a walk with pleasure. After breakfast, we found out from Count Benkendorf that we are to be sent, not to Crimea, but to one of the faraway provincial towns three or four days' journey to the east! But where exactly they don't say—even the commandant doesn't know. And we were still counting on a long stay in Livadia! Chopped down and sawed up a large fir by the path at the forest clearing. A short, warm rain fell.

In the evening, I'll read aloud Conan Doyle's "A Study in Scarlet."

29 July. Saturday.   The same marvelous weather. During the morning walk, as we passed the gates of the road leading straight to the greenhouses, we noticed a guard sleeping on the grass. The noncommissioned off. accompanying us walked up to him and took the guard's rifle away from him.

During the day, we chopped down nine trees and sawed up one fir—all of them right by the road. It was sweltering, the clouds gathered and thunder could be heard, but by evening the sky had cleared. After vigil, Aleksei got presents.

Put away and packed all my things, so the rooms have an empty look.

30 July. Sunday.   Today dear Aleksei turned 13. May God grant him health, patience, and strength of spirit and flesh in these hard times!

Went to liturgy and, after breakfast, to the service to which they brought the icon of Our Lady of the Sign. Somehow it was especially moving to pray to her holy image together with all the people closest to us. She was brought and taken out through the garden by the guards of the Third Regiment.

We worked at the same clearing; we cut down one fir and started to saw apart another two. It was terribly hot. Everything is packed up now, except the paintings we have left on the walls. I saw Benkendorf before supper and the commandant in the evening.

31 July. Monday.   The last day of our stay at Tsarskoe Selo. The weather stayed marvelous. During the day, we worked at the same spot; chopped down three trees and sawed up yesterday's. After supper, we waited for our constantly postponed hour of departure to be set. Kerensky came unexpectedly and said that Misha [Grand Duke Mikhail Aleksandrovich] would show up soon. Truly, around 10:30 dear Misha came in accompanied by Ker. and the chief of the guards. It was very pleasant to meet, but to talk in front of strangers was awkward. When he left, riflemen from the guard's staff began to pull our baggage into the round hall. That's where Benkendorf, the ladies-in-waiting, the girls, and our people were sitting. We paced back and forth waiting for the trucks to be made available. The secret about our departure was so well kept until then that both the cars and the train were ordered to come after the appointed hour of our departure. The vexation turned out to be colossal. Aleksei wanted to sleep, but as soon as he would lie down, he would be gotten up. A false alarm was raised a few times: we put on our coats, walked out onto the balcony, and returned to the halls again. It was completely light out. We drank tea and, finally, at 5:15 Ker. showed up and said that we could go. We sat down in our two cars and went to the Aleksand. station. We entered the train by the crossing. Some sort of caval. regiment came galloping after us straight from the park. I. [Ilia] Tatishchev[3] and two govt. commissars who were to accompany us to Tobolsk met us by the door. The sunrise was beautiful when we started our trip to Petrograd and, via a connect. railway branch,

came out onto the north. R.R. line. At 6:10 in the morning, we left Ts.S. behind.

1. These are the same graves mentioned by Archpriest Beliaev in his diary on 30 March 1917.

2. On 6 July 1917, in the wake of the July Days, the Provisional Government ruled that individuals convicted of "publicly calling for disobedience to the legal orders of the government" shall be sentenced in peacetime to a maximum of three years' imprisonment and that in wartime such actions shall be considered treason. The death penalty was restored at the front on 12 July 1917.

3. Ilia Leonidovich Tatishchev, count, adjutant general in the imperial suite. Tatishchev followed the tsar's family into exile in Tobolsk.

· 57 ·

Letter from Alexandra to Anna Vyrubova, [1 August 1917]. Original English text.[1]

My sweet beloved Precious childy, wee one, Darling Martyr. I cant write, heart **far too** full. I love you, we love you, I love you—we thank you & bless you. I bow down before you & kiss the wound on yr. forehead,[2] the eyes of suffering & inner light I cant find words—you **know all & I know all**—no distance changes the love—the souls are ever together & through suffering understand each other yet more—mine are all well & with me kiss, kiss & bless you & pray for you without end. I know yr. new anguish with this great distance between us—one does not tell us where we go (in the train only shall know) nor for how long—but we think it is where you & ours[3] were last summer—our Saint [Ioann Tobolsky] calls us there & our friend [Rasputin]—wonderful, is it not—and you know the place. Beloved the misery of having everything packed up—empty rooms—such pain—the house of 23 years—yet you suffered yet far more, my angel. Sweetheart farewell. Somehow make L. know you got this—we prayed before Znameni [icon of the Virgin] & I remembered the last time on yr. bed. My Childy, my treasure, *Mami*[4] is ever, forever, near her precious Child—heart and soul tear to go so fr home & fr you—to be again for months without news is terrible. God is *milostiv i miloserden* [gracious and merciful]. He wont forsake you—& will bring us together again, I fully believe it, in sunny times. Thanks for Baby's image [icon for Aleksei].+++

1. Although the original text is undated, it was written immediately prior to Alexandra's departure from Tsarskoe Selo on the morning of 1 August 1917.

2. This wound was caused when one of the soldiers guarding Vyrubova in the Peter and Paul Fortress, where she was held after her arrest on 21 March, pushed her against the edge of her iron cell door.

3. In 1915, Vyrubova and Lili Den traveled to Tobolsk to visit the holy man Ioann Tobolsky.

DOCUMENT 57. Letter from Alexandra to her close friend Anna Vyrubova,
[1 August 1917].

4. Mami (Mommy), written in Cyrillic script, was an affectionate name Alexandra sometimes used for herself in letters to Vyrubova. She usually signed her letters to Vyrubova with the abbreviation "M."

· 58 ·

Diary of Yelizaveta A. Naryshkina, chief comptroller of the household of the empress,
1 August 1917.

I cried all morning. They took them away! And with what complications! They had to wait until six in the morning, sitting on their suitcases! Kerensky was beside himself hurrying everyone: he was embarrassed that he couldn't organize what was done so well under the old regime. Mikhail arrived; Kerensky let him in, sat down in the corner, stopped up his ears and said: "Talk!" The Sovereign was terribly upset. They didn't say anything serious to each other, but he was very moved. The empress wrote a wonderful farewell note to me; it ends like this: "Farewell, my sweet, dear friend; my heart is too full to write more."

The Benkendorfs returned to their lodgings; they very much want me to come to them this evening, but I am in no condition to go such a long way. Tomorrow I will be taken to them in a chair. Iza [Buksgevden] spent the whole day with me. It was finally revealed: they are taking them to Tobolsk. Iliusha Tatishchev is accompanying them instead of Benkendorf. The Sovereign has lost a lot of weight and grown pale. The empress is in control of herself and continues to hope! Despite everything, she is glad to be going to the domestic reaches of their "dear friend" [Rasputin]. And Ania [Vyrubova] is a saint before whom one should kneel down. Nothing has changed in her mentality! Nastenka [Gendrikova] is great. They are being accompanied by a few train cars full of soldiers of the guard, together with members of the Soviet of Soldiers' and Workers' Deputies. The trip will take five days. The commandant is going with them and will stay on; he took over the cash box from Valia [Dolgorukov] and will manage the expenses himself. They told no one, not even the Sovereign, where they are taking them. Earlier there was talk of Crimea, which was what they were packing for, but two days before departure it was announced that they were not going south and that they needed to take all warm things with them. It was also said that they had to stock up with five days' worth of provisions. Only by these signs was it possible to guess that the trip's destination was Siberia. What a trial and what humiliation! And they take it all with the determination and meekness of saints. Mme. Geringer came to see me; it was she who brought the empress's precious note.

❧ 3 ❧

Siberian Captivity

T dawn on 1 August 1917, the former tsar and his family left their palace at Tsarskoe Selo for the last time and, under heavy guard, boarded a train to Siberia. Although Minister President Aleksandr Kerensky stated that Nicholas, his family, and those who voluntarily accompanied them were to be treated as "under arrest" (Document 59), conditions en route and in exile were no harsher than at Tsarskoe Selo. The journey to Siberia was made in comfortable sleeper cars of the International Wagon-Lits Company and with a restaurant car serving—according to the evaluation that Nicholas noted in his diary on 1 August—the "very tasty cuisine of the Chinese-Eastern [Trans-Siberian] R.R." Thirty-nine courtiers, retainers, and servants traveled with the imperial family (several others joined them in Tobolsk). A sizable armed guard, numbering more than three hundred, was freshly armed with machine guns and other new weapons. Its function, however, seems to have been more to protect the prisoners from external threats than to keep them from escaping. To prevent interference, the train was marked Red Cross Mission and flew a Japanese flag.[1] When passing any populated area, and especially when going through a station, curtains were pulled down and doors locked. Nicholas, evidently not understanding the fears of his captors, judged this order to be "stupid and tedious."[2]

These precautions notwithstanding, troubles soon arose. Just outside the town of Perm—according to Colonel Yevgeny Kobylinsky, commandant of the Tsarskoe Selo garrison, who was in charge of the transfer—"some person with a big gray beard, evidently representing some sort of low-level railroad employees, came into my coach and, calling himself chairman of the railway workers, declared that the 'comrade' railway workers wished to know the purpose of this train, and until they were told, they would not let the train pass."[3] This person was mollified when shown a letter signed by Kerensky stating that the train was on a special mission. But the incident was a reminder of social forces that would increasingly affect the lives of the captive tsar and his family. The revolution had mobilized lower-class groups throughout the country; they felt a new sense of power and legitimacy to pursue directly whatever they considered to be their interests and goals.

Whether or not these local workers suspected that the train carried the former tsar and his family is not clear. But other groups were certainly aware of its cargo. Newspaper articles and speeches at factory meetings contained reports that the tsar had been "secreted away" from Tsarskoe Selo "without the knowledge of the people," as well as demands that the government reveal where the family was being taken.[4] Rumors quickly identified the Red Cross train heading east as carrying the former tsar and his family. It was said that the train was on its way to Harbin, Manchuria. Telegrams from cities and stations along the line arrived at the offices of the Petrograd Soviet and at the Petrograd offices of the All-Russian Central Executive Committee of Soviets (VTsIK), warning that these rumors were "exciting ferment" in the population, and asking whether the train should be stopped (Document 60).[5] Popular opinion and rumor about the fate of the tsar and his family would continue to influence the circumstances of their captivity.

At Tiumen, the family, suite, and guards boarded two steamers on the Tura River, sailed to the Tobol River and then on to Tobolsk. In unpopulated areas the family was allowed walks on the shore. Along the way, the boats passed the village of Pokrovskoe—Rasputin's home village. The family stood on deck and stared at his

large two-story house. According to the children's tutor, Pierre Gilliard, the family believed that seeing the house was a sign of inescapable destiny: "Rasputin had foretold that it would be so, and chance
once more seemed to confirm his prophetic words."[6]

After arriving in Tobolsk on the evening of 6 August, the family
had to remain aboard the boats for a few days until their lodgings
were ready. The former Governor's House was still, Nicholas noted,
"empty, unfurnished, dirty, and hence impossible to move into." A
security fence and sentry posts also had to be built. The family
"joked about the amazing inability of people to arrange even for
lodgings."[7]

The governor's mansion, into which the family and part of their
suite moved (the larger part of the suite resided across the road in a
house that had belonged to a merchant named Kornilov), was located on a street that in the revolutionary spirit of the times was
renamed Freedom Street. Accordingly, the governor's mansion was
sometimes called Freedom House. But now it was undeniably a
prison: armed guards stood at the entrances, and a tall wooden
palisade enclosed the garden, greenhouse, and service buildings;
guards periodically marched around the perimeter of the com-
pound, and the guards' barracks overlooked the grounds. In September, when Vasily Pankratov arrived to take charge of the imprisonment of the family, they and their suite were photographed, in
full face and profile, and required to carry identity cards. "It was
forced on us in the old days; now it's their turn," explained Pankratov's deputy, Aleksandr Nikolsky, who, like Pankratov, had been
a political prisoner under the tsarist government.[8]

The family's imprisonment was relatively luxurious, however.
According to Yevgeny Kobylinsky, the head of the guard, as the
family and their retinue were leaving Tsarskoe Selo, Kerensky had
instructed him, "Don't forget that this is the former emperor. Neither he nor his family should experience any deprivation."[9] Indeed,
all accounts agree about the comfort in which the former imperial
family was held captive in Tobolsk. Although walks outside the
fenced yard were denied them—evidently for fear that they might
be liberated by monarchists, captured by radicals, or simply assaulted in the streets (Documents 68, 70, 123)—the tsar and his
family were eventually allowed to attend some services in a nearby

church; servants and members of the suite were allowed to go into town freely; and local nuns and townspeople were permitted to bring food, cakes, and sweets to the house. Commandant Kobylinsky personally did much to promote the well-being of the prisoners, and most of the soldiers of the guard, as Nicholas informed his sister, were "completely different" from the hostile reservists who had guarded the family at Tsarskoe Selo—so much so that the family became "acquainted" with many of the soldiers (with "the real soldiers") and often visited their barracks to talk and play checkers (Document 72).[10] The townspeople were also comparatively sympathetic. When the family sat on the balcony, passersby often bowed, raised their caps, or made the sign of the cross over them.[11] At worst, people in the street stared silently and curiously at the once-powerful and distant imperial family—hence the family's preference for sunning themselves upon a platform that Nicholas constructed on top of the sheltered greenhouse.

The greatest burden of their confinement was boredom, although the family made every effort to avoid idleness and ennui. They cut and sawed wood; Alexandra, sometimes joined by her daughters, did needlework; they played checkers and cards; they read; the children were given lessons; and the family performed plays, mainly English and French. As many of the documents attest, Nicholas and Alexandra also frequently thought about, and undoubtedly discussed, the past, the revolution, foreign and domestic politics, the Russian people, and their own fate.

This tranquil but tedious existence was the object of intricate conspiracies, political pressures, and official anxiety. The government received reports, evidently false, that crowds were demonstrating outside Freedom House waving nationalist flags and singing the old national anthem, "God Save the Tsar." By midsummer 1917 a number of influential monarchists, some of them in contact with Alexandra's intimate friends Anna Vyrubova and Lili Den in Petrograd, were known to be organizing to free Nicholas and his family and restore the monarchy. Worried by the various conspiracies, the government arrested and deported suspected counter-revolutionaries, including Grand Dukes Mikhail Aleksandrovich and Pavel Aleksandrovich, General Vasily Gurko, and Anna Vyrubova and other "*rasputintsy*" (Rasputinites). The exiling of suspected reactionaries was halted when the Central Executive Committee of Soviets had trains stopped in Finland and the deportees arrested (Document 62).[12] It was also at this time, in late August 1917, that Kerensky ordered Vasily Pankratov, a trusted Socialist Revolutionary and former political prisoner, to go to Tobolsk and take command of the imprisonment of the former imperial family.

The Provisional Government's fear of counterrevolution in the late summer of 1917 was the product of not merely the looming conspiracies to free the former tsar but also the larger political threat that a resurgent right posed to its authority. Since the Bolshevik uprising in early July, military commanders and civic and political leaders were calling publicly for a restoration of "iron discipline" and "strong state power" in order to "save the motherland and freedom."[13] A spokesman for this point of view and a hero to its proponents was General Lavr Kornilov, whom Kerensky had appointed commander in chief of the Russian army on 24 July. In the name of saving Russia from social disorder and defeat in the war, Kornilov demanded such reforms as the extension of the death penalty to undisciplined troops in the rear and the application of martial law to workers in military industry. At national meetings of representatives of business, industry, the professions, the military, and conservative and liberal political parties—the Conference of Public Figures, held in Moscow on 8–10 August, and the State Conference, held in Moscow on 12–15 August—Kornilov was lauded and cheered. Meanwhile, to protest what was perceived as the reactionary politics of the State Conference, workers virtually shut down Moscow in a general strike. Class and ideological polarization had never been so stark. Rumors of a military coup were rampant.[14]

On 26 August, General Kornilov took the step that many seemed to be calling for: he demanded that all civil and military authority be placed in his hands. Having gained what he thought was Kerensky's agreement, he sent troops toward the capital, but Kerensky publicly accused him of treason. Kornilov responded by completely rejecting the authority of the Provisional Government, which, in his words, "under the pressure of the Bolshevik majority in the soviets acts in complete accord with the plans of the German Staff Headquarters."[15] Fighting for his and the Provisional Government's political life, Kerensky appealed to the Central Executive Committee of Soviets to help organize armed resistance against the troops approaching the capital, authorized the distribution of arms to Petrograd workers, and freed many Bolshevik leaders from prison. Faced with armed workers' detachments, garrison troops loyal to the Provisional Government and the soviets, and the direct action of railway workers to slow the advance of Kornilov's troops, the mutiny collapsed within days. Nicholas, who had followed events from Tobolsk, was disappointed. According to Gilliard, Nicholas saw Kornilov's effort to install a military dictatorship "as the only means that remained of perhaps avoiding the imminent catastrophe. I then for the first time heard the Czar regret his abdication. He had made this decision in the hope that those who had wished to get rid of him would be capable of making a success of the war and saving Russia."[16]

Vasily Pankratov, whose recollections conclude this chapter (Document 123), arrived in Tobolsk on 1 September carrying Kerensky's orders to take charge of the imperial family's captivity. Somewhat contemptuously, Nicholas thought that he looked like "a workman or an impoverished schoolteacher."[17] The impression was not inappropriate. Pankratov viewed himself, in many ways justifiably, as representing the social and moral spirit of the revolution. In social background he was the epitome of what radicals called the democracy. An uneducated son of poor peasants, he became a skilled lathe operator at the famous Semiannikov shipbuilding and machine works in St. Petersburg and pursued what knowledge and culture he could in his spare hours. Politically, he had a history as a revolutionary that brought him considerable esteem in left-wing circles. Besides being a veteran of populist study circles of the early 1880s and later participating in the first efforts to spread socialist ideas among workers in St. Petersburg, Moscow, and other Russian cities, he had, in an act of revolutionary gallantry, killed a gendarme to defend the honor of a woman (or so he told Kobylinsky). When arrested, he had resisted violently and was sentenced to fourteen years in the notorious Shlisselburg prison (sharing confinement with a number of famous revolutionaries), followed by many years of exile in Siberia. Freed in 1905, Pankratov immediately became active again in the revolutionary movement and joined the Socialist Revolutionary Party, though in the quieter and more repressive years that followed the 1905 revolution he studied geology and worked professionally as a geologist.[18]

Most important, Pankratov saw himself as bringing the righteous moral spirit of the revolutionary movement to his job as the tsar's jailer. He agreed with Yekaterina Breshko-Breshkovskaia, one of the senior leaders of the Socialist Revolutionary Party, that he should take the appointment because his experiences in the movement, prison, and exile would allow him "to carry out the task nobly and with dignity."[19] Thus, when he arrived in Tobolsk, Pankratov instructed the guards that it was a matter of revolutionary honor to be polite and respectful to the former tsar and his family. Rudeness and deliberate offense, he insisted, "is not worthy of us" (Document 123). Members of the imperial suite, Kobylinsky, and other witnesses all later testified before the White army commission investigating Nicholas's murder that Pankratov was personally "kind," "gentle," "warm," "honest," and "decent."[20] In Gilliard's words, he was "the typical enlightened fanatic."[21]

Aleksandr Nikolsky, the deputy commissar who arrived with Pankratov, represented another moral aspect of the revolution— resentment, plebeian rage, and retribution. He was, by all accounts, "rude," "uncultivated," "obstinate as a bull," "rough and distant."[22] The Romanov family had already encountered this hostile and defiant spirit while imprisoned at Tsarskoe Selo, and they would later feel it much more intensely. It continued to inspire groups of workers and soldiers to call on the government to imprison Nicholas the Bloody (Document 64). On 25 October 1917 this social anger and impatience helped topple the Provisional Government and bring the Bolsheviks to power.

The Bolshevik seizure of state power occurred in the midst of continuing social upheaval. Even more than in the first months after the February Revolution, demands by the lower classes for greater power in both society and the state were combined with direct assertions of popular power and defiance of existing authority. Growing numbers of factory workers demanded control over wages and work rules and stopped work to achieve it. And they continued to take control over their everyday lives, whether by being insolent and insubordinate with foremen and employers or by taking part in more elaborate rituals of power and reversal, such as carting supervisors or owners out of factories in wheelbarrows. Soldiers and sailors continued to defy orders, assault officers, sometimes elect new ones, and desert in rising numbers. Peasants, increasingly impatient with advice that they wait for the government to enact legal land reform, were also likely to simply seize the land they believed they needed and deserved. And on the streets of every major town, crowds of workers, soldiers, students, and other townspeople seized public squares, boulevards, and streets for meetings, funeral processions, demonstrations, and riots.[23]

By the fall of 1917 a huge proportion of urban workers and soldiers were demanding control of the state. The Bolsheviks constituted the only major political party to champion this demand unambiguously. As a result, they began to be elected in increasingly predominant numbers to local soviets, factory committees, trade union boards, soldiers' committees, and other organizations. Distrust and resentment of the privileged classes, poverty (worsened by the war), influential ideas about the natural equality and dignity of all human beings, religious notions of apocalyptic salvation and final judgment, and a serious fear that the Provisional Government was too weak to resist the growing threat of counterrevolution that would undo even the gains of February combined to encourage lower-class Russians to abandon the liberal-socialist Provisional Government and support the Bolshevik call for "all power to the soviets."[24]

With the Bolsheviks in power, the Russian Revolution was transformed into a radical social upheaval in which the struggle between classes became a matter of state policy. The fall of the Provisional Government and the proclamation of "soviet power" unleashed further rank-and-file radicalism, class revenge and reversal, and utopian visions of breaking with every inheritance and symbol of the past to build a new order. The Romanovs fell victim not merely to decisions made by the new regime (the conventional story of their fate) but also to this popular social revolution.

"It's nauseating to read the newspapers' description of what happened two weeks ago in Petrograd and Moscow!" Nicholas wrote in his diary on 17 November when news of the revolution finally reached Tobolsk (Document 75). Formally, Tobolsk remained outside the revolution for some time. The city was run by its old city council for several months, and the Provisional Government's commissar was left in charge of the imperial family until January 1918. Even the Tobolsk Soviet—unlike the soviets in Moscow and Petrograd and in nearby Yekaterinburg and Omsk—retained its Menshevik and Socialist Revolutionary majority until April 1918. But before soviet power and Bolshevik rule arrived in Tobolsk, the revolution was felt in Freedom House.

The local soldiers of the guard began to act as self-appointed representatives of the new order. The Second Rifle Regiment, considered from the start less sympathetic toward the family than were the two other regiments brought from Tsarskoe Selo to guard them, became more and more defiant and assertive. In late November a soldiers' committee was formed, which took the lead in pressuring Pankratov and Kobylinsky to be stricter with the family. By January 1918 this committee felt sufficiently strong to dismiss, on its own self-proclaimed authority, the commissars Pankratov and Nikolsky and to ask the Bolshevik-led Soviet government to appoint replacements.[25] By February 1918, as Alexandra wrote to Anna Vyrubova, the situation had so deteriorated that "everything depends on the soldiers."[26]

In the eyes of hostile witnesses, the soldiers—provoked, in Nicholas's view, by "bad ringleaders" (Document 88)—"became cruder," "began to act like hooligans," and complained increasingly that "Nikolashka" (as they derisively called Nicholas) was being treated too gently.[27] A variety of trivial but menacing incidents occurred, very often focused on the remaining symbols of the authority and hierarchy of the old order. In September a shipment of wine sent from Tsarskoe Selo to the former imperial family had to be poured into the Irtysh River after soldiers (some of whom suspected it was for their officers) angrily demanded its disposal (Documents 68, 70).[28] In December a meeting of the soldiers' committee lodged a formal protest against the priest and deacon of a local church, where the family were attending Christmas services, for addressing the family by their former titles, an act that the soldiers saw (possibly justifiably) as connected to the growth of monarchist agitation and conspiracy in and around Tobolsk (Document 85). A week later the soldiers' committee resolved to demand that all of the guards and their officers remove their epaulettes (Documents

87, 88). Nicholas and his son, Aleksei, were pressured to stop wearing their customary epaulettes as well, to avoid provoking the men.[29] In late February, after the tsar and his children were seen on top of a "snow mountain" that they had built in the yard for tobogganing, where they were waving good-bye to some of the "good" soldiers who were returning home, the soldiers' committee ordered the mountain demolished ("motivated solely by feelings of vain spite," Kobylinsky believed).[30] The behavior of the guards, according to Gilliard, became positively "indecent" by the spring of 1918: on the board of the swing used mainly by the daughters appeared "filthy, stupid, crude words carved with a soldier's bayonet."[31]

The changing composition of the guard strengthened the radical element. The Bolshevik Revolution and peace negotiations with Germany set in motion a massive demobilization of the army. In Tobolsk, soldiers of the guard who had served their terms left and were replaced by younger men sent from the Tsarskoe Selo reserves. As Commandant Kobylinsky later noted, the arrivals had clearly been "more corrupted by being there in the very cauldron of political struggle." In the eyes of the suite, as Gilliard wrote in his diary on 17 March, "those who have left have been replaced by a pack of blackguardly-looking young men."[32]

These radical soldiers saw signs that the central government supported their imposition of a stricter and more revolutionary regimen on the former tsar and his family and suite. On 27 February (new style: the Russian calendar was advanced thirteen days on 1 February 1918 to bring it into conformity with the Gregorian calendar in use in most of the rest of the world), Kobylinsky, who was still formally head of the guard, received notice that Nicholas and his family must be put on "soldiers' rations" and that the family would be receiving a much smaller monetary allowance from the state. To manage the adjustment Nicholas organized what he jokingly called, in the spirit of the times, a "committee," which decided to dismiss ten servants and exclude such "luxuries" as butter and coffee from the table (though "good people" continued to bring funds and provisions to the family).[33]

In April, with a new Bolshevik commissar on his way, further restrictions were implemented. Some were ordered by the Soviet government—which had moved to Moscow in March—and others were enacted locally and then sanctioned by the government: walks in the yard were reduced in frequency and duration; servants and members of the suite living in Freedom House were no longer allowed to go into town; the remaining members of the suite were moved in with the family as voluntary prisoners (only the doctors were allowed to come and go); Nicholas and Aleksei were forced to remove the epaulettes from their uniforms or hide them under coats when in public ("swinishness," Nicholas wrote); and after Nicholas was seen wearing a traditional cossack dagger (*kinzhal*) on his cossack uniform, it was confiscated and a search for other weapons was carried out at the insistence of the guard (Documents 103, 110).[34]

Yet these were minor matters compared with the changes that external pressures would bring about. During these early months of 1918, a regional struggle for control of Tobolsk and of the imperial family pitted the Bolsheviks of the Western Siberian Regional Soviet, based in Omsk, against the Bolsheviks of the Ural Regional Soviet, based in Yekaterinburg. Both groups sent commissars and armed detachments to Tobolsk, got their representatives into the local soviet, and tried to take control of guarding the former imperial family. As Nicholas noted with contempt in his diary and as other documents confirm, these actions caused a great deal of anxiety, distrust, and fear among both the prisoners and their guards (Documents 67, 98, 106, 110). At the beginning of April, new elections to the Tobolsk Soviet resulted in a Bolshevik majority led by Pavel Khokhriakov, who had been sent to Tobolsk with an armed detachment by the Ural Soviet. Among the first acts of the new Bolshevik soviet was the demand that the guard hand Nicholas over for confinement in the local prison (Document 106). The local guard refused, arguing that the fate of the former tsar and his family was a national matter that could not be decided locally.[35]

In addition to political and social hostility, one reason that the soldiers' committee of the guard and Bolsheviks from Yekaterinburg and Omsk (and in the government in Moscow) were demanding stricter control over Nicholas and his family was the fear that monarchists might free them. The concern was justified. In the country as a whole, former tsarist officers were organizing armies to resist Bolshevik power, which were soon dubbed White armies. In and around Tobolsk, monarchists gathered in growing numbers to bring money and provisions to the tsar and his family and to prepare to free them.

Accurately identifying the various monarchist conspiracies to free the tsar is nearly impossible—much of what has passed for documentation amounts to rumors, accusations, self-serving émigré recollections, and vague allusions. To be sure, rumors and fears of monarchist plots influenced the fate of the family more than any actual efforts to free them and thus were themselves historically important. Still, a number of actual conspiracies were afoot, especially by the spring of 1918. All failed, for they were generally flawed by amateurishness and fractious relationships among the conspirators. The lack of success resulted in years of mutually accusatory polemics among Russian émigrés.

Nicholas's and especially Alexandra's letters and diaries repeatedly mention sightings—from their balcony or out windows—of known supporters walking about the street in front of the old Governor's House, as well as the receipt of a wide variety of gifts from friends and well-wishers who had come to town or sent emissaries.[36] Many of the visiting friends—most of them military officers—were involved in conspiracies to free the tsar and his family. An officer named K. Sokolov described one plot led by an unnamed lawyer with links to the clergy and involving a set of officers like himself. The plan was to free the family on one of the Sundays when they were allowed to attend church services in town; the conspirators intended to hide on the altar, behind the iconostasis, and burst out during the service, overpowering the guard and taking the family to safety. The conspiracy, which Sokolov admitted "had the smell of a Dumas novel," was broken by arrests soon after the group arrived in Tobolsk in early January 1918.[37] Associates of another group, organized by a former member of the Senate, were also operating in Tobolsk by the late fall of 1917 and were allegedly negotiating with the English and French embassies for support of their plans to free the tsar and his family.[38] Yet another effort was led by Nikolai Markov (known as Markov II), a well-known rightist politician and former Duma deputy, who maintained connections to the family through Anna Vyrubova and Lili Den.[39] In the spring of 1918 an influential group of Moscow monarchists (led by former high-ranking tsarist officials), who had successfully raised a large amount of money for the imprisoned family, turned to the German ambassador, Count Wilhelm von Mirbach, seeking his government's help in protecting and perhaps rescuing the family, and made contacts with the main Petrograd organization of monarchists to work jointly to save the family.[40] There are also accounts of a rescue plan in the early months of 1918 that was supported by the British royal family and by senior British politicians and intelligence officers.[41]

The rescue operation that was apparently best known to the family itself and had its confidence was led by Boris Solovyov, who had been a member of Rasputin's circle in Petrograd and who, in September 1917, married Rasputin's oldest daughter, Maria (Matryona). Solovyov contacted Vyrubova, who had enough faith in him to let him serve as her personal courier in delivering correspondence, money, and gifts to and from the family in Tobolsk. After marrying Maria Rasputina, Solovyov spent some time in Rasputin's home in Pokrovskoe—on his honeymoon, Solovyov later told White army investigators—and while based there (and later in Tiumen), Solovyov tried to bring the various efforts to free the tsar and his family under his control. He was in close contact with Father Aleksei Vasiliev, the family's priest in Tobolsk, whose use of the family's former titles had created a minor scandal in December.

Many émigrés—including the chief White army investigator of the execution of the tsar and his family—were later convinced that Solovyov was a provocateur, acting on behalf of the Bolsheviks in order to expose and sabotage efforts to free the family. Their suspicions are not entirely implausible—Bolshevik intelligence did succeed in arresting many conspirators (including Solovyov in late March), and much evidence suggests that Solovyov was using his marriage to Rasputin's daughter to advance his credibility. The accusations against Solovyov more likely reflected the need to find a scapegoat, someone to blame for the monarchists' failure to save the tsar. Whatever the truth about Solovyov's intentions, Nicholas and Alexandra apparently believed his claims (in messages smuggled to them) that he had assembled a force of three hundred loyal officers,

disguised as ordinary soldiers and pretending to support the Bolsheviks, who were on their way from Tiumen to free the family
(Document 91).[42]

The profusion of real and rumored plots to free the captives was
echoed by recurrent rumors of escape from Tobolsk and by still
more demands for stricter confinement. Newspaper articles frequently reported that the guard at Tobolsk was weak and unreliable
and that Nicholas or other members of the family had fled or been
freed (Documents 74, 78, 79, 80, 123). Official denials notwithstanding, these fears gave rise to frequent public demands to tighten
security, imprison "Nicholas the Bloody Romanov" in the fortress
at Kronstadt, replace the guards with soldiers from the newly
formed Red Army, and bring Nicholas to the capital for trial (Documents 93, 98).[43]

The more dangers the new Bolshevik state faced—and thus the
more the leadership feared the former tsar's potential authority and
freedom—the more seriously they considered incarcerating him in a
proper prison and putting him on trial. In late February 1918 a new
danger imperiled the regime: after weeks of Russian refusals to
either accept or reject Germany's harsh peace terms, German and
Austrian armies resumed their offensive on 18 February (new style)
and made rapid advances into Russian territory. Declaring on 21
February that "the socialist fatherland is in danger," the Council of
People's Commissars (Sovnarkom) approved Lenin's resolution
calling for "revolutionary defense" against the aggressors "to the
last drop of blood," along with repressive violence against a wide
range of enemies: "Hostile agents, speculators, looters, hooligans,
counterrevolutionary agitators, and German spies are to be shot on
the spot."[44] On the preceding day, the Sovnarkom had demanded
that preparations be made to put Nicholas on trial (Document 95).
On 23 February the Bolshevik party newspaper, *Pravda,* published
a call for "extreme measures" in dealing with the tsar at this time of
crisis: "It is necessary to move Romanov to a secure place. It is
necessary to deprive him of all free contact with any persons whatsoever. It is necessary to confine him in prison and immediately
bring him to trial."[45] Although the immediate crisis passed with the
signing of the peace treaty at Brest-Litovsk on 3 March, civil war

was on the horizon. Opponents of the regime were building up their armed forces, and the Bolsheviks established their own Red Army.

In the middle of all these efforts by the right to free the tsar and his family and by the left to tighten or seize control of them, a representative of the Tobolsk soldiers' committee went to Moscow to discuss the situation with the party and state leadership (Documents 99, 126). The Presidium of the Central Executive Committee of Soviets responded by ordering that security at Freedom House be tightened, that armed reinforcements (bearing "money, guns, and grenades" for the guard) be dispatched, and that the family be transferred to Moscow as soon as possible (Document 100). Several days later, the Executive Committee reversed this last decision and ordered instead that Nicholas and his family be sent to the Urals (Document 101). No document tells what caused Moscow to reconsider. The most likely explanation is that the Soviet leadership bowed to pressure from militants in the Ural Regional Soviet in Yekaterinburg. Apparently, an influential representative of the Ural Soviet—Filipp Goloshchekin, head of the Ural branch of the party as well as a member of the Presidium of the Ural Soviet—was in Moscow negotiating with Soviet and party leaders at this time.[46] An alternative explanation—intriguing and plausible but unproven— is that the second decision was intended to deceive Yekaterinburg so that Moscow could bring the Romanovs to the capital without local interference. Whatever the plan, taking the Romanovs from Tobolsk, given the monarchist plots and the demands and threats from both Yekaterinburg and Omsk, required a man trusted by the center and skilled in conspiracy. That person was Vasily Yakovlev, who left Moscow for Tobolsk on 9 April carrying letters from the Central Executive Committee of Soviets signed by its chairman, Yakov Sverdlov (Document 102).[47]

An aura of mystery, rumor, and speculation has long surrounded the person of Yakovlev. According to various accounts, he was an agent of the Germans pretending to serve the Bolsheviks but in fact planning to free the family; an agent of the Bolsheviks, who were themselves bringing the family to Moscow to hand over to the Germans as part of a deal worked out after the Brest-Litovsk treaty; a dupe in a game of deceit that the Bolsheviks were playing with the

Germans, in which they were pretending to bring the family to Moscow to hand over to the Germans but were in fact arranging with the Ural Bolsheviks to prevent this; an agent of monarchist organizations planning to lead the family to freedom via Japan; an English secret agent; or even a double agent serving several masters. Yakovlev's hidden intentions were supposedly perceptible in various gestures—saluting the tsar; addressing him as Your Majesty; being polite and showing concern for Nicholas's and Alexandra's comfort on their journey from Tobolsk; defecting to anti-Bolshevik forces later in 1918.[48]

With the opening of the archives in Russia, scholars now know much more about Yakovlev than earlier historians did. But although he is now a less mysterious figure, he remains an extravagant one. The son of a peasant, Yakovlev (whose real name was Konstantin Miachin) became a professional revolutionary after a number of years in various working-class jobs. He was active mainly in the Urals and was inclined to take part in the most militant and romantic actions—throwing bombs at and engaging in shoot-outs with police, "expropriating" type for underground printing shops, organizing armed workers' groups, and robbing mail trains and safes at railroad stations for the revolutionary cause. Even among Bolsheviks he was an extremist, although his radicalism was less unusual in the Urals than in the center. After 1905, he joined those who opposed Lenin's insistence that party members participate in legal organizations like trade unions and the Duma. After several years in European exile—to avoid certain arrest—he returned to Russia in 1917, serving in various powerful party positions in Petrograd and in his native Urals, including as a member of the directing committee of the Cheka, the "extraordinary commission" for fighting counterrevolution.[49] As the original Russian texts of the documents in this chapter show, he was close enough to Yakov Sverdlov, chairman of the Central Executive Committee of Soviets, for the two to address each other in the familiar second person.

After transferring the tsar and his family to Yekaterinburg, Yakovlev was made a commander of the Second Army of the eastern front in the civil war, even though the Yekaterinburg Bolsheviks still considered him a counterrevolutionary for the way he handled the transfer. At this point, his career took another dramatic turn, one that has incited much speculation about his true political convictions: he defected to anticommunist forces favoring a restoration of the Constituent Assembly (which the Bolsheviks had forcibly closed after a Socialist Revolutionary majority was elected). When this movement collapsed, Yakovlev fled to China, where, he claimed, he became involved in the revolutionary movement. Then, in 1928— when the Chinese nationalists had turned against their Communist allies—Yakovlev returned to the USSR, partly to defend his record against the official account, which presented him as a counter-revolutionary. He was soon arrested, however, and sentenced to a labor camp. Freed in 1933 but soon confronted with renewed accusations, he appealed to Stalin and to the security police to "defend" him. In 1938 he was arrested again and shot.[50]

Whatever the actual purpose of Yakovlev's mission to Tobolsk, archival documents that have come to light in the past few years (the most important of which are presented below) make it clear that the operation was closely directed and explicitly approved by Moscow, in particular by Sverdlov. If there was a purpose other than the stated one of transferring the former tsar and his family to the Urals, Moscow likely approved it.

Yakovlev arrived in Tobolsk on 22 April, slowed by slush, ice, and mud on the road from Tiumen. He bore letters from the Central Executive Committee of Soviets giving him full authority over all local institutions (Documents 102, 105) and authorizing a "revolutionary tribunal" and execution by shooting of anyone who refused to obey his instructions.[51] Yakovlev was determined to evacuate the family from Tobolsk immediately: the roads were already nearly impassable, and once the frozen river thawed, the risk of a counter-revolutionary assault to free Nicholas was much greater. But Aleksei's illness forced Yakovlev to secure Moscow's permission to alter the original plan and take only Nicholas and then, after Alexandra protested, to take her and Maria as well (Documents 108, 109, 110, 122).[52]

For security reasons the destination was kept a secret from the family and the local guards, although everyone in the family believed that they were going to Moscow.[53] Indeed, this expectation was a large part of the reason Alexandra was so insistent on going along. To Gilliard she said: "I can't let the Czar go alone. They want to separate him from his family as they did before. They're going to try to force his hand by making him anxious about his family. The Czar is necessary to them; they feel that he alone represents Russia. Together we shall be in a better position to resist them, and I ought to be at his side in the time of trial."[54] Recalling the last time they were apart, when, in Alexandra's view, anxiety over the family and distance from her advice and strength had allowed Nicholas to abdicate, Alexandra was determined to prevent any such weakness again. She was evidently convinced that the Bolshevik government wanted Nicholas to sign the Brest-Litovsk treaty with Germany, for "he alone represents Russia." Her political naïveté remained intact.

Sverdlov, in his personal instructions to Yakovlev and in his letter to the Ural Soviet (Document 102) insisted particularly on one thing: Nicholas was to be brought to Yekaterinburg alive.[55] The point was not superfluous. Yakovlev well knew the Ural tradition of autonomy, militance, and direct and violent action. In Moscow, too, the Soviet leadership was aware of what official reports from early 1918 called the "irregularities," "excesses," "disorganization," and "indiscipline" of armed Bolshevik groups in the Urals.[56] Many local Bolsheviks were evidently talking about "finishing off the butcher" Nicholas II.[57]

When Yakovlev arrived in Tobolsk, he found himself and his operation threatened by this radical propensity toward direct revolutionary justice. As he informed Sverdlov by telegraph on 27 April, he had just learned of a recent attack by forces from Yekaterinburg, who had allegedly planned to capture and kill the tsar; the guard had repulsed the attack (Document 114). The attackers were probably the same "Tiumen brigand-Bolsheviks" whose arrival "on 15 troikas, with bells, whistles, and whoops," and whose rapid forced departure from town Nicholas noted in his diary on 22 March (Document 110 [4 April]). But for the Yekaterinburg radicals the setback was only temporary. In the following days they hinted to Yakovlev that they still intended to execute Nicholas and warned him not to interfere. At least some of these Yekaterinburg Bolsheviks suspected that Moscow planned to deport Nicholas, and they were determined to prevent it. Yakovlev learned that a detachment from Yekaterinburg had arranged a massive ambush on the road to Tiumen and, when that failed, were preparing to attack him along the railroad between Tiumen and Yekaterinburg (Documents 111, 114, 121). To avoid ambush Yakovlev requested permission from Sverdlov to reverse his course and head eastward toward Omsk and away from Yekaterinburg (Documents 112–114, 116); permission was granted, but Yakovlev's reversal of course provoked angry accusations of treason from Yekaterinburg (Document 115, 117). After clarifications and lengthy telegraph negotiations between Moscow and Yekaterinburg—the details of which, unfortunately, are not known—Sverdlov ordered Yakovlev to bring his "baggage" to Yekaterinburg, assuring him that the Yekaterinburg Bolsheviks had guaranteed the former tsar's safety (Documents 118, 119). Yakovlev conceded but felt it to be his duty to offer a final warning to Sverdlov: once the family were in the hands of the Bolsheviks of Yekaterinburg, Moscow would never be able to get them back, and their lives would be in constant danger. "Thus, we warn you one last time and free ourselves from any moral responsibility for the future consequences" (Document 120).

· 59 ·

Kerensky's "Instructions" to persons accompanying the former emperor and his family to their new place of residence, 31 July 1917.

———————

1. En route, the former emperor and empress, as well as their family and the persons who are willing to accompany them, are to be treated as under arrest.

2. En route, persons indicated in point 1 can have no contact with anyone except persons I have assigned to accompany them.

3. When passing through towns and large settlements, all shades must be drawn and all doors must be locked in the railcars housing persons indicated in point 1.

4. The train is allowed to stop to switch engines, take on water, inspect railcars, and attend to other technical needs only at smaller stations and depots.

5. During stops, the train must be stationed on sidings farthest away from residences and must be surrounded by guards.

6. Once every 24 hours at double-track sections of single-track railways or at small stations, a half-hour stop is allowed for persons indicated

in point 1 to take a walk, providing the necessary measures for guarding them are followed.

7. At all times en route, in each railcar where persons indicated in point 1 are to be found, sentries (no fewer than four persons) must be posted at both sides of the entrances, and an officer must be present. Doors along the corridors inside the railcars should not be closed so that the sentries at either end of the railcars can see each other. Every half hour the officer on duty, accompanied by one of the sentries, is to walk along the railcar corridor to verify the number of all those lodged within.

8. En route, the rules of internal order established during the stay of the arrested persons in the Aleks. Palace at Tsarskoe Selo should be maintained as much as possible.

9. Each day, morning and evening, the train commandant, the aide to the commissar of the former Court Ministry, and member of the State Duma [Vasily] Vershinin, ~~morning and evening~~ jointly inform me by telegraph about developments and, if necessary, also immediately notify me of anything urgent. Communications to be made by military telegraph.

10. By their mutual agreement, persons indicated in point 9, may, if necessary, request the assistance of local military and civil authorities as well as call for additional medical help.

11. Prior to the transfer of persons indicated in point 1 from the train to the ship, measures must be enacted so that ~~on~~ the streets are cleared of passersby.

12. The transfers are to take place as far as possible in closed carriages.

13. The same rules are followed aboard the ship, with the only exception being the length of walks. Specifically: persons indicated in point 1 may be on deck the entire time of the passage except when passing settlements and stopping at docks.

14. For transfer into the town designated as their residence, the same conditions on the streets must be observed as indicated in points 11 and 12.

15. From the moment the persons indicated in point 1 are accommodated in the new place of residence, the same rules apply that were followed in the Aleksandrovsky Palace of Tsarskoe Selo. A journal of the transfer is to be kept for the duration of the trip, which is to be read upon arrival by the former emperor, who may make his notations, and after this it is to be signed by the persons indicated in point 9, as well as by representatives of the Tsarskoe Selo garrison, and is to be sent to me.

16. One copy of the present instructions is to be handed over for the guidance of persons indicated in point 9, and the other is to be kept by me.

I have crossed out "morning and evening" in point 9; "on" in point 11.

Minister President,
Minister of War and Navy,
A. Kerensky

· 60 ·

The Yekaterinburg District Soviet's inquiry to the Petrograd Soviet concerning the transfer
of Nicholas II to Tobolsk, 5 August 1917.

A special train carrying the former tsar and his family went through Yekaterinburg on the way to Tiumen on 4 August of this year. According to newspaper accounts, the former tsar is being transferred to Tobolsk. In town and along the railway line, the rumor is going around that the train is under orders to go to Novo-Nikolaevsk and on to Harbin. This rumor is exciting ferment in the population. The district committee has sent telegrams to the Krasnoiarsk, Novo-Nikolaevsk, and Irkutsk soviets of deputies and suggests that these rumors be checked and, if they are accurate, that measures be taken.

We ask you to inform us whether the Central [Executive] Committee knows of the circumstances behind the Provisional Government's dispatch of the former tsar into exile in Tobolsk and whether the Soviets of Workers', Soldiers', and Peasants' Deputies participated in the decision.

On behalf of the chairman of the
Executive Committee of the
Soviets of Workers' and Soldiers'
Deputies, M. Medvedev
Secretary, S. Derzhavin

· 61 ·

Diary of Alexandra, 6–7 August 1917. Original English text.

o.b. [on board] *"Rus"* on the river.

August	[Festival of the] *Transfiguration* [of Christ]
6	
Sun.	After 9 from *Tura* on to *Tobol:*
	Stopped twice, for food & wood
	Children walked once in the wood

Got up about 3, as too hot in my cabin
After 6 arrived at *Tobolsk,* on the *Irtysh* [River]
All things taken over
House empty, dirty & nothing arranged
To spend night—on board again, till
everything arranged in our & the other
houses.

o.b. *"Rus"* at *Tobolsk,* on the river

August
7   Cold grey & windy, poured, later sunshine
Mon.   Spent the day in bed—at anchor

· 62 ·

"A Counterrevolutionary Plot," *Izvestiia* (Petrograd), 25 August 1917.

————

THE PROGRESS OF THE INVESTIGATION

The investigation into the matter of a counterrevolutionary plot, which
is being conducted by P. A. Aleksandrov, the investigator for especially
important cases at the Petrograd district court, is moving at an accelerated
pace.

According to information obtained from the preliminary investigation,
the participants seem to have a deep faith in their purely political aims of
restoring the monarchist regime in Russia.

An interrogation of the arrested and a general examination of all documents did not yield specific information about whether the plotters
wanted to return the abdicated Nicholas Romanov to the throne. Also not
established is whether the plotters unanimously desired that Gr.D. [Grand
Dukes] Mikhail Aleksandrovich or Pavel Aleksandrovich or someone else
be monarch of Russia.

The plot was exposed at the moment when they had recognized only
the necessity for Russia to return to a monarchist regime.

THE INTERROGATION OF L. V. KHITROVO

Yesterday at 4 o'clock in the afternoon, Liubov Vladimirovna Khitrovo, the mother of a lady-in-waiting, was arrested in Yelabuga on the

orders of A. F. Stal, procurator of Moscow district's judicial chambers, and was delivered to the judicial procedures building for interrogation.

She came to Petrograd accompanied by an inspector from the Moscow criminal police.

The interrogation was conducted by P. A. Aleksandrov, the judicial investigator for especially important cases, and A. F. Stal, chief supervisor for the investigation. The interrogation lasted for 4 hours and yielded much incriminating information.

At the end of the interrogation, house arrest was prescribed for L. V. Khitrovo as a way to limit her activities.

The now-arrested General [Pyotr] Frolov, former commander of the troops in the Petrograd [military] district, was sent from Moscow to Petrograd.

MARGARITA KHITROVO[1]

Lady-in-waiting Margarita Khitrovo is also on the way to Petrograd. A. F. Kerensky and A. F. Stal received extensive enciphered telegrams about the full circumstances of her arrest, but they have not yet been deciphered because of incorrect transmission.

All the arrested are to be delivered to Petrograd, where the entire case will be concentrated.

A. F. Stal, chief supervisor for the investigation, left yesterday for Moscow, where he will spend a week. He has been entrusted with all further investigation of the plot.

The first irrefutable information about the plot was received by the public prosecutor's office from one highly respected citizen in Nizhny Novgorod.

The public prosecutor's office believes it is still not possible to determine the role and significance of each of the arrested and of all persons implicated in the case.

OFFICIAL LIST OF THOSE BEING EXILED FROM RUSSIA

Drawing on official information, we are able to provide the complete list of persons exiled abroad on the basis of the law on ostracism. This list includes retired general V. I. Gurko; former lady-in-waiting A. A. Vyrubova; S. Glinka-Yanchevsky, editor of *Zemshchina* [a right-wing journal];

Doctor Badmaev;[2] I. F. Manasevich-Manuilov;[3] and G. Elvengrem, senior captain of the Guards.

Elvengrem played a rather active role in the Union of the Holders of the St. George Cross. In his deposition, which was recorded during the interrogation by investigating authorities, Elvengrem stated that he was vice-chairman of this union. Elvengrem was assigned to the general staff. Being very popular in the union, he took an active part in all the union's activities.

All those being exiled are presented with the text of the order: "On the basis of point 2 of the Prov. Govt.'s order from 2 August, which assigned extraordinary powers to the ministers of war and internal affairs, the said individual, whose activities especially threaten the defense of the state, internal security, and the gains of the revolution, is, by mutual agreement of the ministers, required to leave the bounds of the Russian state immediately."

The departure of the above-listed persons is to take place today, 25 August. The majority of them declared the command impracticable because of a lack of [financial] means and the impossibility of bringing their personal affairs to a close in such short order. In addition, complications arose in the preparation of foreign passports. As a result, all will be exiled on Saturday. A special convoy, as well as representatives of military and civilian power, will accompany them to Torneo [in Finland at the Russian imperial border with Sweden].

1. Margarita Sergeevna Khitrovo (Rita), former lady-in-waiting to Alexandra, companion of Olga's. Suspected of involvement in a monarchist plot, Khitrovo was arrested after she traveled to Tobolsk and tried to contact the imperial family; she was later released for lack of evidence.

2. Pyotr Aleksandrovich Badmaev (prior to baptism, Zhamsarain), by origin a Buriat (a largely Buddhist people in the Russian imperial Far East), was Alexander III's godson and a hereditary aristocrat. Starting in 1875, Badmaev served in the Asiatic department of the Ministry of Foreign Affairs. He was a doctor of Tibetan medicine, belonged to Rasputin's circle, and was popular at court.

3. Ivan Fyodorovich Manasevich-Manuilov (1869–1918), a journalist and alleged police informant. Arrested in August 1916 for blackmailing a bank director, he was convicted in February 1917 and jailed, but he was freed when the prison was burned down by revolutionary crowds on 27 February 1917.

· 63 ·

Monarchists' letter to Nicholas II, [August 1917].

Tsar—Martyr!

HUNDREDS and thousands of loving hearts offer up a prayer to the Lord God for You, dear one, and send You greetings. We do not know whether the cry of our heart will reach You, but we have the right to hope since we now have "freedom of speech," and, moreover, we are not armed.

Monarchists, Your admirers

· 64 ·

Resolution passed by the general assembly of the crew of the gunboat *Bobr* (Beaver), 6 September 1917.[1]

The gunboat *Beaver*'s crew protests the dispatch of Nicholas the Bloody to no one knows where and why and without the knowledge, it turns out, of the revolutionary centers of democracy, the S.W.S.D. [Soviets of Workers' and Soldiers' Deputies]; the crew protests the inaction of the Soviets' leaders, by whose negligence this came to pass. The resolutions of the forces of revolutionary democracy demanding that Nicholas be sent to Kronstadt have been disregarded on the grounds that there was no basis for worrying that he would be freed by counterrevolutionaries. And now, completely unknown to the Soviets, the bourgeoisie is sending him no one knows where or for what purpose, plainly with the idea of trying to return to the old regime.

We protest the systematic release from prison of leading figures from the old regime, traitors such as Shtiurmer [the former chairman of the Council of Ministers], Vyrubova, and others.

We protest the improper actions of the commanders who are kicking out generals who sympathize with the ideas of democracy and appointing obvious lackeys of Nicholas to responsible posts.

We protest the introduction of the death penalty and the repression against our comrades. We remind you that you will achieve nothing by repressing your political opponents.

We declare that POWER MUST BE TAKEN INTO THE HANDS OF THE

S.W.S.P.D. [Soviets of Workers', Soldiers', and Peasants' Deputies], which the country and the democractic forces UNQUESTIONABLY TRUST.

> Chairman of the General
> Assembly, A. Boiko
> Secretary, Lilazovsky

1. This document is stamped with the following seal: "Liberty, Equality, Fraternity. Ship's Committee of the gunboat *Beaver*."

· 65 ·

Deciphered telegram from commissar Vasily Pankratov[1] to Minister President Aleksandr Kerensky on the situation of the tsar and his family in Tobolsk, 14 September 1917.

Nicholas asked permission for Doctor Derevenko's son,[2] the boy, to visit Aleksei on holidays, and for Bitter [Bitner],[3] the teacher from the Tsarskoe Selo gymnasium, to give the younger daughters lessons. Kobylinsky knows the teacher well. I allowed it, but turned down the request to go beyond the fence.

1. On 1 September 1917, on Aleksandr Kerensky's instruction, Vasily Semyonovich Pankratov, a Socialist Revolutionary who had spent many years in prison and exile, was appointed commissar in charge of the imperial family in Tobolsk by the Provisional Government. Colonel Yevgeny Kobylinsky and the special purpose detachment guarding the tsar and his family were subordinate to him. The commissar's aide, Aleksandr Vladimirovich Nikolsky, was an ensign and former political exile.

2. Nikolai Vladimirovich Derevenko (Kolia), son of the court surgeon Vladimir Derevenko, pupil at the Imperial Nikolaevsky Gymnasium (secondary school) in Tsarskoe Selo, and one of Aleksei's few childhood friends. Derevenko accompanied his father to Tobolsk and Yekaterinburg.

3. Klavdia Mikhailovna Bitner, former teacher at the Mariinsky women's gymnasium in Tsarskoe Selo, also worked as a nurse at the Lianozovsky infirmary in Tsarskoe Selo. In Tobolsk she taught the tsar's children Russian and mathematics.

· 66 ·

Message to Doctor Yevgeny Botkin from V. Somov, head of chancellery for the minister president of the Provisional Government, concerning permission for the tsar and his family to attend church and take walks outside town, 15 September 1917.

Yevg. Serg. [Yevgeny Sergeevich],

On the instructions of the minister pres., I inform you that the minister president has granted the request made in your letter of 26 August to allow the former tsar and his family to take walks outside of town and to attend church services.[1]

H. [Head] of chanc. for the
minister president, V. Somov

1. Doctor Botkin's request was denied by commissar Pankratov (Document 68).

· 67 ·

Deciphered telegram from commissar Vasily Pankratov to Minister President Aleksandr Kerensky on the Omsk Soviet's interference in the affairs of the regiment guarding Nicholas, 20 September 1917.

Sent on 20 September 1917 at 11:16
Received on 21 September 1917

Inquiries from localities [concerning] the organization of affairs have alarmed the local Executive Committee; misunderstandings have been cleared up by explanations given. The Omsk Executive Committee is causing alarm, as it wants to secure participation; I declined, considering this unnecessary.[1]

1. Rumors published in newspapers concerning the escape of Nicholas and his children provoked local soviets into trying to interfere in the guarding of the tsar and his family.

· 68 ·

Commissar Vasily Pankratov's report to Minister President Aleksandr Kerensky on the problems of guarding the imperial family in Tobolsk, 30 September 1917.

To Minister President A. F. Kerensky:

The special purpose detachment has still not calmed down and insists on an explanation: among the things that were sent here by the court ministry was wine (six crates)—who exactly sent this, on whose orders, and to whom?

I implore you to give a very detailed answer to avoid suspicion and to calm the detachment. Two delegates, I. I. Burikhin and the senior noncommissioned officer Nikolai Alekseevich Kusiakin, are being sent to you with this purpose in mind.

For this reason, I ask that I. I. Burikhin be supplied with papers stating that you assigned him here. During the past few days, the riflemen have asked him about such papers, and he did not have any.

I must say that the discovery of the wine instantly spoiled the riflemen's mood and, especially, their attitude toward the officers. Great effort is being expended to smooth over and dispel the suspicion. Some have suspected that the wine was sent for the officers (?). Once again, I implore you to explain to the delegates, Burikhin and Kusiakin, that the episode with the delivered wine in no way gives the detachment a black mark. This last concern worries the detachment more than anything else. It turns out that my assurances are not enough for them. They are waiting for your explanation.

In the document that V. Somov sent to me on 15 September of this year, numbered 3352 [Document 66], it is proposed that the f. [former] tsar and his family be allowed to walk outside town and to attend church. The latter is already being done. As for walks, we would have to do this with the help of carters since at the present, troubled time there is no other means of transport, neither automobiles nor carriages. A whole cavalcade will be needed for this, for the riflemen will also need carters, and this is too noisy and complicated. So far, I have refused the f. ts., who lives in comfort enough, these walks out of town. The yard where he and his family walk is large enough, and there is more than enough air. But, as soon as everything calms down and the opportunity arises to arrange these out-of-town walks safely, I will do so.

The document sent by V. Somov was not signed by you, Aleksandr Fyodorovich. I would ask that you send me another one with your signature.

The former tsar asked my permission to allow Father Aleksei, priest at the Blagoveshchensky Church, to serve as a religious teacher to his younger daughters. I answered that Miss Bitner, about whom I have already informed the minister president, could teach religion just as well. The former tsar declared that this was unacceptable. But for my part, I found it impossible to allow a priest to be a religious teacher, justifying my refusal by the fact that any outsider visiting the lodgings of the f. ts. complicates conditions of guarding him.

Yours faithfully,
V. Pankratov

· 69 ·
Letter from Alexandra to Maria Syroboiarskaia,[1] 17 October 1917.

————

Tobolsk   17 October 1917

MY thoughts are with you much of the time. So many months I've known nothing about you, and you never got my 7 letters. Only 2. The last letter was at the end of July. I have almost completely stopped writing, do so only rarely. Am afraid of bringing harm to others. They'll think up some foolishness again.

No one trusts anybody, everyone watches one another. Everyone sees something terrible and dangerous in everything. Oh, people, people! Petty dishrags. Without character, without love for their motherland, for God. This is why He punishes the country.

But I do not want to, and will not, believe that He will allow her to die. Just as parents punish their disobedient children, so He acts with Russia. She sins and has sinned before Him and is not deserving of His love. But He is all-powerful—can do everything. He will hear, finally, the prayers of the suffering, will forgive and save when it seems that an end has come to everything. Whoever loves their motherland more than anything should not lose faith that she will be saved from death, even though everything is getting worse. One must believe without wavering.

It's sad that his arm [that of Aleksandr Vladimirovich Syroboiarsky, her son] hasn't properly healed and that he won't be returning to his former place—but that's better. It would be impossibly depressing, and he wouldn't be up to it. Be cheerful. Don't either of you lose heart. What can we do? We'll have to suffer, and the more we suffer in this world, the better it will be in the next. After the rain comes sun; one must only bear it and believe. God is merciful; He won't abandon His own. And you will see better days. Aleksandr Vladim. is young—he has much ahead of him. One must survive a terrible illness, then the organism is strengthened and it is easier and more joyful to live. I pray with all my heart and tenderly embrace you.

Sister A.

1. Maria Martianovna Syroboiarskaia, wife of artillery colonel Vladimir Syroboiarsky, mother of Aleksandr Syroboiarsky (Document 52, note 1); she later emigrated to the United States.

· 70 ·

Diary of Nicholas II, 5 September–22 October 1917.

---

5 September. Tuesday.　Telegrams arrive here twice a day; many are so unclearly written that it's difficult to believe them. It appears that there is a vast muddle in Petrograd, a change in the govt.'s composition again. Apparently, nothing came of General Kornilov's undertaking.[1] He and the majority of the other generals and officers siding with him are under arrest, and the troop units that were marching on Petrograd are retreating.

The weather stayed marvelous and hot.

. . .

22 September. Friday.　A lot of snow covered the ground again in the morning; it was overcast, toward evening it all melted. We walked twice, as usual. The other day, our kind Baron Bode [a palace official] arrived with a load of additional household items and some of our things from Ts. Selo.

23 September. Saturday.　Three or four crates of wine were among these things; and when the militia unit soldiers here learned of this during the day, there was an uproar. They began to demand the destruction of all the bottles [stored] in the Kornilov house. After a long exhortation on the part of the commissar and others it was decided to take all the wine away and pour it into the Irtysh. Before tea, from the windows we observed the departure of the cart with the crates of wine, upon which sat the asst. comm. [commissar] with an axe in his hands, followed by the whole convoy of armed riflemen. It rained in the morning, after an hour it cleared up, and fine weather began: 11 degrees [51°F] in the shade.

. . .

29 September. Friday.　The other day, Ye. S. Botkin received a document from Kerensky stating that walks outside town are permitted. In response to Botkin's question about when they might begin, Pankratov, the rascal, answered that there can't even be any discussion about it now because of some sort of incomprehensible fear for our safety. Everyone was extremely upset by this answer. The weather has turned cooler. Finished *Ramuntcho*.

. . .

2 October. Monday.　A warm day; around 4 o'clock it rained briefly. Now all of our people who wish to take walks must go about town accompanied by riflemen.

. . .

20 October. Saturday. Today is already the 23d anniversary of dear Papa's death and these are the circumstances in which we are forced to live through it! Lord, how sad I am for poor Russia. Yesterday, before supper, an evening requiem was held.

. . .

22 October. Sunday. At 8 o'clock, went to liturgy and the whole family received communion. What spiritual comfort at a trying time! The weather stayed mild; snow fell all day. We spent a long time in the garden.

1. General Lavr Kornilov, commander in chief of the Russian army, attempted a military putsch on 26–30 August 1917.

· 71 ·

Letter from Tatiana to Pyotr Petrov, 23 October 1917.

Tobolsk   23 October 1917

Dear Pyotr Vasilievich,

I AM quite embarrassed that I haven't written you until now. Can you please get my books by A. [Aleksei] Tolstoy; they always stood on the 1st shelf of my bookshelf, but I don't know what it's like now. I will be very grateful to you if you get them, although I know how hard it is. Send them with Iza if you can manage it, or by mail in the name of commissar Pankratov for delivery to me!

Now then! We remember you often, I hope that you are completely better. Here we have a lot of snow but it isn't very cold. The lessons are going well, so that almost all the time is filled up and the day goes by very quickly—mainly because it is monotonous.

Yesterday we partook of the Blessed Sacrament in church. This was very good.

What are you doing? How is brother doctor and nephew? And where is his former superior, Pavel Pavlovich? I hope that at least for them everything is going well. Do you see Mr. Conrad [a former teacher at Tsarskoe Selo] and Konstantin Alekseevich? Give them all [my] regards.

24 October. Yesterday I didn't get a chance to finish, so I continue today. The weather was divine all day, bright sun, which makes my mood immediately better, so don't think that it is always bad. Not at all. As you know,

we don't get dejected easily! Were you amazed when you found out about the wedding of your very 1st pupil———?!!

We didn't expect that at all. And did Mr. Conrad see the young ones? How do they look now and where are they? Does he continue to give lessons there? Did his family arrive? How did K. A. settle into the new house? Forgive me for so many questions, but I hope that you will answer them all. All the best to you. Everyone sends heartfelt regards. May God protect you. I do not envy your proximity to the repulsive and vile Petrograd.

Your student No. 2, Tatiana

· 72 ·

Letter from Nicholas to his sister Ksenia Aleksandrovna, 5 November 1917.

Tobolsk   5 November 1917

My dear, darling Ksenia,

I THANK you with all my heart for the kind letter from 15 October, which gave me great pleasure.

Everything you write about Mama's health has calmed me down. May God grant that she regain her strength completely and that she take care of herself.

We just returned from liturgy, which begins for us at 8 o'clock, when it is completely dark.

In order to get into our church we must pass by the town garden and cross the street—about 500 paces in all from the house. The riflemen stand in a loose chain along the right and left; when we begin to go home, they gradually leave their places and walk behind us while others remain off in the distance and to the side—all this reminds us of the end of a roundup, so that we laugh every time we walk through our gate.

I am very glad that they reduced your guard—both you and they understand it's "extremely tiresome."

Poor, confused people. I'll try to write Misha [Mikhail Aleksandrovich, their brother]; I've heard no news of him except from you.

Real winter just can't seem to set in; it's been snowing for two days with some frost, then everything melts and starts over again. But the air is incredibly pure and good to breathe.

We live here as though on a ship at sea, and the days all resemble one another; for that reason I'll describe our life in Ts. Selo to you.

As you know, when I arrived from Mogilyov, I found all the children quite sick, especially Maria and Anastasia. Naturally, I spent the whole day with them dressed in a white smock. The doctors came to see them in the morning and the evening, accompanied at first by a guard officer. Some of them entered the bedroom and were present during the doctor's exams. Later, the officers stopped accompanying the doctors.

I took walks with Valia D. [Dolgorukov] and with one of the officers or with the chief of the guard himself. Since, after the end of February, they no longer cleared the park, there was no place to walk because of the masses of snow—so excellent work turned up for me: clearing paths.

A chain of guards stood around the house and another around the pond and the railing of the small garden across from the windows of Mama's rooms.

We could walk only inside and along the length of this second chain.

When the ice melted and it became warm, the former commandant, Colonel Korovichenko, said that he would push the chain out a little farther.

Three weeks went by without a change. One fine day, four riflemen with their guns followed me; I made use of this and went farther into the park. Ever since, long daily walks in the park have been allowed, as has the chopping down and sawing up of dry trees. All of us would exit through the doors of the round hall, to which the chief of the guard kept the key.

We never used the balcony, since the door to it was locked.

Our exit together with all of our people into the garden, to work either in the vegetable garden or in the woods, must have recalled the animals' abandonment of Noah's Ark: next to the sentry box at the bottom of the stairs from the round balcony a crowd of riflemen gathered to observe this procession in a mocking manner. The return home also took place in a group, since the door was instantly locked. At first, I would greet them out of habit, but I soon stopped because they answered unpleasantly or not at all.

During the summer, we were allowed to take the air until 8 o'clock in the evening. I rode bicycles with my daughters and watered the vegetables, since it was very dry. Evenings, we sat by the windows and watched how the riflemen rested on the grass, smoked, read, horsed around, and sang.

The riflemen who came here with us are completely different— practically all of them have been at the front; very many are wounded and have the Georg. Cr. [St. George Cross] and medals—the great majority are real soldiers. We've gotten acquainted with many of them.

I forgot to mention that on the holidays in March and April there were processions (demonstrations) in the streets with musicians playing the "Marseillaise" and the same-old "Funeral March" by Chopin.

These processions invariably ended in our park by the grave to the "Victims in the Revolution," which they dug on the avenue opposite the round balcony. Because of these ceremonies, they let us out for a walk later than usual; [we had to wait] until they had left the park.

This intolerable "Funeral March" haunted us long afterward and we spontaneously whistled and sang it until we went totally silly.

The soldiers told us that they, too, were quite sick of the demonstrations, which usually ended in bad weather and snow.

Naturally, during this long period of time there were many trifling and amusing, but sometimes unpleasant, episodes. But everything can't be described, and someday, should God grant it, we'll tell you in person.

I'm afraid that I have bored you, darling Ksenia, with this overly lengthy letter, and what's more, my hand has grown numb.

My thoughts are continually with you, with dear Mother, and with your family. I tightly embrace you and all of them; how I love you.

The Bepuatons kiss you tenderly.

May God preserve and bless all of you.

How I would like for us to be together.

Good-bye, my dear.

                                                With all my heart,
                                                Your old Niki

[On a separate page, included with this letter:][1]

Lenin	Ulianov (Tsederblium)
Steklov	Nakhamkes
Zinoviev	Apfelbaum
Trotsky	Bronshtein
Kamenev	Rosenfeld
Gorev	Goldman
Mekhovsky	Goldenberg
Martov	Tsederbaum
Sukhanov	Gimmer
Zagorsky	Krakhman
Meshkovsky	Gollender

1. This list of revolutionaries includes selected leaders in the Bolshevik government, Mensheviks who had helped lead the soviets before October but opposed the Bolshevik Revolution, as well as individuals who held no major political office but had Jewish-sounding names. Because of police repression in tsarist Russia, socialist activists all used pseudonyms.

This list identifies only some of the real names correctly. Lenin was Ulianov but not Tsederblium. Zinoviev was Radomyslsky. Zagorsky was Lybotsky. Mekhovsky and Meshkovsky appear to be a bifurcation of one person—the pseudonym was Meshkovsky and the real name Goldenberg. Gorev/Goldman is unknown.

· 73 ·

Letter from Olga to Pyotr Petrov, 23 November 1917.

——————

Tobolsk   23 November 1917

THANK YOU, dear old Pyotr Vasilievich, for the letter that I got today, a month after you sent it. It arrived in Tobolsk on 31 Oct. (I saw the date on the postmark), and I don't understand what was happening with it here until now. What a fashionable color I'm using to write you with, eh?[1] Almost everyone here with us now read your letter and asked especially to send you greetings. Sig [Sidney Gibbs] already wrote you from here. He lives in another house. I can't tell you anything interesting, as we live quietly and monotonously. On Sundays we go to church at 8:30 in the morning; vigil is held in our hall. An amateur choir sings; the voices aren't bad but they sing in a concertlike manner that I can't stand, although many praise it. They scared us, scared us with this severe climate, but winter still hasn't completely set in. One day there's frost with a slight wind, and the next there are 2 degrees of warmth [36°F], everything melts, and it's incredibly slippery. Sunrises are always very clear and beautiful despite the overcast days. The Irtysh [River] came to a halt long ago. I think that's all the news.

We just read about the death of poor Vasia Ageev in the papers.[2] Could it really be he? Pyotr Vasilievich, could you find out from Zhenia Mak.'s mother whether it's true?[3] She probably knows and, if yes, let her tell his mother how brother and all of us sympathize and grieve with her. Finally, Conrad has news of his people. I can imagine how he worried. Send him and all those who remember us greetings. We are getting ready to build a hill, but there is still too little snow. P. [Papa] usually saws and stacks firewood, and M. [Mama] comes out when it's not cold; otherwise it's difficult for her to breathe. Joy, Ortino, and Jimmy are thriving.[4] The first two have to be chased from the yard all day, where they take pleasure in the refuse pit and eat all kinds of filth.

Well, it's time to end. All of ours send warm greetings and wish you good health. How is Father? All the best to you.

Pupil No. 1, Olga

1. This letter is written in red ink.

2. Vasia Ageev, military school pupil, Aleksei's childhood friend. His nickname, Glina, was often used in correspondence and in Aleksei's diary.

3. Zhenia (Yevgeny) Makarov, military school pupil. In 1916, Makarov often played with Aleksei at Headquarters in Mogilyov.

4. Joy, Ortino, and Jimmy were family dogs.

· 74 ·

"Rumors about the Escape of Nicholas Romanov's Second Daughter," *Vecherniaia pochta* (Evening post [Petrograd]), 23 November 1917.

———

Telegram from our correspondent.

Copenhagen, 20 November. London telegraphs that a rumor is circulating there to the effect that the former tsar Nicholas Romanov's second daughter escaped from Tobolsk and has now arrived in America.

It appears that Tatiana Nikolaevna plans to give lectures on Russian events and to open a school in the United States.

According to these same rumors, Tatiana Nikolaevna is said to have married Count Frederiks, son of the former minister of the court.

Note: Probably all these rumors are a sensation having no basis in fact.

The same for Count Frederiks—there is and was no son; there are only daughters.

· 75 ·

Diary of Nicholas II, 11–26 November 1917.

———

11 November. Saturday. A lot of snow fell. It's been a long time since we've received any newspapers from Petrograd; the same with telegrams. At such a difficult time this is hard. The daughters played on the swings and jumped from them into the snow. There was vigil at 9 o'clock.

. . .

17 November. Friday. The same unpleasant weather with a piercing wind.

It's nauseating to read the newspapers' description of what happened two weeks ago in Petrograd and Moscow!

It's much worse and more disgraceful than the Time of Troubles.[1]

18 November. Saturday. The most astounding news came: three parliamentarians from our Fifth Army went to the Germans outside Dvinsk and

signed off on preliminary terms for a truce! I never expected such a night-mare. How did these Bolshevik scoundrels have the nerve to fulfill their secret dream of concluding peace with the enemy without asking the people for their opinion and while the adversary is occupying a large swath of the country?

. . .

26 November. Sunday.   We went to evening service at 8 o'clock.

Today is St. George's Day. The town organized a lunch and other festivities in the People's House for the holders of the St. George Cross. But among our guards from the Second Regiment were a few holders whom their comrades without the cross did not want to relieve, instead ordering them to go on performing their duty—even on a day like this! Freedom!!! We walked far and for a long time; the weather is mild.

1. The Time of Troubles (*smutnoe vremia*) was a turbulent period in Russian history at the beginning of the seventeenth century. It was marked by dynastic crisis, external threats to Russia's national independence, and unprecedented social upheaval and breakdown. The establishment of the Romanov dynasty marked its end.

· 76 ·

Letter from Pierre Gilliard to Pyotr Petrov, 26 November 1917. Original in French.

———

Tobolsk   Sunday, 26 November 1917

Dear *Pyotr Vasilievich,*

I JUST received your card dated the 15th and I thank you for it. I showed it to A. N. [Aleksei], who was very sad to know that you were grieved by his long silence; he will write to you tomorrow. His only excuse is that he really is very busy: 28 hours of lessons each week, not counting the preparations. He will write to you tomorrow during my French lesson, and he will bless you since, thanks to you, he will get to skip a dictation. I am so happy to learn that you are well. If you are sleeping badly, you are not alone. Who is not suffering from insomnia? The anxiety that has pursued you for weeks wears on the nervous system; Gibbes [Gibbs] himself feels the effects of it, despite his British imperturbability. Nothing new here; everyone is healthy. We suffer morally, as in the rest of Russia; suffering and anxiety are unfortunately not enough to save a country. You know, during the twelve years that I have been living in Russia, I have begun to love its sad and dreamy, idealistic, and sometimes childish nature, but what crazy wind has blown upon this people? What devastation! What sorrow! Please tell M. Conrad that I was very happy to learn that his wife and children had arrived safely in Switzerland. I did receive the letter from Mme Conrad and I showed it; Gibbes also spoke about M. Conrad, but it seems impossible to have him come here.

Everyone sends greetings to you, as well as to M. Conrad. With fondest love, and please do not forget your [illegible],

Pierre Gilliard

· 77 ·

Letter from Alexandra to Aleksandr Syroboiarsky, 29 November 1917.

————

Tobolsk   29 November 1917

I RECEIVED a postcard from mother [Maria Syroboiarskaia] today; she writes after receiving your letter from Vologda. Yes, the Lord God saved you once again and henceforward will never leave you. A heartfelt thanks for the postcard from Irkutsk. Unfortunately, not everything has been sent from Tiumen yet—how tedious! It's hard for Mama [Alexandra] that you are so far away and that she will learn nothing of you for a long time.

I can imagine how horrible everything is that they lived through there [the October Revolution in Moscow]. Unbelievably difficult, sad, offensive, embarrassing; but don't lose faith in God's mercy—He will not let the motherland perish. All this humiliation, filth, and horror must be borne with humility (as it is not within our power to help). And He will save, ever-patient and merciful—He does not stay angry forever. I know that you do not believe this, and this is painful and sad. It would be impossible to live without this faith.

Many already recognize that all this was utopia, a chimera. Their ideals collapsed, are covered with dirt and disgrace; they did not do a single good thing for the motherland—freedom—ruin—total anarchy: that's what things have come to. I pity even these idealists (when they are kind), but will thank God when their eyes are opened. They thought only of themselves, forgot the motherland—all words and noise. But many will wake up; the lie will be exposed, all the falsity; but the people [*narod*] aren't all damaged, they got lost, were tempted. An uncultured, wild people, but the Lord won't abandon them, and the Holy Mother of God will stand up for our poor Rus.

I hope that this letter reaches you safely; write now.

Good-bye. I wish you all the best. The Lord be with you. Be cheerful. The most heartfelt regards.

Sister

· 78 ·

"The Escape of Nicholas II," *Petrogradskii golos* (Petrograd voice), 2 December 1917.

The news reached Smolny last night that Nicholas II had managed to steal away from Tobolsk.

In response, the military-revolutionary committee[1] appealed to the Nikolaevsky R.R. line with the urgent demand that a 15-car train be immediately readied to dispatch 500 sailors to Cheliabinsk and proposed that the railroad take all measures to ensure that nothing holds the train up on its way.

The railroad communicated with "Vikzhel,"[2] which ordered that the military-revolutionary committee be given every possible assistance.

1. Military-Revolutionary Committees (VRKs) were combat organizations belonging to the soviets of workers' and soldiers' deputies. In many areas, these committees organized and coordinated the armed uprisings establishing Soviet power. The Petrograd VRK played a central role in the Bolshevik seizure of power in the capital.

2. Vikzhel—the All-Russian Executive Committee of the Union of Railroad Employees— was established at the first All-Russian Congress of Railroad Employees, which met in Moscow in July and August 1917. The Vikzhel leaders were mainly Mensheviks and Socialist Revolutionaries.

· 79 ·

Telegram from the special purpose detachment to the "Chairman of the People's Army of Socialists" at Smolny, 3 December 1917.

Received on 3 December 1917 at 2:14
From Tobolsk

Rumors about the escape of Nicholas Romanov are false [and] provocative.

Captain Aksiuta[1]

1. Fyodor Alekseevich Aksiuta, captain with the special purpose detachment on guard in Tobolsk.

· 80 ·

Report by the delegates to the third Western Siberian Congress of Soviets of Workers' and Soldiers' Deputies concerning the vigilant guarding of the overthrown tsar in Tobolsk, 10 December 1917.

———

Comrade Dronin (Bolshevik) raises the question of more vigilantly guarding Nicholas II in Tobolsk.

Comrade Mitkevich declares, after speaking over the direct [telegraph] line with the commissar assigned by Omsk to monitor the attitude of the inhabitants of the town of Tobolsk toward Nicholas II, that the mansion where the Romanovs are held is strictly guarded and that fears about the possibility of the former tsar's flight are unfounded.

Zinoviev, chairman of the Tobolsk Soviet of Workers' and Soldiers' Deputies, says that the Romanovs' guard consists of 350 people, mainly holders of the St. George Cross, chosen from among three regiments of the Tsarskoe Selo garrison. There is strict discipline and complete unanimity in the detachment.

A tall fence surrounds the house in which Romanov is held. Guards are everywhere, inside and out, and at night a few more patrols make the rounds. Absolutely no one is allowed inside the house; likewise, only servants are allowed to leave the house to receive provisions. Each one of them carries the commandant's identification card with a photo, and these are strictly examined when they leave and return to the house.

All the Romanovs' correspondence is examined by the detachment headed by commissar Pankratov, a Shlisselburger.[1]

The Romanovs have no money at their disposal; the detachment commandant has it and takes care of all the Romanovs' bills.

All persons residing in Tobolsk are strictly controlled. Thus, only individuals who are completely ignorant of the rules for guarding the Romanovs can talk about their escape or their having any kind of personal contacts with anyone.

Recently, in the papers—mainly in the bourgeois press—every conceivable piece of provocative information is appearing about the Romanovs in order to inflame the minds of the people.

The most serious attention must be paid to this information.

1. In 1884, Pankratov was sentenced to fourteen years' confinement in the notorious Shlisselburg prison for his involvement in the revolutionary socialist underground in St. Petersburg. To be known as a Shlisselburger was a badge of honor in revolutionary circles.

· 81 ·

Letter from Alexandra to Aleksandr Syroboiarsky, 10 December [1917].

————

10 December

WHAT sad holidays these are now! I remember letters from the front last winter—how they decorated the tree, a concert, and presents from the old unit. Yes—it's good that we don't know in advance what fate readies for us!

Yes, one lives in the past and in the hope of better days. You shouldn't look at it all so gloomily—chin up—look more cheerily into everyone's eyes—never lose your hope—steadfastly believe that this nightmare will pass. Not all is lost—the country is young—just as the body grows stronger after a very serious illness, so it will be with the dear motherland. Remember my words—I have lived through so much, have suffered—I'm old in comparison with you—nevertheless, I believe more strongly and have more hope than you.

The Lord tests and later will relieve—will heal all the terrible wounds. Not much is left to withstand; with the new year there will be better days—although there is still much ahead that is difficult; it hurts, so much bloodshed, it hurts terribly! But truth must finally prevail. You are young in years; everyone still has much work ahead, this critical period will pass and then we'll have to work with all our strength again, to build, create, fix—to strengthen the motherland. There are times when you worry terribly, but I haven't experienced that yet; I was always busy with something, thank God, with official duties before, and now with the children. For you, of course it's a hundred times worse, but believe me, it can't be bad forever. I can't convince you as I know nothing of you, but I believe deeply in God's mercy and fairness—one must suffer for a great sin, atone for one's guilt—later you'll understand.

We'll talk about all this, but where, when, how—only God knows. How to live without hope? One must be cheerful and then God will grant spiritual peace.

You feel hurt, vexed, offended, ashamed; you suffer; everything hurts, aches; but your soul is at rest; there is calm faith and love in God, Who won't abandon His own and will hear the persistent prayers, have mercy, and save.

Look at beloved nature—the sun shines brightly there, and so it must shine within the soul and disperse the black clouds.

I worry for my very dear ones in Petrograd. It is very bad there. They say there are great disorders and horrors again—and yet the soul keeps a vigil; it is the Lord God who gives hope and serenity. I've worried for more than 3 years for the ones dear to me. My heart is tired, but I pray endlessly and believe.

I write you boring things, but I so want to help my former wounded friend and again I am thwarted—I can't find words; but try to understand that God is above everything and for Him everything is possible, accessible. People can do nothing. He alone will save; for this reason we must unceasingly ask Him, beg Him, to save our dear long-suffering motherland.

How glad I am that we are not abroad but instead are living through everything with her [Russia]. How I would like to share everything with my beloved ill person, to live through it together and to look after him, as well as the motherland, with love and concern.

I felt myself her mother for too long to lose this feeling—we make up one whole and share sorrow and happiness. She hurt us, offended us, slandered us, and so forth, but we love her deeply just the same and want to see her regain her health; just as with a sick child who has bad but also good qualities, so with our dear motherland. But enough of that. Yes, nature is the best of all, but, nevertheless, it changes in summer and in winter: fog, storm, squalls, and so forth; so it is with a person and with a country—everything repeats itself but the dimensions are different.

That other countries have it better: I don't think that you could live there. You must first find tranquility and peace within yourself; then you can live anywhere—in freedom, in bonds. It's hard, maybe terrifying, but the soul must remain untroubled: strong, intense, hard as stone. How cruelly others are destroying everything that one built with courage and love—it hurts, but a person must survive it. If you saw His pain and meekness you would understand Him [Nicholas].

It's 4 months since we've been here in captivity. Remember the evenings at the field hospital and at our place. So many indelible memories for our whole lives. May God grant that we meet in the new year—I very much hope so. It is so hard to be far from all friends.

I wish you good health, spiritual peace, work, and happiness in the new year. We send very warm regards and wishes. Good-bye! May God protect (I make the sign of the cross over you). All the very best; get better fast.[1] We are waiting for news.

Sister

1. Aleksandr Syroboiarsky was preparing for an appendectomy.

· 82 ·

Letter from Aleksei to Pyotr Petrov, 19 December 1917.

———————

Tobolsk   19 December 1917

My dear Pyotr Vasilievich,

I WISH you all the best for the coming holiday and new year. I hope that you received
my first letter. How is your health? So far
we have very little snow, and that is why it is hard to build a hill. Joy
[Aleksei's dog] is growing fatter by the day because he eats various filth
from the refuse pit. Everyone uses sticks to chase him away. He has lots of
acquaintances in town, and that is why he always runs away. I am writing
you during my French lesson because I have almost no free time, but when
I have a vacation I will write you more often. Greetings and best wishes to
the teachers. May the Lord protect you!

Your fifth pupil, Aleksei

· 83 ·

Letter from Alexandra to Anna Vyrubova, [16 December 1917]. Original written
in English.

———————

M Y own precious child: It seems strange writing in English after
nine weary months. We are doing a risky thing sending this
parcel, but we profit through Anushka[1] who is still on the
outside. Only promise to burn all we write as it could do you endless harm
if they discovered that you were still in contact with us. After all, people are
still quite mad. Therefore dont judge those who are afraid to visit you, just
leave time for people to quiet down. You cant imagine the joy of getting
your sweet letters. I have read them over and over to myself & to the
others. We all share the anguish, & the misery, & the joy to know that you
are free at last. I wont speak of what you have gone through. Forget it, with
the old name you have thrown away.[2] Now live again.

One has so much to say that one ends by saying nothing. I am unac-
customed to writing in English, just short letters or cards, nothing of
consequence. Your perfume quite overcame us. It went the round of our
tea table, & we all saw you quite clearly before us. I have no "white rose"
to send you, and could only scent the shawl with vervaine. Thanks for your
own mauve bottle, the lovely blue silk jacket, & the excellent pastilles. The

children and Father were so touched with the things you sent, which we remember so well, & packed up at Tsarskoe. We have none of such things with us, so alas, we have nothing to send you. I hope you got the food through the Lotkarevs & Mme. Krarup. I have sent you at least five painted cards, always to be recognized by my sign 卐. I have always to be imagining new things!

Yes, God is wonderful & has sent you (as always) in great sorrow a new friend. I bless him for all that he has done for you, & I cannot refrain from sending him an image, as to all who are kind to you. Excuse this bad writing, but my pen is bad, & my fingers are stiff from cold. We had the blessing of going to church at eight o'clock this morning. They dont always allow us to go. The maids are not yet let in as they have no papers so the odious Kommissar [Pankratov] doesn't admit them & the commandant [Kobylinsky] can do nothing. The soldiers think we already have too many people with us. Well, thanks to all this we can still write to you. Something good always comes out of everything.

Many things are very hard—& then we remember you. Our hearts are ready to burst at times. Happily there is nothing in this place that reminds us of you. This is better than it was at home where every corner was full of you. Ah, child, I am proud of you. Hard lessons, hard school of suffering, but you have passed your examinations so well. Thanks, child, for all you have said for us, for standing up for us, & for having borne all for our own & for Russia's sake. God alone can recompense you, for if He has let you see horrors He has permitted you to gaze a little into yonder world. Our souls are nearer now than before. I feel especially near you when I am reading the Bible. The children also are always finding texts suiting you. I am so contented with their souls. I hope God will bless my lessons with Baby. The ground is rich, but is the seed ripe enough? I do try my utmost, for all my life lies in this.

Dear, I carry you always with me. I never am separated from your ring, but at night I wear it on my bracelet as it is so loose on my finger. After we received our Friend's cross we got also this cross to bear. God knows it is painful being cut off from the lives of those dear to us, after being accustomed for years to share every thought. But my child has grown self-dependent with time. In your love we are always together. I wish we were so in fact, but God knows best. One learns to forget personal desires. God is merciful & will never forsake His children who trust Him.

I do hope this letter and parcel will reach you safely, only you had better write & tell Anushka that you get everything safely. Nobody here must dream that we evade them, otherwise it would injure the kind commandant and they might remove him.

I keep myself occupied ceaselessly. Lessons begin at nine (in bed). Up at noon for religious lessons with Tatiana, Marie, Anastasia, and Alexei. I have a German lesson three times a week with Tatiana & once with Marie, besides reading with Tatiana. Also I sew, embroider, & paint, with spectacles on because my eyes have become too weak to do without them. I read "good books" a great deal, love the Bible, & from time to time read novels. I am so sad because they are allowed no walks except before the house and behind a high fence. But at least they have fresh air, and we are grateful for anything. He [Nicholas] is simply marvelous. Such meekness while all the time suffering intensely for the country. A real marvel. The others are all good & brave & uncomplaining, and Alexei is an angel. He & I dine *à deux* & generally lunch so, but sometimes downstairs with the others.

They don't allow the priest to come to us for lessons, & even during services officers, commandant & Kommissar, stand near by to prevent any conversation between us. The priest is very good, loyal. Strangely enough Germogen[3] is Bishop here, but at present he is in Moscow. We have had no news from my old home or from England. All are well, we hear, in the Crimea, but the Empress Dowager has grown old and very sad and tearful. As for me my heart is better as I lead such a quiet life. I feel utter trust & faith that all will be well, that this is the worst, & that soon the sun will be shining brightly. But oh, the victims, & the innocent blood yet to be shed! We fear that Baby's other little friend from Mogiloff who was at M. has been killed, as his name was included among cadets killed at Moscow. Oh, God, save Russia! That is the cry of one's soul, morning, noon and night. Only not that shameless peace.[4]

I hope you got yesterday's letter through Maria Feod.'s son-in-law. How nice that you have him in charge of your affairs. Today my mind is full of Novgorod & the awful 17th.[5] Russia must suffer for that murder too. Everyone must suffer for all they have done, but no one understands this. Dear I am glad you see me in your dreams. I have seen you only twice, vaguely, but some day we shall be together again. When? I do not ask. He alone knows. How can one ask more? We simply give thanks for every day safely ended. I hope nobody will ever see these letters, as the smallest thing makes them react upon us with severity. That is to say we get no church services outside or in. The suite and the maids may leave the house only if guarded by soldiers, so of course they avoid going. Some of the soldiers are kind, others horrid.

Forgive this mess, but I am in a hurry & the table is crowded with painting materials. So glad you liked my old blue book. I have not a line of yours—burnt everything—all the past is a dream. One keeps only tears & grateful memories. One by one all earthly things slip away, houses and possessions ruined, friends vanished. One lives from day to day. But God is in all, & nature never changes. I can see all around me churches (long to go to them), & hills, the lovely world. Wolkoff[6] wheels me in my chair to church across the street from the public garden. Some of the people bow and bless us, but others don't dare. All our letters and parcels are examined, but this one today is contraband. Father and Alexei are sad to think they have nothing to send you, & I can only clasp my weary child in my arms and hold her there as of old. I feel old, oh, so old, but I am still the mother of this country, & I suffer its pains as my own child's pains, & I love it in spite of all its sins and horrors. No one can tear a child from its mother's heart, & neither can you tear away one's country, although Russia's black ingratitude to the Emperor breaks my heart. Not that it is the **whole** country, though. God have mercy & save Russia. Suffering all around. How long without news from my family. And here separation from dear ones, from you. But the world of the spirit is surprising, endless faith, given by God, and thus I hope always. We also shall meet—with our love that shatters walls.

Little friend, Christmas without me—up in the sixth story! My beloved child, long ago I took you to hold in my heart & never to be separated. In my heart is love and forgiveness for everything, though at times I am not as patient as I ought to be. I get angry when people are dishonest, or when they unnecessarily hurt & offend those I love. Father, on the other hand, bears everything. He wrote to you of his own accord. I did not ask him. Please thank everybody who wrote to us in English. But the less **they** know we correspond the better, otherwise they may stop all letters.

Ever your own, M.

1. Anushka was one of Alexandra's personal maids.

2. Although her marriage had ended many years earlier, Vyrubova did not begin to use her family name, Taneeva, again until 1917.

3. Germogen (Hermogen) became bishop of Tobolsk on 7 March 1917. A former supporter of Rasputin who then tried to expose him, Germogen endeavored to help the imperial family while they were in Tobolsk.

4. On 20 November (3 December) armistice negotiations began between Germany and Soviet Russia at Brest-Litovsk. In their proposals for peace, the Germans demanded that extensive western territories be separated from Russia.

5. Anniversary of Rasputin's assassination.

6. Aleksei Nikolaevich Volkov was Alexandra's valet. He accompanied the family to Tobolsk and then to Yekaterinburg, where he was separated from the family and put in prison. He later escaped.

· 84 ·

Diary of Alexandra, 24–25 December 1917. Original English text.

———————

December	*Tobolsk*
24.	Xmas Eve
Sunday	Arranged presents.
	12 o'clock. Service in the house.
	Lunched downstairs.
	Dressed the trees, placed the presents—
	4½ [4:30] tea—Then went to the guard *14th rif.*
	reg.—
	Malyshev 20 men. I brought them a small
	Xmas tree & eatables—& a gospel each with
	a bookmarker I had painted—sat **there**
	7½ Dined downstairs with all, *Kolia* [Derevenko]
	too
	One has forbidden Isa to come to us, or leave her
	house.
	9. Xmas tree for the suite—all our people.
	9½. Evening service: a large choir sang
	soldiers came too.

December	11. [°C; 52°F] *Tobolsk*
25.	Xmas Day.
Monday	Got up at 6¼.
	7¼ Went to Church. After mass, *service*
	before the *miracle-work. Icon of the Abal.*
	[Abalaksky] *Mother of G.*
	Painted & rested.
	12. lunched downstairs.
	Saw Isa at the window.
	Sat for 10 m. on the balkony
	whilst N. [Nicholas] cleared the snow away.
	4½ tea—*Kolia* too.
	6. The others had their repetition. I looked
	on, then rested.
	8. Dined downstairs—*Kolia* too.
	N. read to us.

· 85 ·

Report in the newspaper *Tobol'skii rabochii* (Tobolsk worker) concerning the matter of
addressing the Romanov family by title, 27 December 1917.

———

On 27 December, the general meeting of the special purpose detachment delivered a statement to the Executive Committee of the [Tobolsk]
Soviet of W., S., and P. [Workers', Soldiers' and Peasants'] Deputies revealing that on 25 December, Deacon [Aleksandr] Yevdokimov, with the consent of the priest [Aleksei] Vasiliev, called the former tsar and tsaritsa by
the title "Their Majesties," and the children "Highnesses," during the
Yektenii[1] portion of the liturgy at the Blagoveshchensky Church. The
detachment demanded the immediate arrest of both. The mood was tense
and threatened to spill over into mob justice [*samosud*]. The Soviet's Ex.
Comm., together with representatives from all the revolutionary organizations and the city government, decided to summon both persons and to
clarify the circumstances of the matter. The interrogation did not clarify
who was guilty because each person's testimony contradicted both itself
and that of the other person.

For this reason, the decision was made to inform the procurator and
the bishop about what had occurred and to put the deacon and the priest
under house arrest to avoid mob justice, with the aim of guaranteeing an
inquiry. In addition, the highly unusual importation of the Abalaksky icon
to Tobolsk, and specifically to the Blagoveshchensky Church, was also
brought to light. All this, together with the detachment's anxious mood
and rumors about the growth of monarchist agitation in Tobolsk, gave the
procurator the chance to institute proceedings on the basis of article 129
on the charge of attempting to overthrow the existing order.

While the matter of the classification of the crime was being decided,
the deacon and the priest violated their own signed statement that they
would not leave their homes: the former went to higher members of the
clergy, and the latter left for Abalak. The Soviet found an official court
investigation to be insufficient and resolved to form a committee of revolutionary inquiry, which was instructed to determine the roots of monarchist agitation in Tobolsk and its environs. Having vested this committee
with plenary powers, the Soviet placed it under the jurisdiction of the
Revolutionary-Democratic Committee. Zhelkovsky, Ivanitsky, Koganitsky, and candidates Nikolsky and Filippov formed the committee.[2]

———

1. Yektenii, from the Greek for "zeal," is a collection of prayers that are read by the
deacon or priest at each service in the name of the faithful and that contain requests and
appeals to God.

2. Isaak Yakovlevich Koganitsky was a native of Tobolsk and had been a member of the Bolshevik party since 1904. The Moscow party committee sent him to Tobolsk to keep watch over the tsar and his family, and he became a member of the Presidium of the Executive Committee of the Tobolsk Soviet.

Aleksandr Vladimirovich Nikolsky, ensign, Socialist Revolutionary, and assistant to commissar Vasily Pankratov in Tobolsk.

Nothing further is known about Zhelkovsky, Ivanitsky, and Filippov.

· 86 ·

Letter from Tatiana to Pyotr Petrov, 27 December 1917.

Tobolsk   27 December 1917

Hello, sweet Pyotr Vasilievich,

THANK YOU for the postcard with the congratulations. May God grant you all good things in the new year. Did you have a tree this year? We had a good tree; it smelled divine. I don't remember such a strong scent anywhere else. I think they call it "balsam fir." I hope things are going well for you under the direction of an illiterate janitor! In my opinion, this is so sweet, and the main thing is that this is so madly sensible; if it is the same everywhere and in the same spirit then it is understandable what a great benefit it is to our poor mother-land!!!

Please give regards to Yury I., Mr. Conrad, and K. A. And how is the Father's health?

It isn't too cold here. On average it is minus 15 to 16 degrees [5°F]. We live as before. Lessons stopped because of the holidays. Well, good-bye, all the best. May God preserve you. Heartfelt regards.

Tatiana

· 87 ·

Diary of Nicholas II, 31 December 1917–3 January 1918.

31 December. Sunday.   Not too cold a day with a gusty wind. Toward evening, Aleksei got up, for he could put his boot on.

After tea, we all went our separate ways until the coming of the New Year. Lord! Save Russia✝!

. . .

2 January. Tuesday.   It was confirmed that both of them have rubella, but, fortunately, today they felt better; there is a fair amount of rash.

The day stayed gray, not too cold, and with a strong wind. Today walking in the garden but having no work was intolerable boredom!

3 January. Wednesday.   Aleksei also came down with rubella, but very mild. Olga and Tatiana felt well; the latter even got up. Snow fell all day. The committee of the rifle detachment decreed the removal of epaulettes in order not to be subjected to insults and attacks in town. Incomprehensible!

· 88 ·

Letter from Nicholas to Ksenia Aleksandrovna, 7 January 1918.

———

Tobolsk   7 January 1918

My dear sweet Ksenia,

YOU made me **very** happy with your let-ter—a heartfelt thank-you for it.

We are also so pleased to get letters from all of you. I liked the plan for organizing a hotel and dividing future duties between us—but will this really be in your home?

It is exceedingly difficult to live without news—telegraph bulletins do not arrive here and are not sold on the street every day, and you find out about new horrors and outrages taking place in our unlucky Russia only from them. It is nauseating to think how our allies must despise us.

For me, night is the best part of the day—at least you forget yourself for a while.

In recent days the question of removing epaulettes and other insignia was discussed in our riflemen's detachment committee, and it was decided by a very paltry majority not to wear epaulettes. There were two reasons: their regiments in Ts. Selo did this, and, the other circumstance, local soldiers and hooligans attack individual riflemen in the streets with the aim of tearing off their epaulettes.

All real soldiers who spent three years at the front had to indignantly submit to this ridiculous resolution. The best two platoons from the rifle regiments live amicably. But recently, the [other] platoon has gotten much worse, and their attitude toward those two is becoming strained.

The same story is happening everywhere—two or three bad ring-leaders stir things up and lead all the rest astray.

At the start of the new year, the children, with the exception of Anastasia, had rubella. Now all of them are over it.

The weather remains excellent; there is almost always sunshine; very cold weather doesn't last long. Wish you happy returns on the 24th [her name day], dear Ksenia.

I embrace you, dear Mama, and the rest of you tightly.

I remain with you.

Warmly,
Your Niki

· 89 ·

Letter from Alexandra to Anna Vyrubova, 9 January 1918.

————

No. 1   9 January 1918

MY own sweet, dear Child, thank you, darling, for the various letters, which deeply gladdened us. I received the letter and perfume that you had sent back in October, Dear Child, on Christm. Eve. Then, one more time, perfume through little N.; it's a shame that I didn't see her. But we all saw one person who could be the brother of our dear little Daddy. Also his movements—were quite [the same]; the soul rejoiced and trembled. Papa [Nicholas] noticed him from a distance, handsome, tall, without a hat—they still hadn't seen one another—with red felt boots as they wear them here. He crossed himself, made a bow to the ground, threw his hat in the air, and jumped for joy; he reminded us of our meeting in Kiev. Tell me, did you get the different packages of sausage, flour, coffee, tea, and noodles and the presents through various acquaintances? Letters and photographs through *beau-fils* M. F. G? I worry, for they say that packages with edibles are opened. They also say it's better not to send them "registered," for they pay more attention to them, and that's why they get lost. I am beginning to mark down numbers as of today, and you should watch for them. They still haven't been able to deliver us that package of your pict. cards, the silv. dish, and Lili's bell. We all warmly wish you happy returns on your name day—may God + bless you, console, strengthen, and gladden you. I tenderly embrace you, tenderly stroke your dear little head, and kiss your sufferer's brow. Believe, my dear, that the Lord God won't leave you now—He is merciful, He will save our dear, beloved motherland—and will never become altogether angered. Remember the Old Testament and all the sufferings of the Israelites for their sins. And didn't they forget the Lord God, and for this reason they have no happiness and success? They lack good sense. Oh, how I prayed on the 6th [Christ's Baptism] so that the Lord would send down the spirit of reason, the spirit of the fear of God. Everyone has lost their head—the Kingdom of Evil is not yet past, but the suffering of the innocent is what torments. What do people live on now? They take away everything—houses, pensions, money. The Heavenly Father punishes his children because we have all sinned so. But I firmly believe, unshakably, that He will save everything; He alone can do this. What is strange in the Russian character is that a person quickly becomes nasty, bad, cruel, reckless, but can just as quickly become different. This is called lack of character, in essence—grown, ignorant children. It is common knowledge that during long wars passions rise all the more. It's terrible what goes on, how they kill, lie, steal, send people to prison, etc.—but it has to be endured, we must be cleansed, changed. I write boringly—forgive me, darling, my little one. I very frequently wear your jackets, the mauve and light blue ones, because it is cold in the rooms. But very cold weather doesn't last long; it rarely drops to 15–20 [below] [$-4°F$ to $+5°F$]. Sometimes I go out, even sit on the balcony. The children just got over rubella (except Anast., who was not infected). They caught it from Kolia Der. [Derevenko]—thus both the older ones began the new year in bed, and Maria's temperature of course rose to 39.5 [°C; 103°F]. Their hair is growing well. Now lessons have started again, and I gave three yesterday in the morning. Today I'm free, so I'm writing. I thought a lot about you on the 2d, sent someone to put a candle in front of the icon of St. Seraphim. I am also giving notes for requests for prayers on behalf of all you dear ones—to our church and to the cathedral where the relics are—and this will partially cleanse. Just think, that Ts.S. wanderer was here in the fall—walked with his staff—and delivered communion bread to me through others. I've begun to read your books; the style is a bit different from the usual. We have also got hold of some good books here, but there is little time for reading, for I embroider, knit, draw, [give] lessons, and my eyes are growing weak so that I cannot any longer do things without glasses. You'll see an old woman. Did you know that Nik. D. has appendicitis? He is in O. [Odessa] at the hospital. And Syr. [Syroboiarsky] also had an appendicitis operation only a month ago—he is bored, very depressed, with his mother; and in his correspondence he is such a sweet, tender, and passionately believing soul. . . . A new life must be led and yourself forgotten. I have to end, my darling. Christ be with you. + Regards to all of yours. I kiss Mama. Again, I tenderly congratulate you. I want to hurry and finish the drawing and include it. I am afraid that you are having horrible days—the rumors also reach us about the officers' murder in Sev. [Sevastopol]. I'm afraid for N. N. [Rodionov]—he's there with his brother.

Your old Mami

· 90 ·

Postcard from Alexandra to Aleksandr Syroboiarsky, 11 January 1918.[1]

+

O Lord, send us patience
During these dark, tumultuous days
To stand the people's persecution
And the tortures of our executioners.

Give us strength, O God so righteous,
To forgive our neighbors' wickedness
And to greet the bloody, heavy cross
With Your meekness.

In these days of mutinous unrest
When our enemies rob us,
Christ the Saviour, help us
Bear insult and disgrace.

Lord of the world, God of the universe,
Bless us with prayer
And grant peace to the humble soul
In this unbearable and fearful hour.

And at the threshold of the grave
Breathe a power that is beyond man
Into the lips of Your slaves
To pray meekly for their enemies.

11 Jan. 1918   卐

1. On the front of the card is a reproduction of an Italian painting of Christ wearing a crown of thorns and gazing toward heaven.

· 91 ·

Note from Alexandra to Boris Solovyov,[1] [24 January 1918].

––––––––

I see by your tradesman's clothing that contact with Us is not safe. I am grateful to God for the fulfillment of Father's and My personal wish: you are Matryosha's [Maria Rasputina's] husband: may God bless your marriage and send you both happiness. I believe that you will protect Matryosha and guard her against evil people in an evil time. Let me know what you think about our situation. Our common wish is to achieve the possibility of living tranquilly, like an ordinary family, outside politics, struggle, and intrigues. Write frankly, for I will accept your letter with faith in your sincerity. I am especially glad that it is you who has come to us. Get to know F. [Father] Vasiliev without fail—this is a person deeply devoted to us. And how long do you intend to stay here? Warn us beforehand of your departure.

1. Boris Nikolaevich Solovyov, lieutenant. In September 1917 he married Maria (Matryona), Grigory Rasputin's daughter. At Anna Vyrubova's request, Solovyov maintained contact, via Petrograd, with the imperial family in Tobolsk; he also brought them money and correspondence and was planning their escape.

· 92 ·

Letter from Tatiana to Pyotr Petrov, 26 January 1918.

––––––––

Tobolsk   26 January 1918

Hello, sweet Pyotr Vasilievich,

THANK YOU very much for your two letters. I was very touched that you wrote so much. We are in complete health, thank God, live quietly as before, and strangely enough, so far none among us has fought with anyone else. In the morning we have lessons for two hours, from 9 to 11, walk for an hour, and study for another hour. After lunch we walk again—usually until 4, and if it's really good weather, then for longer. Before tea, we work or occupy ourselves for a while with something. After tea and before supper there are often rehearsals of some play. We have already put on three. All the same, we're still practicing another little diversion, and it's good for conversation.

A small [snow and ice] hill has been built in our yard. When we get bored with walking back and forth, then we slide down it, and often we take very funny falls. Once Zhilik [Gilliard] ended up sitting on my head. I begged him to get up, but he couldn't because he had sprained his ankle and it hurt. Somehow I crawled out. It was terribly silly and funny, but he still had to lie down for a few days because of his ankle. Another time I was going down the hill backwards and banged the back of my head really hard against the ice. I thought nothing would be left of the hill, but it turned out that neither it nor my head burst, and my head didn't even hurt. I've got a hard head, don't I? Eh?

We also had very cold weather with a particularly strong wind—it sliced terribly at my face. It was very cold in the rooms. In the hall it was $5\frac{3}{4}°$ [42°F]. Not far from Mr. Conrad's. Please console him at least a little bit. Does he get letters from his wife? How can it be that you still haven't gone to the show in the Chinese theater? Oh! What famous things you are missing!

Did Yury Petrovich get my postcard? All the best. We send greetings to his sister, too.

Be well. We send everyone heartfelt regards.

Tatiana

· 93 ·

From the protocol of a session of the Council of People's Commissars, 29 January 1918.

————

HEARD: 21. Concerning the transfer of Nicholas Romanov to Petrograd to bring him to trial.

([Report by] N. Alekseev)

RESOLVED: 21. Alekseev is charged with presenting all resolutions of the peas. [peasant] congress on this matter to the Counc. of Peop. Commiss. by Wednesday.

· 94 ·

Portion of letter from Alexandra to Aleksandr Syroboiarsky, 13 [26] February [1918].

————

13 February

I'VE received a long letter here from mama and also a postcard from 6 January, but I still don't have the registered letter, and now it's doubtful that I will. Lord knows what goes on. The post office accepts nothing for Petrograd and Moscow. They say a massacre is going on there. The Germans are at Pskov. The peace will be concluded on the most terrible, disgraceful, and disastrous terms for Russia. One's hair stands on end, but God will save. We will see His justice. It seems this "infectious disease" will spread to Germany, but there it will be much more dangerous and worse, and in this I see Russia's only salvation. It's hard, very hard, not to know anything that goes on there. God have mercy and help and save us. But the soul is not dejected, it feels support from above, the sun is shining behind the clouds. What they are doing with the churches! One will no longer [be allowed to] pay priests for lessons.

In general, it's chaos, a nightmare, but other countries survived such times in other centuries and came out of it. Everything repeats itself. There is nothing new. There, people are cultured; here they are not. Pride has long ago been trampled underfoot. But we believe that the motherland is young: it will survive this terrible illness and the whole organism will be strengthened, but if everything ends thus, then in a few years there will be a new war. Everything draws one to church, to unburden everything there, but it is impossible. You also don't attend? Likely we will form our own choir, because I can't support a real choir any longer. At first it won't be so good, but later it will do. In the Crimea we sang three times at vigil; Olga and Tatiana were small then—12, 14 years old—but they helped. I have to get ready for the first week of fasting—in both the morning and the evening. The sun shines marvelously and warms us all. I didn't go out yesterday; it was windy and I was very busy.

· 95 ·

From the protocol of a session of the Council of People's Commissars, on preparing evidence in the case against Nicholas and deciding on his transfer from Tobolsk, 20 February 1918.

Chaired by: Vl. Ilich Lenin.

Present: Trutovsky, Algasov, Uritsky, Alekseev, Proshian, Kolegaev, Shteinberg, Karelin, Pokrovsky, Vinogradov, Lomov, Olminsky, Raskolnikov, Shliapnikov, Menzhinsky, Bogolepov, Akselrod, Bonch-Bruevich, Kozmin, Alt-fater, Lomov, Sokolnikov, Berens, Stalin, Krasikov, Brilliantov, Kozlovsky, Krylenko, Pravdin, Petrovsky, Sverdlov.

HEARD: 1. Protocol of the session of the commission under the Council of People's Commissars from 20 February 1918.

RESOLVED: 1. To approve [the decisions].

Point 1: To charge the Commissariat of Justice and two representatives of the peasant congress with preparing evidence in the case of Nicholas Romanov. Delay the question of transferring Nicholas Romanov until a reexamination of this question in the Council of People's Commissars. Do not preassign a place for the trial of Nicholas Romanov as yet.

· 96 ·

Portion of a letter from Alexandra to Anna Vyrubova, 2 (15) March 1918.

———

No. 9   2 (14) [*sic*] March 1918

MY dear sweet Child! How do I thank you for everything? A big, tender thank-you from Papa, Mama, and the children. You spoil us terribly with all the presents and expensive letters. I was worried that I didn't get anything for a long time; there were rumors that you had left. . . . I cannot write as I would like, and I am afraid to write as you do in English, in case they fall into other hands—I write nothing bad or compromising. My wonderful perfume! little icons— books! It is all expensive. And [illegible] a big thank-you. We still haven't seen everything—little by little. As a joke, I call it contraband. Only protect yourself, my Joy. . . .

Thank you for the work, the chocolate—we have yet to see it. The weather was marvelous, springlike—they even got suntanned. Now it is 20 [°C; 68°F], 17 in the sun. Twice I sat on the balcony, otherwise in the yard (when there is a slight frost), for the sun is very warm. My health was fine the whole time, but it is now a week since my heart has been bothering me again, and it has ached for a few days. It really hurts me. . . . God, how the motherland suffers. You know I love it far more strongly and tenderly than you do. . . . The poor motherland. They have tormented it from the inside, and the Germans have crippled it from the outside—they gave away a huge piece, as during the time of Al. Mikh. [Tsar Aleksei Mikhailovich]—and without a fight during the time of the rev. [revolution] that they prepared from abroad. Yes, they will bring order—but what could be more insulting and humiliating than being obligated to an enemy—God save us! Only they shouldn't dare to speak to Papa and Mama.[1] We hope to fast next week if they allow us to attend ch. [church]—we haven't been since 6 January [the Festival of the Lord's Baptism]. Maybe now it will work out, the ch. draws [me] so strongly. I'll be precise just as you say, [illegible] only praying to the Lord Jesus Christ to pardon my sins. . . . Soon it will be a year since we parted from you, but what is time? Nothing—life is vanity, eternity is everything. We ready ourselves in our thoughts for admission to the Kingdom of Heaven. Then there is nothing terrible—everything can be taken away from a person, but no one can take away the soul. The Devil trips a person up at every step; he is sly, but he also is fulfilling his duty. Still, we must fight hard against him. He knows our weaknesses better than we do and uses this. But our business is to be on guard, to do battle, not to sleep. All of life is a battle; otherwise there would be no achievements or rewards. You see, all tests sent down by Him, calamities—everything is for the best. One sees His hand everywhere. People do bad to you, and without a murmur you accept it. And He will send down a guardian angel, His comforter. We are never alone—He is omnipresent—all-knowing—Love itself. How can one not believe in Him? The sun shines brightly, although the world sins and we sin; darkness and evil reign, but the sun of truth will shine again. Just open your eyes and keep the doors to the soul unlocked so that the rays of that sun can be accepted within yourself. You see, we love Him, my Child, and we know that "that's the way it should be." Just bear it a little longer, darling, and these sufferings will pass and we will forget the tortures. Later we will be grateful for everything—it is a great school. Lord help those who do not hold the love of God in their hardened hearts, who see only the bad and do not try to understand that all this will pass, that it cannot be otherwise: the Saviour came and showed us the example. He who follows along His path of love and suffering understands all the greatness of the Kingdom of Heaven. I cannot write, am not able in words to say what fills my heart, but you, my little martyr, understand all this better than I—you are already further and higher on that staircase than I. But all His children are now apathetic. One lives as though here but not here—one sees much with different eyes—and sometimes it is difficult being with people, even though they are religious—but something is missing. It isn't that we are better; the opposite is true—we should be more tolerant of them. It isn't their fault that they did not have such a mentor. Nevertheless, I become irritated—this is my big sin, an incredible stupidity. . . . Yesterday, on 1 M. [March],[2] we had a requiem and I fervently prayed in my thoughts for your father, too. The 2d was the day of my father's death 26 y. [years] ago, and the day that the sweet, wounded one, Komenshev [?] lay in the big pal. [palace]; he took a little piece of me with him, the bright hero— completely unknown, but a radiant soul beckoned my soul to bring a ray of light. . . . I cannot but bless another soul—he wanted to be warmed so. There are those close by from whom one doesn't draw warmth; I am not drawn to them and that is bad. I give to them in words—it is a matter of obligation—but not from within. The fire doesn't burn inside when meeting; I feel cold with them—and again this isn't kind on my part. Warm kisses.

Your M.

+

1. That is, with Nicholas and herself, who would oppose such a peace with Germany.
2. Liturgy in memory of the assassination of Alexander II on 1 March 1881.

· 97 ·
Diary of Nicholas II, 9 (22) January–2 (15) March 1918.

---

9 January. Tuesday. An excellent, quiet day with a light frost, minus 6–10 degrees [21–14°F]. The last two days I have been reading a book from the local gymnasium library full of absorbing historical facts: *Tobolsk and Its Environs,* by Golodnikov.

I worked well during the day—cleaned the little square and, after that, filled the shed with firewood; Orlov, a good old rifleman from the First Regiment and former member of the Preobrazhensky Regiment, helped me.

. . .

13 January. Saturday. The same excellent weather. In the morning I warmed myself in the sun while sitting on the greenhouse roof. In the daytime, after tea, we held a big rehearsal in the appropriate costumes.

At 9 o'clock another priest officiated at vigil.

. . .

26 January. Friday. I finished reading the twelve volumes of the works of Leskov and started reading *The Garden of Allah* in Russian translation. During the day I put in some good work on the firewood and sawing.

By decision of the detachment committee, Pankratov and his aide are relieved of their positions and are departing from the Kornilov house!

. . .

1 (14) February. Thursday. We discovered that in the mail instructions were received to change the [calendar] style to match up to the foreign one, starting from 1 February. In other words, today already turns out to be 14 February. There will be no end to the misunderstandings and mix-ups!

In the morning, from the little hill, we saw the farewells and departures of many riflemen from among the older conscripts. It was warm, but a blizzard added a lot of snow, wh. [which] I cleaned from the yard. Aleksei spent another day lying down. Vigil was held at 9 o'clock.

. . .

7 (20) February. Wednesday. 8 (21) February. The same unchangingly marvelous weather with a warm sun and with an amazingly bright moon at night.

Judging from the telegraph bulletins, it seems that the war with Germany was renewed when the truce ran out; and it seems that we have nothing at the front: the army has been demobilized, and cannon and ammunition have been abandoned to the mercy of fate and the advancing enemy! Disgrace and horror!!

. . .

12 (25) February. Monday. Telegrams arrived today with notification that the Bolsheviks, or, as they call themselves, the Sovnarkom [Council of People's Commissars], must agree to peace on the humiliating terms of the Ger. [German] govt., because the enemy troops are moving ahead and there is no way to keep them back! What a nightmare!

. . .

14 (27) February. Wednesday. We are having to significantly curtail our expenditures on provisions and a servant because the department of the marshal of the court is closing as of 1 March, and besides this, the use of personal capital is limited to receiving 600 rubles each a month. These last few days we were busy calculating the minimum that will allow us to make ends meet.

. . .

28 February (13 March). Wednesday. The same kind of day with minus 12 degrees [10°F]. I finished *Anna Karenina* and started to read Lermontov.

I sawed a lot with Tatiana.

Recently we have started to receive meat, coffee, biscuits for tea, and jam from various good people who found out about the curtailment of our expenditures on provisions. How touching!

. . .

2 (15) March. Friday. I recall these same days last year in Pskov and on the train!

How much longer will our unfortunate motherland be torn and ripped apart by internal and external enemies? Sometimes it seems as if one has no more strength to stand it; one doesn't even know what to hope for, what to desire.

And still there is none like God!

May His holy will be done!

· 98 ·

Telegram from the Western Siberian Soviet to Lenin and Trotsky[1] on the need to replace
the detachment guarding Nicholas in Tobolsk, 28 March 1918.

Sent on 28 March 1918 at 15:05
Received on 28 March 1918
From Omsk

The Red Army should replace the soldiers guarding Nicholas Romanov in Tobolsk after these have been disbanded. The Western Siber. Committee [Executive Committee of the Western Siberian Soviet] sent a Red Army detachment from Omsk [with] a commissar empowered to effect this replacement. We ask that a decree be published immediately noting that the old guard has been disbanded and replaced at the discretion of the Western Siberian Committee. Entrust the establishment of a guard for Romanov to the Western Siberian Committee of Soviets, giving the committee the right to put responsible guard commissars in charge. A decree on the Red security detail taking over the guarding of the tsar from the old detachment must be urgently sent by telegraph [to] Tobolsk to I. Demianov, commissar of the Western Siberian Committee.

Chairman of the Westsibsovdep
[Western Siberian Soviet of
Deputies], Kosarev
Secretary, Karpov

1. At the time, Trotsky was a member of the Central Committee of the Bolshevik party and people's commissar of foreign affairs.

· 99 ·

Memorandum by Vladimir Bonch-Bruevich, secretary of the Sovnarkom, to the
Secretariat of the All-Russian Central Executive Committee of Soviets (VTsIK) on
receiving a delegate from the detachment guarding Nicholas, [no later than 1 April 1918].

A com. [comrade] soldier[1] from the detachment guarding the former tsar came from Tobolsk. There are many disturbances there; many have left the detachment, don't get salaries, etc. Talk with him in depth and find out everything. This is a serious matter. Sverdlov asked that this soldier be sent to him.

Vlad. Bonch-Bruevich

1. The soldier Lukin (Lupin, according to other sources) was the delegate from the special purpose detachment guarding the former imperial family. He was received by Yakov Sverdlov and addressed a meeting of the Presidium of the Central Executive Committee on 1 April.

· 100 ·

From the protocol of a session of the Presidium of the VTsIK, on guarding Nicholas in Tobolsk, 1 April 1918.

HEARD:

11. Report on the former tsar's guard:
    1. concerning expanding the guard;
    2. concerning salaries;
    3. concerning machine guns and hand grenades;
    4. concerning the arrested: Dolgorukov, Tatishchev, Gendrikov [Gendrikova], and the English-language teacher [Gibbs]. (Verbal report by special purpose detachment's delegate).[1]

RESOLVED:

I. To inform the special purpose detachment guarding the former tsar, Nicholas Romanov, of the following order:
    1. To ask the detachment to continue guarding [Nicholas] until reinforcements are dispatched.
    2. To instruct the detachment to remain at its post under all circumstances until the arrival of the reinforcements appointed by the VTsIK.
    3. To step up the surveillance over those under arrest, to consider citizens Dolgorukov, Tatishchev, and Gendrikov[a] under arrest, and, until special instructions are received, to offer the English-language teacher a choice of either living with the arrested or ceasing all relations with them.
    4. The detachment from the VTsIK will immediately bring money, machine guns, and grenades to the detachment [guarding Nicholas].
II. To authorize the commissar of war to immediately form a detachment of 200 per. [persons] (30 of these per. from the VTsIK partisan detachment, 20 per. from the detachment of Left SRs [Socialist Revolutionaries]), to send them to Tobolsk to reinforce the guards, and, should the possibility arise, to immediately transport all the arrested to Moscow.

(The present decree is not to be made public.)

> Chairman of the VTsIK,
> Ya. Sverdlov
> Secretary of the VTsIK,
> V. Avanesov

1. The soldier Lukin; see Document 99.

· 101 ·

From the protocol of a session of the Presidium of the VTsIK, on assigning reinforcements to the detachment guarding Nicholas and on transferring the Romanovs to the Urals, 6 April 1918.

———

Those present: M. N. Pokrovsky, Ya. M. Sverdlov, M. F. Vladimirsky, A. I. Okulov, V. A. Avanesov, G. I. Teodorovich, and [A. S.] Yenukidze, chief of the military section. . . .

HEARD: 13. Concerning the former tsar, Nicholas Romanov.

RESOLVED: As a supplement to the previously adopted resolution, to charge c. [comrade] Sverdlov with communicating with Yekaterinburg and Omsk over the direct [telegraph] line about the appointment of reinforcements for the detachment guarding Nicholas Romanov and about the transfer of all the arrested to the Urals.

To inform the Sovnarkom about the present resolution and to ask about the immediate fulfillment of the resolution. . . .

> Chairman of the VTsIK,
> Ya. M. Sverdlov
> Secretary, V. A. Avanesov

· 102 ·

Letter from Yakov Sverdlov, VTsIK chairman, to the Ural Regional Soviet concerning the transfer of the imperial family to Yekaterinburg, 9 April 1918.

———

9 April 1918

Dear comrades!

Today via the direct line I am informing you in advance of a messenger coming to you, c. [comrade] Yakovlev.[1] We charged him with transferring Nicholas to the Urals. Our opinion is that you should settle him in Yekaterinburg for now. Decide for yourselves whether to place him in prison or

Российская
Соціалистическая Федеративная
Совѣтская Республика.

Всероссійскій Центральный
Исполнительн. Комитет
Совѣтовъ Раб., Солд. и Кр. Деп.

9/IV—18г.

DOCUMENT 102. Letter from Yakov Sverdlov, VTsIK chairman, to the Ural Regional Soviet, 9 April 1918.

to outfit some mansion. Do not take him anywhere outside Yekaterinburg without our direct order. Yakovlev's assignment is to deliver Nicholas to Yekat. alive and to hand him over either to Chair. Beloborodov[2] or to Goloshchekin.[3] Yakovlev has been given the most precise and detailed instructions. Do everything that is necessary. Talk over the details with Yakovlev.

> With com. [comradely] reg.
> [regards],
> Ya. Sverdlov

1. Vasily Vasilievich Yakovlev, special commissar appointed by the VTsIK and the Sovnarkom and charged with transferring Nicholas and his family from Tobolsk.
2. Aleksandr Georgievich Beloborodov, chairman of the Ural Regional Soviet starting in January 1918.
3. Filipp Isaevich Goloshchekin, member of the presidium of the Ural Regional Soviet Executive Committee and the military commissar for the Ural Soviet.

· 103 ·

Telegram from Tobolsk to the VTsIK about removing the epaulettes from the uniforms of the former tsar and heir, 17 April 1918.

> Received on 17 April 1918 at 22:37
> From Tobolsk.

The detachment resolved to remove the epaulettes from the former emperor and former heir. We ask that this be sanctioned on paper.

> Chairman of the committee,
> Matveev
> Commander of the detachment,
> Kobylinsky

[On the document is written the resolution:] Inform [Tobolsk] that the f. [former] ts. [tsar] is under arrest and the detachment's decision is correct.

> V. Avanesov

· 104 ·

"The Trial of Nicholas Romanov," from the newspaper of the Kungursky Soviet of Peasants', Workers', and Soldiers' Deputies (Perm province), 17 April 1918.

Nashe slovo [Our word] reports that the Supreme Investigatory Commission[1] has prepared a series of trials of prominent figures of the old regime. The trial of Nicholas II will be held first.

The Supreme Investigatory Commission has divided Romanov's entire reign into two periods: prior to 17 October [1905] and after the granting of a constitution. Crimes by the former emperor in the first period of his reign are being ignored by the commission. As an absolute monarch, Nicholas II could do as he pleased prior to 1905. The law had no force. After 1905, the former emperor is incriminated in a whole series of criminal acts committed when he was constrained by a bad constitution, but a constitution nonetheless.

Nicholas is accused of (1) the coup d'état of 3 June [1907], when the law on elections to the State Duma was altered, and (2) improper spending of the people's means and a number of smaller matters.

1. The Supreme Investigatory Commission was an alternate name for the Extraordinary Investigatory Commission (ChSK), which the Provisional Government established in March 1917 to consider whether former tsarist officials had violated the law in their political activities. It ceased to meet after December 1917.

· 105 ·

Telegram from Filipp Goloshchekin, military commissar for the Ural Regional Soviet, to Pavel Khokhriakov,[1] chairman of the Tobolsk Soviet, on the subordination of detachments to commissar Vasily Yakovlev, 21 April 1918.

Sent on 21 April 1918 at 9:30
From Yekaterinburg

To the Chairman of the Tobolsk S. [Soviet], Khokhriakov

I found out [about] your conversation yesterday with Ditkovsky [Didkovsky].[2] Your mildness is not permissible. I am sending three detachments, one under the command of Gusakov. There are roughly 1,000 troops. Announce to the whole town that artillery is to be used and the nest of counterrevolutionaries mercilessly razed upon the least resistance or insubordination to Yakovlev's orders. 2225.

Military commissar of the Ural
region, Goloshchekin

1. Pavel Danilovich Khokhriakov, who was closely associated with the Yekaterinburg Bolsheviks, became chairman of the Tobolsk Soviet on 9 April 1918.
2. Boris Vladimirovich Didkovsky, Bolshevik party activist, member of the Presidium of the Ural Regional Soviet Executive Committee. In 1918 he participated in the transfer of Nicholas II and his family from Tobolsk to Yekaterinburg.

· 106 ·

General meeting of the special detachment guarding Nicholas in Tobolsk, 22 April 1918.

———

Present at the meeting: extraordinary commissar Yakovlev and commissar Zaslavsky.[1]

Chaired by: c. [comrade] Matveev.

c. [comrade] YAKOVLEV: Comrades, your delegate Lukin was in Moscow and reported on the material situation, after which the Sovnarkom issued a decree about which I will speak, and now I ask [you] to hear my mandate (the secretary reads documents). As you see, comrades, I am given broad authority; therefore everyone should be under my direction and nothing should be done without me. I have already discussed the material question of a subsistence allowance with your committee. It will be resolved tomorrow or the day after, as soon as the office readies the list.

Concerning the demobilization of the detachment, c. Yakovlev said: You remain and continue to serve as a fragment of the old army. I propose that those who want to can stay and serve. Anyone who doesn't want to can leave. Each chooses for himself. Of course, this has to be handled in an organized way and not just by dropping everything and walking off.

Misunderstandings that arose in connection with the invasion of detachments and commissars with demands have been smoothed over now that all the Tobolsk detachments are completely subordinated to myself alone. I invited c. Zaslavsky and members of the Tobolsk [Soviet] Executive Committee in order for it to be clearer to you that this muddle was the result of a misunderstanding.

PSHENKOV: Expresses gratitude for the response by Soviet power and expresses readiness to continue serving with comrade Yakovlev in the detachment's name.

YAKOVLEV: Points out the difficulties and pressures of the national work of the wor.-peas. [worker-peasant] government and the circumstances that forced the government to be concerned with the detachment only now that the building of a new life has begun.

It was asked on what terms the Red Army is being formed. Next, c. Yakovlev gave an answer about general conditions. Thereupon, c. Grinkov expressed displeasure with the c. soldiers of the guard in relation to the complicated situation with the Tobolsk Executive Committee and the commissars appointed by Yekaterinburg and Omsk. He protests the unfounded rumor that the guard does not submit to Soviet power. Although he considers the matter closed, he does not consider it out of place to find out the purposes of the commissars who are not from the central authorities, who caused misunderstandings between detachments that could have had sad consequences, for at one time, people in the special guard expected a fight and lay awake at night with rifles in their hands.

C. YAKOVLEV: I have invited c. Zaslavsky and members of the Tobolsk Executive Committee here. They will answer the question posed.

ZASLAVSKY: Reports that he acted according to instructions and calls over the [direct telegraph] apparatus from the Ural Regional Soviet, the accuracy of which can be confirmed right now on the basis of documents at the post and telegraph [office]. "Much was explained by the insufficient isolation of the former tsar in the 'Freedom House.' But since there turned out to be dissent in the Tobol. Executive Committee concerning the orders for the prisoners, nothing specific was decided and the question stayed open until c. Yakovlev arrived." Further, c. Zaslavsky blames commissar Demianov [commissar from Omsk] for acting according to his personal views and not informing other commissars, which led to the creation of a tense situation; moreover, a 36-hour ultimatum to transfer Nicholas Romanov to the local prison was set by Demianov and no one else.

DEKTIAROV (member of [Tobolsk] Executive Committee): Paints a general picture of the state of affairs, which were confused, thanks to the conservative actions of Zaslavsky. Dektiarov's impression is that Zaslavsky acted conspiratorially, judging perhaps by his outward appearance, and the same can be said of c. Demianov, who was new to this business and let slip about the introduction of a state of siege, which created mutual distrust and slowed down the common cause.

He argues that things will settle down with the arrival of c. Yakovlev, who is, moreover, personally sent by the [Central] Executive Committee for purposes of accord and reconciliation.

ZASLAVSKY: Announces that he did nothing suspicious and did not act in a conspiratorial manner, because without the permission of the Executive Committee he could not have talked over the [direct telegraph] apparatus. And if anyone is guilty of the muddle caused, it's Demianov.

GRINKOV: Draws conclusions as to why they did not fulfill the orders of the Tobolsk Executive Committee concerning the delivery of the former tsar to prison. The basic reason was the guards' principled decision to recognize only those orders on the situation of the former tsar's family that were made by the central authorities. Recognizing that they were right to do this, for the family under guard is of interest not to Tobolsk alone but to all Russia, the entire staff of the special guard detachment was very disturbed when com. Zaslavsky responded to their refusal with punitive measures—the denial of bread and money to the soldiers—and, on top of that, with repression coming in the form of an ultimatum. C. Grinkov considers it tactless that these orders were supported by the members of the Executive Committee, and he spoke ill of the former membership of the Executive Committee: "The former membership of the Tob. Executive Committee occupied themselves with empty chatter rather than with governing, and this is why these misunderstandings arose."

Further, the speaker thanks God that with the arrival of c. Yakovlev, with extraordinary plenipotentiary authority, all the detachments are coming under his, Yakovlev's, command.

In conclusion, he adds descriptions of all the regional and local commissars.

C. Zaslavsky said that Nicholas Romanov would be transferred to Verkhneudinsk [in eastern Siberia] and that a decree on this would soon be issued.

ZASLAVSKY: Denies such announcements, for he did not make them to anybody. Next he demonstrates again that everything he did was done on the basis of decrees from the Regional [Executive] C. [Committee] and the local Executive Committee acting in unison.

AKSIUTA: Finds that c. Sverdlov's telegram granting full powers to the Tob. Executive Committee in the matter of guarding the for. [former] tsar prior to the arrival of c. Yakovlev is a stain on the whole membership of the special guard. He argues, as does the whole guard, that the Romanov family had state significance, and thus to submit to the Executive Committee's thoughtless decision would mean making a martyr out of Nicholas Romanov, which can hardly be to anyone's advantage.

YAKOVLEV: Proposes to forget the misunderstandings of past days and finds that the detachment acted properly in not allowing the realization of what the TsIK [Central Executive Committee] did not sanction.

The assembly was brought to a close after c. Yakovlev's answers to questions regarding small housekeeping matters.

1. Semyon Zaslavsky. In the spring of 1918 the Ural Regional Soviet Executive Committee sent Zaslavsky to Tobolsk to keep watch over the guarding of the imperial family. Zaslavsky also headed a Red Guard detachment and was elected to the Executive Committee of the Tobolsk Soviet.

· 107 ·

An inspection of Freedom House, 23 April 1918.

———

Thus have the residents of Tobolsk named the former Governor's House where the former tsar's family is now imprisoned. A spacious white building [on a hill] with two floors facing the street and three the court-yard, it is surrounded by a high plank fence and guarded by sentries. In the big yard is a collection of firewood that the house inhabitants split and saw as they wish for the sake of appetite and amusement, with Nicholas being especially successful at it.

Commission members—the Sovnarkom commissar Yakovlev; his sec-retary, Galkin; house commandant Kobylinsky; the chairman of the guards' committee, Matveev; the representative of the Yekaterinburg Ex-ecutive Committee, Avdeev;[1] and the officer on duty—came in through the front entrance and into the first room on the right, which serves as the duty officer's room. Having looked through the duty journal, the commis-sion set out to examine the rooms.

To the right and left of the corridor are a dining room and rows of rooms where Tatishchev, Dolgorukov, Shneider together with two hangers-on, Gendrikova together with the nanny, Gilliard, and Gips [Gibbs] are lodged. The Romanovs are lodged on the second floor. Here are the hall and study of the former "autocrat," who is not deprived of comforts. The low-ceilinged rooms at the top are densely populated by servants. Many trunks block the corridor.

The commission met Nicholas and three of his daughters in the hall.

Com. Yakovlev greeted everyone and asked Romanov: "Does the guard satisfy you? Do you have any complaints?"

To which Nicholas, rubbing his hands and grinning stupidly, answered: "Very pleased, very pleased."

The commissar expressed the desire to see Aleksei. Nicholas stumbled: "Aleksei Nikolaevich is very ill."

"It is necessary for me to see him," the commissar persisted.

"All right, perhaps you alone," Romanov agreed.

Com. Yakovlev and Nicholas went into Aleksei's room.

The daughters scrutinized the Communist government's representative with curiosity during the conversation.

Aleksei really did seem very ill from a bruise, a hereditary illness of the House of Hesse. The yellow-complexioned, haggard boy seemed to be passing away.

During the commission's examination of the other lodgings, footmen humbly bowed, and withered grandees respectfully got to their feet.

The former tsaritsa was not ready for a visit at this time.

Com. Yakovlev visited [her] alone afterward.

Alexandra, appearing in a royal manner, met him grandly, politely answered questions, and often smiled.

Aleksei was visited one more time.

1. Aleksandr Dmitrievich Avdeev, a worker in the Yekaterinburg factory belonging to the Zlokazov brothers and a member of the Executive Committee of the Ural Regional Soviet. He participated in transferring Nicholas and his family from Tobolsk to Yekaterinburg and served as commandant at the House of Special Purpose (Ipatiev house).

· 108 ·

Negotiations by telegraph between G. I. Teodorovich, VTsIK secretary, and commissar Yakovlev on the arrangements for transferring Nicholas from Tobolsk, [24 April 1918.]

———

Secretary Teodorovich speaking according to Sverdlov's instructions.
My answer: It is possible that only the main part [Nicholas] will have to be transported out. You and comrade Sverdlov foresaw this much earlier. He fully approves your intentions to transport out the main part. We'll give approp. [appropriate] orders to c. Nevsky, commiss. [commissar] for post and telegr. What else do you have to say?
[Yakovlev:] [From] Yekat. Did Goloshchekin send for Zaslavsky? Call Yakovlev in the Kornilov house and inform Galkin.

· 109 ·

Diary of Alexandra, 10–12 (23–25) April 1918. Original English text.

———

Tobolsk.

10 April.
———
23 Tuesday.

Baby had a bad night because of strong pains. 36.6 [°C; 97°F]. Snowing again. In the morning the new *commissar Yakovlev* came to see us (impression of an inteligent highly nervous workman, engeneer, etc.). 10½ [10:30]. Spent the day with Baby. Gay, played cards, read to him. Slept fr. 5–7¼.—37.4 [°C; 99°F]
N. read to us in the evening.

. . .

Tobolsk.

12 April
———
25 Thursday.

Baby had a better night 36 [°C; 97°F].
9.10–10. *Anastasia: Isaiah* 38–42.
Sat with Baby, played cards & worked.
12¼–1. *Maria: J. Sirach* [Ecclesiasticus] 18–26.

After luncheon the *Com. Yakovlev* came as I wanted to arrange about the *walk:* Church for Passion week. Instead of that he anounced by the order of his government (*bolsheviks*) that he has to take us all away (*where?*) Seeing Baby is too ill wished to take N. alone (if not willing then obliged to use force) I had to decide to stay with Baby or accompany him. Settled to accompany him as can be of more need & too risky not knowing where & for what. (we imagine Moscow) Horrible suffering. Marie comes with us, Olga will look after Baby, Tatiana the household & *Anastasia* will cheer all up. Take *Valia* [Dolgorukov], *Niuta* [Demidova],[1] *Yevg. Serg.* [Botkin] offered to go. *Chemod.* [Chemodurov, a valet] & *Sednyov.* Took meals with Baby, put few things together, quite small luggage. $10\frac{1}{2}$. Took leave of all our people after evening tea with all. Sat all night with the Children. Baby slept & at 3 went to him til we left. Started at $4\frac{1}{2}$ in the morning. Horrid to leave precious children. 3 of our rifles went with us.

   1. Anna Stepanovna Demidova, one of Alexandra's personal maids.

· 110 ·

Diary of Nicholas II, 14 (27) March–16 (29) April.

14 (27) March. Wednesday.   The detachment here was disbanded when they completed their term of service. But because the guard details must still run around town, they sent a detachment from Omsk for this purpose. The arrival of these Red Guards, as any armed unit is now called, aroused all sorts of talk and fears. It is amusing to hear what has been said about this in recent days. The commandant and our detachment, it seems, were also upset, because for two nights already the guard has been reinforced and a machine gun brought when evening comes! This is the kind of trust in one another that has come about these days.

. . .

22 March.[1] Thursday.   The weather remained gray, but there was a good thaw. In the morning, we heard from the yard how the Tiumen brigand-Bolsheviks departed from Tobolsk on 15 troikas, with bells, whistles, and whoops. The Omsk detachment ran them out of town!

23 March. Friday.   A very good day; the morning was clear and warm. From 10 o'clock to 5 o'clock the singing of the riflemen and the sound of bala-

laikas could be heard from the open windows of the barracks—[this was] because of boredom and the lack of anything better to do!

We spent all of four and a half hours outdoors, including on the balcony.

. . .

27 March. Tuesday. The cold came upon us quickly with a north wind. The day remained clear. Yesterday I started to read aloud Nilus's book on the Antichrist, to which have been added the "protocols" of the Jews and Masons—very timely reading matter.[2]

28 March. Wednesday. An excellent sunny day without wind. Yesterday there was disquiet in our detachment brought about by rumors of the arrival of more Red Guards from Yekaterinburg. The guard was doubled by nightfall, the patrols were reinforced, and pickets were put up on the street. We talked of the alleged danger for us in this house and the need to move to the archbishop's house on the hill. All day the conversation was about this in committees and so forth; finally in the evening everything calmed down. Kobylinsky came and reported about all this to me. They even asked Alix not to sit on the balcony for a period of three days!

. . .

30 March. Friday. A new surprise every day!

Today Kobylinsky brought a document that he received last night, sent from the Centr. Exec. Committee in Moscow to our detachment, about transferring all our people living in the other [Kornilov] house to us and considering us arrested once again as in Ts. Selo. Immediately the servant women began to move from one room to another to make room for the new arrivals.

Aleksei's groin began to hurt from coughing, and he stayed in bed the whole day.

. . .

1 April. Sunday. Carrying out orders from Moscow, the detachment committee today resolved that people living in our house not go out into the street anymore, that is, into town. Thus, all day the conversation was about how to fit into this already-overcrowded house the seven people who were supposed to move in. All this is done in haste because of the arrival soon of a new detachment with a commissar who is bringing instructions with him. That is why our riflemen want to protect themselves

from possible reprimand by setting a strict new regimen into effect at our place!

At 11:30 *obednitsa* [liturgy without communion] was finished. Aleksei lay down all day; the pain continued but at long intervals. The weather was gray, windy.

2 April. Monday.   In the morning the commandant, together with a commission composed of officers and two riflemen, looked over part of the lodgings of our house. The result of this "search" was the confiscation of sabres from Valia and *Mr. Gilliard* and a kinzhal [traditional dagger worn with cossack uniforms] from me! Again, Kobylinsky explained this measure simply as necessary to calm the riflemen!

Aleksei felt better, and he fell soundly asleep at 7 o'clock in the evening. The weather remained gray and calm.

. . .

8 April. Sunday.   The twenty-fourth anniversary of our engagement! The day remained sunny with a cold wind; all the snow melted.

Obednitsa was at 11:30. Afterward, Kobylinsky showed me a telegram from Moscow in which the detachment committee's decree on the removal of epaulettes from myself and Aleksei is confirmed! That was why I decided not to put them on for walks but only at home. I won't let **them** forget this swinishness! I worked in the garden for two hours. In the evening I read aloud *The Soothsayers*—also by Vsevolod Solovyov.

9 April. Monday.   We found out about the arrival of Yakovlev with special plenipotentiary powers from Moscow; he moved into the Kornilov house. The children imagined that he would come today to perform a search and burned all letters; Maria and Anastasia even burned their diaries. The weather was vile and cold, and there was a wet snow. Aleksei felt better and even slept two or three hours during the day.

10 April. Tuesday.   At 10:30 in the morning Kobylinsky showed up with Yakovlev and his suite.

I received him in the hall with my daughters. We were expecting him around 11 o'clock; that was why Alix wasn't ready yet. He came in with shaven face, smiling and embarrassed, and asked whether I was pleased with the guard and lodgings. After that, he went into Aleksei's room at almost a run and without stopping went to inspect the rest of the rooms, apologized for the trouble, and went downstairs. He stopped in to check others on the rest of the floors in the same rush.

After half an hour he appeared again to introduce himself to Alix, again rushed to see Aleksei, and went downstairs. The inspection of the house stopped there for now. We walked as usual; the weather remained changeable: first sun, then snow.

11 April. Wednesday. The day was good and relatively warm. I sat a lot on my favorite greenhouse roof; the sun warms one well there. I worked at the hill and on cleaning the deep ditch along the inside fence.

12 April. Thursday. After breakfast Yakovlev came with Kobylinsky and announced that he had received orders to take me away, not saying where. Alix decided to go with me and to take Maria; protesting wasn't worth it. Leaving behind the rest of the children and Aleksei hurts, and in the present circumstances it was more than difficult! We immediately started packing what was most essential. Later Yakovlev said that he would return for O., T., An., and Al. and that we would probably see them in three weeks. We passed the evening sadly; no one slept during the night, of course.

13 April. Friday. At 4 in the morning we said farewell to the dear children and sat down in the tarantasses [springless carriages]: I with Yakovlev, Alix with Maria, and Valia with Botkin. From among our people, Niuta Demidova, Chemodurov, and Sednyov went with us, as did eight riflemen and a mounted convoy (Red Army) of ten people. The weather was cold, and there was an unpleasant wind; the road was very difficult, and we shook terribly from the frozen ruts. We crossed the Irtysh over rather deep water. We had four changes of horses and went 130 versts [about 86 miles] the first day. We came to the town of **Ievlevo,** where we spent the night. We were housed in a large, clean house and slept soundly in our cots.

14 April. Saturday. We got up at 4 o'clock because we had to leave at 5 o'clock, but there turned out to be a delay because Yakovlev overslept, and besides that he was waiting for a lost package. We crossed the Tobol over planks on foot; we had to be ferried only about 10 sazhens [70 feet] on the other side. We got to know Yakovlev's aide—Guzakov, who headed up the whole guard on the trip to Tiumen. When the day dawned, it was excellent and very warm. The road became softer, but we still shook terribly and I feared for Alix. It was very dusty in the open places and dirty in the forests. There was a switch of horses in the village of Pokrovskoe; for a long time we stood right before Grigory's [Rasputin's] house and saw his whole family looking through the window. The last switch of horses was in the

village of Borki. Here Ye. S. Botkin started having bad kidney pains; he was put to bed in the house for an hour and a half, and after that he set out without hurrying. We drank tea and snacked with our people and the riflemen in the village school building. We took the last leg slowly and with all possible military precautions. We arrived in **Tiumen** at 9:15 under a beautiful moon and with a whole squadron surrounding our carriage as we came into town. It was pleasant to get into the **train,** although it wasn't very clean; we ourselves and our things had a desperately dirty look. We went to bed at 10 o'clock without undressing; I was above Alix's bunk, and Maria and Niuta were in the next compartment.

15 April. Sunday.   We all got a good night's rest. We guessed by the name of the station that we were going in the direction of **Omsk.** We started to guess: Where will they take us after Omsk—to Moscow or Vladivostok? The commissars said nothing, of course. Maria often went to the riflemen; their compartment, which accommodated four, was at the end of the railcar, and the rest were in the neighboring car. Our lunch at the Vagai station stop at 11 o'clock was delicious. At the stations they covered the windows because there were a lot of people out owing to the holiday. After a cold snack with tea we went to sleep early.

16 April. Monday.   In the morning we noticed that we were going back. It turned out that they didn't want to let us into Omsk! But then we were freer; we even walked twice, the first time along the length of the train and the second time rather far into the field together with Yakovlev himself. Everyone was in a cheerful mood.

1. On 19 March (1 April) 1918, Nicholas ceased writing both new- and old-style dates in his diary, as he had begun to do on 1 (14) February, when the Gregorian calendar became the legal norm in Russia, and resumed his use of only old-style dates.

2. Sergei Nilus, *Velikoe v malom i Antikhrist, kak blizkaia politicheskaia vozmozhnost': Zapiski pravoslavnogo* (Great things in small things and the Antichrist as an immediate political possibility: Notes of an Orthodox believer) (Tsarskoe Selo, 1905). This book, which describes a supposed international Jewish-Masonic conspiracy to destroy Russia, includes the text of the notorious fabrication "Protocols of the Elders of Zion." A friend sent a copy to Alexandra in Tobolsk; she read it "with interest" and then recommended it to Nicholas (letter from Alexandra to Anna Vyrubova, 20 March [2 April] 1918, Beinecke Rare Book and Manuscript Library, Yale University, Romanov collection, container 1). White army investigators who entered the Ipatiev house after the deaths of the Romanovs found this book on a pedestal for flowers together with the first volume of Tolstoy's *War and Peace* and a Russian Bible (A. Nametkin, Report of the examination of the Ipat'ev house, 2–8 August 1918, Documents of the Investigation into the Death of Nicholas II [Sokolov Archive], Houghton Library, Harvard University, vol. 1, doc. 9).

· 111 ·

Telegram from commissar Yakovlev to Filipp Goloshchekin, the military commissar for the Ural Regional Soviet, on the impermissible attempts to seize Nicholas undertaken by the Ural detachments, [27 April 1918].

To Goloshchekin. Your detachments have only the single wish of destroying that baggage for which I was sent. The initiators: Zaslavsky, Khokhriakov, and Kusiatsky [Gusiatsky]. They undertook a series of measures to get their way in Tobolsk and also on the road, but my detachments are still rather strong, and they weren't successful. I have one prisoner from Gusiatsky's detachment who admitted everything. I won't tell everything now, only the most pertinent, which consists of the following. Zaslavsky hid a day before I set out, saying that you had summoned him to Yekaterinburg. He set out in order to ready the Fifth and Sixth companies near Yekaterinburg to attack my train. That was their plan. Do you have knowledge of this? It seems to me that you are being deceived, and their constant mockery of you in conversations makes me suspect that you are being deceived. They decided that if I don't give them the baggage, then they will finish off the whole detachment, along with me.

I am convinced, of course, that I will break these lads of their nasty intentions. But there is among the detachments you have in Yekaterinburg a strong inclination to destroy the baggage. Do you guarantee the preservation of this baggage? Remember that the Council of Commissars vowed to keep me safe. Answer in detail personally. I am sitting at the station with the main part of the baggage, and as soon as I get an answer, I depart. Make a place ready.

Yakovlev, Guzakov

· 112 ·

Negotiations over the direct telegraph line between commissar Yakovlev and Yakov Sverdlov, VTsIK chairman, on transferring Nicholas from Tobolsk, 27 April 1918.

Received on 27 April 1918 at 20:50
From Tiumen

The route remains the same, or did you change it? Inform Tiumen immediately. I am going by the old route. An immediate answer is necessary.

Yakovlev

The route is the old one; tell me whether you are carrying the baggage [Nicholas] or not.

Sverdlov

· 113 ·

Negotiations by telegraph between Sverdlov and Yakovlev in Tiumen concerning the transfer of Nicholas, [27 April 1918].

Sverdlov at the apparatus. Is Yakovlev at the apparatus? (Interval) Let me know whether you are too nervous; perhaps fears are exaggerated and the old route can be retained. Waiting for an answer?? (Interval)

Yes, yes, I read it. (Interval)

It's quite clear. (A small interval)

Do you consider it possible to go to Omsk and wait there for further instructions? (Interval)[1]

Go to Omsk, telegraph when you get there. Appear before the chairman of the soviet, Vladimir Kosarev. Transport everything secretly; I'll give further instructions in Omsk. Get going. Out. (Interval)

It will be done; all instructions will be given. Out. Good-bye.

1. Omsk lies east of Yekaterinburg along the Trans-Siberian Railroad. An eastbound train reaching Omsk from Tiumen can continue east, head west on a separate line toward Moscow bypassing Yekaterinburg, or go back to Yekaterinburg—hence the suspicions about Yakovlev's destination (Map 3).

· 114 ·

Communication by telegraph from commissar Yakovlev in Tiumen to Sverdlov concerning the need to alter the plan for transferring Nicholas in response to efforts to kill him, [27 April 1918].

I have just brought part of the baggage [Nicholas, Alexandra, and Maria] here. I want to change the route because of the following extremely important circumstances. Certain people arrived in Tobolsk from Yekaterinburg before I did in order to destroy the baggage. The special purpose detachment repulsed their attack—barely avoiding bloodshed.

When I arrived, the Yekaterinburg people hinted to me that the baggage need not be delivered to its destination. I also rebuffed them. I took a series of measures, and they decided not to tear it away from me. They asked me not to sit next to the baggage. (Petrov.) This was a direct warning that I might be destroyed. Naturally, in keeping with my goal of delivering everything intact, I sat next to the baggage.

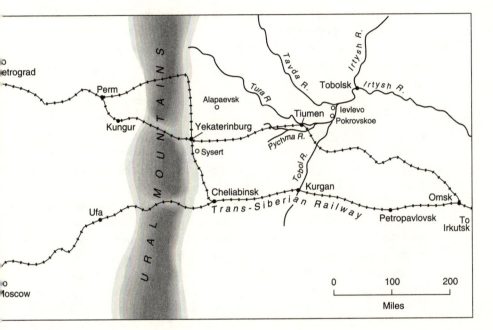

Map 3. The Urals and western Siberia.

Knowing that all the Yekaterinburg detachments are striving toward the single goal of destroying the baggage, I summoned Guzakov with a detachment. The entire route from Tobolsk to Tiumen was guarded by my detachments. Having failed to achieve their goal in Tobolsk, on the road, and in Tiumen, the Yekaterinburg detachments decided to prepare to ambush me outside Yekaterinburg. They decided that if I didn't hand over the baggage to them without a fight, they would massacre us. I, Guzakov, and my whole detachment know all this from evidence supplied by someone from the Yekaterinburg detachment whom we arrested. And also by those actions and facts that I happened to come upon.

Yekaterinburg, with the exception of Goloshchekin, has one desire: to finish off the baggage at all costs. The Fourth, Fifth, and Sixth Red Army companies are organizing an ambush. If this conflicts with the thinking from the center [Moscow], then it is mad to transport the baggage to Yekaterinburg. Guzakov and I propose transporting everything to Simsky Gorny district [Ufa province], where we can save it from the right wing as well as from the left. I offer my services as the permanent commissar for guarding the baggage right up to the end. I state in my name, and also in Guzakov's name, that we cannot vouch for Yekaterinburg under any circumstances. To send [the baggage] there under the guard of those detachments that strove to achieve that one goal and didn't achieve it because I took stern enough measures would be madness. I have warned you; now decide: either I take the baggage to Simsky Gorny district immediately, where there are good places in the mountains that are exactly and purposely suited for this, or I head to Yekaterinburg. It is up to you. And I cannot vouch for the consequences. If the baggage falls into hands [of the Yekaterinburg detachment], it will be destroyed. Since they've gone so far in preparing to wipe out me and my detachment, then of course the end result will be the same. So answer: do I go to Yekaterinburg or through Omsk to Simsky Gorny district?

I'm waiting for an answer. I'm at the station with the baggage.

Yakovlev, Guzakov

· 115 ·

An inquiry by telegraph from the Ural Regional Soviet to Lenin and Sverdlov on the actions of commissar Yakovlev in transferring Nicholas from Tobolsk, 28 April 1918.

Received on 28 April 1918 at 18:50
From Yekaterinburg. Secret

Your commissar Yakovlev brought Romanov to Tiumen, put him on the train, and made for Yekaterinburg. Having driven halfway to the next station, he changed direction. He went back. Now the train with Nicholas is near Omsk. We do not know what the purpose of this is. We consider such an act traitorous. According to your letter of 9 April, Nicholas is supposed to be in Yekaterinburg. What does this mean? In accordance with the decision adopted by the regional soviet and the regional party committee, an order has been given to hold up Yakovlev and the train at all costs, to arrest and deliver both him and Nicholas to Yekaterinburg. We are waiting by the apparatus for an answer.

Beloborodov and Safarov[1]

1. Georgy Ivanovich Safarov, member of the Presidium of the Executive Committee of the Ural Regional Soviet and editor of the newspaper *Ural'skii rabochii* (Ural worker).

· 116 ·

Orders telegraphed from Sverdlov to the Omsk Soviet on assisting commissar Yakovlev in fulfilling his mission, [28 April 1918].

To Vladimir Kosarev, chairman of the soviet, Omsk.

Yakovlev, [about] whose powers I informed you, will arrive [in] Omsk with the baggage; trust [him] completely. Follow only our orders [and] no one else's. I place full responsibility on you; conspiracy is necessary. Yakovlev is acting in accordance with our direct orders. Send an order immediately up the Omsk-Tiumen line: assistance must be rendered in every possible way to Yakovlev.

Sverdlov

· 117 ·

Telegram from Aleksandr Beloborodov, chairman of the Ural Regional Soviet, to Sverdlov
on the provocative actions of commissar Yakovlev while transferring Nicholas to
Yekaterinburg, 29 April 1918.

Received on 29 April 1918 at 13:40

From Omsk. Top military priority

On 28 April, a special train number 8 VA set out along the Omsk line under the command of commissar Yakovlev, who was escorting the former tsar, Nicholas Romanov. Commissar Yakovlev was under orders from the All-Russian Sovnarkom to deliver the former tsar from Tobolsk [to] Yekaterinburg, to turn him [over] to the control of the Ural Regional Soviet of W.P.S. [Workers', Peasants', and Soldiers'] Deputies. According to letters from Sverdlov, chairman of the TsIK [Central Executive Committee], dated 9 April, the former tsar was not to be taken [to] any other place without direct orders from the center—and we received no such orders. Having taken Romanov [from] Tobolsk, commissar Yakovlev rushed [to] Tiumen, directed the train [to] Yekaterinburg, but [at] the next closest switching point, turned the train [in] the opposite direction, east toward Omsk. Having discussed commissar Yakovlev's behavior, the Ural Regional Soviet of Workers, Peasants, and Soldiers, by unanimous verdict, sees [in] him outright betrayal of the revolution, a desire to transport the former tsar [beyond] the bounds of the revolutionary Urals for reasons unknown and contrary to the exact written instructions of the TsIK chairman. This is an act that puts commissar Yakovlev outside the ranks of revolutionaries. The Ural Regional Soviet suggests that all revolutionary organizations, [in] particular the Omsk Soviet, take the most decisive special measures, including the application of armed force, to stop the former tsar's train. Commissar Yakovlev has [under] his command an armed force of approximately 100 people. Commissar Yakovlev must be arrested together [with] those persons in his detachment who will resist; the whole convoy must be replaced with new, completely dependable people; the arrested, together [with] Nicholas Romanov, must be delivered to Yekaterinburg and turned over to the regional soviet. We propose not to pay attention [to] various documents that Yakovlev will present or cite, since all his former steps indisputably attest [to] the criminal scheme Yakovlev implemented, possibly on the instructions of other persons. The regional committees of the parties of Communist Bolsheviks, Left SRs, and Maximalists consider the fulfillment of the regional soviet's resolution obligatory for members of these parties. We ask [you] to immediately telegraph the regional soviet in Yekaterinburg [about] adopted measures, [as well as about] the consequences.

> Chairman of the Ural Regional
> Soviet of Workers', Peasants',
> [and] Soldiers' Deputies,
> Aleksandr Beloborodov

· 118 ·

Telegram from Sverdlov to the Yekaterinburg regional committee of the Bolshevik party
and the Ural Regional Soviet stressing his complete trust in commissar Yakovlev,
[29 April 1918].

> Yekaterinburg: To the [Ural] Regional Soviet. To the Regional
> Committee of Bolsheviks—Beloborodov, Goloshchekin

Everything being done by Yakovlev—concerning Preobrazhensky, Didkovsky, Safarov—is in direct fulfillment of an order I have given. I will inform [you] of the details by special courier. Issue no orders concerning Yakovlev. He is acting in accordance with an order rec. [received] from me today at 4 o'clock in the morning. Undertake absolutely nothing without our agreement. Yakovlev is to be trusted completely. Once again, no interference.

> Sverdlov

· 119 ·

Telegram from Sverdlov to commissar Yakovlev in Omsk about the need to transfer
Nicholas to Yekaterinburg, [29 April 1918].

> Omsk, special train: To extraordinary commissar of the Central
> Executive Committee and the Sovnarkom Yakovlev

Immediately go back [to] Tiumen; I reached an understanding [with the] Uralites; they adopted measures [and] guaranteed that they will be personally responsible for the actions of the regional men; hand all the baggage over [in] Tiumen to the chairman of the Ural regional committee; this is essential. Go together [with them] yourself; render the chairman assistance. The mission stays the same. You accomplished the main thing. [In] Yekaterinburg you will receive a detailed proposal, [also] inform me [of] your departure [from] Omsk to Tiumen [with] a copy to Beloborodov, Ural regional committee; if necessary, take reinforcements from Vladimir

Kosarev, chairman of the soviet in Omsk; I am convinced that all orders will be precisely fulfilled. Regards.

Sverdlov

· 120 ·

Negotiations over the direct telegraph line between commissar Yakovlev and Sverdlov on the transfer of Nicholas to Yekaterinburg, [29 April 1918].

From Omsk

Without question I submit to all orders from the center. I will deliver the baggage wherever you say. But I consider it my duty to warn the Council of Peop. Commissars once more that the danger is entirely well founded, which both Tiumen and Omsk can confirm. One more thought: if you send the baggage to Simsky district, then you can always transport it to Moscow or wherever you want. If the baggage is taken by the first route [to Yekaterinburg], then I doubt that you will be able to drag it out of there. None of us—not I, not Guzakov, not Avdeev from Yekaterinburg—doubt this; nor do we doubt that the baggage will be in utter danger at all times. Thus, we warn you one last time and free ourselves from any moral responsibility for the future consequences. I am going by the first route. We are departing at once. I remind you that there were constant misunderstandings during negotiations over the [telegraph] apparatus. Podbelsky,[1] it seems, forbade negotiations; but for me they are quite essential, as you can see. Also let Nevsky[2] know that he is to send strict orders by telegram to all railway authorities to give no other information by telegraph except that our train is to proceed without interruption and with stops for technical repairs only. So then, I am going by the first route. I'll hand over the baggage. [Then] I'll go for the other part of it. Farewell. Be well.

Yakovlev, Guzakov

1. Vladimir Nikolaevich Podbelsky, people's commissar of post and telegraph.
2. Vladimir Ivanovich Nevsky, deputy people's commissar of communications from November 1917 to July 1918 and people's commissar of communications from July 1918 to March 1919.

· 121 ·

Statement to commissar Yakovlev by Aleksandr Nevolin, member of the Ural detachment
of the Red Army, concerning the proposed attack on the convoy escorting Nicholas,
[3 May 1918].

———————

I am Aleksandr Ivanovich Nevolin, a worker in Perm prov. [province],
Usolsky region, Aleksandrovsky factory.

In Yekaterinburg, I joined the Red Army in the Fourth Company.

At precisely 4 o'clock yesterday, 16 April, Gusiatsky, aide to the chief
of staff, comes to the company and announces that we must be ready to
march in half an hour. At 6 o'clock we reach the station. The chief of staff
says to us: "You have the following assignment: to bring one person, dead
or alive, to Yekaterinburg." He says nothing more.

We arrive in Tiumen. Gusiatsky says: "Now we go on horseback."
When we've gone roughly halfway on horseback, Gusiatsky makes us stop
in a village. He says that commissar Yakovlev is coming with a Moscow
detachment and we have to wait for him. Soon a detachment actually
comes through and we follow it. We get to Tobolsk and spend two nights
there. Gusiatsky comes to us and says: "So commissar Yakovlev has arrived here and wants to take Romanov to Moscow, and then it seems
they've decided to send him abroad. We have the following task: to deliver
him to Yekaterinburg at all costs. To accomplish this, we propose the
following: Yakovlev has nine machine guns and two gunners. I recom-
mend my gunners to him for his machine guns, and we go together. When I
give a prearranged signal, you must attack them and seize all their
weapons and Romanov."

Naturally, none of my comrades objected to any of his words. I was the
only one who protested, and I dissuaded my comrades; when this idea of
theirs didn't fly, they left.

Two or three hours later, I hear they are calling a meeting again. I go, of
course. I hear instructor's aide Ponomarev and instructor Bogdanov begin:

"We have already abandoned that plan and have decided this: We'll
ambush them on the road to Tiumen. As soon as Yakovlev and Romanov
are even with us, you must completely cut Yakovlev's detachment to shreds
using machine guns and rifles.

"And say nothing to anyone. If anyone starts asking which detachment
this is, say that it's Moscow's and don't say who your chief is, because this
must be done by bypassing the regional soviet and in general all soviets."

Then I asked him a question: ["]So we're to be brigands? I myself am
not in agreement with your plans. If you need to kill Romanov, then you

may make that personal decision, but I won't allow such a thought to enter my head. I know that all our armed forces stand guard to defend Soviet power and not to benefit personally, and if commissar Yakovlev and the people dispatched with him are from the Council of People's Commissars, then they should deliver him where they were told. And we are not and cannot be brigands killing Red Army comrades like ourselves because of one Romanov.["]

They, of course, argued that I, Nevolin, am always poking my nose into everything and upsetting everybody. But nonetheless, I convinced the comrades that we couldn't do this, and others also started to argue, and all their plans came to naught.

After the meeting, Gusiatsky, Bogdanov, and Ponomarev severely reprimanded me and started to put more and more pressure on me. When we got to the Tobol River, we stopped in the village there and waited for Yakovlev to arrive with Romanov. When Yakovlev came to the village, then Gusiatsky said if we couldn't do anything, all of us should keep silent. What could you do? Well, if the Fifth and Sixth companies were in Yekaterinburg, he [Yakovlev] couldn't be stopped, and that meant that Romanov got away. Then I told him that it makes no difference to us where; it isn't our business, they know better what to do with him. After that, Gusiatsky got even madder at me. I felt that my life was at stake. Looking for a way out, I finally decided to flee with Yakovlev's detachment.

In the morning, around 8 o'clock, they began crossing the Tobol River. At the same time, I was among those in Yakovlev's detachment crossing to the other side. Gusiatsky found out that I had fled and sent two people, but they wouldn't let them up to shore. And so I went with commissar Yakovlev to the town of Ufa. I could not return to Yekaterinburg—Gusiatsky's allies might have shot me.

I think they'll take action against me at home at the factory. If possible, I ask that documents be sent from the high Council of People's Commissars. I have been a member of the Bolshevik party since the beginning of March 1917. Before that, I worked at the Aleksandrovsky factory.

I put my name to the above,
Aleksandr Ivanovich Nevolin

· 122 ·

"On the Transfer of the Former Tsar from Tobolsk to Yekaterinburg,"[1] interview with
Yakovlev in *Izvestiia*, 16 May 1918.

———

Commissar Yakovlev, who was assigned the task of fulfilling the Council of People's Commissars' order to transfer the former tsar from Tobolsk to Yekaterinburg and who has just been appointed commander on the Ural-Orenburg front, tells how he accomplished this responsible assignment in a conversation with our reporter.

Having readied everything for the move I had set for 27 April,[2] I came on the eve of that day to the Governor's House in Tobolsk, where Nicholas Romanov lived with his family and the people close to him.

Romanov had been warned of my arrival but knew only that I was an official representative of Soviet power. He knew nothing about the goal of my visit.

When I saw the former tsar, I stated to him:

"Citizen Romanov, I have been assigned by the Council of People's Commissars to remove you from Tobolsk. The departure is set for 4 o'clock in the morning tomorrow. Be ready by that time."

Romanov was startled and anxiously asked:

"And where am I being transferred?"

I answered that I did not know the precise destination myself and that I would receive orders only after I was on the road.

Romanov thought a bit and said:

"I won't go."

At that moment, Alexandra Fyodorovna walked into the room. Having discovered what the conversation was about, she cried:

"What are you doing with him! You want to tear him away from his family. How can you? He has an ill son. No, he can't go, he must stay with us!"

I responded by saying that I had a specific order that I would precisely fulfill. (At that moment, there was still no discussion about any separation and it was assumed that the whole family would be transferred together with Nicholas Romanov. The transfer was rife with well-known difficulties, however, and, for this reason, it was decided to leave the ill Aleksei in Tobolsk until the spring when the ice would melt and he could be transported from Tobolsk to Tiumen by ship. They had to decide for themselves who among the rest of the members of the Romanov family would set out together with him [Nicholas] and who would stay until spring with Aleksei.)

Romanov heard me out, but he did not seem to fully understand and literally repeated what Alexandra Fyodorovna had just said:

"I have an ill son! How can I be separated from my family? I can't go."

I thought it unnecessary to start some kind of argument, and briefly repeating that the departure was scheduled for 4 o'clock in the morning, I left. As I was leaving, Alexandra Fyodorovna nervously cried out after me:

"This is too cruel; I don't believe that you'll do this!"

I went to Kobylinsky, the head of the guard in Tobolsk, and told him that my orders to leave on the appointed day and at the appointed hour would be fulfilled one way or the other. If Nicholas Romanov wasn't ready to depart by that time, he would have to go without baggage. Kobylinsky thought it necessary to go to Romanov to let him know that it was not possible to defy in any way the orders to leave.

Romanov discussed the question of leaving with his family and friends for two or two and a half hours. During that time, this family council changed its decision several times: first, they decided that Nicholas would go with all the daughters and Tatishchev, and Alexandra Fyodorovna would stay, then that Alexandra Fyodorovna would go and all the daughters would stay, etc. Finally, Kobylinsky was told that Alexandra Fyodorovna, daughter Maria, Prince Dolgoruky [Dolgorukov], Professor Botkin, lady-in-waiting [personal maid] Demidova, one footman, and one valet would be going. The rest of the daughters, Aleksei, Tatishchev, and so forth—forty people altogether—would be staying in Tobolsk until spring.

I was slightly surprised that Alexandra Fyodorovna decided to separate from her son and leave Tobolsk together with her husband. But Kobylinsky told me that he had heard Alexandra Fyodorovna's casual remark to Tatishchev that throws some light on this decision.

Alexandra Fyodorovna said to Tatishchev, "I am afraid that left alone he may do something stupid."

It seems that Alexandra Fyodorovna did not have a very high opinion of her husband's intellect and discretion.

The next day, 27 April, at exactly 4 o'clock in the morning, everything was ready and we started on our way. We had to go 260 versts [172 miles] on horseback from Tobolsk to Tiumen. For the first 30 versts [20 miles], the road was all bumpy. We had to cross three rivers, the Irshan [Irtysh], Tobol, and Tura. The spring flooding of rivers was beginning; the ice cracked and rose. On the bridge across the Irshan, we had to ride in water that came up to the horses' bellies. It was already risky to cross the Tobol in carriages; we had to get out and walk across the ice. We also had to cross the Tura in water.

Thanks to the measures we adopted, the whole trip was accomplished extremely quickly. There were eight stops in all, and we were met everywhere with harnessed troikas placed in a row; we left our carriages parallel to this row, and thanks to this, the transfer was accomplished in some ten minutes. We spent the night in Vyiavlevo [Ievlevo]. The next day at 9 P.M. we were already in Tiumen.

The detachment I had taken was composed of only 35 people: 15 mounted and 20 infantry. In addition, small patrols were posted at all the transfer points.

This difficult and quick journey did not tire Romanov much. Generally speaking, he's grown noticeably healthier in the past year. He has worked a lot in the fresh air—chopped wood, cleared snow, and so on. His hands are calloused, he is cheerful and feels marvelous. It looks as if he's made peace with his situation.

Alexandra Fyodorovna has gotten a good deal more tired but tried not to show it. In general, she tried to maintain a proud and reserved manner.

Our attitude toward them greatly puzzled them. Apparently, they at first feared rudeness, violence, and insults from our side. But the whole detachment behaved entirely properly toward the Romanovs, not allowing a single impolite or insulting word. At the same time, relations were quite unpretentious, the same as they might be with any other citizen.

Alexandra Fyodorovna looked at us with wide eyes, but Nicholas quickly adjusted and also began to behave unpretentiously.

We set out from Tiumen by train. Here the guard was expanded to 160 men. The trip from Tiumen to Yekaterinburg was completed without incident.

Romanov felt good on the way, just as before. Apparently, he was most interested in three things: his family, the weather, and food. He really does love his family and cares about them very much.

We did not discuss politics at all. I, of course, didn't think it possible to carry on any discussions about political topics with the former tsar. But it is characteristic of him that he is apparently completely disinterested in political questions. All of his thoughts revolve around extremely narrow [*obyvatelskie*] and very family-oriented interests.

Only once did our conversation go beyond the bounds of family, weather, and food. We were riding past some church. Romanov, a very religious person, always crosses himself in these instances. When we rode past the church and he said something about religion—right now I don't remember what—I answered that I personally wasn't religious but that I accepted the principle of full freedom of conscience: let all people believe as they wish.

To this Romanov exclaimed: "Fancy, I hold exactly the same point of view! I also recognize complete freedom of conscience!" I looked at him not knowing whether he was joking or dissembling. But his face expressed such sincere simple-heartedness that not a doubt remained about the absence of any ulterior motive.

In general, I came away from this trip with a very definite impression about the surprising and phenomenal narrow-mindedness of Nicholas Romanov.

Alexandra Fyodorovna is quite different. She is very wily and proud. She has a strong influence on her husband. The entire trip she kept completely to herself and for whole days did not come out of her compartment. She did not want to accept even the shadow of a favor from us. This went to extremes. It's well known that the corridors in the railway cars are very narrow, and when two people meet in them, one must stand aside. Alexandra Fyodorovna did not wish for one of us to have to stand aside and let her pass. So she got up every day at 4 or 5 o'clock in the morning to walk to the bathroom to wash. If she saw a sentry in the corridor upon exiting the bathroom, she would go back and lock herself in until the sentry left the corridor.

Maria, the Romanovs' daughter, is a young girl completely immature for her years. She has no understanding at all of life in the broad sense of the word. She is under the strong influence of her mother.

A big crowd had gathered at the train station by the time we arrived in Yekaterinburg. Apparently, the railwaymen had disclosed that we were coming. The crowd was high-strung. The train stopped, not right at the platform, but some distance from it. Just in case, even before we arrived in Yekaterinburg, I had given orders to firmly lock all the windows in the railway cars and to pull the curtains.

The train had barely come to a stop when my detachment stepped out of the railway cars and cordoned off the train, not allowing the crowd to approach it. Shouts could be heard from the crowd:

"Show us this bloodsucker!" etc.

I answered that if the crowd didn't disperse, I would show them machine guns. This had no effect, however. The crowd grew and pressed against the patrols that I had posted.

Then I gave orders to move a freight train that was standing on a siding to a track between the platform and my train. When this was done, under the cover of the freight train, I moved my train away to another station—Yekaterinburg 2, where no one was waiting. From there, I let the local soviet know about my arrival. The chairman of the soviet and members of the Presidium came. I handed Nicholas Romanov over to them, and they gave me a signed document to that effect.

In Yekaterinburg, Romanov and family have been lodged in an ordinary private house surrounded by a large fence made of planks. This house does not remind one at all of the Governor's House in Tobolsk, which could have been a country palace by the size of its rooms and hall.

Romanov's guard in Yekaterinburg has been strengthened, and a regime stricter than the one at Tobolsk established.

1. This article appeared in connection with commissar Vasily Yakovlev's appeal that the accusation against him for counterrevolutionary actions during the transfer of Nicholas be dropped.

2. They departed on 26 April 1918. Yakovlev omitted from this account one day and, with it, the conflicts and route changes that were at the center of the accusations against him.

· 123 ·

From the recollections of commissar Vasily Pankratov, "With the Tsar in Tobolsk," concerning events from September through December 1917.

I left for the Governor's House on 2 September. Not wanting to violate decorum, I told the former tsar's valet that he should announce my arrival and that I desired to see the former tsar. The valet immediately fulfilled the task, opening the door to the former tsar's study.

"Hello," said Nicholas Aleksandrovich, offering me his hand, "did you arrive safely?"

"Yes, thank you," I answered, offering my hand.

"How is the health of Aleksandr Fyodorovich Kerensky?" the former tsar asked.

In this question I detected a sort of genuine sincerity, mixed with sympathy, even gratitude. I gave a brief answer to the question and asked after the health of the former tsar and his family.

"Fine, thank God," he answered, smiling.

It must be noted that the former tsar smiled during the entire time of our discussion.

"Have you gotten settled and comfortable?"

"Not bad, although there are some inconveniences, but still not bad," answered the former tsar. "Why aren't we allowed in the church or on walks to town? Are they really afraid that I might run off? I will never leave my family."

"I daresay that such an attempt would only worsen your situation and the situation of your family," I answered. "Escorting you to church will be possible. I have permission for that. But concerning walks in town, I doubt that is possible for now."

"Why?" asked Nicholas Aleksandrovich.

"I am not empowered to allow this. Later, we'll see. We have to ascertain the surrounding conditions."

The former tsar expressed incomprehension. He did not understand what I meant by surrounding conditions. He understood them only in the sense of being kept isolated from them—and that was all.

"Can you allow me to saw firewood?" he suddenly asked. "I love such work."

"Perhaps you would like to have a joiner's workshop? That is more interesting work," I offered.

"No, I don't like such work; better that you order wood brought to the yard and give me a saw," objected Nicholas Aleksandrovich.

"Tomorrow, all this will be done."

"Can I correspond with my relatives?"

"Of course. Do you have books?"

"A lot, in fact, but for some reason we don't get foreign journals. Are we forbidden to have them?"

"That is probably the fault of the post office. I will find out. In any case, your newspapers and journals won't be held up."

"I would like to be acquainted with your family," I said.

"Certainly. Excuse me. I'll be right back," answered the former tsar, going out of his office and leaving me alone for a few minutes.

The former tsar's office was a well-furnished room; a rug covered the floor; there were two tables, one a writing desk with books and papers, the other a simple one on which a number of pocket watches and smoking pipes of various sizes lay; there were a few pictures on the walls and curtains over the windows.

I thought to myself involuntarily: Does he have some feeling of being a former autocrat, ruler of a huge state, an absolute monarch, in these new surroundings? During our meeting he had such good self-control, as if he did not feel that the new situation sharply affected him, as if it did not entail huge deprivations and restrictions. Yes, people's fates are a mystery. But who is to blame for life's changes? These thoughts came incoherently one after the other and put me in a special mood, a type of peacefulness, probably as they would anyone who happens to be in a completely new role.

"This way, Mr. Commissar," said Nicholas Aleksandrovich as he reappeared.

I walked into the big hall, and to my horror I saw the following picture: the tsar's entire family had formed an orderly line and was standing at attention: Alexandra Fyodorovna stood closest to the entrance to the hall, next to her Aleksei, then the princesses.

What is this, a demonstration?—the question flashed through my mind and for a second confused me. That is how those under arrest are lined up for the warden's rounds. But I immediately put that thought out of my mind and began to greet them.

The former empress and her children briefly answered my salutations and all my questions. Alexandra Fyodorovna pronounced Russian words with a strong accent, and it was noticeable that she had a hard time with the spoken Russian language. But all her children spoke excellent Russian.

"How is your health, Aleksei Nikolaevich?" I addressed the former heir.

"Good, thank you."

"Have you ever been to Siberia before?" I addressed the daughters of the former tsar and received a negative answer.

"It's not as terrible as many say. The climate here is good, the weather marvelous," interrupted Nicholas Aleksandrovich, "and there are almost always sunny days."

"Which Petersburg lacks."

"Yes, the Petersburg climate could envy that of Tobolsk," the former tsar added. "Won't it be cold to live here in winter? The hall is large."

"We'll have to try to make it not so. We'll examine and fix all the stoves. And there is enough fuel here," I answered. "There are no other appropriate lodgings in this town."

"Do you have books?" I asked the princesses.

"We brought our library," one of them answered.

"If you need anything, I ask that you let me know," I said, leaving.

With that, my first meeting with the family of the former tsar ended. I do not know what impression I made, but as for me, the first impression that I came away with was that if this family had lived in a different situation and not at court with endless ceremonies and rules of etiquette dulling minds and fettering everything healthy and free, completely different people could have been made out of them, except, of course, Alexandra Fyodorovna. The latter made a very specific impression upon me. I immediately detected in her something completely alien to Russian women. . . .

THE SPECIAL PURPOSE DETACHMENT: GUARDING THE FORMER TSAR AND HIS FAMILY

Before I departed, I was informed that this detachment under the direction of Colonel Kobylinsky was composed of select soldiers from three Guards Rifle Regiments: the First, Second, and Fourth, numbering 337 men with 7 officers.

The very first day I arrived in Tobolsk, I proposed to Colonel Kobylinsky that he gather the whole detachment so that I could meet the men
and familiarize them with the instructions.

"We have been assigned a critical responsibility on behalf of the motherland. Before the calling of the Constituent Assembly, which will decide
the future of the former tsar, you must behave with dignity; do not allow
the former tsar and his family to be insulted or treated rudely. Any indiscre-
tions on our part will only disgrace us. Acting rudely to unarmed prisoners
is not worthy of us. Thus," I said at the end of my speech, "I call on all of
you to follow this rule: We will have to answer for any of our actions. We
do not have the right to act as judges over the former tsar and his family,
who have been entrusted to us."

The detachment completely understood my statement and proved it by
not once acting boorish during the entire five months that I was commissar. The behavior of the detachment was almost knightly.

The majority of the detachment soldiers made a pleasing impression on
me with their inner discipline and tidy military appearance. With the
exception of a few, our detachment comprised real fighting men who had
spent two years breaking through positions under German fire; many had
two golden crosses of St. George. These were real fighting men—not rear
Guards—tall, handsome, and disciplined. And I felt a deep responsibility
and obligation to help them preserve these qualities. To do this it was
necessary to create a more or less healthy atmosphere, to fill their time with
work and education. The situation was far from perfect: the barracks were
poorly equipped and adapted. Major repairs were needed. When naviga-
tion was possible, our soldiers found work on the docks, where the boat-
men gladly let them load and unload the barges and ships. During their free
time, part of the detachment worked on the docks. Such work could not be
counted on in wintertime. I decided to arrange a school for illiterate and
semi-literate soldiers and lectures and reports for everyone, figuring that
this would manage to occupy the detachment with useful, intelligent work.
Three officers offered to help me in these efforts.

I divided all the work concerning the guard with Colonel Kobylinsky in
the following manner: he took upon himself the financial and housekeeping part, and I the rest. Apropos of this, I have to note that all those
"opinions and comments" about Kobylinsky that I had to listen to in
Petrograd were, to my great satisfaction, completely unjustified.

Military circles had a negative attitude toward him. But I found in him
a good, noble, conscientious coworker. Yevgeny Stepanovich Kobylinsky
is an officer of the Guards. Having taken part in the war with the Germans,
he was badly wounded in one battle and was kept alive thanks only to

skillful medical treatment. He never belonged to any political parties and did not aspire to join; he was simply a human being in the best sense of the word. Noble and honest by nature, well brought up and intellectually mature, he always demonstrated discretion and dignity in his relationships with people; hardworking and unselfish, he won trust and respect for himself. I quickly became close to him and grew to love him from the heart. Our mutual relations became very frank. . . .

VIGIL

Before I met them, I often heard it said that Nicholas II's family was very religious and that this explained the influence that Grigory Rasputin had on the imperial family. But religiosity is understood very differently by people, and in this case making a judgment is exceedingly difficult. The spiritual-moral need of the royal prisoners was initially satisfied by holding services in the hall of the Governor's House, that is, in the same house where the former tsar's family lived. And on the next Saturday, I happened to attend vigil for the first time.

Alexandra Fyodorovna took upon herself all the work of setting up and readying the hall for worship. She placed the icon of the saviour in the hall, covered the wooden icon stand, decorated them both with her embroidery, etc. At 8 o'clock in the evening the priest from the Blagoveschensky Church and four nuns from the Ivanovsky Monastery came. The suite gathered in the hall, arranging themselves by rank in a precise order; the servants arranged themselves to the side, also by rank. Whenever the former tsar and family came through the side doors, they also arranged themselves in the same exact order: Nicholas II to the right, next to him Alexandra Fyodorovna, then Aleksei, and then the princesses. All those present met them with deep bows. The priest and nuns too. Candles were lit around the icon stand. The service began. The whole family piously crossed themselves; the suite and the servants followed the movements of their former masters. I remember that this whole situation made a profound first impression upon me. The priest in garments, the black nuns, flickering candles, the weak singing of the nuns, the visible religiosity of the prayerful, the image of the saviour. A string of thoughts gave way one to another.

"What are they praying about, what does this former royal family ask for? What do they feel?" I asked myself.

The nuns began to sing, "Glory to God in the highest and on earth, peace, goodwill toward men." Nicholas II's whole family got on their knees and fervently crossed themselves. Following suit, all the rest fell on their knees as well. At the time it seemed to me that the former tsar's whole family sincerely immersed themselves in religious feeling and mood.

The service is ending. The anointing with oil begins. The priest turns to face the former imperial family. Nicholas II walks up to him first, then Alexandra Fyodorovna, then the heir, daughters, suite, and servants according to rank. And after that, the hall empties.

Prince Dolgorukov comes up to me.

"Mr. Commissar, when will we be allowed to go to church? Nicholas Aleksandrovich and Alexandra Fyodorovna asked me to find out," he asked me.

"As soon as everything is ready. I have not the slightest intention of depriving them of visiting church," I answered.

"What preparations are necessary?"

"Those that avert any unpleasantness and misunderstanding."

"I don't understand," the prince answers, chagrined.

"Don't think that unpleasantness that has only to do with me personally is what worries me; unpleasantness of an entirely different order is possible and I can't let that happen," I explained to the prince. But once again he did not understand me.

The point was that I was less afraid of efforts to run away or anything of that nature than I was of possible attacks by individual Tobolskites, who had already managed to send completely uncensored anonymous letters to Alexandra Fyodorovna, Nicholas, and even his daughters, though I held these up. All correspondence for the imperial family went through my hands.

And what if one of these authors took it into his head to toss out some joke while they were walking into church—to cast stones, shout an uncensored obscenity, and so forth? There would have to be a response, in any event. It is best to eliminate the possibility of such incidents well in advance.

And Kobylinsky and I tried to adopt all precautions against such possibilities.

Although the Blagoveshchensky Church was located only several hundred yards from the house where Nicholas II lived, without eliminating the inconveniences mentioned above we could not satisfy the family's requests. In fact, within a week everything was arranged.

THE POPULATION'S ATTITUDE TOWARD THE FORMER TSAR

Rumors were circulating in the press that "patriotic" demonstrations by huge crowds were going on in front of the Governor's House, that pilgrimages to this house are undertaken, and so forth. All these rumors were false from beginning to end. Never had there been nor could there be any patriotic demonstrations or pilgrimages. Perhaps they would have taken place if not for the notorious Grigory Rasputin, who had already discredited this family back in 1915 with his behavior and cynical bragging about being close to the imperial family. This impudent rascal behaved himself so shamelessly on his last visit to Tobolsk, so scandalously and brazenly, that he removed the last vestiges of the halo from the tsar's family. He was constantly drunk here, on drunken business he pestered women with dirty propositions and demanded that one of the local police officers to whom he had taken a liking be made a priest. Thanks to Rasputin, the notorious Varnava, whose negative side is well known to Tobolsk townspeople, was made bishop. "I made a bishop of you," Rasputin once wrote him. During my time in Tobolsk I had heard so much about Rasputin's dirty escapades that I do not know whether to believe them all. Rasputin, more than anyone, utterly ruined the imperial family's prestige in the eyes of the people of Tobolsk (and in theirs only?), though it was supposedly to bolster their authority that the family kept him at their court so long and made him so all-powerful. . . .

PASSING THE TIME

Before the onset of cold weather, the curiosity of the Tobolskites found satisfaction in the fact that they could see the imperial family on the balcony. On clear days the entire family, most often after lunch, would frequently come out onto the balcony, from which a view opened onto the city garden, the hilly part of town, and Freedom Street. At first the passersby on the street stared at Nicholas Aleksandrovich's family with great curiosity. A completely understandable and natural curiosity. The female inhabitants were most surprised by the princesses' hair: Why is their hair cut short like boys'? Alexandra Fyodorovna most often came out onto the balcony with knitting or sewing. Having sat down in a chair, she would get to work. Only from time to time would she admire the view of the town, which she would never have seen if it had not been for "fate." Nicholas Aleksandrovich visited the balcony least frequently of all. From the very first day that logs and a crosscut saw were brought, he spent a large part of the day sawing logs into firewood. This was one of his favorite ways of passing the time. I was astounded by his physical stamina and even strength. His usual coworkers in this work were the princesses, Aleksei, Count Tatishchev, and Prince Dolgorukov, but they all quickly tired and kept relieving one another while Nicholas II continued working. The same thing could be observed in games of *gorodki* [a type of skittles]: everyone would quickly tire while he remained indefatigable. In general, the former tsar was physically very healthy and loved movement. Sometimes he would walk around in the yard for hours, [alone] or accompanied by his daughters. In this sense, Alexandra Fyodorovna was his exact opposite. She displayed altogether little mobility. There was also a noticeable and significant difference between her and Nicholas II in terms of sociability. The children took walks more often with their father than with her. Alexandra Fyodorovna's reserve and inclination to solitude were striking. Perhaps one explanation was that she took the situation and the new surroundings much harder, but in any case, as far as I was able to tell, she was by her very nature Nicholas II's complete opposite. She preserved in herself all the qualities of a German—and a German with megalomania and an air of superiority. Her attitude toward her surroundings displayed itself in all of her movements. While Nicholas II readily, simply, and easily talked with each of the servants, callousness and arrogance were noticeable in Alexandra Fyodorovna's relationships. She never participated in games of *gorodki* or in sawing logs. Sometimes, however, she would express interest in the chickens and ducks that the cook had started raising in the backyard garden. There she felt herself to be somehow freer. I talked to her more than once there, but the topics were always chickens and ducks. But in the evening, the former imperial family gathered in the hall, where Doctor Botkin, Dolgorukov, Tatishchev, and Gendrikova together with Shneider joined them and spent time in conversation. Sometimes someone would read aloud. But this reading was not always successful, for the listeners got tired of remaining silent and started up a conversation, and some even fell asleep to the monotonous sound of it.

"Mr. Commissar, we frequently bring up the question of walking in town and even beyond it," Doctor Botkin said to me, recounting how the long evenings were spent in the Governor's House.

"We still haven't finished with the business of going to church. You know what that entails," I answered.

"It seems to me that your fears are unfounded. Their majesties don't have any thoughts of escape." (Botkin always used their titles like this.)

"I am afraid of that least of all," I objected. "There are many other reasons, but I don't have the right to divulge them."

"Then I will petition the Provisional Government myself."

"I don't object. You take it up."

After a few days the tsar asks me to see him. I appear. He excuses himself for the trouble.

"I would like to ask you to allow us to see the town. Why do you fear for us?"

"I don't have permission for that from the Provisional Government. Besides, there are other reasons."

"When will the permission come? We are interested in seeing the town, the churches. The town is quite old and historic."

"It seems you were here?" I asked.

"On the way somewhere—for a few hours," the former tsar answered somewhat reluctantly.

I personally had nothing against satisfying the former tsar's request to see the town, but, first of all, the instructions given me by the Provisional Government, and, second, the developing situation—and that was the biggest hindrance—on the whole ruled out this possibility. Something terrible was advancing on Russia following the events [mutiny] connected with General Kornilov. The Russian Revolution was entering a new phase.

THE SURROUNDING ATMOSPHERE

On the instructions of the Provisional Government, all correspondence of the former tsar, his family, and the suite was supposed to go through me. I admit that the obligation was entirely unpleasant and even disgusting. The point was that the Russian "patriots" apparently thought that all their letters addressed to the members of the former imperial family, no matter how smutty their content, would be immediately given to the addressees. Never in my life had I had to read such repulsive pornographic letters as at that time. And all this vileness was directed either toward Alexandra Fyodorovna or toward Nicholas II. Some letters with pornographically dirty pictures, crude to the point of outrage, I handed over to Colonel Kobylinsky. I said these were the letters of Russian "patriots," for I was deeply convinced that many of the authors of these letters were ready to grovel before Nicholas II and his family before the overthrow, when he was still all-powerful, and now composed such repulsive anonymous letters thinking that this was very good and witty. There were many sealed letters in revolutionary red envelopes with the revolutionary motto, "Long live the Russian Revolution." All the letters, and there were often very many, had to be carefully read through and then thrown into the fire; there were more than a few letters of a threatening nature. Such authors were to be found even in America, for letters in English were also received from there addressed to the daughters of the former tsar and containing proposals.

Sometimes so many such letters came that the entire morning was spent on this vileness.

Nicholas II himself and his family corresponded with very few of their relatives. The former tsar wrote only to his mother and to his sister Ksenia Aleksandrovna. The children corresponded with a wider circle and apparently this gave them great pleasure, for every time I came to the house where Nicholas's family was lodged I was almost always met by one of the princesses with a question: Were there any letters? It is interesting to note that Alexandra Fyodorovna and her children never wrote to Maria Fyodorovna. Even the children developed somewhat cold relationships with their grandmother thanks to the notorious known relationship between the latter and Alexandra Fyodorovna.

In addition to Russian newspapers, Nicholas II received English and French newspapers and journals. Someone who apparently knew the former tsar's tastes sent him rather cheerful little magazines. Nicholas Aleksandrovich liked reading these little magazines. There were no obstacles in delivering the newspapers and magazines, although this pleasure sometimes also caused distress: sometimes rumors were reported in the newspapers that strongly upset the former tsar's family.

"Tell us please, Mr. Commissar, why do the papers write what isn't true about us?" one of the princesses asked me once.

"What?"

"About the escape. You know that isn't true. You read it, of course."

"That is how some of our newspapers got used to doing things long ago. They want to make more money," I answered.

Novoe vremia [New times] and some other newspaper had actually published a lie about Nicholas II's escape, and I had to send an urgent telegram with a denial. But while this denial was on the way (and sometimes denials were not even published in newspapers) the canard had already flown through all of Russia and even made it to the front, stirring up the population. I even received inquiries and threats. Rumors about the detachment guarding the tsar being out of hand were circulating, causing, in a word, alarm and animosity.

The Tobolsk Soviet under the chairmanship of Doctor Varnakov asked me to stop in sometime "on a very important matter."

I stop in the next day.

"What's the matter?" I ask.

Those present are somehow at a loss, looking for a precise way to begin. After a brief silence, Varnakov is the first to speak.

"As far as we've managed to familiarize ourselves with the detachment, it seems not to be very politically developed."

"That means unreliable," Pisarevskaia and Kiselevich interrupted. "We can send for reliable people from Omsk, workers who are fully politically conscious."

"Omsk will send real men. Your detachment—" Pisarevskaia was the one to speak again. I did not let her finish but stated that any effort to replace the detachment with anyone else should once and for all be forgotten. ["]The consequences would be very unpleasant for you if I told the detachment about this. I won't allow interference while I am here. I ask you not to disturb me further with such conversations. I would like to see everywhere the same sort of discipline and level of development as in our detachment," I finished and left.

From that time on, the Tobolsk Soviet practically loathed me.

I would like to state for the record that the detachment (as initially constituted) presented itself as a military unit preserving all discipline. It stood out sharply from the local garrison soldiers for its neatness, sobriety, and exemplary behavior. While the local garrison soldiers could often be seen drunk, dirty, inconceivably dressed, our Guardsmen dressed cleanly, behaved themselves, and quickly began to win the hearts of the local women and servants. On these grounds, hatred, enmity, and jealousy of our Guardsmen had already surfaced among the local garrison soldiers. If there were no outright conflicts, it was because the local soldiers feared our Guardsmen.

THE EDUCATION AND INTELLECTUAL DEVELOPMENT
OF THE FORMER TSAR'S CHILDREN

Winter neared. Nicholas II and Alexandra Fyodorovna decided that Maria, Anastasia, and Aleksei must continue their education, which remained incomplete. Russian language, history, geography, arithmetic, and other lessons began soon thereafter. The teaching staff consisted of Countess Gendrikova, Shneider, Doctor Botkin, the Frenchman Gilliard, the Englishman Gibbs, and Nicholas II himself, who taught the children history. From my frequent encounters with and observations of this entire staff of teachers, I was amazed that such a family, which possessed all the means, did not surround the children with the best possible teachers, who could have given the children a real education and fostered their intellectual growth. With the exception of the Frenchman Gilliard and the Englishman Gibbs, the rest were just courtiers; even Doctor Botkin had acquired all the qualities of a courtier, and it went without saying that Gendrikova and Shneider had.

I was confirmed in this opinion more than once. Just how little attention was paid to the children's development could be judged by the interest with which they listened to the most ordinary things, as though they had never seen, read, or heard about anything. At first I thought this was simple bashfulness. But soon I came to realize that the situation concerning their education and intellectual development was very bad. Once, the former tsar asked me: "Could one more teacher be invited?"

Colonel Kobylinsky and I decided to suggest a teacher we knew.

"I have to confer with Alexandra Fyodorovna," the former tsar answered, thanking me for the offer. "Alexandra Fyodorovna and I together discuss all questions concerning the children's upbringing."

I raised no objection.

"Do you know this teacher well?" Nicholas Aleksandrovich asked.

"Colonel Kobylinsky knows her better than I do, and Alexandra Fyodorovna knows her from the Tsarskoe Selo infirmary and from the gymnasium where she taught for almost eight years," I answered.

"I am very, very grateful to you. I'll talk it over with Alexandra Fyodorovna and she will likely agree. We really have a shortage of teachers. I teach Russian history myself. I love Russian history."

"Unfortunately, history is taught one-sidedly in our schools, and the majority of teachers stick to the same old hackneyed routine. Only an independent reading gives a real understanding of history."

"Yes, yes. I love military history," Nicholas Aleksandrovich interrupted me. "Military history has always interested me."

It became clear in further conversation that the former tsar really did know Russian military history, but his general knowledge of the history of the Russian people was very weak: he had either forgotten or simply poorly understood the periods of Russian history and their significance. All of his discourse on these matters was reduced to a history of wars. Could such preparation make a teacher out of him even for children?

After a few days, the new teacher, Klavdia Mikhailovna Bitner, began giving lessons.

"What is the children's preparation like?" I asked her.

"There is a lot to be desired. I never expected to find what I did. Such grown children and they know so little of Russian literature, are so little developed. They have read little Pushkin, even less Lermontov, and have never even heard of Nekrasov, not to even mention any others. Aleksei hasn't learned the declension of numbers when used with words and has a hazy concept of Russian geography. What does this mean? How were they taught? There was every opportunity to arrange for the best professors and teachers—and this wasn't done."

"What are they most interested in, if they are interested at all? Perhaps court life killed everything inside them," I asked.

"They are interested in absolutely everything. They like it very much when one reads aloud to them. And I have to give you a compliment, Vasily Semyonovich: they like your tales about your travels very much."

"I didn't tell them anything special."

"Nevertheless, they love listening to your stories."

"You can already judge their development by that. You told them about the northern lights, about the Yakut, the Tungus. Didn't they even ask whether you had any written accounts of your trips?"

"You ought to read aloud to them Nekrasov's *Russian Women* and *Red-Nosed Frost*," I suggested to Klavdia Mikhailovna.[1]

"It will be interesting to see what impressions these poems make on them. I adore these poems myself. I'll do it right away tomorrow."

The next day Klavdia Mikhailovna told me what an astonishing impression the poems of Nekrasov made on all the children.

"How is it no one told us that we had such a wonderful poet?" the princesses asked.

"Everyone listened," Klavdia Mikhailovna recounted. "Even the former tsar and Alexandra Fyodorovna came. The children were delighted. Strange. How little they bothered about their development and education."

"There was no time to devote to their own children, to surround them with a healthy atmosphere and real people and not courtiers," Colonel Kobylinsky said. "Even a poor, ordinary family from the intelligentsia made better arrangements for their children. In those families, at this age the children are far more developed and better educated. . . ."

THE OCTOBER REVOLUTION OF 1917

News of this revolution reached Tobolsk in bits and pieces. It was impossible to get a true picture of what was happening in the capital cities. Kerensky's telegrams were very short and one-sided; the newspaper reports were notable for their strong partisanship and sparkled only with polemics. My position in Tobolsk had become extremely vulnerable, and I wanted more than anything for the Constituent Assembly to meet quickly and to relieve me of this difficult obligation. The October Revolution had a depressing effect, not just on the former tsar, but also on the suite. From the newspapers they saw what was happening in Petrograd. For a long time, Nicholas II suffered silently and never talked to me about this. But when newspaper accounts were received about the stealing of wine from the basements of the Winter Palace, he nervously asked me: "Can it be that Kerensky can't stop this willfulness?"

"Apparently, he can't. After all, a mob is a mob everywhere and at all times."

"How can that be? Aleksander Fyodorovich was chosen by the people. The people should submit, not act willfully. Kerensky is the soldiers' beloved," the former tsar said somewhat peevishly.

"We are too far from everything here; it's hard for us to judge the events in Russia. But for me all the excesses of the mob are understandable and not unexpected. Remember the Japanese war. You, Nicholas Aleksandrovich, remember the mobilization of 1914 in Kuznetsk, Barnaul, and other towns—how the recruits destroyed the buildings of the liquor monopoly, how they smashed the wineshops, the outrages they committed. For some reason, nothing like this happened in Germany and Austria. It would seem that there were no mobs there."

Apparently, my explanation was completely incomprehensible to the former tsar. After remaining silent for a few minutes, he said:

"But why ravage the palace? Why not stop the mob? Why allow the stealing and destruction of riches?"

The tsar pronounced these last words in a trembling voice. His face paled, the fire of indignation flashed in his eyes. Just at that moment, Tatishchev and one of the daughters walked up. The conversation on this topic was cut short. Later, I very much regretted this. I really wanted to find out for myself how the former tsar actually saw the unfolding events. Does he recognize that the "willful" mob was not prepared and reared yesterday, or this year, but by the preceding centuries of a bureaucratic regime that sooner or later had to provoke the mob to "willfulness"? Apparently, Nicholas II had poorly understood this willfulness in March 1917, but he pictured it even more poorly in October of the same year. For this, one had to know not just military history, which he taught his son, but the history of the people, the history of the mob. The rebellions of Stenka Razin, of Pugachev, the rebellions of military settlements were obviously forgotten by the former ruler. Apparently, he never asked himself the question, Why is it that nowhere else—not in Germany, France, or Austria—did the people and troops stir up such rebellions during wartime? Why was it possible only in our country, in Russia, where tsarist and bureaucratic power seemed so stable, indestructible? And yet it collapsed to its very foundation in the space of two or three days. Perhaps this is the fate of any despotic regime? We have seen many such examples in history. . . .

Even before I left Petrograd, I had told Kerensky and Kuzmin[2] that it would be necessary to arrange a school for the detachment, to present lectures so that the soldiers would not pine away and get out of hand from being bored and having nothing to do. Tobolsk is a godforsaken, small provincial town with a long, cold winter. Kerensky and Kuzmin were in complete agreement with me. As soon as I arrived in Tobolsk, I immediately took up this matter. There were many illiterate and semi-illiterate soldiers in the detachment. Some officers also agreed to help them study; I gave lessons myself to the ones who were more prepared: I read them lectures on natural history, geography, the history of culture, and so on. My aide, A. V. Nikolsky, taught accounting. In addition, I repeatedly gave talks and read lectures on different topics in the People's House for everyone who went there and for our detachment soldiers. Prior to the October events, the lessons went well and the soldiers eagerly attended the school. At the beginning of November, some completely stopped going to the school: evidently, they thought their educations were complete. Sometimes, they appeared at school and cracked stupid jokes about the senior groups who were learning geometry.

"Everyone wants to be a seminarian, a scholar," one of them once blurted out.

"You are interfering with studies," I said.

"Let the seminarians study, then."

"Get out of here," one of the students loudly shouted, "or you'll hear from me."

There were more than a few like this in the detachment.

In the barracks, they often prevented people from studying, provoking angry frustration and bitter gibes. The detachment's internal discord grew each day. All my efforts to reconcile the groups of soldiers came to nothing. I merely managed to soften the sharpness of the enmity between them. But even that was only temporary.

Finally, the dentist who was considered the former imperial family's regular dentist returned from the Crimea. Now I have forgotten his surname. I put him up with me, and he would go to the Governor's House to treat members of the former royal family. I do not know what convictions he had previously held, but in Tobolsk he told me that he was a Tolstoyan. It turned out that we knew some doctors in common. In the evenings we often talked a long time about Nicholas II's past. His stories fully confirmed my observations of the imperial family. They suffocated in the monotonous court atmosphere. They felt real spiritual hunger, a thirst to meet people from another milieu. But traditions pulled them down like a lead weight and made them slaves to etiquette. Whenever a noncourtier managed to show up in the royal family circle, that person instantly became an object of general attention—that is, if the clique of courtiers did not manage to get rid of him in time. That was the way it was with Grigory Rasputin. . . .

I received anonymous threatening letters from the front, from Omsk, Krasnoiarsk, Yekaterinburg, and even from Tobolsk residents themselves. Some letters even threatened to send a whole division because we had "let the royal family get out of hand" and had even let the tsar run away with one of his daughters. All these threats and accusations were based on the type of newspaper speculation that always distinguished those Russian press organs that only desired to sell more papers. Oh, how these newspaper lies poisoned my life! Not only were my telegrams with refutations not always published in these newspapers, but sometimes the post and telegraph office tried to prevent them from reaching the editorial offices of these mendacious newspapers. . . .

The natural world of Siberia apparently made a good impression on the imperial family. They often asked me about it. Their eyes were used to the soft, tender pictures of the south. The Russian dynasty was hardly interested in Russia's north. Every year they either went abroad or to the Crimea and the Caucasus. Having ended up in Tobolsk against their will— a place they would never have visited, of course, and knew about only by hearsay—they themselves now observed the particulars of these severe natural surroundings.

Siberia is my second home. After fourteen years of solitary confinement in the Shlisselburg Fortress and after a whole year of being moved among Siberian prisons and overnight stops on the way to exile under strict escort, I wound up free in Viliuisk at the end of February. At that time of year, despite the severe frosts, the sun stays on the horizon longer and its colors are so diverse, soft, and intricate that for whole hours I would admire the wonderful sky. I must admit that I fell deeply in love with northern nature the very first time I saw it. I felt close to it and started to study it and learn from it. It is understandable that in meetings with Nicholas's family the theme of our conversation was often Siberia and its natural surroundings. How little they knew! How little interested they had been in it previously! Their notion of Siberia differed little from the notions of Italian beauties who think that wolves and bears run along the streets of Siberian towns and that there are eternal snows and frosts in Siberia.

Under the influence of these stories, Nicholas Aleksandrovich often repeated his request to walk beyond town, and I had to refuse him every time.

"You have nothing to fear. If you think that I will decide to run away, appoint an escort," he would say.

"I already explained to you that that is the least of the obstacles."

"And if we take it up ourselves with the government?"

"Please do. Have I put any obstacles in your way on that score?"

"But we are appealing to you as a representative of the government. Alexandra Fyodorovna and I have now talked it over and decided to petition the government directly. But it seems to us that you could grant this request on your own authority."

Oh, how little Nicholas knew about what was happening all around, despite the fact that I gave him all the newspapers, from which it was evident that the Provisional Government had already fallen and been scattered and been replaced by the Soviets. Only here in Tobolsk province had the local soviet not taken power completely. The provincial commissar still held power, the town still had self-rule, and elections were held to the zemstvo [elective district council]. But the soviets, especially the Omsk Regional Soviet, had begun an insistent onslaught. Twice the Omsk Soviet's military commissar had given orders to transfer the former tsar and his family to a hard-labor prison and to arrest the provincial commissar. I did not see the necessity for resorting to such a measure. . . .

The preelection campaign for the Constituent Assembly had begun. The residents of Tobolsk turned to me to give a talk in the People's House in which I would set out the Constituent Assembly's program. I ended up having to give talks to the detachment and local garrison as well as in the People's House. It was as if, for a time, the preelection campaign distracted the provincial population from deep anger.

One morning, when I went to the Governor's House to hand over letters and journals, one of the princesses asked me:

"Could it really be true that the Constituent Assembly will send us all abroad?"

"Where did you get such information?"

"They write it in the newspapers."

"What does it matter what they write in the papers? The Constituent Assembly hasn't been convened yet, and nobody knows how they will decide this question," I answer.

The princess became embarrassed, and after a few minutes, she suddenly said, "It would be better if they sent us someplace else in Siberia but not abroad."

I looked at the princess and involuntarily asked myself what she meant.

"You don't want to leave Russia?"

"It's best if we stay in Russia. Let them send us deeper into Siberia. Have you also been elected to the Constituent Assembly?"

"Yes," I said.

"And will you leave soon? You could not go. Who will stay here in your place?"

I answered that if they did not send a replacement, I would have to stay but that I was making every effort to be at the Constituent Assembly.

I do not know why, but Nicholas II's family definitely didn't want me to go. The ladies-in-waiting, Botkin, and the others told me this more than once. . . .

1. Nikolai Nekrasov (1821–1878) was one of the most popular poets in Russia in the late nineteenth and early twentieth centuries. Most of his poems, including those mentioned here, dwelled on the sufferings of the Russian peasants and expressed, in a richly lyrical and innovative voice, strong moral criticism of the Russian social order.

2. Captain A. I. Kuzmin was deputy commander of the Petrograd military district and a close associate of Kerensky's. He was Pankratov's superior in the summer of 1917 when Pankratov was working as an organizer and lecturer in the cultural enlightenment department of the Petrograd garrison. Kuzmin was partly responsible for selecting Pankratov to serve as commissar in Tobolsk.

4

Death in Yekaterinburg

CCORDING to Pavel Matveev, a member of the guard that accompanied Nicholas on his journey from Tobolsk, when Nicholas realized that his destination was Yekaterinburg, not Moscow, he commented, "I would go anywhere at all, only not to the Urals," where, he had heard, the "mood" was "harshly against" him.[1] The comment may be apocryphal, like so much of the testimony of witnesses that has served as evidence, but even the fact that it was reported reflects the Urals' well-deserved reputation as a bastion of left-wing radicalism. This reputation was reconfirmed, according to other recollections, the moment of the group's arrival in Yekaterinburg, the capital of the "Red Urals." When the train approached the station on the morning of 30 April 1918, a huge crowd stood waiting on the platform. As the train pulled in, people began shouting for Nicholas and his family to be shown to them. Many yelled threats: "We ought to throttle them!" "Finally they're in our hands!" Even the station commissar called out, "Yakovlev! Bring the Romanovs out of the car. Let me spit in his dirty face."[2] Only the threat of force, supported by the local Communist authorities, ensured the safe transfer of the three Romanovs and their company to their place of confinement: the requisitioned home of a wealthy merchant named Ipatiev.

Upon entering the Ipatiev house, Alexandra penciled onto the window jamb her talismanic sign, the counterclockwise swastika, and the date, "17/30 Apr. 1918."[3] Three servants and Doctor Yevgeny Botkin joined the Romanovs in the house. Prince Dolgorukov, who accompanied the tsar as his aide, was arrested immediately after arriving in Yekaterinburg and placed in a local prison on suspicion that he had links to counterrevolutionary plots to free the former imperial family (Document 129).[4] The rest of the family, together with their tutors and other servants, were brought to Yekaterinburg under guard in late May. Arrests reduced that party as well: Nicholas's aide General Ilia Tatishchev, the lady-in-waiting Countess Anastasia Gendrikova, the children's language tutor and reader Yekaterina Shneider, and several others. The remaining servants and members of the suite—including the teachers Pierre Gilliard and Sidney Gibbs, and Alexandra's friend Sofia Buksgevden—were told to return to Tiumen and from there to go wherever they wished (many chose to remain in Yekaterinburg).[5] Most of the arrested would be shot shortly before or soon after the execution of the tsar and his family.

Every effort was made to ensure that the tsar and his family were guarded against attempts to free them. Concern about security was the primary reason they were moved to Yekaterinburg, and it remained a preoccupying theme in the correspondence between Moscow and Yekaterinburg and in the many rules and procedures stipulated for their confinement (Documents 126, 128, 129, 136). A high fence was built around the house, and later, when it was believed that the family might be signaling to people outside, the windows were whitewashed and, for added security, a second, higher fence was built.[6]

Guards were stationed both outside the house and within. In place of the Tsarskoe Selo soldiers who had guarded them in Tobolsk, a special Red Guard was recruited from among local factory workers, mainly from the large Sysert and Zlakozov plants. In early July the internal guard was replaced by a squad of men from the Cheka—the Extraordinary Commission for the Struggle with Counterrevolution and Sabotage.[7] Many of these guards viewed the assignment with pride and honor. One guard, the thirty-one-year-old metal turner Anatoly Yakimov, boldly admitted this before the White court that was accusing him of crimes against the tsar: "You ask me why I went to guard the tsar? I saw nothing wrong in this. . . . It seemed to me, and I still think, that there will be a 'good' and 'just' life only when there aren't any rich and poor, as there are now, and this will happen only when all of the people understand through education that such a life does not yet exist. I viewed the tsar as the number one capitalist, who always will be holding hands with the capitalists and not with the workers. For that reason, I did not want a tsar and thought it was necessary to keep him under guard, imprisoned for the safety of the revolution."[8]

The symbolic and expressive aspects of captivity in Yekaterinburg were as important as the practical. More than ever before, the men responsible for the family treated them as defeated political prisoners. Immediately after arriving in Yekaterinburg, the family were subjected to a strict search of their belongings. Nicholas "blew up at this," he wrote in his diary (Document 147, entry of 17 [30] April). According to his valet, who was present, Nicholas declared, "Until now I have dealt only with honorable and decent people." Boris Didkovsky, a member of the Presidium of the Ural Regional Soviet Executive Committee who supervised the search, responded bluntly, "I ask you not to forget that you are under investigation and arrest."[9] Letters and diaries written by the captives described the new, harsh conditions: intrusive sentries posted inside the house, even by the bathrooms, and living downstairs; refusal to allow the prisoners to keep their own money (they had to make specific requests); confiscation of their photographic equipment, which had given the family much pleasure over the years but might be used to supply information to conspirators; denial of requests that additional members of the royal suite who had accompanied them voluntarily to Yekaterinburg be allowed to join them in the Ipatiev house; severe restrictions on the frequency and length of walks in the garden, "so that this resembles a prison regime," Nicholas was told (Document 147, entry of 1 [14] May); orders forbidding guards to converse with the prisoners; a plain diet of black bread, tea, soup, stewed meat, noodles, and cutlets, served without linen or silver; the sealing and whitewashing of the windows, with only a single window remaining open during the hot weather, and that was allowed only after weeks of pleading and was soon covered with an iron grating (Documents 132, 135, 136, 147).[10]

At an everyday, personal level, many members of the guard behaved in a manner that further emphasized the reversal of power and status represented by the confinement of the tsar and his family. The persistent and blatant pilfering of personal belongings from the storage shed was part of a larger pattern of contempt for the prisoners. According to the valet, Terenty Chemodurov, "The behavior and the appearance of the guard were absolutely indecent: they were rude and unrestrained, with cigarettes between their teeth, and impudent in their manners; they inspired disgust and revulsion."[11] Other witnesses described the guards forcing the princesses to play revolutionary songs on the piano and making lewd remarks as the young women walked to the bathroom.[12] According to one worker-guard at his interrogation by the White army investigatory commission, the commandant in charge of the Ipatiev house, Aleksandr Avdeev—a worker who had headed the factory committee at the Zlakozov works—was "a real Bolshevik" who "often talked openly about how the Bolsheviks destroyed the bourgeois fat cats and took power from Nicholas 'the Bloody.' . . . He talked about the tsar with spite. He cursed him as much as he could and never called him anything but 'the bloody one' and 'the bloodsucker.'"[13]

Some of these stories may be exaggerations and even fabrications —they were told to White investigators by survivors from the tsar's suite or by former guards who had been arrested by the Whites and were on trial during the civil war for their role in persecuting and killing the tsar. The White investigators themselves posed questions and wrote reports that clearly sought to adduce every possible instance of the moral suffering of the tsar and his family at the hands of the Bolsheviks. Tales were solicited and readily believed, for they confirmed the perception of adherents to the old order that the revolution had brought rough and resentful plebeians to power. Though prejudiced in construction, this particular narrative of the revolution was in many ways justified.

Investigators who examined the house after the Czechs and Whites took Yekaterinburg found a great deal of "crude and cynical" graffiti in the downstairs guards' rooms, at sentry posts, on fences, in bathrooms, and on the outside walls of the house, including in areas where the family had walked. They found extensive doggerel about sexual relations between "Grishka and Sashura" (Rasputin and Alexandra), sometimes portraying Nicholas sitting nearby drinking, observations about the size of Rasputin's genitals, and numerous lewd drawings showing Rasputin and Alexandra in various poses. Nicholas was the target mainly of more explicitly political, but no less demeaning, graffiti. Much of it was in rhyme.

> To all of the peoples Nicholas said
> As for a Republic, go fuck yourselves instead

> Our Russian Tsar called Nick
> We dragged off the throne by his prick

> *Tsaria russkogo Nikolu*
> *za khui sdernuli s prestolu*

Nicholas was accused of "drinking the people's blood" and poisoning them with alcohol out of greed and laziness. Also scrawled were names and nicknames of guards, miscellaneous obscene exclamations and ditties, and pornographic drawings (sketches of genitalia and such) having no explicit reference to the Romanovs. There were also a couple of sentimental love poems ("Do you remember / sweet spring / on that aromatic / day in May . . . ") and a few Communist slogans ("Down with International Imperialism and capital and to hell with all monarchy").[14]

The emerging Bolshevik political culture nurtured a belligerent and plebeian tone and manner, especially as the fragile authority of the new regime was questioned and threatened. After the first couple of months in power—as the challenges of effective governing became more difficult and opponents became more vocal and organized—Lenin and other Bolsheviks began increasingly to use the language of class violence and terror. In an essay written (though not published) in late December 1917, Lenin declared (perhaps too bluntly for general publication) that there should be "no mercy toward the enemies of the people," but "war to the death against the rich and their lickspittles the bourgeois intellectuals, war against criminals, idlers, and hooligans," and a policy of "shooting on the spot one out of every ten idlers."[15]

Militant rhetoric like this became ever more pervasive and public. Talk about dictatorship, iron discipline, and shooting enemies became the norm among Bolsheviks. By late June 1918 "mass terror" in the fight against counterrevolution was explicitly on the agenda.[16] During the civil war years that followed, the leather-jacketed commissar, commanding and self-righteous in manner and with a Mauser at his hip, became the archetype of the Bolshevik.[17] The images and metaphors that infused Bolshevik rhetoric were increasingly martial and often evoked images of harsh combat between good and evil. As described in the 1920s by a Soviet linguist, the speeches of revolutionary activists were filled with "images of the avenger of the oppressed, images of iron and blood, rapacious beasts, hydras, hydras with millions of tentacles, and enormous fires spread over the earth by whirlwinds."[18] Verses written by a young working-class poet in 1918 typify the militant vision that many had of their revolution:

> Explode,
> Chop apart
> The old world!
> In the heat
> Of universal combat
> And in the red gleam of fires
> Be
> Merciless!
> Strangle
> The bony body of destiny!
> Slaves!
> With your teeth
> Tear to shreds
> The regal mantle,
> Trample
> The crowns of rulers![19]

Nicholas and other Romanovs, as symbols and representatives of the "old world" and the old authorities, were often the targets of such verbal assault. And the aggression escalated. Whereas in the early months after the abdication, demands in popular resolutions and appeals tended to be that Nicholas and perhaps Alexandra be imprisoned in a fortress and tried for their crimes, workers and soldiers were now inclined to demand that they be immediately "destroyed" and even to threaten direct action to assure this (Document 144).

By all accounts, this spirit was especially strong in the Urals, even before the onset of open civil war. Ural Bolsheviks had a well-established reputation for radical leftism, with a noted tendency toward autonomous action, social and political extremism, and violence.[20] Given this extremist tradition, we must admit the plausibility of the long-standing argument that the Ural Bolsheviks themselves decided to murder the tsar and his family and servants or, at least, that they overstepped Moscow's more limited authorization. We shall return to this question.

The Urals were a stronghold of not just extremist Bolsheviks but also radical socialists and anarchists who, by the early summer of 1918, were openly seeking the execution of the tsar. The commandant of the Ipatiev house, Avdeev, reported that from the moment Nicholas arrived in Yekaterinburg "anarchists were demanding immediate execution of the former tsar and insisting that we hand him over so that they might mete out his punishment."[21] There was apparently at least one armed attempt, in the middle of June, to raid the Ipatiev house in order to abduct and kill the tsar.[22] Word of the planned assault—which had the guards ready to evacuate the Romanovs from the house—and of the preemptive arrests of the "anarchist" conspirators reached Nicholas and Alexandra on 13 June (Document 147).[23] Clearly, the many rumors that the family had been killed, which had to be publicly denied over and over again, reflected real threats against them (Document 143).[24]

Nicholas's guards also had to worry about attempts to free the former tsar and his family. In émigré memoirs and in testimony before White jurists investigating Nicholas's murder, there are indications that rescue efforts were under way in June and July 1918. Various groups of monarchist officers and political figures were involved in these conspiracies, with the support, in some cases, of the German and the English governments. Doctor Vladimir Derevenko, who until late June was still allowed to come and go from the Ipatiev house to treat Aleksei, appears to have been the primary contact between the conspirators and the former imperial family.[25]

In late June the family received the first of several secret letters from "a group of officers in the Russian army" who were prepared, they claimed, to free them (Documents 137–142, 146). Depending on which sources one believes, the letters arrived and the answers were returned either hidden in the cork of a bottle of cream delivered with food that nuns from the nearby Novotikhvinsky Convent were allowed to bring to the family or carried by a guard claiming to be loyal to the tsar. Recent writers have judged the letters an elaborate fabrication, basing their conclusion on skepticism about the likelihood of such an effort and on the 1960s testimony of a former member of the Ural Cheka. The purpose of this elaborate and cruel charade, it is alleged, was to provide an opportunity to murder the family while they were fleeing (such as apparently occurred in Perm, where Grand Duke Mikhail was killed on the night of 12–13 June in an escape apparently staged by the local Cheka)[26] or, more likely, to provide evidence of a plot to rescue the family that could be used (and indeed was used) to justify their execution (Documents 151, 156).[27]

Whatever the true source of these offers of help, the family clung to them with hope, lying awake fully dressed on the designated night, waiting for their deliverers (Document 147, entry of 14 [27] June). The commissars and soldiers of the guard, upon discovering (or being told of) the secret letters, also seem to have treated the plan as real. According to Alexandra's diary, they grew more nervous; they guarded the one open window more closely and soon had a metal grating put across it (Document 150).[28] To the very end of their lives the Romanovs apparently hoped that they would be freed. When, after their execution, their bodies were stripped for burial, eighteen pounds of diamonds and jewelry were found sewn into their clothing and underwear (Documents 159, 160)—the financial resources they would have needed to survive in exile or until their restoration to power.

At the beginning of July, partly in response to these threats of rescue and assassination, responsibility for guarding the family was transferred to the local Cheka, the political security police. The commandant Avdeev and his deputy Aleksandr Moshkin were dismissed, and the latter was arrested for stealing from the Romanovs. The entire inner guard was replaced. The new commissar in charge was Yakov Yurovsky. According to his autobiography, he was a former watchmaker, photographer, and medical assistant who had been active in the social-democratic underground in the Urals and western Siberia since 1904.[29] According to testimonies given before White investigators by some of Yurovsky's family members (who as arrested relatives of the tsar's alleged murderer and as Jews facing a monarchist court certainly had reason to ingratiate themselves with their interrogators), Yurovsky was the son of a glassmaker and suspected thief, a convert to Lutheranism (while living in Berlin during the time of the 1905 revolution in Russia), and (according to his sister-in-law) an arrogant, greedy, and cruel despot who liked to say, "Those who are not with us are against us." The White investigator Nikolai Sokolov, in his book on the death of the imperial family, added his belief that Yurovsky's grandfather had been a rabbi in Poland.[30] Sorting out truth, deception, and prejudice in this evidence is more than difficult. What is certain is that after October 1917, Yurovsky was a leading figure in Yekaterinburg politics—a member of the Executive Committee of the Ural Regional Soviet, deputy commissar of justice for the region, chief of security for the city of Yekaterinburg, and a member of the collegium of the Ural regional Cheka, whose offices were in the American Hotel in Yekaterinburg. On 4 July 1918 he was named commandant of the House of Special Purpose, the Ipatiev house (Document 145), though in Yekaterinburg he remained subordinate to the authority of Filipp Goloshchekin, the regional military commissar, and Aleksandr Beloborodov, the chairman of the Ural Soviet, who were also regional party leaders.

Nicholas viewed the replacement of Avdeev and Moshkin and the inner guard as a response to the constant stealing of family belongings; and Yurovsky's immediate solicitude for the security of their property seemed to confirm this. The petty thievery ended, and, Nicholas noted, provisions brought to them by local nuns, which the previous guards had also pilfered, now began arriving in full (Document 147, entries of 21 and 23 June [4 and 6 July]). Although the worker-guards remained posted outside the house, they were expelled from the house itself and replaced with ten men who were unknown to the locals and were reportedly from the Cheka.[31] Nicholas and the local worker-guards referred to the new men as Latvians—a term often used to describe non-Russian Communists active in Soviet Russia but also, perhaps, a reference to the important role that ethnic Latvians played in the Cheka. In fact, the new men seem to have been a mixture of Magyars, Germans, Austrians, and Russians. Whatever their background, in the eyes of locals they all were outsiders and remained aloof.[32]

Yurovsky made increasing discipline and security a high priority. Upon taking command at the Ipatiev house, he immediately raised the number of guard posts around the house and drew up strict rules for both the internal and external guards: do not engage in conversations or read newspapers or books while on duty; march in single file when changing shifts; keep bunks carefully made and clean; put waste only in proper containers, and strictly maintain general cleanliness; and watch the prisoners carefully to be certain that they cannot run away or throw messages through a window into the street.[33] Even though the many petty abuses that the family had endured under the old guard ceased, Nicholas judged that under Yurovsky "life has not changed one bit" (Document 147, entry of 25 June [8 July]). The prison regime was more rigorous than ever.

Yurovsky's measures to augment security and regimentation at the Ipatiev house were practical, but they also reflected ideals of order and discipline that inspired Bolshevik and especially Cheka activists during these years. Plebeian crudeness and brutality had no place in the conduct of the model revolutionary. The founder and head of the Cheka, Feliks Dzerzhinsky, constantly reiterated his ideal of the Chekist as the most honest, just, and disciplined of people, as the most "pure in spirit," no matter how lethal his work.[34] This moralization of killing—offensive though it may sound now—is important to understand. Soon it would produce a vocabulary in which a political execution was a "purge" (*chistka*), a "cleansing." This was not a euphemism but the deliberate expression of a certain moral understanding. We can fairly assume that the same spirit inspired the executioners of the former tsar and his family and servants. Yurovsky's own cold-blooded recounting of that night's work (Documents 159, 160) reflected his personal ideal of doing the work of the revolution in a disciplined, professional manner; it probably also reflected his temperament and inclinations. That the course of events, as Yurovsky himself recalls, was so chaotic and filled with mishap—achieving moments of absurd burlesque amid horrible tragedy—must have been a troubling blow to his self-image.

Although security was much tighter after the Romanovs' transfer from Tobolsk to Yekaterinburg, it is not clear that anyone in authority decided exactly what to do with them until very shortly before their execution. On 19 May 1918, Yakov Sverdlov, chairman of the All-Russian Central Executive Committee of the Soviets and secretary of the Bolshevik party, reported to the party's Central Committee that the Presidium of the Central Executive Committee of Soviets had begun discussing the future of Nicholas Romanov. He added—for it magnified the urgency of a decision at the center —that the question was also being discussed independently by Bolsheviks and Socialist Revolutionaries in the Urals. "We must decide what is to be done with Nicholas. Decisions made so far have resolved nothing about our attitude toward Nicholas but have only instituted necessary precautionary measures." It was time, in other words, to move from a defensive to a proactive policy concerning the former tsar. In answer, the Central Committee authorized Sverdlov to begin discussions about the fate of the Romanovs with the Ural Bolsheviks.[35] Unfortunately, no available document reveals the content of these discussions. Nor do we know what decisions, if any, were reached by the party's Central Committee, or the Central Executive Committee of Soviets, or the Council of People's Commissars (Sovnarkom). The available protocols of the meetings of these bodies—some of which have been lost or remain classified—contain no mention of discussions about the fate of the Romanovs.[36] But some evidence points to further discussions in Moscow and to possible decisions.

Plans for a trial were clearly at the forefront of these discussions. The idea had been raised repeatedly from the moment the Bolsheviks came to power, and the growing threat to their power in the spring and summer of 1918 probably brought it onto the immediate agenda. Yurovsky recalled that plans to put Nicholas on trial were discussed in May 1918 (Documents 159, 160). Lev Trotsky, then people's commissar of war, by his own account, suggested in late

June or early July that because of the "bad situation in the Urals" the Soviet government ought to take steps to put Nicholas on trial immediately. He proposed "an open trial that would reveal a picture of the entire reign (policies concerning peasants, workers, nationalities, culture, the two wars, etc.). The trial ought to be broadcast to the whole country by radio. Reports on the trial ought to be read aloud and commented on daily in every rural district." Trotsky recalled that Lenin liked the idea of a public trial but felt that "there might not be time enough." And Trotsky himself was "preoccupied with other matters."[37]

Word of these discussions evidently reached a former tsarist minister imprisoned in Petrograd, who was told in early July by the head of the Petrograd Cheka that "Soviet power has decided to bring the actions of the former emperor before a people's court" and that the minister would be made to testify.[38] Also in early July, according to a deputy in the Ural Soviet, a member of the soviet's Presidium, Filipp Goloshchekin, while in Moscow discussing the military defense of the region, was told that the Ural Communists should prepare a local trial to which Trotsky could come as prosecutor.[39] All accounts agree that the various plans were scuttled by circumstances.

The Bolsheviks were facing a desperate crisis of authority and control. Armed counterrevolution and serious dissent within the revolutionary camp (which was viewed and treated as counterrevolution) were gathering strength. In the wake of the Brest-Litovsk treaty with Germany in March 1918, which many revolutionaries viewed as a cowardly sellout to militarism, the left wing of the Socialist Revolutionary Party (the Left SRs), which had initially formed a coalition government with the Bolsheviks, quit the Sovnarkom in protest and began a campaign of agitation against the Bolshevik "commissarocracy." At the same time, growing numbers of workers, soldiers, and peasants began to voice their opposition to Bolshevik policies and practices: the signing of the "treasonous" peace with Germany (Lenin admitted that its terms were "obscene" but insisted on the need for peace at any price); the failure to restore order to the economy and thus to end the "people's suffering"; the closure of even many socialist newspapers; and both political repression and too much freedom for enemies.[40] Often with Menshevik or Socialist Revolutionary support, an active minority of workers demonstrated and even went on strike against Communist policies, demanding new elections to the soviets and, in Moscow and Petrograd, organizing new anti-Bolshevik workers' councils.[41] So-called Left Communists also criticized many of Lenin's policies, and even influential allies like the writer and publicist Maksim Gorky openly denounced the Bolshevik leaders for betraying the humane ideals of socialism.[42] At the Fifth Congress of Soviets, which opened in Moscow on 4 July 1918, the Left SRs called for a vote of no confidence in the government and, when unsuccessful, walked out. On 5–6 July armed insurrections by SRs broke out in Moscow and other cities; in the turmoil an SR assassinated the German ambassador to Soviet Russia, Count Wilhelm von Mirbach, igniting a diplomatic crisis.

These challenges from the left appeared especially dangerous— and treasonous—against the background of foreign intervention and counterrevolution from the right. Allied troops had landed at Murmansk in March, and the Japanese took Vladivostok in April. In the middle of May 1918 the forces of the Czech Legion mutinied when the Communist authorities ordered them disarmed after a violent incident while they were leaving Russia. The legion was an army of thirty thousand former prisoners of war and defectors from the Austro-Hungarian army who had been fighting on the Russian side since 1917. According to a plan worked out between the Bolshevik government and Thomas Masaryk, the president of the Czechoslovak National Council, the legion had been traveling east on the Trans-Siberian Railroad toward Vladivostok, where ships were to pick the soldiers up and take them back to Europe to fight on the western front. Now in rebellion, they seized control of cities along the railroad line and allowed dissident socialists, liberals, and monarchists to establish anti-Bolshevik regional governments and armies under their protection. In the important Volga town of Samara, which fell to the Czech Legion in early June, the SR-led Committee of the Constituent Assembly (Komuch) formed a government and an anti-Bolshevik People's Army. In the western Siberian capital of Omsk a Provisional Siberian Government was formed, also in June, by a diverse mixture of Kadets, SRs, and monarchists.[43] Yekaterinburg, which lay midway between Omsk and Samara, was temporarily saved from falling into enemy hands chiefly because it was located on a rail route that ran north of the main trans-Siberian line. But Yekaterinburg was clearly a target. "The Revolutionary Red Urals are in mortal danger," read a proclamation in local newspapers on 28 June; workers and poor peasants were called on to "take up arms."[44] By the end of June, the Bolsheviks faced the likelihood that Yekaterinburg would soon fall, putting the tsar in the hands of counterrevolutionaries.

This threatening situation made a trial, at least of the sort that Trotsky envisioned, difficult and unlikely. But was there a further decision in Moscow? At the time and until the late 1980s, the official Soviet answer was that the Ural Bolsheviks decided to execute Nicholas and his family and staff on their own authority, receiving Moscow's endorsement only after the fact (Documents 151–156).[45] In the West, and now generally among writers in Russia, the virtual consensus is that "the command came from Lenin personally and from the top party leadership" and that recent evidence proves this "conclusively."[46] This scenario is plausible, but the evidence (even the recently declassified evidence) is circumstantial and indirect at best.

We know that at the very end of June and the beginning of July, Filipp Goloshchekin was in Moscow discussing the military defense of the Urals with state and party leaders. According to Pavel Bykov, a member of the Ural Regional Soviet, Goloshchekin was also sent to the capital to seek Moscow's approval for a decision to execute Nicholas made by the Ural Soviet. But Goloshchekin was rebuffed; the central authorities still wanted to hold a public trial and told Goloshchekin to return and prepare one.[47]

In fact, we do not know, and likely will never know, what was agreed upon when Goloshchekin was in Moscow. Even if Bykov's account is true as far as it goes, the possibility remains that a contingency plan was discussed. As military commissar for the Ural region, Goloshchekin certainly would have described the insecurity of Bolshevik power in Yekaterinburg and thus the difficulties and risks in arranging a public trial. There is some indication that a contingency plan was discussed. In the 1930s, Yurovsky stated that while Goloshchekin was in Moscow in early July "the center" decided "what to do if abandoning Yekaterinburg became unavoidable"—implying that this was a decision in favor of executing the former tsar (Document 160). Yurovsky's assistant, Grigory Nikulin, also later claimed that Sverdlov had told Goloshchekin, "If you can organize a trial, then organize it, but if not, well, you know what that means."[48]

We do know that on 16 July, four days after Goloshchekin's return to Yekaterinburg and the day on which the Ural Communists were making preparations for an execution at the Ipatiev house, Goloshchekin sent a telegram to Grigory Zinoviev—the Communist leader who was then head of the Petrograd Soviet—asking that he inform Moscow that the "trial" that had been agreed on when Goloshchekin was in Moscow "cannot be put off" owing to the military threat against Yekaterinburg (Document 149). Was "trial" a prearranged code word for *execution,* as Edvard Radzinsky and other writers have assumed? Or might the term have referred to plans for an actual trial that—perhaps as earlier agreed upon in Moscow—now had to be turned into summary justice?

Did Moscow respond with a direct order? If a decision to execute the former tsar and his family had already been made in Moscow, no such order would have been necessary. According to Yurovsky, however, an order to "exterminate the R——ovs" did arrive in Yekaterinburg sometime before 6:00 in the evening on 16 July (Document 159). Yurovsky's testimony that an order was given is important, especially because, when he wrote this as a confidential document in 1920, it contradicted the official line that Moscow only affirmed a decision made in Yekaterinburg. But Yurovsky's statement is not proof. It also raises more questions.

First, according to Yurovsky, the order came from the city of Perm, not Moscow. This is difficult to explain. On 7 July, Lenin had ordered that the head of the Ural Soviet, Aleksandr Beloborodov, be given direct wire access to the Kremlin.[49] This connection had already been used several times to send coded telegrams between Moscow and Yekaterinburg concerning military defense and was still in use on the day after the killings (Document 152).[50] Perm itself was an important administrative center in the Urals. During the preceding month, Beloborodov had been in regular telegraphic communication with Fyodor Lukoianov, head of the regional Cheka, and with other officials and representatives of the Ural Soviet who were then in Perm, concerning the Romanovs and other matters.[51] Perhaps *they* secured the order from Moscow, although it is not clear why this would have been necessary. Perhaps, as Radzinsky claimed, the order came through Reingold Berzin, the commander of the front against the Czech Legion.[52] These are speculations, of course, attractive because they point to Moscow as the source of the command. But there is another equally plausible possibility: the message from Perm was not an order from Moscow at all, but confirmation by leading members of the Ural Soviet (and Cheka) who were out of town that they supported the vote for execution. There may have been another, later telegram from Moscow, however.

The main evidence that a telegram ordering execution came from Moscow is a statement made in the 1960s by a member of the Kremlin guard who claimed that he had personally carried Lenin's message to the telegraph office "confirming" the "decision" of the Ural party committee to execute the former tsar and his family.[53] If such a telegram existed, all traces of it have vanished. Moreover, if there was such a telegram, it cannot have been the order that Yurovsky said was received before 6:00 P.M., for the telegram that Goloshchekin sent to Zinoviev asking for Moscow's approval (the only extant telegram between Yekaterinburg and the center from that day) was not forwarded to Moscow until 9:22 P.M. (Document 149). Perhaps another, earlier telegram had been sent directly to Moscow, or perhaps Lenin sent a later answer. Again, what little material evidence exists remains ambiguous and contradictory.

There is other testimony, however. Writing from exile in 1935, Lev Trotsky dismissed with contempt the official Soviet claim that the Ural Soviet's Executive Committee acted independently of Moscow. He recalled a casual conversation that he had had with Sverdlov, sometime after Yekaterinburg had fallen to the Czechs, in which Sverdlov told Trotsky that Nicholas and his whole family had been executed. Because Trotsky had been away from Moscow at the time, according to his own account, he asked Sverdlov, "Who decided this?" Sverdlov answered, "We decided it here. Ilich [Lenin] thought that we could not leave them a living banner, especially in the present difficult circumstances."[54] The historian Richard Pipes, like many other writers, has judged Trotsky's statement to be "incontrovertible positive evidence" that the order came from Moscow.[55] But there is a serious problem with Trotsky's testimony: Trotsky's claim that he was not in Moscow at the time of the decision. Trotsky wrote that he was away from Moscow from early July until after the fall of Yekaterinburg on 25 July and thus that he first heard the news of the execution in a conversation with Sverdlov during a later visit to Moscow. Yet in the official minutes of the meeting of the Sovnarkom on 18 July 1918, at which Sverdlov reported the execution of the tsar, Trotsky is listed as present (Document 154). Was Trotsky lying—part of his assault on Stalin's version of Soviet history—or confused? Or is the official record of the meeting in error? Again, the evidence is dubious and contradictory.

Finally, some circumstantial evidence suggests that Moscow may have approved the execution in advance. At a meeting on 2 July, the Sovnarkom appointed a committee to draft a decree nationalizing the properties of the Romanovs, which was approved by the Sovnarkom on 13 July but not published until the day the execution of the Romanovs was also announced, the 19th.[56] Richard Pipes speculates that this was the echo of a secret decision to execute the tsar. Another possible echo of this decision was heard two days later, on 4 July, when the commissars at the Ipatiev house and the inside guard were replaced by men associated with the local Cheka, the political police. "This was the execution squad."[57] And so it turned out to be, but to conclude from the results that execution was their mission from the start is speculation—and, as we have seen, there are other explanations for why the inside guard was replaced by disciplined Cheka men.

If the evidence points with any degree of consistency and reliability to a single story, that story is not the one repeated most often: that Moscow—indeed, Lenin personally—gave the order to execute the former tsar and his family and suite. The scenario more in keeping with the evidence is that the party and state leaders in Moscow, in discussions with Goloshchekin, the Urals' representative, in early July, ordered that a trial—to be held in Yekaterinburg—be prepared immediately; but if the military situation forced the evacuation of Yekaterinburg and if Nicholas and his family could not be safely removed to a secure location, then execution without trial would be necessary. This version of events stays closest to the evidence in hand, including documents and testimony long kept secret. Still, any author—including myself—who concludes that the truth can be stated with certainty, is overconfident in his or her omniscience or overzealous in the desire to tell a good story. Every answer to the question of who gave the order—and, indeed, to many questions about the Romanovs' final days—is based on a fair measure of deduction and imaginative speculation.

An official announcement appeared in the national press two days after the killing of the former tsar, his family, and what remained of their suite. It informed the nation that Nicholas had been executed on the order of the Presidium of the Ural Regional Soviet to prevent the tsar from being freed by White Guards, whose plot (Documents 137–142, 146) had been uncovered, and under pressure of the dangers posed by the rapid approach of "Czechoslovak bands." His "wife and son have been sent to a secure place" (Documents 155, 156).

This official announcement is now generally seen as disinformation: the entire family had been killed and Moscow knew it. But even if we assume a deliberate lie, questions remain about what sort of disinformation it was, about the meaning of the lie. Most authors have judged that the official claim that only Nicholas had been killed reflected Bolshevik anxiety about how popular opinion would react to the murder of innocent women and children. Questions can certainly be raised about this reading of public opinion and especially this view of Bolshevik sensibilities. One also has to wonder why there was no mention in the official announcements of the daughters —certainly the most innocent victims. It is worth considering another explanation of this apparent public lie.

Even if we find convincing the indirect evidence that the leadership in Moscow gave preliminary approval for an execution, we must contend with the virtual silence in this evidence about precisely who the intended victims were. It is altogether possible that the Ural Soviet had been authorized, either directly or in case of necessity, to execute only Nicholas. Hence the need for Beloborodov to inform Moscow that "the entire family suffered the same fate as its head" (Document 152). Hence the official story that Yekaterinburg had taken matters into its own hands. Hence the claim that the family had been evacuated—reflecting, perhaps, confusion over what had actually occurred or an attempt to cover up what Moscow had not intended. This possible scenario is no less consistent with the evidence—fragmentary, vague, inconsistent, and often unreliable—and the political dynamics of the time than the generally accepted story that Moscow ordered the execution of the entire family and that Yekaterinburg did what it was told.

Speculation in the face of very imperfect evidence has flourished around stories about the survival of part or all of the imperial family. The testimonies of men who participated in the execution and in the destruction and burial of the bodies, the recovery of the remains in 1991, genetic and anthropological tests on the remains, and DNA tests on a portion of the remains of Anna Anderson (the most plausible claimant to be the surviving Anastasia, until recent DNA tests precluded any genetic link to the royal family) all strongly suggest that stories of survival are fictive.[58] But the stories themselves are not so easily dismissed.

Contemporary testimony by a large number of witnesses still stands as baffling counterevidence. Immediately after the family was allegedly killed, witnesses began coming forward with stories of a train on which Alexandra and her children were seen traveling to Perm and, most often, of a young woman, clearly injured and traumatized, who claimed to be one of the tsar's daughters. She had presumably escaped from the Ipatiev house before the execution, fled during the transfer of the family to Perm (if that story was true), or survived the execution attempt (protected by her diamond-filled corset) and fled or been helped to escape during the mishap-filled transport of the bodies for secret burial. Now in the hands of Cheka guards, she had evidently been beaten by local police and possibly raped and was apparently killed soon after these reported sightings. Much of this testimony concerning the train to Perm and the mysterious battered young woman was recorded by White investigators compiling evidence concerning the murder of the tsar and his family. The first of these investigators, Aleksandr Kirsta (chief of criminal investigations in Yekaterinburg under the Whites) and Ivan Sergeev (a justice in the Yekaterinburg circuit court), considered the evidence convincing enough to conclude that only Nicholas and perhaps the heir had been executed.[59]

The evidence that the whole family was killed is itself problematic. Official Soviet documents reproduced in a book published in

1974 by the Holy Trinity Orthodox Monastery in Jordanville, New York, show that the entire family and their servants were killed.[60] But these documents are almost certainly forgeries.[61] A more convincing document is the coded telegram that Beloborodov sent to Moscow on 17 July reporting that "the entire family suffered the same fate as its head" (Document 152). Because it was found by White investigators in the Yekaterinburg telegraph office, some researchers have argued that it, too, is a forgery, fabricated by the investigators, who needed the story of the entire family's execution for political reasons.[62]

The discovery of the bodies in 1976 and their exhumation in 1991 appear to provide the strongest material support for the case that the whole family was massacred. Mitochondrial DNA studies of the remains and computer imaging of the skulls and bones have confirmed that the bodies of Nicholas and Alexandra and three of their children (together with Doctor Botkin and three servants) were just where Yurovsky had said they would be. But the bodies of two members of the family—eventually identified as Aleksei and Maria—were missing. Yurovsky had explained this: two of the corpses were burned and the remains buried apart from the main grave (Documents 159, 160). It is conceivable that he might have said this to cover up the embarrassing fact that two of the victims, discovered to be alive, protected by their jeweled corsets (Aleksei was also likely wearing one), had been removed from the truck by sympathetic soldiers while it was halted for a time en route to the burial site.[63] Again we turn to speculation and rumor to account for the inadequacies of the evidence. Complicating matters further are the doubts about the forensic tests and their results recently expressed by Russian officials involved in the investigation of the remains. Among the problems: investigators are still not certain which bones belong to Nicholas II and which to his cook, Kharitonov.[64]

Even if all of the stories of survival are eventually proven false, the fact that they have been believed for so long should remind us not only of the inadequacies and contradictions of the evidence but also of the power of assumptions, motives, and imagination to shape the way we make sense of the "facts" that come to us from the past. One of the witnesses to survival, Boris Solovyov (the husband of Rasputin's daughter), recognized this when he told investigators that although he was among those who believed that the family still lived, such beliefs were inspired less by facts than by "faith and feeling."[65]

The "true" story of the death of the last tsar and his family, which the documents presented here tell, is not a simple or straightforward tale. The varied evidence and claims will provoke different readings and judgments as readers think about the documents interpretively and react to them emotionally, morally, and politically. The stories themselves are contradictory and multidimensional. The testimonies are shaped by perceptions and memories of a traumatic time and by a mixture of judgment, desire, and intention. The official documents—telegrams, minutes of meetings, reports— are shaped and sometimes distorted by assumptions and purposes. Readers should not allow their own judgment to obstruct their ability to see the conflicting and uncertain stories and meanings these documents contain. The death of the Romanovs may be seen as tragic martyrdom, or the first bloody signpost of twentieth-century totalitarianism and state terror, or an act of bloody retribution for past abuses, or even the pursuit of justice. But these events are also filled with doubt, confusion, misadventure, farce, and quite ordinary human responses to extraordinary times and events.

· 124 ·

Telegram from Aleksandr Beloborodov, chairman of the Ural Regional Soviet, to V. I. Lenin, chairman of the Council of People's Commissars (Sovnarkom), and Yakov Sverdlov, chairman of the All-Russian Central Executive Committee of Soviets (VTsIK), on the transfer of Nicholas to Yekaterinburg, 30 April 1918.

Military priority
2 addresses. Moscow.
To Lenin, Sovnarkom chairman. To Sverdlov, TsIK chairman
From Yekaterinburg.

I received the former tsar Nicholas Romanov, the former tsaritsa Alexandra, and their daughter Maria Nikolaevna from commissar Yakovlev today, 30 April [at] 11 o'clock Petrograd [time]. They are all situated in a private house under guard. Telegraph me your inquiries [and] clarifications.

> Chairman of the Ural Regional
> Soviet, Beloborodov

· 125 ·

Letter from Maria in Yekaterinburg, with postscripts from Alexandra and Nicholas,
to Olga in Tobolsk, 1 May 1918.

———

Yekaterinburg 18 April (1 May) 1918

Christ is risen!

IN my thoughts I kiss you thrice, my dear Olga, and greet you on this joyous holiday. I hope that you will have a quiet holiday. Give our greeting to all of our people. I write you while sitting on Papa's cot. Mama is still in bed as she got very tired and her heart is no. 3 [*sic*]. We slept, the three of us, in a cozy white room with four big windows. The sun shines as it does in our hall. The upper pane is open and the chirping of birds can be heard; the elec. [electric] streetcar too. It's quiet on the whole. A demonstration was held in the morning: May Day. We heard music. We live on the lower floor; around us is a wooden fence; we can see only the crosses on the cupolas of the churches on the square. Niuta [Demidova] sleeps in the dining room, and Yev. Serg. [Yevgeny Sergeevich Botkin], Sednyov, and Chemodurov sleep in the big drawing room. The prince [Dolgorukov] has still not been allowed in. I don't understand why and feel very bad for him. Everyone is sleeping on cots that were brought last night for them and the guards. The house owners are the Ipatievs.[1] I kiss you warmly and bless you, my beloved little dear.

Your old mother is always with you in her thoughts, my dear Olga. The three of us are constantly talking about you and wonder what all of you are doing. The beginning of the trip was unpleasant and depressing; it was better after we got into the train. It's not clear how things will be here. [Alexandra]

The Lord protect you. I embrace you thrice, my dear. Papa

Niuta darns stockings. We made beds together in the morning. Christ be with you. We kiss the ladies and nannies.

> Your M. [Maria]

1. While the former imperial family was in residence, the Ipatiev house was often officially called the House of Special Purpose. It was named after its last owner, Nikolai

Nikolaevich Ipatiev, a retired captain of the army corps of engineers and a prominent Yekaterinburg merchant (he emigrated and died in Prague on 22 April 1923). Prior to 1945, the house bore a memorial plaque and served as a museum for displaying belongings of the executed imperial family. In 1977, while Boris Yeltsin was Communist party leader in Yekaterinburg, the Ipatiev house was razed, presumably because pilgrimages to the site, which had begun in the 1960s, were increasing in frequency.

· 126 ·

From the protocol of a session of the Sovnarkom, on the transfer of Nicholas and his family to Yekaterinburg, 2 May 1918.

Chaired by: V. I. Ulianov (Lenin).

Those present: Lenin, Shliapnikov, Larin, Vinogradov, Vinokurov, Sereda, Rozin, Petrovsky, Latsis, Kozmin, Nevsky, Khodorovsky, Kritsman, Chicherin, Gukovsky, Shelomovich, Nogin, Smirnov, Pravdin, Rykov, Karakhan, Podbelsky.

. . .

HEARD: 4. A special report by Sverdlov.

RESOLVED: 4. To submit for publication the following announcement by Sverdlov.

"In November or December of last year, the question of the former tsar was raised in the Presidium of the Central Executive Committee [TsIK]. A whole series of events caused this question to be deferred. A month ago, a delegate from the tsar's guard appeared at the TsIK Presidium and reported that things were far from well with the guard: some of the guards had run away; the neighboring peasants had received payment. By all reports coming from Tobolsk, there was no certainty that Nicholas Romanov would not get the chance to escape from Tobolsk. Different reports indicated that various monarchist groups were undertaking some preliminary steps in this direction. Because of these reports, the Presidium of the All-Russian Central Executive Committee of Soviets ordered that former tsar Nicholas Romanov be transferred to a more secure location, which was done. At present, Nicholas Romanov, his wife, and one daughter are in Yekaterinburg, Perm province, and the task of guarding them has been assigned to the Ural Regional Soviet."

Chairman of the Council of
People's Commissars,
V. Ulianov (Lenin)
Secretary of the Council [of
People's Commissars], L. Fotieva

· 127 ·

Letter from Alexandra and Maria to Olga in Tobolsk, 2 May 1918.

————

Yekaterinburg   19 April (2 May) 1918

Christ is risen!

I KISS you warmly thrice, my little dear. My health is better today, but I'm still in bed. The others walked for an hour in the tiny garden and were very glad for it. A barrel full of water was brought so that Father can have a bath of nine l. [liters] before lunch. [Alexandra]

I swung on an American swing with Niuta and walked to and fro with Papa. Mama is lying down on a cot today and is a bit better, but her head and heart ache. We asked that a list be drawn up of all those coming with you. I hope they didn't forget anyone. I don't know who Iza will bring. We have to explain the reason for each person being with us. Oh, how difficult it all is again. We lived in peace for 8 m. [months], and now it's starting all over again. I feel so sorry that you must pack and arrange everything by yourselves. I hope Stupel[1] will help. If only we could get news from you more quickly. May the Lord protect you.

Masha

1. Stupel (only his family name is known), court cloakroom attendant who remained with the imperial family during their Siberian exile.

· 128 ·

Telephonegram from Yakov Sverdlov, VTsIK chairman, to Aleksandr Beloborodov, chairman of the Ural Regional Soviet, on the conditions of the imperial family's confinement, 3 May 1918.

————

Received on 3 May 1918 at 23:50
From Moscow, Kremlin.

Note.

I propose maintaining Nicholas in the strictest way. Yakovlev is charged with transporting the others.[1] I propose sending an estimate of all expenses, including the cost of the guards. Notify me of the details of the new conditions under which they will live.

VTsIK Chairman, Sverdlov

1. Because the Executive Committee of the Ural Regional Soviet had accused special commissar Yakovlev of a counterrevolutionary attempt to remove the former tsar without its

approval, Yakovlev refused the further assignment of transferring the tsar's children from Tobolsk to Yekaterinburg. Yakovlev returned to Moscow to report to Sverdlov, and Khokhriakov was given the task of completing the transfer of the Romanov family to Yekaterinburg.

· 129 ·

Telegram from Beloborodov to Sverdlov on adopting stricter procedures for guarding Nicholas and his family, [4 May 1918].

_____

From Yekaterinburg.

Secret.

Response to your note [Document 128]. To maintain [conditions of] strict arrest, meetings with unauthorized persons [are] absolutely not allowed. Cheliad [Chemodurov] and Botkin are [in] the same position as the arrested. Prince Vasily Dolgorukov [and] Bishop Germogen were arrested by us; do not respond to any of their mediators' declarations [and] complaints. Papers taken from Dolgorukov clearly show the existence of a plan of escape. There were rather major disagreements [with] Yakovlev, and, as a result, we parted coldly. By resolution, we rehabilitated him [from] accusations [of] counterrevolutionary activity, recognizing the influence of excessive nervousness. He is now at the Ashabalashevsky factory. Today we are telegraphing him to set out for the final fulfillment of the mission. Telegraph the special purpose detachment in Tobolsk not to worry, their comrades are in Yekaterinburg. We'll take care of paying salaries to the disbanded soldiers in the special purpose detachment ourselves through Yakovlev. We'll send an estimate.

Beloborodov

· 130 ·

Letter from Beloborodov to plenipotentiary representative Pavel Khokhriakov on the transfer of the imperial family and the need to arrest counterrevolutionaries in Tobolsk, 6 May 1918.

_____

Yekaterinburg   6 May 1918

Comrade Khokhriakov!

You will receive this letter together with an authorization from Com. Rodionov,[1] a Left SR [Socialist Revolutionary] who has been assigned to

Tobolsk to replace the drunken head of the detachment and [instructed] to hand the authorization over to you.

We had a small misunderstanding here with Matveev,[2] the chair. of the detach. comm.: we arrested all eight of these persons [soldiers in the detachment committee] for refusing to follow the [Ural] Regional Soviet's orders. Later we reached agreement, however, and we parted friends. They promised to help fulfill the mission. We think it makes no sense not to trust them, especially since a large portion of the task has been accomplished.

In addition to this, you are requested to levy taxes on Tobolsk and to deal with counterrevolutionaries in the most merciless manner. Arrest whomever you think should be arrested. If information of a serious nature is exposed, bring them to Yekat. as you did concerning Germogen.

A letter has been sent to the chair. of the Tiumen Soviet with the proposal that a detachment not be sent.

With com. [comradely] greetings,
A. Beloborodov

1. Rodionov (possibly a pseudonym) was chief of the Red Army detachment of "Latvians" who arrived in Tobolsk to transfer the imperial family, and he succeeded Kobylinsky as the last commandant of the Governor's House. Together with commissar Khokhriakov, he oversaw the transfer of the tsar's children from Tobolsk to Yekaterinburg.

2. Pavel Matveevich Matveev, a Bolshevik, was chairman of the soldiers' committee of the special purpose detachment responsible for guarding the imperial family in Tobolsk. As a member of the detachment headed by Yakovlev, he escorted Nicholas from Tobolsk to Yekaterinburg.

· 131 ·

Letter from Anastasia to her sister and parents in Yekaterinburg, 7 May 1918.

———

Tobolsk   24 April 1918 (7 May) 6:00 P.M.

Truly He is risen!
My dear, sweet Mashka,

WE were so terribly happy to get news [in your letter], and [we] shared our impressions! I apologize for writing crookedly on the paper, but this is just my stupidity. What we rec. [received] from An. Pav. was very sweet; [sends] regards, etc., to you. How are you all? Sashka and so on? You see, of course, that there are always a huge number of rumors; well, and you understand how hard it is and one doesn't know whom to believe and sometimes it's all so disgusting! As they only tell you the half of it, but not the rest, and that's why we think he's lying. Ks. Mikh. [Ksenia, actually Klavdia, Mikhailovna] Bitner comes and spends time with the little one. Aleksei is so sweet; he eats and tries so (remember how it was at the little bench when you were here?). We take turns having breakfast with Aleks. [Aleksei] and making him eat, although there are days when he eats without needing to be told. Dear ones, in our thoughts we are with you all the time. It is terribly sad and empty; I really don't know what possesses me. The baptismal cross is with us, of course, and we got your news. So. The Lord will help and does help. We arranged the iconostasis terribly nicely for Easter, all in spruce, which is the way they do it here, and flowers. We took pictures. I hope they come out. I continue to draw, not too badly they say; it's very pleasant. We swung on the swing; boy, did I laugh when I fell off so splendidly! Yes, quite! I told the sisters so many times last night that they are sick of hearing about it, but I could tell it again and again, although there is no one left to tell. In general, there is a whole trainload of things to tell you all. My Jim[1] has caught cold, and coughs, so he sits at home and sends regards. There was such incredible weather! One could shout from the pleasantness of it. Strangely enough, I tanned more deeply than anyone else, a regular Arab woman!? But these days I am boring and not pretty. It's cold, and this morning we froze, although we were inside, of course, and didn't go out. I very much apologize: I forgot to extend good wishes to all you dear ones on the holiday; I kiss you all not thrice but heaps of times. My dear, all of us thank you for the letters. There were demonstrations here too, but they weren't much of anything. We sit here together as always, but you are missed. Tell precious Papa that we are very grateful for the figs; we are savoring them. I apologize, of course, that this is such a jumbled letter; you understand that my thoughts are flying and I can't write everything and so put down whatever comes into my head. Soon we'll go for a walk; summer hasn't come yet and nothing is blooming, but things are starting to come up.

You know, I want to see you so much it's sad. I go for walks and then I'm back. It's boring whether you go out or not. I swung. The sun came out, but it's cold and my hand can barely write.

Your regards were transmitted to us word for word, and we send you a big thanks and the same. In the evenings we sit around; yesterday we told fortunes using the book. You know which one. Sometimes we work.

We do everything they ask.

A kiss to you [Maria] and to you dear ones and much else I won't enlarge on, for you will understand. Thought about it already some time ago. Russa [?], although sweet, is strange and makes one angry, for she doesn't understand and simply can't bear it. Once I was almost rude, a real cretin. Well, it looks as if I've written enough silliness. Right now I'll write some more, and then I'll read it later, during free time, that is. For now, good-bye. I wish you the best, happiness, and all good things. We constantly pray for you and think, Help us Lord. Christ be with you, precious ones. I embrace all of you tightly and kiss you.

A. [Anastasia]

1. Jim (Jimmy), Anastasia's pet dog. After the imperial family was executed, the dog was also apparently killed. White Guards discovered the dog's corpse, together with various small objects that had belonged to the Romanovs and their suite, in a mine near Yekaterinburg.

· 132 ·

Letter from Maria with a note by Alexandra to the children in Tobolsk, 10–11 May 1918.

No. 16   Yekaterinburg   27 Apr. (10 May) 1918

WE miss the quiet and calm life in Tobolsk. We get nasty surprises here almost every day. Members of the regional committee [Executive Committee of the Ural Regional Soviet] were just here and asked each of us how much money we have with us. We had to sign our names to it. As you know, Papa and Mama haven't got a cent with them; they signed that they had nothing, and I signed that I had 16 rubles and 17 kopeks that Anastasia had given me for the trip. They took all the money away from everyone else for safekeeping by the committee; they left everyone a little bit—gave them a receipt. They warned us that there are no guarantees that we won't be searched again. Who would think that after 14 months of imprisonment we would be treated like this? We hope you have it better—the way it was when we were there.

28 Apr. (11 May)

Good morning, my dears. We just got up and lit the stove, for it has gotten cold in the rooms. The firewood crackles invitingly; it reminds me of a frosty day in T. [Tobolsk]. Today we gave our dirty linen to the laundress. Niuta has also become a laundress, and [she] washed Mama's kerchief and the dust rags very well indeed. We have had Latvians as part of the guard for a few days now. It's probably not very cozy at your place [with] everything packed. Were my things packed? If they didn't pack the birthday book, then ask N. T. to write. If it doesn't work out, that's all right. You must be coming soon now. We know nothing about you and very much await letters. I continue to draw according to Bem.'s book. If possible, you might buy some white paint. We have very little of it. In the fall, Zhilik got some good paint, flat and full. Who knows, maybe this letter will reach you the day before your departure. May God bless your trip and protect you from all evil. I so want to know who will accompany you. Tender thoughts and prayers surround you. Only to be together again quickly. I kiss you warmly, sweet, dear ones, and bless you.

Sincere regards to all and to those staying as well. I hope that Al. [Aleksei] is feeling stronger again and that the trip won't tire him out too much. Mama

We'll go walking today, for it's warm. They still haven't let us see Valia [Dolgorukov]. Regards to Vl. Vas. and the others.[1] I very much regretted that I didn't have time to say good-bye. It will probably be very sad for you all to leave T. [Tobolsk], the cozy house, and so on. I remember all the cozy rooms and the garden. Do you swing on the swings, or has the board broken? Papa and I kiss you sweet ones warmly. May God protect you. I send regards to everyone in the house. Does Tolia come to play? All the best and have a good trip if you are already leaving.

Your M. [Maria]

1. Most likely a reference to members of the guard with whom the children had become friendly.

· 133 ·

Diary of Maria Grigorievna Solovyova (Rasputina),[1] 22 May 1918.

———

9 [22] May

What happiness has befallen me! Today I saw the imperial children entirely by accident. I went [to Tiumen] to the pier for tickets and saw a ship docked there; but no one was allowed [near]. I miraculously got through to the cashier's and suddenly Nastia [Gendrikova] and the little one [Aleksei] saw me through a ship's window; they were terribly happy. [Saint] Nicholas the Miracle Worker arranged this. Now Boria[2] and I are going to Abalak.[3] Boria is in a very good mood, which makes me happy. What a pity that I couldn't say a word to them! They were like angels.

1. Maria (Matryona) Grigorievna Solovyova (Rasputina), daughter of Grigory Rasputin. After September 1917, she lived in her native village of Pokrovskoe in Tobolsk province.
2. Maria Solovyova's husband, Boris Solovyov. He was involved in efforts to free the tsar and his family.
3. Abalakovsky Monastery, which was located near Tobolsk. Representatives from the monastery maintained contact with the tsar and his family in exile.

· 134 ·

Document given to the Ural Regional Soviet and signed by Klementy Nagorny[1] expressing
his willingness to serve the imperial family and submit to the prison regime of the
Ipatiev house, 24 May 1918.

I, the undersigned cit. [citizen] Klementy Grigoriev. [Grigorievich]
Nagorny, from Kiev prov. [province], Svirsk district, Antonovsk section of
the village of Pustovarova, sign this document stating that I wish to continue to be of service to the former tsar Nicholas Romanov and pledge to
submit to and fulfill all orders of the Ural Regional Soviet issued by the
house commandant and to consider myself in the same circumstances as
the rest of the Romanov family.

K. Nagorny

24 May 1918

1. Klementy [Klim] Grigorievich Nagorny, former sailor with the imperial yacht *Shtandart*. Nagorny protected and looked after Aleksei in Tobolsk and Yekaterinburg, then was
arrested at the Ipatiev house, imprisoned, and shot by the Cheka together with Ivan Sednyov.

· 135 ·

Letter from Doctor Yevgeny Botkin to the Ural Regional Soviet Executive Committee
requesting that Pierre Gilliard and Sidney Gibbs be allowed into the Ipatiev house to care
for the patient Aleksei Romanov, 24 May 1918.

To Mr. Chairman:

As the doctor who has, for the past ten years, looked after the health
of the Romanov family generally and of Aleksei Nikolaevich in particular,
I appeal to you, Mr. Chairman, with the following most fervent request,
since the Romanov family is now under the jurisdiction of the [Ural]
Regional [Soviet] Executive Committee. Aleksei Nikolaevich, whose treatment is directed by Doctor Vl. Nik. Derevenko, is subject to trauma to the
joints caused by bruises, inescapable for boys of his age, which result in the
pooling of fluid in the joints and produce severe pain. In these instances,
the boy is in such indescribable pain day and night that no one from among
his closest relatives, though they do not spare themselves, has the strength
to bear looking after him for long, not to mention his mother, with her
chronically ill heart. Nor is my declining strength sufficient. His attendant,
Klim Grigorievich Nagorny, after a few sleepless nights filled with agony,
becomes totally worn out and wouldn't be able to take it at all if Aleksei
Nikolaevich's teachers, Mr. Gibbs and particularly Mr. Gilliard, did not
come to relieve and to help him. Calm and composed, they trade off,

reading to him and talking with him and thus diverting the patient from his sufferings during the course of the day, easing them for him and, at the same time, giving his relatives and Nagorny the opportunity to sleep and gather their strength to replace them by turns. Aleksei Nikolaevich is especially used to and attached to Mr. Gilliard as he has been with him constantly for the past seven years. Mr. Gilliard sometimes spends whole nights by Aleksei's side, letting the tormented Nagorny get some sleep. Both teachers, and especially, I repeat, Mr. Gilliard, are completely irreplaceable for Aleksei Nikolaevich, and I, as a doctor, must admit that they sometimes bring more relief to the patient than medical means, which in these instances of self-treatment are extremely limited.

In light of all of the above-mentioned reasons, I decided, as a supplement to the request of the patient's parents, to disturb the [Ural] Regional [Soviet] Executive Committee with the fervent plea that Mr. Gibbs and Mr. Gilliard be allowed to continue their selfless service to Aleksei Nikolaevich Romanov because the boy, as it happens, is currently having one of the worst attacks of his illness, which is especially difficult for him to endure as a result of overexhaustion from the trip. Do not refuse admittance to them. As a last resort, at least allow Mr. Gilliard alone to go to him tomorrow.

Doctor Yev. Botkin

City of Yekaterinburg
24 May 1918

Resolution: Having examined the present request of Doctor Botkin, I think that even one servant would be one too many, because the children are all [illegible] and can look after the patient, and so I suggest that the chairman of the Reg. [Ural Regional Soviet] immediately notify these ladies and gentlemen that they have overstepped their bounds.

Commandant Avdeev

· 136 ·

Instructions to the commandant of the House of Special Purpose, [May 1918].

GENERAL RULES

The commandant must bear in mind that two main goals are being pursued in keeping Nicholas under guard: (1) [this section left blank]

A. The commandant's rights and obligations
    1. The [Ural] Regional Soviet has given the commandant the

responsibility for keeping Nicholas Romanov and his family under guard. The commandant bears exclusive responsibility in the event the former tsar or any one of those who are under guard with him escape or are abducted.

2. The guards present in the house shall unquestioningly fulfill all the commandant's orders relating to the establishment of a defined regimen. The commandant's orders to the guards are given to the chief of the guards in oral or written form at the commandant's discretion.

3. The Regional Soviet is responsible to the Council of People's Commissars for keeping the tsar under guard. By decree of the Regional Soviet, supervision of the tsar's imprisonment is given to the Presidium [of the Ural Regional Soviet] and is handled by the chairman; thus the commandant executes only those orders issued by the chairman. The commandant must be able to recognize by sight the chairman of the Regional Soviet and, in cases where written orders are given, must know his signature, as well as the signatures of members of the Presidium, and, for verification purposes, the orders must have the seal of the Regional Soviet. . . .

THE REGIME

The commandant must bear in mind that Nicholas Romanov and his family are under Soviet arrest and thus the conditions of his confinement must correspond to this status. Subject to this regime are (a) the former tsar himself and his family and (b) those persons who express their desire to share his situation. . . .

From the moment that the persons indicated in article [left blank] come under the jurisdiction of the regional soviet, all their free contact with the outside ceases. Indeed, for persons at liberty it will be exactly the same: they can no longer freely communicate with the Romanovs.

HOW THE PRISONERS ARE TO BE TREATED

The commandant must be absolutely polite when dealing with the prisoners.

Conversations with the prisoners may have only the following content: (1) listening to every possible oral statement of theirs; (2) imparting orders from the Regional Soviet to them; (3) providing clarification to their questions concerning the conditions of confinement, (4) concerning the delivery of provisions, foodstuffs, and necessities, [and] (5) concerning the rendering of medical help.

No conversations whatsoever on general political themes are allowed with any of the prisoners.

The commandant must strictly ensure that the guards make absolutely no remarks concerning the prisoners in the prisoners' presence.

Notation I: The prisoners do not have the right to talk with the guards. If they make such efforts, the guard must answer that no conversations are allowed.

Notation II: For their part, the guards do not have the right to initiate conversations with the prisoners.

ADMITTING OUTSIDERS TO SEĖ THE PRISONERS

As a general rule, no meetings are allowed between outsiders and the prisoners. If permission for a meeting is granted, however, it shall be conveyed in written form and signed by the Presidium of the [Ural] Regional Soviet and should be confirmed by telephone or in person.

When a meeting is allowed, the written permission shall indicate precisely with whom the meeting is permitted and what its duration shall be.

The commandant must be present during meetings and shall ensure that the visitor is not given anything that is not permitted. If such an effort is made, the commandant shall end the meeting.

Only a language that the commandant understands may be used for conversing during meetings. The commandant shall end the meeting if an effort is made to talk in a different language.

WALKS

The prisoners are allowed daily walks for a duration set by the regional soviet.

Those wishing to go for a walk must all go out together.

Before taking the prisoners out for a walk, the commandant shall order the guard to be reinforced where the prisoners will walk by posting sentries in all corners of the yard where they will walk and also on the balcony.

The commandant shall try, as much as possible, not to start walks at the same time every day, varying the time between 12 and 4 o'clock in the afternoon.

CORRESPONDENCE

All prisoners' correspondence is to be examined by a person specially authorized for this purpose by the Presidium of the [Ural] Regional Soviet.

The prisoners shall give the commandant the letters and telegrams they want to send, and the commandant shall send them to the person assigned to examine the correspondence.

Letters and telegrams addressed to those indicated in article [left blank] and received directly by the commandant are to be sent to the person who is to examine them.

The commandant shall see to it that the prisoners do not attempt to evade these rules by passing letters to the outside through guards or other persons also living in the House of Special Purpose.

The commandant shall warn the prisoners that if such attempts are discovered and proven, they will lose the right of correspondence.

Only Russian, Fr. [French], and Ger. [German] are to be used in letters.

· 137 ·

Letter from an "officer of the Russian army" to the imperial family, [19 or 20 June 1918].
Original in French.[1]

────────

Friends are no longer sleeping and hope that the hour so long awaited has come. The revolt of the Czechoslovaks threatens the Bolsheviks ever more seriously. Samara, Cheliabinsk, and all of eastern and western Siberia are in the hands of the provisional national government. The army of Slavic friends is eighty kilometers [50 miles] from Yekaterinburg. The soldiers of the Red Army cannot effectively resist. Be attentive to any movement from the outside; wait and hope. But at the same time, I beg you, be careful, because the Bolsheviks, before being **vanquished, represent real and serious danger for you.** Be ready at every hour, day and night. Make a drawing of your ~~two~~ three[2] bedrooms [showing] the position of the furniture, the beds. Write the hour that you all go to bed [in margin: 11:30].[3] One of you must not sleep between 2:00 and 3:00 on all the following nights. Answer with a few words, but, please, give all the useful information for your friends from outside. You must give your answer **in writing** to the same soldier who transmits this note to you, **but do not say a single word.**

> From someone who is ready to
> die for you,
> Officer of the Russian Army

Les amis ne dorment plus et
espèrent que l'heure si longtemps
attendue est arrivée. La revolte
des tschekoslovaques menace
les bolcheviks de plus en plus
serieusement Samara Tschela-
binsk et toute la Sibirie orien-
tale et occidentale est au pou-
voir de gouvernement national
provisoir. L'armée des amis
slaves est à quatre-vingt
kilometres d'Ezaterinbourg,
les le soldats de l'armée rouge
ne resistent pas efficassement.
Soyez attentifs au tout mouve-
ment de dehors, attendez et
espérez. Mais en même temps,
je vous supplie, soyez prudents
parce que les bolcheviks avant

DOCUMENTS 137 and 138. Letter from an "officer of the Russian army" to
the imperial family, [19 or 20 June 1918] and their response, [between 21 and
23 June 1918].

d'être vaincus représent pour vous le péril réel et sérieux. Soyez prêts toutes les heures, la journée et la nuit. Faites le croquis de vos ~~deux~~ chambres, les places, des meubles, des lits. Écrivez bien l'heure quand vous allez coucher vous tous. L'un de vous ne doit dormir de 2 à 3 heure toutes les nuits qui suivent. Répondez par quelques mots mais donnez, je vous en prie, tous les renseignements utiles pour vos amis de dehors. C'est au même soldat qui vous transmet cette note qu'il

à 11 ½

faut donner votre reponse
par ecrit mais dites pas
un seul mot.

    Un qui est prêt à mourir
       pour vous.
L'officier de l'armée Russe

du coin jusqu'au balcon.
5 fenêtres donnent sur la
rue, 2 sur la place.
Toutes les fenêtres sont
fermées collées et
peintes en blanc. Le
Petit est encore malade
au lit, et ne peut pas
marcher du tout. —
chaque secousse lui
cause des douleurs

Il y a une semaine
Qu'à cause des anarchis[tes]
on pensait à nous fai[re]
partir à Moscou la nuit.
Il ne faut rien risque[r]
sans être absolumen[t]
sûr du résultat.
Sommes presque tout le
temps sous observa-
tion attentive.

1. It is now widely believed that this letter and the following letters from an "officer" (Documents 139, 141, 146) were part of a plan by local authorities to engineer the imperial family's "escape" in order either to execute them while they were trying to flee or to create a pretext for execution. In the 1960s, a former member of the Ural Cheka, I. Rodzinsky, testified that Pyotr Voikov, a graduate of the University of Geneva and a member of the Ural Regional Soviet Executive Committee, drafted the letters, which Rodzinsky then copied.

2. This correction from "two" to "three" was made by a member of the tsar's family as part of the response (Document 138), which was written directly on the received letter.

3. The addition in the margin was also made by a member of the tsar's family.

· 138 ·

Response to the "officer's" letter, [between 21 and 23 June 1918]. Original in French.[1]

———

From the corner up to the balcony, there are 5 windows on the street side, 2 on the square. All of the windows are glued shut and painted white. The little one is still sick and in bed and cannot walk at all—every jolt causes him pain. A week ago, because of the anarchists, we were supposed to leave for Moscow at night. No risk whatsoever must be taken without being **absolutely** certain of the result. We are almost always under close observation.

1. Although most accounts state that Nicholas wrote this and the following responses (Documents 140, 142), the handwriting does not resemble his or Alexandra's. It closely resembles Olga's script, however. Olga, who knew French fairly well, very likely wrote the letters on behalf of the family.

· 139 ·

Letter from the "officer" to the imperial family, [25 June 1918]. Original in French.

———

With the help of God and your sangfroid, we hope to succeed without taking any risk. One of your windows must be unglued so that you can open it at the right time. Indicate which window, please.

The fact that the little tsarevich cannot walk complicates matters, but we have taken that into account, and I don't think it will be too great an inconvenience. Write if you need two people to carry him in their arms or [if] one of you can take care of that. If you know the exact time in advance, is it possible to make sure the little one will be asleep for one or two hours [before the escape]?

The doctor must give his opinion, but in case of need we can provide something for that.

Do not worry: no attempt will be made without being absolutely sure of the result.

Before God, before history, and before our conscience, we give you this solemn promise.

An officer

· 140 ·

Response to the "officer's" letter, [25 June 1918]. Original in French.

———

The second window from the corner facing the square has been opened for 2 days—day and night. The seventh and eighth windows facing the square next to the main entrance are always open. The room is occupied by the commandant and his aides, who are also the inside guards—up to 13 persons at least—armed with rifles, revolvers, and bombs. None of the doors have keys (except ours). The commandant or his aides come into our room whenever they want. The one who is on duty does the outside rounds twice every hour of the night, and we hear him chatting with the sentry beneath our windows. There is a machine gun on the balcony and another downstairs in case of alarm. If there are others, we do not know about them. Do not forget that we have the doctor, a maid, 2 men, and a little boy who is a cook with us. It would be ignoble of us (although they do not want to inconvenience us) to leave them alone after they have followed us voluntarily into exile. The doctor has been in bed for three days with kidney trouble, but he is getting better. We are constantly awaiting the return of two of our men [Ivan Sednyov and Klementy Nagorny], young and robust, who have been shut up in the city for a month—we do not know where or why. In their absence, the little one is carried by his father in order to move about the rooms [or] to go out into the garden. Our surgeon, D. [Derevenko], who comes almost daily at 5:00 to see the little one, lives in the city; do not forget. We never see him alone. The guards are in a little house across from our five windows on the other side of the street, 50 men. The only things that we still have are in crates in the shed (in the interior courtyard). We are especially worried about A. F. [Alexandra Fyodorovna] no. 9, a small black crate, and a large black crate no. 13 N. A. [Nicholas Aleksandrovich] with his old letters and *diaries*. Naturally the bedrooms are filled with crates, beds, and things, all at the mercy of the thieves who surround us. All the keys and, separately, no. 9 are with the commandant, who has behaved well toward us. In any case, warn us if you can, and answer if you can also bring our people. In front of the entrance, there is **always** an automobile. There are bells at each sentry post, in the command. room, and some wires also go to the guardhouse and elsewhere. If our other people remain, can we be sure that nothing will happen to them??? Doctor B. [Botkin] begs you not to think about him and the other men, so that your task will not be more difficult. Count on the seven of us and the woman. May God help you; you can count on our sangfroid.

· 141 ·

Letter from the "officer" to the imperial family, [26 June 1918]. Original in French.

————

Do not worry about the fifty or so men who are in a little house across from your windows—they will not be dangerous when it comes time to act. Say something more precise about your commandant to make the beginning easier for us. It is impossible to tell you now if we can take all your people; we hope so, but in any case they will not be with you after your departure from the house, except the doctor. Are taking steps for Doctor D. [Derevenko]. Hoping before Sunday to indicate the detailed plan of the operation. As of now it is like this: once the signal comes, you close and barricade with furniture the door that separates you from the guards, who will be blocked and terror-stricken inside the house. With a rope especially made for that purpose, you climb out through the window —we will be waiting for you at the bottom. The rest is not difficult; there are many means of transportation and the hiding place is as good as ever. The big question is getting the little one down: is it possible? Answer after thinking carefully. In any case, the father, the mother, and the son come down first; the girls, and then the doctor, follow them. Answer if this is possible in your opinion, and whether you can make the appropriate rope, because to have the rope brought to you is very difficult at this time.

An officer

comme jamais. Les gros de
question c'est descendre
le petit, est ce possible,
répondez en reflichissant
bien. En tout cas c'est
le père, la mère et le fils
qui descendent les premiers,
les filles après le docteur
les suit. Répondez si
cela est possible à votre avis
et si vous pouvez faire la
corde approprié étant donné
que faire venire la corde à
vous est bien difficile ce
moment si

Un officier

Nous ne voulons et ne pouvons pas fuire.
Nous pouvons seulement être enlevés par
force, comme c'est la force, qui nous a
emmenés de Tobolsk. Ainsi, ne comptez
sur aucune aide de votre part. Le commandant
active

DOCUMENT 142. Response to the "officer," [27 June 1918].

souvent

a beaucoup d'aides, ils changent et sont devenu soucieux. Ils gardent notre emprisonnement aigu que nos très consciencieusement et sont bien avec nous. Nous ne voulons pas qu'ils souffrent a cause de nous et ni voir pour nous, surtout au nom de Dieu éviter l'effusion de sang. Renseignez vous sur eux vous même. Une descente de ces fenêtres sans escalier est complètement impossible. Même descendu on est encore en grand danger à cause de la fenêtre ouverte de la chambre des commandants et la mitrailleuse de l'étage d'embas, où l'on pénètre de la cour intérieure. ~~Revenez donc à l'idée de nous enlever.~~ Si vous veillez sur nous vous pourrez toujours venir nous sauver en cas de danger imminent et réel. — Nous ignorons complètement ce qui se passe à l'extérieur, ne recevant ni journaux ni lettres — Depuis qu'on a fermé d'ouvrir la fenêtre, la surveillance a augmenté et on défend même de sortir la tête, au risque de recevoir une balle dans la figure.

· 142 ·

Response to the "officer," [27 June 1918]. Original in French.

We do not want to, nor can we, **escape**. We can only be **carried off** by force, just as it was force that was used to carry us from Tobolsk. Thus, do not count on **any active help** from us. The commandant has many aides; they change often and have become **worried**. They guard our imprisonment and our lives conscientiously and are kind to us. We do not want them to suffer because of us, nor you for us; in the name of God, avoid bloodshed above all. Find out about them yourself. Coming down from the window without a ladder is completely impossible. Even once we are down, we are still in great danger because of the open window of the commandant's bedroom and the machine gun downstairs, where one enters from the inner courtyard. ~~Give up, then, on the idea of carrying us off.~~ If you watch us, you can always come save us **in case of** real and imminent danger. We are completely unaware of what is going on outside, for we receive no newspapers or letters. Since we have been allowed to open the window, surveillance has increased, and we are forbidden even to stick our heads [out], at the risk of getting shot in the face.

· 143 ·

Telegram from Commander Mikhail Muravyov[1] to the Sovnarkom concerning Reingold Berzin's[2] investigation of rumors about the murder of Nicholas, 28 June 1918.

Received on 28 June 1918 at 10:11
From Kazan

I inform you of the telegram I received from Commander Berzin.

"I have received Moscow newspapers that carry an item on the murder of Nicholas Romanov at some railway stop outside Yekaterinburg by Red Army men. I officially inform you that on 12 June, I, together with members of the military inspectorate and the military commissar of the Ural military district and member of the All-Russian Investigatory Commission[3] examined the house to ascertain how Nicholas Romanov is being confined with his family and to inspect the sentries and guards. All members of the family and Nicholas himself are alive, and all information about his murder and so forth is a provocation.

> Commander of the Northern
> Ural-Siberian Front, Berzin"

> Commander Muravyov
> Ch. [Chief] of St. [Staff] at the
> Front, Ogloblin

1. Mikhail Artemievich Muravyov, lieutenant colonel in the tsarist army. During the February Revolution, Muravyov was associated with the Socialist Revolutionary Party. After the October Revolution, he supported the Soviet government. In June 1918, he was appointed commander of forces fighting against the Czech Legion. On 11 July, however, he incited a mutiny in support of the Left Socialist Revolutionary uprising and was killed when he reportedly resisted arrest.

2. Reingold Iosifovich Berzin, commander and political officer in the Red Army. Beginning in January 1918, he commanded the Second Revolutionary Army. From February to March 1918, he was commander of the western revolutionary front in the fight against counterrevolution. In June 1918, he became chairman of the Higher Military Inspectorate in Siberia and commander of the northern Ural-Siberian front. At the request of the Council of People's Commissars, he evaluated the situation of the tsar and his family in Yekaterinburg.

3. The All-Russian Investigatory Commission is presumably a misnomer for the All-Russian Extraordinary Commission, the Cheka. The military commissar of the Ural military district was Filipp Goloshchekin; he was also a member of the Cheka.

· 144 ·

Telegram from the Kolomna district organization of Bolsheviks to the Sovnarkom
demanding that Nicholas and his relatives be executed, 3 July 1918.

Received on 4 July 1918 at 10:06
From Petrograd, Kolomna

The Kolomna organization of Bolsheviks unanimously resolved to demand that the Sovnarkom immediately destroy him [Nicholas] and the family and relatives of the former tsar, because the German bourgeoisie, together with the Russian bourgeoisie, is restoring the tsarist regime in captured towns. [In] case [the Sovnarkom] refuses [to do] this, we have decided to carry out this decree using our own forces.

> Kolomna district committee of
> Bolsheviks

· 145 ·

Telegram from Beloborodov to Sverdlov and Filipp Goloshchekin on changing the
internal guard in the House of Special Purpose, 4 July 1918.

———————

Moscow. To Chairman of the VTsIK Sverdlov for Goloshchekin

Syromolotov[1] has just left to organize the matter according to the
Center's [Moscow's] instructions; misgivings are unfounded. Avdeev has
been replaced; his assistant Moshkin[2] has been arrested; Yurovsky[3] [has
been appointed] in place of Avdeev; the internal guard has all been
changed and is being replaced with others.

Beloborodov

1. Fyodor Fyodorovich Syromolotov, former mining engineer. In 1918, he was a member
of the Ural Regional Soviet Executive Committee and regional commissar of finances.

2. Aleksandr Mikhailovich Moshkin, former worker at the Zlokazov factory, aide to
Avdeev, commandant at the Ipatiev house. For stealing the personal belongings of the imperial family, Moshkin was fired and sent to the front.

3. Yakov Mikhailovich Yurovsky, member of the Bolshevik Party since 1905, member of
the Ural Regional Soviet Executive Committee, deputy regional commissar of justice, member of the collegium of the Ural Regional Cheka. Yurovsky was appointed commissar of the
House of Special Purpose on 4 July 1918.

· 146 ·

Letter from the "officer" to the imperial family, [after 4 July 1918]. Original in French.

———————

The change in the guards and in the commandant prevented us from
writing to you. Do you know what the cause of this was? We answer your
questions. We are a group of officers in the Russian army who have not lost
consciousness of our duty before Tsar and Country.[1]

We are not informing you in detail about ourselves for reasons that you
can understand, but your friends D. and T.,[2] who are already safe, know
us.

The hour of deliberation is approaching, and the days of the usurpers
are numbered. In any case, the Slavic armies are advancing toward
Yekaterinburg. They are a few versts from the city. The moment is becoming critical, and now bloodshed must not be feared. Do not forget that the
Bolsheviks will, in the end, be ready to commit any crime. The moment has
come. We must act. Rest assured that the machine gun downstairs will not
be dangerous. As for the commandant, we will know how to take him
away. Await the whistle around midnight. That will be the signal.

An officer

1. The letter writer initially misspelled the word *Country,* writing *Parti* (party) and then correcting it to *Patrie.*

2. Most likely Dolgorukov and Tatishchev, who had already been executed by the Cheka.

· 147 ·

Diary of Nicholas II, 17 (30) April–30 June (13 July) 1918.

———

17 [30] April.[1] Tuesday. Another wonderful, warm day. At 8:40 we arrived in Yekaterinburg. The train stood for about three hours at one station. There was great friction between the locals and our commissars. Finally, the former won out and the train moved to another freight station. We got out of the train after an hour and a half's wait. Yakovlev put us in the hands of the regional commissar here and the three of us sat down in a motorcar and drove through deserted streets to the house that had been readied for us— Ipatiev's. Our people and also our things arrived little by little, but Valia [Dolgorukov] wasn't allowed in.

The house is nice and clean. Four large rooms were set aside for us: the corner bedroom, the bathroom, the dining room next door with a view onto the little garden and the low-lying part of town, and, finally, a spacious hall with an arch and no doors. We couldn't unpack our things for a long time because the commissar, commandant, and guard officer just couldn't find time to inspect the trunks. And later the inspection was like at customs: very strict, right down to the last little vial in Alix's medicine kit. I blew up at this and harshly told the commissar my opinion. Finally, by 9 o'clock, everything was settled. We had dinner in the dining room at 4:30, and after cleaning up, we had a snack with tea.

We arranged ourselves the foll. [following] way: Alix, Maria, and I— the three of us—together in the bedroom; the bathroom shared; N. Demidova in the dining room; Botkin, Chemodurov, and Sednyov[2] in the hall. The room for the officer of the guard was near the entrance to the house. The guards were housed in two rooms by the dining room. In order to go to the bath and W.C., one has to walk by the sentry standing at the door of the guards' rooms. A very tall plank fence has been built around the house 2 sazhens [14 feet] from the windows; a chain of sentries stands there and in the garden, too.

. . .

25 April [8 May]. Wednesday. We got up at 9 o'clock. The weather was slightly warmer—reaching 5 degrees [41°F]. Today a guard that is eccentric in both personality and dress took up its post. The guard is composed of a

few former officers, and the majority are Latvians dressed in different sorts of jackets with all possible types of headgear. The officers stood guard with sabers and rifles. When we went out to walk, all the soldiers who had free time also came to the garden to look at us; they talked among themselves, walked, and horsed around. Before dinner, I talked a long time with a former officer, a native of the Baikal area; he told me many interesting things; the little chief of the guard [was] also standing there; he was born in Riga. Before supper, Ukraintsev[3] brought us the first telegram from Olga. The house came somewhat alive thanks to all of this. Besides this, the sounds of singing and playing on the piano, which had recently been dragged there from our hall, resounded from the [guards'] duty room. The food was excellent, plentiful, and served on time.

26 April [9 May]. Thursday. Today, all around us, that is, in the duty and guards' rooms, some sort of big fuss began in the morning; the telephone rang all the time. Ukraintsev was gone all day, although it was his duty day. We weren't told what happened, of course; perhaps the arrival here of some detachment caused confusion among the locals! But the guards' mood was cheerful and very obliging. My enemy "the pop-eyed one"—on duty instead of Ukraintsev—came out walking with us. He was silent the whole time, for no one talked to him. In the evening, while we played bezique, he brought some other character, made the rounds of the rooms together with him, and left.

27 April [10 May]. Friday. At half past eight we were supposed to get up and get dressed in order to receive yesterday's deputy commandant, who had handed us over to a new one—with a kind face reminiscent of an artist's. Snow fell thickly in the morning, and in the afternoon the sun came out. The walking was good. After tea, the "pop-eyed one" came again and asked each of us how much money we had. After that, he asked [us] to note down the exact figures and [then] took people's money from them for safekeeping by the [Ural] Regional Soviet's treasurer! A most unpleasant incident. During last night's game, the kind little chief of the guards sat with us, watched the game, and talked a lot.

. . .

29 April [12 May]. Sunday. Good sunny weather, rather cool. This past evening, the chief of the guards was absent for about three hours to dance at a ball! That was why he walked around looking funny and sleepy all day.

Alix sat in the garden on a bench during our walk. Dinner and supper were served on time.

. . .

1 [14] May. Tuesday. We were gladdened by the receipt of letters from To-bolsk; I got one from Tatiana. We read them to each other all morning. The weather stayed marvelous, warm. By noon, there was a change in the guard using the same special crew of frontline soldiers—Russians and Latvians. The [new] chief of the guards is a young, imposing person [Pavel Medvedev]. Today we were told, via Botkin, that we are allowed only one hour a day to walk; to the question "Why?" the person act. [acting] as commandant answered: "So that this resembles a prison regime." The food was served at the normal time. A samovar was purchased for us—at least we won't be dependent on the guards. I had four beziques during the evening game.

2 [15] May. Wednesday. The application of a "prison regime" continued, manifesting itself in the fact that an old housepainter came and white-washed all the windows. Now it is like looking at fog through the windows. We went out to walk at 3:30, and at 4:10 they herded us home. There wasn't a single extra soldier in the yard. The chief of the guards didn't talk with us because the whole time one or another of the commissars was in the garden watching us, him, and the sentries! The weather was very good, but in the rooms it had become dim. Only the dining room was improved, because the rug covering the windows was removed!

Sednyov has a cold with a fever.

. . .

6 May [19 May]. Sunday. I have made it to the age of 50; it even seems strange to me! The weather remained marvelous, as though made to order. At 11:30 the same priest and deacon officiated at a very good service. I took a walk with Maria before dinner. During the day, we sat for an hour and a quarter in the garden, warming ourselves in the gentle sunshine. We get no news from the children and are starting to doubt whether they have left Tobolsk.

. . .

10 [23] May. Thursday. During the course of an hour in the morning we were told, step by step, that the children were a few hours from town, that they had arrived at the station, and finally that they had arrived at the house,

although their train had been standing here since 2 o'clock in the morning! What an enormous joy it was to see them again and to embrace them after the four-week separation and the uncertainty.

There was no end to the mutual questions and answers. Very few letters had reached them or had been received from them. The poor things had endured a lot of personal, spiritual suffering both in Tobolsk and during the three-day trip. Snow fell during the night and stayed on the ground all day. Out of all those who had arrived with them, only Kharitonov and Sednyov's nephew[4] were allowed in. During the day, we went into the garden for about 20 minutes—it was cold and desperately dirty. We waited through the evening for the delivery of our beds and other necessary things from the train station, but in vain, and all the daughters ended up having to sleep on the floor. Aleksei spent the night on Maria's cot. In the evening, as if on purpose, he bumped his knee and suffered terribly all night, disturbing our sleep.

. . .

13 [26] May. Sunday.   We slept excellently, except Aleksei. His pains continued, but at greater intervals. He stayed in bed in our bedroom. There was no service. The weather was the same; snow covered the rooftops. Just as in recent days, V. N. Derevenko came to examine Aleksei; today he was accompanied by the dark-complexioned gentleman wh. [whom] we took to be a doctor [Yakov Yurovsky]. After a brief walk, we, together with Comm. [commandant] Avdeev, stopped in at the shed wh. [where] all of our considerable baggage was stored. Some trunks were opened and the examination [of our things] continued. I started reading the works of Saltykov (Shchedrin),[5] which I found among the books belonging to the house's owner. We played bezique in the evening.

. . .

14 [27] May. Monday.   The weather remained warm. I read a lot. Aleksei felt generally better.

We walked for an hour during the day. After tea, Sednyov and Nagorny were called to the reg. [regional] soviet for interrogation. In the evening, an examination of the daughters' things continued in their presence. The sentry standing under our window shot into our house because he thought something moved by the window (after 10 o'clock at night)—it seems to me that he was just amusing himself with his rifle, as sentries always do.

. . .

20 May [2 June]. Sunday. *Obednitsa* [liturgy without communion] was held at 11 o'clock; Aleksei was present, lying in bed. The weather remained marvelous, hot. We walked after the service and during the day before tea. It's unbearable to sit locked up like this and not be able to go out into the yard when one wants to and to spend a nice evening in the fresh air! The prison regime!

21 May [3 June]. Monday. A wonderful, warm day. We walked twice. Downstairs in the guards' quarters another shot rang out; the commandant came to ask whether the bullet had come through the floor. Aleksei had no pain at all; as usual he spends the day in bed in our room. I finished Saltykov's second volume. We played bezique in the evening.

22 May [4 June]. Tuesday. The rooms are hot and stuffy. We only walked during the day. Around 5 o'clock, a strong rainstorm passed through and another one [came] in the evening. Aleksei is much better, and the swelling in his knee has gone down a great deal. My legs and lower back hurt, and I slept poorly.

23 May [5 June]. Wednesday. They moved the clock forward two hours. Today Aleksei got dressed and was carried out into the fresh air through the main entrance. The weather remained marvelous. Alix and Tatiana sat with him for an hour and a half. We took our time walking in the garden. I was in a sour mood. We went to bed when it was still light out.

24 May [6 June]. Thursday. My hemorrhoids gave me terrible pain all day, so I lay down on the bed because it is more comfortable to apply compresses that way. Alix and Aleksei spent half an hour in the fresh air, and after they returned, we went [out] for an hour.
The weather remained marvelous.

25 May [7 June]. Friday. I spent dear Alix's birthday in bed with strong pains in my legs and in oth. [other] places.
The next two days I felt better and could eat sitting in an armchair.

27 May [9 June]. Sunday.[6] Finally, I got up and left the cot. It was a summery day. We walked in two turns: Alix, Aleksei, Olga, and Maria before dinner; me, Tatiana, and Anastasia before tea. The greenery is very nice and lush, with a pleasant smell. I am reading Saltykov's twelfth v. [volume], *Poshekhonskaia starina* [Old days in Poshekhon'e], with interest.

28 May [10 June]. Monday. It's a very warm day. They are constantly opening our trunks in the shed and taking out various objects and provisions from Tobolsk. And there is no explanation for doing so. All this leads one to the thought that the things that they like could be taken home very easily and, consequently, lost to us! How loathsome! External relationships have also changed in recent weeks: the prison guards try not to talk with us—as though they are not quite themselves; it's as though one senses some sort of uneasiness or apprehension in them! Incomprehensible!

29 May [11 June]. Tuesday. Dear Tatiana turned 21 years old! Starting at night, a strong wind blew right through the ventilation window, thanks to which the air in our bedroom was finally clean and rather cool. We read a lot. We walked again in two turns.

Kharitonov served a compote for breakfast, to the great joy of all. In the evening, bezique as usual.

31 May [13 June]. Ascension. We waited a long time, fruitlessly, for the arrival of the priest to officiate at the service: everyone was busy at the churches. They didn't let us out into the garden during the day for some reason. Avdeev came and talked with Yev. Serg. [Botkin] for a long time. According to what he said, he and the regional soviet fear the actions of anarchists, and for that reason we might have to leave soon, probably for Moscow! He asked that we prepare ourselves for departure. We've slowly started packing, but quietly, at Avdeev's special request, to avoid attracting the attention of the guard officers.

Around 11 o'clock at night, he returned and said that there were still a few days left. Thus, even on 1 June we stayed bivouacked and unable to put anything away.

The weather remained good; as always, the walk took place in two turns. Finally, after supper, Avdeev, slightly tipsy, announced to Botkin that the anarchists have been captured and that the danger is past and our departure has been canceled! After all the preparations, it was even depressing! In the evening, we played bezique.

3 [16] June. Sunday. Again, there was no service performed at our place. All week I read, and today finished, Shilder's history *Imp. Pavel I* [Emperor Paul I]—it was very interesting.

We keep waiting for Sednyov and Nagorny, wh. [whom] they promised to release today.

5 [18] June. Tuesday.   Dear Anastasia has already turned 17. It was extremely hot outside and in. I am continuing to read Saltykov's third volume—it is engaging and clever.

The whole family took a walk before tea. Kharitonov makes us food from leftovers; provisions are brought once every two days. The daughters are learning how to cook from him; in the evenings they knead dough, and in the mornings they bake bread! Not bad!

9 [22] June. Saturday.   The weather has been wonderful the last few days, but very hot; our rooms were terribly stuffy, especially at night. By Botkin's written request, we were allowed 1½-hour walks. Today at teatime six persons, probably from the regional soviet, came to see which windows should be opened. The resolution of this matter has been going on for two weeks! Different characters have often come and silently inspected the windows in our presence.

The aroma from all the gardens in town is amazing.

10 [23] June. Trinity.   Was commemorated with different events: one window was opened here this morning; Yev. Serg. [Botkin] had kidney pains and suffered terribly; at 11:30 a real liturgy and vespers was held; and at the end of the day, Alix and Aleksei dined with us in the dining room. In addition, we walked for two hours! The day was marvelous. It turns out that yesterday's visitors were commissars from Petrograd. The air in the room became fresh, and toward evening it even became cooler.

12 [25] June. Tuesday.   Yesterday and today were astoundingly hot. The rooms too, although the windows were open the whole time! We walked for two hours during the day. Two big thunderstorms passed through during dinner and freshened the air! Yev. Serg. [Botkin] is much better but is still lying down.

14 [27] June. Thursday.   Our dear Maria turned 19 years old. The same tropical weather held, 26° [78°F] in the shade and 24° [75°F] in the rooms; one can hardly stand it! We spent an anxious night and sat up dressed.

All this was because we had received two letters in the last few days, one after the other, in wh. we were told that we should get ready to be abducted by some sort of people loyal to us! The days passed and nothing happened, but the waiting and uncertainty were quite torturous.

21 June [4 July]. Thursday.   Today the commandants were changed. During dinner, Beloborodov and others came and said that the one wh. we believed to be a doctor—Yurovsky—had been appointed instead of Avdeev. In the daytime, before tea, he and his aide made a list of the gold things—ours and the children's. They took the majority of them (rings, bracelets, etc.) with them. They explained this by saying that an unpleasant incident had taken place in our house, mentioning the disappearance of some of our things. So wh. I wrote about my concern on 28 May was confirmed. I pity Avdeev, but he is to blame for not restraining his people from stealing from the trunks in the shed.

23 June [6 July]. Saturday.   Yesterday, commandant Yu. [Yurovsky] brought a box containing all the precious objects that had been taken, asked that we check the contents, and sealed the box in our presence, leaving it with us for safekeeping. The weather became cooler, and it was easier to breathe in the bedroom. Yu. and his aide are beginning to understand what sort of people were surrounding and protecting us while stealing from us.

And not only our belongings—they even withheld a large portion of the supplies brought from the convent. We discovered this only after the latest changes, because now the entire amount of the provisions has begun reaching the kitchen.

As usual, I've read a lot these past days; today I began Saltykov's seventh volume. I like his stories, tales, and essays very much.

It was a rainy day; we walked for an hour and a half and returned home dry.

25 June [8 July]. Monday.   Our life has not changed one bit with Yu. He comes into the bedroom to check that the seal on the box is undisturbed and looks through the open window. All morning today and until 4 o'clock they checked and fixed the elec. lights. New Latvians are standing guard inside the house, and the same ones are there outside—some are soldiers, some are workers! Rumor has it that some of Avdeev's men are already under arrest and in prison!

The door to the shed with our baggage is sealed. If only this had been done a month ago!

There was a thunderstorm during the night, and it became even cooler.

28 June [11 July]. Thursday.   Around 10:30 in the morning, three workers came to the open window, lifted a heavy grating, and attached it to the

outside of the window frame without any warning from Yu. We like this type less and less!

I began reading Saltykov's eighth volume.

30 June [13 July]. Saturday.   Aleksei took his first bath since Tobolsk; his knee is getting better, but he can't completely straighten it yet. The weather is warm and pleasant. We have no news from the outside.

1. On 19 March (1 April) 1918, Nicholas resumed using only old-style dates.

2. Terenty Ivanovich Chemodurov, Nicholas's valet since December 1908. On 24 May 1918, because of illness, Chemodurov left the Ipatiev house and entered a local prison hospital; he was freed by White soldiers on 25 July 1918.

Ivan Dmitrievich Sednyov, former crewman aboard the imperial yacht *Shtandart* and a servant to Nicholas and Alexandra's daughters. Sednyov voluntarily accompanied the family to Tobolsk and Yekaterinburg. He was arrested on 27 May and was later shot together with Klementy Nagorny.

3. Ukraintsev was a guard at the Ipatiev house. The imperial family believed they recognized him as their former hunting beater for imperial animal hunts.

4. Ivan Mikhailovich Kharitonov, cook to the imperial family in Tobolsk and Yekaterinburg. He was executed together with the Romanovs on the night of 16–17 July 1918.

Leonid (Lenka) Sednyov was a fourteen-year-old kitchen-boy who was with the Romanovs in Tobolsk and Yekaterinburg. On the night before their execution he was taken from the house and, it appears, sent to relatives in Kaluga province.

5. Mikhail Yevgrafovich Saltykov (1826–1879), who wrote under the pseudonym N. Shchedrin, is considered Russia's greatest satirical writer and polemicist. His works satirized Russian bureaucrats, bureaucratic government, the old landed gentry, and rising capitalist entrepreneurs.

6. On 26 May (8 June) 1918, for the first time, Nicholas failed to make a daily entry in his diary. Days without entries occur frequently during the following month and a half. In this translation, all entries from 20 May (2 June) on have been included; gaps are in the original.

· 148 ·

Telegram to V. I. Lenin from the editors of the *National Tidende* (Copenhagen) and Lenin's response, 16 July 1918. Original English text.

Received on 16 July 1918 at 13:27

Rumour here going that the exczar has been murdered. Kindly wire facts.
National Tidende

[To] National Tidende, Kjobenhavn
16 July at 16:00

Rumour not true   exczar safe. All rumours are only lie of capitalist press.
Lenin

ТЕЛЕГРАФЪ ВЪ МОСКВѢ

ТЕЛЕГРАММА

НМОСКВУ ЛЕНИНУ

ПЕТРОГРАДА СМОЛЬНАГО НР 142,28,16/7,17;50,

НМОСКВУ КРЕМЛ СВЕРДЛОВУ КОПИЯ ЛЕНИНУ НИЗ ЕКАТЕРИНБУРГА ПО ПРЯМОМУ
ПРОВОДУ ПЕРЕДАЮТ СЛЕДУЮЩЕЕ СООБЩИТЕ МОСКВУ ЧТО УСЛОВЛЕННОГО С
ФИЛИППОВЫМ СУДА ПО ВОЕННЫМ ОБСТОЯТЕЛЬСТВАМ НЕ ТЕРПИТ ОТЛАГАТЕЛЬСТВА ЖДАТ
НЕ МОЖЕМ ЕСЛИ ВАШИ МНЕНИЯ ПРОТИВОПОЛОЖНЫ СЕИЧАС ЖЕ ВНЕ ВСЯКОЙ ОЧЕРЕДИ
СООБЩИТЕ ГОЛОЩЕКИН САФАРОВ СНЕСИТЕС ПО ЕТОМУ ПОВОДУ САМИ С
ЕКАТЕРИНБУРГОМНЗИНОВЬЕВ

DOCUMENT 149. Telegram from Grigory Zinoviev to Lenin and Sverdlov on
the receipt of information from Yekaterinburg concerning the fate of the
imperial family, 16 July 1918.

· 149 ·

Telegram from Grigory Zinoviev[1] to Lenin and Sverdlov on the receipt of information
from Yekaterinburg concerning the fate of the imperial family, 16 July 1918.

———————

Sent on 16 July 1918 at 17:50
Received on 16 July 1918 at 21:22
To Moscow. To Lenin.
From Petrograd. Smolny

To Moscow, Kremlin, to Sverdlov, copy to Lenin.

The following has been transmitted over the direct line from Yekaterinburg: ["]Let Moscow know that for military reasons the trial agreed upon
with Filipp [Goloshchekin] cannot be put off; we cannot wait. If your
opinions differ, then immediately notify without delay.

Goloshchekin, Safarov.["]

Get in touch with Yekaterinburg on this matter yourselves.

Zinoviev

1. Grigory Yevseevich Zinoviev, chairman of the Petrograd Soviet and member of the
Central Committee of the Bolshevik party.

· 150 ·

Diary of Alexandra, 11–16 July 1918. Original English text.

———————

Yekaterinburg.

12.[°C; 54°F]   *28. June.*   Irenes B.D. 52

11. Thursday

The Ox Commandant [Yurovsky] insisted to see us all at 10, but kept us
waiting 20 m. [minutes] as was breakfasting & eating cheese. wont permit
us to have any more any cream. 10½ [10:30] Workmen turned up outside &
began putting up iron railings before our only open window. Always fright
of our climbing out no doubt or getting into contact with the sentry. Strong
pains continue. Greyish weather. Brought me [meat] for 6 days, but so little
only suffices for putting in the soup. *The Bull* [Nikolsky] very rude to
Kharitonov. Remained in bed all day. Lunched only, as they brought the
meat so late.—Anastasia read to me whilst the others went out. Lovely
weather.

Yekaterinburg.

13.[°C; 56°F]   29. June   [Feast of] *Sts. Peter*

                                _____   *and Paul the Apostles*

                                12. Friday.

Bright sunshine—in the afternoon there were severel showers & short thunderstorms. The others went out twice,—M. [Maria] remained with me, I spent the day on my bed & got into it again at 9½. Lovely evening. Every day one of the girls reads to me *Spiritual Readings*, i.e. *Complete Yearly Cycle of Brief Homilies for Each Day of the Year. (Grig. Diachenko).—*

Constantly hear artillery passing, infantry & twice cavalry during the course of this week. Also troops marching with music—twice it seems to have been the Austrian prisoners who are marching against the Chechs (also our former prisoners) who are with the troops coming through Siberia & not far fr. here now. Wounded daily arrive to the town.—

Yekaterinburg.

11.[°C; 52°F]   30. June.   Louise's 29 B.D.

                                _____

                                13. Saturday.

Beautiful morning. I spent the day as yesterday lying on the bed, as back ached when move about. Others went out twice. Anastasia remained with me in the afternoon. One says *Nagorny* & *Sednyov* have been sent out of this government [province], instead of giving them back to us. At 6½ Baby had his first bath since *Tobolsk*. He managed to get in & out alone, climbs also alone in & out of bed, but can only stand on one foot as yet. 9¾ I went to bed again.—

Rained in the night. Heard three revolver shots in the night.

Yekaterinburg.

12.[°C; 54°F]   1. July.

                                _____

                                14. Sunday.

Beautiful summer morning. Scarcely slept because of back & legs.

10½. Had the joy on an *obednitsa* [liturgy without communion]—the young Priest for the 2nd time.

11½. The others walked—O. with me. Spend the day on the bed again. T. stayed with me in the afternoon. *Spir. Readings. Book of the Prophet Hosea chap. 4–14, Pr. [Prophet] Joel* 1–the end.

4½. tea—tatted all day & laid patiences. Played a little bezique in the eveing, they put my long straw couch in the big room so it was less tiring for me.

10 o'clock. Took a bath—& went to bed.

	Yekaterinburg.	
11.[°C; 52°F]	2. July.	4th week of Pentecost.
	15. Monday.	Marie E.'s B.D.

Greyish morning. Later sunshine. Lunched on the couch in the big room, as women came to clean the floors, then lay on my bed again & read with *Maria J. Sirach.* [Ecclesiasticus] 26–31. They went out twice as usual. In the morning T. read to me *Spir. Readings.* Still no *Vl. Nik.* [Derevenko]— at 6½ Baby had his second bath—Bezique. Went to bed at 10¼.—

11¼. of warmth at 10½ evening. Heard the report of an artillery shot in the night & several revolver shots.

	Yekaterinburg.	
11.[°C; 52°F]	3. July.	Irina's 23rd B.D.
	16. Tuesday.	

Grey morning, later lovely sunshine. Baby has a slight cold. All went out ½ hour in the morning, Olga & I arranged our medicines [jewelry]. T. read *Spir. Readings.* 3. They went out, T. stayed with me & we read: *Book of the Pr. Amos & Pr. Obadiah.* Tatted. Every moring the *Command.* comes to our rooms, at last after a week brought eggs again for Baby.

8 o'clock Supper.

Suddenly *Lenka Sednyov* was fetched to go & see his Uncle & flew off— wonder whether its true & we shall see the boy back again!

Played bezique with N.

10½ to bed. **15** degrees. [59°F]

· 151 ·

Telegram from the Ural Regional Soviet to Lenin and Sverdlov on the execution of Nicholas, 17 July 1918.

———

Received on 17 July 1918 at 2 o'clock

To chairman of the Sovnarkom, comrade Lenin, and chairman [of VTsIK,] Sverdlov

From Yekaterinburg

The Presidium of the [Ural] Regional Soviet of the Workers' and Peasants' Government is at the [telegraph] apparatus.

ТЕЛЕГРАФЪ ВЪ МОСКВѢ. №9 ТЕЛЕГРАММА

ПРЕДСѢДАТЕЛЮ СОВНАРКОМА ТОВ ЛЕНИНУ
ПРЕДСѢДАТЕЛЮ М. Ц. СВЕРДЛОВУ

ИЗЪ ЕКАТЕРИНБУРГА У АППАРАТА ПРЕЗИДИУМЪ ОБЛАСТНОГО СОВЕТА РАБОЧАГО
КРЕСТЬЯНСКАГО ПРАВИТЕЛЬСТВА ТОЧКА

Служебныя отмѣтки.

ВВИДУ ПРИБЛИЖЕНИЯ НЕПРІЯТЕЛЯ КЪ ЕКАТЕРИНБУРГУ И РАСКРЫТИЯ ЧРЕЗВЫЧАЙНОЙ
КОМИССІЕЙ БОЛЬШОГО БѢЛОГВАРДЕЙСКАГО ЗАГОВОРА ИМѢВШАГО ЦѢЛЬЮ
ПОХИЩЕНИЯ БЫВШАГО ЦАРЯ И ЕГО СЕМЬИ ТОЧКА ДОКУМЕНТЫ В НАШИХ РУКАХ ТОЧКА
ПОСТАНОВЛЕНІЮ ПРЕЗИДИУМА ОБЛАСТНОГО СОВѢТА В НОЧЬ НА
ШЕСТНАДЦАТОЕ ИЮЛЯ РАЗСТРѢЛЯН НИКОЛАЙ РОМАНОВ
ТОЧКА СЕМЬЯ ЕГО ЭВАКУИРОВАНА В НАДЕЖНОЕ МѢСТО ТОЧКА ПО ЭТОМУ ПОВОДУ НАМИ
ВЫПУСКАЕТСЯ СЛѢДУЮЩЕЕ ИЗВѢЩЕНІЕ ТОЧКА ВВИДУ ПРИБЛИЖЕНИЯ КОНТР
РЕВОЛЮЦІОННЫХ БАНД КРАСНОЙ СТОЛИЦѢ УРАЛА И ВОЗМОЖНОСТИ ТОГО ЧТО
КОРОНОВАННЫЙ ПАЛАЧ ИЗБѢЖИТ НАРОДНАГО СУДА СКОБКИ РАСКРЫТ ЗАГОВОР
БѢЛОГВАРДЕЙЦЕВ ПЫТАВШИХСЯ ПОХИТИТЬ ЕГО И ЕГО САМОГО И НАЙДЕНЫ

*) Въ служебномъ заголовкѣ телеграммы, принятой на КОМПРОМЕНТИРУЮЩІЕ ДОКУМЕНТЫ
порядку, слѣдующее: 1) номеръ телеграммы, 2) число словъ, 3)

БУДУТ ОПУБЛИКОВАНЫ СКОБКИ ПРЕЗИДИУМ ОБЛАСТНОГО СОВѢТА ИСПОЛНЯЯ ВОЛЮ
РЕВОЛЮЦІИ ПОСТАНОВИЛЪ РАЗСТРѢЛЯТЬ БЫВШАГО ЦАРЯ НИКОЛАЯ РОМАНОВА ЗАПЯТАЯ
ВИНОВНАГО В В БЕЗЧИСЛЕННЫХ КРОВАВЫХ НАСИЛІИ РУССКАГО НАРОДА В НОЧЬ НА 16
ИЮЛЯ 1918 ГОДА ПРИГОВОРЪ ЭТОТ ПРИВЕДЕН ИСПОЛНЕНІЕ СЕМЬЯ РОМАНОВА
СОДЕРЖИТЬСЯ ВМѢСТѢ СЪ НИМ ПОД СТРАЖЕЙ ИНТЕРЕСАХ ОХРАНЫ ОБЩЕСТВЕННОЙ
БЕЗОПАСТНОСТИ ЭВАКУИРОВАННЫЕ ИЗ ГОРОДА ЕКАТЕРИНБУРГА ТОЧКА
ИЗ ПРЕЗИДИУМ ОБЛАСТНОГО СОВѢТА ТОЧКА ПРОСИМ ВАШИХ САНКЦИИ РЕДАКЦИИ ДАННАГО
РАЗ ДОКУМЕНТЫ ЗАГОВОРА ВЫСЫЛАЮТСЯ СРОЧНО КУРЬЕРОМ СОВНАРКОМУ И ЦК
ИЗВѢЩЕНІЯ ОЖИДАЕМ У АППАРАТА ПРОСИМ ДАТ ОТВѢТ ЭКСТРЕННО ЖДЕМ У АППАРАТА

*) Въ служебномъ заголовкѣ телеграммы, принятой за буквенномъ аппаратѣ, значеніе чиселъ по
порядку, слѣдующее: 1) номеръ телеграммы, 2) число словъ, 3) число письма и 4) часы и минуты подачи.

DOCUMENT 151. Telegram from the Ural Regional Soviet to Lenin and Sverdlov on the execution of Nicholas, 17 July 1918.

In view of the enemy's proximity to Yekaterinburg and the exposure by the Extraordinary Commission [Cheka] of a serious White Guard plot with the goal of abducting the former tsar and his family. The documents are in our hands. Nicholas Romanov was shot on the night of the sixteenth of July by decree of the Presidium of the [Ural] Regional Soviet. His family has been evacuated to a safe place. For this reason, we are issuing the following notification: ["]In light of the approach of counterrevolutionary bands toward the Red capital of the Urals and the possibility of the crowned executioner escaping trial by the people (a plot among White Guards to try to abduct him and his [family] was exposed and compromising documents have been found [and] will be published), the Presidium of the [Ural] Regional Soviet, fulfilling the will of the revolution, resolved to shoot the former tsar, Nicholas Romanov, [who is] guilty of countless bloody, violent acts against the Russian people. This sentence was carried out on the night of 16 July 1918. The Romanov family, kept with him under guard, has been evacuated from the city of Yekaterinburg in the interest of maintaining public security.

> Presidium of the [Ural]
> Regional Soviet["]

We ask for your sanction [of] the wording of this[.] The documents concerning the plot are being expedited by courier to the Sovnarkom [and] the TsIK [Central Executive Committee]. We are waiting by the apparatus for advice. We urgently request an answer[;] we are waiting by the apparatus.

· 152 ·

Deciphered telegram from Beloborodov to Secretary to the Sovnarkom Nikolai Gorbunov[1] on the fate of the imperial family, 17 July 1918.

[Sent on] 17 July 21:00
MOSCOW. Kremlin.
To Sovnarkom Secretary GORBUNOV with verification of receipt requested

Inform Sverdlov that the entire family suffered the same fate as its head. Officially the family will die during evacuation.

> Beloborodov

1. Nikolai Petrovich Gorbunov, secretary to the Sovnarkom and V. I. Lenin's personal secretary.

DOCUMENT 152. Encoded telegram from Beloborodov to secretary to the Sovnarkom Nikolai Gorbunov on the fate of the imperial family, 17 July 1918.

· 153 ·

From the protocol of a session of the VTsIK Presidium, on the execution of the former
tsar Nicholas II, 18 July 1918.

Present: Ya. M. Sverdlov, L. S. Sosnovsky, A. P. Rozengolts, [K. G.]
Maksimov, M. F. Vladimirsky, [A. Kh.] Mitrofanov, N. G. Smidovich, G. I.
Teodorovich, [F. A.] Rozin, and V. A. Avanesov.

HEARD: News of Nicholas Romanov's execution. (Telegram from Yekaterinburg.)

RESOLVED: The following resolution is adopted after discussion: The
VTsIK, represented by its Presidium, recognizes that the Ural Regional
Soviet's decision was correct.

Instructs comrades Sverdlov, Sosnovsky, and Avanesov to compose a
suitable announcement for publication. It must be published that the TsIK
has in its possession documents (diary, letters, etc.) that belonged to tsar N.
Romanov. Comrade Sverdlov is instructed to assemble a special commission to examine and publish these papers.[1]

> VTsIK Chairman, Ya. M.
> Sverdlov
> VTsIK Secretary, V. Avanesov

1. A commission to select Romanov documents for publication was established under
the People's Commissariat of Enlightenment. Selections from Nicholas's diaries, letters, and
other documents, with corresponding commentaries, were published in *Izvestiia,* in other
newspapers, in journals, and in separate volumes.

· 154 ·

From the protocol of a session of the Sovnarkom, on Yakov Sverdlov's announcement of
Nicholas II's execution, 18 July 1918.

Chaired by: Vl. Ilich Ulianov (Lenin).

Present: Gukovsky, V. M. Bonch-Bruevich, Petrovsky, Semashko, Vinokurov, Solovyov, Kozlovsky, Galkin, Smirnov, Dauge, Svidersky, Pravdin, Trotsky, Popov, Altfater, Stuchka, Rykov, Nogin, Skliansky, Pestkovsky, Nevsky, Sereda, Podbelsky, Skorniakov, Yuriev, Briukhanov, Nikolaev,
Miliutin, Popov (statistician), Prof. Sirinov (relating to point 8), Chicherin,
Karakhan.

. . .

HEARD: 3. Special announcement by comrade Sverdlov, chairman of the
TsIK, on the execution of former tsar Nicholas II according to the sentence

Разстрѣлъ Николая Романова.

Въ послѣдніе дни столицѣ Краснаго Урала Екатеринбургу серьезно угрожала опасность приближенія Чехо Словацкихъ бандъ, въ тоже время былъ раскрытъ новый заговоръ контръ-револлюціонеровъ имѣвшихъ цѣлью вырвать изъ рукъ совѣтской власти Коронованнаго палача. Въ виду этого Уральскій областной комитетъ постановилъ разстрѣлять Николая Романова, что и было приведено въ исполненіе шестнадцатаго іюля. Жена и сынъ Николая Романова въ надежномъ мѣстѣ.

Всероссійскій Центр. Испол. Комит. признавъ рѣшеніе Уральскаго областного совѣта правильнымъ.

DOCUMENT 155. "Nicholas Romanov's Execution," VTsIK leaflet, [no earlier than 18 July 1918].

passed by the Yekaterinburg Soviet and on the TsIK Presidium's confirmation of the sentence.

DECREED: 3. To record the information.

. . .

> Chairman of the Council of
> People's Commissars,
> V. Ulianov (Lenin)
> Council Secretary, N. Gorbunov

· 155 ·

"Nicholas Romanov's Execution," VTsIK leaflet, [no earlier than 18 July 1918].

In the last few days, Yekaterinburg, the capital of the Red Urals, was seriously threatened by the approaching Czecho-Slovak bands. At the same time, a new counterrevolutionary plot was exposed that had as its goal tearing the Crowned executioner from the hands of soviet power. In view of this, the Ural Regional [Executive] Committee resolved to shoot Nicholas Romanov, and this was carried out on the sixteenth of July. Nicholas Romanov's wife and son are in a secure place.

The All-Russian Cent. Exec. Comm. recognized that the Ural Regional Soviet's decision was correct.

· 156 ·

Pravda editorial and report on the shooting of Nicholas Romanov, 19 July 1918.

Nicholas Romanov

"We need a tsar!" the loquacious Rodzianko recently proclaimed. But rifle shots cut short Nicholas Romanov's life journey when this inveterate landowner's Czechoslovak friends, who had already freed Mikhail Romanov,[1] began to sneak up to the former bearer of the crown in order to steal him out from under the vigilant guard of the Yekaterinburg proletariat and, painting the shabby crown with workers' blood, to hoist that crown back onto that empty head. He is no longer, and he cannot be resurrected—no matter how much the holy church fathers pray for his health.

Nicholas Romanov was essentially a pitiful figure. But, having been chosen for the position of autocratic despot by the will of history during an epoch characterized by the cruelest breakdown of all social relationships, he became the inescapable symbol of a brutal regime of blood and violence against the people, a regime of the whip, cane, gallows, torture, and the refined depravity of religious phrasemongering, military adventurism, and hypocritical support for peace, a regime in which the brothel and divine worship were both elevated to the throne.

He was anointed sovereign in the year 1894 [1896], anointed simultaneously with rose-colored oil in church and with the red blood of crushed workers and peasants on Khodynka field.[2] Within ten years after the start of his royal career, Nicholas II threw Russia into the maelstrom of war. He imitated his true Russian papa, who shot the best sons of the Russian people, and, most likely because of this, Nicholas pinned the label "Peacemaker" onto himself, extending an olive branch at the Hague Conference while feverishly readying the slaughter. The domestic regime of this protégé of savage landowners was so good that even gentlemen liberals were astounded, and Pavel Miliukov himself met with Azef[3] at terrorist conferences abroad. Only the Judas of liberalism, Pyotr Struve, shouted "Long live the army!" then. All the rest waited with impatience for the crushing defeat of the tsarist troops.

This crushing defeat unleashed the forces of the revolution. The last hopes for the tsar were shot to death on 9 January [1905].[4] The bloody dictatorship of a cowardly and malicious landowner who could feel the ground giving way beneath his feet was unmasked before the whole country. Frightened, Nicholas turned to his relative Wilhelm [the German emperor] for help. His agents laid siege to Parisian bankers' offices. Everything possible was put into motion: deception, perjury, surreptitious murder, provocations, bullets, gunpowder, the hard cash of foreign stockbrokers. In December 1905, blood flowed all over Russia, and gallows went up like landmarks of the autocracy. Nicholas strangled the revolution. Punitive expeditions to Latvia and the exploits of tsarist desperadoes and executioners are beyond description. They even put saws to living people, these agents of the most devout tsar!

This autocratic band, with Nicholas at its head running everything in Russia, left an indelible memory in its wake: Stolypin the Hangman, who practically whipped peasants personally, created Azef, and was later killed by one of the little Azefs; Purishkevich and Markov the Second, who, in the capacity of "parliamentary representatives" of the autocracy, proved that "we have no parliament" by their unparliamentary cursing in the elaborate and obscene true Russian manner; the likes of Sashka Kosoi and Sashka Polovnev in their thieves' dens, who organized the murder of their political opponents; the Greguses, who outdid the holy agents of the Spanish Inquisition in the matter of torture; the dashing generals Renenkampf and Min, who chopped off the heads of workers and peasants and handed their bloodied swords over to the "external enemy." These are the heroes of autocracy who were blessed by metropolitans, the higher orders of the clergy, and the priests as "God-fearing warriors" and "upholders of authority."

Having sent tens of thousands of his subjects to sleep underneath the damp ground, Nicholas resurrected the regime of the Middle Ages with all its charms. The Beilis affair,[5] in which the "yids" were accused of using Christian blood, inspired thugs and pimps to rip open the stomachs of an entire people. The unprecedented trial excellently illustrates what a pitiful scoundrel sat on the tsarist throne.

The war of 1914, into which Nicholas threw Russia after furious preparations on land and at sea, once again delivered a blow against tsarist autocracy.

In its death throes, the bloody regime clung to the greasy boots of the charlatan Rasputin, who raised his drunken eyes to the sky, cried, prayed, engaged in debauchery, and choked, ruined, and tormented the Russian people once again. Everything was caving in. Everything was collapsing. Disaster was inevitable, and the time for history's judgment had come.

The March [February] Revolution killed the autocracy politically. When they wanted to resurrect it, the bearer of this base "order" was executed physically.

Nicholas II was not just the personification of the barbarian-landowner, of this ignoramus, dimwit, and bloodthirsty savage. The "noble" blood of English kings and German emperors also ran in his veins.

He was tied from two sides to the imperialism of the brigand states of Europe. They will cry for him there. Russian workers and peasants have only one desire: to drive a good aspen-wood stake into this grave cursed by the people.

In the Presidium of the All-Russian TsIK

The first session of the Presidium of the TsIK's fifth convocation, chaired by comrade Sverdlov, took place on 18 July. Presidium members Avanesov, Sosnovsky, Teodorovich, Vladimirsky, Maksimov, Smidovich, Rozengolts, Mitrofanov, and Rozin were present.

ROMANOV'S EXECUTION

The chairman, comrade Sverdlov, announced the news just received over the direct line from the Ural Regional Soviet concerning former tsar Nicholas Romanov's execution.

In the last few days, Yekaterinburg, the capital of the Red Urals, was seriously threatened by the advancing Czechoslovak bands. At the same time, a new counterrevolutionary plot was exposed that had as its goal tearing the crowned executioner from the hands of Soviet power. In view of all these circumstances, the Presidium of the Ural Regional Soviet resolved to shoot Nicholas Romanov, and this was carried out on 16 July.

Nicholas Romanov's wife and son have been sent to a secure place. The documents on the exposed plot have been sent to Moscow by special courier.

Having made this announcement, comrade Sverdlov recalled the history of Nicholas Romanov's transfer from Tobolsk to Yekaterinburg after the discovery of the same kind of White Guard organization that was attempting to organize Nicholas Romanov's escape. Recently, the intention was to put the former tsar on trial for all his crimes against the people; only current developments interfered with bringing this about.

Having discussed all the circumstances that forced the Ural Regional Soviet to decide to have Nicholas Romanov shot, the Presidium of the Central Executive Committee made the following resolution: The All-Russian TsIK, represented by its Presidium, recognizes that the Ural Regional Soviet's decision was correct.

MATERIALS

Then the chairman reported that the TsIK now has at its disposal extremely important materials and documents that belonged to Nicholas Romanov: his personal diaries, which he kept from the time of his youth up until recently; his wife's and childrens' diaries; Romanov's correspondence, etc.

By the way, it also has letters from Grigory Rasputin to Romanov and his family. All these materials will be examined and published in the near future.

1. The Bolsheviks had executed Mikhail in June 1918.

2. In the morning of 18 (30) May 1896, four days after Nicholas II was anointed and crowned in the Uspensky Cathedral in the Moscow Kremlin, hundreds of thousands of ordinary Russians gathered on Khodynka field on the outskirts of Moscow for an officially sponsored celebration. When the free food and souvenirs began to be distributed, the crowds began pushing toward the booths. Many fell and were trampled. Official reports recorded 1,350 dead.

3. Yevno Azef was the leader of the terrorist Battle Organization of the Socialist Revolutionary Party, which organized assassinations of a number of government officials in the early years of the twentieth century. In 1908, Azef was exposed as a paid informant of the tsarist secret police.

4. On Sunday, 9 January 1905, police fired upon crowds of workers and their families

marching to the Winter Palace in St. Petersburg to present a petition of social grievances and desires to Nicholas II. Hundreds were wounded and killed, sparking the Revolution of 1905. Many Russians viewed "Bloody Sunday" as a moral and political touchstone, revealing the utter rottenness of the old regime.

5. In 1913 in Kiev, the Russian government charged a Jew, Mendel Beilis, with murdering a Christian boy and using his blood in a religious ritual. The trial incited both anti-Jewish pogroms and anti-government protests by liberals and socialists. Beilis was acquitted.

· 157 ·

"The Funeral of Nicholas the Bloody,"[1] a report by the newspaper *Ural'skii rabochii* (Ural worker), 26 September 1918.

Vlast' naroda [People's power], published in Cheliabinsk, prints the description received from Yekaterinburg of the solemn funeral of the former tsar arranged by military units of the People's Army [the anticommunist army linked to the Czech Legion].

The f. [former] tsar's corpse, buried on the spot of his execution in the forest, was exhumed from the grave that was found by following the instructions of individuals who knew the circumstances of the execution. The corpse was exhumed in the presence of Western Siberia's religious authorities, local clergy, and delegates from among the People's Army, the cossacks, and the Czechoslovaks.

The tsar's corpse was transferred to a zinc coffin encased in lavish wooden paneling of Siberian pine.

This coffin was placed in the Yekaterinburg cathedral under the protection of an honor guard drawn from the highest officers of the People's Army. From there, the coffin will be temporarily buried in a special sarcophagus in Omsk (*Priazovskii krai* [Priazov region], no. 131, 10 September).

Let them have their day! A new wave of the revolution will scatter to the winds the White Guards' power in Siberia, at the same time scattering the ashes of Nicholas the Bloody.

1. This report is obviously false, though it is not clear whether it was intentional disinformation or a reflection of false rumors and reports (soon after Yekaterinburg fell to the Whites in July 1918, investigators did in fact find the initial burial site in the woods and dug up evidence of the murder, though not the bodies themselves). There is no evidence that the story cited in the Bolshevik newspaper was actually printed in the indicated White newspaper. Whether an intentional fabrication or not, the story served to highlight the efforts by the White army to restore the hated old order and provided an occasion to underscore their inevitable failure.

· 158 ·

From the examination record of the interrogation of the defendant Pavel Medvedev,
commander of the guard at the Ipatiev house, 21–22 February 1919.

In the year 1919, on 21 and 22 February, in the town of Yekaterinburg, I. A. Sergeev, member of the Yekaterinburg regional court, interrogated in his chambers the following person in the capacity of defendant pursuant to articles 403–405 of the Code of Juridical Procedures, having charged him with crimes stipulated in articles 13 [conspiracy] and 1453 [aggravated and premeditated murder] of the Penal Code as formulated in my ruling of this February, during which the defendant testified:

I, Pavel Spiridonovich Medvedev, 31 years of age, am Orthodox, literate, have never been charged with breaking the law, am of peasant origin, come from Sysert factory, Sysert district, Yekaterinburg region, Perm province, am married, have a wife, Maria Danilovna, an eight-year-old daughter, Zoia, a six-year-old son, Andrei, and a one-year-old son, Ivan, and have my house and homestead in Sysert; I worked in the Sysert factory welding shop and earned extra money as a shoemaker in my spare time.

I had only two years of elementary schooling and left school not having finished out the year. I was mobilized as a fighter in the first-class irregulars and was conscripted into militia detachment no. 2, stationed in the town of Verkhotur. I spent a total of two months in the detachment and was then discharged from military service as a factory worker working for national defense.

After the February Revolution, I think it was in April 1917, I, like the majority of factory workers, joined the Bolshevik party and, in the course of three months, paid party dues of 1 percent of my pay; then I stopped paying money, for I did not wish to engage in party work.

After the October overthrow, in January 1918, I was conscripted into the Red Army, and by February I had already been sent to the Dutovsk front. Commissar Sergei Vitalievich Mrachkovsky was head of the detachment to which I was assigned. We fought outside the town of Troitsk, but we were not very fortunate in the war, and we spent more time "wandering" the steppe than we did in battle. In the month of April, I returned home from the front to rest here for three weeks.

In the second half of May, the above-named commissar, Mrachkovsky, came to our factory and began to assemble a detachment from among the workers to guard the house where the f. [former] emperor Nicholas II was confined with his family. The terms of employment seemed to suit me, and

I signed up for this detachment. Altogether, thirty men were assembled: [names follow].

. . .

We lived in the Ipatiev house for two to three weeks, and then we were given lodgings in the Popov house located opposite it. A few days after this, fifteen workers from the Zlokazov factory in Yekaterinburg were added to the detachment's composition. I do not remember the names and surnames of these workers. The Zlokazov workers also chose a "chief" (guard commander) from among themselves by the last name of Yakimov. I think his name was Leonid, but, in any case, he was called Lenka. There were only eleven guard positions, and of these, two guarded inside the house, two manned the machine guns, and four guarded outside.

The imperial family took a daily walk in the garden. The heir was sick the whole time, and the sovereign would bring him out carrying the wheelchair in his arms. The family's dinner was first served from a soviet dining hall, and then later they were allowed to cook dinner in a kitchen set up on the second floor.

The guard commander's duties were to manage household affairs and weapons for the detachment, to put men on duty, and to watch them at their posts. While on duty, the guard commander was to be in the commandant's office. At first, the guard commander was on duty for 12 hours, and then later a third guard commander was chosen—Konstantin Dobrynin—and we started being on duty for 8 hours.

At the end of June or the beginning of July, I don't remember exactly, Commandant Avdeev and his assistant, Moshkin, were replaced (I think they were caught stealing things belonging to the tsar's family), and a new commandant was appointed by the name of Yurovsky—the same man who is depicted on the photograph you have shown (a photograph of Yurovsky is shown). A new assistant commandant came with him, whose name and surname I cannot remember. His distinguishing characteristics are the following: about 30 or 32 years of age, heavyset, above average height, dark brown hair, with a smallish mustache, no beard; he speaks somehow through his nose (nasally).

I took up duty the night of 16 July, and around 8 o'clock the same evening, Commandant Yurovsky ordered me to confiscate all the Nagant revolvers in the detachment and to bring them to him. I took revolvers from those at their posts and from some others, a total of twelve revolvers, and brought them to the commandant's office. Then Yurovsky said to me: "Today we'll have to shoot everybody. Warn the detachment so they won't worry if they hear shots." I guessed that Yurovsky was talking about the shooting of the entire imperial family and the doctor and servants who lived with them, but [I] didn't ask who decided on the execution or when it would take place. I must tell you that the kitchen boy who had been in the house was transferred to the guard detachment's lodgings (the Popov house) that morning on Yurovsky's orders. Latvians from the "Latvian commune" were on the lower floor of the Ipatiev house, having moved in there after Yurovsky took up his post as commandant. There were ten of them. I don't know any of them by name or surname. Around 10 o'clock at night I warned the detachment as Yurovsky had ordered, telling them not to worry if they heard shots. I told Ivan Starkov that the shooting of the imperial family was at hand. I cannot positively remember and I cannot name who exactly from the detachment were then at their posts. I cannot remember from whom I took revolvers either.

Around midnight Yurovsky woke up the imperial family. I don't know whether he told them why he was waking them and where they had to go. I confirm that it was indeed Yurovsky who went into the rooms where the imperial family were. Yurovsky gave neither me nor Konstantin Dobrynin orders to wake up those sleeping. Roughly within an hour the whole imperial family, the doctor, the maid, and two servants got up, washed, and dressed. Even before Yurovsky went to wake the family, two members from the Extraordinary Commission [Cheka] came to the Ipatiev house: the first, as it turned out subsequently, was Pyotr Yermakov, and the other was someone I did not know by name or surname—tall, blond, and with a small mustache, age 25 or 26. I know Valentin Sakharov, but this was someone else and not him. Around 2 o'clock in the morning the tsar, tsaritsa, four royal daughters, the maid, the doctor, cook, and footman came out of their rooms. The tsar carried the heir in his arms. The sovereign and heir were dressed in soldiers' shirts and caps. Her Majesty and the daughters were in dresses with no outerwear and uncovered heads. The sovereign walked ahead with the heir—behind them came the tsaritsa, the daughters, and the others. Yurovsky, his assistant, and the two members of the Extraordinary Commission that I mentioned, accompanied them. I was also there.

None of the members of the imperial family asked anybody any questions in my presence. There were no tears, no sobbing, either. Having descended the stairs leading from the second entrance hall to the lower floor, we went into the courtyard and from there through a second door (counting from the gates) into the inner lodgings of the lower floor. Yurovsky showed the way. They were brought into the corner room on the lower floor adjacent to the sealed storage room. Yurovsky ordered that chairs be brought: his assistant brought three chairs. One chair was given to Her Majesty, the other to the sovereign, the third to the heir. Her Majesty sat by the wall with a window, closer to the back pillar of the arch. Behind her stood three daughters (I know them all very well by sight, as I saw each of them taking walks nearly every day, but I don't really know them by name). The heir and His Majesty sat side by side, almost in the middle of the room. Behind the heir's chair stood Doctor Botkin. The maid (I do not know her name—a tall woman) stood to the left of the door leading to the sealed storage room. One of the imperial daughters (the fourth one) stood with her. Two servants stood in the left-hand corner (from the entrance), by the wall adjacent to the storage room.

The maid had a pillow in her hands. The daughters brought little pillows with them also. One of the little pillows was put on the seat of Her Majesty's chair, the other on the heir's seat. It seems that all of them suspected the fate that was about to befall them, but no one made a single sound. Simultaneously, eleven people walked into the same room: Yurovsky, his assistant, two members of the Extraordinary Commission, and seven Latvian men. Yurovsky sent me out, saying, "Go to the street, to see whether anybody's there and whether the shots will be heard."[1] I walked out into the courtyard enclosed by a tall fence, and I heard the sound of shots before I had reached the street. I immediately returned to the house (only 2 or 3 minutes had gone by), and when I entered that room where the shooting had taken place, I saw that all the members of the imperial family—tsar, tsaritsa, four daughters, and the heir—were already lying on the floor with multiple wounds to their bodies. The blood flowed in streams. The doctor, the maid, and the two servants were also dead. When I entered the room, the heir was still alive—moaning. Yurovsky walked up to him and shot him point-blank two or three times. The heir fell silent. The murder scene, the smell and the sight of blood, made me nauseous. Before the murder, Yurovsky passed out Nagant revolvers to everyone and gave a revolver to me, but, I repeat, I did not take part in the shooting. Yurovsky had a Mauser in addition to a Nagant.

When the murder was over, Yurovsky sent me to the detachment to get people to wash off the blood in the room. On the way to the Popov house, I ran into the guard commanders Ivan Starkov and Konstantin Dobrynin, who had come running from the detachment. The latter asked me: "Did they shoot Nicholas II? Watch out that they don't shoot someone else in place of him: you'll have to answer for it." I answered that Nicholas II and his whole family were killed. I brought back twelve to fifteen people from the detachment, but who exactly I can't remember at all and can't name you a single name. The people I brought first busied themselves with loading the corpses of the dead onto a truck that had been brought up to the front entrance. The corpses were brought out on stretchers made of sheets wrapped around harness beams taken from sleighs in the courtyard. The corpses piled into the truck were covered with part of a soldier's blanket taken from the small storage room located in the corridor of the lower floor. Liukhanov, a worker from the Zlokazov factory, was the chauffeur. Pyotr Yermakov and the other member of the Extraordinary Commission climbed into the truck and took the corpses away. I do not know what direction they went or what they did with the corpses. We washed off the blood in the room and the courtyard and put everything in order. By 3 o'clock in the morning it was all over, and Yurovsky went to his office, and I went home to the detachment.

. . .

On 24 July I left Yekaterinburg with commissar Mrachkovsky. In Perm, commissar Goloshchekin assigned me to the guard outfitted to blow up the Kamsk Bridge in case the "White Guards" showed up. I didn't manage to blow up the bridge according to orders given, and I didn't even want to, having decided to give myself up willingly. I got orders to blow up the bridge when the Siberian troops had already begun shooting up the bridge, and I went and gave myself up willingly. I soon became a medical orderly at evacuation aid post no. 139 in the town of Perm, where I remained until the moment of my arrest. There I somehow started talking with one of the nurses. In response to one of her remarks that the newspapers write about how nastily the imperial family was treated, I told her that all this wasn't true. Moreover, I told her, in just the detail I told you earlier, that I had served in the Ipatiev house guard detachment, and [I] told her how the imperial family lived there and how the shooting took place. I explained everything to her about Yurovsky, his assistant, the two members of the Extraordinary Commission, and the Latvians, told her who did the shooting, how the blood was washed off, and how the corpses were carried out to the truck. This conversation took place soon after I joined the aid post. This was the nurse whom the official you sent later pointed out to me from a distance.

I know only this about where the corpses are hidden: as I was leaving Yekaterinburg, I met Pyotr Yermakov at the Alapaevsk station and asked him where they had taken the corpses. Yermakov explained that the corpses had been thrown into a mine beyond the Upper Isetsk factory and that the mine had been blown up with bombs to cave it in. I know nothing about and heard nothing about burnt-out fires near the mines. I have no further knowledge about where the corpses can be found.

I never expressed an interest in who determined the fate of the tsar and his family or who had the right to do so, for I was only carrying out orders given by those whom I served. Beloborodov and Goloshchekin were the ones from among the Soviet authorities who frequently came to the house. Before the shooting, I did not see or hear Yurovsky read any sort of document to the tsar or say anything about the impending execution. From among the men named by me who served in the Sysert detachment the day of the shooting, those absent were Ivan Kotov, Viktor Lugovoi, Andrei Starkov, Grigory Kesarev, and Vasily Semyonov; Aleksei Nikiforov was discharged for medical reasons about three weeks before this. I don't know exactly where all those named in my deposition are to be found. Some of those from the detachment were at the Levshinsk pier until Perm was taken; some serve in the Red Army.

This is all that I can tell you about the accusations made against me. I repeat that I did not directly participate in the shooting. Filipp Proskuriakov, whom you have shown me, was in the detachment until recently, but I don't remember whether he took part in cleaning up the room and carrying the corpses.

I do recollect that Yurovsky allowed me to take a small suitcase belonging to Botkin before my departure for Sysert. I am not able to explain anything more.

> This has been read and correctly
> recorded, Medvedev
> Member of the Yekaterinburg
> regional court, I. Sergeev

1. Medvedev's statement that he did not participate in the shooting is suspect, though understandable considering that he was facing a White court. Several months earlier, Medvedev's wife had testified that before her husband went into hiding he had told her in detail about his direct participation in the shooting (Mariia Medvedeva, testimony of 9–10 November 1918, Houghton Library, Harvard University, Sokolov Archive, vol. 1, doc. 57).

· 159 ·

Yakov Yurovsky's note on the execution of the imperial family and the concealment of the corpses, 1920.

On 16 July [1918], a telegram in previously agreed-upon language came from Perm containing the order to exterminate the R-ovs [Romanovs]. At first (in May), the intention was to bring Nicholas to trial, but this was prevented by the advancing Whites. On the 16th at 6 o'clock in the eve., Filipp G-n [Goloshchekin] decreed that the order be carried out. A car was to arrive at midnight to take away the corpses. At 6 o'clock, the boy [Leonid Sednyov] was taken away, which very much upset the R-ovs and their people. Doctor Botkin even came to ask why this was called for?

It was explained that the boy's uncle, who had been arrested, had escaped and then returned and wanted to see his nephew.[1] The boy was sent the next day to his birthplace (in Tula province, I think). The truck did not arrive at 12 o'clock; it came only at half past one. This delayed carrying out the order. By that time everything was ready: 12 people with revolvers (including 5 Latvians) were selected who were supposed to carry out the sentence; 2 of the Latvians refused to shoot at girls.

Everyone was asleep when the car came. Botkin was woken up, and he woke up all the rest. The explanation was as follows: "The R-ov family must be moved from upstairs to downstairs as all is not calm in town." They dressed in half an hour. A downstairs room was selected that had walls of plastered wood (to prevent [the bullets from] ricocheting); all the furniture was removed. The detachment was at the ready in the next room. The R-ovs suspected nothing. The comm. [commandant][2] went to get them personally, alone, and led them downstairs to the room below. Nich. was carrying A. [Aleksei] in his arms; the rest carried little pillows and other small things with them. Walking into the empty room, A. F. [Alexandra Fyodorovna] asked: "What, there isn't even a chair? One isn't even allowed to sit down?" The comm. ordered two chairs to be brought. Nich. seated A. on one, and A. F. sat down on the other. The commandant ordered the rest to stand in a row.

When they had taken their places, he called in the detachment. When the detachment came in, the commandant told the R-ovs that, in light of the fact that their relatives in Europe were continuing their aggression against Soviet Russia, the Ural [Regional Soviet] Executive Committee had decreed that they were to be shot. Nicholas turned his back to the detachment, his face toward his family, then, as though collecting himself, turned to the commandant with the question: "What? What?" The comm. hurriedly repeated his statement and ordered the detachment to get ready. The detachment had been given instructions earlier on whom to shoot and were ordered to aim directly for the heart to avoid a large amount of blood and to finish them off more quickly. Nicholas, again turning to the family, said nothing more; the others made a few incoherent exclamations; this all lasted a few seconds. Then the shooting started; [it] lasted for two to three minutes. Nich. was killed on the spot by the comm. himself. A. F. died immediately after that and the other R-ovs (altogether 12 people were shot [in fact, 11 people were shot]): N., A. F., four daughters (Tatiana, Olga, Maria, and Anastasia), Doctor Botkin, the footman Trupp,[3] the cook Tikhomirov [actually, Kharitonov], another cook,[4] and a lady-in-waiting whose last name the commandant has forgotten [actually, Alexandra's personal maid, Anna Demidova]. A., three of his sisters, the lady-in-waiting, and Botkin were still alive. They had to be shot again. This surprised the comm. because they had aimed for the heart. It was also surprising that the bullets from the pistols ricocheted off something and jumped about the room like hail. When they tried to finish off one of the girls with bayonets, the bayonet could not pierce the corset. Thanks to all of this, the entire procedure, including "verification" (feeling the pulse, etc.), took around 20 minutes.

Then they started carrying out the corpses and putting them into the car, which had been covered with heavy blankets so the blood wouldn't seep out. At this point, the stealing began: three reliable comrades had to be assigned to guard the corpses while the procedure continued (the corpses were brought out one by one). All of the stolen goods were returned under the threat of execution (a gold watch, a cigarette case with diamonds, and so on). The comm. was only assigned to carry out the sentence; the removal of corpses and so on was comrade Yermakov's responsibility (a worker from the Upper Isetsk factory, a party comrade, ex-prisoner).[5] He was supposed to come with the car and be admitted by using the agreed-upon password, "chimney sweep." The car's late arrival caused the commandant to doubt Ye-v's [Yermakov's] thoroughness, and the comm. decided to stay with the whole operation to the end.

Around 3 o'clock in the morning, we departed for the place that Ye-v was to have prepared (beyond the Upper Isetsk factory). First it was assumed that they [the corpses] would be brought by car and then, beginning at a certain point, on horseback, since the car could go no further. The place selected was an abandoned mine. After driving a little more than 3 miles[6] past the Upper Isetsk factory, we bumped into a whole encampment—about 25 people—on horseback, in light, horse-drawn carts, etc. These were workers (members of the soviet, of the Executive Committee, etc.) whom Ye-v had prepared. The first thing they exclaimed was: "Why didn't you bring them to us alive?!" They thought the Romanovs' execution would be entrusted to them. They began to load the corpses into the light carts, but wagons were needed. This was very inconvenient. They immediately began to clean out [the corpses'] pockets—it was necessary to threaten them with being shot and to post sentries here as well. Then it was discovered that Tatiana, Olga, and Anastasia were dressed in some kind of special corsets. It was decided to strip the corpses bare, but not here, only at the place of burial. But it turned out that no one knew where the mine was that had been selected for this purpose.

It was growing light. The comm. sent men on horseback to find the place, but no one found anything. It turned out that nothing had been readied at all: there were no shovels and so on. The car had gotten stuck between two trees, so it was abandoned, and, after the corpses were covered with blankets, the carts were moved in single file. We drove about 11 miles from Yekaterinburg and stopped a mile from the village of Koptiaki; this was around 6 or 7 o'clock in the morning. In the forest, an abandoned prospector's mine about eight feet deep was found (gold was once mined there). The mine had a couple of feet of water. The comm. ordered the corpses undressed and a fire built so that everything could be burnt. Men on horseback were posted everywhere to drive away all passersby.

When one of the girls was being undressed, it was noticed that the bullets had torn the corset in places, and diamonds could be seen in the holes. The eyes of those all around began burning brightly. The comm. immediately decided to dismiss the whole group, leaving on guard a few men on horseback and five from the detachment. The rest dispersed. The detachment began to undress and burn the corpses. A. F. was wearing a whole pearl belt made of several strands and sewn into cloth. Around each girl's neck, it turned out, was a portrait of Rasputin with the text of his prayer sewn into the amulets. The diamonds were instantly removed. They (things made of diamonds, that is) amounted to about eighteen pounds. These were buried in the cellar of one of the little houses at the Alapaevsk factory; in 1919 they were dug up and brought to Moscow.

After we put everything valuable into bags, the rest of what was found on the corpses was burnt and the corpses themselves were lowered into the mine. While this was going on, a few of the valuables (someone's brooch, Botkin's dentures) were dropped, and in the effort to cave in the mine with the help of hand grenades, it was evident that the corpses were damaged and that certain parts were torn off some of them—that is how the commandant explains how the Whites (who discovered it) came to find a ripped-off finger and so forth at this spot. But it was not planned to leave the R-ovs here—the mine had earlier been designated only a temporary burial spot.

Having completed the operation and left the guard, around 10 to 11 o'clock in the morning (already 17 July), the comm. went to report to the Ural [Regional Soviet] Executive Committee, where he found Safarov and Beloborodov. The comm. told them what had been found and expressed his regret that they had not allowed him to conduct a timely search of the R-ovs. The comm. found out from Chutskaev (chairman of the Executive Committee of the city soviet) that at mile 6 along the Moscow highway there are very deep, abandoned mines suitable for burying the R-ovs. The comm. left for that spot but did not arrive immediately because his car broke down. He [eventually] reached the mines on foot and actually found three very deep mines filled with water, where he decided to submerge the corpses by tying rocks to them. Guards were there who served as inconvenient witnesses, so it was decided to send, together with the truck containing the corpses, a car with Cheka security officers, who would arrest everyone there under the pretext of a search. To make his way back, the comm. appropriated a pair of horses that happened to come along. Those who had been by chance detained [for being in the area] were sent on. After setting out [for town] on horseback, together with another Chekist [member of the Cheka], to organize the whole matter, the comm. fell from his horse and badly hurt himself (afterwards, the Chekist fell as well). In case the plan with the mines didn't work, it was decided to burn the corpses or to bury them in clay pits filled with water, after first disfiguring the corpses beyond recognition with sulfuric acid.

Finally, having returned to town around 8 o'clock in the evening on the 17th, everything necessary began to be gathered: the kerosene, the sulfuric acid. Horse-drawn carts without drivers were taken from the prison. It had been planned to leave at 11 o'clock at night, but the incident with the Chekist held things up, and we left for the mine, together with ropes to drag out the corpses and so on, only around 12:30 on the night of the 17th to the 18th. In order to isolate the mine (the first prospector's mine) for the duration of the operation, it was announced to the village of Koptiaki that Czechs were hiding in the forest, that the forest would be searched, and that on no account should anyone from the village go anywhere. It was ordered to shoot on the spot anyone who happened to break into the cordoned-off area.

Meanwhile, dawn came (this was already the third day, the 18th). The thought was to bury some of the corpses right then and there by the mine. We began to dig a pit and almost finished digging it out. But just then a peasant acquaintance of Yermakov's drove up, and it turned out he had been able to see the pit. That effort had to be abandoned. It was decided to take the corpses to the deep mines. Because the carts were flimsy and falling apart, the comm. left for town to get motor vehicles (a truck and two motorcars, one for the Chekists). The carts had broken down earlier, and the vehicles were needed for transport to the deep mines, but in fact the vehicles could not make it to the place of temporary burial and that was why the carts still had to be used. When the vehicles arrived, the carts were already moving—the vehicles met them a quarter of a mile closer to Koptiaki. We could not begin the trip until 9 o'clock at night. We crossed the railroad tracks and, a quarter of a mile later, we moved the corpses onto the truck. We drove with difficulty, paving the hazardous places with railway ties, but we still got stuck a few times. Around 4:30 in the morning of the 19th, one of the vehicles got completely stuck. Since we had not reached the mine, it was necessary to either bury or burn the corpses. One comrade, whose last name the comm. has forgotten, promised to take the latter upon himself but left without carrying out his promise.

We wanted to burn A. [Aleksei] and A. F., but by mistake the lady-in-waiting [the maid Demidova] was burnt with A. instead. We then immediately buried the remains under the fire and lit the fire again, which completely covered up traces of the digging. Meanwhile, we dug a common grave for the rest. A pit around 6 feet deep and 8 feet square was ready by around 7 o'clock in the morning. We piled the corpses in the pit, poured sulfuric acid onto their faces and generally over their whole bodies to prevent them both from being recognized and from stinking as a result of decomposition (the pit was not deep). Having thrown dirt and brushwood on top, we put down railroad ties and drove over them a few times—no traces of the pit were left. The secret was completely safe; the Whites didn't find this burial place.

Koptiaki is 12 miles from Yekaterinburg. The R.R. crosses mile 6 between Koptiaki and the Upper Isetsk factory to the northwest [of town]. The burial place is 700 feet closer to the U. Isetsk factory from the point of intersection.

1. In fact, the uncle, Ivan Sednyov, had already been executed.
2. This account is written in the third person by Yurovsky, who calls himself the commandant.
3. Aleksei Yegorovich Trupp, a footman to the imperial family, was with the Romanovs in Tobolsk and Yekaterinburg.
4. Yurovsky was inaccurate here: there was no other cook.
5. Pyotr Zakharovich Yermakov, military commissar for Upper Isetsk, a long-time associate of Goloshchekin's in the revolutionary movement.
6. Russian measurements in this document have been converted to U.S. measurements.

· 160 ·

From Yurovsky's account of the execution of the tsar and his family as told at a meeting of old Bolsheviks in Sverdlovsk (formerly Yekaterinburg), 1 February 1934.

———

. . . It was presumed that a trial would have been organized for them had time permitted. But as I have already said above, the front had been moving closer and closer since the beginning of July and was then only about 25 miles[1] away, inevitably hastening a denouement.

This was a question of great political significance then and could not be resolved without a decision by the center, because the situation at the front also depended not only on the Urals but also on the center's possibilities (by this time, you see, the Red Army was becoming more and more centralized and concentrated). There were continual contacts and conversations with the center about this. Around 10 July, the decision had already been made about what to do if abandoning Yekaterinburg became unavoidable. You see, only this can explain why execution without a trial was put off until 16 July, with Yekaterinburg being finally abandoned on 25–26 July; moreover, Yekaterinburg's evacuation was conducted in a completely, so to speak, orderly and timely way. Around 10 or 11 July, Filipp [Golosh-chekin] told me that Nicholas would have to be liquidated and that it was necessary to prepare for this.

When it came to liquidation methods, we had no experience in such matters, since we hadn't engaged in such things before, and thus it was no wonder that there was a lot that was rushed in putting this matter into effect, especially because all sorts of dangers and the proximity of the front intensified the problem. He told me that individual comrades thought that to pull this off more securely and quietly it should be done at night, right in their beds as they sleep. That seemed inconvenient to me, and I said that we would think about how to do it and would get prepared.

On the morning of 15 July, Filipp arrived and said that things had to be finished off tomorrow. Sednyov the kitchen boy (a boy of thirteen) was to be taken away and sent to his former birthplace or to somewhere in central Russia. It was also said that Nicholas was to be executed and that we should officially announce it, but when it came to the family, then perhaps it would be announced, but no one knew yet how, when, and in what manner. Thus, everything demanded the utmost care and as few people as possible—moreover, absolutely dependable ones.

On the 15th I immediately undertook preparations, for everything had to be done quickly. I decided to assemble the same number of men as there were people to be shot, gathered them all together, and told them what was happening—that they all had to prepare themselves for this, that as soon as we got the final order everything was going to have to be ably handled. You see, it has to be said that shooting people isn't the easy matter that it might seem to some. After all, this wasn't going on at the front but in a "peaceful" situation. You see, these weren't bloodthirsty people, but people performing the difficult duty of the revolution. That was why it wasn't mere chance that, at the last minute, the situation arose that two Latvians refused [to participate]—they didn't have it in them.

On the morning of the 16th, I sent away the kitchen boy Sednyov under the pretext of a meeting with his uncle who had come to Sverdlovsk. This caused anxiety among the arrested. Botkin, the devoted intermediary, and then one of the daughters asked where and why they had taken Sednyov and for how long. Aleksei missed him, they said. Having gotten an explanation, they left, seemingly calmed. I prepared 12 Nagant revolvers and determined who would shoot whom. Comrade Filipp warned me that a truck would arrive at 12 o'clock at night. Those who arrived would give a password; they would be allowed in and would be given the corpses, which they would take away for burial. Around 11 o'clock at night on the 16th I gathered the men together again, gave out the revolvers, and stated that we would soon have to start liquidating the arrested. I warned Pavel Medvedev about the thorough check of the sentries outside and in, about how he and the guard commander should be on watch themselves in the area around the house and at the house where the external guard was lodged, and about how they should keep in contact with me. Only at the last minute, when everything was ready for the shooting, were they to warn all the sentries as well as the rest of the detachment that if they heard shots coming from the house they shouldn't worry and shouldn't come out of their lodgings, and that if something was especially worrisome they should let me know through the established channel.

The truck did not show up until half past one in the morning; the fact that we waited longer than expected couldn't help but create anxiety, in addition to the anxiety of waiting in general, but the main thing was that the [summer] nights were so short. Only after the truck came—or after I learned by telephone that the truck was on its way—did I go to wake the arrested.

Botkin was asleep in the room closest to the entrance; he came out and asked what the matter was. I told him that everyone had to be woken up right away as the town was uneasy, that staying upstairs was dangerous for them, and that I would transfer them to another place. Preparations took a lot of time, around 40 minutes. When the family was dressed, I led them to a room previously selected in the downstairs part of the house. We had thought this plan through with comrade Nikulin.[2] Here I have to say that we didn't think in advance about the fact that the windows could not contain the noise; second, that the wall against which those to be shot were to be lined up was made of stone; and, finally, that the shooting would take on a chaotic character, but this was impossible to foresee. This last thing wasn't supposed to occur because each man was going to shoot one person, and so everything was to be orderly. The reasons for the chaos—that is, disorderly and confused shooting—became clear later. Although I warned them through Botkin that they didn't need to bring anything with them, they nevertheless gathered up various little things—pillows, little bags, and so forth—and, I believe, a little dog.

Once they had descended to the room (at the entrance to the room on the right is a very wide window, almost the size of the whole wall), I suggested they stand by the wall. Apparently, at that moment they still did not imagine anything of what was in store for them. Alexandra Fyodorovna said: "There aren't even chairs here." Nicholas was carrying Aleksei in his arms. And he continued to stand with him like that in the room. Then I ordered a pair of chairs to be brought. Alexandra Fyodorovna sat on one of them to the right of the entrance, almost in the corner and by the window. Next to her, toward the left side of the entrance, stood the daughters and Demidova. Here Aleksei was set down beside them on a chair; after him came Doctor Botkin, the cook, and others, and Nicholas was left standing opposite Aleksei. Simultaneously, I ordered the people to come down and ordered that everyone be ready and that each be at his place when the command was given. Nicholas, having seated Aleksei, stood so that he was blocking him. Aleksei sat in the left-hand corner of the room from the entrance, and I immediately, as I recall it, told Nicholas approximately the following: that his imperial relatives and close associates both inside the country and abroad had tried to free him and that the Soviet of Workers' Deputies had decreed that they be shot. He asked: "What?" and turned to face Aleksei. Right then, I shot him and killed him on the spot. He didn't manage to turn to face us to get an answer. Now, instead of order, chaotic shooting began. The room was very small, but still everyone could have entered the room and performed the shooting in an orderly way. But, apparently, many shot across the threshold, and the bullets began to ricochet, since the wall was made of stone. Moreover, the firing intensified when those being shot began to scream. It took a great effort on my part to stop the shooting. A bullet from one of those shooting behind me whizzed by my head, and I can't remember whether it was the palm, hand, or finger of someone else that was hit and pierced by a bullet. When the shooting stopped, it turned out that the daughters, Alexandra Fyodorovna, the lady-in-waiting [actually, the personal maid] Demidova, I think, and also Aleksei were alive. I thought that they had fallen out of fear or perhaps on purpose and that was why they were still alive. Then we began to finish them off (I had earlier suggested that they be shot in the region of the heart so that there would be less blood.) Aleksei remained seated, petrified, and I finished him off. They shot the daughters but nothing happened, then Yermakov set the bayonet in motion and that didn't help, then they were finished off by being shot in the head. Only in the forest did I discover what hampered the shooting of the daughters and Alexandra Fyodorovna.

Now that the shooting was over, the corpses had to be moved, and it was rather a long way. How could they be carried? Here someone thought of stretchers (they didn't think of it at the proper time). They took harness beams from sleighs and stretched sheets over them, I think. Having checked that everyone was dead, we began to carry them. Then we realized that bloodstains would be everywhere. I immediately ordered that the stretchers be lined with available soldiers' blankets and that the truck be covered with them. I assigned Mikhail Medvedev[3] to remove the corpses. He is a former member of the Cheka and, at present, an employee of the GPU [security police]. He and Pyotr Zakharovich Yermakov were supposed to take the corpses and drive away with them. When the first corpses were taken away, someone, I can't remember who, told me that one of the men had appropriated some valuables for himself. I then understood that there were valuables among the things the family had brought with them. I immediately stopped the carrying of the corpses, gathered the men together, and demanded that the stolen valuables be handed over. After a certain amount of denial, two men returned valuables they had stolen. Threatening anyone who looted with execution, I dismissed these two and, as I recall, assigned comrade Nikulin to supervise the carrying of the corpses, having warned them that valuables were present on the bodies of those shot. I gathered together all the items containing objects that they had seized, in addition to the objects themselves, and sent them to the commandant's office. Comrade Filipp [Goloshchekin], apparently sparing me (as my health wasn't the best), warned me that I shouldn't go to the "funeral," but I was very worried about how well the corpses would be hidden. That was why I decided to go myself, and I did the right thing as it turned out; otherwise, all the corpses would have certainly fallen into the hands of the Whites. It is easy to see how they would have used this matter to their advantage.

Having ordered that everything be washed and cleaned up, we departed around 3 o'clock or a little later. I took a few people from the internal guard along with me. I did not know where they were planning to bury the corpses. As I said above, Filipp had apparently assigned this matter to comrade Yermakov, who took us somewhere near the Upper Isetsk factory (by the way, I think it was Pavel Medvedev who told me the same night that, when he was running to the detachment, he saw comrade Filipp walking by the house the whole time and looking more than a little worried about how things would go there). I hadn't been to these parts and wasn't familiar with them. About 1 or 2 miles or maybe more from the Upper Isetsk factory, we were met by a whole convoy of people on horseback and in light horse-drawn carts. I asked Yermakov who these people were, why they were here, and he answered that these were the people he had prepared. I don't know to this day why there were so many. I heard only isolated shouts: "We thought that you would deliver them to us alive, and now it turns out they're dead." Then, I think it was 2 or 3 miles farther on, the truck got stuck between two trees.

During this stop, some of Yermakov's people started to pull at the girls' blouses where they discovered the valuables. The stealing was starting up again. Then I ordered that people be posted so that no one could come near the truck. The truck was stuck and couldn't budge. I asked Yermakov, "And is the place chosen for them far?" He said, "It's not far, beyond the railway embankment." And, on top of being stuck between the trees, this was a marshy place. No matter where we went, it was swampy. I thought to myself, He brought so many people and horses; at least there should have been wagons instead of lightweight carts. But there was nothing to be done. We had to unload and lighten the truck; but even this didn't help. Then I ordered the bodies loaded onto the horse-drawn carts, since we couldn't wait any longer: dawn was coming.

Only when it was already beginning to be light did we reach the well-known "clearing." Peasants were sitting by the fire about 20 paces or so from the mine selected for the burial site, apparently having spent the night there after haymaking. Along the way, lone people could also be seen at a distance, and it became utterly impossible to continue working within sight of people. I have to say that the situation was becoming difficult and everything could have been ruined. I still didn't know then that the mine wasn't worth a damn for our purposes. And then there were those cursed valuables. I didn't know then that there were rather a lot of them. The people that Yermakov had gathered weren't at all right for this sort of job, and there were so many of them, too. I decided that the people had to be gotten rid of. I immediately found out that we were about 10 or 11 miles outside town and about 1 or 2 miles outside the village of Koptiaki. A large-enough area had to be cordoned off, which I ordered done. I selected people and instructed them to surround a certain area. In addition, I sent people to the village to advise the villagers not to go anywhere, saying that Czechoslovaks were nearby, that our units had been brought here, and that it was dangerous. Then [I said] to send anyone they saw back to the village and, if nothing else worked, to shoot those who were stubbornly disobedient. I sent the other group of people back to the village, because they were no longer necessary.

Having done this, I ordered the corpses [un]loaded and the clothing removed and burned. That is, I ordered the things destroyed without a trace, and saw to it that any incriminating evidence was removed, in case someone were to discover the corpses. I ordered bonfires built. Things that had been sewn into the daughters' and Alexandra's clothing were discovered when the corpses began to be undressed; I can't remember exactly what was discovered on the latter or if it was simply the same sort of things as were sewn into the daughters' clothing. The daughters had bodices made up of solid diamonds and other precious stones that served not just as receptacles for valuables but also as protective armor. That was why neither bullets nor bayonets yielded results during the shooting and bayonet blows. No one is responsible for their death agonies but themselves, it has to be said. There turned out to be about 18 pounds of such valuables. By the way, their greed turned out to be so great that on Alexandra Fyodorovna there was a simply huge piece of gold wire bent into the shape of a bracelet of around a pound in weight. All these valuables were immediately ripped out so that we wouldn't have to drag the bloody clothing with us. Those valuables that the Whites discovered when they excavated were undoubtedly part of the things that had been individually sewn into the clothing and that remained in the ashes of the fire when the clothing was burned. The next day, comrades gave me a few diamonds that they had found there. How could they have overlooked other valuables? They had enough time to look. The most likely thing is that they just didn't think of it. By the way, some valuables are being returned to us through Torgsin stores,[4] for it is likely that the peasants from Koptiaki village picked some valuables up after our departure. We gathered the valuables, burned the things, and threw the stark-naked corpses into the mine.

And here another muddle ensued. The water barely covered the bodies; what to do? We thought of blowing up the mine with bombs to cave it in. But nothing came of this, of course. I saw that we were getting nowhere with the burial and that the bodies couldn't be left as is and that everything had to be started all over again. But what to do? Where to put them? Around 2 o'clock in the afternoon I decided to go to town because it was clear that the corpses had to be extracted from the mine and transferred to a different place. Besides, even a blind man could find them with the place being so churned up. People had seen that something was going on there. I posted sentries and guards at the spot, took the valuables, and left.

I went to the Regional [Soviet] Executive Committee and told the authorities how badly things had gone. Comrade Safarov, and I can't remember who else, listened and had nothing to say. Then I found Filipp [Goloshchekin] and pointed out the necessity of transferring the corpses to another place. When he agreed, I suggested that people be sent immediately to pull out the corpses. I would concern myself with finding another place. Filipp summoned Yermakov, severely reprimanded him, and sent him to dig up the corpses. I simultaneously instructed him to take bread and dinner, as the men had been there almost 24 hours without sleep and were hungry and worn out. They were supposed to wait there until I arrived. It turned out not to be so easy to pull out the corpses, and we suffered rather a lot over it. We had set out late, and we fiddled with it all night.

I went to Sergei Yegorovich Chutskaev, then chairman of the [Yekaterinburg] City Soviet Executive Committee, to ask whether he perhaps knew of a place. He recommended some very deep abandoned mines on the Moscow highway. I got a car, took someone from the regional Cheka with me, Polushin, I think, and someone else, and we left. About a mile short of the designated spot, the car broke down, so we left the driver to fix it and set out on foot, looked the place over, and found that it would do. The only thing was making sure there weren't extra, watchful eyes. Some people lived not far from there, and we decided we would go and remove them and send them to town. At the end of the operation we would free them; that was what we decided on. When we got back to the car, the car itself needed towing. I decided to wait for a chance passerby. Some time later, some people were tearing along, driving a pair of horses. I stopped them, and it turned out that the boys knew me and were hurrying to get to their factory. They weren't very keen on it, but they gave the horses up.

While we rode, another plan came to mind: to burn the corpses. But no one knew how. It seems to me Polushin said he knew how, which was fine, since no one really knew how it would turn out. I still had the mines along the Moscow highway in mind and consequently decided to obtain carts to use for transport. Besides, in case of bad luck, I thought of burying them in groups in different places along the thoroughfare. The road leading to Koptiaki, which is next to the clearing, is clayey, so if they could be buried there without anyone seeing, not a living soul would ever guess. They could be buried and carts could be driven over [the site]. The result would be a rough pathway and nothing more. And so, three plans.

There was no form of transportation, no car. I went to the director of the military transport garage to find out if they had any cars. There turned out to be a car, but the director, whose surname I forget, later turned out to be a scoundrel, and I think they shot him in Perm. Comrade Pavel Petrovich Gorbunov was the garage director or deputy director, I can't remember exactly, and is currently the deputy [chairman] of the State Bank. I told him that I needed a car quickly. He said, "And I know what for." And he gave me the director's car. I went to Voikov,[5] supply director for the Urals, to obtain gasoline or kerosene, sulfuric acid for disfiguring the faces, and a shovel. I obtained all of these. As deputy commissar of justice of the Ural region, I saw to it that ten carts without drivers were taken from the prisons. Everything was loaded up, and they left. The truck was directed to

the same place. I myself stayed to wait for Polushin, "specialist" in burning, who had disappeared. I waited for him at Voikov's. Even though I
waited until 11 o'clock at night, I didn't find him. Later they told me that
he was on his way to me but fell from his horse, hurt his leg, and couldn't
make it. I could have used the car again, but around 12 o'clock at night I
mounted a horse with a comrade whose name I don't remember now and
departed for the place where the corpses were. Misfortune befell me too.
The horse stumbled, rose to its knees, and somehow fell awkwardly on its
side, crushing my leg. I spent an hour or more lying down before I could
mount my horse again. We arrived late during the night and went to work
extracting [the corpses]. I decided to bury a few corpses on the road. We
started digging a pit. It was almost ready by dawn when one comrade came
up to me and said that, despite the ban on allowing anyone near, a person
had shown up from somewhere, an acquaintance of Yermakov's, whom
Yermakov permitted to remain at a distance. The person could see that
people were digging around here since piles of clay were lying around.
Although Yermakov assured us that this person couldn't see anything,
other comrades started to illustrate, that is, to show, where the person had
been standing and how he undoubtedly couldn't help seeing.

    That was how this plan was ruined too. It was decided to fill in the pit.
We piled everything onto the cart as evening fell. The truck was waiting in
a spot where it was pretty nearly guaranteed that it would not get stuck
(the driver was Liukhanov, the worker from the Zlokazov factory). We
headed for the Siberian highway. Having crossed the railway embankment, we loaded the corpses into the truck again and quickly got in. We
had been struggling for two hours, so it was getting close to midnight, and I
decided that we had to bury them somewhere around here because at this
late hour it was certain that no one at all could see us. I had sent for
railroad ties to be brought to cover the place where the corpses would be
piled, so there was only one person who might see a few of the men—the
railroad night watchman. I had in mind that if anyone found the ties, they
might guess that they were put down to let a truck pass through. I forgot to
say that during that evening or, more precisely, during the night, we got
stuck twice. Having unloaded everything, we got out, but then we got
hopelessly stuck a second time. Two months ago, I saw a picture of these
ties as I leafed through the book by Sokolov, [the White army commander]
Kolchak's investigator for exceptionally important cases.[6] There it was
noted that the railway ties were put down at that spot to let a truck drive
through. So, having dug up a whole area, they never thought to look
beneath the ties.

    I have to say that we were all so devilishly exhausted that we didn't want to dig new graves, but, as always happens in these cases, two or three began doing it and then others joined in. We immediately lit fires, and while the grave was being readied, we burned two corpses: Aleksei and, apparently, Demidova, instead of Alexandra Fyodorovna, as we had intended. We dug a pit by the spot where they were burned, piled in the bones, evened it over, lit another big fire, and covered all traces with ashes. Before putting the rest of the corpses in the pit, we poured sulfuric acid on them; then we filled in the pit, covered it with railway ties, drove the empty truck over them, tamped the ties down a little, and were done with it. At 5 or 6 o'clock in the morning, we gathered everyone together, explained the importance of what we had accomplished, warned everyone to forget about what they had seen and never speak of it with anyone, and left for town. The boys from the regional Cheka who had lost track of us—comrades Isai Rodzinsky, Gorin, and someone else—arrived when we had already finished with everything.

I left with a report for Moscow on the night of the 19th. It was then that I gave the valuables to Trifonov, member of the Third Army's Revolutionary Council. I think Beloborodov, Novoselov, and someone else buried them in a basement in the earthen floor of a worker's house in Lysev. In 1919, when a Central Committee commission was on its way to the liberated Urals to establish Soviet power there, I was also coming there to work. The same Novoselov, together with someone else whose name I can't remember, extracted [the valuables]. N. N. Krestinsky, who was returning to Moscow, took them with him. In 1921–1923, when I worked in the republic's State Depository putting the valuables in order, I remember that one of Alexandra Fyodorovna's pearl strands was valued at 600,000 gold rubles.[7]

In Perm, when I was sorting through things that had belonged to the former imperial family, a number of valuables—more than a wagonload —were again discovered, hidden in things down to their underwear.

---

1. Russian measurements in this document have been converted to U.S. measurements.

2. Grigory (Petrovich?) Nikulin was a former factory worker from the Yekaterinburg area. Starting in March 1918, he worked for the Ural Regional Cheka. In July 1918, he was aide to Yakov Yurovsky, commandant of the Ipatiev house, and participated in the execution of the tsar and his family.

3. Mikhail Aleksandrovich Medvedev (real family name: Kudrin) was a former sailor and political prisoner. Since January 1918, he had worked for the Yekaterinburg Cheka, and he participated in the execution of the tsar and his family.

4. In the early 1930s, the Soviet government opened Torgsin stores to raise hard currency by selling scarce goods to foreigners. Soviet citizens could use the shops by bringing gold, silver, and other valuables to special exchanges where they would receive coupons honored at the stores.

5. Pyotr Lazarevich Voikov, a member of the Yekaterinburg Soviet and the Bolshevik party, commissar for supplies for the Ural region from January to December 1918.

6. N. Sokolov, *Ubiistvo tsarskoi sem'i* (Murder of the imperial family) (Berlin, 1925).

7. At the time, this amount was several hundred times the average annual salary for an industrial worker in the Soviet Union.

Chronology

Until 1 February 1918, Russia used the Julian calendar, which was twelve days behind the Gregorian calendar until 1 March 1900 and thirteen days behind thereafter.

6 (18) May 1868	Nicholas (Nikolai Aleksandrovich) born.
6 June (25 May on the Russian calendar) 1872	Alix of Hesse-Darmstadt (the future Empress Alexandra) born.
1878	Alix's mother dies.
1 (13) March 1881	Alexander II killed by a bomb thrown by members of a revolutionary organization, People's Will. Alexander III, Nicholas's father, takes the throne.
8 (20) May 1887	The older brother of Vladimir Ilich Ulianov (Lenin) executed for participating in an attempt on the life of Alexander III.
April 1894	Nicholas and Alix engaged to be married.
20 October (1 November) 1894	Alexander III dies. Nicholas becomes emperor.
21 October (2 November) 1894	Alix converts to Russian Orthodoxy and takes the name Alexandra (Aleksandra) Fyodorovna.

14 (26) November 1894	Nicholas and Alexandra married.
3 (15) November 1895	Their first daughter, Olga, born.
14 (26) May 1896	Nicholas II's coronation in Moscow.
18 (30) May 1896	Hundreds trampled to death in coronation celebrations on Khodynka field in Moscow.
29 May (10 June) 1897	Tatiana, the second daughter of Nicholas and Alexandra, born.
February–March 1899	Student strikes and riots.
14 (26) June 1899	Maria, the third daughter of Nicholas and Alexandra, born.
5 (18) June 1901	Anastasia, their fourth daughter, born.
Winter 1901–1902	Establishment of Socialist Revolutionary Party.
July–August 1903	Second Congress of Russian Social-Democratic Workers' Party. Separate factions, Bolsheviks and Mensheviks, emerge.
1903–1904	Union of Liberation, a liberal organization, established.
February 1904	Beginning of Russo-Japanese War. After devastating Russian defeats, armistice in June 1905 and peace treaty in November 1905.
15 (28) July 1904	Assassination of Viacheslav Pleve (von Plehve), minister of internal affairs.
30 July (12 August) 1904	Aleksei, the first son of Nicholas and Alexandra and heir to the throne, born.
August 1904	Prince Pyotr Sviatopolk-Mirsky named minister of internal affairs. He proposes program of political reforms, which is rejected.
9 (22) January 1905 (Bloody Sunday)	Crowds of lower-class people petitioning the tsar, led by the priest and police agent Georgy Gapon, are fired upon by police.
January–October 1905	Growing wave of strikes, demonstrations, civic organizing, and demands for political reform and social change.
[February 1905]	Nicholas agrees to elections for a national representative assembly (Duma).
12–18 (25–31) October 1905	Constitutional Democratic (Kadet) Party formed.
17 (30) October 1905	Nicholas signs October Manifesto promising reform.

1 (14) November 1905	Grigory Rasputin first mentioned in Nicholas's diary: "We have met a man of God, Grigory of Tobolsk province."
April–July 1906	First State Duma. Dissolved by Nicholas II because of strong oppositional mood in the Duma. Pyotr Stolypin named chairman of the Council of Ministers.
February–June 1907	Second State Duma. After its dissolution, electoral law is changed.
November 1907	Third Duma opens—the first allowed to complete its five-year term.
September 1911	Stolypin assassinated. Vladimir Kokovtsev named chairman of the Council of Ministers.
November 1912	Fourth State Duma opens.
1913	Celebration of the Tercentenary of the Romanov dynasty.
January 1914	Ivan Goremykin named chairman of the Council of Ministers.
19 July (1 August) 1914	Germany declares war on Russia.
Summer 1915	Progressive Bloc forms in the Duma and demands the establishment of a cabinet enjoying "public confidence."
21 August (3 September) 1915	Majority of ministers favors forming a new government in consultation with the Duma.
22 August (4 September) 1915	Nicholas II takes personal command of the armed forces. Leaves for General Headquarters at Mogilyov.
3 (16) September 1915	Duma prorogued.
20 January (2 February) 1916	Nicholas appoints Boris Shtiurmer chairman of the Council of Ministers in place of Goremykin.
13 (26) March 1916	New minister of war, Dmitry Shuraev, appointed.
18 September (1 October) 1916	Aleksandr Protopopov appointed minister of internal affairs.
1 (14) November 1916	Duma reconvenes. Deputies frequently criticize government.
19 November (2 December) 1916	Aleksandr Trepov appointed chairman of the Council of Ministers.
17 (30) December 1916	Murder of Rasputin.
18 (31) December 1916	Nicholas leaves Headquarters and returns to Tsarskoe Selo, his home near St. Petersburg.

27 December 1916 (9 January 1917)	Nikolai Golitsyn appointed chairman of the Council of Ministers.

1917

14 (27) February	Duma reconvenes. Resists pressures to act openly against the tsar's government.
22 February (7 March)	Nicholas returns to Mogilyov.
23 February (8 March)	International Women's Day. Strikes and demonstrations in Petrograd, the capital, grow over the next few days.
25 February (10 March)	Nicholas orders commander of Petrograd military district to suppress unrest.
26 February (11 March)	Duma prorogued.
27 February (12 March) (February Revolution)	Petrograd garrison mutinies. Formation of Provisional Committee of the Duma and Petrograd Soviet of Workers' Deputies. Council of Ministers submits resignation to Nicholas, who refuses to accept it.
28 February (13 March)	Nicholas tries to return to Tsarskoe Selo. Train blocked, so goes to Pskov, where he arrives on 1 (14) March.
28 February–2 March (13–15 March)	Political strikes and demonstrations spread to Moscow and provincial capitals. Soviets (workers' councils) form in many Russian cities. Military and civic leaders appeal to Nicholas to form a government responsible to the Duma.
1–2 (14–15) March	Provisional Government established after agreement between Duma Committee and Petrograd Soviet. Asks for Nicholas II's abdication.
2 (15) March	Nicholas abdicates for himself and his heir, Aleksei, in favor of his brother, Mikhail.
3 (16) March	Mikhail, after meeting with representatives of the Provisional Government, refuses the throne.
4 (17) March	Nicholas requests that the government allow him and his family to reside at Tsarskoe Selo until the children recover from their illness, and then allow them safe passage to the port of Romanov (Murmansk).

7 (20) March	Provisional Government orders that Nicholas and Alexandra be deprived of freedom and confined at Tsarskoe Selo.
8 (21) March	Nicholas bids farewell to the army and departs for Tsarskoe Selo with a government escort.
9 (22) March	British foreign secretary agrees to Provisional Government's request to give Nicholas and his family asylum in England for the duration of World War I. The offer is later withdrawn.
3–4 (16–17) April	Lenin returns to Petrograd from exile in Switzerland and issues his April Theses, in which he calls for revolution against the "bourgeois" Provisional Government, political power to the soviets, an end to the war, nationalization of land and its distribution to peasants, and placing industry under the control of workers' councils.
20–21 April (3–4 May) (April Days)	Demonstrations by workers, soldiers, and others in the streets of Petrograd and Moscow after leak to the public of a diplomatic note to the Allies from Foreign Minister Pavel Miliukov expressing annexationist war aims.
5 (18) May	First coalition government: six socialist ministers (Mensheviks and Socialist Revolutionaries) join Provisional Government.
Spring and summer	Continuing labor strikes amid inflation and shortages of fuel and food; agrarian unrest, including direct violations of gentry property rights (illegal woodcutting, theft of seed and tools, land seizures); the strengthening of national independence movements; growing Bolshevik success in elections to factory committees, soldiers' and sailors' committees, and neighborhood soviets.
3–24 June (16 June–7 July)	First All-Russian Congress of Soviets of Workers' and Soldiers' Deputies

	elects the Central Executive Committee (VTsIK), headed by Mensheviks and Socialist Revolutionaries.
16 (29) June	Beginning of Russian offensive on Austrian front. Within days, turns into a Russian rout.
18 June (1 July)	Street demonstration in Petrograd, organized by Congress of Soviets, at which Bolshevik slogans unexpectedly prevail: "Down with the ten capitalist ministers," "Down with the offensive," "All power to the soviets."
3–5 (16–18) July (July Days)	Mass armed demonstrations in Petrograd, encouraged by the Bolsheviks. Main demand: "All power to the soviets." Bolshevik leaders are arrested or go into hiding.
7 (20) July	Minister President Georgy Lvov accepts resignations of the Kadet ministers; then he himself resigns. Aleksandr Kerensky is asked to form a new government.
11 (24) July	Minister President Kerensky goes to Tsarskoe Selo to inform the former imperial family that they will be evacuated for their safety.
1 (14) August	The family, accompanied by a sizable suite, leaves Tsarskoe Selo under heavy guard and boards a train that takes them to Tiumen, where they board boats for Tobolsk.
6 (19) August	The family arrives in Tobolsk and, after a few days' delay, takes up residence in the former governor's mansion.
8–10 (21–23) August	Conference of Public Figures in Moscow presents demands that social order be restored.
12–15 (25–28) August	State Conference in Moscow brings together representatives from a wide range of civic organizations and parties (Bolsheviks refuse to participate). Conference fails to unite society in support of Provisional Government but reveals widely held sentiments in favor of

	firm authority and order. General strike virtually shuts down Moscow.
25 August (7 September)	Government attempts to deport suspected counterrevolutionary conspirators associated with the imperial family, including Anna Vyrubova. Petrograd Soviet, preferring their imprisonment, prevents deportation.
26–30 August (8–12 September)	The commander in chief of the Russian army, General Lavr Kornilov, after his demand that the government give him all civil and military authority is rebuffed, attempts military putsch.
31 August (13 September)	Bolsheviks win majority in elections to Petrograd Soviet.
1 (14) September	Socialist Revolutionary Vasily Pankratov arrives as new commissar in charge of imperial family.
5 (18) September	Bolsheviks win majority in Moscow Soviet.
14–22 September (27 September–5 October)	Democratic State Conference in Petrograd—composed of representatives of urban and rural soviets, town councils, soldiers' committees, trade unions, and other organizations—refuses to support Bolshevik appeals to form a Soviet government.
24–25 October (6–7 November) (October Revolution)	Bolshevik Military-Revolutionary Committee overthrows Provisional Government.
25–26 October (7–8 November)	Second Congress of Soviets meets and endorses Bolshevik seizure of power. Mensheviks and Socialist Revolutionaries walk out in protest.
26 October (8 November)	Congress of Soviets approves formation of all-Bolshevik government, the Council of People's Commissars (Sovnarkom), headed by Lenin.
31 October–2 November (13–15 November)	Fighting in Moscow ends in Bolshevik victory.
2 (15) November	Bolshevik party rejects demands made by Union of Railroad Employees (Vikzhel) and supported by several leading Bolsheviks, including Lev

	Kamenev and Grigory Zinoviev, for a multiparty socialist government.
12 (25) November	Elections to Constituent Assembly begin, as scheduled by Provisional Government. Bolsheviks, who win in most cities and garrisons, win far fewer seats than the Socialist Revolutionaries.
17 (30) November	News of the Bolshevik Revolution reaches Tobolsk.
20 November (3 December)	Armistice negotiations with Germany begin at Brest-Litovsk.
28 November (11 December)	Constitutional Democratic Party banned and leaders arrested as "enemies of the people."
7 (20) December	Cheka (Extraordinary Commission) established to fight counterrevolution and sabotage.
9–10 (22–23) December	Agreement on cooperation with Left Socialist Revolutionaries (Left SRs), who enter the Council of People's Commissars and the Collegium of the All-Russian Cheka.
16 (29) December	Decree abolishes all ranks and titles in the army, recognizes authority of soldiers' committees and councils, and requires democratic election of officers.
Late December	Tsarist generals Mikhail Alekseev and Lavr Kornilov establish Volunteer Army to fight against the Bolshevik government.

1918

1 (14) January	Attempt to assassinate Lenin.
5 (18) January	Constituent Assembly meets in Petrograd. Fifty thousand demonstrate in support, despite ban on demonstrations. Dispersed with force; between eight and twenty-one people are killed.
6 (19) January	Constituent Assembly disbanded. Some protests.
19 January (1 February)	Patriarch Tikhon anathematizes the Bolsheviks for bringing harm to the Russian Orthodox Church and for "sowing the seeds of hatred, enmity,

	and fratricidal strife." He calls on believers to defend the church.
24 January (6 February)	Decision to adopt new calendar beginning after January 31 (old style) in order that Russia "calculate time" in same way as "almost all cultured nations."
18 February	After unsuccessful peace negotiations, German and Austrian troops resume offensive against Russia. Following rapid successes, Germans add further territorial demands to peace terms.
20 February	Sovnarkom decides to prepare a trial of Nicholas II.
23 February	Bolshevik party newspaper, *Pravda*, calls for stricter and more secure terms of imprisonment for the former tsar and his family and for a trial.
27 February	Nicholas and his family are put on "soldiers' rations" by order of the VTsIK.
3 March	At Brest-Litovsk, Russians agree to peace terms that Lenin describes as "obscene" but necessary. Treaty provokes widespread dissent in party and society.
Early March	Capital moved to Moscow.
8 March	Russian Social-Democratic Workers' Party (Bolshevik) renamed All-Russian Communist Party (Bolshevik).
9 March	Allied forces land in Murmansk.
13 March–3 April	Meetings of factory deputies in Petrograd—organized by Menshevik-led Assembly of Factory Plenipotentiaries—protest worsening economic conditions and Bolshevik rule.
14 March	Left SRs quit government, mainly in protest against Brest-Litovsk treaty. During April–June, SRs increasingly critical of Bolshevik policies.
4 April	"Left Communists," based in Moscow party organization, issue manifesto criticizing Soviet foreign and

	economic policies as insufficiently revolutionary and democratic.
6 April	The Presidium of the VTsIK orders Nicholas and his family transferred to the Urals.
22 April	Vasily Yakovlev arrives in Tobolsk with letters from the VTsIK giving him plenipotentiary powers over all matters concerning the former imperial family.
26 April	Yakovlev and armed detachment transport Nicholas, Alexandra, and Maria, accompanied by Doctor Botkin, Nicholas's aide, and three servants, away from Tobolsk. Because of Aleksei's illness, the rest of the family are to be moved later.
30 April	Yakovlev and his prisoners arrive in Yekaterinburg. They take up residence in the Ipatiev house (except for Nicholas's aide, Vasily Dolgorukov, who is arrested and put in prison).
22 May	Rebellion of Czech Legion begins after government attempts to disarm the soldiers.
23 May	The rest of the family arrive in Yekaterinburg. Several members of the imperial suite arrested. Most not allowed to join the family in the Ipatiev house.
May–June	Meetings of workers' representatives in Petrograd and Moscow protest economic breakdown and Bolshevik authoritarianism toward workers and peasants and demand reconvening of Constituent Assembly and new elections to soviets.
Early June	British troops land at Archangel in the north.
7–8 June	Czech Legion takes Samara, after which deputies to Constituent Assembly form an anti-Bolshevik socialist government (Committee of Members of the Constituent Assembly, or Komuch).

11 June	Committees of the Village Poor established by Soviet government to intensify class struggle in villages.
Night of 12–13 June	Grand Duke Mikhail killed in an escape attempt evidently staged by the local Cheka.
14 June	After new elections bring large numbers of Mensheviks and right SRs into local soviets, the VTsIK expels these parties from its ranks and advises local soviets to do the same.
16 June	Capital punishment reintroduced.
28 June	Nationalization of industry ordered.
Late June–early July	Ural Soviet representative Filipp Goloshchekin is in Moscow discussing military defense of the Urals and policy toward the imperial family. He returns to Yekaterinburg on 12 July.
2 July	Unsuccessful political strike in Petrograd called by Assembly of Factory Plenipotentiaries.
4 July	Fifth Congress of Soviets opens in Moscow. Left SRs unsuccessfully call for vote of no confidence in the government and then walk out.
5–6 July	Armed insurrections by SRs in Moscow and other cities.
6 July	Assassination of the German ambassador Wilhelm von Mirbach.
Night of 16–17 July	Execution of the former tsar Nicholas II, his family, their physician, and three servants in Yekaterinburg.
17 July	Several grand dukes executed in the town of Alapaevsk in the Urals, where they were held in prison.

Glossary of Personal and Institutional Names

Dates conform to the calendar in use at the time: the Julian calendar until 1 February 1918, the Gregorian calendar thereafter, which was thirteen days ahead of the old calendar in the twentieth century. Sometimes both old- and new-style dates are given. Accent marks indicate stressed syllables in Russian names. Members of the Romanov dynasty are listed by their first names and patronymics.

Aleksándr Mikháilovich (Sandro) (1866–1933). Grand duke, grandson of Nicholas I, husband of Grand Duchess Ksenia Aleksandrovna, adjutant general in the imperial suite, vice-admiral. Served in the navy beginning in 1885. In charge of organizing aviation for the army during World War I. Discharged on 22 March 1917. Lived in exile in the Crimea with his family and the dowager empress Maria Fyodorovna. Emigrated in late March 1919.

Alekséev, Mikhaíl Vasílievich (1857–1918). Adjutant general, infantry general. Took part in the Russo-Japanese War (1904–1905) and World War I. Chief of staff on the southwestern front and commander of the northwestern front, 1914–1915. Chief of staff to the commander in chief of the Russian army from August 1915 to March 1917. Commander in chief, following the February Revolution, until 21 May (3 June) 1917. At the end of December 1917, helped to organize the anti-Bolshevik Volunteer Army in southern Russia, sharing its leadership with General Lavr Kornilov. Became "supreme director" of the Volunteer Army and head of state in the associated political movement in March 1918. Died in Yekaterinodar in October 1918. Buried in Belgrade.

Alekséi Nikoláevich (Baby, Little One, Sunshine, Sunbeam) (30 July 1904–17 July 1918). Tsarevich (heir to the throne), son of Nicholas II and Alexandra Fyodorovna. Hemophiliac. Executed in Yekaterinburg together with his parents and sisters on the night of 16–17 July 1918.

Alexandra (in Russian: Aleksándra) Fyódorovna (Alix, Sunny). Born on 6 June (25 May by the old Russian calendar) 1872 in Darmstadt as Alix Victoria Helena Louise Beatrice, princess of Hesse-Darmstadt. In 1894, in order to marry the future Nicholas II, she converted from Lutheranism to Russian Orthodoxy, becoming Alexandra Fyodorovna. Executed together with her family in Yekaterinburg on the night of 16–17 July 1918.

Anastasía Nikoláevna (5 June 1901–17 July 1918). Grand duchess, fourth daughter of Nicholas II and Alexandra Fyodorovna. Executed in Yekaterinburg together with her family on the night of 16–17 July 1918.

Andréi Vladímirovich (1879–1956). Grand duke, youngest son of Grand Duke Vladimir Aleksandrovich and Grand Duchess Maria Pavlovna (the elder), cousin of Nicholas II. Graduated from Mikhailovsky Artillery School (1902) and Aleksandrovsky Academy of Military Law. Served in the Senate from 1911. In World War I, was major general in the imperial suite and commander of the Life Guards Horse Artillery. Married the ballerina Matilda Kseshinskaia, with whom Nicholas II had been romantically involved before his marriage. Under house arrest in Kislovodsk during the February Revolution. Emigrated.

Avdéev, Aleksándr Dmítrievich. Worker at the Zlokazov brothers' factory in Yekaterinburg, political exile, Bolshevik. A member of the Executive Committee of the Ural Regional Soviet. Took part in transferring Nicholas II from Tobolsk to Yekaterinburg. Commandant of the House of Special Purpose (Ipatiev house), where the imperial family was imprisoned. Dismissed on 4 July 1918 and sent to the front. Author of memoirs.

Beloboródov, Aleksándr Geórgievich (1891–1938). Son of a worker at the Aleksandrovsky factory near Solikamsk. Worked in Ural factories as clerk and electrician. Member of the Bolshevik wing of the Russian Social-Democratic Workers' Party from 1907. Arrested in 1908, he served about four years in prison. A deputy to the sixth Bolshevik party congress, July 1917. Member of the Ural Regional Committee of the Bolshevik party. Became chairman of the Ural Regional Soviet in late January 1918 and helped to organize the execution of the Romanovs. A member of the Central Committee of the Bolshevik party, 1920–1921. People's commissar of internal affairs, 1923–1927. In 1927, expelled from the party and dismissed from all posts as a Trotskyist. Rehabilitated in 1930 but again arrested in August 1936. Convicted in February 1938, he died in prison. Conviction overturned in 1958.

Benkendórf (Benckendorff), Pável Konstantínovich (1833–1921). Count, adjutant general in the imperial suite, cavalry general, chief marshal of the court, master of ceremonies, member of the State Council. Part of the imperial family's inner circle. Author of memoirs.

Bérzin (Bérzinsh), Reingóld Iósifovich (1888–1939). Commander and political officer in the Red Army. Member of the Bolshevik party from 1905. Lieutenant and political activist in the army during World War I. In January 1918, became commander of the Second Revolutionary Army. From February to March 1918, commander of the western revolutionary front. In June 1918, became chairman of the Higher Military Inspectorate in Siberia and commander of the northern Ural-Siberian front. Asked by the Council of People's Commissars (Sovnarkom) to evaluate the situation of the imperial family in Yekaterinburg. In the late 1920s, worked mainly in military industry and agriculture. Arrested and executed in 1939; rehabilitated posthumously.

Bítner, Klávdia Mikháilovna (b. 1878). Hereditary noblewoman. Former teacher at the Mariinsky women's gymnasium (secondary school) in Tsarskoe Selo. During the war, nurse in the Lianozovsky infirmary in Tsarskoe Selo. Tutored the imperial children while they were in Tobolsk. Later married Yevgeny Kobylinsky.

Borís Vladímirovich (1877–1943). Grand duke, cousin of Nicholas II, major general in the imperial suite. Graduated from Nikolaevsky Cavalry School (1896). Took part in the Russo-Japanese War (1904–1905) and World War I. Commanded the Life Guards Ataman Regiment of Cossacks and was afterward field *ataman* (commander) of cossack forces attached to Staff Headquarters at Mogilyov. Discharged after the February Revolution; lived in exile in the northern Caucasus, then in Livadia (in the Crimea). Emigrated in 1919.

Bótkin, Yevgény Sergéevich (1865–1918). Personal doctor of Nicholas II and his family. Lecturer at the Military Medical Academy. Took part in the Russo-Japanese War (1904–1905). Joined the imperial family as a voluntary prisoner in Tobolsk and Yekaterinburg. Executed with the family on the night of 16–17 July 1918.

Buksgevden (Buxhoeveden), Sófia Kárlovna (Isa, Iza) (1884–1956). Baroness, lady-in-waiting to Alexandra. Voluntarily followed the imperial family to Tobolsk but was not allowed to join them, and lived separately. Allowed to accompany the children on the journey to Yekaterinburg but not to join them in the Ipatiev house. Died in London. Author of memoirs.

Central Executive Committee of Soviets of Workers', Soldiers', and Peasants' Deputies, All-Russian (VTsIK, TsIK). Established at the First All-Russian Congress of Soviets in June 1917. After the Second Congress (25–26 October [7–8 November] 1917), the Central Executive Committee was headed by a Presidium. See also Soviets.

Cheká (ChK, VChK, Vecheka), the All-Russian Extraordinary Commission for the Struggle with Counterrevolution and Sabotage. Established on 7 (20) December 1917, headed by Feliks Dzerzhinsky. Its role combined the fight against banditry, against looting, and against financial corruption with the tasks of a political police. During 1918 a network of provincial and district Chekas was established. The first national congress of Chekas was held in June 1918. During the civil war, the Cheka was the primary organ of the Red Terror. Replaced by the GPU, the OGPU and, in later years, by the NKVD and the KGB.

Chemodúrov, Terénty Ivánovich (1849–1919). Valet to Nicholas II from 1 December 1908. Followed the imperial family into exile in Tobolsk and Yekaterinburg. In May 1918, because of illness, left the Ipatiev house and entered a local prison hospital. Freed by White soldiers on 25 July. Died in Tobolsk in 1919.

Council of Ministers (Sovét minístrov). The name of the cabinet in Russia from the mid-nineteenth century until the Bolshevik revolution of October 1917. In the tsarist government, the Council of Ministers became especially influential after the abolition of the parallel Committee of Ministers in 1906; the council met daily to coordinate administration and discuss general policy. Although the tsar retained ultimate authority on all questions of policy and had absolute authority to appoint and dismiss ministers, day-to-day political power was in the hands of the ministers, even after the establishment of the State Duma in 1906. The demand for a "responsible ministry"—for ministers subject to the approval and censure of the elected State Duma—was a major demand of liberals on the eve of the February Revolution. Beginning in 1905, the Council of Ministers was headed by a chairman appointed by the tsar (previously, the tsar had chaired its meetings). At the beginning of March 1917, the Provisional Committee of the State Duma selected a new cabinet and appointed a minister president to chair the new Council of Ministers. This council was replaced by the Council of People's Commissars (Sovnarkom) after the Bolshevik Revolution.

Council of People's Commissars (Sovnarkom [Sovét naródnykh komissárov]). Established on 26 October (8 November) 1917 to replace the Council of Ministers of the tsarist and Provisional governments. Headed by Vladimir Lenin until his death in 1924. It was the executive and administrative branch of the Soviet government, formally subordinate to the legislative authority of the All-Russian Central Executive Committee of Soviets; in practice, it was the dominant structure of state power.

Den (Dehn, born Smonskaia), Yúlia Aleksándrovna (Lili). Wife of Captain Karl Akimovich Den, commander of the cruiser *Variag* (Varangian). A close friend of Alexandra's and Anna Vyrubova's. Under arrest with the imperial family in the Aleksandrovsky Palace until she and Vyrubova were removed on orders of the Provisional Government. Took part in organizing communications between sympathizers in Petrograd and the imperial family in Tobolsk. Emigrated to England. Author of memoirs.

Derevénko, Nikolái Vladímirovich (Kólia). Son of the court surgeon Vladimir Derevenko and pupil at the Imperial Nikolaevsky Gymnasium. One of the small circle of Tsarevich Aleksei's friends who was regularly invited to play with him. Accompanied his father to Tobolsk and Yekaterinburg.

Derevénko, Vladímir Nikoláevich. Physician treating the tsarevich Aleksei from 1912. Court surgeon. The only person authorized to come and go from the Ipatiev house, in order to attend the ailing Aleksei.

Didkóvsky, Borís Vladímirovich (1883–1938). Bolshevik party activist. After graduating from the University of Geneva in 1913, worked as a geologist in the Urals. Member of the Presidium of the Ural Regional Soviet Executive Committee. Participated in the transfer of Nicholas II and his family from Tobolsk to Yekaterinburg. Held various responsible party, governmental, and economic positions in the Urals. Rector of Ural State University from 1921 to 1923. Arrested and executed in 1938.

Dmítry Pávlovich (1891–1942). Grand duke, son of Grand Duke Pavel Aleksandrovich and Aleksandra Georgievna of Greece, aide-de-camp in the imperial suite, staff major in the Life Guards Horse Regiment. Took part in the killing of Grigory Rasputin, for which he was exiled to Persia.

Dolgorúkov (in some sources: Dolgoruky), Vasíly Aleksándrovich (Vália) (1868–

1918). Prince, major general in the imperial suite, chief marshal of the court. During World War I, served at Staff Headquarters under Nicholas II. Followed the abdicated tsar to Tobolsk. During the transfer of the imperial family from Tobolsk to Yekaterinburg, accused of possessing weapons and plotting an escape. He was imprisoned; together with Ilia Tatishchev, he was executed, on 10 July 1918.

Dúma, State. A national representative assembly established in 1906. Empowered to initiate and approve legislation, though limited in its authority. Day-to-day political power was in the hands of the Council of Ministers, whom the tsar appointed and who were not responsible to the Duma. The tsar could veto legislation, as could the State Council, half of whose members were appointed by the tsar. Much of the budget (especially for the military and for foreign policy) was not under the control of the Duma. In 1907 the voting law was changed to reduce representation of the peasantry, urban workers, and national minorities and to increase that of the gentry.

Extraordinary Commission for the Struggle with Counterrevolution and Sabotage, All-Russian. See Cheka.

Frederíks (Fredericks), Vladímir Borísovich (1838–1927). Count, adjutant general in the imperial suite, cavalry general, large landowner, member of the State Council, minister of the imperial court and domain (from 1897), chancellor of the Russian imperial and tsarist orders, head of the imperial household, and one of Nicholas II's most trusted associates. During the February Revolution, deported from Staff Headquarters by orders of the Provisional Government and then arrested. Emigrated after the Bolshevik Revolution.

Fyódorov, Sergéi Petróvich (1869–1936). Privy councilor, court surgeon, professor. Served at Staff Headquarters from the autumn of 1915 as physician to the tsar and the heir. Head of the faculty of surgery of the Military Medical Academy from 1903 to 1936. Director of the Leningrad Institute of Surgical Neuropathology from 1926 to 1936.

Géndrikova (Hendrikova), Anastasía Vasílievna (Nastenka, Nastinka, Nastia). Countess, lady-in-waiting to Alexandra. Voluntarily followed the imperial family into exile. Executed together with Yekaterina Shneider in Perm on 4 September 1918. Their bodies were discovered by White soldiers on 7 May 1919.

Geórgy Mikháilovich (1863–1919). Grand duke, son of Grand Duke Mikhail Nikolaevich, infantry general, adjutant general in the imperial suite. During World War I, served at the headquarters of the commander in chief of the Russian army. Traveled to Japan on a special mission in 1915–1916. Curator of the Russian Museum, numismatist. Executed at the Peter and Paul Fortress on 27 January 1919.

Germogén (Hermogen) (secular name: Geórgy Yefrémovich Dolganyóv) (1858–1918). Bishop of Tobolsk and Siberia. Graduated from the Department of Law at Novorossiisk University and from the St. Petersburg Ecclesiastical Academy with a degree in theology. Took monastic vows in 1890. Rector of Tiflis Ecclesiastical Seminary and archimandrite (abbot) beginning in 1908. Became bishop of Volsk and suffragan (bishop) of Saratov in 1901. Germogen was at first a devotee of Rasputin's but later denounced him, for which he was expelled from the Holy Synod. Bishop of Tobolsk from 7 March 1917. Aided the Romanovs during their exile in Tobolsk and was in contact with monarchist groups that were organizing their escape. Pronounced an anathema on the Bolsheviks in 1918. Was arrested and killed by drowning in the Tobol River in June 1918.

Gibbs, Sidney (Sídnei Ivánovich) (Sidney Gibbes) (Sig) (1876–1963). English citizen, invited to instruct Nicholas and Alexandra's daughters in the English language in 1908. Tutored the heir, Aleksei, in English from 1913 until 1918. Separated from the imperial family in Yekaterinburg and sent to Tiumen; from there he made his way back to Tobolsk. Returned to Yekaterinburg in August 1918 to assist in the White investigation of the execution of the Romanovs. Became a secretary at the British High Commission in Omsk in January 1919. In 1919, moved to Harbin, Manchuria, where he worked in the British-run Chinese Maritime Customs. In 1934, converted to Russian Orthodoxy and became a monk, initially taking the name Aleksei. Ordained into the Orthodox priesthood and rechristened Nicholas. Returned to England in 1937. After World War II, established an Orthodox congregation in Oxford, where he kept a number of icons and other items that had belonged to the imperial family.

Gilliard, Pierre (Pyótr Andréevich Zhiliar) (Zhílik) (1879–1962). Swiss citizen, tutor, French-language instructor and governor to the heir, Aleksei. Followed the imperial family into exile in Tobolsk. During the transfer of the Romanovs to Yekaterinburg, was separated from them and sent to Tiumen. Left Soviet Russia in 1920. Married A. A. Tegleva in Geneva in 1922. Author of memoirs.

Goloshchékin (pronounced Goloshchókin), Filípp Isáevich (1876–1941). Born in the town of Nevel in Vitebsk province. Member of the Bolshevik party from 1903 and graduate of a dentistry school in Riga. Known in the party simply as comrade Filipp. Spent over six years in exile, making repeated escapes. In 1912, he represented the Moscow Bolshevik party organization at the Prague party conference, together with Grigory Zinoviev. After the February Revolution, was sent to do party work in the Urals, where he became head of the regional party. A delegate to the sixth party congress in July–August 1917. Military commissar of the Ural Regional Soviet from December 1917 and, after May 1918, district (*okrug*) military commissar. In late June and early July, as a member of the Presidium of the Ural Regional Soviet Executive Committee, discussed the security situation in the Urals and the fate of the imperial family with party and state leaders in Moscow. A member of the leftist "military opposition" in 1919. Member of the Central Committee of the Communist Party from 1924 through 1934. Also served as a member of the collegium of the security police (Cheka, GPU, and NKVD). Chief arbiter of the Council of People's Commissars (Sovnarkom) from 1933. Arrested on 15 June 1941 and executed on 28 October 1941 in the NKVD internal prison in the Kuibyshev region. Rehabilitated posthumously.

Guchkóv, Aleksándr Ivánovich (1862–1936). Major industrialist. Founder and leader of the Union of 17 October (known as the Octobrist Party). Member of the third State Duma from 1907 to 1912, Duma chairman from 1903 to 1911, and member of the State Council from 1915. From 1915 to 1917, chairman of the Central Military-Industrial Committee and member of the Special Defense Council. During the February Revolution as members of the Provisional Committee of the State Duma, he and Vasily Shulgin negotiated Nicholas II's abdication on 2 March 1917. Served as minister of war and navy in the first Provisional Government (March–May 1917). Opposed to Soviet power, he emigrated to Germany in 1918 and died in Paris.

Gúrko, Vasíly Iósifovich (1864–1937). Cavalry general. During World War I, commanded the First Caucasus Division and, when General P. A. Pleve was named commander of the northern front, took over command of the Fifth Army from Pleve. In August 1916, was appointed commander of the "special army." During the illness of General Mikhail Alekseev, became acting chief of staff to the commander in chief of the Russian army. After the February Revolution, was briefly commander of the western front but was removed after criticizing the government for the collapse of discipline. Subsequently emigrated. Author of memoirs.

Ivánov, Nikolái Iúdovich (1851–1919). Adjutant general, artillery general, member of the State Council; commander of the southwestern front from July 1914 to March 1916, he then served at Staff Headquarters under Nicholas II. Appointed commander of the Petrograd military district on 27 February (12 March) 1917. Arrested by the Extraordinary Investigatory Commission (ChSK) in March 1917 but released by Kerensky. After the October Revolution, fled to Kiev, then to the Don region. Commanded the White cossack southern army.

Kalínin, General. See Protopopov, Aleksandr Dmitrievich.

Kérensky, Aleksándr Fyódorovich (1881–1970). Politician, lawyer, deputy to the fourth State Duma, leader of the Trudovik (Laborist) faction in the Duma. A Socialist Revolutionary from March 1917. During the February Revolution, member of the Provisional Committee of the State Duma and deputy chairman of the Executive Committee of the Petrograd Soviet. Minister of justice in the Provisional Government from 2 March to 5 May 1917. War and navy minister in the first and second coalition governments of May–September, minister president from 8 July to 25 October 1917, simultaneously commander in chief of the Russian army from 30 August. Emigrated in 1918, living in Paris first and in the United States after 1940. Author of many memoirs.

Khabálov, Sergéi Semyónovich (1855–1924). Lieutenant general, military governor of the Ural region, *ataman* (commander) of the Ural cossack host. From June 1916, chief of the Petrograd military district; from 5 to 28 February, commander. Organized the use of armed force against insurgents in Petrograd in late February 1917, provoking the February Revolution. Arrested on 28 February and imprisoned in the Peter and Paul Fortress. Freed by the Provisional Government in September. Discharged from the army on 11 November 1917. Emigrated.

Khitrovó, Margaríta Sergéevna (Rita) (1895–1952). Graduate of the Smolny Institute. Former lady-in-waiting to Empress Alexandra, companion of Nicholas and Alexandra's daughter Olga. During the war, a nurse at Tsarskoe Selo infirmary. Arrested after she traveled to Tobolsk on her own initiative and tried to contact the imperial family; accused of plotting a monarchist coup but released for lack of evidence. Emigrated, eventually settling in the United States.

Khokhriakóv, Pável Danílovich (1893–1918). Sailor in the Baltic fleet, stoker, member of the Bolshevik party from 1916. Closely associated with Yekaterinburg Bolsheviks in early 1918. Chairman of the Tobolsk Soviet from 9 April

1918. After Nicholas, Alexandra, and Maria had left Tobolsk, he was in charge of transferring the remaining children and the rest of the Romanov suite from Tobolsk to Yekaterinburg. Participated in the killing of Bishop Germogen. Died on 17 August 1918 fighting the Whites in the civil war.

Kiríll Vladímirovich (1876–1938). Grand duke, first cousin of Nicholas II, rear admiral in the imperial suite. Took part in the Russo-Japanese War (1904–1905) and World War I. Commander of the naval Guards Equipage, which, during the February Revolution, before Nicholas II's abdication, he led to the State Duma to pledge allegiance to the Provisional Government. Left Russia for Finland in the summer of 1917 and subsequently emigrated. After emigrating, he was a claimant to the Russian throne, proclaiming himself Kirill I, Emperor of All the Russias.

Kobylínsky, Yevgény Stepánovich (1879–1927). Colonel, commander of the Tsarskoe Selo guard in March 1917, commandant of Tsarskoe Selo palace garrison from May. In Tobolsk, commander of the special purpose detachment guarding the imperial family from 1 August and commandant of the Governor's House, where they were imprisoned, until 2 May 1918. After the transfer of the family from Tobolsk to Yekaterinburg, joined the White army. Married Klavdia Bitner. Served on the staff of Admiral Aleksandr Kolchak's Siberian army as quartermaster. Taken prisoner at Krasnoiarsk during the civil war. Later, convicted of involvement in an anti-Soviet conspiracy and executed in 1927.

Koganítsky, Isaák Yákovlevich (1884–1954). Native of Tobolsk, member of the Bolshevik party from 1904. Took part in World War I. On instructions of the Moscow party committee, sent to Tobolsk to keep watch over the imperial family. Organized a Bolshevik faction in the Tobolsk Soviet. Elected to the presidium of the Executive Committee of the Tobolsk Soviet. In Siberia, took part in the civil war. Author of memoirs.

Kornílov, Lavr Geórgievich (1870–1918). Lieutenant general, infantry general. Took part in the Russo-Japanese War (1904–1905) and World War I. After the February Revolution, was appointed commander of the Petrograd military district by the Provisional Government and assigned to arrest Empress Alexandra at Tsarskoe Selo. Following the resignation of General Mikhail Alekseev on 21 May (3 June) 1917, promoted to commander in chief of the Russian army. On 26 August, began moving troops against Petrograd to establish a military dictatorship. The "Kornilov mutiny" was suppressed with the help of armed worker Red Guards and loyal soldiers. Removed from his post and arraigned on 29 August. Escaped from the Bykhovsky prison and fled to Novocherkassk, where he and General Alekseev took joint command of the anti-Bolshevik Volunteer Army. Killed during the first Kuban campaign at Yekaterinodar on 31 March 1918.

Korovichenko, Pável Aleksándrovich. Colonel, military lawyer, attorney by training. Friend of Aleksandr Kerensky's and commandant of the Aleksandrovsky Palace in Tsarskoe Selo from 21 March to 27 May 1917. Subsequently commanded forces of the Kazan and Tashkent military districts. Was killed fighting against Red forces in central Asia in late 1917.

Ksénia Aleksándrovna (Xenia) (1875–1960). Grand duchess, daughter of Alexander III, elder sister of Nicholas II; married Grand Duke Aleksandr Mikhailovich in 1894. After the February Revolution, lived as an exile in the Crimea together with her family and the dowager empress Maria Fyodorovna. Lived in London after 1919.

Lvov, Geórgy Yevgénievich (1861–1925). Prince, lawyer. During World War I, head of the All-Russian Union of Zemstvos and Town Councils for Relief to Wounded and Sick Soldiers, member of the Supreme Council for the Support of Conscripts' Families, and member of the Moscow City Duma. After the February Revolution, minister president in the first two cabinets of the Provisional Government (until July 1917). Emigrated to France.

María Fyódorovna (1847–1928). Born Princess Dagmar of Denmark, daughter of Christian IX; married the future Alexander III in 1866. Mother of Nicholas II. Under her authority and name a network of charitable and educational institutions was established. After the February Revolution she lived as an exile in the Crimea together with her daughter Ksenia Aleksandrovna and Grand Duke Aleksandr Mikhailovich. Emigrated to Denmark in late March 1919.

María Nikoláevna (14 June 1899–17 July 1918). Grand duchess, third daughter of Nicholas II and Alexandra Fyodorovna. Executed along with her family in Yekaterinburg on the night of 16–17 July 1918.

Matvéev, Pável Matvéevich. Ensign in the Life Guards Second Tsarskoe Selo Rifle Regiment, Bolshevik, chairman of the soldiers' committee of the special purpose detachment, which guarded the imperial family in Tobolsk. Member of the detachment transferring Nicholas from Tobolsk to Yekaterinburg. Author of memoirs.

Medvédev, Pável Spiridónovich. Worker at the Sysert factory in the Urals, commander of the guard at the Ipatiev house in Yekaterinburg, where the imperial family was imprisoned. Arrested by Whites in Perm on 11 February 1919 and interrogated on the killing of the family. Died of typhus while in custody.

Mikhaíl Aleksándrovich (Mísha) (1878–1918). Grand duke, youngest brother of Nicholas II, adjutant general in the imperial suite, major general, member of the State Council, heir to the throne from 1899 to 1904, when the tsarevich, Aleksei, was born. In 1912, was officially censured for marrying, against the will of Nicholas II, the commoner and divorcée Natalia Vulfert (later, Brasova). Made to renounce any rights he might have had to the throne. Pardoned in 1915 and restored to his ranks. During World War I, commanded the so-called native (or "savage") Caucasus Division and the Second Cavalry Corps, decorated with the St. George Cross, appointed inspector general of the cavalry. On 2 March 1917, Nicholas II abdicated in his favor, but Mikhail refused to assume the throne. Arrested by the Provisional Government during the "Kornilov mutiny" and again during the October Revolution. Exiled to Perm by decision of the Council of People's Commissars (Sovnarkom) in March 1918. Killed on the outskirts of Perm on the night of 12–13 June 1918 in an escape evidently staged by the local Cheka.

Miliukóv, Pável Nikoláevich (1859–1943). Historian, professor, political activist, publicist. One of the organizers of the Kadet Party, chairman of its Central Committee from 1907, and editor of the newspaper *Rech* (Speech). A member of the third and fourth State Dumas. During the February Revolution he advocated preserving the monarchy. Minister of foreign affairs in the first cabinet of the

Provisional Government (until 2 May 1917). After the Bolshevik revolution of October 1917, joined anti-Bolshevik armed forces in the south. In 1918, tried to convince German authorities in occupied Ukraine to support White efforts against the Bolsheviks. Emigrated at the end of 1918, remaining politically outspoken concerning Soviet politics. Wrote many memoirs, essays, and historical studies.

Nagórny, Kleménty Grigórievich (Klim) (d. 1918). Former sailor in the Guards Equipage. Served on the imperial yacht *Shtandart*. Joined family in Tobolsk as personal caretaker (*diad'ka*) to Aleksei. Accompanied Aleksei to Yekaterinburg but was taken from the Ipatiev house on 27 May 1918, arrested, and, in June, shot by the Cheka, together with Ivan Sednyov.

Naryshkin, Kiríll Anatólievich (Kira) (b. 1868). Aide-de-camp in the imperial suite, major general, boyhood friend of Nicholas II's. After Nicholas's abdication he chose not to remain with the imperial family.

Naryshkina, Yelizavéta Alekséevna (Zizi) (b. 1840). Born Princess Kuragina, chief comptroller (*ober-gofmeisterina*) of the empress's household, *stats-dama* (lady-in-waiting of the highest rank), *kavaler-dama* (Dame of the Order of St. Catherine). Director of a number of charitable committees and institutions aiding female ex-convicts and the families of convicts and exiles. Shared the imperial family's confinement in the Aleksandrovsky Palace in Tsarskoe Selo.

Nicholas II (Niki, Nicky) (civil name after abdication: Nikolái Aleksándrovich Románov). Born on 6 (18) May 1868 to Alexander III and Maria Fyodorovna. Married Alix of Hesse-Darmstadt on 14 (26) November 1894. Succeeded to the Russian throne after the death of his father on 20 October (1 November) 1894. Crowned in Moscow on 14 (26) May 1896. Abdicated on 2 (15) March 1917. Executed with his family in Yekaterinburg on the night of 16–17 July 1918.

Nikolái Nikoláevich (the younger; Nikolasha) (1856–1929). Grand duke, grandson of Nicholas I, first cousin once removed of Nicholas II, adjutant general in the imperial suite. Took part in the Russo-Turkish War (1877–1878). Cavalry general (1895–1905), chairman of the State Defense Council (1905–1909), commander of the Life Guards corps and of the St. Petersburg military district (1904–1914). Commander in chief of the Russian army from the outbreak of World War I until 23 August 1915, when he was replaced by Nicholas II and made commander of the Caucasus armies. When abdicating, Nicholas II again appointed him commander in chief (2–11 March 1917), but pressure from the Petrograd Soviet and the Provisional Government compelled him to resign. Retired to his estate in the Crimea. Emigrated to Italy in March 1919 and lived in southern France from 1922. A portion of the White émigré community viewed him as the true claimant to the Russian throne. From December 1924 until his death, he headed Russian émigré military organizations.

Nikólsky, Aleksándr Vladímirovich. Ensign, Socialist Revolutionary, former political exile, aide to commissar Vasily Pankratov in Tobolsk. Dismissed from that post by the soldiers' committee of the special purpose detachment on 26 January 1918 because he represented the overthrown Provisional Government.

Ólga Nikoláevna (3 November 1895–17 July 1918). Grand duchess, eldest daughter of Nicholas II and Alexandra Fyodorovna. Executed together with her family in Yekaterinburg on the night of 16–17 July 1918.

Pankrátov, Vasíly Semyónovich (1864–1925). A child of peasants, he became a skilled lathe operator at the Semiannikov shipbuilding and machine works in St. Petersburg. During the early 1880s he was involved in populist study circles. Propagandized workers in St. Petersburg and other Russian cities. For the murder of a gendarme in Kiev in 1884, he was arrested and sentenced to fourteen years in the Shlisselburg prison, followed by twenty-seven years in exile in Siberia. Freed in 1905, became active in the revolutionary movement and joined the Socialist Revolutionary Party. Before World War I, studied geology and worked as a geologist. Organizer and lecturer in the cultural-enlightenment department of the Petrograd garrison in the summer of 1917. Appointed commissar in charge of the imperial family in Tobolsk by the Provisional Government on 21 August 1917. Dismissed on 26 January 1918. Author of memoirs.

Pável Aleksándrovich (Paul) (1860–1919). Grand duke, youngest son of Alexander II, adjutant general in the imperial suite, cavalry general. Appointed commander of the Life Guards corps on 28 May 1916; later became inspector of the Guards. For distinction in battle, decorated with the St. George Cross. Married Aleksandra Georgievna of Greece in 1889. After her death, he entered into a morganatic marriage with Princess Olga Valerianovna Palei (born Karnovich), a situation that required him to live abroad for a number of years. He returned to Russia at the start of World War I. Executed in the Peter and Paul Fortress on 27 January 1919.

Petróv, Pyótr Vasílievich. Hereditary nobleman, official for special commissions attached to the Main Directorate of Military Training Institutions. Tutor to the tsar's children in Russian language and literature.

Protopópov, Aleksándr Dmítrievich (nickname at Tsarskoe Selo: General Kalínin) (1866–1918). Industrialist, landowner, hereditary nobleman, Simbirsk provincial marshal of the gentry, member of the Octobrist Party, deputy to the third State Duma, deputy chairman of the fourth State Duma. Owing mainly to Rasputin's endorsement, he was appointed acting minister of internal affairs on 18 September 1916 and minister on 20 December 1916. A member of Nicholas and Alexandra's trusted inner circle. Executed by the Cheka in 1918.

Raspútin (adopted the name Nóvykh in 1907), Grigóry Yefímovich (1864–1916). Born a peasant in Tobolsk province, Siberia. Gained considerable influence at court as a seer and healer, but his alleged debauchery tarnished the reputation of the imperial family. Killed in December 1916 by Prince Feliks Yusupov, the hereditary nobleman Vladimir Purishkevich, and Grand Duke Dmitry Pavlovich.

Rodziánko, Mikhaíl Vladímirovich (1859–1924). A landowner in Yekaterinoslav province, a leader of the Octobrist Party, member of the State Council from 1906 to 1907, deputy to the third State Duma, chairman of the third State Duma (from March 1911), chairman of the fourth State Duma (1912–1917). Leader of the Provisional Committee of the State Duma during the February Revolution. After the October Revolution, active in the White cause, serving with the army of General A. I. Denikin from 1918 to 1920. Emigrated to Yugoslavia. Author of memoirs.

Rúzsky, Nikolái Vladímirovich (1854–1918). Adjutant general in the imperial suite, infantry general, member of the Military Council of the War Ministry

(1909–1914), commander of the northern front from August 1915 to April 1917. Refused to support either side in the civil war. Taken hostage and killed by the Caucasus Red Army in Piatigorsk in October 1918.

Safárov (Vóldin), Geórgy Ivánovich (1891–1941). A member of the Bolshevik party from 1908. Returned to Russia together with Lenin in April 1917 after many years in exile. Together with Filipp Goloshchekin, he was the party official responsible for planning and carrying out the execution of the imperial family. Member of the presidium of the Ural Regional Soviet Executive Committee and editor of the newspaper *Ural'skii rabochii* (Ural worker). A leader of the leftist "military opposition" in 1919, he belonged to the Central Committee of the Communist Party, the leadership of the Communist Youth League (Komsomol) and the Communist International (Comintern). In 1927, as a member of the United Opposition, which was associated with Lev Trotsky, he was dismissed from all posts. Readmitted to the party but arrested again in the 1930s. Executed in 1941. Rehabilitated posthumously.

Sednyóv, Iván Dmítrievich (1886–1918). Former crewman aboard the imperial yacht *Shtandart*, servant to Nicholas and Alexandra's daughters. Joined the family voluntarily in Tobolsk and Yekaterinburg. Arrested on 27 May 1918 and executed in June 1918.

Senate (also known as the Ruling or Governing Senate). An institution composed of notables appointed by the tsar, responsible mainly for the administration of justice. Abolished on 22 November 1917.

Sergéi Mikháilovich (1865–1918). Grand duke, son of Grand Duke Mikhail Nikolaevich and Grand Duchess Olga Fyodorovna (of Baden). Artillery general in the Life Guards Horse Artillery, adjutant general in the imperial suite. Appointed the commander in chief's inspector general of field artillery in January 1916. Retired after the February Revolution. Killed with other Romanov grand dukes and the Grand Duchess Yelizaveta Fyodorovna on the outskirts of Alapaevsk in the Urals on the night of 17–18 July 1918.

Shnéider, Yekaterína Adólfovna (Trina). Language tutor and reader (*lectrice*) to the imperial children. Voluntarily followed the imperial family into exile. Executed together with Anastasia Gendrikova in Perm on 4 September 1918. Their bodies were discovered by White soldiers on 7 May 1919.

Shulgín, Vasíly Vitálievich (1878–1976). Publicist, deputy to the second through fourth State Dumas, a leader of the Nationalists and the Progressive Nationalists in the Duma. During the February Revolution, as members of the Provisional Committee of the Duma, he and Aleksandr Guchkov negotiated Nicholas II's abdication. After the October Revolution he helped establish the anti-Bolshevik Volunteer Army and was head of the Southern Russian National Center. Emigrated after the civil war. Arrested by the Soviet secret police (NKVD) in Yugoslavia in 1944 and sentenced to a prison term, which he served in Vladimir, in the Soviet Union. Freed in 1956, he settled in Vladimir, where he died. Author of memoirs.

Solovyóv, Borís Nikoláevich (b. 1893). Lieutenant, son of the treasurer of the Holy Synod N. V. Solovyov, member of Rasputin's circle in Petrograd, officer for commissions and adjutant to the chairman of the Military Commission of the

State Duma Committee. In September 1917, married the daughter of Grigory Rasputin, Maria (Matryona). Served as Anna Vyrubova's courier, delivering correspondence, money, and gifts to and from the imperial family in Tobolsk and planning the family's escape. While living in Pokrovskoe and later in Tiumen, he tried to bring the various efforts to free the tsar and his family under his own control. Stayed in close contact with Father Aleksei Vasiliev, the family's priest in Tobolsk, and with one of the family's maids. Arrested in March 1918. Many émigrés later maintained that Solovyov was a provocateur, acting on behalf of the Bolsheviks in order to expose and abort genuine plans to free the tsar and his family. Died abroad.

Soviets. Councils of deputies elected by urban workers and soldiers but also including representatives of leftist parties, trade unions, and other organizations. Ranging from neighborhood soviets in large cities like Moscow to regional soviets. Initiative and leadership were generally in the hands of members of the socialist parties—Mensheviks, Socialist Revolutionaries, Bolsheviks—who were mainly intellectuals. First established during the 1905 revolution, they arose again in Petrograd in February 1917, then in most other Russian cities. The Petrograd Soviet, which shared the Tauride Palace with the Provisional Government, and especially the Executive Committee of the Petrograd Soviet, functioned as a national political center for the left until the First All-Russian Congress of Soviets of Workers' and Soldiers' Deputies established the All-Russian Central Executive Committee of Soviets (VTsIK) in early June 1917. After October 1917, the Congress of Soviets was formally the supreme organ of state power; between sessions, the VTsIK was.

Sovnarkom. See Council of People's Commissars.

State Council. Until 1906, an appointed advisory body composed of Russia's oldest aristocratic families; from 1906, the upper house in the new bicameral legislative system. Half the members were appointed by the tsar and half elected by major corporative groups in Russian society—provincial rural assemblies (zemstvos), the nobility, merchants and industrialists, the clergy, the Academy of Sciences and the universities, and the Finnish Diet.

Sverdlóv, Yákov Mikháilovich (1885–1919). A leading figure in the Bolshevik party and Soviet state. Member of the Russian Social-Democratic Workers' Party from 1901 and, from 1912, of the Central Committee of the Bolshevik party, where, as secretary, he was in charge of assignments of party members, establishing liaisons with local organizations, and managing the party press. In 1917, sent to Yekaterinburg, where he directed the work of the Ural Regional Party Conference. Chairman of the All-Russian Central Executive Committee of Soviets (VTsIK) from 8 (21) November 1917 until his death from illness on 16 March 1919. The city of Yekaterinburg bore the name Sverdlovsk in his honor from 1924 to 1991.

Syroboiárskaia, María Martiánovna. Wife of artillery colonel V. A. Syroboiarsky. Mother of A. V. Syroboiarsky. Emigrated to the United States.

Syroboiár#sky, Aleksándr Vladímirovich (1888–1946). An officer in the Russian army, served at the front throughout World War I, first as a sergeant in the artillery and later as a commander of an armored division; he was promoted to colonel in 1916. Seriously injured, he met Alexandra when he was a patient in the infirmary at Tsarskoe Selo. From that time, had an extensive correspondence with Alexandra and other members of the imperial family. During the civil war, joined the anti-Bolshevik army of Admiral Aleksandr Kolchak, who promoted him to major general. Emigrated to the United States in 1923. Published letters sent to him by members of the imperial family in a book titled *Skorbnaia pamiatka* (A mournful memento) (New York, 1928). Died in Lakewood, New Jersey.

Syromólotov, Fyódor Fyódorovich (1877–1949). Former mining engineer. In 1918, a member of the Ural Regional Soviet Executive Committee and regional commissar for finances. While the Romanovs were being killed, Syromolotov was in Perm on assignment from the Council of People's Commissars (Sovnarkom) to recover imperial valuables.

Tatiána Nikoláevna (29 May 1897–17 July 1918). Grand duchess, second daughter of Nicholas II and Alexandra Fyodorovna. Executed together with her family in Yekaterinburg on the night of 16–17 July 1918.

Tatíshchev, Iliá Leonídovich (1859–1918). Count, adjutant general in the imperial suite, lieutenant general with the Life Guards Horse Regiment, major general while serving Kaiser Wilhelm II (1905–1914). Tatishchev followed the imperial family into exile in Tobolsk. Arrested after the transfer of the family to Yekaterinburg (23 May 1918). Executed together with V. A. Dolgorukov on 10 July.

Tegleva, Aleksándra Aleksándrovna (Shura). Hereditary noblewoman; nanny to Nicholas and Alexandra's children. She was with the family in exile in Tobolsk. After emigrating, she married Pierre Gilliard.

TsIK. See Central Executive Committee of Soviets, All-Russian.

Vóikov, Pyótr Lázarevich (1888–1927). Born to a teacher's family. A member of the Bolshevik party from 1903. Studied at the Universities of Geneva and Paris and married the wealthy daughter of a Polish factory owner; returned to Russia after the February Revolution. A member of the Yekaterinburg Soviet and the Military-Revolutionary Committee in 1917. Ural regional commissar for supplies from January to December 1918. Worked in the People's Commissariat for Provisions from December 1918 to July 1919, in the Central Union of Consumers' Cooperatives from March 1919, in the collegium of the People's Commissariat for Foreign Trade from October 1920. Soviet diplomatic representative to Poland from 1924. Killed in Warsaw on 7 July 1927 by a Russian monarchist.

VTsIK. See Central Executive Committee of Soviets, All-Russian.

Výrubova (born Tanéeva), Ánna Aleksándrovna (Ania, the Cow) (1884–1964). Lady-in-waiting (*freilina*) and closest friend of Alexandra Fyodorovna. Spent the period of the February Revolution in the Aleksandrovsky Palace and contracted measles from Nicholas and Alexandra's children. After recovering, was separated from the imperial family by order of Aleksandr Kerensky and confined in the Peter and Paul Fortress. After an investigation, she was released for lack of evidence. Vyrubova organized and maintained clandestine communications with the imperial family in Tobolsk. After their death she fled to Finland, where she became a nun. Author of memoirs.

Yákovlev, Vasíly Vasílievich (Konstantín Alekséevich Miáchin) (1886–1938). Son of a peasant. Became a full-time Bolshevik revolutionary after working a number of years in various industrial jobs. Active mainly in the Urals. Participated in "expropriating" type for underground printing shops, organizing armed workers' groups, and robbing mail trains and safes at railroad stations. Before World War I, a left-wing dissident within the Bolshevik party, opposing Lenin's insistence that party members participate in legal organizations. After several years in European exile he returned to Russia in 1917, serving in various important party positions in Petrograd and in his native Urals, including a post as a member of the directing committee of the Cheka. In the spring of 1918, the All-Russian Central Executive Committee of Soviets (VTsIK) and the Council of People's Commissars (Sovnarkom) named him extraordinary commissar in charge of transferring the imperial family from Tobolsk to Yekaterinburg. In May 1918, after returning to Moscow, he was appointed commander of the Second Army on the eastern front (Ural-Orenburg front) in the civil war, but he defected to supporters of the government of the Constituent Assembly (Komuch) the following autumn. After this movement was crushed by Admiral Kolchak, Yakovlev fled to Harbin, in central Manchuria, where he took the name Stoianovich. After he submitted a "letter of repentance" to Stalin in March 1928, he was permitted to return to the Soviet Union. An inquiry into his case was conducted and a sentence pronounced—execution—which was subsequently commuted to ten years of prison and convict labor. He was granted early release in August 1933 and a restoration of civil rights for exemplary work and was employed for a time by local NKVD organs. Another arrest ensued, however, and on 16 September 1938 he was executed.

Yermakóv, Pyótr Zakhárovich (1884–1952). Former factory clerk in the Upper Isetsk works in the Urals; Bolshevik involved in terrorist acts and "expropriations" in 1905. Close to Filipp Goloshchekin. Arrested in 1911 and sent into exile, returning only after the February Revolution. After the October Revolution, became the Upper Isetsk military commissar and took an active role in suppressing counterrevolution. Served in the militia (police) during the 1920s. A director of prison institutions of the Ural region beginning in 1927. Died in 1952. A street in the city of Sverdlovsk (Yekaterinburg) was named after him.

Yuróvsky, Yákov Mikháilovich (1878–1938). Born in Klinsk, in Tomsk province. His father was a glassworker, his mother a seamstress. Received an elementary education and was apprenticed to a watchmaker. Active in the socialist underground in the Urals and western Siberia from 1904. A Bolshevik from 1905. Arrested in 1912 for revolutionary activities and deported to Yekaterinburg, where he opened his own photographic studio. Drafted into the army during World War I, he enrolled in a medical training college and, after graduating, remained in Yekaterinburg as a medical assistant (*feldsher*) at an army field hospital. After the February Revolution, Yurovsky was elected to the Yekaterinburg Soviet. After the October Revolution, became a member of the Executive Committee of the Ural Regional Soviet, taking the position of deputy regional commissar of justice. Also chief of security for the city of Yekaterinburg and a member of the collegium of the Ural regional Cheka. Appointed commandant of the House of Special Purpose (Ipatiev house), where the imperial family was imprisoned, on 4 July 1918. After the execution of the Romanovs and the fall of Yekaterinburg, he was appointed head of the Moscow regional Cheka and a member of the collegium of the Moscow city Cheka and worked in the Viatka Cheka. Became chairman of the Yekaterinburg provincial Cheka in 1919. Subsequently, he held responsible economic and party posts. Gave lectures on the execution of the Romanovs at gatherings of old Bolsheviks. Died in the Kremlin Hospital in 1938.

Yusúpov, Felíks Felíksovich (Count Sumarókov-Élston, the younger) (1887– 1967). Prince. From an old aristocratic line whose motto was "By a single path, with no twists." Married Princess Irina Aleksandrovna, Nicholas II's niece, in 1914. One of the organizers and accomplices in the murder of Grigory Rasputin in 1916, for which he was deported to live under police supervision at one of his estates in Kursk province. After the February Revolution he resided with his family in the Crimea. After emigrating he wrote a variety of memoirs.

Zaslávsky, Semyón. A member of the Bolshevik party from 1905. Sent by the Ural Regional Soviet Executive Committee to Tobolsk in the spring of 1918 to keep watch over the guarding of the imperial family. Commanded a Red Guard detachment. Was elected a member of the Executive Committee of the Tobolsk Soviet. Opposed commissar Yakovlev in the matter of transferring the imperial family from Tobolsk.

Zémstvos. Provincial rural assemblies established in 1864; representatives elected by the local population. Included peasants, but franchise was weighted so that larger landowners would be dominant. Hired professionals played an increasingly large role in the zemstvos. Zemstvos were responsible for education, road building, health care, and improvements in agricultural technique. Became organizing centers for Russian liberalism and a source of demands for a more representative national government.

Genealogy of the Imperial Family

Members of the Romanov family are usually identified in the documents by their title, such as grand duke, and their name and patronymic. Thus, Mikhail Aleksandrovich is the son of Aleksandr.

This table is only a partial listing of dynastic relatives.

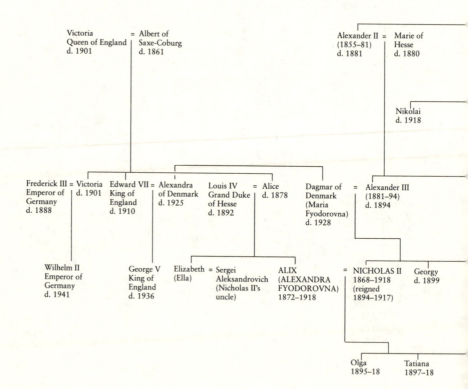

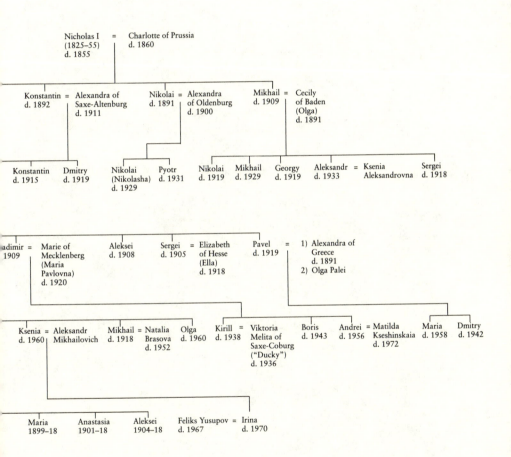

Nicholas I = Charlotte of Prussia
(1825–55)   d. 1860
d. 1855

Konstantin = Alexandra of   Nikolai = Alexandra   Mikhail = Cecily
d. 1892   Saxe-Altenburg   d. 1891   of Oldenburg   d. 1909   of Baden
         d. 1911   d. 1900   (Olga)
                                               d. 1891

Konstantin   Dmitry   Nikolai   Pyotr   Nikolai   Mikhail   Georgy   Aleksandr = Ksenia   Sergei
d. 1915   d. 1919   (Nikolasha) d. 1931   d. 1919   d. 1929   d. 1919   d. 1933   Aleksandrovna   d. 1918
                      d. 1929

…adimir = Marie of   Aleksei   Sergei   = Elizabeth   Pavel   =   1) Alexandra of
…1909   Mecklenberg   d. 1908   d. 1905   of Hesse   d. 1919   Greece
       (Maria   (Ella)   d. 1891
       Pavlovna)   d. 1918   2) Olga Palei
       d. 1920

Ksenia = Aleksandr   Mikhail = Natalia   Olga   Kirill   = Viktoria   Boris   Andrei = Matilda   Maria   Dmitry
d. 1960   Mikhailovich   d. 1918   Brasova   d. 1960   d. 1938   Melita of   d. 1943   d. 1956   Kseshinskaia   d. 1958   d. 1942
                       d. 1952   Saxe-Coburg   d. 1972
                                       ("Ducky")
                                       d. 1936

Maria   Anastasia   Aleksei   Feliks Yusupov = Irina
1899–18   1901–18   1904–18   d. 1967   d. 1970

Notes

Introduction: Nicholas and Alexandra, an Intellectual Portrait

1. See the bibliography for a listing of the most important publications in Russia and the West.

2. The dramatic qualities of this story and its use for moral and political judgment are strongly evident in the account by the playwright Edvard Radzinsky, published in the United States as *The Last Tsar: The Life and Death of Nicholas II* (New York, 1992). Other recent works that have made use of the newly available documents are Genrikh Ioffe, *Revoliutsiia i sud'ba Romanovykh* (The revolution and the fate of the Romanovs) (Moscow, 1992); Iu. Baranov and V. Khrustalëv, *Gibel' imperatorskogo doma, 1917–1919 gg.* (The destruction of the imperial house, 1917–1919) (Moscow, 1992); Veniamin A. Alekseev, *Gibel' tsarskoi sem'i: Mify i real'nost' (novye dokumenty o tragedii na Urale)* (The destruction of the imperial family: Myths and realities [new documents about the tragedy in the Urals]) (Yekaterinburg, 1993).

3. Richard Pipes, *The Russian Revolution* (New York, 1990), 787–788.

4. There are important exceptions, notably are Andrew M. Verner, *The Crisis of the Russian Autocracy: Nicholas II and the 1905 Revolution* (Princeton, 1990); and Dominic Lieven, *Nicholas II: Emperor of All the Russias* (London, 1993). Verner's book, though focused on the years 1905–1906, contains a thoughtful and complex portrait of Nicholas's political values and personality; his main argument, that Nicholas never identified with his role as Russia's autocratic ruler, is not convincing, however. Lieven's book, an excellent and sympathetic biography, is mainly a factual narrative of Nicholas II's reign rather than a systematic examination of his life and mentality; still, there are insights into Nicholas's thought and values. Also exploring the mental world of Nicholas and Alexandra is Robert K. Massie, *Nicholas and Alexandra* (New York, 1967), though this account is preoccupied with the effects of the tsarevich's hemophilia and the influence of Rasputin, too focused on events within narrow court circles, dependent on translated sources, and uncritically trusting of testimonies in émigré memoirs. A Soviet study of value is L. G. Zakharova, "Krizis samoderzhaviia nakanune revoliutsii 1905 goda" (The crisis of the autocracy on the eve of the 1905 revolution), *Voprosy istorii* (Problems of history), 1972, no. 8 (August): 119–140.

5. See the introduction to Chapter 4.

6. For an early example of Nicholas's complaints about the burdens of office, see his letter of 21 November 1898 to his mother, the dowager empress Mariia Fëdorovna, in Gosudarstvennyi arkhiv Rossiiskoi Federatsii (State Archive of the Russian Federation, henceforth GARF), f. 642, op. 1, d. 2325, l. 66. English translations of much of Nicholas's correspondence with his mother appear in *The Letters of Tsar Nicholas and Empress Marie,* ed. Edward J. Bing (London, 1937), 139. The Russian texts of many of these letters were published in "Perepiska Nikolaia II i Marii Fëdorovny (1905–1906 gg.)" (The correspondence of Nicholas II and Mariia Fëdorovna, 1905–1906), *Krasnyi arkhiv* (Red archive) 22 (1927): 153–209; and in "Iz perepiski Nikolaia i Marii Romanovykh v 1907–1910 gg." (From the correspondence of Nicholas and Mariia Romanov, 1907–1910), *Krasnyi arkhiv* 50–51 (1932): 161–193. My quotations are from the archival originals, a number of which remain unpublished.

7. S. Iu. Vitte, *Izbrannye vospominaniia, 1849–1911* (Selected recollections, 1849–1911) (Moscow, 1991), 125.

8. *Dnevnik V. N. Lamsdorfa (1886–1890)* (The diary of V. N. Lamsdorf, 1886–1890) (Moscow and Leningrad, 1926), 231; Lieven, *Nicholas II,* 24–28.

9. Lieven, *Nicholas II,* 40.

10. Verner, *Crisis,* 8.

11. Lieven, *Nicholas II,* 60.

12. Baroness Sophie Buxhoeveden [Buksgevden], *The Life and Tragedy of Alexandra Fedorovna, Empress of Russia: A Biography* (London, 1928), 276. See also Anna Viroubova [Vyrubova], *Memories of the Russian Court* (London, 1923), 55–56, 58. See also Lieven, *Nicholas II,* 35.

13. Nicholas to Alexandra, 3 September 1902, GARF, f. 640, op. 1, d. 102, l. 600b. The correspondence between Nicholas and his wife was entirely in English. Russian translations of letters written in 1914–1917 were published in *Perepiska Nikolaia i Aleksandry Romanovykh* (The correspondence of Nicholas and Alexandra Romanov), vols. 3–5 [vols. 1–2 were planned but never published] (Moscow and Leningrad, 1923–1927). English translations of the Russian translations of Nicholas's letters were published in *The Letters of the Tsar to the Tsaritsa, 1914–1917,* trans. E. L. Hynes (London, 1929); Transcriptions of the English originals of Alexandra's letters were published as an addendum to *Pis'ma imperatritsy Aleksandry Fëdorovny k imperatoru Nikolaiu II* (Letters of Empress Alexandra Fëdorovna to Emperor Nicholas II [1914–1916]), 2 vols. (Berlin, 1922); however, they contain many errors. My quotations are from the original English texts, held in the State Archive of the Russian Federation.

14. For example, Nicholas to Mariia Fëdorovna, 21 November 1898, GARF, f. 642, op. 1, d. 2325, l. 64.

15. Nicholas to Alexandra, 31 August 1902, GARF, f. 640, op. 1, d. 102, l. 53; Nicholas to Mariia Fëdorovna, 29 December 1905, GARF, f. 642, op. 1, d. 2328, l. 32–320b. Nicholas, in a further revelation of his tastes and values, also announced at this celebration that he was restoring a number of the battalion's lost traditions, such as their original grand uniforms. See also Nicholas to Mariia Fëdorovna, 13 September 1901, GARF, f. 642, op. 1, d. 2327, l. 120b.

16. Nicholas to Alexandra, 2 May 1904, GARF, f. 640, op. 1, d. 102, l. 630b–64; Nicholas's speech of 16 April 1904, *Pravitel'stvennyi vestnik* (Government herald), 17 (30) April 1904. This and other speeches by Nicholas may also be found in *Polnoe sobranie rechei Imperatora Nikolaia II (1894–1906 gg.)* (The complete collected speeches of Emperor Nicholas II [1894–1906]) (St. Petersburg, 1906).

17. Viroubova, *Memories,* 104.

18. Nicholas to Alexandra, 31 March 1916, GARF, f. 640, op. 1, d. 109, l. 59–600b. The regiment of cossacks mentioned here was His Majesty's Own Convoy, a unit of the Life Guards. Colonel A. S. Zhukov committed suicide in June 1916.

19. See Anna Vyrubova's comments on the importance of this issue for Nicholas, who decided on prohibition on his own initiative. Viroubova, *Memories*, 127.

20. See the description by Nicholas's sister in Ian Vorres, *The Last Grand Duchess: Her Imperial Highness Grand Duchess Olga Alexandrovna* (New York, 1965), 24. See also Lieven, *Nicholas II*, 24–29.

21. Nicholas to Mariia Fëdorovna, 27 September 1909, GARF, f. 642, op. 1, d. 2330, l. 97.

22. Nicholas to Alexandra, 3 January 1916, GARF, f. 640, op. 1, d. 109, l. 4.

23. For example, see Nicholas to his mother, Mariia Fëdorovna, 10 October 1900, 21 July 1906, and 22 March 1907, GARF, f. 642, op. 1, d. 2326, l. 86; d. 2328, l. 45; d. 2330, l. 90b; and Nicholas to Alexandra, 10 January and 26 April 1916, GARF, f. 640, op. 1, d. 109, l. 170b; d. 110, l. 180b–190b. See also Verner, *Crisis*, 11.

24. A. Elchaninov, *Tsarstvovanie Gosudaria Imperatora Nikolaia Aleksandrovicha* (The reign of His Imperial Majesty Nicholas Aleksandrovich) (St. Petersburg and Moscow, 1913), 31 and generally chap. 2. The book appeared in an English translation, *The Tsar and His People* (London, [1913?]). Nicholas approved, read, and authorized the book. See Lieven, *Nicholas II*, 268n37.

25. "V gostiakh khorosho, a doma luchshe." Nicholas quoted this, for example, in his letter to his mother on 31 October 1909, GARF, f. 642, op. 1, d. 2330, l. 102.

26. See, for example, Nicholas to Mariia Fëdorovna, 20 October 1902, GARF, f. 642, op. 1, d. 2327, l. 57–590b.

27. See, for example, Alexandra to Nicholas, 26 March 1916, GARF, f. 601, op. 1, d. 1150, l. 329–330.

28. Nicholas to Alexandra, 26 June 1904, GARF, f. 640, op. 1, d. 102, l. 65; Alexandra to Nicholas, 3 April 1916, GARF, f. 601, op. 1, d. 1151, l. 7–70b.

29. Nicholas to Alexandra, 16 June 1916, GARF, f. 640, op. 1, d. 111, l. 29 (emphasis in the original). In original: "B . . . y"

30. Nicholas to Mariia Fëdorovna, 27 September 1906, GARF, f. 642, op. 1, d. 2329, l. 110b.

31. Nicholas to Mariia Fëdorovna, 27 September 1906, GARF, f. 642, op. 1, d. 329, l. 13; speeches of 1 September 1902, 12 September 1902, 19 January 1905, *Pravitel'stvennyi vestnik*, 3 (16) September 1902, 17 (30) September 1902, 20 January (2 February) 1905.

32. "Dnevnik kn. Ekateriny Alekseevny Sviatopolk Mirskoi za 1904–1905 gg." (Diary of Princess Yekaterina Alekseevna Sviatopolk-Mirskaia for 1904–1905), *Istoricheskie zapiski* (Historical notes) 77 (1965): 247.

33. For example, his speech of 21 February 1905, in *Pravitel'stvennyi vestnik*, 22 February (7 March) 1905.

34. See, for example, his first speech after assuming the throne in 1894, in *Pravitel'stvennyi vestnik*, 1 (13) November 1894.

35. *Pravitel'stvennyi vestnik*, 25 June (8 July) 1905.

36. Nicholas to Mariia Fëdorovna, 22 September 1904, GARF, f. 642, op. 1, d. 2327, l. 100–1000b.

37. See Buxhoeveden, *Life and Tragedy*, 207–208.

38. Nicholas to Alexandra, 24 November 1915, in GARF, f. 640, op. 1, d. 106, l. 95 (emphasis in the original); Nicholas to Alexandra, 4 January 1916, GARF, f. 640, op. 1, d. 109, l. 6 (emphasis in the original).

39. See also Nicholas's comments about his motives noted in the diary of Pierre Gilliard (Aleksei's tutor), 5 August 1914, quoted in Gilliard, *Thirteen Years at the Russian Court* (New York, 1921), 243–244.

40. Nicholas to Mariia Fëdorovna, 5 April 1900, GARF, f. 642, op. 1, d. 2326, l. 560b. (emphasis in the original).

41. Nicholas to Alexandra, 28 and 29 May 1916, GARF, f. 640, op. 1, d. 110, l. 47–480b. See also Nicholas's telegram of 28 May 1916, GARF, f. 640, op. 1, d. 107, l. 97.

42. Viroubova, *Memories,* 151.

43. Buxhoeveden, *Life and Tragedy,* 136; Maurice Paléologue, *An Ambassador's Memoirs,* 2 vols. (London, 1924), 1: 203–210 (entry dated 30 November 1914). Paléologue was told that Philippe communicated to Nicholas "innumerable decisions . . . by the ghost of his father, Alexander III." Paléologue, *Ambassador's Memoirs,* 1: 206. During the war Alexandra still occasionally reminded Nicholas of Philippe's prophecies and teachings.

44. See, for example, Nicholas to Alexandra, 29 August 1902, GARF, f. 640, op. 1, d. 102, l. 470b.

45. Rasputin to Nicholas, Beinecke Rare Book and Manuscript Library, Yale University, Romanov collection, container 1. A photograph of the original letter is in N. Sokolov, *Ubiistvo tsarskoi sem'i* (Murder of the imperial family) (Berlin, 1925), facing 96. An English translation appears in Massie, *Nicholas and Alexandra,* 268.

46. Nicholas to Alexandra, 9 September 1916, GARF, f. 640, op. 1, d. 114, l. 110b; Nicholas to Alexandra, 24 September 1916, GARF, f. 640, op. 1, d. 114, l. 400b–410b.

47. For example, Nicholas's letters to Alexandra of 25 November 1914 and 28 February 1915 and his telegram of 6 May 1915, GARF, f. 640, op. 1, d. 102, l. 1030b.; d. 104, l. 52; d. 105, l. 5.

48. Said to the French ambassador Maurice Paléologue, *Ambassador's Memoirs,* 2: 93 (entry dated 12 October 1915).

49. "Dnevnik E. A. Sviatopolk Mirskoi," 251 (1 November 1904), quoting her husband, the minister of internal affairs, Prince P. D. Sviatopolk-Mirskii.

50. Lieven, *Nicholas II,* 33.

51. Nicholas to Alexandra, 29 August 1902, GARF, f. 640, op. 1, d. 102, l. 470b.

52. A. Iswolsky, "Souvenirs de mon ministère," *Revue des deux mondes* (1 July 1919): 105. See also Nicholas's comments to his mother that faith in God gave him strength and "spiritual peace" and the knowledge that Russia's sufferings (in 1905) were "God's will" and that "we have to patiently submit to our misfortunes to the end." Nicholas to Mariia Fëdorovna, 8 and 15 December 1905, GARF, f. 642, op. 1, d. 2328, l. 230b., 280b. These assurances likely reinforced the dowager empress's opinion that her son was exceptionally fatalistic, as she told the chairman of the Council of Ministers earlier in 1905: "Je ne puis pas comprendre quelquefois que ce soit mon fils, il est tout à fait calme et content." Quoted in "Dnevnik E. A. Sviatopolk Mirskoi," 279 (19 January 1905). For further discussion and other examples, see V. N. Kokovtsov, *Iz moego proshlogo: Vospominaniia 1903–1919* (From my past: Recollections, 1903–1919), 2 vols. (Paris, 1933), 2: 171–172; Verner, *Crisis,* 146–147.

53. Diary of Sergei Aleksandrovich, 15 November 1904, quoted in Verner, *Crisis,* 117.

54. Diary of Nicholas II, 18 October, 20 October, 25 October 1894. Because there are many editions of parts of Nicholas's diary, I cite only entry dates here and in other notes. Quotations are from the original manuscript diaries for 1917–1918 or from published editions: *Dnevniki imperatora Nikolaia II* (Diaries of Emperor Nicholas II [1894–1918]) (Moscow, 1991); and *Dnevnik imperatora Nikolaia II, 1890–1906* (Diary of Emperor Nicholas II, 1890–1906) (Berlin, 1923).

55. Diary of Nicholas II, 11 (24) March 1918, 19 April (2 May) 1918.

56. For discussions of these coexisting and competing political myths, see Michael Cherniavsky, *Tsar and People: Studies in Russian Myths* (New Haven, 1961), chaps. 2–3; and Verner, *Crisis,* chap. 3, esp. 72–79.

57. These ideas are elaborated in K. P. Pobedonostsev, *Moskovskii sbornik* (Moscow collection) (Moscow, 1896), translated into English as *Reflections of a Russian Statesman* (London, 1896; reprint: Ann Arbor, Mich., 1965). See also *Pis'ma Pobedonostseva k Aleksandru III* (Letters of Pobedonostsev to Alexander III) (Moscow, 1925–1926); and discussions in Robert F. Byrnes, *Podedonostsev: His Life and Thought* (Bloomington, Ind., 1968); Byrnes, "Russian Conservative Thought before the Revolution," in *Russia under the Last Tsar,* ed. Theofanis George Stavrou (Minneapolis, 1969), 42–68; and Verner, *Crisis,* 84–88.

58. Lieven, *Nicholas II,* 64. In addition to examples that follow in the text, see Nicholas's letter to his mother of 21 October 1902, GARF, f. 642, op. 1, d. 2327, l. 61–610b. See also the observation of General A. Mosolov, chief of the Court Chancellery, that one reason Nicholas had no secretary was that "he wished to be alone before his own conscience." A. Mosolov, *Pri dvore imperatora* (At the court of the emperor) (Riga, [1935]), 12. For an English translation, see A. A. Mossolov, *At the Court of the Last Tsar* (London, 1935).

59. Elchaninov, *Tsarstvovanie,* 28 (English edition, 22–23).

60. "Perepiska N. A. Romanova i P. A. Stolypina" (Correspondence of N. A. Romanov and P. A. Stolypin), *Krasnyi arkhiv* 5 (1924): 105 (10 December 1906) (emphasis in the original). Nicholas is quoting a Russian saying that also forms part of the prayer spoken by the tsar at his coronation. The prayer is in turn based on a passage in Ecclesiastes 9:1, "The righteous and the wise and their works are in the hand of God."

61. Nicholas to Alexandra, 8 August 1916, GARF, f. 640, op. 1, d. 112, l. 390b; Nicholas to Alexandra, 25 August 1915, GARF, f. 640, op. 1, d. 106, l. 47.

62. Diary of Nicholas II, 20 October 1894. Nicholas also observed that the expression on his dead father's face was "marvelous [*chudnoe*], smiling, as if he wants to laugh!" Diary, 21 October 1894.

63. [Aleksandr Izvolskii], *The Memoirs of Alexander Iswolsky* (London, 1920), 264.

64. Cherniavsky, *Tsar and People,* chap. 2.

65. Grand Duke Alexander, *Once a Grand Duke* (New York, 1932), 169 (I have made a slight correction in this translation). See similar recollections by Nicholas's sister Olga, in Vorres, *Last Grand Duchess,* 54–55.

66. Cherniavsky, *Tsar and People,* chaps. 1–2.

67. Nicholas to Alexandra, 30 August 1902, GARF, f. 640, op. 1, d. 102, l. 51–510b. See also his letters of 1 and 2 September 1902, GARF, f. 640, op. 1, d. 102, l. 56–58.

68. Diary of General Aleksandr Kireev, Manuscript Section of the Russian State Library, f. 126, quoted in Lieven, *Nicholas II,* 109.

69. Lieven, *Nicholas II,* 99, 106–110, 113; Verner, *Crisis,* 82–84.

70. Speech to representatives of the nobility, zemstvos, and cities, 17 January 1895, *Pravitel'stvennyi vestnik,* 18 (30) January 1895. On Sviatopolk-Mirsky's proposals, see Verner, *Crisis,* 118–140, esp. 125.

71. *Pravitel'stvennyi vestnik,* 8 (21) June 1905. See also Elchaninov, *Tsarstvovanie,* 117 (English edition, 124); and Verner, *Crisis,* 180–183.

72. "Perepiska N. A. Romanova i P. A. Stolypina," 102 (undated letter of late June or early July 1906); speeches of 18 January and 27 April 1906, *Pravitel'stvennyi vestnik,* 20 January (2 February) 1906 and 28 April (11 May) 1906.

73. "Perepiska N. A. Romanova i P. A. Stolypina," 122 (2 February 1911).

74. Nicholas to Alexandra, 27 August 1915, GARF, f. 640, op. 1, d. 106, l. 52.

75. For an account of this national "pilgrimage" in which the sacred bond between tsar and *narod* is the leitmotif, see [Evgenii Vasil'evich Bogdanovich], *Istoricheskoe palomnichestvo nashego Tsaria v 1913 godu* (The historical pilgrimage of our Tsar in 1913) (St. Petersburg, 1914).

76. Vladimir N. Kokovtsov, *Out of My Past: The Memoirs of Count Kokovtsov* (Stanford, 1935), 360–361.

77. "Tsar' i narod" (Tsar and people), *Novoe vremia,* 21 July 1914; diary of Nicholas II, 20 July 1914; Alexandre Spiridovich, *Les dernières années de la cour de Tzarskoié-sélo 1910–1914,* 2 vols. (Paris, 1928–1929), 2: 483–484.

78. Testimony of Klavdiia Bitner (a teacher at the Tsarskoe Selo gymnasium who taught the imperial children at Tobolsk), to a White army investigatory commission, 4 August 1919, in *Gibel' tsarskoi sem'i* (The destruction of the imperial family), ed. Nikolai Ross (Frankfurt, 1987), 422.

79. Mosolov, *Pri dvore imperatora,* 15–16. See also the recollections of A. F. Girs, quoted in Verner, *Crisis,* 22.

80. Speeches of 6 June and 31 December 1905, *Pravitel'stvennyi vestnik*, 8 (21) June 1905 and 1 (14) February 1906.

81. Elchaninov, *Tsarstvovanie*, 26, 38, 53–54, 92 (English edition, 22, 34, 50–51, 97).

82. Speeches of 8 May 1904 and 19 January 1905, *Pravitel'stvennyi vestnik*, 9 (22) May 1904 and 20 January (2 February) 1905.

83. Nicholas to Alexandra, 9 September 1915, GARF, f. 640, op. 1, d. 106, l. 66.

84. *Styd* and *pozor* were among the terms he commonly applied to such actions. See, for example, Nicholas to Mariia Fëdorovna, 30 August 1906, GARF, f. 642, op. 1, d. 2329, l. 50b.

85. Even the usually naive and apologetic Anna Vyrubova realized that Nicholas's contempt for political opposition caused him to "underestimate its importance" and danger. Viroubova, *Memories*, 136.

86. Nicholas was not particularly tolerant of non-Christians in general—he customarily spoke of all Japanese, for example, as "monkeys"—although the important Jewish presence in the Russian Empire made Jews a special case.

87. Nicholas to Mariia Fëdorovna, 27 October 1905, GARF, f. 642, op. 1, d. 2328, l. 15–150b.

88. Nicholas to Mariia Fëdorovna, 12 January 1906, GARF, f. 642, op. 1, d. 2328, l. 34–340b; 2 November 1906, GARF, f. 642, op. 1, d. 2329, l. 25.

89. See, for example, Nicholas's letter to his mother on 1 March 1907, GARF, f. 642, op. 1, d. 2330, l. 2.

90. "Perepiska N. A. Romanova i P. A. Stolypina," 105–106.

91. Nilus published several editions of the "Protocols" in Russia between 1905 and 1917, together with his own views on the Jewish conspiracy. A copy of the 1905 edition—S. A. Nilus, *Velikoe v malom i Antikhrist, kak blizkaia politicheskaia vozmozhnost': Zapiski pravoslavnogo* (Great things in small things and the Antichrist as a near political possibility: Notes of an Orthodox believer) (Tsarskoe Selo, 1905)—was found with Alexandra's books in Yekaterinburg after the family was killed. Sokolov, *Ubiistvo*, 291. It was sent by a friend to Alexandra in Tobolsk. See Document 110, note 2. Klavdiia Bitner, who spent time with the captive family in 1917–1918 as a teacher, told White investigators that Nicholas blamed the "yids" for inciting and misleading the people and causing the revolution. Bitner testimony, 4 August 1919, in *Gibel' tsarskoi sem'i*, 422.

92. For an insightful discussion on the symbolic significance of the two capitals in Russian political culture, see Richard Wortman, "Moscow and St. Petersburg: The Problem of Political Center in Tsarist Russia, 1881–1914," in *Rites of Power: Symbolism, Ritual, and Politics since the Middle Ages*, ed. Sean Wilentz (Philadelphia, 1985), 244–271.

93. Wortman, "Moscow and St. Petersburg," 251.

94. Elchaninov, *Tsarstvovanie*, 54.

95. Wortman, "Moscow and St. Petersburg," 251–254.

96. *Tsarskoe prebyvanie v Moskve v aprele 1900 goda* (The tsar's visit to Moscow in April 1900) (St. Petersburg, 1900), 55–56, quoted in Wortman, "Moscow and St. Petersburg," 261; diary of General Aleksandr Kireev, quoted in Zakharova, "Krizis samoderzhaviia," 131.

97. Nicholas to Mariia Fëdorovna, 12 January 1906, GARF, f. 642, op. 1, d. 2328, l. 34.

98. See also Nicholas's letter to his mother on 29 December 1905, GARF, f. 642, op. 1, d. 2328, l. 31–310b.

99. Nicholas to Alexandra, 5 November 1916, GARF, f. 640, op. 1, d. 115, l. 100b. See also his comments on specific ministers or ministerial recommendations in his letters of 26 September 1916 and 10 November 1916, GARF, f. 640, op. 1, d. 114, l. 440b (concerning a candidate for Petrograd police chief, who was "an honest man, but awfully weak, a real pancake"); and d. 115, l. 190b–20.

100. Nicholas to Alexandra, 4 December, 8 December, and 9 December 1916, GARF, f. 640, op. 1, d. 115, l. 22, 27, 29.

101. Nicholas to Mariia Fëdorovna, 15 December 1905 and 27 September 1906, GARF, f. 642, op. 1, d. 2328, l. 270b., d. 2329, l. 13.

102. Speech of 1 December 1905, *Pravitel'stvennyi vestnik,* 2 (15) December 1905.

103. Alexandra to Nicholas, 22 July 1902, GARF, f. 601, op. 1, d. 1148, l. 32 (emphasis in the original).

104. Alexandra to Nicholas, 27 September 1916 and 22 August 1915, GARF, f. 601, op. 1, d. 1151, l. 329–3290b; d. 1149, l. 230. Many other examples could be cited, such as those in her letters of 16 and 17 June 1915.

105. Alexandra to Nicholas, 22 August 1915, 8 March 1916, and 5 November 1916, GARF, f. 601, op. 1, d. 1149, l. 230; d. 1150, l. 287; d. 1151, l. 393.

106. Alexandra to Nicholas, 22 June 1915, 4 December 1916, and 14 December 1916, GARF, f. 601, op. 1, d. 1149, l. 2040b, 2060b; d. 1151, l. 418–419; l. 4570b (emphasis in the original).

107. Nicholas to Alexandra, 29 September 1916, GARF, f. 640, op. 1, d. 114, l. 500b.

108. Nicholas to Alexandra, 14 December 1916 and 15 December 1916, GARF, f. 640, op. 1, d. 115, l. 37; l. 400b.

109. Nicholas to Alexandra, 14 December 1916, GARF, f. 640, op. 1, d. 115, l. 370b.

110. Gilliard, *Thirteen Years,* 109–110. See also Alexandra's comments on the "*Schadenfreude* [gleeful cruelty] of Germany," in Alexandra to Nicholas, 12 June 1915, GARF, f. 601, op. 1, d. 1149, l. 1490b. In 1917–1918, according to witnesses, Alexandra continued to voice "hatred" for Wilhelm and the Germans. Bitner testimony, 4 August 1919, in *Gibel' tsarskoi sem'i,* 423.

111. Alexandra to Nicholas, 24 September 1914, GARF, f. 601, op. 1, d. 1148, l. 268–2680b.

112. Alexandra's early life and education are discussed in Buxhoeveden, *Life and Tragedy,* 1–20.

113. Alexandra to Nicholas, 25 June 1915, GARF, f. 601, op. 1, d. 1149, l. 224–2240b.

114. Viroubova, *Memories,* 73.

115. Diary of General Aleksandr Kireev, cited in Lieven, *Nicholas II,* 163.

116. Alice to Queen Victoria, 29 August 1866, quoted in Buxhoeveden, *Life and Tragedy,* 2–3.

117. Viroubova, *Memories,* 5, 58.

118. Alexandra to Nicholas, 28 October 1914, GARF, f. 601, op. 1, d. 1148, l. 2960b.

119. Viroubova, *Memories,* 108–112; Buxhoeveden, *Life and Tragedy,* 192.

120. Viroubova, *Memories,* 109–110.

121. Viroubova, *Memories,* 5, 79.

122. Alexandra to Nicholas, 8 March 1916 and 3 April 1916, GARF, f. 601, op. 1, d. 1150, l. 2860b; d. 1151, l. 8. See also her letter of 26 March 1916, GARF, f. 601, op. 1, d. 1150, l. 329–330.

123. Buxhoeveden, *Life and Tragedy,* 173; Viroubova, *Memories,* 67.

124. Viroubova, *Memories,* 3, 67; Buxhoeveden, *Life and Tragedy,* 166 (quoting a 1905 letter from Alexandra), 173.

125. Alexandra to Nicholas, 23 November 1914, GARF, f. 601, op. 1, d. 1148, l. 319.

126. Alexandra to Nicholas, 21 October 1914, GARF, f. 601, op. 1, d. 1148, l. 276.

127. Alexandra to Nicholas, 8 March 1916, GARF, f. 601, op. 1, d. 1150, l. 2860b.

128. "With God's help . . . it has lifted up the spirits, cleansed the many stagnant minds, brought unity in feelings & is a 'healthy war' in the moral sense." Alexandra to Nicholas, 24 September 1914, GARF, f. 601, op. 1, d. 1148, l. 268–2680b.

129. Alexandra to Nicholas, 27 October 1914, GARF, f. 601, op. 1, d. 1148, l. 2940b.

130. Alexandra to Nicholas, 16 June 1915 and 13 March 1916, GARF, f. 601, op. 1, d. 1149, l. 175; d. 1150, l. 306–3060b.

131. Nicholas describes these events in his diary entries of 5–8 April 1894 and in a letter

to his mother of 10 April 1894, GARF, f. 642, op. 1, d. 2322, l. 2–50b. See also Massie, *Nicholas and Alexandra,* 33–35.

132. Nicholas Zernov, *The Russian Religious Renaissance of the Twentieth Century* (New York, 1963); George L. Kline, *Religious and Anti-Religious Thought in Russia* (Chicago, 1968); Christopher Read, *Religion, Revolution and the Russian Intelligentsia, 1900–1912* (London, 1979); V. F. Botsianovskii, *Bogoiskateli* (Godseekers) (St. Petersburg and Moscow, 1911).

133. Viroubova, *Memories,* 151.

134. Viroubova, *Memories,* 151.

135. Alexandra to Nicholas, 22 July 1902, GARF, f. 601, op. 1, d. 1148, l. 320b.

136. See Chapter 4.

137. Lili Dehn [Den], *The Real Tsaritsa* (London, 1922), 63.

138. See Ol'ga to Anna Vyrubova, quoted in Viroubova, *Memories,* 324.

139. For example, Alexandra to Nicholas, 8 and 11 November 1916, GARF, f. 601, op. 1, d. 1151, l. 3980b, 409.

140. Alexandra to Nicholas, 16 June 1915, GARF, f. 601, op. 1, d. 1149, l. 173.

141. Alexandra to Nicholas, 15 June 1915, 16 June 1915, 11 November 1916, GARF, f. 601, op. 1, d. 1149, l. 165; d. 1149, l. 173; d. 1151, l. 409.

142. Alexandra to Nicholas, 5 February 1916 and 24 September 1916, GARF, f. 601, op. 1, d. 1150, l. 2340b; d. 1151, l. 318.

143. Alexandra to Nicholas, 7 September 1916, GARF, f. 601, op. 1, d. 1151, l. 2630b. See also the letters of 30 October 1916 and 11 November 1916, GARF, f. 601, op. 1, d. 1151, l. 370, 3710b, 410–411.

144. Alexandra to Nicholas, 14 December 1916, GARF, f. 601, op. 1, d. 1151, l. 459.

145. Alexandra to Nicholas, 30 October 1916 and 14 December 1916, GARF, f. 601, op. 1, d. 1151, l. 3710b, 458–4590b.

146. Alexandra to Nicholas, 8 November 1916 and 14 December 1916, GARF, f. 601, op. 1, d. 1151, l. 400; l. 4580b, 4590b.

147. Buxhoeveden, *Life and Tragedy,* 55.

148. Alexandra to Victoria, princess of Battenberg, 14 (27) January 1905, quoted in Buxhoeveden, *Life and Tragedy,* 109.

149. Alexandra to Nicholas, 14 December 1916, GARF, f. 601, op. 1, d. 1151, l. 4590b.

150. Ibid., 458–4580b.

151. Alexandra to Nicholas, 13 December 1916, GARF, f. 601, op. 1, d. 1151, l. 454. See also the letter of 6 March 1916, GARF, f. 601, op. 1, d. 1150, l. 2710b.

152. Alexandra to Victoria, princess of Battenberg, 14 (27) January 1905, quoted in Buxhoeveden, *Life and Tragedy,* 109.

153. Nicholas to Alexandra, 30 August 1902, GARF, f. 640, op. 1, d. 102, l. 51–510b.

Chapter 1: Revolution

1. Speech to representatives of nobility, zemstvos, and cities, 17 January 1895, *Pravitel'stvennyi vestnik,* 18 (30) January 1895.

2. See especially R. V. Ivanov-Razumnik, *Istoriia russkoi obshchestvennoi mysli* (History of Russian social thought), 2d ed. (St. Petersburg, 1914), vols. 1–2; Nicholas Riasanovsky, *A Parting of Ways: Government and the Educated Public in Russia* (Oxford, 1976); Isaiah Berlin, *Russian Thinkers* (New York, 1978); Edith Clowes, Samuel Kassow, and James West, eds., *Between Tsar and People: Educated Society and the Quest for Public Identity in Late Imperial Russia* (Princeton, 1991).

3. For a bibliography of important recent works on lower-class attitudes, culture, and rebellion, see Stephen P. Frank and Mark D. Steinberg, eds., *Cultures in Flux: Lower-Class Values, Practices, and Resistance in Late Imperial Russia* (Princeton, 1994).

4. See, for example, Gerald Surh, *1905 in St. Petersburg* (Stanford, 1989); Charters Wynn, *Workers, Strikes, and Pogroms* (Princeton, 1992); Robert Weinberg, *The Revolution*

of 1905 in Odessa (Bloomington, Ind., 1993); S. A. Smith, *Red Petrograd: Revolution in the Factories, 1917–1918* (Cambridge, Eng., 1983).

5. Many works explore aspects of the history of Russian socialism. See especially Leopold H. Haimson, *The Russian Marxists and the Origins of Bolshevism* (Cambridge, Mass., 1955); Oliver Radkey, *The Agrarian Foes of Bolshevism* (New York, 1958); Abraham Ascher, *Pavel Axelrod and the Development of Menshevism* (Cambridge, Mass., 1972); Robert C. Williams, *The Other Bolsheviks* (Bloomington, Ind., 1986).

6. On the general history of Russian liberalism, see George Fischer, *Russian Liberalism* (Cambridge, Mass., 1958); Charles Timberlake, ed., *Essays on Russian Liberalism* (Columbia, Mo., 1972); S. Galai, *The Liberation Movement in Russia, 1900–1905* (Cambridge, Eng., 1973).

7. Geoffrey Hosking, *The Russian Constitutional Experiment* (New York, 1973).

8. William G. Rosenberg, *Liberals in the Russian Revolution: The Constitutional Democratic Party, 1917–1921* (Princeton, 1974).

9. The following discussion of Russian wartime politics and of the February 1917 revolution draws upon a variety of sources and accounts. The best general histories are Tsuyoshi Hasegawa, *The February Revolution: Petrograd, 1917* (Seattle, 1981); and Richard Pipes, *The Russian Revolution* (New York, 1990).

10. "Tiazhelye dni (sekretnye zasedaniia Soveta Ministrov, 16 iiulia–2 sentiabria 1915 goda)" (Harsh days [the secret meetings of the Council of Ministers, 16 July–2 September 1915]), recorded by A. N. Iakhontov, *Arkhiv russkoi revoliutsii* (Archive of the Russian Revolution) (Berlin) 18 (1926): 136. An English translation of this document has been published as *Prologue to Revolution,* ed. Michael Cherniavsky (Englewood Cliffs, N.J., 1967).

11. Nicholas Riasanovsky, *A History of Russia,* 5th ed. (New York, 1993), 421.

12. Nicholas to Alexandra, 20 September 1916, GARF, f. 640, op. 1, d. 114, l. 33.

13. For example, "Doklad petrogradskogo okhrannogo otdeleniia osobomu otdelu departamenta politsii" (Report of the Petrograd Okhrana to the Special Section of the Department of the Police), dated October 1916, *Krasnyi arkhiv* 17 (1926): 4–35. This report warned of "the possibility of riots in the near future by the lower classes of the empire enraged by the burdens of daily existence." Ibid., 4.

14. "Delo s doneseniiami i telefonnymi soobshcheniiami P.O.O. ob obshchestvennom dvizhenii" (Reports and telephone information from the Petrograd Okhrana on the social movement), 2 January–26 February 1917, GARF, f. 111, op. 1, d. 669, l. 1–386; Major General Konstantin Globachev (head of the Petrograd Okhrana), "Dopolnenie k doneseniiu (sovershenno-sekretno)" (Addendum to report [top secret]), 26 January 1917, GARF, f. 111, op. 1, d. 669, l. 112–113; Hasegawa, *February Revolution,* 201.

15. The various plots are described and assessed in Hasegawa, *February Revolution,* chaps. 7, 10, and in S. Mel'gunov, *Na putiakh k dvortsovomu perevorotu* (On the road to a palace revolution) (Paris, 1931).

16. Letter from Anatolii Savenko (a nationalist member of the Progressive Bloc), 18 February 1917, GARF, f. 102, op. 265, d. 1070, l. 62. The letters of other Duma deputies in mid-February (read by the police, who copied down passages before sending the letters on) also mention the war of words that flourished amid the deepening malaise and uncertainty. GARF, f. 102, op. 265, d. 1070, l. 60, 66, 70.

17. Diary of Z. V. Arapov, 15 February 1917, Manuscript Division, Russian State Library, f. 12, folder 1, d. 9, l. 85–87, quoted in E. D. Chermenskii, *IV gosudarstvennaia duma i sverzhenie tsarizma v Rossii* (The fourth State Duma and the overthrow of tsarism in Russia) (Moscow, 1976), 274.

18. Telegram from Protopopov to the general staff, 25 February 1917, *Proletar'skaia revoliutsiia* (Proletarian revolution) 13 (1923): 290; telegram from Khabalov to Chief of Staff Alekseev, 25 February 1917, *Krasnyi arkhiv* 21 (1927): 4–5 (although this telegram was received at Headquarters at 6:08 P.M. on 25 February, a handwritten notation by Alekseev

indicates that he did not report it to the tsar until the 26th); E. I. Martynov, *Tsarskaia armiia v fevral'skom perevorote* (The imperial army in the February Revolution) (Leningrad, 1927), 80–81.

19. Quoted by Khabalov in his testimony of 22 March 1917, in *Padenie tsarskogo rezhima: Stenograficheskie otchety doprosov i pokazanii, dannykh v 1917 g. v Chrezvychainoi Sledstvennoi Komissii Vremennogo Pravitel'stva* (The fall of the imperial regime: Stenographic reports of interrogations and testimony given in 1917 to the Extraordinary Investigatory Commission of the Provisional Government), ed. P. E. Shchegolev, 7 vols. (Moscow and Leningrad, 1924–1927), 1: 190–191. The original text of Nicholas's telegram was not preserved, although other testimony confirms the substance of Khabalov's statement. Martynov quotes a slightly different text, citing, but not identifying the location of, an original in Nicholas's own hand. Martynov, *Tsarskaia armiia*, 81.

20. Testimony of Khabalov, in *Padenie tsarskogo rezhima*, 1: 191–194; testimony of War Minister Mikhail Beliaev, in *Padenie tsarskogo rezhima*, 2: 231–233.

21. See, for example, the memoir by the Bolshevik V. Kaiurov, "Shest' dnei fevral'skoi revoliutsii" (Six days of the February Revolution), *Proletarskaia revoliutsiia* 13 (1923): 165–166.

22. Testimony of Count Frederiks (minister of the imperial court), *Padenie tsarskogo rezhima*, 5: 38.

23. Telegram from Khabalov to Nicholas II, 27 February 1917, 12:10 P.M., *Krasnyi arkhiv* 21 (1927): 8.

24. Telegram from Beliaev to Alekseev, 27 February 1917, 7:22 P.M., *Krasnyi arkhiv* 21 (1927): 9.

25. Testimony of Beliaev, in *Padenie tsarskogo rezhima*, 2: 239; supplementary written testimony from Nikolai Golitsyn, chairman of the Council of Ministers, in *Padenie tsarskogo rezhima*, 4: 9; telegram from Beliaev to Alekseev, 27 February 1917, 7:29 P.M., *Krasnyi arkhiv* 21 (1927): 9.

26. *Krasnyi arkhiv* 21 (1927): 11–13; GARF, f. 601, op. 1, d. 2089, l. 2.

27. Telegram from Brusilov to Alekseev, 27 February 1917, received at 1:00 P.M. and shown to Nicholas II, *Krasnyi arkhiv* 21 (1927): 7; telegram from Ruzskii to Nicholas II, 27 February 1917, 9:15 P.M., *Krasnyi arkhiv* 21 (1927): 13; telegram from Rodzianko to Nicholas II, 27 February 1917, 12:40 P.M., *Krasnyi arkhiv* 21 (1927): 6–7.

28. Communication by direct telegraph between Grand Duke Mikhail Aleksandrovich and Nicholas II, 27 February 1917, *Krasnyi arkhiv* 21 (1927): 11–12.

29. A. S. Lukomskii, "Iz vospominanii" (Reminiscences), in *Arkhiv russkoi revoliutsii* 2 (1922): 21–22. In his conversation by direct telegraph with Grand Duke Mikhail, Alekseev also suggested that he would propose a political solution in his report to the tsar on the morning of the 28th.

30. Hasegawa, *February Revolution*, 366–367.

31. "Zhurnal [No. 1] Soveta Ministrov Vremennogo Pravitel'stva" (Journal [No. 1] of the Council of Ministers of the Provisional Government), 2 March 1917, GARF, f. 601, op. 1, d. 2103, l. 1.

32. *Izvestiia* [komiteta Petrogradskikh zhurnalistov] (News [of the Committee of Petrograd Journalists]), 27 February 1917.

33. N. N. Sukhanov, *The Russian Revolution: A Personal Record*, ed. and trans. Joel Carmichael (Oxford, 1955; originally published in Russian in 1922), 101–108.

34. "Zhurnal Soveta Ministrov Vremennogo Pravitel'stva," 2 March 1917, GARF, f. 601, op. 1, d. 2103, l. 1.

35. *Izvestiia Petrogradskogo Soveta rabochikh i soldatskikh deputatov* (News of the Petrograd Soviet of Workers' and Soldiers' Deputies), henceforth, *Izvestiia*, 2 and 3 March 1917; Sukhanov, *Russian Revolution*, 118–125; Hasegawa, *February Revolution*, 417–418.

36. See Hasegawa, *February Revolution*, 446–454.

37. D. N. Dubenskii, "Kak proizoshel perevorot v Rossii: Zapiski-dnevniki" (How the

revolution in Russia occurred: Notes and diaries), *Russkaia letopis'* (Russian chronicle) 3 (1922): 46–47.

38. Hasegawa, *February Revolution*, 492.

39. S. N. Vil'chkovskii, "Prebyvanie Gosudaria Imperatora v Pskove 1 i 2 Marta 1917 goda, po razskazu general-ad"iutanta N. V. Ruzskogo" (His Majesty the Emperor in Pskov, 1–2 March 1917, according to the account of Adjutant General N. V. Ruzskii), *Russkaia letopis'* 3 (1922): 169. In a communication by direct telegraph with Rodzianko the following morning, Ruzskii also mentioned Nicholas's willingness to allow Rodzianko to form a government. *Krasnyi arkhiv* 21 (1927): 56.

40. Telegram from Alekseev to Ivanov, 28 February 1917, received at Tsarskoe Selo on 1 March at 1:15 A.M.), *Krasnyi arkhiv* 21 (1927): 31. Alekseev sent copies to all of the front commanders.

41. Telegram from Nicholas II to Ivanov, 2 March 1917, 12:20 A.M., *Krasnyi arkhiv* 21 (1927): 53. Later that day, on the tsar's instructions, Alekseev sent orders to the front commanders canceling the order for reinforcements to be sent from the front to support Ivanov. Telegram from Alekseev to Generals Evert and Brusilov, 2 March 1917, *Krasnyi arkhiv* 21 (1927): 64.

42. Communication by direct telegraph between Ruzskii and Rodzianko, 2 March 1917, 3:30–7:30 A.M., Rossiiskii gosudarstvennyi voenno-istoricheskii arkhiv (Russian State Military-Historical Archive, henceforth RGVIA), f. 2031/s, op. 1, d. 9, l. 99–101, published in *Revoliutsionnoe dvizhenie v Rossii posle sverzheniia samoderzhaviia* (The revolutionary movement in Russia after the overthrow of the autocracy) (Moscow, 1957), 405–409 (quotation 406).

43. Telegram from Alekseev to front commanders, 2 March 1917, 10:15 A.M., *Russkaia letopis'* 3 (1922): 135–136; *Krasnyi arkhiv* 21 (1927): 67–69.

44. *Krasnyi arkhiv* 21 (1927): 75.

45. Ruzskii's account in Vil'chkovskii, "Prebyvanie," *Russkaia letopis'* 3 (1922): 178.

46. *Russkaia letopis'* 3 (1922): 140. A reproduction of the original telegram to Rodzianko is in Martynov, *Tsarskaia armiia*, 159.

47. Draft manifesto of abdication, *Krasnyi arkhiv* 22 (1927): 7; Nicolas de Basily [Nikolai Bazili], *Memoirs* (Stanford, 1973), 116–117, 122–125 (including photograph of Basily's final draft). This publication is a translation of the French original, which is in the Basily Papers in the Archives of the Hoover Institution, Stanford, California.

48. Basily, *Memoirs*, 125; recollections by Guchkov, in Basily Papers, Archives of the Hoover Institution, translated in Basily, *Memoirs*, 129–130; telegram from Guchkov and Shul'gin to Alekseev, 3 March 1917, RGVIA, f. 2031/s, op. 1, d. 9, l. 223, published in *Revoliutsionnoe dvizhenie v Rossii posle sverzheniia samoderzhaviia*, 416–417.

49. Basily, *Memoirs*, 119–120.

50. Shulgin and Guchkov both mentioned his serenity in their recollections of the meeting: Guchkov in Basily, *Memoirs*, 127–128, and Shulgin in V. V. Shul'gin, *Dni* (Days) (Belgrade, 1925), 266–268.

51. V. N. Voeikov, *S tsarem i bez tsaria* (With the tsar and without the tsar) (Helsingfors, 1936), 212.

52. Speech by Miliukov, *Izvestiia*, 3 March 1917.

53. Guchkov remembered thinking that "a beautiful myth could have been created around this innocent and pure child. His charm would have helped to calm the anger of the masses." Quoted in Basily, *Memoirs*, 128.

54. Telegram from Grand Duke Nikolai Nikolaevich to General Alekseev, 3 March 1917, 6:22 P.M., *Krasnyi arkhiv* 22 (1927): 25.

55. These meetings have been described in the memoirs of most of the participants, notably Shul'gin, *Dni*, 295–307; P. N. Miliukov, *Istoriia vtoroi russkoi revoliutsii* (The history of the second Russian Revolution), vol. 1 (Sofia, 1921), 53–55; Miliukov, *Vospominaniia* (Memoirs), vol. 2 (New York, 1955), 316–318.

Chapter 2: Under Arrest at Tsarskoe Selo

1. Telegram from General Alekseev to Prince L'vov, 4 March 1917, *Krasnyi arkhiv* 22 (1927): 54; telegram from L'vov to Alekseev, 6 March 1917, GARF, f. 601, op. 1, d. 2107, l. 1, reprinted in *Krasnyi arkhiv* 22 (1927): 55.

2. Correspondence between Ambassador George Buchanan and the British Foreign Office, 18–22 March 1917, Public Record Office, FO 371, vol. 2995, pp. 415–416; vol. 2998, pp. 90–93, 98, 106–112, 120–121.

3. George Buchanan, *My Mission to Russia* (London, 1923), 2: 104–105.

4. For examples, see GARF f. 1235, op. 53, d. 19, l. 58; *Krasnyi arkhiv* 22 (1927): 67.

5. Arthur Stamfordham to Foreign Secretary Arthur Balfour, 6 April 1917, Public Record Office, FO 800, vol. 205, and in the Lloyd George Papers, Record Office, House of Lords. These letters are quoted in Kenneth Rose, *King George V* (London, 1983), 212–213, and in Anthony Summers and Tom Mangold, *The File on the Tsar* (New York, 1976), 249–250. See also Stamfordham's letter to Balfour, dated 30 March, concerning the king's reluctance to admit the tsar and his family into Britain. Public Record Office, FO 800, vol. 205, quoted in Summers and Mangold, *File on the Tsar,* 248.

6. See Rose, *George V,* 209–210.

7. Foreign Office to Buchanan, 13 April 1917, Public Record Office, FO 800, vol. 205, cited in Rose, *George V,* 213–214, and in Summers and Mangold, *File on the Tsar,* 250–251. See also Robert D. Warth, *The Allies and the Russian Revolution* (Durham, N.C., 1954), 34–37.

8. Alexander Kerensky, *The Catastrophe: Kerensky's Own Story of the Russian Revolution* (New York, 1927), 261.

9. The following discussion of the conditions of the family's confinement at Tsarskoe Selo is based on the documents in this chapter and on diaries (of Nicholas, Alexandra, and Aleksei's tutor Gilliard), memoirs, and letters. Valuable letters, in addition to those included in this book, can be found in *Pis'ma tsarskoi sem'i iz zatocheniia* (Letters of the imperial family from captivity) (Jordanville, N.Y., 1974). I have also made use of letters from Pierre Gilliard, in GARF, f. 611, op. 1, d. 50. The most reliable memoirs for this period—judged by their mutual consistency and general accuracy about events that can be otherwise documented—are Paul Benckendorff [Pavel Benkendorf], *Last Days at Tsarskoe Selo* (London, 1927); Sophie Buxhoeveden, *The Life and Tragedy of Alexandra Feodorovna* (London, 1928); and Pierre Gilliard, *Thirteen Years at the Russian Court* (New York, 1921).

10. Benckendorff, *Last Days at Tsarskoe Selo,* 31–34.

11. See also the diary of Nicholas II, 27 May 1917; Alexandra to A. V. Syroboiarskii, 28 May 1917, *Pis'ma tsarskoi sem'i iz zatocheniia,* 62; Benckendorff, *Last Days at Tsarskoe Selo,* 91.

12. Gilliard, *Thirteen Years,* 232 (11 [24] June).

13. Gilliard, *Thirteen Years,* 229; "Zapros sobraniia predstavitelei fronta" (Inquiry of a meeting of representatives of the front), 12 April 1917, GARF, f. 1235, op. 53, d. 19, l. 71.

14. Benckendorff, *Last Days at Tsarskoe Selo,* 38; Buxhoeveden, *Life and Tragedy,* 283.

15. Buxhoeveden, *Life and Tragedy,* 298; Benckendorff, *Last Days at Tsarskoe Selo,* 84.

16. Benckendorff, *Last Days at Tsarskoe Selo,* 43.

17. Diary of Nicholas II, 30 March and 18 April 1917; Buxhoeveden, *Life and Tragedy,* 283–284, 299; Benckendorff, *Last Days at Tsarskoe Selo,* 67–68, 86; Documents 46, 72. On the basis of interviews conducted during 1918–1919, the White investigator Nikolai Sokolov described other examples of soldiers' "humiliating" and "hooliganistic" behavior toward the former tsar and his family. N. Sokolov, *Ubiistvo tsarskoi sem'i* (Berlin, 1925), 15–16.

18. See also "Prizyvy k mesti" (Calls for revenge), *Izvestiia,* 28 May 1917; Kerensky, *Catastrophe,* 262. In the Russian archives are also many telegrams, letters, and petitions sent during the spring and summer of 1917 to the Petrograd Soviet and to the Central Executive

Committee of Soviets, which was formed in June at the national congress of soviets. Some examples were published in *Krasnyi arkhiv* 81 (1937): 121–127. See also GARF, f. 1235, op. 53, d. 20, l. 2, 7, 12, 15; and f. 1235, op. 53, d. 19, l. 79.

19. See also the letter to the press from the commandants Korovichenko and Kobylinskii, "Kak soderzhit'sia Nikolai Romanov s sem'eiu v Tsarskom sele" (How Nicholas Romanov and his family are being maintained in Tsarskoe Selo), *Izvestiia,* 21 May 1917; and the article "V Tsarskom sele" (In Tsarskoe Selo), *Izvestiia,* 28 May 1917.

20. "Prizyvy k mesti," *Izvestiia,* 28 May 1917.

21. *Rech'* (Speech [a Kadet Party newspaper]), 28 April 1917, translated in *The Russian Provisional Government, 1917: Documents,* ed. Robert Browder and Alexander Kerensky, 3 vols. (Stanford, 1961), 2: 1098.

22. *Rech',* 28 March 1917, translated in *Russian Provisional Government,* 2: 1045–1046.

23. No adequate history yet exists of Russian society during the revolution. Good partial accounts can be found in Marc Ferro, *The Russian Revolution of 1917* (London, 1972); Ferro, *The Bolshevik Revolution* (London, 1980); Diane Koenker, *Moscow Workers and the 1917 Revolution* (Princeton, 1981); Diane Koenker and William G. Rosenberg, *Strikes and Revolution in Russia, 1917* (Princeton, 1989); Tim McDaniel, *Autocracy, Capitalism, and Revolution in Russia* (Berkeley, 1988); S. A. Smith, *Red Petrograd: Revolution in the Factories, 1917–1918* (Cambridge, Eng., 1983); and Allan K. Wildman, *The End of the Russian Imperial Army,* 2 vols. (Princeton, 1980, 1987).

24. Speech by L'vov, *Russkiia vedomosti,* 9 July 1917, translated in *Russian Provisional Government,* 3: 1388.

25. Alexander Kerensky, "The Road to the Tragedy," in *The Murder of the Romanovs* (London, 1935), 120.

Chapter 3: Siberian Captivity

1. Evgenii Kobylinskii, testimony of 6–10 April 1919, Documents of the Investigation into the Death of Nicholas II (Sokolov Archive), Houghton Library, Harvard University, Kilgour collection, MS Russian 35, vol. 3, doc. 29. Parts of Kobylinskii's testimony are published in *Gibel' tsarskoi sem'i* (The destruction of the imperial family), ed. Nikolai Ross (Frankfurt, 1987). See also quotations from Kobylinskii's journal, in Alexander Kerensky, "The Road to the Tragedy," in *The Murder of the Romanovs* (London, 1935), 130–133.

2. Diary of Nicholas II, 2 August 1917.

3. Kobylinskii, testimony of 6–10 April 1919, Houghton Library, Sokolov Archive, vol. 3, doc. 29, and in *Gibel' tsarskoi sem'i,* 293.

4. For example, resolution of workers of the railroad construction shop of the Putilov works in Petrograd, 4 August 1917, *Rabochii i soldat* (Worker and soldier [temporary successor to the banned *Pravda*]), 10 August 1917.

5. See also telegram from the Irkutsk Soviet, 5 August 1917, GARF, f. 1235, op. 53, d. 19, l. 92.

6. Pierre Gilliard, *Thirteen Years at the Russian Court* (New York, 1921), 239–240.

7. Diary of Nicholas II, 6 August 1917.

8. Gilliard, *Thirteen Years,* 239–241; Kobylinskii, testimony of 6–10 April 1919, Houghton Library, Sokolov Archive, vol. 3, doc. 29, and in *Gibel' tsarskoi sem'i,* 295–296.

9. Gilliard, testimony of 12–14 September 1918, Houghton Library, Sokolov Archive, vol. 1, doc. 36, and in *Gibel' tsarskoi sem'i,* 103; Kobylinskii, testimony of 6–10 April 1919, Sokolov Archive, vol. 3, doc. 29, and in *Gibel' tsarskoi sem'i,* 295.

10. Gilliard testimony of 12–14 September 1918, Houghton Library, Sokolov Archive, vol. 1, doc. 36; testimony of the nanny Aleksandra Tegleva, 5–6 July 1919, Sokolov Archive, vol. 5, doc. 36; Gilliard, diary entry of 30 January 1918, in Gilliard, *Thirteen Years,* 252–253.

11. Gilliard, testimony of 5–6 March 1919, Houghton Library, Sokolov Archive, vol. 2, doc. 55, and in *Gibel' tsarskoi sem'i*, 230; Gilliard, *Thirteen Years*, 242; N. Sokolov, *Ubiistvo tsarskoi sem'i* (Berlin, 1925), 30–31; Document 123.

12. Genrikh Ioffe, *Revoliutsiia i sud'ba Romanovykh* (Moscow, 1992), 94–96, 106–111; RGVIA, f. 366, op. 2, d. 15, l. 45–49, 61, cited in Ioffe, *Revoliutsiia*, 108–109; *Izvestiia*, 22 and 23 August 1917, 10 September 1917.

13. See especially speeches and resolutions at the Conference of Public Figures (8–10 August) and at the State Conference (12–15 August), both held in Moscow, as reported in *Rech'*, 12–17 (25–30) August 1917.

14. Alexander Rabinowitch, *The Bolsheviks Come to Power* (New York, 1976), 100–115; Richard Pipes, *The Russian Revolution* (New York, 1990), 442–448; *Revoliutsionnoe dvizhenie v Rossii v avguste 1917 g.* (The revolutionary movement in Russia in August 1917) (Moscow, 1959), 359–377.

15. *Revoliutsionnoe dvizhenie v Rossii v avguste 1917 g.*, 441–443, 445–446; Rabinowitch, *Bolsheviks Come to Power*, 117–127; Pipes, *Russian Revolution*, 448–464.

16. Gilliard, *Thirteen Years*, 243.

17. Diary of Nicholas II, 1 September 1917.

18. "Pamiati Vasiliia Semenovicha Pankratova" (In memory of Vasilii Semenovich Pankratov), preface to V. S. Pankratov, *S tsarem v Tobol'ske* (With the tsar in Tobolsk) (Leningrad, 1925), 7–10; Kobylinskii, testimony of 6–10 April 1919, Houghton Library, Sokolov Archive, vol. 3, doc. 29, and in *Gibel' tsarskoi sem'i*, 295.

19. Pankratov, *S tsarem*, 12.

20. Testimonies of Kobylinskii (6–10 April 1919), Aleksandra Tegleva (5–6 July 1919), and Elizaveta Ersberg (6 July 1919), Houghton Library, Sokolov Archive, vol. 3, doc. 29, vol. 5, docs. 36–37; testimonies of Klavdiia Bitner (4 August 1919) and Aleksei Volkov (20–23 August 1919)—both missing from the Houghton collection—in *Gibel' tsarskoi sem'i*, 425, 448.

21. Gilliard, *Thirteen Years*, 241. Klavdiia Bitner, a teacher from the Tsarskoe Selo gymnasium who taught the imperial children in Tobolsk, called Pankratov "a real revolutionary idealist." Testimony in *Gibel' tsarskoi sem'i*, 425.

22. Testimonies of Kobylinskii (6–10 April 1919), Tegleva (5–6 July 1919), and Ersberg (6 July 1919), Houghton Library, Sokolov Archive, vol. 3, doc. 29, and vol. 5, docs. 36–37; Bitner, testimony of 4 August 1919, in *Gibel' tsarskoi sem'i*, 425.

23. See Marc Ferro, *The Bolshevik Revolution* (London, 1980); Diane Koenker, *Moscow Workers and the 1917 Revolution* (Princeton, 1981); Diane Koenker and William G. Rosenberg, *Strikes and Revolution in Russia, 1917* (Princeton, 1989); Tim McDaniel, *Autocracy, Capitalism, and Revolution in Russia* (Berkeley, 1988); S. A. Smith, *Red Petrograd: Revolution in the Factories, 1917–1918* (Cambridge, Eng., 1983); and Allan K. Wildman, *The End of the Russian Imperial Army*, vol. 2 (Princeton, 1987).

24. In addition to the studies cited in the previous note, my discussion of popular upheavals and attitudes in 1917 is based on hundreds of petitions, letters, and other unpublished archival documents sent by lower-class Russians to various political authorities in 1917, located in the State Archive of the Russian Federation (GARF), fonds 1244 (*Izvestiia*); 1235 (All-Russian Central Executive Committee [VTsIK] of the Second All-Russian Congress of Soviets); 1778 (Chancellery of the Minister President of the Provisional Government); 1796 (Main Land Committee); 6978 (VTsIK, first session).

25. Telegram from the soldiers' committee of the guard, 26 January 1918, GARF, f. 393, op. 2, d. 94, l. 8; telegram from the Tobol'sk provincial commissar, 26 January 1918, *Bor'ba za vlast' Sovetov v Tobol'skoi (Tiumenskoi) gubernii (1917–1920 gg.): Sbornik dokumentov* (Struggle for Soviet power in Tobol'sk province: A collection of documents) (Sverdlovsk, 1967), 146; telegram from the people's commissar for internal affairs promising a new appointment, 31 January 1918, GARF, f. 393, op. 2, d. 94, l. 7; Gilliard, diary entries of 6 and 8 February 1918, in Gilliard, *Thirteen Years*, 253.

26. Alexandra to Vyrubova, 23 February 1918, Beinecke Rare Book and Manuscript Library, Yale University, MS Vault, Shelves, Romanov collection, container 1.

27. Kobylinskii, testimony of 6–10 April 1919, Houghton Library, Sokolov Archive, vol. 3, doc. 29, and in *Gibel' tsarskoi sem'i,* 296–297; Gilliard, testimony of 5–6 March 1919, Sokolov Archive, vol. 2, doc. 55; *Gibel' tsarskoi sem'i,* 230.

28. Telegrams from Pankratov to Kerensky, 23 September 1917, GARF, f. 1778, op. 1, d. 279, l. 1, 4.

29. Gilliard, diary entries of 18 and 19 January 1918, in Gilliard, *Thirteen Years,* 252; Gilliard, testimony of 5–6 March 1919, Houghton Library, Sokolov Archive, vol. 2, doc. 55.

30. Kobylinskii, testimony of 6–10 April 1919, Houghton Library, Sokolov Archive, vol. 3, doc. 29, and in *Gibel' tsarskoi sem'i,* 298; Gilliard, testimony of 5–6 March 1919, Sokolov Archive, vol. 2, doc. 55; Gilliard, diary entries of 4–5 March 1918, in Gilliard, *Thirteen Years,* 255; diary of Nicholas II, 20 February (5 March) 1918.

31. Gilliard, testimony of 5–6 March 1919, Houghton Library, Sokolov Archive, vol. 2, doc. 55; see also Tegleva, testimony of 5–6 July 1919, Sokolov Archive, vol. 5, doc. 36.

32. Kobylinskii, testimony of 6–10 April 1919, Houghton Library, Sokolov Archive, vol. 3, doc. 29, and in *Gibel' tsarskoi sem'i,* 298; Gilliard, *Thirteen Years,* 256.

33. Kobylinskii, testimony of 6–10 April 1919, Houghton Library, Sokolov Archive, vol. 3, doc. 29, and in *Gibel' tsarskoi sem'i,* 299; Gilliard, diary entries of 25 February–1 March 1918, in Gilliard, *Thirteen Years,* 254–255; diary of Nicholas II, 14–15 (27–28) February and 12 (25) March 1918.

34. Kobylinskii, testimony of 6–10 April 1919, Houghton Library, Sokolov Archive, vol. 3, doc. 29, and in *Gibel' tsarskoi sem'i,* 298–299; telegram from VTsIK to Kobylinskii, 19 April 1918, GARF, f. 601, op. 2, d. 35, l. 3; protocol of VTsIK Presidium, 18 April 1918, GARF, f. 1235, op. 34, d. 36, l. 128–134 (point 20).

35. Kobylinskii, testimony of 6–10 April 1919, Houghton Library, Sokolov Archive, vol. 3, doc. 29, and in *Gibel' tsarskoi sem'i,* 300; P. M. Bykov, *Poslednie dni Romanovykh* (Last days of the Romanovs) (Alma-Ata, 1991; originally published in Sverdlovsk, 1926), 71.

36. Besides documents in this collection, see Alexandra's letters to Anna Vyrubova of 22 and 23 January, 3 (16) March, 13 (26) March, and 20 March (2 April) 1918, Beinecke Rare Book and Manuscript Library, Yale University, MS Vault, Shelves, Romanov collection, container 1. Although most of these letters were published by Vyrubova in the 1920s (later reprinted in *Pis'ma tsarskoi sem'i iz zatocheniia* [Letters from the imperial family in captivity] [Jordanville, N.Y., 1974]), Vyrubova expurgated the letters to remove, among other things, many of the references to the arrival and presence in Tobolsk of familiar monarchist officers.

37. K. Sokolov, "Popytka osvobozhdeniia Tsarskoi Sem'i (Dekabr' 1917 g.–Fevral' 1918 g.)" (An attempt to free the imperial family [December 1918–February 1918]), *Arkhiv russkoi revoliutsii* 17 (1927): 280–287.

38. S. Markov, *Pokinutaia tsarskaia sem'ia, 1917–1918* (The forsaken imperial family) (Vienna, 1928), 195–196.

39. N. Markov, "Popytka spaseniia Tsarskoi Sem'i" (An attempt to save the imperial family), *Vestnik Vysshego monarkhicheskogo soveta* (Herald of the Supreme Monarchist Council) (Berlin), 28 April (11 May) 1924, reprinted in Markov, *Pokinutaia tsarskaia sem'ia,* 424–429; Markov, *Pokinutaia tsarskaia sem'ia,* 194–197; B. Markov, "K perevodu tsaria iz Tobol'ska v monastyr'" (Toward the transfer of the tsar from Tobol'sk to a monastery), GARF, f. 601, op. 1, d. 2471; Ioffe, *Revoliutsiia i sud'ba Romanovykh,* 152; *Pis'ma tsarskoi sem'i iz zatocheniia,* 238–239.

40. Testimonies of A. V. Krivoshein (17 January 1921 and 6 February 1921), D. B. Neigart (27 and 29 January 1921 and 29 May 1921), and A. F. Trepov (16 February 1921), quoted in Sokolov, *Ubiistvo,* 104–107.

41. Anthony Summers and Tom Mangold, *The File on the Tsar* (New York, 1976), 253–260.

42. Testimonies of Boris Solov'ev (29 December 1919 and 1 January 1920), Matrëna

Solov'eva (Mariia Rasputina) ([26–27] December 1919), Evgenii Loginov (24 October 1919), Konstantin Mel'nik (2 November 1919), and Viktor Botkin (2 November 1919), Houghton Library, Sokolov Archive, vol. 7; Nikolai Sedov, testimony of 22 November 1918, Sokolov Archive, vol. 1, doc. 46, and in *Gibel' tsarskoi sem'i,* 117–118; N. Markov, "Popytki spaseniia," 428; Sokolov, *Ubiistvo,* 87–104; S. Markov, *Pokinutaia tsarskaia sem'ia,* 197, 218, 240, 413–415; Ioffe, *Revoliutsiia i sud'ba Romanovykh,* 153–163; Alexandra to Boris Solov'ev, 26 January 1918, in Markov, *Pokinutaia tsarskaia sem'ia,* 263; Gilliard, diary entry of 23 March 1918, in Gilliard, *Thirteen Years,* 257–258 (on Nicholas's confidence in these stories).

43. The archives contain many such resolutions—for example, the resolution of the Congress of the Baltic Navy, 22 November 1917, GARF, f. 130, op. 23, d. 2, l. 99.

44. [V. I. Lenin], "Sotsalisticheskoe otechestvo v opasnotsi!" (The socialist fatherland is in danger!), *Pravda,* 22 (9) February 1918. All editions of his collected works identify Lenin as the author.

45. "Nemetskii imperator i russkii tsar'" (The German emperor and the Russian tsar), *Pravda,* 23 (10) February 1918 (evening edition).

46. Bykov, *Poslednie dni,* 72.

47. Telegram from the Tobol'sk guard and the response from VTsIK, 16 April 1918, GARF, f. 601, op. 2, d. 35, l. 1.

48. Sokolov, *Ubiistvo,* 49–54, 108–109; Summers and Mangold, *File on the Tsar,* 262–270; Ioffe, *Revoliutsiia i sud'ba Romanovykh,* 163–164; Edvard Radzinsky, *The Last Tsar* (New York, 1992), 256–284; Tegleva, testimony of 5–6 July 1919, Houghton Library, Sokolov Archive, vol. 5, doc. 36.

49. Ioffe, *Revoliutsiia i sud'ba Romanovykh,* 167–175; declaration from K. Stoianovich (Iakovlev) to Stalin and Yezhov, 27 June 1937, Family archive of V. V. Iakovlev, in Veniamin Alekseev, *Gibel' tsarskoi sem'i* (The destruction of the imperial family) (Ekaterinburg, 1993), 80.

50. Letters and declarations from Iakovlev, 1931–1937, Family archive of V. V. Iakovlev, in Alekseev, *Gibel' tsarskoi sem'i,* 72–82; N. Leshkin, "Poslednii reis Romanovykh" (The last journey of the Romanovs), *Leninets* (Ufa), October–November 1976, quoted in Radzinsky, *Last Tsar,* 282–284; Ioffe, *Revoliutsiia i sud'ba Romanovykh,* 199–207.

51. Kobylinskii, testimony of 6–10 April 1919, Houghton Library, Sokolov Archive, vol. 3, doc. 29, and in *Gibel' tsarskoi sem'i,* 301.

52. Notes and telegraph reports from Iakovlev to VTsIK, 25 April 1918, GARF, f. 601, op. 2, d. 4, l. 88, 98–99.

53. Kobylinskii, testimony of 6–10 April 1919, Houghton Library, Sokolov Archive, vol. 3, doc. 29; *Gibel' tsarskoi sem'i,* 303.

54. Gilliard, diary entry of 25 April 1918, in Gilliard, *Thirteen Years,* 260–261. See also Document 122.

55. V. Iakovlev, "Poslednii reis Romanovykh" (The last journey of the Romanovs), *Ural* 1988 (no. 7): 151–152.

56. Report by M. Tukhachevskii to VTsIK, GARF, f. 1235, op. 79, d. 7, l. 29–290b., quoted in Ioffe, *Revoliutsiia i sud'ba Romanovykh,* 180–181.

57. Ioffe, *Revoliutsiia i sud'ba Romanovykh,* 180–181.

Chapter 4: Death in Yekaterinburg

1. P. M. Matveev, "Tsarskoe selo—Tobol'sk—Ekaterinburg" (manuscript in Yekaterinburg Communist Party archive), published as "Vospominaniia P. M. Matveeva" (Memoirs of P. M. Matveev), *Ural'skii rabochii,* 16 September 1990, quoted in P. M. Bykov, *Poslednie dni Romanovykh* (Alma-Ata, 1991; originally published in Sverdlovsk, 1926), 83–84, and in Genrikh Ioffe, *Revoliutsiia i sud'ba Romanovykh* (Moscow, 1992), 196.

2. V. Iakovlev, "Poslednii reis Romanovykh" (The last journey of the Romanovs), *Ural*

1988 (no. 7): 163, quoted in Ioffe, *Revoliutsiia i sud'ba Romanovykh,* 196. These memoirs were written by Yakovlev shortly after his return to the USSR in 1928. They were also reprinted in *Poslednie dni Romanovykh: Dokumenty, materialy sledstviia, dnevniki, versii* (The last days of the Romanovs: Documents, investigative materials, diaries, versions) (Sverdlovsk, 1991), 44–74.

3. Investigators who entered the house after Yekaterinburg was taken by the Czech Legion and the Whites saw and photographed this mark (noting also a swastika above one of the beds). N. A. Sokolov, report on the inspection of the Ipat'ev house, 15–25 April 1919, Documents of the Investigation into the Death of Nicholas II (Sokolov Archive), Houghton Library, Harvard University, Kilgour collection, MS Russ 35, vol. 3, doc. 42, and in *Gibel' tsarskoi sem'i,* ed. Nikolai Ross (Frankfurt, 1987), 316; Pierre Gilliard, testimony of 5–6 March 1919, Houghton Library, Sokolov Archive, vol. 2, doc. 55, and in *Gibel' tsarskoi sem'i,* 235. A photograph, an original print of which is in the Sokolov Archive at Harvard, is reprinted in N. Sokolov, *Ubiistvo tsarskoi sem'i* (Berlin, 1925), facing 49.

4. Arrest order signed by Aleksandr Beloborodov, 30 April 1918, GARF, f. 601, op. 2, d. 4, l. 343.

5. Resolutions of Presidium of the Ural Soviet on arrests, 23 May 1918, GARF, f. 601, op. 2, d. 3, l. 5, 8, 134–135; Pierre Gilliard, testimony of 12–14 September 1918, Houghton Library, Sokolov Archive, vol. 1, doc. 36, and in *Gibel' tsarskoi sem'i,* 105.

6. Diary of Alexandra, 23 May (5 June) 1918, GARF, f. 640, op. 1, d. 326, l. 72.

7. M. I. Letemin (a worker-guard from the Sysert factory), testimony of 18–19 October 1918, in *Gibel' tsarskoi sem'i,* 108–109; F. P. Proskuriakov (a worker-guard from the Sysert factory), testimony of 1–3 April 1919, in *Gibel' tsarskoi sem'i,* 271–273.

8. A. A. Iakimov, testimony of 7–11 May 1919, Houghton Library, Sokolov Archive, vol. 4, doc. 18, and in *Gibel' tsarskoi sem'i,* 338.

9. T. I. Chemodurov, testimony of 15–16 August 1918, Houghton Library, Sokolov Archive, vol. 1, doc. 23, and in *Gibel' tsarskoi sem'i,* 61–62.

10. See also Chemodurov, testimony of 15–16 August 1918, Houghton Library, Sokolov Archive, vol. 1, doc. 23, and in *Gibel' tsarskoi sem'i,* 62.

11. Chemodurov, testimony of 15–16 August 1918, Houghton Library, Sokolov Archive, vol. 1, doc. 23, and in *Gibel' tsarskoi sem'i,* 62; Sokolov, *Ubiistvo,* 127–129.

12. Prince L'vov's account of what he was told by Ivan Sednëv and Nagornyi (with whom he shared a cell), quoted in Sokolov, *Ubiistvo,* 129–130.

13. Iakimov, testimony of 7–11 May 1919, Houghton Library, Sokolov Archive, vol. 4, doc. 18, and in *Gibel' tsarskoi sem'i,* 335.

14. I. A. Sergeev, report on inspection of the Ipat'ev house, 11–14 August 1918, Houghton Library, Sokolov Archive, vol. 1, doc. 19; N. A. Sokolov, report on inspection of the Ipat'ev house, 15–25 April 1919, Sokolov Archive, vol. 3, doc. 42; Sokolov, report on inspection of materials removed from Ipat'ev house by the investigator Sergeev, 19 May 1919, Sokolov Archive, vol. 4, doc. 37. These reports are also in *Gibel' tsarskoi sem'i,* 51–59, 314–320, 348–349.

15. V. I. Lenin, "Kak organizovat' sorevnovanie?" (How to organize competition), in *Izbrannye proizvedeniia v chetyrekh tomakh* (Selected works in four volumes) (Moscow, 1988), 3: 52. The essay was written on 24–27 December 1917 but not published until 1929.

16. V. I. Lenin to G. E. Zinov'ev, 26 June 1918, in *Polnoe sobranie sochinenii,* 5th ed., vol. 50 (Moscow, 1965), 106.

17. Superb literary expressions of this cultural style are in Boris Pilniak, *The Naked Year* (1921) and in Isaak Babel's stories about the civil war, *Red Cavalry* (1926).

18. A. M. Selishchev, *Iazyk revoliutsionnoi epokhi,* 2d ed. (Moscow, 1928), 85–87, 133 (quotation).

19. V. Aleksandrovskii, "Sev" (Sowing), *Pravda,* 14 November 1918.

20. See the discussion of Ural Bolshevik "*levachestvo*" (leftism) in Ioffe, *Revoliutsiia i sud'ba Romanovykh,* 303.

21. A. D. Avdeev, "Nikolai Romanov v Tobol'ske i v Ekaterinburge" (Nicholas Romanov in Tobolsk and Yekaterinburg), *Krasnaia nov'* (Red virgin soil) 1928, no. 5 (May): 202.

22. Bykov, *Poslednie dni Romanovykh,* 97.

23. Diary of Alexandra, 31 May (13 June), GARF, f. 640, op. 1, d. 326, l. 77.

24. For denials in addition to those in the documents, see the telegram from the Yekaterinburg Soviet, published in *Izvestiia,* 25 June 1918; telegram from P. I. Berzin to Sovnarkom, 27 June 1918, GARF, f. 130, op. 2, d. 111, l. 106, published in *Izvestiia,* 28 June 1918; *Svobodnyi put'* (The free path) (Perm), 2 July (19 June) 1918.

25. Dmitrii Malinovskii, testimony of 17 June 1919, Houghton Library, Sokolov Archive, vol. 5, doc. 8; Kirill Sobolev, testimony of 30 August 1919, in *Gibel' tsarskoi sem'i,* 457–458; Paul Bulygin, "The Sorrowful Quest," in *The Murder of the Romanovs* (London, 1935), 161–165; A. Mosolov, *Pri dvore imperatora* (At the court of the emperor) (Riga, [1935]), 221–222.

26. Ioffe, *Revoliutsiia i sud'ba Romanovykh,* chap. 8. Ioffe's discussion is based extensively on newly declassified materials.

27. Avdeev, "Nikolai Romanov v Tobol'ske i v Ekaterinburge," 202; Bykov, *Poslednie dni Romanovykh,* 92–94; Edvard Radzinsky, *The Last Tsar* (New York, 1992), 320–322; Ioffe, *Revoliutsiia i sud'ba Romanovykh,* 294–296; Richard Pipes, *The Russian Revolution* (New York, 1990), 767–768.

28. Diary of Alexandra, 15 (28) June 1918, GARF, f. 640, op. 1, d. 326, l. 840b.

29. Ioffe, *Revoliutsiia i sud'ba Romanovykh,* 317–319.

30. Testimonies of Iurovskii's brother, sister, and sister-in-law, Houghton Library, Sokolov Archive, vol. 7, docs. 1–3; Sokolov, *Ubiistvo,* 134–135.

31. Iakimov, testimony of 7–11 May 1919, Houghton Library, Sokolov Archive, vol. 4, doc. 18, and in *Gibel' tsarskoi sem'i,* 337–338.

32. Ibid.; Sokolov, *Ubiistvo,* 138.

33. Rules for the guards at Ipat'ev house drawn up by Iurovskii, 4 July 1918, GARF, f. 601, op. 2, d. 23, l. 5–17.

34. A. F. Khatskevich, *Soldat velikikh boev: Zhizn' i deiatel'nost F. E. Dzerzhinskogo* (Soldier of great battles: The life and work of F. E. Dzerzhinskii) (Minsk, 1987), 230, 246.

35. Sverdlov's report to the Central Committee of the Communist Party, 19 May 1918, RTsKhIDNI (Russian Center for the Preservation and Study of Documents of Recent History), f. 17, op. 2, d. 1, reprinted in *Izvestiia TsK KPSS* (News of the Central Committee of the Communist Party of the Soviet Union) 1989, no. 4 (April): 147.

36. Ioffe, *Revoliutsiia i sud'ba Romanovykh,* 298–299.

37. Lev Trotsky, diary entry of 9 April 1935, Houghton Library, Harvard University, Trotsky Archive, bMS Russ 13, T-3731, p. 110.

38. V. N. Kokovtsov, *Iz moego proshlogo: Vospominaniia 1903–1919* (From my past: Recollections, 1903–1919), 2 vols. (Paris, 1933), 2: 461.

39. Bykov, *Poslednie dni Romanovykh,* 89–90.

40. A valuable source of evidence for lower-class discontent is the previously classified collection of "anti-Bolshevik" correspondence from the population sent to the Central Executive Committee of Soviets. GARF, f. 1235, op. 140, d. 8 and 10.

41. GARF, f. 9550 (Soviet-era leaflets), op. 11 ("counterrevolutionary" materials), d. 303–315 (materials from the assemblies of worker plenipotentiaries, March–June 1918); M. S. Bernshtam, *Nezavisimoe rabochee dvizhenie v 1918 godu* (The independent workers' movement in 1918) (Paris, 1981), chaps. 1–2; William G. Rosenberg, "Russian Labor and Bolshevik Power after October," *Slavic Review* (Summer 1985): 228–238; Vladimir Brovkin, *The Mensheviks after October* (Ithaca, N.Y., 1987).

42. Maxim Gorky, *Untimely Thoughts: Essays on Revolution, Culture and the Bolsheviks, 1917–1918,* trans. Herman Ermolaev (New Haven, 1995).

43. Ioffe, *Revoliutsiia i sud'ba Romanovykh,* 231–239; Pipes, *Russian Revolution,* 624–

631; James Bunyan, *Intervention, Civil War, and Communism in Russia, April–December 1918: Documents and Materials* (Baltimore, 1936).

44. *Ural'skii rabochii,* 15 (28) June 1918.

45. Bykov, *Poslednie dni Romanovykh,* 98–101.

46. Dominic Lieven, *Nicholas II* (London, 1993). See very similar statements in Pipes, *Russian Revolution,* 770; and Radzinsky, *Last Tsar,* 324–331.

47. Bykov, *Poslednie dni Romanovykh,* 89, 98.

48. G. Nikulin, unpublished autobiography, written in May 1964, RTsKhIDNI, f. 558, op. 3, d. 13, l. 1–70, quoted in Ioffe, *Revoliutsiia i sud'ba Romanovykh,* 333.

49. Order from Lenin, 7 July 1918, GARF, f. 130, op. 2, d. 787, l. 11–12, cited in Vladimir Il'ich Lenin, *Biograficheskaia khronika,* vol. 5 (Moscow, 1974), 616.

50. Sokolov, record of examination of material evidence, 23 February 1919, Houghton Library, Sokolov Archive, vol. 2, doc. 41. Sokolov stated that he found many such telegrams. Sokolov, *Ubiistvo,* 249.

51. Many of these telegrams were found later in Yekaterinburg. Houghton Library, Sokolov Archive, vol. 1, doc. 30, vol. 2, doc. 41; *Gibel' tsarskoi sem'i,* 214–219.

52. Radzinsky, *Last Tsar,* 342–344.

53. Quoted in Radzinsky, *Last Tsar,* 345–346.

54. Trotsky, diary entry of 9 April 1935, Houghton Library, Harvard University, Trotsky Archive, bMS Russ 13, T-3731, p. 111.

55. Pipes, *Russian Revolution,* 770.

56. *Dekrety sovetskoi vlasti* (Decrees of Soviet Power), vol. 3 (Moscow, 1964), 21–22; *Izvestiia,* 19 July 1918.

57. Pipes, *Russian Revolution,* 771.

58. The findings have been reported in scores of news stories. See, for example, John Darnton, "Scientists Confirm Identification of Bones as Czar's," *New York Times,* 10 July 1993; Josie Glausiusz, "Royal D-Loops," *Discover* (January 1994): 90; Rebecca Fowler, "Anastasia: The Mystery Resolved," *Washington Post,* 6 October 1994; interview with Veniamin Alekseev, Federal Information Systems Corp. (Russia), broadcast of 17 April 1995.

59. Report by A. Kirsta and testimonies of Pavel Utkin, Natal'ia Mutnykh, and many others (taken in 1918–1919), in Houghton Library, Sokolov Archive, vol. 4, doc. 5, and in *Gibel' tsarskoi sem'i,* 77, 86–87, 172–191. Other reports, testimonies, and evidence are described in Anthony Summers and Tom Mangold, *The File on the Tsar* (New York, 1976), 188–239, 273–354; and Marc Ferro, *Nicholas II: The Last of the Tsars* (London, 1991), 234–287.

60. *Pis'ma tsarskoi sem'i iz zatocheniia* (Letters of the imperial family from captivity) (Jordanville,N.Y., 1974), 399, 408–409.

61. Ioffe, *Revoliutsiia i sud'ba Romanovykh,* 320–321. Among the suspicious indications in these documents are mistitled institutions, unknown individuals, and the misspelling of Goloshchekin's name and signature (appearing as Golochekin).

62. Summers and Mangold, *File on the Tsar,* 106–117; Ferro, *Nicholas II,* 254–255.

63. Radzinsky, *Last Tsar,* 414–415.

64. TASS news service, 18 August 1994; Russian Federation Press Release (Federal Information News Broadcast Corp.), 18 August 1994; Reuters North American Wire, 23 February 1995.

65. Boris Solov'ev, testimony of 1 January 1920, Houghton Library, Sokolov Archive, vol. 7 [no document number or pagination].

Select Bibliography

ARCHIVAL SOURCES

State Archive of the Russian Federation (Gosudarstvennyi arkhiv Rossiiskoi Federatsii, or GARF)
- f. (fond) 130. Council of People's Commissars (Sovnarkom)
- f. 601. Nicholas II
- f. 611. Petrov, Pëtr Vasil'evich
- f. 640. Alexandra Fëdorovna
- f. 644. Pavel Aleksandrovich
- f. 673. Ol'ga Nikolaevna
- f. 685. Mariia Nikolaevna
- f. 1235. All-Russian Central Executive Committee (VTsIK) of the Second All-Russian Congress of Soviets
- f. 1244. *Izvestiia*
- f. 1778. Chancellery of the Minister President of the Provisional Government
- f. 1799. Chancellery of the Provisional Government
- f. 5881. Collection of Russian émigré memoirs
- f. 6978. All-Russian Central Executive Committee (VTsIK) of the First All-Russian Congress of Soviets
- f. 9550. Collection of leaflets of the Soviet period

Russian Center for the Preservation and Study of Documents of Recent History (RTsKhIDNI), the former Central Party Archive of the Institute of Marxism-Leninism
- f. 2. Lenin, Vladimir Il'ich
- f. 5. Secretariat of Lenin
- f. 19. Council of People's Commissars (Sovnarkom)
- f. 588. Collection of documents on Russian history

PUBLISHED SOURCES AND STUDIES

Alekseev, Veniamin A. *Gibel' tsarskoi sem'i: Mify i real'nost' (novye dokumenty o tragedii na Urale)*. Yekaterinburg, 1993.

Alexander [Mikhailovich], Grand Duke. *Once a Grand Duke*. New York, 1932.

Alexandra Fëdorovna. *Letters of the Tsaritsa to the Tsar*. London, 1923.

———. *Pis'ma imperatritsy Aleksandry Fëdorovny k imperatoru Nikolaiu II [1914–1916]*. 2 vols. Berlin, 1922.

Avdeev, A. D. "Nikolai Romanov v Tobol'ske i v Ekaterinburge." *Krasnaia nov'*, 1928, no. 5.

Basily [Bazili], Nicolas de. *Memoirs*. Stanford, 1973.

Benckendorff [Benkendorf], Paul. *Last Days at Tsarskoe Selo*. London, 1927.

[Bogdanovich, Evgenii Vasil'evich]. *Istoricheskoe palomnichestvo nashego Tsaria v 1913 godu*. St. Petersburg, 1914.

Bor'ba za vlast' Sovetov v Tobol'skoi (Tiumenskoi) gubernii (1917–1920 gg.): Sbornik dokumentov. Sverdlovsk, 1967.

Buchanan, George. *My Mission to Russia*. 2 vols. London, 1923.

Bulygin, Paul. "The Sorrowful Quest." In *The Murder of the Romanovs: The Authentic Account*. London, 1935.

Buranov, Iu. A., and V. M. Khrustalëv. *Gibel' imperatorskogo doma, 1917–1919 gg*. Moscow, 1992.

Buxhoeveden [Buksgevden], Sophie. *The Life and Tragedy of Alexandra Fedorovna, Empress of Russia: A Biography*. London, 1928.

Bykov, P. M. *The Last Days of Tsardom*. London, 1937.

———. *Poslednie dni Romanovykh*. Sverdlovsk, 1926.

Dehn [Den], Lili. *The Real Tsaritsa*. London, 1922.

Diteriks, M. K. *Ubiistvo tsarskoi sem'i i chlenov doma Romanovykh na Urale*. 2 vols. Vladivostok, 1922.

Elchaninov, A. *The Tsar and His People*. London, [1913?].

———. *Tsarstvovanie Gosudaria Imperatora Nikolaia Aleksandrovicha*. St. Petersburg and Moscow, 1913.

Eugénie de Grèce. *Le tsarevich: Enfant martyr*. Paris, 1990.

Ferro, Marc. *Nicholas II: The Last of the Tsars*. London, 1991.

Gibel' tsarskoi sem'i: Materialy sledstviia po delu ob ubiistve Tsarskoi sem'i (avgust 1918–fevral' 1920). Ed. Nikolai Ross. Frankfurt, 1987.

Gilliard, Pierre. *Thirteen Years at the Russian Court*. New York, 1921.

———. *Le tragique destin de Nicolas II et de sa famille*. Paris, 1922.

Gurko, V. *Tsar i tsaritsa*. Paris, 1927.

Iakovlev, V. [K. Miachin]. "Poslednii reis Romanovykh: Vospominaniia." *Ural*, 1988, no. 8.

Ioffe, Genrikh. *Revoliutsiia i sud'ba Romanovykh*. Moscow, 1992.

———. *Velikii Oktiabr' i epilog tsarizma*. Moscow, 1987.

Iroshnikov, Mikhail, Liudmila Protsai, and Yuri Shelayev. *The Sunset of the Romanov Dynasty*. Moscow, 1992.

Iusupov, F. F. *Konets Rasputina: Vospominaniia*. Paris, 1927.

"Iz perepiski Nikolaia i Marii Romanovykh v 1907–1910 gg." *Krasnyi arkhiv*, 50–51 (1932).

[Izvol'skii, Aleksandr]. *The Memoirs of Alexander Iswolsky*. London, 1920.

Kerensky, Alexander. *The Catastrophe: Kerensky's Own Story of the Russian Revolution*. New York, 1927.

———. "The Road to the Tragedy." In *The Murder of the Romanovs: The Authentic Account*. London, 1935.

Khrustalëv, V. M. "Taina 'missii' chrezvychainogo komissara Iakovleva." *Rossiiane*, 1993, nos. 10–12.

———. "Tainoe ubiistvo velikikh kniazei v Alapaevske." *Rossiiane*, 1993, nos. 10–12.

Koganitskii, I. "1917–1918 gg. v Tobol'ske: Nikolai Romanov; Germogenovshchina." *Proletarskaia revoliutsiia*, 1922, no. 4.

Kokovtsov, Vladimir N. *Iz moego proshlogo: Vospominaniia 1903–1919.* 2 vols. Paris, 1933.

———. *Out of My Past: The Memoirs of Count Kokovtsov.* Stanford, 1935.

Leshkin, N. "Poslednii reis Romanovykh." *Leninets* (Ufa), October–November 1976.

Lieven, Dominic. *Nicholas II: Emperor of All the Russias.* London, 1993.

Markov, N. "Popytka spaseniia Tsarskoi Sem'i." *Vestnik Vysshego monarkhicheskogo soveta* (Berlin), 28 April (11 May) 1924.

Markov, S. *Pokinutaia tsarskaia sem'ia, 1917–1918.* Vienna, 1928.

Martynov, E. I. *Tsarskaia armiia v fevral'skom perevorote.* Leningrad, 1927.

Massie, Robert K. *Nicholas and Alexandra.* New York, 1967.

Matveev, P. M. "Vospominaniia P. M. Matveeva." *Ural'skii rabochii,* 16 September 1990.

Mel'gunov, S. P. *Poslednii samoderzhets.* Moscow, 1917.

———. *Sud'ba Imperatora Nikolaia II posle otrecheniia"* Paris, 1957.

Mel'nik [Botkina], Tat'iana. *Vospominaniia o tsarskoi sem'e i ee zhizn' do i posle revoliutsii.* Belgrade, 1921.

Monarkhiia pered krusheniem, 1914–1917: Bumagi Nikolaia II i drugie dokumenty. Moscow and Leningrad, 1927.

Mosolov, A. A. *Pri dvore imperatora.* Riga, [1935].

———. *Pri dvore poslednego Rossiiskogo imperatora.* Paris, 1934.

Mossolov [Mosolov], A. A. *At the Court of the Last Tsar.* London, 1935.

Nemtsov, N. M. "Poslednii pereezd polkovnika Romanova." *Krasnaia niva,* 1928, no. 27.

Nicholas II. *Dnevniki imperatora Nikolai II.* Moscow, 1991.

———. *Dnevnik imperatora Nikolaia II [1890–1906].* Berlin, 1923.

———. "Dnevnik Nikolaia Romanova" *Krasnyi arkhiv,* 20–22 (1927).

———. *Letters of the Tsar to the Tsaritsa, 1914–1917.* Trans. E. L. Hynes [from Russian translations of the original English]. London, 1929.

———. *Polnoe sobranie rechei Imperatora Nikolaia II (1894–1906 gg.).* St. Petersburg, 1906.

Nicholas II and Alexandra Fëdorovna. *Nicky-Sunny Letters: Correspondence of the Tsar and Tsaritsa, 1914–1917.* Hattiesburg, Miss., 1970.

———. *Perepiska Nikolaia i Aleksandry Romanovykh.* Vols. 3–5. Moscow and Leningrad, 1923–1927.

Nicholas II and Mariia Fëdorovna. *Letters of Tsar Nicholas and Empress Marie.* Ed. Edward J. Bing. London, 1937.

———. "Perepiska Nikolaia II i Marii Fedorovny (1905–1906 gg.)." *Krasnyi arkhiv* 22 (1927).

———. *The Secret Letters of the Last Tsar: Being the Confidential Correspondence between Nicholas II and His Mother, Dowager Empress Maria Feodorovna.* Ed. Edward J. Bing. New York, 1938.

Nicholas II and Wilhelm II. *Willy-Nicky Correspondence: Being the Secret and Intimate Telegrams Exchanged between the Kaiser and the Tsar.* Ed. Herman Bernstein. New York, 1917.

Nikolai II i velikie kniaz'ia. Moscow and Leningrad, 1925.

Obninskii, V. P. *Poslednii samoderzhets.* Moscow, 1917.

Otrechenie Nikolaia II: Vospominaniia ochevidtsev, dokumenty. Ed. P. E. Shchegolev. 2d ed. Leningrad, 1927.

Padenie tsarskogo rezhima: Stenograficheskie otchëty doprosov i pokazanii, dannykh v 1917 g. v Chrezvychainoi sledstvennoi komissii Vremennogo Pravitel'stva. Ed. P. E. Shchegolev. 7 vols. Moscow and Leningrad, 1924–1927.

Paléologue, Maurice. *An Ambassador's Memoirs.* 2 vols. London, 1924.

Pankratov, V. S. *S tsarem v Tobol'ske: Iz vospominanii.* Leningrad, 1925.

Pipes, Richard. *The Russian Revolution.* New York, 1990.

Pis'ma tsarskoi sem'i iz zatocheniia. Ed. E. E. Al'ferev. Jordanville, N.Y., 1974.

Poslednie dni poslednego tsaria. Saratov, 1922.

Poslednie dni Romanovykh: Dokumenty, materialy sledstviia, dnevniki, versii. Sverdlovsk, 1991.

Radzinsky, Edvard. *The Last Tsar: The Life and Death of Nicholas II.* New York, 1992.

Riabov, G., and G. Ioffe. "Prinuzhdeny Vas rasstreliat'." *Rodina,* 1989, nos. 4–5.

Shchegolov, P. E. *Poslednii reis Nikolaia vtorogo.* Moscow and Leningrad, 1928.

Skorbnaia pamiatka. [Ed. A. V. Syroboiarskii] New York, 1928.

Sokolov, K. "Popytka osvobozhdeniia Tsarskoi Sem'i (Dekabr' 1917 g.–Fevral' 1918 g.)." *Arkhiv russkoi revoliutsii* 17 (1927).

Sokolov, N. *Ubiistvo tsarskoi sem'i.* Berlin, 1925.

Summers, Anthony, and Tom Mangold. *The File on the Tsar.* New York, 1976.

Taneeva [Vyrubova], A. *Stranitsy iz moei zhizn'.* N.p., 1923.

"Trebovaniia naroda o zakliuchenii Nikolaia Romanova v krepost' (publikatsiia dokumentov)." *Krasnyi arkhiv* 81 (1937).

Tsarskoe prebyvanie v Moskve v aprele 1900 goda. St. Petersburg, 1900.

Verner, Andrew M. *The Crisis of the Russian Autocracy: Nicholas II and the 1905 Revolution.* Princeton, 1990.

Vil'chkovskii, S. N. "Prebyvanie Gosudaria Imperatora v Pskove 1 i 2 Marta 1917 goda, po razskazu general-ad"iutanta N. V. Ruzskago." *Russkaia letopis'* 3 (1922).

Vil'ton, Robert. *Poslednie dni Romanovykh.* Paris, 1923.

Viroubova [Vyrubova], Anna. *Memories of the Russian Court.* London, 1923.

Voeikov, V. N. *S tsarëm i bez tsaria.* Helsingfors, Finland, 1936.

Volkov, A. A. *Okolo tsarskoi sem'i.* Paris, 1928.

Vorob'ev, V. "Konets Romanovykh." *Prozhektor,* 15 July 1928.

Vorres, Ian. *The Last Grand Duchess: Her Imperial Highness Grand Duchess Olga Alexandrovna.* New York, 1965.

Wilton, Robert. *The Last Days of the Romanovs.* London, 1920.

Wortman, Richard. "Moscow and St. Petersburg: The Problem of Political Center in Tsarist Russia, 1881–1914." In *Rites of Power: Symbolism, Ritual, and Politics since the Middle Ages,* ed. Sean Wilentz. Philadelphia, 1985.

Zakharova, L. G. "Krizis samoderzhaviia nakanune revoliutsii 1905 goda." *Voprosy istorii,* 1972, no. 8.

Zentsov, G. "Poezdka za Nikolaem Romanovom v Tobol'ske." *Ufimskii oktiabr'skoi sbornik,* 1920, no. 2.

Document and Illustration Credits

Documents

1. Letter from Alexandra to Nicholas, 22 February 1917. GARF (Gosudarstvennyi arkhiv Rossiiskoi Federatsii [State Archive of the Russian Federation]), f. 601, op. 1, d. 1151, l. 479–483ob. Manuscript. Original English text.
2. Letter from Nicholas to Alexandra, 23–24 February 1917. GARF, f. 640, op. 1, d. 115, l. 45–48ob. Manuscript. Original English text.
3. Letter from Alexandra to Nicholas, 24 February 1917. GARF, f. 601, op. 1, d. 1151, l. 486–489. Manuscript. Original English text.
4. Letter from Nicholas to Alexandra, 24–25 February 1917. GARF, f. 640, op. 1, d. 115, l. 49–51ob. Manuscript. Original English text.
5. Letter from Alexandra to Nicholas, 25 February 1917. GARF, f. 601, op. 1, d. 1151, l. 490–493ob. Manuscript. Original English text.
6. Telegram from Rodzianko to Nicholas, 26 February 1917. GARF, f. 601, op. 1, d. 2089, l. 1–1ob.
7. Letter from Alexandra to Nicholas, 26 February 1917. GARF, f. 601, op. 1, d. 1151, l. 494–499. Manuscript. Original English text.
8. Letter from Nicholas to Alexandra, 26 February 1917. GARF, f. 640, op. 1, d. 115, l. 52–53ob. Manuscript. Original English text.
9. Telegram from Beliaev to Alekseev, 27 February 1917. *Krasnyi arkhiv* 21 (1927): 8.
10. Telegram from Nicholas to Golitsyn, 27 February 1917. GARF, f. 601, op. 1, d. 2089, l. 2.
11. Letter from Nicholas to Alexandra, 27 February 1917. GARF, f. 640, op. 1, d. 115, l. 54–54ob. Manuscript. Original English text.
12. Telegram from Nicholas to Alexandra, 27 February 1917. GARF, f. 640, op. 1, d. 108, l. 130. Message in English.
13. Declaration by Provisional Committee of the State Duma, 28 February 1917. *Izvestiia Petrogradskogo Soveta rabochikh deputatov,* no. 1, 28 February 1917.

14. Telegram from elected members of the State Council to Nicholas, 28 February 1917. GARF, f. 601, op. 1, d. 2091, l. 1–10b. Copy.

15. Telegram from Nicholas to Alexandra, 28 February 1917. GARF, f. 640, op. 1, d. 108, l. 131. Original English text.

16. Diary of Alexandra, 28 February 1917. GARF, f. 640, op. 1, d. 333, l. 300b. Copy (original has been lost). Manuscript. Original English text.

17. Telegram from Alexandra to Nicholas, 1 March 1917. GARF, f. 1779, op. 1, d. 1722, l. 15.

18. Manifesto of the grand dukes, 1 March 1917. GARF, f. 5881, op. 1, d. 367, l. 10–11. Copy.

19. Telegram from Alekseev to Nicholas, 1 March 1917. *Krasnyi arkhiv* 21 (1927): 53–54. The text was written by Nikolai Bazili, a lawyer and chief of the diplomatic chancellery at Headquarters; it was corrected in a couple of places by General Aleksandr Lukomskii and signed by General Alekseev.

20. Portion of telegram from Alekseev to Nicholas, 2 March 1917. GARF, f. 601, op. 1, d. 2102, l. 1–2. Copy.

21. Letter from Pavel Aleksandrovich to Rodzianko, [2 March] 1917. GARF, f. 644, op. 1, d. 161, l. 1–10b. Manuscript. Written in the hand of Ol'ga Palei, wife of Pavel Aleksandrovich.

22. Letter from Pavel Aleksandrovich to Kirill Vladimirovich, 2 March 1917. GARF, f. 644, op. 1, d. 174, l. 1–10b. Manuscript. Written in the hand of Ol'ga Palei, wife of Pavel Aleksandrovich.

23. Letter from Kirill Vladimirovich to Pavel Aleksandrovich, 2 March 1917. GARF, f. 644, op. 1, d. 410, l. 1. Manuscript.

24. Letter from Alexandra to Nicholas, 2 March 1917. GARF, f. 601, op. 1, d. 1151, l. 500–5000b. Manuscript. Original English text.

25. Protocol of talks between Guchkov, Shul'gin, and Nicholas, 2 March 1917. GARF, f. 601, op. 1, d. 2099, l. 1–30b. Copy.

26. Nicholas II's manifesto of abdication, 2 March 1917. GARF, f. 601, op. 1, d. 2100(a), l. 5, and d. 2101(b), l. 1. See Document 25 on the intentionally inaccurate time recorded for the signing.

27. From the minutes of the first meeting of the Council of Ministers of the Provisional Government, 2 March 1917. GARF, f. 601, op. 1, d. 2103, l. 10b.

28. Conversation by direct telegraph between Ruzskii and Rodzianko, 3 March 1917. GARF, f. 5881, op. 2, d. 84, l. 1–4.

29. Act of abdication of Mikhail Aleksandrovich, 3 March 1917. Facsimile: GARF, f. 601, op. 1, d. 2101(b), l. 2. Printed copy: GARF, f. 668, op. 1, d. 131, l. 1.

30. Diary of Nicholas II, 27 February–3 March 1917. GARF, f. 601, op. 1, d. 265, l. 64–68. Manuscript.

31. Letter from Alexandra to Nicholas, 3 March 1917. GARF, f. 601, op. 1, d. 1151, l. 502–504. Manuscript. Original English text.

32. From the protocol of a session of the Executive Committee of the Petrograd Soviet, 3 March 1917. TsGA SPb (Tsentral'nyi gosudarstvennyi arkhiv Sankt-Peterburga [Central State Archive of St. Petersburg]), f. 7384, op. 9, d. 2, l. 1–2. Copy. Published in *Petrogradskii Sovet rabochikh i soldatskikh deputatov v 1917 g.*, vol. 1 (Leningrad, 1991): 81–82.

33. Note from Nicholas to Alekseev, 4 March 1917. *Krasnyi arkhiv* 22 (1927): 53–54. Manuscript. Dated on the basis of Alekseev's telegram to L'vov, ibid., 54.

34. Letter from Alexandra to Nicholas, 4 March 1917. GARF, f. 601, op. 1, d. 1151, l. 505–506. Manuscript. Original English text.

35. From the protocol of a session of the Executive Committee of the Petrograd Soviet, 6 March 1917. TsGA SPb, f. 7384, op. 9, d. 5, l. 1–4. Copy. Published in *Petrograd-*

skii Sovet rabochikh i soldatskikh deputatov v 1917 g., vol. 1 (Leningrad, 1991): 153–156.

36. Declaration by eighty-five members of the Petrograd Soviet, 7 March 1917. GARF, f. 1235, op. 53, d. 19, l. 60.
37. From the minutes of the tenth session of the Provisional Government, 7 March 1917. GARF, f. 1779, op. 2, d. 1, ch. 1, l. 15. Printed copy.
38. Kerenskii's speech to the Moscow Soviet, [7 March 1917]. From *Malenkaia gazeta* (Petrograd), 10 March 1917. Dated according to Kerenskii's memoirs.
39. Nicholas II's parting words to the troops, 8 March 1917. GARF, f. 5827, op. 1, d. 10, l. 1. Printed copy.
40. Diary of Nicholas II, 8 March 1917. GARF, f. 601, op. 1, d. 265, l. 73. Manuscript.
41. From the protocol of a session of the Executive Committee of the Petrograd Soviet, 9 March 1917. TsGA SPb, f. 7384, op. 9, d. 8, l. 7–11. Copy. Published in *Petrogradskii Sovet rabochikh i soldatskikh deputatov v 1917 g.*, vol. 1 (Leningrad, 1991), 218–221. In point 3 "Nicholas II," a title that the revolutionaries eschewed, was changed by hand to "Nicholas Rom." (Romanov).
42. Diary of Alexandra, 8–9 March 1917. GARF, f. 640, op. 1, d. 333, l. 340b–35. Manuscript copy. Original English text.
43. Telegram from Soviet of Workers' Deputies at the Konstantinovsky factories to Chkheidze, 13 March 1917. GARF, f. 1235, op. 53, d. 19, l. 63.
44. Instructions to head of the garrison at Tsarskoe Selo, 17 March 1917. GARF, f. 1778, op. 1, d. 14, l. 3–30b. Verified copy.
45. "A. F. Kerenskii before the Soviet of Soldiers' Deputies," 29 March 1917. *Kavkazskii krai*, 29 March 1917.
46. Diary of Archpriest Afansii Beliaev, 2–31 March 1917. GARF, f. 601, op. 1, d. 2077, l. 1–280b. Manuscript.
47. Telegram from Kuragino to Kerenskii, 5 April 1917. GARF, f. 1235, op. 53, d. 20, l. 1.
48. Statement by Danilov, 7 April 1917. GARF, f. 6978, op. 1, d. 714, l. 101–102. Manuscript.
49. Poem by Ol'ga, 23 April 1917. GARF, f. 673, op. 1, d. 73, l. 1. Manuscript. On the reverse of the card is a portrait of the baby Jesus and the Virgin Mary under the words "Peace on Earth."
50. Resolution from the crew of the cruiser *Rossiia*, 20 May 1917. GARF, f. 1235, op. 33, d. 12, l. 81.
51. Telegram from soldiers of the Nikolaevskii Maritime Battery, 21 May 1917. GARF, f. 1235, op. 53, d. 2, l. 11.
52. Letter from Alexandra to Syroboiarskii, 29 May 1917. Private collection. Published in *Skorbnaia pamiatka* (New York, 1928): 44–50, and *Pis'ma tsarskoi sem'i iz zatocheniia* (Jordanville, N.Y., 1974), 63–66.
53. Letter from Ol'ga to Petrov, 19 June 1917. GARF, f. 611, op. 1, d. 70, l. 93–940b. Manuscript.
54. Letter from Ol'ga to her aunt Ol'ga, 21 June 1917. GARF, f. 643, op. 1, d. 214, l. 28–29. Manuscript.
55. Deciphered telegrams from George Buchanan to London, 11 (24) and 12 (25) July 1917. Public Record Office, F.O. 371 (British Foreign Office Records of General Political Correspondence from Russia), vol. 3015, pp. 2, 4–5.
56. Diary of Nicholas II, 9 March–31 July 1917. GARF, f. 601, op. 1, d. 265, l. 73–174. Manuscript.
57. Letter from Alexandra to Vyrubova, [1 August 1917]. Beinecke Rare Book and Manuscript Library, Yale University, MS Vault, Shelves, Romanov collection, container 1. Manuscript. Original English text.

58. Diary of Naryshkina, 1 August 1917. *Poslednie novosti* (Paris), 10 May 1936.
59. Kerenskii's "Instructions" to the guard, 31 July 1917. GARF, f. 601, op. 2, d. 14, l. 1–10b. Portion of document preserved. On the document is the notation: "Copy 2 A. Kerenskii."
60. The Ekaterinburg District Soviet's inquiry to the Petrograd Soviet, 5 August 1917. GARF, f. 1235, op. 53, d. 19, l. 91.
61. Diary of Alexandra, 6–7 August 1917. GARF, f. 640, op. 1, d. 333, l. 111ob–112. Manuscript. Original English text.
62. "A Counterrevolutionary Plot," *Izvestiia* (Petrograd), 25 August 1917.
63. Monarchists' letter to Nicholas II, [August 1917]. GARF, f. 601, op. 2, d. 22, l. 1. Manuscript. Dated by location among documents in archive.
64. Resolution passed by the general assembly of the crew of the gunboat *Bobr*, 6 September 1917. GARF, f. 1244, op. 2, d. 10, l. 7.
65. Deciphered telegram from Pankratov to Kerenskii, 14 September 1917. GARF, f. 1778, op. 1, d. 279, l. 2. Verified copy. Mistakenly dated 14 August 1917.
66. Message from Somov to Botkin, 15 September 1917. GARF, f. 601, op. 2, d. 23, l. 38. Manuscript.
67. Deciphered telegram from Pankratov to Kerenskii, 20 September 1917. GARF, f. 1778, op. 1, d. 279, l. 3. Verified copy.
68. Report from Pankratov to Kerenskii, 30 September 1917. GARF, f. 601, op. 2, d. 20, l. 1–4. Manuscript.
69. Letter from Alexandra to Syroboiarskaia, 17 October 1917. Private collection. Published in *Skorbnaia pamiatka*, 54–55, and *Pis'ma tsarskoi sem'i iz zatocheniia*, 135–136.
70. Diary of Nicholas II, 5 September–22 October 1917. GARF, f. 601, op. 1, d. 265, l. 196, d. 266, l. 2–14. Manuscript.
71. Letter from Tat'iana to Petrov, 23 October 1917. GARF, f. 611, op. 1, d. 71, l. 124–125ob.
72. Letter from Nicholas to Kseniia Aleksandrovna, 5 November 1917. Private collection. Published in *Pravoslavnaia zhizn'*, January 1961: 6–9, and *Pis'ma tsarskoi sem'i iz zatocheniia*, 143–145.
73. Letter from Ol'ga to Petrov, 23 November 1917. GARF, f. 611, op. 1, d. 70, l. 102–103ob. Manuscript.
74. "Rumors about the Escape of Nicholas Romanov's Second Daughter," *Vecherniaia pochta* (Petrograd), 23 November 1917.
75. Diary of Nicholas II, 11–26 November 1917. GARF, f. 601, op. 1, d. 266, l. 21–27. Manuscript.
76. Letter from Gilliard to Petrov, 26 November 1917. GARF, f. 611, op. 1, d. 50, l. 25–25ob. Manuscript. Written in French.
77. Letter from Alexandra to Syroboiarskii, 29 November 1917. Private collection. Published in *Skorbnaia pamiatka*, 56–58, and *Pis'ma tsarskoi sem'i iz zatocheniia*, 156.
78. "The Escape of Nicholas II," *Petrogradskii golos*, 2 December 1917.
79. Telegram from the special purpose detachment to Smolny, 3 December 1917. GARF, f. 1235, op. 53, d. 20, l. 18. Notation on document: "Immediately to the press."
80. Report by the delegates to the third Western Siberian Congress of Soviets of Workers' and Soldiers' Deputies, 10 December 1917. GAOO (Gosudarstvennyi arkhiv Omskoi oblasti), f. 658, op. 1, d. 1, l. 109–110. Reprinted in *Protokoly zasedanii III Zapadno-Sibirskogo s"ezda Sovetov rabochikh deputatov* (Omsk, 1917): 108, and in *Bor'ba za vlast' Sovetov v Tobol'skoi (Tiumenskoi) gubernii (1917–1920 gg.): Sbornik dokumental'nykh materialov* (Sverdlovsk, 1967): 128–129.
81. Letter from Alexandra to Syroboiarskii, 10 December 1917. Private collection. Published in *Skorbnaia pamiatka*, 59–60, and *Pis'ma tsarskoi sem'i iz zatocheniia*, 176–178.

82. Letter from Aleksei to Petrov, 19 December 1917. GARF, f. 601, op. 1, d. 66, l. 11. Manuscript.
83. Letter from Alexandra to Anna Vyrubova, [16 December 1917]. Original English text. A version of the original was published in Anna Viroubova, *Memories of the Russian Court* (London, 1923), 309–313, and in Russian translation in *Russkaia letopis'* 4 (1922): 207–210, and in *Stranitsy iz moei zhizni* (N.p., 1923), 153–156. The original document cannot be located. Unfortunately, the English versions of Alexandra's letters that Vyrubova published are not reliable transcriptions; on the basis of letters whose originals are extant it appears that either Vyrubova or an editor often corrected Alexandra's syntax and grammar and omitted many names, phrases, and even entire passages, even though they were included in the Russian translations of the letters that Vyrubova published in the early 1920s. Thus, the text here is a hybrid, correcting Vyrubova's English version with translations from the published Russian versions. Although the content of this letter is accurate, the exact style is necessarily approximate. Dated by content. Published version dated 10 December.
84. Diary of Alexandra, 24–25 December 1917. GARF, f. 640, op. 1, d. 333, l. 1820b.–183. Manuscript. Original English text.
85. Report in the newspaper *Tobol'skii rabochii*, 27 December 1917. *Tobol'skii rabochii*, 6 January 1918.
86. Letter from Tat'iana to Petrov, 27 December 1917. GARF, f. 611, op. 1, d. 71, l. 127–128. Manuscript.
87. Diary of Nicholas II, 31 December 1917–3 January 1918. GARF, f. 601, op. 1, d. 266, l. 40–42. Manuscript.
88. Letter from Nicholas to Kseniia Aleksandrovna, 7 January 1918. Private collection. Published in *Pravoslavnaia zhizn'*, January 1961: 9–10 and *Pis'ma tsarskoi sem'i iz zatocheniia*, 209–210.
89. Letter from Alexandra to Vyrubova, 9 January 1918. Beinecke Rare Book and Manuscript Library, Yale University, MS Vault, Shelves, Romanov collection, container 1. Manuscript.
90. Postcard from Alexandra to Syroboiarskii, 11 January 1918. Private collection. Published in *Skorbnaia pamiatka*, 82–83, and *Pis'ma tsarskoi sem'i iz zatocheniia*, 220. Both sides of the postcard are reproduced in *Pis'ma tsarskoi sem'i iz zatocheniia*, 446–447.
91. Note from Alexandra to Solov'ev, [24 January 1918]. From a deciphered copy of the coded original, which the recipient burned. Private collection. Published in S. Markov, *Pokinutaia tsarskaia sem'ia, 1917–1918* (Vienna, 1928), 255–256, and *Pis'ma tsarskoi sem'i iz zatocheniia*, 260.
92. Letter from Tat'iana to Petrov, 26 January 1918. GARF, f. 611, op. 1, d. 71, l. 130–1310b. Manuscript.
93. From the protocol of a session of the Sovnarkom, 29 January 1918. GARF, f. 130, op. 23, d. 7, l. 170(a). Verified copy.
94. Portion of letter from Alexandra to Syroboiarskii, 13 February 1918. Private collection. Published in *Skorbnaia pamiatka*, 64–66, and *Pis'ma tsarskoi sem'i iz zatocheniia*, 278.
95. From the protocol of a session of the Sovnarkom, 20 February 1918 (excerpt). GARF, f. 130, op. 23, d. 8, l. 204. Verified copy.
96. Portion of a letter from Alexandra to Anna Vyrubova, 2 (15) March 1918. Beinecke Rare Book and Manuscript Library, Yale University, MS Vault, Shelves, Romanov collection, container 1. Manuscript.
97. Diary of Nicholas II, 9 January 1918–2 (15) March 1918. GARF, f. 601, op. 1, d. 266, l. 44–66. Manuscript.
98. Telegram from the Western Siberian Soviet to Lenin and Trotsky, 28 March 1918. GARF, f. 130, op. 2, d. 1109, l. 5–6.

99. Memorandum by Bonch-Bruevich, [no later than 1 April 1918]. GARF, f. 1235, op. 93, d. 77, l. 185. Manuscript. Dated in relation to Document 100.

100. From the protocol of a session of the Presidium of the VTsIK, 1 April 1918. GARF, f. 1235, op. 34, d. 36, l. 7–13.

101. From the protocol of a session of the Presidium of the VTsIK, 6 April 1918. GARF, f. 1235, op. 34, d. 36, l. 29–31.

102. Letter from Sverdlov to the Ural Regional Soviet, 9 April 1918. GARF, f. 601, op. 2, d. 33, l. 1. Manuscript.

103. Telegram from Tobol'sk to the VTsIK, 17 April 1918. GARF, f. 601, op. 2, d. 27, l. 2.

104. "The Trial of Nicholas Romanov," from *Golos Kungurskogo Soveta K., R. i S. D.* (Perm province), 17 April 1918.

105. Telegram from Goloshchekin to Khokhriakov, 21 April 1918. GARF, f. 601, op. 2, d. 33, l. 9–90b. Handwritten on telegraph form.

106. General meeting of the special detachment guarding Nicholas in Tobol'sk, 22 April 1918. GARF, f. 601, op. 2, d. 33, l. 27–28. Manuscript.

107. An inspection of Freedom House, 23 April 1918. GARF, f. 601, op. 2, d. 33, l. 54–540b. Manuscript.

108. Negotiations by telegraph between VTsIK and Iakovlev, [24 April 1918]. GARF, f. 601, op. 2, d. 33, l. 67–670b. Handwritten on telegraph form. Dated by content.

109. Diary of Alexandra, 10–12 (23–25) April 1918. GARF, f. 640, op. 1, d. 326, l. 510b–520b. Manuscript. Original English text.

110. Diary of Nicholas II, 14 (27) March–16 (29) April 1918. GARF, f. 601, op. 1, d. 266, l. 71–92. Manuscript.

111. Telegram from Iakovlev to Goloshchekin, [27 April 1918]. GARF, f. 601, op. 2, d. 33, l. 44–48. Handwritten on telegraph form. Dated by content.

112. Negotiations over the direct telegraph line between Iakovlev and Sverdlov, 27 April 1918. GARF, f. 130, op. 2, d. 1109, l. 54–540b. Handwritten on telegraph form. On the document is the notation: "Taken by telephone. Fisher."

113. Negotiations by telegraph between Sverdlov and Iakovlev, [27 April 1918]. GARF, f. 601, op. 2, d. 32, l. 2. Decoded translation of telegraph tape in Morse code. Manuscript. Dated by content.

114. Communication by telegraph from Iakovlev to Sverdlov, [27 April 1918]. GARF, f. 601, op. 2, d. 32, l. 170b, 880b., 99–100. Handwritten on telegraph form. Dated by content.

115. An inquiry by telegraph from Ural Regional Soviet to Lenin and Sverdlov, 28 April 1918. GARF, f. 130, op. 2, d. 1109, l. 19–20. Handwritten on telegraph form.

116. Orders telegraphed from Sverdlov to the Omsk Soviet, [28 April 1918]. GARF, f. 601, op. 2, d. 32, l. 7. Decoded translation of telegraph tape in Morse code. Manuscript. Dated by content.

117. Telegram from Beloborodov to Sverdlov, 29 April 1918. GARF, f. 601, op. 2, d. 27, l. 5.

118. Telegram from Sverdlov to Yekaterinburg regional committee of the Bolshevik party, [29 April 1918]. GARF, f. 130, op. 2, d. 1109, l. 22. Copy. Dated by content and relation to other documents in archive.

119. Telegram from Sverdlov to Iakovlev, [29 April 1918]. GARF, f. 601, op. 2, d. 32, l. 71. Decoded translation of telegraph tape in Morse code. Dated by content.

120. Negotiations over the direct telegraph line between Iakovlev and Sverdlov, [29 April 1918]. GARF, f. 130, op. 2, d. 1109, l. 16–160b. Handwritten on telegraph form. Dated according to when Iakovlev was in Omsk.

121. Statement to commissar Iakovlev by Nevolin, [3 May 1918]. GARF, f. 601, op. 2, d. 33, l. 84–850b. Manuscript. Dated by content.

122. "On the Transfer of the Former Tsar from Tobol'sk to Ekaterinburg," interview with Iakovlev in *Izvestiia* (Petrograd), 16 May 1918.

123. From the recollections of commissar Pankratov, September through December 1917. Published as V. S. Pankratov, *S tsarem v Tobol'ske: Iz vospominanii* (With the tsar in Tobolsk: Recollections) (Leningrad, 1925). The date applies to the events discussed.

124. Telegram from Beloborodov to Lenin and Sverdlov, 30 April 1918. GARF, f. 601, op. 2, d. 27, l. 6.

125. Letter from Mariia, with notes from Alexandra and Nicholas, to Ol'ga in Tobol'sk, 1 May 1918. GARF, f. 673, op. 1, d. 78, l. 1–10b. Manuscript.

126. From the protocol of a session of the Sovnarkom, 2 May 1918 (excerpt). GARF, f. 130, op. 23, d. 13, ll. 56–62. Verified copy.

127. Letter from Alexandra and Mariia to Ol'ga in Tobol'sk, 2 May 1918. GARF, f. 673, op. 1, d. 78, l. 2. Manuscript.

128. Telephonegram from Sverdlov to Beloborodov, 3 May 1918. GARF, f. 601, op. 2, d. 32, l. 136. Handwritten on telegraph form. On the document is the notation: "Personally transmitted by telephone at 24:00. Sibirev."

129. Telegram from Beloborodov to Sverdlov, [4 May 1918]. GARF, f. 1235, op. 79, d. 5, l. 176–178. Handwritten on telegraph form. Dated by content.

130. Letter from Beloborodov to Khokhriakov, 6 May 1918. GARF, f. 601, op. 2, d. 32, l. 149. Manuscript.

131. Letter from Anastasiia to sister and parents in Ekaterinburg, 7 May 1918. GARF, f. 685, op. 1, d. 40, l. 4–60b. Manuscript.

132. Letter from Mariia with a note by Alexandra to the children in Tobol'sk, 10–11 May 1918. GARF, f. 673, op. 1, d. 276, l. 1–20b. Manuscript.

133. Diary of Mariia Solov'eva [Rasputina], 22 May 1918. GARF, f. 601, op. 2, d. 75, l. 20. Verified copy.

134. Document given to the Ural Regional Soviet and signed by Nagornyi, 24 May 1918. GARF, f. 601, op. 2, d. 38, l. 2. Manuscript.

135. Letter from Botkin to Ural Regional Soviet Executive Committee, 24 May 1918. GARF, f. 601, op. 2, d. 37, l. 1–10b. Manuscript.

136. Instructions to the commandant of the House of Special Purpose, [May 1918]. GARF, f. 601, op. 2, d. 34, l. 3–8. Manuscript draft. Dated by content.

137. Letter from an "officer of the Russian army" to the imperial family, [19 or 20 June 1918]. GARF, f. 601, op. 2, d. 27, l. 25–26. Manuscript. Written in French. This and the subsequent letters between the "officer" and the family are dated by content, that is, in relation to known events and to references in Nicholas's and Alexandra's diaries. See the discussion in Pipes, *Russian Revolution*, 767–770.

138. Response to the "officer's" letter, [between 21 and 23 June 1918]. GARF, f. 601, op. 2, d. 27, l. 26–260b. Manuscript. Written in French. This note was written directly on the letter received (Document 137). This and the following responses from the imperial family appear to be written in Ol'ga's hand.

139. Letter from the "officer" to the imperial family, [25 June 1918]. GARF, f. 601, op. 2, d. 27, l. 19–20. Manuscript. Written in French.

140. Response to the "officer's" letter, [25 June 1918]. GARF, f. 601, op. 2, d. 27, l. 20–200b. Manuscript. Written in French. Written directly on the letter received (Document 139).

141. Letter from the "officer" to the imperial family, [26 June 1918]. GARF, f. 601, op. 2, d. 27, l. 22–23. Manuscript. Written in French.

142. Response to the "officer," [27 June 1918]. GARF, f. 601, op. 2, d. 27, l. 23–230b. Manuscript. Written in French. Written directly on the letter received (Document 141).

143. Telegram from Murav'ev to the Sovnarkom, 28 June 1918. GARF, f. 130, op. 2, d. 1109, l. 38.

144. Telegram from the Kolomna district organization of Bolsheviks to the Sovnarkom, 3 July 1918. GARF, f. 130, op. 2, d. 1109, l. 2.

145. Telegram from Beloborodov to Sverdlov and Goloshchekin, 4 July 1918. GARF, f. 1235, op. 1, d. 6, l. 10.

146. Letter from the "officer" to the imperial family, [after 4 July 1918]. GARF, f. 601, op. 2, d. 27, l. 28–28ob. Manuscript. Written in French.

147. Diary of Nicholas II, 17 (30) April–30 June (13 July) 1918. GARF, f. 601, op. 1, d. 266, l. 92–134. Manuscript.

148. Telegram to Lenin from the *National Tidende* (Copenhagen), and Lenin's response, 16 July 1918. GARF, f. 130, op. 2, d. 1109, l. 40–41. RTsKhIDNI (Rossiiskii tsentr khraneniia i izucheniia dokumentov noveishei istorii [Russian Center for the Preservation and Study of Documents of Recent History]), f. 2, op. 1, d. 6601, l. 1. Manuscript. Original English text. Reply is in Lenin's hand. On reply is the note, in Russian: "Returned from telegraph [office]. Connection could not be made."

149. Telegram from Zinov'ev to Lenin and Sverdlov, 16 July 1918. GARF, f. 130, op. 2, d. 653, l. 12.

150. Diary of Alexandra, 11–16 July 1918. GARF, f. 640, op. 1, d. 326, l. 91–93ob. Manuscript. Original English text.

151. Telegram from the Ural Regional Soviet to Lenin and Sverdlov, 17 July 1918. GARF, f. 601, op. 2, d. 27, l. 8–9.

152. Deciphered telegram from Beloborodov to Gorbunov, 17 July 1918. A photograph of the original document was printed in N. Sokolov, *Ubiistvo tsarskoi sem'i* (Murder of the imperial family) (Berlin, 1925), facing page 249. The text is deciphered ibid., 247–248. The original was found by White army investigators in the Ekaterinburg telegraph office.

153. From the protocol of a session of the VTsIK Presidium, 18 July 1918. GARF, f. 1235, op. 28, d. 24, l. 1.

154. From the protocol of a session of the Sovnarkom, 18 July 1918. RTsKhIDNI, f. 19, op. 1, d. 158, l. 8. GARF, f. 130, op. 23, d. 17, l. 62–65. Verified copy.

155. "Nicholas Romanov's Execution," VTsIK leaflet, [no earlier than 18 July]. GARF, f. 9550, op. 2, d. 421, l. 1. Printed.

156. *Pravda* editorial and report, 19 July 1918.

157. "The Funeral of Nicholas the Bloody," *Ural'skii rabochii* (Ekaterinburg), 26 September 1918.

158. From the examination record of the interrogation of Medvedev, 21–22 February 1919. Documents of the Investigation into the Death of Nicholas II (Sokolov Archive), Houghton Library, Harvard University, Kilgour Collection, MS Russian 35, vol. 2, doc. 86. Verified copy. Paragraph breaks have been added.

159. Iurovskii's note on the execution of the imperial family and the concealment of the corpses, 1920. GARF, f. 601, op. 2, d. 27, l. 31–34. Written at the request of the historian M. N. Pokrovskii. Typed with handwritten corrections and additions.

160. From Iurovskii's account as told at a meeting of old Bolsheviks, 1 February 1934. TsDOOSO (Tsentr dokumentatsii obshchestvennykh organizatsii Sverdlovskoi oblasti [Center for the Documentation of Social Organizations of Sverdlov Region]), f. 41, op. 1, d. 151, l. 10–22.

Photographs

1. Nicholas II in seventeenth-century dress for a masked ball, St. Petersburg, 1903. *Al'bom kostiumirovnogo bala v Zimnem dvortse v fevral'ia 1903 goda* (St. Petersburg, 1904). New York Public Library. Astor, Lenox, and Tilden Foundations.

2. Nicholas II posing by a tennis court near the coast of Finland, 1912. Photograph by Anna Vyrubova. Beinecke Rare Book and Manuscript Library, Yale University, Romanov Collection, album 2.

3. Alexandra writing a letter in bed, Tsarskoe Selo, 1910 or 1911. Photograph by Anna

Vyrubova. Beinecke Rare Book and Manuscript Library, Yale University, Romanov Collection, album 7.

4. Nicholas II in cossack uniform at Spala, 1912. Photograph by Anna Vyrubova. Beinecke Rare Book and Manuscript Library, Yale University, Romanov Collection, album 2.

5. Nicholas II blessing troops leaving for the front in the Russo-Japanese War, Peterhof, 1905. Mikhail Iroshnikov et al., *Sunset of the Romanov Dynasty* (Moscow, 1992), 141.

6. Nicholas II receiving bread and salt from representatives of the people during celebrations for the tercentenary of the House of Romanov, Kostroma, 1913. Mikhail Iroshnikov et al., *Sunset of the Romanov Dynasty* (Moscow, 1992), 297.

7. Nicholas and Alexandra on board the yacht *Shtandart,* 1914. Beinecke Rare Book and Manuscript Library, Yale University, Romanov Collection, album 3.

8. Alexandra as war nurse with recovering soldiers, Tsarskoe Selo, 1914 or 1915. Beinecke Rare Book and Manuscript Library, Yale University, Romanov Collection, album 3.

9. Alexandra and Nicholas under arrest in the palace at Tsarskoe Selo, 1917. GARF, f. 683, op. 1, d. 125, l. 23.

10. Alexandra in bed amid her icons, Tsarskoe Selo, 1917. GARF, f. 683, op. 1, d. 125, l. 23.

11. Nicholas clearing snow from a pathway, Tsarskoe Selo, March 1917. GARF, f. 611, op. 1, d. 102, l. 177.

12. Aleksei and Nicholas breaking ice in front of the palace at Tsarskoe Selo, March 1917. GARF, f. 683, op. 1, d. 125, l. 23.

13. Aleksei in uniform, Tsarskoe Selo, March 1917. GARF, f. 683, op. 1, d. 125, l. 23.

14. Ol'ga, Aleksei, Anastasiia, and Tat'iana resting from working in the garden, Tsarskoe Selo, March 1917. GARF, f. 611, op. 1, d. 102, l. 147.

15. Alexandra embroidering while the family (not shown) prepares a vegetable garden, Tsarskoe Selo, April 1917. Beinecke Rare Book and Manuscript Library, Yale University, Romanov Collection, album 3.

16. Tat'iana, holding a pet dog, and Anastasiia with a guard and servants in the background, Tsarskoe Selo, June 1917. Photograph by Mariia. GARF, f. 611, op. 1, d. 102, l. 157.

17. Nicholas and Alexandra in the palace garden, Tsarskoe Selo, June 1917. Photograph by Mariia. GARF, f. 611, op. 1, d. 102, l. 164.

18. Nicholas smoking in the palace park, Tsarskoe Selo, June 1917. Photograph by Mariia. GARF, f. 611, op. 1, d. 102, l. 163.

19. The children with their heads shaved after measles caused hair loss, June 1917. Photograph by Pierre Gilliard. GARF, f. 611, op. 1, d. 102, l. 166.

20. Aleksei swimming near the "children's island" in the palace pond, Tsarskoe Selo, July 1917. Photograph by Mariia. GARF, f. 611, op. 1, d. 102, l. 158.

21. Tat'iana and Anastasiia with guards, Tsarskoe Selo, July 1917. GARF, f. 683, op. 1, d. 125, l. 25.

22. Aleksei with a guard, Tsarskoe Selo, July 1917. GARF, f. 683, op. 1, d. 125, l. 250b.

23. Nicholas posing by the stump of a tree that he helped fell, with guards standing behind him, Tsarskoe Selo, July 1917. GARF, f. 683, op. 1, d. 125, l. 240b.

24. Former Governor's House in Tobol'sk, with palisade fence under construction, August 1917. GARF, f. 601, op. 1, d. 2110, l. 33.

25. Soldier of the guard posing by the front entrance of the Governor's House, Tobol'sk, winter 1917–1918. GARF, f. 601, op. 1, d. 2110, l. 20.

26. Soldiers of the guard posing beside the Governor's House, Tobol'sk, winter 1917–1918. GARF, f. 601, op. 1, d. 2110, l. 26.

27. Nicholas and Aleksei sawing wood, Tobol'sk, winter 1917–1918. Beinecke Rare Book and Manuscript Library, Yale University, Romanov Collection, album 1.

28. Nicholas with daughters on the roof of the greenhouse at the Governor's House, Tobol'sk, early 1918. Beinecke Rare Book and Manuscript Library, Yale University, Romanov collection, album 1.
29. Ipat'ev house in Ekaterinburg during the first days that Nicholas and his family were imprisoned there, spring 1918, before the construction of the second fence. Houghton Library, Harvard University, Sokolov Archive, vol. 3.
30. Ural Regional Soviet of Workers' and Soldiers' Deputies, Ekaterinburg, 1917. *The Murder of the Romanovs* (London, 1935), facing page 181.
31. Filipp Goloshchekin, military commissar of the Ural Regional Soviet. Houghton Library, Harvard University, Sokolov Archive, vol. 3.
32. Aleksandr Beloborodov, chairman of the Ural Regional Soviet. Houghton Library, Harvard University, Sokolov Archive, vol. 3.
33. Iakov Iurovsky, commandant of the House of Special Purpose (Ipat'ev house), July 1918. *The Murder of the Romanovs* (London, 1935), facing page 261.

Index

References to N. are to Nicholas II; references to A. are to Alexandra.

Abalakovsky Monastery, 305, 305n3
Abdication: act of, 96–100; manifesto of Mikhail Aleksandrovich, 105, 108; manifesto of N., 100–102, 107; N. agrees to abdicate, 60–63, 97; N.'s sense of duty requiring, 11–12, 100–101, 145–146, 174
Ageev, Vasily (Vasia), 80, 80n2, 203, 204n2
Aksiuta, Fyodor Alekseevich, 207, 207n1
Aleksandr Mikhailovich, 115, 115n1, 379
Aleksandrovsky Palace, 67n1, 121, 131, 133, 134, 138, 141, 143–144, 147, 156, 188
Alekseev, Mikhail Vasilievich, 47, 52, 53, 59–61, 66, 67n7, 68, 83, 88–89, 91, 107, 108, 114, 118, 224, 379, 385
Aleksei (Father), 196
Aleksei (Tsar), 17, 25
Aleksei Nikolaevich, 7, 30, 65, 67n2, 69–70, 71n13, 94, 240, 261, 379; execution of, 294, 296, 346–366; illnesses suffered by, 13, 33, 62, 69n1, 75, 78–79, 94, 112, 144, 185, 218, 227, 238, 239, 241, 242, 255, 256, 306–307, 326, 335; regency proposals concerning, 56, 60, 61, 92–93, 97–98; at Tobolsk, 178, 179, 211, 212, 240, 265, 303; at Tsarskoe

Selo, 122, 153, 157, 158, 160, 161, 162, 163, 165; at Yekaterinburg, 326, 327, 331, 334, 335
Alexander II, 226, 227n2
Alexander III, 4, 8, 10, 15, 16–17, 199, 342
Anastasia Nikolaevna, 71n12, 240, 380; execution of, 294, 295, 346–366; illnesses suffered by, 70, 112, 144, 201; at Tobolsk, 242, 302–304; at Tsarskoe Selo, 153, 157, 160; at Yekaterinburg, 329
Anderson, Anna, 295
Andrei Vladimirovich, 69, 71n8, 380
Ania. See Vyrubova, Anna
Anti-Semitism. See Jews
Anushka, 211, 212, 214n1
Apraksin, Pyotr Nikolaevich, 75, 94, 95n5
Army: abdication supported by, 60–61; disloyalty to N., 58–60, 64, 93–94; N.'s command of, 11, 16; N.'s farewell address to, 114–115. See also Military values; Red Army; Soldiers; White Army
Arrest of Romanovs, 121–122, 233, 241; declaration by Petrograd Soviet ordering, 113, 117; Executive Committee of Petrograd Soviet on, 130–131; Provisional Government's resolution concerning, 113–114; resolution of Executive Committee of Petrograd Soviet, 110, 112; workers' groups demanding, 133

Autocracy: A.'s belief in, 26, 35; *groznyi* (awesome) tsar, 25–27, 35, 68, 69; N.'s views on, 11, 16–21, 53; as personal authority, 11, 16, 18, 35, 63; *tishaishii* (saintly) tsar, 17, 25–27; and traditional Russian ruler myth, 15–18, 20, 21, 24–27
Avanesov, V. A., 231, 233, 339, 343
Avdeev, Aleksandr Dmitrievich, 238, 239*n1*, 280, 283, 284–285, 322, 326, 328, 330, 347, 380

Baby. *See* Aleksei Nikolaevich
Badmaev, Pyotr Aleksandrovich, 192, 192*n2*
Bazili, Nikolai Aleksandrovich, 61
Beilis affair, 343, 345*n5*
Beliaev, Afanasy Ivanovich (Archpriest), 137–146
Beliaev, Mikhail Alekseevich, 49, 51, 81, 109, 109*n1*
Beloborodov, Aleksandr Georgievich, 233, 233*n2*, 285, 380; and execution of Romanovs, 291–292, 294, 296, 337, 338, 350–351, 354, 365; on internal guard at Yekaterinburg, 322; on transfer to Yekaterinburg, 249–251, 297–298, 301–302
Benkendorf (Benckendorff), Pavel Konstantinovich, 70, 71*n15*, 86, 121, 124, 131, 139, 144, 156, 164, 168, 380
Berzin (Berzinsh), Reingold Iosifovich, 292, 320–321, 321*n2*, 380–381
Birthdays celebrated by Romanovs, 159, 165, 325, 328, 329
Bitner, Klavdia Mikhailovna, 194, 194*n3*, 196, 270–271, 303, 381, 386
"Bloody Sunday," 342, 344*n4*
Bolshevik Party, 41; evaluation of N. by, 341–343; ideals of order and discipline in, 286; and the fate of the Romanovs, 183–184; opposition to, 288–289; political culture and rhetoric of, 280–283, 342–343; popular support for, 128–129, 346. *See also* Lenin
Bolshevik Revolution. *See* October Revolution
Bonch-Bruevich, Vladimir Dmitrievich, 224, 229, 339
Boris Vladimirovich, 94, 95*n1*, 381
Botkin, Yevgeny Sergeevich, 77, 79*n2*, 240, 243, 244, 256, 381; execution of, 296,

352, 353, 358, 359; interceding for Romanovs, 194–195, 198, 306–307; at Tobolsk, 266, 269; at Tsarskoe Selo, 141, 142, 144; at Yekaterinburg, 278, 298, 323, 328, 329, 357
Brasova, Natalia Sergeevna, 92, 92*n1*, 387
Breshko-Breshkovskaia, Yekaterina Konstantinova, 175
Brest-Litovsk treaty, 178, 182, 183, 186; A.'s attitude toward, 213, 214*n4*, 223–224, 225; N.'s attitude toward, 204–205, 228; revolutionaries' attitudes toward, 288
Brusilov, Aleksei Alekseevich, 52, 90, 91*n2*
Bublikov, Aleksandr Aleksandrovich, 114
Buchanan, George, 70, 118–119, 120–121, 154–156
Buksgevden (Buxhoeveden), Sofia Karlovna, 28, 70, 71*n16*, 144, 168, 278, 381
Burial and concealment of corpses and burial site, 345, 350, 353–356, 360–365
Burikhin, I. I., 195, 196
Bykov, Pavel M., 290

Calendar, Julian and Gregorian, xii, 178, 227, 240, 244*n1*, 331*n1*
Central Executive Committee of Soviets of Workers', Soldiers', and Peasants' Deputies, All-Russian (VTsIK, TsIK), 170, 381; congresses of soviets, 289, 391; establishment of, 127–128; on execution of Romanovs, 339–341, 343–344; on guarding N., 229–231; Kerensky's appeals to, 173–174; Presidium of, 183, 230–231, 230*n1*, 287–288, 299; on removing epaulettes, 233; Yakovlev and, 183, 185
Central Military-Industrial Committee, 43–44
Charitable work, by A., 29–30, 75
Cheka, 184, 278–279, 284–285, 286, 288, 293, 320, 321*n3*, 323*n2*, 348, 350, 355, 360, 363, 365, 381
Chemodurov, Terenty Ivanovich, 240, 243, 280, 298, 323, 331*n2*, 381
Chkheidze, Nikolai Semyonovich, 110, 110*n1*, 119–120, 130
Chutskaev, Sergei Yegorovich, 354, 363
Common people (*narod*): A.'s views on, 35–36, 66, 109, 152, 197, 206, 210; at-

titudes and behavior toward the Romanovs, 124, 125, 258, 264–265, 267–268, 274, 277; democratic ideas among, 40; hostility toward the government, 60, 84–85, 97; ideal of bond uniting tsar and, 17–18, 20; N. appeals to, 10; N.'s views on, 18–21, 24, 25, 162; Pankratov's views on, 272; populists' view on, 41; protests against bolshevism, 288–289; social anger of, 40–41, 46, 175–176. *See also* Guards; Peasants; Soldiers; Workers

Conan Doyle, Arthur, 164

Conference of Public Figures, 173

Confinement of Romanovs. *See* Tobolsk imprisonment; Tsarskoe Selo imprisonment; Yekaterinburg imprisonment

Constantinople, 126–127

Constituent Assembly: demands and support for, 54–56, 103, 105, 148, 262; elections to, 275–276; Komuch (Committee of the Constituent Assembly), 289, 393; N.'s views on, 108

Constitutional Democratic Party. *See* Kadet Party

Constitutional monarchy, 56, 91–94

Constitutional reform, 18–19, 20, 35, 36, 42, 44, 46, 59, 103, 105, 145

Coronation of N., 109, 159, 342, 344n2, 403n60

Cossacks, 8, 49, 69, 99, 345

Council of Ministers, 99, 381–382; demands for a popular, 43–44, 49–50, 52–53, 59, 85, 87; and "ministerial leapfrog," 44–45; and N.'s manifesto creating responsible ministry, 59–60; N.'s opposition to changes in, 81; and Petrograd strikes and demonstrations, 50, 52, 53; resignation of, 53, 57

Council of People's Commissars (Sovnarkom), 223, 224–225, 391; and Berzin's investigation of murder rumors, 320–321; and execution of Romanovs, 333, 339, 341; N.'s views on, 228; property of Romanovs nationalized by, 293; on transfer of Romanovs to Yekaterinburg, 299; trial of N. demanded by, 182

Counterrevolution and dissent, 288–290, 302. *See also* Monarchists; White Army

Crimea, 72, 78; memories of, 224, 274; as possible place of exile, 111, 118, 129, 154, 155, 164, 168; as postrevolutionary residence of other Romanovs, 213, 381, 386–387, 388, 394

Czech Legion, 289, 292, 294, 341, 345

Danilov, Aleksandr Petrovich, 147–148

Danilov, Georgy Nikiforovich, 99, 107, 108n1

Danilovich, Grigory, 5

Dardanelles Strait, 126–127

Demianov, I., 229, 236

Demidova, Anna Stepanovna (Niuta), 240, 240n2, 243, 244, 256, 298, 300, 304, 323, 352–353, 356, 359, 365

Democracy, as a social force, 135–137, 174, 193–194

Democratic rights and equality: A.'s rejection of, 36, 66; civic demands for, 5, 39–40, 42, 43, 45, 55–56, 128, 193; in legislation of Provisional Government, 126; N.'s rejection of, 11, 15, 18, 281; and a republic, 55–56, 64, 96, 98, 133, 136, 138, 281

Demonstrations. *See* Strikes and mass demonstrations

Den, Karl Akimovich, 71n6

Den, Yulia Aleksandrovna, 33–34, 69, 71n6, 73, 75, 80, 86, 94, 111, 122, 166n3, 172, 180, 382

Denmark, as possible asylum for Romanovs, 119

Derevenko, Nikolai Vladimirovich, 194, 220, 382

Derevenko, (Doctor) Vladimir Nikolaevich, 382; in Tsarskoe Selo, 77, 79n2, 142, 144, 194n2; in Yekaterinburg, 283–284, 306, 316, 317, 326

Didkovsky, Boris Vladimirovich, 234, 234n2, 251, 279, 382

Discipline and order: A.'s belief in, 150–151; civic demands for, 129, 173; Bolshevik and Cheka ideal, 186, 208, 282, 286; N.'s belief in, 6, 8, 25, 68, 69n2, 164; Pankratov's views on, 262, 269

Dmitry Pavlovich, 135–136, 137n1, 382, 389

Dolgorukov, Vasily Aleksandrovich, 131n1, 382–383; arrest of, 131, 230, 278, 301; execution of, 323n2; at Tobolsk, 201, 240, 256, 264, 266; at Tsarskoe Selo, 156, 157, 168; at Yekaterinburg, 298, 305

Duma, State, 383; A.'s views on, 35, 49, 69, 73, 79, 94; and act of abdication, 87, 96–100; limitations on authority of, 44–45; N. agrees to establish, 18–19, 44; occupation of, 98; proroguing of, 19, 27, 44, 50, 52, 87; restrictions on franchise to, 42, 234. *See also* Progressive Bloc of Duma deputies; Provisional Committee of the State Duma

Dumas, Alexandre, 162, 180

Duty and responsibility: A.'s views on, 30, 66, 226; N.'s sense of, 10–12, 72, 89, 102, 115, 162, 174, 205; revolutionary, 131, 136, 357

Dzerzhinsky, Feliks, 286

Economic hardship, 45–46, 47, 126; A.'s views on, 69, 78; N.'s views on, 72

Education and tutoring, 71n13, 79n3; of A., 28; of lower classes, 40; of N., 4–5; at Tobolsk, 172, 194, 199, 205, 212, 213, 222, 269–271, 273; at Tsarskoe Selo, 123, 153–154, 159, 160, 162

Elizabeth of Hesse-Darmstadt (Ella, A.'s sister), 32

England: A.'s visits to, 28; monarchists' given support of, 283; offer of asylum in, 118–121, 146–147

English culture, in A.'s life, 27–29

Enlightenment, European, 15–16, 39

Ernst of Hesse-Darmstadt (A.'s brother), 92n2

Escape rumors: from Tobolsk, 179, 182, 204, 207, 268, 274, 391; from Yekaterinburg, 283, 295–296. *See also* Rescue efforts

Evert, Aleksei Yermolaevich, 90–91, 91n3

Execution: of German ambassador, 289; of government officials, 344n3; of other members of the court, 278

Execution of Romanovs, 304n1, 332, 333, 335–337, 338; accounts of, 346–366; ambiguities in the evidence, 3, 290–297; central authorities' role in, 3, 286–287, 290–295, 322, 333, 335–341, 344, 355, 356–357; DNA tests on remains, 295, 296; fear of attempts at, 252, 253–254; news reports of, 294, 320–321, 331, 341–344, 345; popular demands for, 283, 321; rescue plots as pretext for, 284, 337, 341; Sovnarkom resolution concerning, 339, 341; stories of survival

of family members, 294–297, 337, 344; Ural Bolsheviks attempting, 186–187, 245, 246, 248, 283, 290; VTsIK Presidium and, 339–341, 343–344

Exile of presumed counterrevolutionaries, 172–173, 191–192

Exile of Romanovs, proposed, 102, 118–121, 146–147, 193–194

Extraordinary Commission for the Struggle with Counterrevolution and Sabotage, All-Russian. *See* Cheka

Extraordinary Investigatory Commission (ChSK), 147, 147n3, 233–234, 234n1

Family life, N.'s delight in, 4, 5, 9–10, 68, 72, 257

Fatalism. *See* Religious practice and faith

February Revolution of 1917, 46–52, 76–77, 84–85, 89–91, 96–99, 114, 116–117, 343; A.'s reaction to, 49, 73, 94; N.'s reaction to, 83, 107

Frederiks, Emma Vladimirovna, 112, 112n1

Frederiks (Fredericks), Vladimir Borisovich, 70, 71n9, 94, 96, 100, 102, 204, 383

Freedom House. *See* Tobolsk imprisonment

Freemasons, presumed conspiracy of, 23, 112, 241, 244n2

French Revolution, comparison of Russian Revolution to, 114, 116–117, 194

Funeral of Romanovs, 345

Fyodorov, (Doctor) Sergei Petrovich, 62, 72, 73n1, 80, 383

Fyodorovsky Cathedral, 16, 24, 137, 141, 146, 146n1

Gendrikova, Anastasia Vasilievna, 383; in Tobolsk, 230, 266, 269; in Tsarskoe Selo, 70, 71n15, 79, 132–133, 144, 168; in Yekaterinburg, 278, 305

George V, 70, 71n10, 118, 120

Georgievsky Battalion, 81, 81n1

Georgy Mikhailovich, 94, 95n2, 383

"German tsaritsa," 27, 45, 261

Germany, 283, 289. *See also* Brest-Litovsk treaty; Prussia; World War I

Germogen (Bishop), 213, 214n3, 301, 383–384, 386

Gibbs, Sidney, 70, 71n13, 109, 203, 205, 230, 269, 278, 306–307, 384

Gilliard, Pierre, 384, 392; in Tobolsk, 132, 153, 171, 174, 175, 178, 205–206, 223, 269; in Tsarskoe Selo, 78, 79*n3*, 109, 122–123; in Yekaterinburg, 278, 306–307

Golitsyn, Nikolai Dmitrievich, 53, 80, 80*n1*, 81

Goloshchekin, Filipp Isaevich, 233*n3*, 285, 321*n3*, 350, 384; and execution of Romanovs, 351, 357, 360, 362; in Moscow, 183, 288; and trial of Romanovs, 288, 290–291, 292, 293, 333; and Yakovlev, 233, 234, 245, 251; and Yurovsky, 285

Gorbunov, Nikolai Petrovich, 337, 337*n1*, 341

Gorbunov, Pavel Petrovich, 363

Gorky, Maksim, 289

Grafitti, by guards, 124, 178, 280–281

Groten, Pavel Pavlovich, 70, 71*n17*, 75, 86

Guards, 131, 182, 229, 235–237, 261, 268–269, 278, 284–285, 293; behavior toward the Romanovs, 123–124, 139, 147, 149, 158, 161, 162, 164, 172, 175, 177–179, 201–202, 213, 262, 279–281; rules for, 133–135, 208, 285, 286; stealing by, 330, 353, 361

Guchkov, Aleksandr Ivanovich, 35, 42, 44, 62, 85, 96–100, 100*n1*, 104, 107, 111–112, 127, 159, 384–385

Gurko, Vasily Iosifovich, 47, 75, 76*n4*, 172–173, 191, 385

Habberton, John, *Helen's Babies*, 69, 70*n2*

Hanbury-Williams, John, 68, 69*n4*

Health of Romanovs: A.'s illnesses, 124, 203, 257, 298, 300, 334; children's illnesses, 13, 33, 62, 68–78, 86, 94, 95, 112, 132, 138, 144, 156, 157, 185, 201, 218, 219, 220, 227, 238, 239, 241, 242, 255, 256, 306–307, 326, 335; N.'s health, 257, 327

History: A.'s views on, 151; children's study of, 153; image of N. in, 2–5; N. teaches, 123, 160, 162, 269; N.'s love of, 25, 227, 328; N.'s views on, 20–21, 23–24, 270; Pankratov teaches, 273

House of Special Purpose. *See* Yekaterinburg imprisonment

Icon of Our Lady of the Sign (*Ikona Znameniia Bozh'ei Materi*), 108, 137–139, 166

Icons and holy relics, 141, 142–144, 216; A.'s veneration of, 34, 67*n8*, 75, 95, 108–109, 137–139, 166, 215, 263; N.'s veneration of, 80, 165

Illnesses. *See* Health of Romanovs

Imprisonment of Romanovs. *See* Tobolsk imprisonment; Tsarskoe Selo imprisonment; Yekaterinburg imprisonment

Investigation into the death of the Romanovs, 175, 181, 279, 280–281, 283, 285, 295–296, 345*n1*, 346, 364, 384

Ipatiev, Nikolai Nikolaevich, 298*n1*

Ipatiev house, razing of, 298*n1*. *See also* Yekaterinburg imprisonment

Isa. *See* Buksgevden, Sofia

Ivanov, Nikolai Iudovich, 51, 56, 59, 68, 69*n3*, 81*n1*, 88*n1*, 94, 135, 136, 385

Ivan the Terrible, 25

Iza. *See* Buksgevden, Sofia

Izvolsky, Aleksandr, 14

Japan: as escape route for Romanovs, 184; N.'s view of Japanese, 404*n86*; Vladivostok seized by, 289

Jewelry and other Romanov valuables, 284, 296, 335, 360–362, 365

Jews, 202*n1*; Beilis affair, 343; beliefs about Masonic-Jewish conspiracy to destroy Russia, 241, 244*n2*; nationalism and anti-Jewish sentiment, 22–23; N.'s suspicions about, 22–23, 24–25, 202, 404*n91*; pogroms against, 22, 25, 343, 345*n5*; recommendations to extend equal rights to, 16

"July Days," 126, 128–129, 162

Kadet Party, 42–43, 44, 129, 289

Kalinin, General. *See* Protopopov, Aleksandr Dmitrievich

Karaulov, Mikhail Aleksandrovich, 131, 131*n1*

Kerensky, Aleksandr Fyodorovich, 53, 64–65, 69, 71*n7*, 127, 163, 272, 385; on humaneness of confinement, 121, 122, 125; and Kornilov's putsch, 173–174; N.'s views on, 156, 157, 160, 164, 165; responds to criticism of government, 135–137; on Russian Revolution, 114, 116–117; and Tobolsk imprisonment, 129, 155, 168, 169, 171, 173, 187–189, 194, 195–196; and Tsarskoe Selo imprisonment, 130

Khabalov, Sergei Semyonovich, 49, 50, 51, 52, 70, 71*n18*, 80, 385
Kharitonov, Ivan Mikhailovich, 296, 328, 331*n4*, 352
Khitrovo, Liubov Vladimirovna, 190–191
Khitrovo, Margarita Sergeevna, 191, 192*n1*, 385
Khodynka field, 342, 344*n2*
Khokhriakov, Pavel Danilovich, 179, 234, 234*n1*, 245, 300*n1*, 301–302, 302*n1*, 385–386
Kireev, Aleksandr Alekseevich, 29
Kirill Vladimirovich, 86–88, 88*n3*, 92*n2*, 93, 94, 111, 386
Klim. *See* Nagorny, Klementy
Kobylinsky, Yevgeny Stepanovich, 133*n2*, 160, 161–162, 194, 194*n1*, 212, 233, 238, 381, 386; and arrest of Romanovs, 121, 122, 132, 151; on education of tsar's children, 271; inspection by, 242–243; and transfer to Tobolsk, 170, 171–172, 177, 178, 261; and transfer to Yekaterinburg, 256
Koganitsky, Isaak Yakovlevich, 216, 217*n2*, 386
Kokovtsov, Vladimir Nikolaevich, 20, 288
Komuch. *See* Constituent Assembly
Koptiaki (village), 354–356, 361, 362, 363
Korf, Pavel Pavlovich, 70, 71*n14*
Kornilov, Lavr Georgievich, 121, 131, 131*n3*, 159, 386; attempted putsch by, 173–174, 198, 199*n1*, 267
Korovichenko, Pavel Aleksandrovich, 122, 135*n1*, 136, 137*n2*, 140–141, 160, 201, 386
Kosarev, Vladimir, 246, 249, 251–252
Kotsebu, Pavel Pavlovich, 121, 134, 135*n1*
Kronstadt naval base and fortress: and the revolution, 14, 162; demands that the Romanovs be imprisoned at, 125, 149, 182, 193
Ksenia Aleksandrovna, 66, 67*n5*, 94, 386–387; N.'s letters to, 200–203, 218–219
Kusiakin, Nikolai Alekseevich, 195, 196
Kutaisov, Konstantin Pavlovich, 69, 71*n8*
Kuzmin, A. I., 272, 276*n1*

Latvians, 286, 302*n1*, 304, 324, 330, 348, 349, 350, 352, 357
Left Communists, 289
Left SRs. *See* Socialist Revolutionary Party

Lelianov, Pavel Ivanovich, 79, 79*n5*
Lenin, Vladimir Ilich, 202, 203*n1*, 382; on Brest-Litovsk treaty, 288; criticism of policies of, 289; and execution of Romanovs, 290, 291, 292, 293, 331, 332, 335–337, 339, 341; and imprisonment of Romanovs, 229, 249, 299; rhetoric used by, 182, 281–282; and trial of N., 224, 288
Liberals, 41, 42–44, 46, 47, 116–117, 127–128
Lieven, Dominic, 16
Lili. *See* Den, Yulia
Linevich, Aleksandr Nikolaevich, 86, 94, 95*n6*
Livadia. *See* Crimea
Lukoianov, Fyodor Nikolaevich, 291–292
Lvov, Georgy Yevgenievich, 35, 43, 52, 61, 62, 65, 98, 99, 100*n4*, 103–105, 129, 163, 387

Maeterlinck, Maurice, 14
Makarov, Yevgeny (Zhenia), 80, 80*n2*, 203, 204*n3*
Manasevich-Manuilov, Ivan Fyodorovich, 192, 192*n3*
Maria Fyodorovna, 8, 9, 12, 22, 25, 63, 99, 113, 153, 202, 268, 387
Maria Nikolaevna, 71*n12*, 94, 240, 258, 387; execution of, 294, 296, 346–366; illnesses suffered by, 70, 144, 156, 201, 220; transfer to Yekaterinburg, 242, 244, 256, 297; at Tsarskoe Selo, 153, 158, 162, 164; at Yekaterinburg, 298, 300, 304–305, 323, 329
Marital relations, between N. and A., 9–10, 256
Markov, Nikolai Yevgenievich (Markov II), 180–181, 342
Maslovsky, Sergei Dmitrievich, 131, 131*n4*
Matveev, Pavel Matveevich, 233, 235, 238, 302, 302*n2*, 387
Maximalists, 250
Medem, Nikolai Nikolaevich, 78, 79*n4*
Medvedev, Mikhail Aleksandrovich, 189, 360, 365*n2*
Medvedev, Pavel Spiridonovich, 346–351, 358, 360, 387
Medvedeva, Maria Danilovna, 351*n1*
Menshevik Party, 41, 54, 127, 177, 202, 202*n1*, 289
Merezhkovsky, Dmitry, 163–164

Miachin, Konstantin Alekseevich. *See* Yakovlev, Vasily

Mikhail (Tsar), 19

Mikhail Aleksandrovich, 52, 88*n2*, 94, 165, 168, 200, 284, 387; proposed regency or assumption of throne of, 56, 60, 61, 62, 64–65, 92–93, 97–98, 99, 102, 103–105, 107, 108, 111; deportation and arrest of, 172–173; execution of, 341, 344*n1*; and manifesto of the grand dukes, 86–88

Military epaulettes and other insignia, efforts to ban wearing of, 177–178, 179, 218, 233, 242

Military-Revolutionary Committees, 207, 207*n1*

Military values, N.'s, 5–8, 114–115

Miliukov, Pavel Nikolaevich, 35, 46–47, 56, 63–64, 65, 88, 88*n4*, 92, 118–120, 126–127, 387–388

Misha. *See* Mikhail Aleksandrovich

Monarchists, 289; arrests and attempted deportations of, 172–173, 191–192, 278, 301; conspiracies of, 177, 190–193, 234, 341, 344. *See also* Investigation into the death of the Romanovs; Rescue efforts; White Army

Moral ideals of Romanovs, 5–9, 15–17, 22–24, 24–25, 29–31

Moscow: as atypical of Russia, 22; N.'s idealization of, 23–24

Moshkin, Aleksandr Mikhailovich, 284–285, 322, 322*n2*, 347

Mrachkovsky, Sergei Vitalievich, 346, 350

Muravyov, Mikhail Artemievich, 320–321, 321*n1*

Nabokov, Vladimir Dmitrievich, 65

Nagorny, Klementy Grigorievich, 306, 307, 316, 328, 331*n2*, 334, 388

Name days celebrated by Romanovs, 158, 163

Narod. See Common people

Naryshkin, Kirill Anatolievich, 96, 100*n3*, 131, 388

Naryshkina, Yelizaveta Alekseevna, 132, 133*n3*, 144, 168, 388

Nastenka, Nastia, Nastinka. *See* Gendrikova, Anastasia

Nationalism, N.'s, 20–24. *See also* Jews: N.'s suspicions about

Nationalization of Romanov's properties, 293

Navy, 14, 148–150, 193–194

Nechvolodov, Aleksandr Dmitrievich, *Tales of the Russian Land*, 154*n1*

Nekrasov, Nikolai, 271, 276*n1*

Nevolin, Aleksandr Ivanovich, 253–254

Nevsky, Vladimir Ivanovich, 239, 254, 254*n2*, 299, 339

Nevsky Prospect, 49, 69, 70*n1*, 138

Newspaper reports, 123, 125; on addressing Romanovs by title, 216; A.'s reaction to, 150; of Bolshevik Revolution, 176; of escape rumors, 182, 204, 207, 268, 274; of execution of Romanovs, 294, 320–321, 331, 341–345; of monarchist plots, 190–192; N.'s comments on, 204; N.'s documents selected for publication, 339*n1*, 344; of N.'s funeral, 345; Provisional Government criticized in, 135; on transfer from Tsarskoe Selo, 170; on transfer to Yekaterinburg, 255–259; on trial of N., 182, 233–234; on war aims, 127

"Nicholas the Bloody," 25, 149, 175, 182, 193, 281

Nikolai Nikolaevich, 62, 63, 64, 89–90, 91*n1*, 99, 104–105, 110, 388

Nikolasha. *See* Nikolai Nikolaevich

Nikolsky, Aleksandr Vladimirovich, 171, 175, 194*n1*, 216, 217*n2*, 333, 388

Nikulin, Grigory, 291, 358, 365*n2*

Nilov, Konstantin Dmitrievich, 115, 115*n4*

Nilus, Sergei, 23, 241, 244*n2*, 404*n91*

Niuta. *See* Demidova, Anna

Nizier-Vachod, Philippe, 12–13, 33

Nolde, Boris Emmanuilovich, 65

Novotikhvinsky Convent, 284, 285, 330

Obolensky, Aleksandr Nikolaevich, 78, 79*n4*

October Revolution of *1917*, 37, 175–176, 271–272, 275, 281–282; A.'s reaction to, 206; N.'s reaction to, 204–205

Octobrist Party, 42, 44

Oldenburgsky, Aleksandr Petrovich, 115, 115*n3*

Olga Aleksandrovna, 154

Olga Nikolaevna, 29, 148, 388; execution of, 294, 346–366; illnesses suffered by, 68, 69*n1*, 75, 112, 144, 157; at Tobolsk, 153–154, 203–204, 218, 240, 388; at Tsarskoe Selo, 156, 157, 160; at Yekaterinburg, 315*n1*, 318, 327

Omsk, 179, 183, 235, 244, 246, 246*n1*, 289
Orchard, Mary Anne, 28

Palace coup, plans for, 46
Pankratov, Vasily Semyonovich, 171, 173, 174–175, 177, 194, 194*n1*, 195–196, 195*n1*, 198, 208, 208*n1*, 212, 259–276, 276*n1*, 389
Party of the People's Freedom. *See* Kadet Party
Pastimes and leisure pursuits: at Tobolsk, 172, 220, 222, 227, 239, 265–266; at Tsarskoe Selo, 123, 161, 172; at Yekaterinburg, 325, 326, 327, 328, 334–335. *See also* Physical activity; Reading
Paul. *See* Pavel Aleksandrovich
Pavel Aleksandrovich, 83, 83*n1*, 86–88, 88*n1*, 91–92, 92–93, 94, 172–173, 389
Peasants: A.'s views of, 147, 151; demands for land, 39–40, 50, 148; disorders and rebellion among, 39–41, 103, 128, 176; holy men, 13; land reform by Provisional Government, 126; N.'s views of, 18–19; Peasant Congress, 223, 224; of Tobolsk, 299; of Yekaterinburg, 361, 362. *See also* Common people
People's Army, 289, 345
Perm, 170, 350; executions in, 284, 383, 387, 390; execution order from, 291–292, 351; and Romanov valuables, 365, 392; rumors of escape or transfer of Romanovs to, 295
Peter and Paul Fortress, 60, 119–120, 124, 130, 149–150
Peter the Great, 17, 21, 23, 26
Petrograd (St. Petersburg), 67*n1*; A.'s hostility toward, 36; N.'s hostility toward, 23–24, 261; unrest in 1917, 47, 49–54, 73, 75, 76–77, 78, 81, 107, 126–129, 138
Petrograd Soviet of Workers' and Soldiers' Deputies, 135, 159, 168; demands arrest of House of Romanov, 113, 119; Executive Committee of, 110, 112, 119–120, 127, 130–131; in the February Revolution, 53, 54, 55–56, 61, 62, 63, 96; political ideology of, 116–117; urges magnanimity toward Romanovs, 125
Petrov, Pyotr Vasilievich, 69, 71*n3*, 153–154, 199–200, 203–204, 205–206, 211, 217, 222–223, 389

Philippe. *See* Nizier-Vachod, Philippe
Physical activity, 122, 257; N.'s enjoyment of, 4, 8–9; at Tobolsk, 172, 198, 201, 203, 222–223, 227, 228, 238, 265–266; at Tsarskoe Selo, 157, 158, 159, 160, 161, 162, 163, 164, 165; at Yekaterinburg, 279, 305, 309, 325, 326, 327, 328, 329, 330
Pipes, Richard, 292–293
Pobedonostsev, Konstantin Petrovich, 12, 15–16, 23–24
Podbelsky, Vladimir Nikolaevich, 254, 254*n1*, 299, 339
Pokrovsky, Mikhail Nikolaevich, 224, 231, 430*n159*
Political philosophy: A.'s, 35–36; N.'s, 5–8, 10–11, 14–27
Progressists, 42, 44
Progressive Bloc of Duma deputies, 19, 44, 46, 53
Progressive Nationalists, 44
Proskuriakov, Filipp Polievktovich, 351
"Protocols of the Elders of Zion." *See* Nilus, Sergei
Protopopov, Aleksandr Dmitrievich, 45, 47, 49, 52, 66, 67*n4*, 80, 93–94, 389
Provisional Committee for the Relief of Wounded and Sick Soldiers, 43
Provisional Committee of the State Duma, 53–56, 58, 61, 62, 64, 84, 96
Provisional Government, 54, 63–64, 82, 84; accomplishments of, 126; Alekseev and others urge acceptance of, 88–91; on arrest of Romanovs, 113–114; criticism of, 135–137; and Kornilov's putsch, 173–174; N.'s views on, 164; overthrow of, 175, 176, 275; political ideology of, 116; protection of Romanovs by, 116–118; rebellion against, 128–129; travel of Romanovs to Tsarskoe Selo, 110–111. *See also* Council of Ministers
Provisional Siberian Government, 289
Prussia, A.'s enmity toward, 27–28
Purishkevich, Vladimir Mitrofanovich, 342, 389
Pushkin, Aleksandr, 270

Radzinsky, Edvard, 291, 292
Rasputin, Grigory Yefimovich, 13, 33, 34–35, 45, 122, 214*n3*, 263, 265, 281, 343, 344, 389; A. remembers, 65, 66, 67*n3*,

79, 166, 212; assassination of, 46, 71*n*8, 136, 213, 274; followers of (*Rasputintsy*), 172, 181; image of, worn by daughters, 354; native village of (Pokrovskoe), 129, 170–171, 181, 243, 305*n1*
Rasputina, Maria. *See* Solovyova (Rasputina), Maria
Rataev, Ivan Dmitrievich, 94, 95*n7*
Reading, 12, 14, 21, 28, 108; anti-Semitic literature, 243, 244*n2*; at Tobolsk, 198, 199, 213, 220, 227, 228, 239, 241, 242, 270–271; at Tsarskoe Selo, 123, 153–154, 158, 161, 162, 163, 164; at Yekaterinburg, 326, 327, 328, 329, 330, 331, 334, 335
Red Army, 183, 229, 235, 243, 257, 351, 356–357
Red Guards, 240, 241, 278
Religious practice and faith, 24, 263–264; of A., 12–13, 30–37, 78–79, 80, 95, 108–109, 112, 150–151, 152, 206, 209–210, 212, 213, 215, 219–220, 221, 224, 225–226; mystics and holy men, 12–13, 33, 34–35; of N., 12–14, 36–37, 66, 157, 228, 257–258; and the revolution, 176; at Tobolsk, 194–195, 199, 200, 203, 303; at Tsarskoe Selo, 137–146, 165; at Yekaterinburg, 327, 329, 334. *See also* Icons and holy relics; Swastikas
Rescue efforts: and justification of execution, 284, 341, 344; from Tobolsk, 172–173, 179–180, 221*n1*; from Yekaterinburg, 278, 283–284, 301, 310, 337; from Yekaterinburg with help of "officer," 284, 310–320, 322–323. *See also* Escape rumors
Resin, Aleksei Alekseevich, 94, 95*n4*
Revolution of *1905*, 10, 14, 18–19, 21, 40, 342
Revolution of *1917*. *See* February Revolution; October Revolution
Rodionov, Nikolai Nikolaevich, 71*n6*, 221, 301, 302*n1*
Rodzianko, Mikhail Vladimirovich, 42, 43, 50, 53, 58, 59, 60–61, 62, 64, 65, 76–77, 84, 88*n1*, 93, 103–105, 389
Rodzinsky, Isai, 315*n1*, 365
Romanov dynasty, tercentenary of, 19–20
Ruler myth. *See* Autocracy
Rural assemblies. *See* Zemstvos

Russian character: A.'s views on, 31, 36, 66, 220; Gilliard's views on, 205–206; N.'s views on, 21
Russo-Japanese War, 7, 11, 21, 342
Ruzsky, Nikolai Vladimirovich, 52, 58, 59, 62, 64, 90, 91*n4*, 96, 97, 99, 103–105, 107, 389–390

Sablin, Nikolai Pavlovich, 69, 71*n6*
Safarov, Georgy Ivanovich, 249, 249*n1*, 251, 354, 362, 390
Saltykov-Shchedrin, Mikhail, 326, 327, 330, 331, 331*n5*
Savvich, Sergei Sergeevich, 107, 108*n1*
Sednyov, Ivan Dmitrievich, 240, 243, 298, 316, 323, 328, 331*n2*, 334, 335, 356*n1*, 357, 390
Sednyov, Leonid, 331*n4*, 351, 357
Senate, 99, 180, 390
Sergeev, Ivan Aleksandrovich, 295, 346. *See also* Investigation into the death of the Romanovs
Sergei Mikhailovich, 14, 32, 115, 115*n2*, 390
Shlisselburg Prison, 174, 208, 208*n1*
Shneider, Yekaterina Adolfovna, 153, 266, 269, 278, 390
Shulgin, Vasily Vitalievich, 62, 96–100, 100*n2*, 111–112, 384–385, 390
Skobolev, Matvei Ivanovich, 110, 110*n1*
Socialism, 41, 289
Socialist Revolutionary Party, 41, 54, 127, 177, 185, 289; left wing of (Left SRs), 250, 288, 289, 301
Socialists, 41, 53, 55, 116–117, 127–128. *See also* Bolshevik Party; Menshevik Party; Socialist Revolutionary Party
Sokolov, K., 180
Sokolov, Nikolai Alekseevich, 285, 364, 366*n6*. *See also* Investigation into the death of the Romanovs
Soldiers: A.'s views on loyalty of, 94–95, 109; demand democratic rights, 54–55, 56, 128; demobilization of, 178, 235; disorders among, 60, 81, 83–85, 96–97, 107, 111, 128, 138, 163; mutiny of, 51, 58–59, 60–61, 96–97, 98, 103. *See also* Guards
Solovyov, Boris Nikolaevich, 181–182, 222, 222*n1*, 296–297, 305, 305*n1*, 339, 390–391

Solovyov, Vsevolod, *The Soothsayers,* 242
Solovyova (Rasputina), Maria Grigorievna, 93, 181, 222, 222*n1*, 305, 305*n1*
Somov, V., 194–195, 196
Soviets of workers', soldiers', and peasants' deputies, 133, 193–194, 229, 391. *See also* Central Executive Committee; Petrograd Soviet
Sovnarkom. *See* Council of People's Commissars
Speransky, Ioann F., 138
Sport and exercise. *See* Physical activity
Stalin, Iosif Vissarionovich, 185, 224
Stamfordham, Arthur, 120
State Conference, 173
State Council, 46, 53, 84–85, 87, 96, 391
Stolypin, Pyotr Arkadievich, 16, 19, 342
St. Petersburg. *See* Petrograd
Strikes and mass demonstrations: during the war, 45; in February *1917,* 47, 49–55, 69, 75, 78, 81, 107, 138; denouncing Miliukov, 126–129; in August *1917,* 173; in October *1917,* 175–176; in opposition to Bolshevik policies, 288–289. *See also* "July Days"
Suffering, 205; A.'s attraction to, 30–31, 148, 150–151, 166, 197, 209, 212, 226; of tsar-saint, 17
Sukhomlinov, Vladimir Aleksandrovich, 147, 147*n2*, 151–152, 153*n3*
Sverdlov, Yakov Mikhailovich, 183, 184, 185, 230*n1*, 391; and fate of Romanovs, 287, 291, 292, 332, 333, 335–337, 339, 343; and transfer to Yekaterinburg, 187, 224, 231–233, 245, 246, 249, 251–252, 300–301
Sviatopolk-Mirsky, Pyotr Dmitrievich, 10, 18
Swastikas, A.'s use of, 33–34, 212, 221, 278
Switzerland, as possible asylum for Romanovs, 119
Syroboiarskaia, Maria Martianovna, 197, 197*n1*, 206, 391
Syroboiarsky, Aleksandr Vladimirovich, 150–153, 153*n1*, 197*n1*, 206–207, 209–210, 210*n1*, 220, 221, 223–224, 391–392
Syromolotov, Fyodor Fyodorovich, 322, 322*n1*, 392

Tatiana Nikolaevna, 29, 71*n11*, 240, 392; execution of, 294, 346–366; illnesses suffered by, 70; at Tobolsk, 199–200, 217, 218, 222–223; at Tsarskoe Selo, 156, 157, 158, 162; at Yekaterinburg, 327, 328
Tatishchev, Ilia Leonidovich, 165, 168, 230, 265, 266, 278, 323*n2*, 392
Tauride Palace, 53, 55, 63–64, 135, 136
Tegleva, Aleksandra Aleksandrovna, 70, 71*n19*, 384, 392
Teodorovich, G. I., 231, 239, 339, 343
Tereshchenko, Mikhail Ivanovich, 127, 155, 156*n1*
Terror, use of, 22, 41, 281–282
Theft of Romanovs' possessions, 330, 347, 353, 361
Time of Troubles (*smutnoe vremia*), 56, 204, 205*n1*
Tiumen, 182, 186, 244, 251
Tobolsk imprisonment, 129, 165, 168; conditions of confinement, 171–172, 177–179, 183, 194–195, 195–196, 197, 198, 199–202, 205–206, 208, 213, 217, 222–223, 227–228, 259–276, 302–304; inspection of Freedom House, 237–238; transfer of Romanovs to, 154–156; travel conditions, 169–171, 184, 187–189, 189–190
Tobolsk Soviet of Workers', Soldiers', and Peasants' Deputies, 177, 179, 268–269; Executive Committee of, 216, 235, 237
Tobolsky, Ioann, 166, 166*n3*
Tolstoy, Aleksei, 199
Tolstoy, Leo, *War and Peace,* 244*n2*
Tomsk, possible transfer of Romanovs to, 155
Trepov, Aleksandr Fyodorovich, 35
Trial of N.: demands for, 146–147, 223; difficulties in arranging, 290–291, 293, 333, 344, 351, 356–357; plans for, 182, 224–225, 233–234, 287–288, 290
Trina. *See* Shneider, Yekaterina
Trotsky, Lev, 202, 229, 229*n1*, 287–288, 292–293, 339
Trudovik (Laborist) faction, 41
Trupp, Aleksei Yegorovich, 352, 356*n3*
Tsar, images of. *See* Autocracy
Tsarskoe Selo, 24, 57, 59, 67*n1*, 99–100, 138
Tsarskoe Selo imprisonment: conditions of confinement, 121–125, 133–135, 153–154, 156–166; education of tsar's children during, 153–154; Executive Committee of Petrograd Soviet on, 130–131;

religious services during, 137–146; transfer from, 125–126, 129; travel of Romanovs to, 110–111, 113–114

TsIK. *See* Central Executive Committee of Soviets of Workers', Soldiers', and Peasants' Deputies, All-Russian

Ukraintsev, 324, 331*n*3
Ulianov, V. I. *See* Lenin, Vladimir Ilich
Union of the Holders of the St. George Cross, 192
Union of the Nobility, 35
Union of the Russian People, 25–26, 36
Unions of town councils and zemstvos, 35, 43. *See also* Zemgor
Ural leftism, 283
Ural Regional Soviet, 179, 183, 231, 250, 302, 307, 308, 335–337; Executive Committee of, 352, 354, 362; Presidium, 294

Valia. *See* Dolgorukov, Vasily
Vasiliev, (Father) Aleksei, 85, 146, 146*n*1, 181, 216, 391
Vershinin, Vasily Mikhailovich, 114, 188
Victims in the Revolution, 124, 146*n*2, 202
Victoria (Queen), 28
Viktoria Fyodorovna, 92, 92*n*2
Vikzhel (Executive Committee of the Union of Railroad Employees), 207, 207*n*2
Violence: A.'s language of, 35, 69; Bolshevik language of, 282, 286–287, 360; popular, 40–41, 49
Voeikov, Vladimir Nikolaevich, 63, 94, 96*n*9
Voeikova, Yevgenia Vladimirovna, 112, 112*n*1
Voikov, Pyotr Lazarevich, 315*n*1, 363, 366*n*5, 392
Volkov, Aleksei Nikolaevich, 214, 214*n*6
von Mirbach, Wilhelm, 181, 289
VTsIK. *See* Central Executive Committee of Soviets of Workers', Soldiers', and Peasants' Deputies, All-Russian
Vyrubova, Anna Aleksandrovna, 28, 29, 30, 69, 71*n*5, 73, 80, 86, 94, 132–133, 166, 166*n*3, 168, 392; A.'s correspondence with, 166, 211–214, 219–221, 225–226; on A.'s spirituality, 33; arrest and attempted deportation of, 172–173;

arrest and imprisonment of, 122, 156; connections with monarchists, 172, 180–181, 191; illnesses suffered by, 69, 70, 72, 75–79, 95, 112, 139; on religious faith of N. and A., 12

Western Siberian Congress of Soviets of Workers' and Soldiers' Deputies, 208
Western Siberian Soviet, 179, 229; Executive Committee of, 229
White Army, 179–182, 294, 345*n*1, 350, 351, 354, 360, 362, 379. *See also* Investigation into the death of the Romanovs
Wilhelm II (Emperor), 112, 342, 392
Winter Palace, 20, 24
Witte, Sergei Yulievich, 4
Work, virtues of, 6, 9, 29–30
Workers, 175–176; A.'s opinion of, 49; attitudes toward Romanovs, 279, 280–282; demands for imprisonment of Romanovs, 124, 182, 283; democratic rights demanded by, 40, 54–55; Yekaterinburg Red Guard recruited from, 278, 347. *See also* Common people; Strikes and mass demonstrations
World War I, 7–8, 20, 21–22, 27–28, 31, 43–44, 114–115, 126–127, 163, 343. *See also* Brest-Litovsk treaty

Xenia. *See* Ksenia Aleksandrovna

Yakimov, Anatoly Aleksandrovich, 279
Yakovlev, Vasily Vasilievich, 183–187, 240, 393; inspection by, 238, 242; subordination of detachments to, 234, 235–237; and transfer to Yekaterinburg, 231, 233*n*1, 239, 243, 245, 246, 249–259, 300, 300*n*1, 323
Yekaterinburg, 179, 183, 186, 235, 289–290, 291, 341, 345*n*1
Yekaterinburg City Soviet Executive Committee, 363
Yekaterinburg District Soviet, 189
Yekaterinburg imprisonment, 239*n*1; conditions of confinement, 279–281, 300–301, 304–305, 320, 323–331, 333–335; instructions to commandant of House of Special Purpose, 307–310; N.'s comments on mood in Urals, 277; transfer to, 184–187, 231, 233, 234*n*2, 239–259, 297–298, 299, 301–302
Yeltsin, Boris, 298*n*1

Yermakov, Pyotr Zakharovich, 348, 350, 353, 356n5, 360–362, 364, 393
Yurovsky, Yakov Mikhailovich, 285, 286, 287, 290–291, 292, 296, 322, 322n3, 326, 330, 333, 347–365, 393–394
Yusupov, Feliks Feliksovich, 67n6, 389, 394

Zaslavsky, Semyon, 235–237, 237n1, 245, 394

Zemgor (Union of Town Councils and Zemstvos, All-Russian), 43
Zemstvos, 18, 35, 43, 394
Zhilik. *See* Gilliard, Pierre
Zinoviev, Grigory Yevseevich, 202, 203n1, 291, 292, 332, 333
Zizi. *See* Naryshkina, Yelizaveta
Znamensky church, 66, 67n8, 75, 78–79, 137–138. *See also* Icon of Our Lady of the Sign